BRITISH PARLIAMENTARY ELECTION RESULTS 1950–1970

POLITICAL REFERENCE PUBLICATIONS

Compiled and Edited by F.W.S. Craig

British Parliamentary Election Results 1918-1949 £8.25 ($24)

British Parliamentary Election Statistics (Second Edition) 1918-1970 £3.75 ($12)

British General Election Manifestos 1918-1966 £3.75 ($12)

Greater London Votes: 1. The Greater London Council 1964-1970 £1.10p ($3)

Greater London Votes: 2. The Greater London Boroughs 1964-1971 (forthcoming)

House of Commons Division Records (forthcoming, annually)

Minor Parties at British Parliamentary Elections 1918-1970 (forthcoming)

The Political Companion (quarterly) £2 ($6) per annum

Prices quoted above are those current at August 1971
and are subject to change without notice.

If you would like a copy of our current catalogue and to be kept informed
of new publications (including the supplement to this volume) please send
us a note of your name and address for inclusion in our mailing list.

BRITISH PARLIAMENTARY ELECTION RESULTS 1950–1970

Compiled and Edited by

F.W.S. CRAIG

POLITICAL REFERENCE PUBLICATIONS

CHICHESTER · 1971

First published 1971

ISBN: 0 900178 02 7

Library of Congress Catalog Card No.: 70-157739

Political Reference Publications,
18 Lincoln Green,
Chichester, Sussex.

Price: £9.50 net in U.K.
$28.00 in U.S.A. and Canada

*Set by Political Reference Publications on
IBM 72 Composer in 8 on 9 point Univers.*

*Printed by offset lithography in Great Britain by
Unwin Brothers Limited, The Gresham Press, Old Woking, Surrey.*

*Bound in Caxton Kingsway bookcloth by
R.J. Acford Limited, Chichester, Sussex.*

To the Martin family—

especially for 1948-1950

CONTENTS

FOREWORD

A two-party system has existed in Britain for only a small portion of this century: all of the election results contained in this volume are from the period when Conservative and Labour candidates together have won the overwhelming bulk of the votes and seats at stake in British general elections. Hence, this volume forms an ideal complement to F.W.S. Craig's *British Parliamentary Election Results 1918-1949*. In the former period, Liberals (plain and hyphenated), National and Coalition candidates often complicated comparison of results in the same constituency across successive general elections. From 1950 to 1970, there is little problem of comparison in England, and the outburst of so-called Celtic nationalism elsewhere was primarily found at the very end of the period.

The publication of F.W.S. Craig's careful verification and, where necessary, correction of the official record of post-war British elections is specially welcome. In theory, the task is a straightforward one, for constituency boundaries were only once substantially altered in the period. In practice, the absence of official party labels on ballots and the discrepancies that enter into many hastily recorded statements of election results make the task of presenting a definitive text a difficult one. That is why amateurs of British politics, as well as professionals, have reason to be grateful to the editor.

In designing this volume for ready and frequent reference, the editor has applied the skills of a typographer as well as those of a psephologist. The result is a volume which has been promptly produced by technically advanced methods of typesetting. It appears in a form that should maximize legibility and convenience.

The book is an innovation in another respect too. The materials contained on the following pages are also stored on magnetic tape convenient for computer analysis at the Survey Research Centre of the University of Strathclyde. Psephologists tired of testing their generalizations by slowly reading off figures from these pages may, upon application, have a computer read and tabulate constituency results for them.

RICHARD ROSE
Professor of Politics

University of Strathclyde
Glasgow
August 1971

PREFACE

With the publication of this second volume of constituency election results I have now completed the coverage of the period from the General Election of 1918 until the summer of 1971. The present volume contains the results of the seven General Elections held between 1950 and 1970 and 238 by-elections up to the end of August 1971. It is intended to publish a small supplement at the end of the present Parliament which will update this book to the next Dissolution when a major redistribution of constituencies will take place. Thereafter an individual volume will be published after each General Election containing constituency results on a cumulative basis.

The very considerable success of *British Parliamentary Election Results 1918-1949* is reflected in the fact that this volume is very similar in style and layout to its predecessor. The minor modifications which have been made are mainly the result of comments made by reviewers and correspondents but I regret that it has not been possible to implement all the suggestions received. To have done so would perhaps have made the book more useful to a small number of people but the increase in pages (and cost) would have outweighed the usefulness of for instance including figures of percentages for the "two-party" vote and swing. For those who may wish special calculations and percentages, the data in this book is stored on magnetic tape at the Survey Research Centre of the University of Strathclyde.

As with previous books in this series, I have had the most willing help of very many people and although it is not possible to mention them all individually, I would especially like to thank David Butler of Nuffield College, Oxford; Professor Richard Rose, Dr. William Miller and Miss Mary Dickie of the Department of Politics, University of Strathclyde; Mrs. Ursula Perry, research assistant, Political Reference Publications; and Alistair B. Cooke of the Institute of Irish Studies, the Queen's University of Belfast.

My wife Phyllis had once again the tedious task of typesetting over 4,600 results and some 7,000 index entries. Her patience when dealing with last minute author's corrections was as usual inexhaustible. My daughter Susan was a most willing helper with indexing and other laborious tasks.

For the convenience of readers a summary table of the votes cast and members elected at each General Election since 1950 has been included as an appendix but I would like to emphasise that this book is primarily a source of definitive constituency data and it is intended that it should be used in conjunction with the cumulative figures which are provided in my book *British Parliamentary Election Statistics 1918-1970*.

With the very thorough checking to which the typescript and proof pages were subjected there should be very few errors but it is inevitable that some will have gone undetected and I must once again rely upon readers to bring these to my attention so that future reprints can be corrected.

Political Reference Publications
Chichester
August 1971

F.W.S. CRAIG
Compiler and Editor

ABBREVIATIONS and SYMBOLS

PARTIES

Agric . . . . Agriculturist/Farmers' candidate/Independent candidate
advocating agricultural policy

Alert P . . . . Alert Party

AP . . . . Anti-Partitionist (candidate of the Anti-Partition of
Ireland League of Great Britain)

APA . . . . All Party Alliance

BCP . . . . British Commonwealth Party

B & CP . . . . British and Commonwealth Party

BEP . . . . British Empire Party

BM . . . . British Movement

BNP. . . . . British National Party

C . . . . Conservative (or Unionist) Party

Com . . . . Communist Party of Great Britain

CS . . . . Christian Socialist

DP . . . . Democratic Party

FP . . . . Fellowship Party

FSL . . . . Fife Socialist League

ILP . . . . Independent Labour Party

Ind . . . . Independent (indicates an unofficial candidate when
placed before a party abbreviation)

INDEC . . . . Independent Nuclear Disarmament Election Committee

IPP . . . . Independent Progressive Party

Irish LP . . . . Labour Party (Dublin)

L . . . . Liberal Party

Lab . . . . Labour Party

Lab/Co-op . . . . Labour Party/Co-operative Party joint candidate

Lan P . . . . Lancastrian Party

L & DBCP . . . . Light and Dark Blue Conservative Party

Loyalist . . . . Independent Loyalist (candidated sponsored by the
League of Empire Loyalists)

MGC . . . . Mudiad Gweriniaethol Cymru—the Welsh Republican
Movement

MK . . . . Mebyon Kernow (Sons of Cornwall)—Cornish home-rule
movement

N . . . . Irish Nationalist/Anti-Partitionist

Nat . . . . National

Nat DP . . . . National Democratic Party (Northern Ireland)

Nat FC . . . . National Fellowship Conservative (candidate of the
National Fellowship)

Nat Party . . . . National Party

NCP . . . . New Conservative Party

N Dem P . . . . National Democratic Party

ABBREVIATIONS AND SYMBOLS

New L . . . . New Liberal (candidate of the New East Islington Liberal Association, subsequently re-named Liberal Party (New Policy) Group)

NF . . . . National Front

NI Ind Lab . . . . Northern Ireland Independent Labour Party

NL & C . . . . National Liberal and Conservative (joint candidate of the Conservative Party and the National Liberal Organization)

NLP . . . . National Labour Party

NTP . . . . National Teenage Party

NUSS . . . . National Union of Small Shopkeepers

Pat P . . . . Patriotic Party

PC . . . . Plaid Cymru (pronounced *Plide Cumree*)—the Welsh (Nationalist) Party

PF . . . . Patriotic Front for Political Action

PL . . . . People's League for the Defence of Freedom

PP . . . . People's Party

Prot U . . . . Protestant Unionist Party

RA . . . . Radical Alliance

Rep . . . . Irish Republican

Rep LP . . . . Republican Labour Party

SCPGB . . . . Social Credit Party of Great Britain

SDLP . . . . Social Democratic and Labour Party

Ser . . . . Serviceman candidate (see Introductory Notes)

SF . . . . Sinn Fein (pronounced *Shin Fane*)—Irish Republican Organisation

SNP . . . . Scottish National Party

Soc . . . . Socialist

SPGB . . . . Socialist Party of Great Britain

TCP . . . . Taxpayers' Coalition Party

UK & DP . . . . United Kingdom and Dominion Party

UM . . . . Union Movement

Unity . . . . Opposition Unity (candidate in Northern Ireland opposed to the Unionist Government and supported by various organisations)

VNP . . . . Vectis (Isle of Wight) Nationalist Party

WGP . . . . World Government Party

WPP . . . . World Parliament Party

WPS . . . . Workers' Party of Scotland

YIP . . . . Young Ideas Party

MISCELLANEOUS

Bt. . . . . Baronet

Dr. . . . . Doctor

H.M. . . . . Her Majesty

Hon. . . . . Honourable

ABBREVIATIONS AND SYMBOLS

MP . . . . Member of Parliament
Prof. . . . . Professor
Rev. . . . . Reverend
Rt. Hon. . . . . Right Honourable (Member of the Privy Council)
Unopp. . . . . Unopposed

SYMBOLS

†   before the name of a candidate in 1950 indicates a member of the previous Parliament.

*   following an electorate indicates that a minor boundary alteration had taken place.

**   following an electorate indicates that a major boundary alteration had taken place.

INTRODUCTORY NOTES

General Note   The name of the constituency at the top of each page is followed, within square brackets, by a consecutive reference number which is used in the indexes to candidates, constituencies and footnotes. The allocation of a distinctive reference number to each constituency was necessary in order to simplify and reduce the time taken for computer processing and indexing. This number should not be confused with the folio number which appears in small type at the foot of each page.

Under the name of each constituency are seven columns with the following headings:

Election   The year of each General Election and the date of any intervening by-election.

Electors   The number of electors on the Register in force at the time of the election.

T'out   Turnout — the number of electors voting expressed as a percentage of the total electorate.

Candidate   The initials and surname of the candidate.

Party   The party affiliation of the candidate.

Votes   The number of votes polled by the candidate.

%   The number of votes polled by the candidate expressed as a percentage of the total votes cast. If necessary the largest percentage has been adjusted to provide an exact total of 100.0%

At the foot of each set of voting figures appears the majority of the successful candidate and this is also expressed as a percentage.

BY-ELECTIONS These are denoted by the year followed by the date (day/month) within round brackets. In the case of an unopposed return the date given is that of the close of nominations. The cause of the by-election is shown within square brackets above the year, and if the MP was elevated or succeeded to the Peerage, his new title is given.

By-elections can only arise for one of the following reasons: (1) death; (2) elevation or succession to the Peerage; (3) acceptance of an office of profit under the Crown (including certain nominal offices to which MPs who wish to resign are appointed); (4) bankruptcy; (5) lunacy; (6) election petition; (7) expulsion from the House of Commons; (8) sitting or voting in the House of Commons without taking the oath or affirmation of allegiance; (9) disqualification from having been elected to the House of Commons.

CHANGE of PARTY ALLEGIANCE When an MP seceded from a party after election and prior to the Dissolution, this is indicated by the new designation being shown within brackets. For example, C (Ind) indicates a change from Conservative to Independent.

CONSTITUENCY BOUNDARIES Details of the area included within constituency boundaries from 1950 will be found in the *Representation of the People Act, 1948* (First Schedule) and Statutory Instruments, 1955, Nos. 2-31 and 165-186. In addition to the changes which took place in 1955 and increased the number of seats in the House of Commons from 625 to 630, minor adjustments to constituency boundaries were made from time-to-time in order to bring them into line with local government boundaries. The following is a complete list of the Statutory Instruments implementing these minor changes:

1949:	Nos. 1439-1441, 2196
1951:	Nos. 320-327, 390, 431-432, 756-758, 1236
1952:	Nos. 452-453, 1347-1350
1953:	Nos. 386-390, 741-746
1956:	Nos. 818-823
1960:	Nos. 449-465, 468-470
1964:	Nos. 273-277

Maps showing constituency boundaries were included with the Boundary Commission reports published in 1947 and 1954.

CO-OPERATIVE PARTY All Co-operative Party candidates are endorsed by the Labour Party and are designated Labour/Co-operative.

DISSOLUTION VACANCIES Seats vacant at the Dissolution of a Parliament are indicated and the cause of the vacancy is given.

ELECTION PETITIONS These are briefly recorded with a note of the outcome but detailed reports will be found in *The Table,* Vol. 24, pp. 59-76 (Fermanagh and South Tyrone; Mid-Ulster); *All England Law Reports,* 1960, Vol. 2, p. 150 and *Weekly Law Reports,* 1960, Vol. 1, p. 762 (Kensington, North); *All England Law Reports,* 1961, Vol. 3, p. 354 and *Weekly Law Reports,* 1961, Vol. 3, p. 577 (Bristol, South-East); *Scots Law Times,* 1965, p. 186 (Perthshire and Kinross-shire, Kinross and West Perthshire).

ELECTORATE STATISTICS The figures of electors at General Elections have been taken from the *Returns of Election Expenses* compiled by the Home Office.

The electorate at by-elections prior to February 1970 has been based on the annual statistics compiled by the Registrar-General for England and Wales, the Registrar-General for Scotland and the Ministry of Home Affairs, Northern Ireland. Since February 1970 when electors reaching eighteen years of age had their birth date printed on the Electoral Register and could vote from that date, it has been necessary to obtain from Returning Officers a statement of the exact electorate on polling day. In a few cases where Returning Officers had not calculated a precise total, the editor has obtained the figure by examining the relevant Electoral Register.

FORFEITED DEPOSITS A candidate forfeits his deposit of £150 if he is not elected and does not poll more than one-eighth of the total votes cast, exclusive of spoilt ballot papers.

GENERAL ELECTION POLLING DATES Polling took place on the following dates:

1950	Thursday, February 23
1951	Thursday, October 25
1955	Thursday, May 26
1959	Thursday, October 8
1964	Thursday, October 15
1966	Thursday, March 31
1970	Thursday, June 18

For a detailed time-table of each General Election see *British Parliamentary Election Statistics 1918-1970* (Political Reference Publications, 1971).

GOVERNMENT PUBLICATIONS For a complete list of bills, acts and papers relating to elections in the United Kingdom since 1950 see the *General Index to Parliamentary Papers, 1950–1958-59* (House of Commons Papers, 1962-63 (96) xxxix, 1) and subsequent Sessional Indexes.

INDEPENDENT CANDIDATES A detailed check has been made on the sponsorship and political background of all Independent candidates and where this revealed close party ties, they have been designated as Independent Conservative, Independent Labour, Independent Liberal, etc.

In all cases where an Independent stood as a representative of either a national or local organisation this is indicated in a footnote. If an Independent contested an election on a specific policy theme this is also noted.

Where an MP was refused re-adoption by his party and contested the seat as an Independent, details are given of the circumstances.

MINISTERS CONTESTING BY-ELECTIONS Candidates who were either Ministers or Junior Ministers at the time they contested by-elections are indicated in footnotes.

NATIONAL LIBERAL AND CONSERVATIVE CANDIDATES In May 1947, recommendations were issued by Lord Woolton, on behalf of the Conservative Party, and Lord Teviot, on behalf of the National Liberal Organization, which advocated that the two parties should come together in constituencies and form combined associations under a mutually agreed title. Owing to local circumstances and preferences, the actual 'labels' used by candidates varied from one constituency to another but for the sake of uniformity the designation National Liberal and Conservative (NL & C) has been used throughout this book. Successful candidates under this agreement joined the Liberal-Unionist Group in the House of Commons.

Between 1955 and 1966 there were seven instances of candidates adopted by joint associations (and included in the official list of candidates issued by the National Liberal Organization) who preferred to run as Conservatives and did not use the National Liberal and Conservative 'label'. The constituencies were: Fife, West, 1955 and 1959; Kirkcaldy Burghs, 1959; Fife, East, 1964; Bradford, North, Brighouse and Spenborough, Dunfermline Burghs, 1966.

In May 1968 the National Liberal Council decided to disband and shortly afterwards the National Liberal Organization was wound-up.

NORTHERN IRELAND PARTIES No distinction is made between candidates of the Northern Ireland Labour Party and Labour candidates in Great Britain. The Northern Ireland Labour Party is an autonomous body but maintains co-operation with the British Labour Party on an informal and ad-hoc basis. Their candidates are endorsed by the National Executive Committee of the Labour Party in London.

With the exception of Sinn Fein (banned in Northern Ireland since 1956) which is the principal republican organisation, the nationalist and anti-partition movement in Northern Ireland comprised (until the formation of a Nationalist Party in 1966) numerous small groups within each constituency. Candidates were selected by ballot at conventions held before each election and attended by representatives of local organisations.

As the result of Sinn Fein being unable to officially operate in Northern Ireland, a Republican Six County Election Directorate was formed in December 1963 which was in effect a sub-committee of Sinn Fein. The purpose of this organisation was to contest elections in Northern Ireland and they sponsored candidates in the General Elections of 1964 and 1966. These candidates have been given the 'label' Republican rather than Sinn Fein but all of them were pledged to accept directives from the Sinn Fein executive in Dublin.

Since 1966 the 'label' Unity has been used to describe candidates selected at 'Unity conventions' and seeking election on an anti-Unionist and pro-nationalist platform.

POSTPONED POLLS Postponed polls at General Elections due to the death of a candidate (Manchester, Moss Side, 1950; Barnsley, 1951) are indicated in footnotes. It should be noted that postponed polls are not considered by-elections but are part of the General Election, no new writ being issued.

SERVICEMEN CANDIDATES At five by-elections between June and November 1962, a total of nine 'Independent Servicemen' candidates were nominated but in most cases took no active part in the election campaigns. By becoming parliamentary candidates they obtained their release from H.M. Forces for the cost of a forfeited deposit. As a result of these candidatures new regulations were introduced which prevented Servicemen from automatically obtaining their discharge.

SURNAMES and INITIALS The surnames and initials of candidates at General Elections are based on the *Returns of Election Expenses* compiled by the Home Office. Every effort has been made to ensure that both the initials and spelling of surnames are correct and many doubtful spellings have been checked against local sources.

The names of candidates at by-elections have in most cases been taken from *The Times* and revised where necessary by extensive checking against other sources.

Degrees, decorations and service ranks have been omitted for reasons of space but members of the Privy Council and Baronets are indicated by a prefix or suffix.

It should be noted that married women frequently seek election under their maiden name, especially if they have been active in politics prior to marriage.

UNIONISTS and ULSTER UNIONISTS Conservative candidates in Scotland stand under the auspices of the Scottish Conservative and Unionist Association and until the association added the word 'Conservative' to its title in April 1965, the majority of candidates ran as Unionists.

In Northern Ireland, Conservative candidates are sponsored by the Ulster Unionist Council and run as Unionists.

Throughout this book, Unionists in Scotland and Northern Ireland are designated as Conservatives.

VOTING STATISTICS The number of votes cast for candidates at General Elections have been taken from the *Returns of Election Expenses* compiled by the Home Office.

By-election figures have in most cases been taken from *The Times* and revised where necessary by extensive checking against other sources.

ENGLAND —— LONDON BOROUGHS

BARONS COURT   [1]

Election	Electors	T'out	Candidate	Party	Votes	%
1955	54,613	75.8	W.T. Williams	Lab/Co-op	20,748	50.2
			Sir K.S. Joseph, Bt.	C	20,623	49.8
					125	0.4
1959	50,032	76.3	W.C. Carr	C	18,658	48.9
			W.T. Williams	Lab/Co-op	17,745	46.5
			S.H.J.A. Knott	Ind L	1,766*	4.6
					913	2.4
1964	46,048	72.9	I.S. Richard	Lab	15,966	47.5
			W.C. Carr	C	14,800	44.1
			S.H.J.A. Knott	L	2,821*	8.4
					1,166	3.4
1966	43,830	75.2	I.S. Richard	Lab	17,021	51.7
			W.C. Carr	C	13,551	41.1
			S.H.J.A. Knott	L	2,384*	7.2
					3,470	10.6
1970	41,375	67.3	I.S. Richard	Lab	13,374	48.0
			R.E. Brum	C	12,269	44.1
			S.H.J.A. Knott	L	2,206*	7.9
					1,105	3.9

Election	Electors	T'out	Candidate	Party	Votes	%
1950	44,101	80.7	†D.P.T. Jay	Lab	24,762	69.6
			W.F.M. Maddan	C	9,084	25.5
			E.R. Handscombe	L	1,090*	3.1
			J. Mahon	Com	655*	1.8
					15,678	44.1
1951	44,478	80.2	D.P.T. Jay	Lab	25,882	72.5
			W.I. Percival	C	9,805	27.5
					16,077	45.0
1955	42,766	69.4	Rt. Hon. D.P.T. Jay	Lab	20,980	70.7
			W.I. Percival	C	8,058	27.2
			E.L. Fenner	Ind	622*	2.1
					12,922	43.5
1959	40,937	70.6	Rt. Hon. D.P.T. Jay	Lab	19,595	67.8
			R.G. Taylor	C	9,289	32.2
					10,306	35.6
1964	35,659	65.7	Rt. Hon. D.P.T. Jay	Lab	14,930	63.8
			R.G. Taylor	C	5,847	24.9
			S.R. Jakobi	L	2,187*	9.3
			Mrs. G.M. Easton	Com	471*	2.0
					9,083	38.9
1966	34,048	63.2	Rt. Hon. D.P.T. Jay	Lab	15,522	72.1
			C.P.M. Davidson	C	5,350	24.9
			Mrs. G.M. Easton	Com	650*	3.0
					10,172	47.2
1970	30,206	58.7	Rt. Hon. D.P.T. Jay	Lab	11,621	65.5
			A.V. Bradbury	C	4,927	27.8
			Mrs. H.M.G. Smallbone	L	1,012*	5.7
			D.J. Welsh	Com	179*	1.0
					6,694	37.7

Note:—

1955: Fenner sought election as a 'Pacifist' candidate. He was opposed to the manufacture of the hydrogen bomb.

BATTERSEA, SOUTH [3]

Election	Electors	T'out	Candidate	Party	Votes	%
1950	40,721	85.6	†Mrs. C.S. Ganley	Lab/Co-op	16,142	46.3
			E. Partridge	C	15,774	45.2
			C.H. Tyers	L	2,949*	8.5
					368	1.1
1951	40,848	85.6	E. Partridge	C	17,731	50.7
			Mrs. C.S. Ganley	Lab/Co-op	17,237	49.3
					494	1.4
1955	39,239	80.6	E. Partridge	C	15,044	47.6
			E.K.I. Hurst	Lab	14,365	45.4
			A.A. Cooper-Smith	L	2,219*	7.0
					679	2.2
1959	37,320	78.9	E. Partridge	C	14,203	48.3
			G.W. Rhodes	Lab/Co-op	12,451	42.3
			W.B. Mattinson	L	2,774*	9.4
					1,752	6.0
1964	36,186	72.3	E.G. Perry	Lab	12,253	46.8
			E. Partridge	C	10,615	40.6
			D. Layton	L	3,294	12.6
					1,638	6.2
1966	35,350	73.0	E.G. Perry	Lab	13,651	53.0
			Dr. I.N. Samuel	C	9,861	38.2
			B. Weekley	L	2,276*	8.8
					3,790	14.8
1970	34,649	63.6	E.G. Perry	Lab	10,925	49.6
			Dr. I.N. Samuel	C	9,227	41.8
			R.A.P. Benad	L	1,183*	5.4
			T. Lamb	NF	716*	3.2
					1,698	7.8

Election	Electors	T'out	Candidate	Party	Votes	%
1950	42,467	79.7	†R.J. Mellish	Lab	26,018	76.9
			F. Warwick	C	5,964	17.6
			Miss B.E. Talbot	L	1,852*	5.5
					20,054	59.3
1951	42,587	78.2	R.J. Mellish	Lab	26,267	78.9
			R.J.D. Manders	C	5,265	15.8
			H. Ball-Wilson	L	1,779*	5.3
					21,002	63.1
1955	40,695	69.5	R.J. Mellish	Lab	21,709	76.8
			Dr. Catherine E. Orr-Ewing	C	4,309	15.2
			H. Ball-Wilson	L	1,554*	5.5
			H.S. Birkett	ILP	715*	2.5
					17,400	61.6
1959	37,921	70.4	R.J. Mellish	Lab	20,528	76.8
			K.P. Payne	C	6,187	23.2
					14,341	53.6
1964	34,845	63.3	R.J. Mellish	Lab	17,481	79.3
			J.G.L.M. Porter	C	4,568	20.7
					12,913	58.6
1966	33,811	60.9	R.J. Mellish	Lab	16,605	80.6
			J.G.L.M. Porter	C	3,990	19.4
					12,615	61.2
1970	34,166	52.9	Rt. Hon. R.J. Mellish	Lab	13,908	76.9
			G.H.J. Nicholson	C	4,172	23.1
					9,736	53.8

Election	Electors	T'out	Candidate	Party	Votes	%
1950	42,172	76.9	†P. Holman	Lab/Co-op	20,519	63.2
			Rt. Hon. Sir P.A. Harris, Bt.	L	9,715	30.0
			Mrs. D.E. Welfare	C	1,582*	4.9
			J.J. Mildwater	Com	610*	1.9
					10,804	33.2
1951	41,829	76.0	P. Holman	Lab/Co-op	22,162	69.7
			R.I. Douglas	L	6,567	20.7
			L. Goodman	C	3,046*	9.6
					15,595	49.0
1955	61,410**	63.9	P. Holman	Lab/Co-op	27,205	69.3
			J.W. Milbourne	C	6,504	16.6
			Dr. R.I. Douglas	L	5,541	14.1
					20,701	52.7
1959	57,617	66.0	P. Holman	Lab/Co-op	24,228	63.6
			R. Roney	C	7,412	19.5
			J. Hart	L	5,508	14.5
			J.L. Read	SPGB	899*	2.4
					16,816	44.1
1964	51,904	59.3	P. Holman	Lab/Co-op	19,914	64.6
			S. Stout-Kerr	C	5,593	18.2
			T.D. Gates	L	5,296	17.2
					14,321	46.4
1966	50,180	57.7	W.S. Hilton	Lab/Co-op	20,178	69.7
			O.S. Henriques	C	4,925	17.0
			T.D. Gates	L	3,841	13.3
					15,253	52.7
1970	47,809	50.4	W.S. Hilton	Lab/Co-op	15,483	64.2
			O.S. Henriques	C	5,578	23.2
			W.O. Smedley	L	3,030	12.6
					9,905	41.0

Election	Electors	T'out	Candidate	Party	Votes	%
1950	65,573	83.3	†W.F. Vernon	Lab	25,511	46.7
			R.C.D. Jenkins	C	24,186	44.3
			P. Baker	L	4,929*	9.0
					1,325	2.4
1951	66,473	83.9	R.C.D. Jenkins	C	26,579	47.7
			W.F. Vernon	Lab	25,888	46.4
			P. Baker	L	3,302*	5.9
					691	1.3
1955	66,495	78.7	R.C.D. Jenkins	C	25,333	48.4
			W.F. Vernon	Lab	23,482	44.9
			D. Phillips	L	3,501*	6.7
					1,851	3.5
1959	66,988	79.2	R.C.D. Jenkins	C	24,991	47.1
			A.L. Hill	Lab	22,740	42.9
			W.J. Searle	L	5,324*	10.0
					2,251	4.2
1964	64,568	73.8	Hon. S.C. Silkin	Lab	22,320	46.8
			M. Stevens	C	19,469	40.8
			F.G. Redman	L	5,627*	11.8
			F.T. Palmer	CS	265*	0.6
					2,851	6.0
1966	63,891	73.7	Hon. S.C. Silkin	Lab	24,469	51.9
			M. Stevens	C	18,173	38.6
			M. Ridd	L	4,458*	9.5
					6,296	13.3
1970	66,265	64.4	Hon. S.C. Silkin	Lab	20,145	47.2
			P.B.B. Mayhew	C	19,250	45.1
			A.N.H. Blackburn	L	3,301*	7.7
					895	2.1

Election	Electors	T'out	Candidate	Party	Votes	%
1950	63,283	77.6	†Mrs. F.K. Corbet	Lab	32,623	66.5
			E.H. Lee	C	13,323	27.1
			K.G.P. Gunnell	L	2,267*	4.6
			T.R. Gibson	Com	886*	1.8
					19,300	39.4
1951	63,815	75.6	Mrs. F.K. Corbet	Lab	33,703	69.8
			C.V. Ford	C	14,557	30.2
					19,146	39.6
1955	61,050	63.7	Mrs. F.K. Corbet	Lab	26,315	67.7
			D.G. Smith	C	12,547	32.3
					13,768	35.4
1959	57,850	64.6	Mrs. F.K. Corbet	Lab	24,389	65.2
			A.F. Lockwood	C	13,007	34.8
					11,382	30.4
1964	53,925	58.1	Mrs. F.K. Corbet	Lab	20,111	64.2
			T.F.H. Jessel	C	11,226	35.8
					8,885	28.4
1966	51,526	55.6	Mrs. F.K. Corbet	Lab	20,630	72.0
			I.J. Lawrence	C	8,023	28.0
					12,607	44.0
1970	50,750	49.9	Mrs. F.K. Corbet	Lab	17,071	67.5
			I.J. Lawrence	C	8,232	32.5
					8,839	35.0

Election	Electors	T'out	Candidate	Party	Votes	%
1950	51,789	70.6	†A.H.P. Noble	C	23,471	64.2
			F.L. Tonge	Lab	9,987	27.3
			L.C. Robertson	L	3,116*	8.5
					13,484	36.9
1951	51,433	69.6	A.H.P. Noble	C	25,034	69.9
			F.L. Tonge	Lab	10,784	30.1
					14,250	39.8
1955	49,049	65.5	A.H.P. Noble	C	23,598	73.4
			S. Fordyce	Lab	8,546	26.6
					15,052	46.8
1959	47,077	65.8	J.S.S. Litchfield	C	20,985	67.8
			L. Goldstone	Lab	6,308	20.4
			K.G. Wellings	L	3,662*	11.8
					14,677	47.4
1964	43,515	62.7	J.S.S. Litchfield	C	16,802	61.5
			J.M.Y. Dickens	Lab	6,868	25.2
			A.C.S. Thomas	L	3,635	13.3
					9,934	36.3
1966	43,336	63.1	W.M.J. Worsley	C	16,377	59.9
			R.N. Tyler	Lab	7,674	28.1
			P. Smith	L	3,285*	12.0
					8,703	31.8
1970	44,038	55.0	W.M.J. Worsley	C	15,852	65.4
			Dr. R.J. Madeley	Lab	5,737	23.7
			A.H.S. Beavan	L	2,136*	8.8
			N.L. Luard	Ind	514*	2.1
					10,115	41.7

Election	Electors	T'out	Candidate	Party	Votes	%
1950	73,316	72.4	†Sir H. Webbe	C	32,672	61.5
			J.E.G. Curthoys	Lab	14,849	28.0
			Dr. J.A. Gorsky	L	4,670*	8.8
			G. Carritt	Com	888*	1.7
					17,823	33.5
1951	78,628	67.2	Sir H. Webbe	C	35,275	66.8
			H.F. Sutherland	Lab	17,537	33.2
					17,738	33.6
1955	74,162	60.1	Sir H. Webbe	C	31,314	70.2
			D.J. Nisbet	Lab	13,270	29.8
					18,044	40.4
1959	68,896	61.3	Rt. Hon. Sir H.B.H. Hylton-Foster	C	27,489	65.2
			W. Howie	Lab	10,301	24.4
			D. Monsey	L	4,409*	10.4
					17,188	40.8
1964	61,988	59.7	Rt. Hon. Sir H.B.H. Hylton-Foster	C	21,588	58.3
			R.G. Wallace	Lab	11,309	30.6
			J.W. Derry	L	4,087*	11.1
					10,279	27.7
[Death]						
1965 (4/11)	60,445	41.8	J.L.E. Smith	C	15,037	59.5
			A.J.S. Pringle	Lab	8,300	32.9
			S.R. Jakobi	L	1,595*	6.3
			D.H.R. Burgess	Ind	326*	1.3
					6,737	26.6
1966	58,630	60.0	J.L.E. Smith	C	19,242	54.7
			A.J.S. Pringle	Lab	12,349	35.1
			T.P.M. Houston	L	3,576*	10.2
					6,893	19.6
1970	58,798	54.7	C.S. Tugendhat	C	19,102	59.4
			A.M. Dubs	Lab	10,062	31.3
			D.A. Nicholson	L	2,708*	8.4
			Dr. W.A. Clark	Ind	157*	0.5
			D.E. Sutch	YIP	142*	0.4
					9,040	28.1

Notes:—

1959-
1964:   Hylton-Foster was the Speaker of the House of Commons from October 20, 1959.

1970:   Clark sought election as a 'Free Liberal Radical' candidate.

Election	Electors	T'out	Candidate	Party	Votes	%
1950	54,838	81.6	J. Cooper	Lab	28,230	63.0
			G.F. Sarjeant	C	13,330	29.8
			E.I. Miller	L	2,637*	5.9
			L.F. Stannard	Com	562*	1.3
					14,900	33.2
1951	55,200	80.3	Sir L.A. Plummer	Lab	28,878	65.2
			Miss I. Dowling	C	15,431	34.8
					13,447	30.4
1955	52,282	69.6	Sir L.A. Plummer	Lab	23,925	65.7
			Miss I. Dowling	C	12,472	34.3
					11,453	31.4
1959	49,412	69.3	Sir L.A. Plummer	Lab	21,226	61.9
			J.D. Brimacombe	C	13,038	38.1
					8,188	23.8
[Death]						
1963 (4/7)	47,576	44.1	Hon. J.E. Silkin	Lab	12,209	58.3
			D.J.H. Penwarden	L	4,726	22.5
			J.D. Brimacombe	C	4,023	19.2
					7,483	35.8
1964	47,124	60.1	Hon. J.E. Silkin	Lab	17,676	62.5
			M.M. Leask	C	8,248	29.1
			C.M.H. Atkins	Ind	2,386*	8.4
					9,428	33.4
1966	44,668	60.1	Hon. J.E. Silkin	Lab	17,893	66.7
			J.R. Giles	C	7,033	26.2
			G. Rowe	BNP	1,906*	7.1
					10,860	40.5
1970	42,570	54.7	Rt. Hon. J.E. Silkin	Lab	14,672	62.9
			M.L. Brotherton	C	7,355	31.6
			M.C. Vaux	NF	1,277*	5.5
					7,317	31.3

Note:—

    1964: Atkins was opposed to coloured immigration.

FULHAM [11]

Election	Electors	T'out	Candidate	Party	Votes	%
1955	55,373	78.6	R.M.M. Stewart	Lab	23,972	55.0
			Mrs. M.L. de la Motte	C	19,578	45.0
					4,394	10.0
1959	52,088	77.0	R.M.M. Stewart	Lab	21,525	53.7
			Mrs. M.L. de la Motte	C	18,581	46.3
					2,944	7.4
1964	48,147	73.2	R.M.M. Stewart	Lab	19,788	56.1
			W.M.J. Grylls	C	14,842	42.1
			A.R. Braybrooke	Pat P	632*	1.8
					4,946	14.0
1966	45,085	76.4	Rt. Hon. R.M.M. Stewart	Lab	20,080	58.3
			W.M.J. Grylls	C	13,094	38.0
			Miss E. Sheriff	Ind L	716*	2.1
			P.T. Robson	Com	256*	0.7
			Miss M.P. Arrowsmith	RA	163*	0.5
			A.R. Braybrooke	Pat P	126*	0.4
					6,986	20.3
1970	43,088	68.8	Rt. Hon. R.M.M. Stewart	Lab	16,312	55.0
			Sir I.A. Mactaggart, Bt.	C	12,807	43.2
			Miss M.P. Arrowsmith	Ind	421*	1.4
			R. Moody	Ind	112*	0.4
					3,505	11.8

Notes:—

1966: Miss Sheriff, a Gibraltarian, was opposed to the Government's policy on Gibraltar.

1970: Miss Arrowsmith sought election as a 'Stop the War in South-East Asia' candidate.

Moody described himself as an 'Anti-Election' candidate and urged electors not to vote for either himself or the other candidates.

FULHAM, EAST [12]

Election	Electors	T'out	Candidate	Party	Votes	%
1950	44,951	84.2	†R.M.M. Stewart	Lab	18,998	50.1
			S.V.T. Adams	C	16,233	42.9
			F.V. Jacoby	L	2,214*	5.9
			R.E. Elsmere	Com	399*	1.1
					2,765	7.2
1951	45,068	84.5	R.M.M. Stewart	Lab	20,279	53.2
			J. Hall	C	17,806	46.8
					2,473	6.4

This constituency was divided in 1955.

Election	Electors	T'out	Candidate	Party	Votes	%
1950	45,687	86.2	†Dr. Rt. Hon. Edith Summerskill	Lab	20,141	51.2
			Dr. W.J. O'Donovan	C	17,292	43.9
			E. Walcot-Bather	L	1,949*	4.9
					2,849	7.3
1951	45,320	86.6	Dr. Rt. Hon. Edith Summerskill	Lab	20,290	51.7
			W.J. Brown	Ind	17,707	45.1
			E. Walcot-Bather	L	1,247*	3.2
					2,583	6.6

This constituency was divided in 1955.

Note:—

1951:   Brown was supported by the local Conservative Association.

GREENWICH [14]

Election	Electors	T'out	Candidate	Party	Votes	%
1950	61,198	83.0	†J. Reeves	Lab	29,379	57.9
			R.D. Gilbey	C	18,255	35.9
			L.M. Dale	L	3,148*	6.2
					11,124	22.0
1951	62,041	81.0	J. Reeves	Lab	30,326	60.4
			W.H. Bishop	C	19,898	39.6
					10,428	20.8
1955	61,314	73.2	J. Reeves	Lab	26,423	58.8
			W.F. Rhodes	C	18,484	41.2
					7,939	17.6
1959	60,561	74.1	R.W. Marsh	Lab	25,204	56.2
			J.R.R. Holmes	C	19,679	43.8
					5,525	12.4
1964	56,741	71.6	R.W. Marsh	Lab	22,814	56.2
			J.S. Gummer	C	12,592	31.0
			M.P.D. Ellman	L	5,205	12.8
					10,222	25.2
1966	55,477	67.7	R.W. Marsh	Lab	24,359	64.9
			J.S. Gummer	C	13,200	35.1
					11,159	29.8
1970	56,746	64.0	Rt. Hon. R.W. Marsh	Lab	20,804	57.3
			J.S. Thom	C	13,197	36.3
			Mrs. P.M. Wylam	L	2,319*	6.4
					7,607	21.0

[Resignation on appointment as Joint Deputy-Chairman of the British Railways Board]

Election	Electors	T'out	Candidate	Party	Votes	%
1971 (8/7)	56,062	39.2	N.G. Barnett	Lab	14,671	66.7
			J.S. Thom	C	6,150	28.0
			R.S. Mallone	FP	792*	3.6
			R.E.G. Simmerson	Ind C	285*	1.3
			D.J.S. Davies	Ind	89*	0.4
					8,521	38.7

Note:—

1971: Simmerson was opposed to Britain entering the Common Market.

HACKNEY, CENTRAL [15]

Election	Electors	T'out	Candidate	Party	Votes	%
1955	66,183	66.1	H.W. Butler	Lab	27,012	61.7
			J.H. Allason	C	15,212	34.8
			J.R. Betteridge	Com	1,530*	3.5
					11,800	26.9
1959	62,561	66.0	H.W. Butler	Lab	25,407	61.5
			J.C.T.T. Waring	C	15,905	38.5
					9,502	23.0
1964	61,036	57.1	H.W. Butler	Lab	23,110	66.3
			H.M.L. Morton	C	11,734	33.7
					11,376	32.6
1966	58,513	57.5	H.W. Butler	Lab	21,466	63.8
			H.M.L. Morton	C	7,440	22.1
			C.V. Gittins	L	4,762	14.1
					14,026	41.7
1970	53,067	50.8	S.C. Davis	Lab	17,380	64.5
			K.S. Lightwood	C	9,339	34.6
			A. Qureshi	Ind	252*	0.9
					8,041	29.9

HACKNEY, SOUTH [16]

Election	Electors	T'out	Candidate	Party	Votes	%
1950	75,828	77.4	†H.W. Butler	Lab	35,821	61.1
			H.P. Brooks	C	15,105	25.7
			F.A. Marlow	L	5,575*	9.5
			J.R. Betteridge	Com	2,199*	3.7
					20,716	35.4
1951	76,552	77.1	H.W. Butler	Lab	39,271	66.5
			P.A.G. Rawlinson	C	18,003	30.5
			J.R. Betteridge	Com	1,744*	3.0
					21,268	36.0

This constituency was divided in 1955.

Election	Electors	T'out	Candidate	Party	Votes	%
1950	41,472	81.0	F. Tomney	Lab	13,346	39.6
			T. Gee	C	10,406	31.0
			†D.N. Pritt	Ind Lab	8,457	25.2
			H.M. Pick	L	1,402*	4.2
					2,940	8.6
1951	42,302	81.2	F. Tomney	Lab	22,709	66.1
			J.M. Howard	C	11,629	33.9
					11,080	32.2
1955	56,677**	70.0	F. Tomney	Lab	24,280	61.2
			A. Bowden	C	15,417	38.8
					8,863	22.4
1959	51,680	69.8	F. Tomney	Lab	21,409	59.4
			W.D.A. Bagnell	C	14,662	40.6
					6,747	18.8
1964	46,718	63.1	F. Tomney	Lab	18,547	62.9
			T.C.G. Stacey	C	10,936	37.1
					7,611	25.8
1966	44,397	63.9	F. Tomney	Lab	19,522	68.8
			M.J. Neubert	C	8,857	31.2
					10,665	37.6
1970	41,362	62.3	F. Tomney	Lab	16,145	62.7
			B.H.I.H. Stewart	C	9,615	37.3
					6,530	25.4

Note:—

1950: Pritt was a member of the Labour Independent Group.

Election	Electors	T'out	Candidate	Party	Votes	%
1950	44,540	81.7	†W.T. Williams	Lab/Co-op	18,825	51.8
			A. Fell	C	16,161	44.4
			J.S. Ritter	L	1,400*	3.8
					2,664	7.4
1951	44,030	80.2	W.T. Williams	Lab/Co-op	19,273	54.6
			R.N.E. Hinton	C	16,038	45.4
					3,235	9.2

This constituency was divided in 1955.

Election	Electors	T'out	Candidate	Party	Votes	%
1950	71,119	80.5	H. Brooke	C	29,949	52.3
			W.F. Hawkins	Lab	17,373	30.3
			W.S. Watson	L	8,336	14.6
			W.R.T. Gore	Com	1,603*	2.8
					12,576	22.0
1951	72,946	78.0	H. Brooke	C	31,346	55.1
			A. Richardson	Lab	19,240	33.8
			W.S. Watson	L	6,302*	11.1
					12,106	21.3
1955	72,423	69.7	H. Brooke	C	28,226	55.9
			A. Richardson	Lab	16,040	31.8
			H.C. Seigal	L	6,222*	12.3
					12,186	24.1
1959	69,438	68.8	Rt. Hon. H. Brooke	C	25,506	53.4
			Dr. D.T. Pitt	Lab	13,500	28.3
			H.C. Seigal	L	8,759	18.3
					12,006	25.1
1964	67,990	67.6	Rt. Hon. H. Brooke	C	19,888	43.3
			J.W.T. Cooper	Lab	18,053	39.3
			Mrs. R.R. Soskin	L	8,019	17.4
					1,835	4.0
1966	67,798	72.4	B.C.G. Whitaker	Lab	22,963	46.8
			Rt. Hon. H. Brooke	C	20,710	42.2
			Mrs. R.R. Soskin	L	5,182*	10.6
			H.G. Baldwin	SPGB	211*	0.4
					2,253	4.6
1970	71,918	63.4	G. Finsberg	C	21,264	46.6
			B.C.G. Whitaker	Lab	20,790	45.6
			J.H.R. Calmann	L	3,550*	7.8
					474	1.0

Election	Electors	T'out	Candidate	Party	Votes	%
1950	54,958	72.1	†Dr. S.W. Jeger	Lab	19,223	48.5
			P.J.F. Chapman-Walker	C	17,993	45.4
			Miss H.M.A. Buckmaster	L	2,411*	6.1
					1,230	3.1
1951	54,978	73.7	Dr. S.W. Jeger	Lab	20,332	50.2
			L.H. Gluckstein	C	18,573	45.8
			I.J. Hyam	L	1,616*	4.0
					1,759	4.4
[Death]						
1953 (19/11)	53,856	56.2	Mrs. L.M. Jeger	Lab	15,784	52.1
			W.T. Donovan	C	13,808	45.6
			I.J. Hyam	L	695*	2.3
					1,976	6.5
1955	51,282	67.3	Mrs. L.M. Jeger	Lab	17,126	49.6
			W.T. Donovan	C	16,195	46.9
			I.J. Hyam	L	1,193*	3.5
					931	2.7
1959	48,504	69.0	G. Johnson Smith	C	17,065	51.0
			Mrs. L.M. Jeger	Lab	16,409	49.0
					656	2.0
1964	43,272	67.5	Mrs. L.M. Jeger	Lab	15,873	54.3
			G. Johnson Smith	C	13,117	44.9
			A.M. Abbas	Ind	226*	0.8
					2,756	9.4
1966	41,366	65.5	Mrs. L.M. Jeger	Lab	16,128	59.5
			J.M.E. Byng	C	10,982	40.5
					5,146	19.0
1970	41,741	54.1	Mrs. L.M. Jeger	Lab	12,448	55.1
			J.M.E. Byng	C	10,125	44.9
					2,323	10.2

Note:—

1953: Hyman was the nominee of the local Liberal Association but his candidature was not supported by the Liberal Party.

Election	Electors	T'out	Candidate	Party	Votes	%
1950	50,644	79.3	†E.G.M. Fletcher	Lab	22,477	56.0
			Mrs. A.K.B. Wilmot	C	14,385	35.8
			T.H.C. Billson	L	3,301*	8.2
					8,092	20.2
1951	50,997	78.2	E.G.M. Fletcher	Lab	23,896	59.9
			Mrs. A.K.B. Wilmot	C	16,000	40.1
					7,896	19.8
1955	49,230	66.1	E.G.M. Fletcher	Lab	19,612	60.3
			G. Finsberg	C	12,910	39.7
					6,702	20.6
1959	48,613	63.5	E.G.M. Fletcher	Lab	17,766	57.6
			K.C. Burden	C	13,097	42.4
					4,669	15.2
1964	47,349	57.1	E.G.M. Fletcher	Lab	14,192	52.5
			K.C. Burden	C	7,715	28.5
			J. Freedman	L	3,081*	11.4
			A.E. Lomas	New L	2,053*	7.6
					6,477	24.0
1966	45,416	57.1	Sir E.G.M. Fletcher	Lab	15,009	58.0
			J.B.W. Holderness	C	7,490	28.9
			J. Freedman	L	2,288*	8.8
			A.E. Lomas	New L	1,127*	4.3
					7,519	29.1
1970	43,674	51.8	J.D. Grant	Lab	13,980	61.7
			R. Devonald-Lewis	C	8,660	38.3
					5,320	23.4

Note:—

1964- Lomas was a founder-member of the New East Islington Liberal Association which was
1966: formed in 1963 following dissensions in the local Liberal Association.

Election	Electors	T'out	Candidate	Party	Votes	%
1950	59,207	76.9	R.M. Hughes	Lab	26,354	57.9
			R.G. Page	C	16,975	37.3
			R.E. Burns	L	2,189*	4.8
					9,379	20.6
1951	59,039	77.8	W. Fienburgh	Lab	27,406	59.6
			R.G. Page	C	18,541	40.4
					8,865	19.2
1955	56,574	64.7	W. Fienburgh	Lab	22,100	60.3
			E. Mackinnon	C	14,522	39.7
					7,578	20.6
[Death]						
1958	54,576	35.6	G.W. Reynolds	Lab	13,159	67.7
(15/5)			R.D. Bartle	C	5,698	29.3
			J. McKie	ILP	576*	3.0
					7,461	38.4
1959	54,120	62.0	G.W. Reynolds	Lab	18,718	55.8
			R.D. Bartle	C	14,820	44.2
					3,898	11.6
1964	51,315	54.7	G.W. Reynolds	Lab	15,525	55.4
			V. Lyon	C	8,912	31.7
			E.G. Thwaites	L	3,634	12.9
					6,613	23.7
1966	50,203	54.2	G.W. Reynolds	Lab	16,188	59.4
			M.W.L. Morris	C	8,357	30.7
			E.G. Thwaites	L	2,682*	9.9
					7,831	28.7
[Death]						
1969	45,180	32.8	M.J. O'Halloran	Lab	7,288	49.2
(30/10)			D.A. Pearce	C	5,754	38.9
			E.G. Thwaites	L	1,514*	10.2
			L.A. Williams	Ind	245*	1.7
					1,534	10.3
1970	45,077	49.0	M.J. O'Halloran	Lab	13,010	58.8
			D.A. Pearce	C	7,862	35.6
			Rev. B. Green	NF	1,232*	5.6
					5,148	23.2

Election	Electors	T'out	Candidate	Party	Votes	%
1950	62,536	74.6	†A. Evans	Lab	30,201	64.7
			T.F. Howard	C	13,012	27.9
			G.W. Waddilove	L	2,602*	5.6
			A. Bender	Com	834*	1.8
					17,189	36.8
1951	61,707	75.2	A. Evans	Lab	31,637	68.2
			T.F. Howard	C	14,750	31.8
					16,887	36.4
1955	58,998	62.0	A. Evans	Lab	24,935	68.1
			C.G.S. Hodgkinson	C	11,667	31.9
					13,268	36.2
1959	56,620	60.6	A. Evans	Lab	22,362	65.1
			N.P. Scott	C	11,974	34.9
					10,388	30.2
1964	52,373	51.5	A. Evans	Lab	17,589	65.2
			N.P. Scott	C	8,023	29.7
			J.F. Moss	Com	1,377*	5.1
					9,566	35.5
1966	48,995	50.9	A. Evans	Lab	16,206	64.9
			A. Hardy	C	5,903	23.7
			H. Weston	Ind	1,271*	5.1
			D.H. Harmston	UM	816*	3.3
			J.F. Moss	Com	756*	3.0
					10,303	41.2
1970	43,282	48.9	G. Cunningham	Lab	12,876	60.9
			J. Szemerey	C	6,601	31.2
			A.E. Lomas	New L	1,161*	5.5
			Mrs. M. Betteridge	Com	509*	2.4
					6,275	29.7

Notes:—

1966: Weston was the nominee of the Islington Council Tenants' Rent Protest Association.

1970: Lomas was a founder-member of the New East Islington Liberal Association which was formed in 1963 following dissensions in the local Liberal Association. At this election he described himself as a candidate of 'The Liberal Party (New Policy Group)'.

Election	Electors	T'out	Candidate	Party	Votes	%
1950	54,480	78.3	†G.H.R. Rogers	Lab	21,615	50.6
			L. Caplan	C	17,991	42.2
			R.R.C. Evans	L	2,522*	5.9
			J.L.R. Eyre	Com	551*	1.3
					3,624	8.4
1951	54,083	79.2	G.H.R. Rogers	Lab	22,686	53.0
			L. Caplan	C	18,543	43.3
			A.G. Gamble	L	1,583*	3.7
					4,143	9.7
1955	53,789	69.7	G.H.R. Rogers	Lab	20,226	53.9
			R.W. Bulbrook	C	17,283	46.1
					2,943	7.8
1959	51,492	67.8	G.H.R. Rogers	Lab	14,925	42.8
			R.W. Bulbrook	C	14,048	40.2
			M.L. Hydleman	L	3,118*	8.9
			Sir O.E. Mosley, Bt.	UM	2,821*	8.1
					877	2.6
1964	50,349	61.3	G.H.R. Rogers	Lab	15,283	49.5
			A. Bowden	C	12,771	41.4
			Miss Y.C. Richardson	L	2,819*	9.1
					2,512	8.1
1966	47,080	62.1	G.H.R. Rogers	Lab	16,012	54.8
			L. Brittan	C	10,749	36.8
			A.C.S. Thomas	L	2,462*	8.4
					5,263	18.0
1970	43,430	57.5	B.L.H. Douglas-Mann	Lab	13,175	52.8
			L. Brittan	C	9,792	39.2
			P.D. Spencer	L	1,990*	8.0
					3,383	13.6

Note:—

1959: A petition was lodged relating to this election but was dismissed.

Election	Electors	T'out	Candidate	Party	Votes	%
1950	63,319	71.0	Sir W.P. Spens	C	32,870	73.1
			P. Picard	Lab	8,002	17.8
			J.B. Frankenburg	L	4,079*	9.1
					24,868	55.3
1951	63,419	68.6	Sir W.P. Spens	C	34,592	79.5
			M.C. Parker	Lab	8,894	20.5
					25,698	59.0
1955	62,724	61.9	Rt. Hon. Sir W.P. Spens	C	32,051	82.5
			Mrs. M.M. Crane	Lab	6,804	17.5
					25,247	65.0

[Seat Vacant at Dissolution (Elevation to the Peerage—Lord Spens)]

Election	Electors	T'out	Candidate	Party	Votes	%
1959	58,023	61.7	W.L. Roots	C	26,606	74.4
			G.C. Hoyer-Millar	L	4,666	13.0
			I.S. Richard	Lab	4,525	12.6
					21,940	61.4
1964	56,157	56.8	W.L. Roots	C	21,668	68.0
			B.J. Stead	Lab	5,300	16.6
			A.A.W. Dix	L	4,916	15.4
					16,368	51.4
1966	55,660	58.1	W.L. Roots	C	21,050	65.1
			J.V. Rosenhead	Lab	6,419	19.8
			T.O. Kellock	L	4,871	15.1
					14,631	45.3

[Resignation]

Election	Electors	T'out	Candidate	Party	Votes	%
1968 (14/3)	54,555	40.0	Sir B.M. Rhys Williams, Bt.	C	16,489	75.4
			T.O. Kellock	L	2,742	12.6
			C. Bradley	Lab	1,874*	8.6
			S. Eustace	Ind	675*	3.1
			W.A. Gold	Ind	59*	0.3
					13,747	62.8
1970	57,130	49.9	Sir B.M. Rhys Williams, Bt.	C	21,591	75.7
			Mrs. F.M. Bridges	Lab	6,928	24.3
					14,663	51.4

LAMBETH, BRIXTON [26]

Election	Electors	T'out	Candidate	Party	Votes	%
1950	56,082	81.1	†M. Lipton	Lab	24,015	52.7
			A.H. Foord	C	18,957	41.7
			Miss E. Lakeman	L	2,527*	5.6
					5,058	11.0
1951	55,362	79.8	M. Lipton	Lab	24,776	56.1
			Mrs. P.M. Marlowe	C	19,423	43.9
					5,353	12.2
1955	53,045	68.2	M. Lipton	Lab	20,594	57.0
			W.L. Roots	C	15,559	43.0
					5,035	14.0
1959	52,262	65.3	M. Lipton	Lab	18,117	53.1
			Dr. H.B.S. Warren	C	16,005	46.9
					2,112	6.2
1964	49,903	57.0	M. Lipton	Lab	16,518	58.1
			K.P. Payne	C	11,934	41.9
					4,584	16.2
1966	47,615	57.0	M. Lipton	Lab	16,634	61.3
			P.J.S. Dixon	C	10,500	38.7
					6,134	22.6
1970	43,346	52.6	M. Lipton	Lab	13,053	57.3
			J.W. Harkess	C	9,727	42.7
					3,326	14.6

Election	Electors	T'out	Candidate	Party	Votes	%
1950	60,961	84.2	J.G. Smyth	C	24,811	48.4
			†R.A. Chamberlain	Lab	22,736	44.3
			R.B. Fredericke	L	3,770*	7.3
					2,075	4.1
1951	62,231	82.7	J.G. Smyth	C	27,200	52.9
			R.A. Chamberlain	Lab	24,251	47.1
					2,949	5.8
1955	59,385	75.2	J.G. Smyth	C	24,831	55.6
			J.A. Joyce	Lab	19,799	44.4
					5,032	11.2
1959	57,807	75.6	Sir J.G. Smyth, Bt.	C	22,958	52.5
			L.L. Reeves	Lab	15,975	36.6
			D.R. Chapman	L	4,744*	10.9
					6,983	15.9
1964	57,090	67.8	Rt. Hon. Sir J.G. Smyth, Bt.	C	17,624	45.6
			J.D. Fraser	Lab	17,173	44.3
			D.R. Chapman	L	3,929*	10.1
					451	1.3
1966	54,592	71.8	J.D. Fraser	Lab	19,103	48.8
			W.D. Wilson	C	16,830	42.9
			M.A. Green	L	3,256*	8.3
					2,273	5.9
1970	53,412	65.7	J.D. Fraser	Lab	16,634	47.5
			P. Temple-Morris	C	16,003	45.6
			E. Hawthorne	L	2,436*	6.9
					631	1.9

Election	Electors	T'out	Candidate	Party	Votes	%
1950	50,673	75.7	†Rt. Hon. G.R. Strauss	Lab	23,988	62.5
			A.F. Lockwood	C	10,618	27.7
			W.S. Dyer	L	3,251*	8.5
			Miss M.C. Heinemann	Com	508*	1.3
					13,370	34.8
1951	49,939	73.7	Rt. Hon. G.R. Strauss	Lab	24,217	65.8
			E.H. Lee	C	12,564	34.2
					11,653	31.6
1955	47,354	62.7	Rt. Hon. G.R. Strauss	Lab	19,220	64.7
			E.H. Lee	C	10,492	35.3
					8,728	29.4
1959	45,802	65.0	Rt. Hon. G.R. Strauss	Lab	18,437	62.0
			Miss A.E.O. Havers	C	11,312	38.0
					7,125	24.0
1964	40,745	59.2	Rt. Hon. G.R. Strauss	Lab	15,458	64.1
			D.W.S.S. Lane	C	8,653	35.9
					6,805	28.2
1966	39,042	58.6	Rt. Hon. G.R. Strauss	Lab	15,233	66.6
			S. Le Marchant	C	7,648	33.4
					7,585	33.2
1970	37,676	54.5	Rt. Hon. G.R. Strauss	Lab	13,046	63.6
			C.W. Jones	C	7,477	36.4
					5,569	27.2

Election	Electors	T'out	Candidate	Party	Votes	%
1950	53,636	84.5	Sir A.U.M. Hudson, Bt.	C	22,465	49.5
			F.B. Copeman	Lab	19,974	44.1
			S.G. Smith	L	2,888*	6.4
					2,491	5.4
1951	54,331	84.0	Sir A.U.M. Hudson, Bt.	C	24,406	53.5
			S.T. Williams	Lab	21,243	46.5
					3,163	7.0
1955	52,485	77.9	Sir A.U.M. Hudson, Bt.	C	22,070	54.0
			S.T. Williams	Lab	18,834	46.0
					3,236	8.0
[Death]						
1957 (14/2)	52,862	70.8	N. MacDermot	Lab	18,516	49.5
			N. Farmer	C	17,406	46.5
			Miss L.M.C. Greene	Loyalist	1,487*	4.0
					1,110	3.0
1959	52,415	81.2	C.J. Chataway	C	22,125	52.0
			N. MacDermot	Lab	17,512	41.1
			K.J. Brookes	L	2,921*	6.9
					4,613	10.9
1964	50,624	74.6	C.J. Chataway	C	17,144	45.4
			Dr. H.J. Collins	Lab	16,801	44.5
			T. Lloyd-Jones	L	3,798*	10.1
					343	0.9
1966	49,532	77.4	R.D. Moyle	Lab	20,352	53.1
			C.J. Chataway	C	17,989	46.9
					2,363	6.2
1970	51,670	68.6	R.D. Moyle	Lab	18,235	51.4
			H.R.L. Samuel	C	17,208	48.6
					1,027	2.8

Election	Electors	T'out	Candidate	Party	Votes	%
1950	56,479	86.5	†Rt. Hon. H.S. Morrison	Lab	26,666	54.5
			C.F.H. Gough	C	18,892	38.7
			G.W. Rouse	L	2,665*	5.5
			J.W. Jones	Com	635*	1.3
					7,774	15.8
1951	57,132	85.2	Rt. Hon. H.S. Morrison	Lab	27,559	56.6
			R.C. Hutchinson	C	20,548	42.2
			J. Mahon	Com	578*	1.2
					7,011	14.4
1955	54,981	77.7	Rt. Hon. H.S. Morrison	Lab	23,821	55.8
			J.C. Arnold	C	17,478	40.9
			J.E. Loverseed	Ind	1,400*	3.3
					6,343	14.9
1959	53,962	78.6	C.A. Johnson	Lab	22,354	52.7
			J.L. Hunt	C	19,273	45.4
			G.A. Forrester	Alert P	788*	1.9
					3,081	7.3
1964	51,175	74.8	C.A. Johnson	Lab	20,078	52.5
			B.J. Hayhoe	C	12,486	32.6
			F.M. Bennett	L	5,706	14.9
					7,592	19.9
1966	49,501	75.1	C.A. Johnson	Lab	21,165	57.0
			G.L. Dixon	C	11,247	30.2
			F.M. Bennett	L	4,779	12.8
					9,918	26.8
1970	51,183	65.8	C.A. Johnson	Lab	19,217	57.1
			G.L. Dixon	C	13,665	40.5
			Miss D. Hart	Ind	821*	2.4
					5,552	16.6

Note:—

1955: Loverseed sought election as a 'Pacifist' candidate. He was opposed to the manufacture of the hydrogen bomb.

LEWISHAM, WEST [31]

Election	Electors	T'out	Candidate	Party	Votes	%
1950	56,007	85.7	H.A. Price	C	23,628	49.2
			†A.M. Skeffington	Lab	21,433	44.7
			A. Pritchard	L	2,939*	6.1
					2,195	4.5
1951	56,214	85.9	H.A. Price	C	25,449	52.7
			A.M. Skeffington	Lab	22,813	47.3
					2,636	5.4
1955	55,056	79.6	H.A. Price	C	24,066	54.9
			T. Sargant	Lab	19,741	45.1
					4,325	9.8
1959	54,069	80.3	H.A. Price	C	22,466	51.7
			R.C. Edmonds	Lab	16,233	37.4
			T.A. Smith	L	4,721*	10.9
					6,233	14.3
1964	54,227	74.8	P.M.E.D. McNair-Wilson	C	18,167	44.8
			Miss J. Lestor	Lab	17,281	42.6
			A.B. Mountain	L	5,123	12.6
					886	2.2
1966	52,858	75.7	J.M.Y. Dickens	Lab	21,018	52.5
			P.M.E.D. McNair-Wilson	C	18,984	47.5
					2,034	5.0
1970	56,625	68.2	J.S. Gummer	C	19,676	51.0
			J.M.Y. Dickens	Lab	18,916	49.0
					760	2.0

Election	Electors	T'out	Candidate	Party	Votes	%
1950	44,486	81.4	†W.J. Field	Lab	18,690	51.6
			H.F.L. Turner	C	14,829	41.0
			J.A. Seabrook	L	2,081*	5.7
			D. Cohen	Com	417*	1.2
			G. McClatchie	SPGB	192*	0.5
					3,861	10.6
1951	44,215	81.0	W.J. Field	Lab	19,923	55.7
			J.E. Ridsdale	C	15,874	44.3
					4,049	11.4
[Resignation]						
1953	44,027	60.3	B.T. Parkin	Lab	14,274	53.8
(3/12)			J.B. Eden	C	12,014	45.3
			W.E. Waters	SPGB	242*	0.9
					2,260	8.5
1955	42,689	72.2	B.T. Parkin	Lab	16,462	53.4
			V.H. Goodhew	C	14,370	46.6
					2,092	6.8
1959	40,952	68.4	B.T. Parkin	Lab	14,397	51.4
			H.H. Sebag-Montefiore	C	13,629	48.6
					768	2.8
1964	38,779	65.1	B.T. Parkin	Lab	14,607	57.9
			J.K.O. Edwards	C	10,639	42.1
					3,968	15.8
1966	37,240	66.4	B.T. Parkin	Lab	14,445	58.4
			J.E. Macdonald	C	7,981	32.3
			D.B. Griffiths	L	2,287*	9.3
					6,464	26.1
[Death]						
1969	33,306	46.3	A.C. Latham	Lab	7,969	51.7
(30/10)			R.S. Price	C	7,452	48.3
					517	3.4
1970	33,926	62.6	A.C. Latham	Lab	11,645	54.8
			R.S. Price	C	8,590	40.4
			M.R. Uziell-Hamilton	L	1,012*	4.8
					3,055	14.4

Election	Electors	T'out	Candidate	Party	Votes	%
1950	48,210	73.9	S.S. de Chair	C	19,964	56.0
			C.F.H. Wegg-Prosser	Lab	13,091	36.7
			S. Myer	L	2,589*	7.3
					6,873	19.3
1951	48,356	71.7	R.A. Allan	C	20,741	59.8
			C.F.H. Wegg-Prosser	Lab	13,932	40.2
					6,809	19.6
1955	46,505	64.3	R.A. Allan	C	18,479	61.8
			C.F.H. Wegg-Prosser	Lab	11,432	38.2
					7,047	23.6
1959	40,951	60.4	R.A. Allan	C	16,006	64.7
			D.J. Nisbet	Lab	8,719	35.3
					7,287	29.4
1964	35,226	58.4	R.A. Allan	C	10,838	52.7
			W. Dow	Lab	7,439	36.2
			P.M.R. Cowen	L	2,278*	11.1
					3,399	16.5
1966	34,181	62.4	N.P. Scott	C	10,297	48.3
			C.S.R. Russell	Lab	8,854	41.5
			D.A.T. Savill	L	2,170*	10.2
					1,443	6.8
1970	34,472	57.5	N.P. Scott	C	10,526	53.1
			R.A. Balfe	Lab	7,913	40.0
			E. Pemberton	L	1,367*	6.9
					2,613	13.1

Election	Electors	T'out	Candidate	Party	Votes	%
1950	50,148	78.4	†Rt. Hon. C.W. Key	Lab	30,756	78.2
			R.T.H. Lonsdale	C	6,088	15.5
			J.F. Purkis	L	1,933*	4.9
			H. Watson	Com	540*	1.4
					24,668	62.7
1951	50,509	75.7	Rt. Hon. C.W. Key	Lab	31,377	82.0
			P.F.H. Emery	C	6,875	18.0
					24,502	64.0
1955	49,038	64.1	Rt. Hon. C.W. Key	Lab	25,642	81.5
			Dr. G.F. Vaughan	C	5,814	18.5
					19,828	63.0
1959	44,412	65.6	Rt. Hon. C.W. Key	Lab	22,506	77.2
			P.B. Black	C	6,635	22.8
					15,871	54.4
1964	44,757	58.3	I. Mikardo	Lab	20,271	77.7
			K.W. Baker	C	5,813	22.3
					14,458	55.4
1966	43,236	57.7	I. Mikardo	Lab	21,071	84.5
			R.G. Holloway	C	3,863	15.5
					17,208	69.0
1970	41,869	49.1	I. Mikardo	Lab	16,520	80.4
			R.C. Denney	C	4,036	19.6
					12,484	60.8

Election	Electors	T'out	Candidate	Party	Votes	%
1950	58,604	74.0	†Sir W.W. Wakefield	C	26,310	60.7
			J.E. Silkin	Lab	12,890	29.7
			B. Guy	L	4,149*	9.6
					13,420	31.0
1951	60,932	70.2	Sir W.W. Wakefield	C	28,783	67.3
			W.C. Balfour	Lab	13,964	32.7
					14,819	34.6
1955	57,648	64.5	Sir W.W. Wakefield	C	26,302	70.7
			I.M. Yates	Lab	10,903	29.3
					15,399	41.4
1959	55,080	65.5	Sir W.W. Wakefield	C	23,278	64.5
			B.A.A. Hooberman	Lab	8,507	23.6
			E.M. Wheeler	L	4,304*	11.9
					14,771	40.9

[Elevation to the Peerage—Lord Wakefield of Kendal]

Election	Electors	T'out	Candidate	Party	Votes	%
1963	51,454	44.2	Rt. Hon. Q.M. Hogg	C	12,495	54.9
(5/12)			P.W. Plouviez	Lab	7,219	31.8
			E.M. Wheeler	L	3,016	13.3
					5,276	23.1
1964	50,003	64.4	Rt. Hon. Q.M. Hogg	C	18,117	56.3
			P.W. Plouviez	Lab	9,324	28.9
			A.W.R. Capel	L	4,776	14.8
					8,793	27.4
1966	47,294	65.1	Rt. Hon. Q.M. Hogg	C	17,443	56.7
			C. Cooper	Lab	9,382	30.5
			A.W.R. Capel	L	3,258*	10.6
			C.N. Frere-Smith	Ind	445*	1.4
			E.J. Miller	Ind	252*	0.8
					8,061	26.2
1970	47,640	59.6	Rt. Hon. Q.M. Hogg	C	17,639	62.1
			K.W. Morrell	Lab	8,325	29.3
			M.J.B. Vann	L	2,443*	8.6
					9,314	32.8

[Resignation on appointment as Lord Chancellor and elevation to a Life Peerage—Lord Hailsham of St. Marylebone]

Election	Electors	T'out	Candidate	Party	Votes	%
1970	47,713	35.3	K.W. Baker	C	10,684	63.4
(22/10)			K.W. Morrell	Lab	4,542	27.0
			M.J.B. Vann	L	1,038*	6.2
			M.E.L. Skeggs	NF	401*	2.4
			J. Papworth	Ind	163*	1.0
					6,142	36.4

Note:—

1966: Frere-Smith was opposed to Britain entering the Common Market.

1970: Papworth was the nominee of the Fourth World Group.
(22/10)

Election	Electors	T'out	Candidate	Party	Votes	%
1950	65,675	79.6	†K. Robinson	Lab	29,163	55.8
			J.E. Harvey	C	19,028	36.4
			P.M.C. Whitton	L	3,148*	6.0
			T. Ahern	Com	967*	1.8
					10,135	19.4
1951	65,840	78.3	K. Robinson	Lab	31,191	60.5
			C.A.B. Borrett	C	20,362	39.5
					10,829	21.0
1955	62,739	69.4	K. Robinson	Lab	24,670	56.6
			A.H.F. Royle	C	17,588	40.4
			J. Nicolson	Com	1,303*	3.0
					7,082	16.2
1959	59,194	69.5	K. Robinson	Lab	22,257	54.1
			D.B. Mitchell	C	15,949	38.8
			W. Webster	NLP	1,685*	4.1
			J. Nicolson	Com	1,230*	3.0
					6,308	15.3
1964	53,670	62.6	K. Robinson	Lab	20,516	61.0
			K.R. Warren	C	11,954	35.6
			J. Nicolson	Com	1,140*	3.4
					8,562	25.4
1966	51,468	63.4	Rt. Hon. K. Robinson	Lab	20,951	64.2
			C.J.O. Moorhouse	C	10,440	32.0
			J. Nicolson	Com	1,253*	3.8
					10,511	32.2
1970	50,108	55.5	A.W. Stallard	Lab	16,497	59.3
			C.J.O. Moorhouse	C	10,648	38.3
			G. McLennan	Com	670*	2.4
					5,849	21.0

Election	Electors	T'out	Candidate	Party	Votes	%
1950	56,848	74.4	†E. Thurtle	Lab	22,510	53.2
			A.G.F. Rippon	C	7,879	18.6
			†J.F.F. Platts-Mills	Ind Lab	7,602	18.0
			G.A. Hensher	L	4,297*	10.2
					14,631	34.6
1951	56,780	73.2	E. Thurtle	Lab	30,162	72.6
			A.G.F. Rippon	C	11,399	27.4
					18,763	45.2
[Death]						
1954	56,888	40.7	V.J. Collins	Lab	18,082	78.2
(21/10)			M.B. Agnew	C	5,043	21.8
					13,039	56.4
1955	56,393	61.6	V.J. Collins	Lab	25,500	73.5
			M.B. Agnew	C	9,216	26.5
					16,284	47.0
[Elevation to a Life Peerage—Lord Stonham]						
1958	54,033	24.9	M. Cliffe	Lab	10,214	76.0
(27/11)			T.H.M. Whipham	C	3,219	24.0
					6,995	52.0
1959	53,210	63.8	M. Cliffe	Lab	22,744	67.0
			T.H.M. Whipham	C	11,178	33.0
					11,566	34.0
[Seat Vacant at Dissolution (Death)]						
1964	47,791	55.7	R.W. Brown	Lab	18,207	68.4
			R.J.L. Bramble	C	8,412	31.6
					9,795	36.8
1966	44,431	55.2	R.W. Brown	Lab	17,456	71.1
			R.E. Sims	C	5,957	24.3
			Sir O.E. Mosley, Bt.	UM	1,126*	4.6
					11,499	46.8
1970	44,372	48.8	R.W. Brown	Lab	14,474	66.9
			R.E. Sims	C	7,166	33.1
					7,308	33.8

Note:—

1950: Platts-Mills was a member of the Labour Independent Group.

Election	Electors	T'out	Candidate	Party	Votes	%
1950	69,384	74.0	†Rt. Hon. G.A. Isaacs	Lab	35,049	68.3
			J.M. Greenwood	C	12,671	24.7
			L.V. Fowler	L	2,950*	5.7
			S.P. Bent	Com	668*	1.3
					22,378	43.6
1951	69,991	72.3	Rt. Hon. G.A. Isaacs	Lab	36,586	72.3
			J.M. Greenwood	C	14,032	27.7
					22,554	44.6
1955	66,592	60.2	Rt. Hon. G.A. Isaacs	Lab	28,174	70.3
			J.M. Greenwood	C	10,944	27.3
			S.P. Bent	Com	959*	2.4
					17,230	43.0
1959	61,747	63.4	R.J. Gunter	Lab	25,036	64.0
			J.M. Greenwood	C	12,696	32.4
			S.P. Bent	Com	1,395*	3.6
					12,340	31.6
1964	58,334	55.9	R.J. Gunter	Lab	22,426	68.8
			A.P.R. Noble	C	8,563	26.3
			S.P. Bent	Com	1,599*	4.9
					13,863	42.5
1966	54,997	54.0	Rt. Hon. R.J. Gunter	Lab	21,855	73.6
			A.P.R. Noble	C	6,454	21.7
			S.P. Bent	Com	1,404*	4.7
					15,401	51.9
1970	51,845	48.2	Rt. Hon. R.J. Gunter	Lab	16,834	67.3
			J. Gordon	C	7,040	28.2
			E. Hume	Com	1,128*	4.5
					9,794	39.1

Election	Electors	T'out	Candidate	Party	Votes	%
1950	65,304	73.2	†W.J. Edwards	Lab	33,475	70.1
			M.H.B. Solomon	C	6,238	13.0
			†P. Piratin	Com	5,991	12.5
			J.H. Maynard	L	2,105*	4.4
					27,237	57.1
1951	66,115	70.9	W.J. Edwards	Lab	35,849	76.5
			M.H.B. Solomon	C	7,586	16.2
			E.F. Bramley	Com	3,436*	7.3
					28,263	60.3
1955	65,601	57.8	W.J. Edwards	Lab	27,677	73.0
			Mrs. L.F. Sutton	C	5,733	15.1
			S. Kaye	Com	2,888*	7.6
			F.C. Winckless	L	1,615*	4.3
					21,944	57.9
1959	63,932	59.4	W.J. Edwards	Lab	26,875	70.8
			P.B. Calwell	C	8,566	22.5
			S. Kaye	Com	2,548*	6.7
					18,309	48.3
1964	60,807	51.3	P.D. Shore	Lab	22,284	71.4
			I.F.H. Davison	C	6,466	20.7
			S. Kaye	Com	2,454*	7.9
					15,818	50.7
1966	59,325	51.2	P.D. Shore	Lab	23,098	76.1
			Miss B.P. Cooper	C	5,049	16.6
			S. Kaye	Com	2,209*	7.3
					18,049	59.5
1970	56,367	45.0	Rt. Hon. P.D. Shore	Lab	18,993	74.8
			H. Greenway	C	4,922	19.4
			S. Kaye	Com	1,468*	5.8
					14,071	55.4

Election	Electors	T'out	Candidate	Party	Votes	%
1950	78,218	78.7	†D. Weitzman	Lab	33,783	54.9
			W.H. Bishop	C	19,469	31.6
			P. Phillips	L	7,740	12.6
			J. Hargrave	SCPGB	551*	0.9
					14,314	23.3
1951	80,221	78.9	D. Weitzman	Lab	37,406	59.1
			T.H.H. Skeet	C	21,369	33.8
			Miss J. Allison	L	4,524*	7.1
					16,037	25.3
1955	65,281**	67.9	D. Weitzman	Lab	25,253	57.0
			L. Defries-Porter	C	15,165	34.2
			B. Ashkenazi	L	2,388*	5.4
			A. Morris	Com	1,525*	3.4
					10,088	22.8
1959	64,723	67.1	D. Weitzman	Lab	22,950	52.8
			R.L. White	C	14,415	33.2
			P. Phillips	L	6,076	14.0
					8,535	19.6
1964	65,191	58.2	D. Weitzman	Lab	21,777	57.4
			R.L. White	C	10,843	28.6
			J. Bright	L	5,324	14.0
					10,934	28.8
1966	64,389	55.8	D. Weitzman	Lab	24,221	67.5
			J.R. Boast	C	10,221	28.4
			M. Goldman	Com	1,491*	4.1
					14,000	39.1
1970	64,904	50.1	D. Weitzman	Lab	20,446	62.9
			J.R. Boast	C	11,298	34.7
			M. Goldman	Com	793*	2.4
					9,148	28.2

Election	Electors	T'out	Candidate	Party	Votes	%
1950	69,206	82.1	†H.R. Adams	Lab	27,582	48.5
			R.G. Grant-Ferris	C	25,533	45.0
			A.H. Rose	L	3,680*	6.5
					2,049	3.5
1951	67,476	83.7	H.R. Adams	Lab	28,844	51.0
			R.G. Grant-Ferris	C	27,661	49.0
					1,183	2.0
1955	64,276	77.6	M.H.C. Hughes-Young	C	25,484	51.1
			Mrs. A.P. Llewelyn Davies	Lab	24,391	48.9
					1,093	2.2
1959	61,831	80.3	M.H.C. Hughes-Young	C	23,655	47.7
			Mrs. A.P. Llewelyn Davies	Lab	21,683	43.7
			R.A. Locke	L	4,287*	8.6
					1,972	4.0
1964	58,338	74.2	Dr. D.L. Kerr	Lab	20,581	47.5
			M.H.C. Hughes-Young	C	18,336	42.4
			R.A. Locke	L	4,369*	10.1
					2,245	5.1
1966	56,521	74.2	Dr. D.L. Kerr	Lab	22,159	52.8
			B.M.D. Cassidy	C	16,331	39.0
			M.R. Uziell-Hamilton	L	3,429*	8.2
					5,828	13.8
1970	58,502	62.6	T.M. Cox	Lab	19,776	54.0
			Mrs. F.P.A. McLaughlin	C	16,830	46.0
					2,946	8.0

Election	Electors	T'out	Candidate	Party	Votes	%
1950	60,866	80.6	†C.W. Gibson	Lab	23,300	47.4
			R.L. Lowndes	C	22,094	45.0
			Mrs. B.A.M. Curtis	L	3,071*	6.3
			Mrs. G. Draper	Com	619*	1.3
					1,206	2.4
1951	59,610	81.9	C.W. Gibson	Lab	25,053	51.3
			R.L. Lowndes	C	23,745	48.7
					1,308	2.6
1955	59,015	75.5	C.W. Gibson	Lab	22,398	50.3
			W.R. van Straubenzee	C	22,173	49.7
					225	0.6
1959	55,894	76.3	Dr. A. Glyn	C	22,266	52.2
			C.W. Gibson	Lab	20,390	47.8
					1,876	4.4
1964	52,826	72.3	Mrs. M. McKay	Lab	17,657	46.3
			Dr. A. Glyn	C	17,101	44.7
			P. Lyden-Cowen	L	2,611*	6.8
			Dr. D. Russell	Ind L	847*	2.2
					556	1.6
1966	51,885	73.1	Mrs. M. McKay	Lab	19,555	51.6
			I.R.E. Gow	C	15,379	40.6
			M.A. Minter	L	2,968*	7.8
					4,176	11.0
1970	52,999	62.9	W.J.M. Shelton	C	16,593	49.8
			Dr. D.T. Pitt	Lab	13,473	40.4
			E.G. Thwaites	L	2,982*	8.9
			F.W. Simkins	SPGB	220*	0.7
			W.G. Boaks	Ind	80*	0.2
					3,120	9.4

Note:—

1964: Russell sought election as a 'Radical Liberal' candidate. He was opposed to Britain entering the Common Market.

Election	Electors	T'out	Candidate	Party	Votes	%
1950	66,158	81.8	†H.N. Linstead	C	28,007	51.8
			Mrs. I. Chaplin	Lab	22,315	41.2
			B. Alton	L	3,785*	7.0
					5,692	10.6
1951	64,932	81.9	H.N. Linstead	C	29,686	55.8
			E.C. Hutchison	Lab/Co-op	23,489	44.2
					6,197	11.6
1955	66,776	76.0	Sir H.N. Linstead	C	28,969	57.1
			B. Bagnari	Lab/Co-op	21,774	42.9
					7,195	14.2
1959	71,772	80.1	Sir H.N. Linstead	C	28,236	49.1
			D. Taverne	Lab	23,115	40.2
			M.F. Burns	L	6,166*	10.7
					5,121	8.9
1964	71,084*	77.0	H.G. Jenkins	Lab	24,581	45.0
			Sir H.N. Linstead	C	23,274	42.5
			A. Cowen	L	6,856	12.5
					1,307	2.5
1966	69,869	78.9	H.G. Jenkins	Lab	26,601	48.3
			Sir H.N. Linstead	C	23,114	41.9
			A.C. Slade	L	5,420*	9.8
					3,487	6.4
1970	76,660	68.9	H.G. Jenkins	Lab	25,162	47.6
			J. Wakeham	C	23,768	45.0
			G. Broughton	L	3,887*	7.4
					1,394	2.6

Election	Electors	T'out	Candidate	Party	Votes	%
1950	57,234	81.0	Rt. Hon. E.D. Sandys	C	26,571	57.3
			P.J.H. Benenson	Lab	15,231	32.9
			A.W. Wilson	L	4,562*	9.8
					11,340	24.4
1951	55,451	81.5	Rt. Hon. E.D. Sandys	C	27,084	60.0
			N.J. Smart	Lab	14,804	32.7
			A.W. Wilson	L	3,319*	7.3
					12,280	27.3
1955	52,727	74.8	Rt. Hon. E.D. Sandys	C	25,862	65.5
			R.E. Prentice	Lab	13,594	34.5
					12,268	31.0
1959	50,916	77.2	Rt. Hon. E.D. Sandys	C	23,479	59.8
			Dr. D.L. Kerr	Lab	10,773	27.4
			R.S. Rubin	L	5,039	12.8
					12,706	32.4
1964	51,910	71.8	Rt. Hon. E.D. Sandys	C	19,408	52.2
			J.L. Walker	Lab	12,085	32.4
			A.H.J. Miller	L	5,261	14.1
			W.A. Brooks	Loyalist	497*	1.3
					7,323	19.8
1966	51,668	70.4	Rt. Hon. E.D. Sandys	C	19,872	54.6
			J.L. Walker	Lab	16,505	45.4
					3,367	9.2
1970	53,146	66.8	Rt. Hon. E.D. Sandys	C	19,215	54.1
			Mrs. A.S. Ward	Lab	13,593	38.3
			D.E. Delaney	L	2,680*	7.6
					5,622	15.8

Election	Electors	T'out	Candidate	Party	Votes	%
1950	51,848	83.3	†Rt. Hon. E. Bevin	Lab	26,604	61.5
			J.D. Campbell	C	14,234	33.0
			A.M. Sage	L	1,504*	3.5
			R.P. Dutt	Com	601*	1.4
			F.R. Hancock	Ind	252*	0.6
					12,370	28.5
[Death]						
1951 (14/6)	51,308	66.8	C.P. Mayhew	Lab	20,801	60.7
			R.J.S. Harvey	C	13,449	39.3
					7,352	21.4
1951	51,679	82.0	C.P. Mayhew	Lab	26,982	63.6
			R.J.S. Harvey	C	15,420	36.4
					11,562	27.2
1955	48,964*	73.9	C.P. Mayhew	Lab	23,275	64.3
			H.C. Crawford	C	12,929	35.7
					10,346	28.6
1959	46,349	75.5	C.P. Mayhew	Lab	22,353	63.9
			E.J. Porter	C	12,638	36.1
					9,715	27.8
1964	47,061	69.0	C.P. Mayhew	Lab	22,158	68.3
			D.W. Clarke	C	10,303	31.7
					11,855	36.6
1966	46,310	67.0	C.P. Mayhew	Lab	22,241	71.7
			A.W. Andrews	C	8,798	28.3
					13,443	43.4
1970	48,887	60.7	C.P. Mayhew	Lab	19,423	65.4
			J.A. Cope	C	10,259	34.6
					9,164	30.8

Note:—

1950: Hancock sought election as a 'Pacifist' candidate.

Election	Electors	T'out	Candidate	Party	Votes	%
1950	52,419	87.1	W.A. Steward	C	21,259	46.5
			†H. Berry	Lab	21,119	46.3
			W.R. Roberts	L	3,279*	7.2
					140	0.2
1951	54,226	87.5	W.A. Steward	C	23,385	49.3
			Hon. J.E. Silkin	Lab	22,041	46.4
			D. Phillips	L	2,040*	4.3
					1,344	2.9
1955	55,329*	83.3	W.A. Steward	C	23,981	52.0
			W. Hamling	Lab	22,101	48.0
					1,880	4.0
1959	54,563	84.7	C.W.C. Turner	C	24,373	52.7
			W. Hamling	Lab	20,678	44.7
			R.S. Mallone	FP	1,189*	2.6
					3,695	8.0
1964	54,359	81.3	W. Hamling	Lab	22,420	50.8
			C.W.C. Turner	C	20,639	46.7
			R.S. Mallone	FP	1,112*	2.5
					1,781	4.1
1966	53,477	81.4	W. Hamling	Lab	23,344	53.6
			M.P. Gaffney	C	19,256	44.3
			R.S. Mallone	FP	906*	2.1
					4,088	9.3
1970	57,508	72.1	W. Hamling	Lab	21,036	50.7
			M.P. Gaffney	C	20,418	49.3
					618	1.4

ENGLAND ——— PROVINCIAL BOROUGHS

ACCRINGTON [47]

Election	Electors	T'out	Candidate	Party	Votes	%
1950	52,431	91.0	†H. Hynd	Lab	23,295	48.8
			H.A. Procter	C	19,022	39.9
			A.K. Blakeman	L	5,403*	11.3
					4,273	8.9
1951	52,705	90.0	H. Hynd	Lab	24,802	52.3
			F.H.G.H. Goodhart	C	22,611	47.7
					2,191	4.6
1955	50,938	85.7	H. Hynd	Lab	22,502	51.5
			D.C. Walls	C	21,157	48.5
					1,345	3.0
1959	49,933	87.9	H. Hynd	Lab	22,242	50.7
			M. Henry	C	21,642	49.3
					600	1.4
1964	48,969	84.5	H. Hynd	Lab	20,561	49.7
			A.V.E.P. Montagu	C	15,143	36.6
			T.A. Maher	L	5,663	13.7
					5,418	13.1
1966	48,412	83.1	A. Davidson	Lab	21,330	53.0
			D.L. Maxwell	C	14,508	36.1
			J.H.S. Gould	L	4,375*	10.9
					6,822	16.9
1970	51,193	80.2	A. Davidson	Lab	20,828	50.7
			Dr. R.C. Webster	C	20,234	49.3
					594	1.4

ACTON [48]

Election	Electors	T'out	Candidate	Party	Votes	%
1950	50,588	87.6	†J.A. Sparks	Lab	21,751	49.1
			G. Willment	C	19,116	43.1
			Miss P.E. Furniss	L	2,781*	6.3
			A.F. Papworth	Com	663*	1.5
					2,635	6.0
1951	51,292	86.9	J.A. Sparks	Lab	23,287	52.2
			L.F. Ramseyer	C	21,296	47.8
					1,991	4.4
1955	49,373	82.6	J.A. Sparks	Lab	20,645	50.6
			J.L. Bott	C	20,120	49.4
					525	1.2
1959	46,835	80.7	P.W. Holland	C	19,358	51.2
			J.A. Sparks	Lab	18,438	48.8
					920	2.4
1964	44,557	77.4	B.F.C. Floud	Lab	17,022	49.4
			P.W. Holland	C	14,423	41.8
			B.N. Martin-Kaye	L	3,049*	8.8
					2,599	7.6
1966	43,464	73.9	B.F.C. Floud	Lab	18,541	57.7
			K.W. Baker	C	13,600	42.3
					4,941	15.4
[Death]						
1968 (28/3)	42,103	59.7	K.W. Baker	C	12,242	48.6
			W.J. Johnson	Lab	8,522	33.9
			F.L. Davis	L	2,868*	11.4
			A. Fountaine	NF	1,400*	5.6
			H.A. Fox	Ind	75*	0.3
			W.A. Gold	Ind	44*	0.2
					3,720	14.7
1970	43,670	66.6	N.J. Spearing	Lab	13,960	48.0
			K.W. Baker	C	13,300	45.7
			D.A. Scherer	L	1,583*	5.4
			M.W. Costin	Com	258*	0.9
					660	2.3

Note:—

1968: Fox sought election as an 'Independent Carnaby Street' candidate.

ALTRINCHAM and SALE [49]

Election	Electors	T'out	Candidate	Party	Votes	%
1950	60,557	88.7	†F.J. Erroll	C	30,843	57.4
			F. Bibby	Lab	16,544	30.8
			L.G. Bayley	L	6,340*	11.8
					14,299	26.6
1951	61,285	84.0	F.J. Erroll	C	33,987	66.1
			J.B. O'Hara	Lab	17,465	33.9
					16,522	32.2
1955	61,525	80.0	F.J. Erroll	C	30,586	62.2
			J.T. Park	Lab	12,174	24.7
			D.F. Burden	L	6,436	13.1
					18,412	37.5
1959	64,860	82.6	F.J. Erroll	C	29,992	56.0
			N. Atkinson	Lab	14,141	26.4
			D.F. Burden	L	9,415	17.6
					15,851	29.6
1964	65,716	81.2	Rt. Hon. F.J. Erroll	C	24,982	46.8
			R.D. Roebuck	Lab	14,945	28.0
			D.F. Burden	L	13,429	25.2
					10,037	18.8

[Elevation to the Peerage—Lord Erroll of Hale]

Election	Electors	T'out	Candidate	Party	Votes	%
1965 (4/2)	65,716	62.0	Rt. Hon. A.P.L. Barber	C	20,380	50.0
			R.D. Roebuck	Lab	11,837	29.0
			D.F. Burden	L	7,898	19.4
			G.O. Symes	Ind	634*	1.6
					8,543	21.0
1966	66,083	78.0	Rt. Hon. A.P.L. Barber	C	24,735	48.0
			Mrs. J. Cope	Lab	17,899	34.7
			A. Cooper	L	8,891	17.3
					6,836	13.3
1970	70,703	74.2	Rt. Hon. A.P.L. Barber	C	27,904	53.2
			Dr. B.E. Jones	Lab	16,671	31.8
			L.G. Bayley	L	7,875	15.0
					11,233	21.4

Note:—

1965: Symes sought election as a 'British Independent Democracy' candidate.

Election	Electors	T'out	Candidate	Party	Votes	%
1950	47,989	86.4	†H. Rhodes	Lab	20,970	50.6
			G.B. Howcroft	C	20,046	48.3
			H.H.H. Blackwell	Com	459*	1.1
					924	2.3
1951	47,558*	86.6	H. Rhodes	Lab	21,424	52.0
			K. Lewis	C	19,740	48.0
					1,684	4.0
1955	62,468**	80.8	H. Rhodes	Lab	26,216	51.9
			E. Hodson	C	24,251	48.1
					1,965	3.8
1959	60,706	81.1	H. Rhodes	Lab	25,991	52.8
			R. Horrocks	C	23,239	47.2
					2,752	5.6

[Seat Vacant at Dissolution (Elevation to a Life Peerage—Lord Rhodes)]

Election	Electors	T'out	Candidate	Party	Votes	%
1964	58,411	77.4	R.E. Sheldon	Lab	24,657	54.5
			H.D. Moore	C	20,550	45.5
					4,107	9.0
1966	57,159	73.7	R.E. Sheldon	Lab	24,728	58.7
			H.D. Moore	C	17,396	41.3
					7,332	17.4
1970	61,402	71.5	R.E. Sheldon	Lab	23,927	54.5
			A.d'A. Fearn	C	19,973	45.5
					3,954	9.0

Election	Electors	T'out	Candidate	Party	Votes	%
1950	54,627	83.6	†Dr. S. Hastings	Lab	30,299	66.3
			K.E.B. Glenny	C	10,269	22.5
			C.H. Willcock	L	5,109*	11.2
					20,030	43.8
1951	55,219	81.9	Dr. S. Hastings	Lab	30,486	67.4
			M.T.B. Underhill	C	11,340	25.1
			N.H. Cork	L	3,387*	7.5
					19,146	42.3
1955	53,314	73.5	Dr. S. Hastings	Lab	27,129	69.2
			B. Massey	C	12,082	30.8
					15,047	38.4
1959	51,654	78.5	T.E.N. Driberg	Lab	23,454	57.9
			K.F. Dibben	C	11,454	28.2
			D.E. Evans	L	5,648	13.9
					12,000	29.7
1964	50,326	73.2	T.E.N. Driberg	Lab	23,055	62.7
			G.C. Waterer	C	8,296	22.5
			N.H. Donohue	L	5,463	14.8
					14,759	40.2
1966	48,281	72.0	T.E.N. Driberg	Lab	22,994	66.2
			G.E. Pattie	C	7,584	21.8
			J.T. Silvey	L	4,181*	12.0
					15,410	44.4
1970	49,317	61.7	T.E.N. Driberg	Lab	21,097	69.4
			G.E. Pattie	C	9,309	30.6
					11,788	38.8

Election	Electors	T'out	Candidate	Party	Votes	%
1950	68,905	88.9	†F. Collindridge	Lab	42,008	68.6
			G.H. Walker	L	10,799	17.6
			C. Gordon-Spencer	NL & C	8,480	13.8
					31,209	51.0
1951	69,694	77.2	S. Schofield	Lab	37,523	69.7
			G. Whitaker	NL & C	9,296	17.3
			G.H. Walker	L	7,002	13.0
					28,227	52.4
[Resignation]						
1953 (31/3)	69,351	57.9	R. Mason	Lab	29,283	72.9
			G. Whitaker	NL & C	10,905	27.1
					18,378	45.8
1955	68,997	78.6	R. Mason	Lab	39,485	72.8
			R.A. Wilson	NL & C	14,776	27.2
					24,709	45.6
1959	69,833	82.7	R. Mason	Lab	42,565	73.7
			J.P.H. Bent	C	15,189	26.3
					27,376	47.4
1964	69,658*	80.0	R. Mason	Lab	37,250	66.8
			Miss J.V. Hall	C	9,417	16.9
			J.H. Dossett	L	9,089	16.3
					27,833	49.9
1966	69,751	73.4	R. Mason	Lab	38,744	75.7
			Miss J.V. Hall	C	12,456	24.3
					26,288	51.4
1970	75,678	71.3	Rt. Hon. R. Mason	Lab	34,956	64.8
			R. Godber	C	10,811	20.0
			J.H. Dossett	L	8,186	15.2
					24,145	44.8

Note:—

1951: Polling was delayed until November 8 owing to the death after nomination of the Labour candidate, F. Collindridge.

Election	Electors	T'out	Candidate	Party	Votes	%
1950	53,300	87.8	†W. Monslow	Lab	26,342	56.2
			Sir W.H. Sugden	C	16,793	35.9
			H.A.A. Jardine	L	3,678*	7.9
					9,549	20.3
1951	54,459	86.2	W. Monslow	Lab	26,709	56.9
			K.F. Lawton	C	20,225	43.1
					6,484	13.8
1955	53,073	80.7	W. Monslow	Lab	22,792	53.2
			E.D.L. du Cann	C	20,033	46.8
					2,759	6.4
1959	51,904	81.7	W. Monslow	Lab	23,194	54.7
			M. Metcalf	C	19,220	45.3
					3,974	9.4
1964	51,601	78.0	W. Monslow	Lab	22,197	55.1
			P. Davies	C	18,068	44.9
					4,129	10.2
1966	50,711	76.8	A.E. Booth	Lab	23,485	60.3
			R.W. Rollins	C	15,453	39.7
					8,032	20.6
1970	54,126	73.8	A.E. Booth	Lab	22,400	56.1
			H.D. Miller	C	17,536	43.9
					4,864	12.2

Election	Electors	T'out	Candidate	Party	Votes	%
1950	56,045	87.3	†I.J. Pitman	C	23,070	47.2
			Dr. H.B.O. Cardew	Lab	19,340	39.5
			P.W. Hopkins	L	6,508	13.3
					3,730	7.7
1951	58,799*	85.6	I.J. Pitman	C	27,826	55.3
			V. Mishcon	Lab	22,530	44.7
					5,296	10.6
1955	57,175	82.5	I.J. Pitman	C	24,489	52.0
			T.W. Richardson	Lab/Co-op	17,646	37.4
			Miss B.S. Burwell	L	5,011*	10.6
					6,843	14.6
1959	57,150	83.6	I.J. Pitman	C	24,048	50.3
			G.E. Mayer	Lab	17,515	36.7
			G.R. Allen	L	6,214	13.0
					6,533	13.6
1964	56,806	80.7	Sir E.J. Brown	C	20,255	44.2
			F.S. Moorhouse	Lab	16,464	35.9
			Dr. B.R. Pamplin	L	8,795	19.2
			S.G. Young	WGP	318*	0.7
					3,791	8.3
1966	55,891	80.5	Sir E.J. Brown	C	19,344	43.0
			F.S. Moorhouse	Lab	18,544	41.2
			R.H. Crowther	L	7,095	15.8
					800	1.8
1970	59,141	77.2	Sir E.J. Brown	C	22,344	49.0
			D.W. Young	Lab	16,493	36.1
			R.H. Crowther	L	5,957	13.1
			S.G. Young	WGP	840*	1.8
					5,851	12.9

Election	Electors	T'out	Candidate	Party	Votes	%
1950	57,066	87.0	†Dr. A.D.D. Broughton	Lab	29,776	60.0
			Mrs. W.C.G. Bremner	C	19,891	40.0
					9,885	20.0
1951	57,453	85.5	Dr. A.D.D. Broughton	Lab	29,326	59.7
			R. Northam	C	19,811	40.3
					9,515	19.4
1955	56,513	79.9	Dr. A.D.D. Broughton	Lab	27,178	60.2
			H. Watson	C	17,970	39.8
					9,208	20.4
1959	56,031	81.9	Dr. A.D.D. Broughton	Lab	26,781	58.4
			Mrs. B.M. Garden	C	19,115	41.6
					7,666	16.8
1964	56,436	78.7	Dr. A.D.D. Broughton	Lab	23,362	52.6
			P.J.D. Marshall	C	13,477	30.4
			I.H. Lester	L	7,564	17.0
					9,885	22.2
1966	56,936	75.3	Dr. A.D.D. Broughton	Lab	24,086	56.2
			P.J.D. Marshall	C	12,435	29.0
			E.A. Berry	L	6,366	14.8
					11,651	27.2
1970	63,035	72.5	Sir A.D.D. Broughton	Lab	23,024	50.4
			D. Thompson	C	15,753	34.5
			P. Wrigley	L	6,893	15.1
					7,271	15.9

Election	Electors	T'out	Candidate	Party	Votes	%
1950	66,178	87.2	H.D. Oakshott	C	25,309	43.8
			†Rt. Hon. Sir F. Soskice	Lab	22,090	38.3
			Rt. Hon. H.G. White	L	10,324	17.9
					3,219	5.5
1951	66,742	85.8	H.D. Oakshott	C	30,611	53.5
			E.W. Harby	Lab/Co-op	22,190	38.7
			T.M. Banks	L	4,477*	7.8
					8,421	14.8
1955	68,186	79.2	H.D. Oakshott	C	31,700	58.7
			T.H. Hockton	Lab	22,277	41.3
					9,423	17.4
1959	70,374	81.8	Sir H.D. Oakshott, Bt.	C	33,705	58.5
			G.J. Oakes	Lab	23,884	41.5
					9,821	17.0

[Seat Vacant at Dissolution (Elevation to a Life Peerage—Lord Oakshott)]

Election	Electors	T'out	Candidate	Party	Votes	%
1964	73,474	80.9	R.E.G. Howe	C	26,943	45.3
			E. Brooks	Lab	24,734	41.6
			M.J.G. Tompkins	L	7,765	13.1
					2,209	3.7
1966	73,593	79.8	E. Brooks	Lab	30,545	52.0
			R.E.G. Howe	C	28,208	48.0
					2,337	4.0
1970	82,101	75.3	E.P. Cockeram	C	31,260	50.6
			E. Brooks	Lab	30,535	49.4
					725	1.2

Election	Electors	T'out	Candidate	Party	Votes	%
1950	73,605	86.5	†P.G.T. Buchan-Hepburn	C	38,102	59.9
			A. Bain	Lab	18,723	29.4
			H.H. Monroe	L	6,834*	10.7
					19,379	30.5
1951	74,370	82.4	P.G.T. Buchan-Hepburn	C	41,282	67.4
			Dr. A.P. Magonet	Lab	19,982	32.6
					21,300	34.8
1955	73,177	76.5	Rt. Hon. P.G.T. Buchan-Hepburn	C	38,614	69.0
			C.F.A. Culling	Lab	17,377	31.0
					21,237	38.0

[Elevation to the Peerage—Lord Hailes]

Election	Electors	T'out	Candidate	Party	Votes	%
1957 (21/3)	72,786	64.7	P.C. Goodhart	C	29,621	62.9
			N.D. Sandelson	Lab	17,445	37.1
					12,176	25.8
1959	73,421	80.8	P.C. Goodhart	C	36,528	61.6
			H. Ferguson	Lab	13,395	22.6
			H.H. Monroe	L	9,365	15.8
					23,133	39.0
1964	72,692	77.4	P.C. Goodhart	C	30,070	53.5
			A.H. Macdonald	Lab	13,338	23.7
			H.H. Monroe	L	12,821	22.8
					16,732	29.8
1966	71,952	77.8	P.C. Goodhart	C	28,837	51.5
			J.D. Grant	Lab	14,972	26.8
			P.A. Golding	L	12,155	21.7
					13,865	24.7
1970	77,385	68.7	P.C. Goodhart	C	30,763	57.8
			I.G. Bing	Lab	13,031	24.5
			P.A. Golding	L	9,404	17.7
					17,732	33.3

Election	Electors	T'out	Candidate	Party	Votes	%
1950	63,429	88.7	E.R.G. Heath	C	25,854	46.0
			†E.A. Bramall	Lab	25,721	45.7
			Miss M.E. Hart	L	4,186*	7.4
			C.C. Job	Com	481*	0.9
					133	0.3
1951	64,343	87.8	E.R.G. Heath	C	29,069	51.5
			E.A. Bramall	Lab	27,430	48.5
					1,639	3.0
1955	63,863	82.6	E.R.G. Heath	C	28,610	54.3
			R.J. Minney	Lab	24,111	45.7
					4,499	8.6
1959	64,906	85.4	Rt. Hon. E.R.G. Heath	C	32,025	57.8
			E.A. Bramall	Lab	23,392	42.2
					8,633	15.6
1964	64,240	84.5	Rt. Hon. E.R.G. Heath	C	25,716	47.4
			L.L. Reeves	Lab	21,127	38.9
			P.L. McArthur	L	6,161*	11.4
			J.A. Paul	Ind	1,263*	2.3
					4,589	8.5
1966	63,886	85.8	Rt. Hon. E.R.G. Heath	C	26,377	48.1
			R.L. Butler	Lab	24,044	43.9
			R.F. Lloyd	L	4,405*	8.0
					2,333	4.2
1970	66,980	76.3	Rt. Hon. E.R.G. Heath	C	27,075	53.1
			J.C. Cartwright	Lab/Co-op	19,017	37.2
			E.P.G. Harrison	L	3,222*	6.3
			E.J.R.L. Heath	Ind C	938*	1.8
			M.P. Coney	Ind C	833*	1.6
					8,058	15.9

Notes:—

1964: Paul was founder and chairman of the Anti-Common Market League and was opposed to Britain entering the Common Market.

1970: E.J.R.L. Heath sought election as a 'Conservative and Consult the People' candidate. His original surname was Lambert but he added the name Heath by Deed Poll before being nominated.

Coney was opposed to Britain entering the Common Market.

BILSTON [59]

Election	Electors	T'out	Candidate	Party	Votes	%
1950	57,612	82.9	†W. Nally	Lab/Co-op	29,919	62.6
			J. Godrich	C	17,858	37.4
					12,061	25.2
1951	61,378	82.7	W. Nally	Lab/Co-op	31,381	61.9
			C. Gordon-Spencer	C	19,352	38.1
					12,029	23.8
1955	61,824*	74.4	R. Edwards	Lab	26,490	57.6
			Miss E.A. Marsh	C	19,482	42.4
					7,008	15.2
1959	65,861	76.8	R. Edwards	Lab/Co-op	27,068	53.5
			F.J. Oxford	C	23,523	46.5
					3,545	7.0
1964	71,005	74.2	R. Edwards	Lab/Co-op	27,986	53.1
			F.J. Oxford	C	24,686	46.9
					3,300	6.2
1966	71,482	73.2	R. Edwards	Lab/Co-op	29,794	56.9
			F.J. Oxford	C	22,541	43.1
					7,253	13.8
1970	77,029	69.4	R. Edwards	Lab/Co-op	27,240	50.9
			C.G. Irving	C	26,240	49.1
					1,000	1.8

BIRKENHEAD [60]

Election	Electors	T'out	Candidate	Party	Votes	%
1950	62,420	84.9	†P.H. Collick	Lab	26,472	49.9
			H.B.T. Cox	C	20,343	38.4
			D.R. Green	L	5,234*	9.9
			S. Coulthard	Com	971*	1.8
					6,129	11.5
1951	63,762	82.8	P.H. Collick	Lab	29,014	55.0
			M. Reney-Smith	C	23,765	45.0
					5,249	10.0
1955	60,587	75.7	P.H. Collick	Lab	24,526	53.5
			H.S. Oddie	C	21,352	46.5
					3,174	7.0
1959	59,960	78.4	P.H. Collick	Lab	22,990	48.9
			K.G. Routledge	C	19,361	41.2
			G.F. Bilson	L	4,658*	9.9
					3,629	7.7
1964	56,594	74.4	E.E. Dell	Lab	23,994	57.0
			R.K. Morland	C	18,133	43.0
					5,861	14.0
1966	55,225	72.8	E.E. Dell	Lab	24,188	60.1
			R.J. Adley	C	15,438	38.4
			A.B. Williams	Com	604*	1.5
					8,750	21.7
1970	58,460	70.8	Rt. Hon. E.E. Dell	Lab	20,980	50.7
			R. Kris	C	15,151	36.6
			D.T.G. Evans	L	4,926*	11.9
			A.B. Williams	Com	351*	0.8
					5,829	14.1

BIRMINGHAM, ALL SAINTS [61]

Election	Electors	T'out	Candidate	Party	Votes	%
1955	51,562	70.6	D.H. Howell	Lab	18,867	51.8
			F.J. Williams	C	17,560	48.2
					1,307	3.6
1959	48,611	70.9	J.H. Hollingworth	C	17,235	50.0
			D.H. Howell	Lab	17,215	50.0
					20	0.0
1964	44,594	66.1	A.B. Walden	Lab	14,975	50.8
			J.H. Hollingworth	C	14,505	49.2
					470	1.6
1966	42,896	65.1	A.B. Walden	Lab	16,350	58.5
			J.H. Hollingworth	C	11,595	41.5
					4,755	17.0
1970	36,290	60.8	A.B. Walden	Lab	12,041	54.5
			J.H. Hollingworth	C	7,762	35.2
			D.G. Minnis	L	2,271*	10.3
					4,279	19.3

Election	Electors	T'out	Candidate	Party	Votes	%
1950	60,628	78.4	†W.L. Wyatt	Lab	28,867	60.8
			C.J.A. Doughty	C	16,826	35.4
			A. Embrey	L	1,487*	3.1
			S.W. Keatley	Ind	338*	0.7
					12,041	25.4
1951	59,777	74.6	W.L. Wyatt	Lab	27,899	62.6
			C. Sweet	C	16,136	36.2
			S.W. Keatley	Ind	545*	1.2
					11,763	26.4
1955	59,889**	71.5	J. Silverman	Lab	25,546	59.6
			Miss F.M. Vale	C	17,284	40.4
					8,262	19.2
1959	57,593	70.3	J. Silverman	Lab	21,518	53.1
			A.M. Beaumont-Dark	C	18,984	46.9
					2,534	6.2
1964	54,544	65.4	J. Silverman	Lab	19,512	54.7
			A.M. Beaumont-Dark	C	16,146	45.3
					3,366	9.4
1966	52,975	64.2	J. Silverman	Lab	20,716	60.9
			J.R. Kinsey	C	13,316	39.1
					7,400	21.8
1970	47,648	58.9	J. Silverman	Lab	15,456	55.1
			A.A. Hill	C	11,894	42.4
			J.C.C. Jordan	BM	704*	2.5
					3,562	12.7

Election	Electors	T'out	Candidate	Party	Votes	%
1950	59,571	78.8	†Sir P.F.B. Bennett	C	29,404	62.7
			J.A. Hobson	Lab	17,512	37.3
					11,892	25.4
1951	60,278	76.1	Sir P.F.B. Bennett	C	29,477	64.3
			W.J.S. Pringle	Lab	16,373	35.7
					13,104	28.6

[Elevation to the Peerage—Lord Bennett of Edgbaston]

Election	Electors	T'out	Candidate	Party	Votes	%
1953 (2/7)	59,326	50.2	Miss E.M. Pitt	C	20,142	67.6
			F.B. Watson	Lab	9,635	32.4
					10,507	35.2
1955	58,469	68.2	Miss E.M. Pitt	C	26,991	67.7
			K.V. Russell	Lab	12,897	32.3
					14,094	35.4
1959	55,719	68.0	Miss E.M. Pitt	C	26,401	69.7
			Mrs. N.F. Hinks	Lab	11,473	30.3
					14,928	39.4
1964	50,966	66.5	Dame Edith Pitt	C	22,818	67.4
			A.J. Kazantzis	Lab	11,059	32.6
					11,759	34.8

[Seat Vacant at Dissolution (Death)]

Election	Electors	T'out	Candidate	Party	Votes	%
1966	51,654	67.8	Mrs. J.C.J. Knight	C	18,869	53.8
			E.O. Smith	Lab	11,335	32.4
			D.J. Badger	L	4,829	13.8
					7,534	21.4
1970	58,832	63.7	Mrs. J.C.J. Knight	C	23,690	63,3
			E.J. Sever	Lab	13,047	34.8
			Miss D.C. Howlett	Ind	725*	1.9
					10,643	28.5

Note:—

1970: Miss Howlett sought election as an 'Independent for Jesus and His Cross' candidate. She was opposed to any reduction in religious education in schools.

BIRMINGHAM, ERDINGTON [64]

Election	Electors	T'out	Candidate	Party	Votes	%
1950	67,755	83.4	†J. Silverman	Lab	29,252	51.8
			J.A.C. Wright	C	23,842	42.2
			S.A. Fitzgerald	L	3,408*	6.0
					5,410	9.6
1951	67,425	82.6	J. Silverman	Lab	29,561	53.1
			D.H. Broome	C	26,153	46.9
					3,408	6.2

This constituency was divided in 1955.

BIRMINGHAM, HALL GREEN [65]

Election	Electors	T'out	Candidate	Party	Votes	%
1950	58,189	83.8	A. Jones	C	24,444	50.2
			T. Crehan	Lab	20,591	42.2
			G.L. Roy	L	3,703*	7.6
					3,853	8.0
1951	58,077	82.9	A. Jones	C	27,289	56.7
			T. Crehan	Lab	20,874	43.3
					6,415	13.4
1955	61,640**	75.3	A. Jones	C	28,543	61.5
			W.J.S. Pringle	Lab	17,846	38.5
					10,697	23.0
1959	61,066	76.2	Rt. Hon. A. Jones	C	29,148	62.6
			D.H.V. Fereday	Lab	15,431	33.2
			H.W. Maynard	Ind C	1,955*	4.2
					13,717	29.4
1964	59,984	75.8	Rt. Hon. A. Jones	C	23,879	52.6
			G.S. Rea	Lab	14,477	31.8
			Mrs. P. Jessel	L	7,113	15.6
					9,402	20.8

[Resignation on appointment as Chairman of the National Board for Prices and Incomes]

Election	Electors	T'out	Candidate	Party	Votes	%
1965 (6/5)	59,647	52.4	R.E. Eyre	C	17,130	54.8
			D. Mumford	Lab	8,980	28.8
			Mrs. P. Jessel	L	5,122	16.4
					8,150	26.0
1966	59,131	73.6	R.E. Eyre	C	20,628	47.4
			G.S. Jonas	Lab	17,295	39.7
			J. Green	L	5,617	12.9
					3,333	7.7
1970	66,748	67.8	R.E. Eyre	C	27,319	60.4
			T.L. Keene	Lab	17,930	39.6
					9,389	20.8

Note:—

1959: Maynard was opposed to the provisions of the Landlord and Tenant Act, 1954.

Election	Electors	T'out	Candidate	Party	Votes	%
1950	57,668	83.1	†H. Roberts	C	24,246	50.5
			C.R. Bence	Lab	18,774	39.2
			R.W. Eades	L	4,926*	10.3
					5,472	11.3
[Death]						
1950	57,549	63.2	Sir E.C.G. Boyle, Bt.	C	22,083	60.7
(16/11)			C.R. Bence	Lab	13,852	38.1
			S.W. Keatley	Ind	453*	1.2
					8,231	22.6
1951	57,830	79.0	Sir E.C.G. Boyle, Bt.	C	27,201	59.5
			R.W. Evely	Lab	18,494	40.5
					8,707	19.0
1955	58,322**	69.5	Sir E.C.G. Boyle, Bt.	C	24,349	60.0
			A. Murie	Lab	14,064	34.7
			S.W. Keatley	Ind	2,148*	5.3
					10,285	25.3
1959	55,596	68.8	Sir E.C.G. Boyle, Bt.	C	23,243	60.8
			A. Murie	Lab	13,116	34.3
			S.W. Keatley	Ind	1,867*	4.9
					10,127	26.5
1964	53,243	66.6	Rt. Hon. Sir E.C.G. Boyle, Bt.	C	16,841	47.5
			Miss S.R.R. Wright	Lab	11,909	33.6
			W.L. Lawler	L	6,249	17.6
			S.W. Keatley	Ind	459*	1.3
					4,932	13.9
1966	51,383	63.2	Rt. Hon. Sir E.C.G. Boyle, Bt.	C	16,225	49.9
			Miss S.R.R. Wright	Lab	14,931	46.0
			E.J. Hamm	UM	1,337*	4.1
					1,294	3.9
1970	46,612	65.3	S.B. Chapman	C	16,122	53.0
			Miss S.R.R. Wright	Lab	14,310	47.0
					1,812	6.0

Election	Electors	T'out	Candidate	Party	Votes	%
1950	64,047	84.3	Rt. Hon. G.W. Lloyd	C	27,308	50.6
			A.F. Bradbeer	Lab	21,715	40.2
			M.E. Beesley	L	4,940*	9.2
					5,593	10.4
1951	64,661	81.6	Rt. Hon. G.W. Lloyd	C	30,456	57.7
			D.H. Howell	Lab	22,325	42.3
					8,131	15.4

This constituency was divided in 1955.

Election	Electors	T'out	Candidate	Party	Votes	%
1950	51,847	80.4	†V.F. Yates	Lab	25,603	61.4
			F.M. Bennett	C	16,071	38.6
					9,532	22.8
1951	52,223	77.2	V.F. Yates	Lab (Ind Lab) (Lab)	24,008	59.5
			L.G. Seymour	C	16,331	40.5
					7,677	19.0
1955	46,904**	60.0	V.F. Yates	Lab	18,476	65.7
			P.W. Hodgens	C	9,665	34.3
					8,811	31.4
1959	39,131	59.1	V.F. Yates	Lab	14,717	63.7
			T.G. John	C	8,393	36.3
					6,324	27.4
1964	29,735	53.7	V.F. Yates	Lab	10,098	63.2
			T.G. John	C	5,879	36.8
					4,219	26.4
1966	25,294	59.7	V.F. Yates	Lab	8,895	58.9
			W.L. Lawler	L	3,580	23.7
			T.G. John	C	2,621	17.4
					5,315	35.2
[Death]						
1969 (26/6)	18,095	51.9	W.L. Lawler	L	5,104	54.3
			Mrs. D.M.G. Fisher	Lab	2,391	25.5
			Dr. L. Glass	C	1,580	16.8
			J.C.C. Jordan	BM	282*	3.0
			A.J.W. Haigh	FP	34*	0.4
					2,713	28.8
1970	18,729	62.3	Mrs. D.M.G. Fisher	Lab	5,067	43.4
			W.L. Lawler	L	4,087	35.0
			C.L. Wade	C	2,523	21.6
					980	8.4

Election	Electors	T'out	Candidate	Party	Votes	%
1950	59,560	84.7	†A.R. Blackburn	Lab (Ind)	26,714	53.0
			T.L.I.S.V. Iremonger	C	19,974	39.6
			E.L.F. Richards	L	3,280*	6.5
			R.A. Etheridge	Com	479*	0.9
					6,740	13.4
1951	60,363	83.3	W.D. Chapman	Lab	26,580	52.8
			M. Chandler	C	23,730	47.2
					2,850	5.6
1955	65,219**	78.6	W.D. Chapman	Lab	27,072	52.8
			C. Sweet	C	24,188	47.2
					2,884	5.6
1959	74,269	78.4	W.D. Chapman	Lab	29,587	50.8
			R.E. Eyre	C	28,647	49.2
					940	1.6
1964	80,377	77.2	W.D. Chapman	Lab	29,301	47.2
			H.B. Adkins	C	25,063	40.4
			R.S. Lewthwaite	L	7,682*	12.4
					4,238	6.8
1966	83,522	75.1	W.D. Chapman	Lab	36,801	58.7
			C.C.H. Chalker	C	24,899	39.7
			D.W. Robinson	Com	1,029*	1.6
					11,902	19.0
1970	96,614	68.4	R.J. Carter	Lab	33,364	50.5
			D.W. Bell	C	32,148	48.6
			D.W. Robinson	Com	605*	0.9
					1,216	1.9

Election	Electors	T'out	Candidate	Party	Votes	%
1950	49,312	83.0	†C.C. Poole	Lab	23,178	56.6
			Sir E.C.G. Boyle, Bt.	C	15,172	37.1
			Mrs. N.F. Hinks	L	2,581*	6.3
					8,006	19.5
1951	49,548	81.1	C.C. Poole	Lab	23,322	58.0
			Mrs. S.A. Ward	C	16,855	42.0
					6,467	16.0
1955	50,500	72.7	C.A. Howell	Lab	18,732	51.1
			F.B. Hingston	C	17,052	46.4
			H. Pearce	Com	928*	2.5
					1,680	4.7
1959	50,306	78.5	C.A. Howell	Lab	16,811	42.6
			S.C. Greatrix	C	16,628	42.1
			W.L. Lawler	L	5,611	14.2
			H. Pearce	Com	424*	1.1
					183	0.5
1964	49,454	74.1	Dr. W.R. Davies	C	18,483	50.4
			C.A. Howell	Lab	18,156	49.6
					327	0.8
1966	48,261	76.2	C. Price	Lab	20,222	55.0
			Dr. W.R. Davies	C	16,557	45.0
					3,665	10.0
1970	49,406	70.6	J.R. Kinsey	C	18,083	51.8
			C. Price	Lab	16,817	48.2
					1,266	3.6

Election	Electors	T'out	Candidate	Party	Votes	%
1955	60,356	74.3	H.E. Gurden	C	25,774	57.5
			H. Watton	Lab	19,054	42.5
					6,720	15.0
1959	58,017	71.6	H.E. Gurden	C	24,950	60.1
			J.O. Rhydderch	Lab	16,594	39.9
					8,356	20.2
1964	56,798	66.3	H.E. Gurden	C	21,443	56.9
			J. Garwell	Lab	16,232	43.1
					5,211	13.8
1966	55,187	66.4	H.E. Gurden	C	16,533	45.2
			J. Garwell	Lab	15,756	43.0
			R.S. Lewthwaite	L	4,333*	11.8
					777	2.2
1970	54,619	64.2	H.E. Gurden	C	18,281	52.2
			M.J. Hartley-Brewer	Lab	16,758	47.8
					1,523	4.4

Election	Electors	T'out	Candidate	Party	Votes	%
1950	64,233	79.3	†F. Longden	Lab/Co-op	31,985	62.8
			J. Pagett	C	15,556	30.6
			F.G. Smith	L	3,365*	6.6
					16,429	32.2
1951	63,504	77.2	F. Longden	Lab/Co-op	31,079	63.4
			F. Irwin	C	15,156	30.9
			F.G. Smith	L	2,779*	5.7
					15,923	32.5
[Death]						
1952 (27/11)	62,459	46.6	W.E. Wheeldon	Lab/Co-op	19,491	67.0
			Miss E.M. Pitt	C	9,614	33.0
					9,877	34.0
1955	56,101**	65.8	W.E. Wheeldon	Lab/Co-op	22,444	60.8
			J.W. Bissell	C	14,484	39.2
					7,960	21.6
1959	51,004	65.7	W.E. Wheeldon	Lab/Co-op	19,213	57.4
			B.C. Owens	C	14,282	42.6
					4,931	14.8
[Death]						
1961 (23/3)	48,318	42.6	D.H. Howell	Lab	12,182	59.2
			B.C. Owens	C	5,923	28.8
			W. Kirk	L	2,476*	12.0
					6,259	30.4
1964	46,268	60.9	D.H. Howell	Lab	17,010	60.4
			A.J. Prescott	C	10,233	36.3
			G. Jelf	Com	926*	3.3
					6,777	24.1
1966	43,686	59.6	D.H. Howell	Lab	18,075	69.5
			F.H.G.H. Goodhart	C	7,471	28.7
			G. Jelf	Com	477*	1.8
					10,604	40.8
1970	38,979	57.9	D.H. Howell	Lab	13,794	61.1
			N.W. Budgen	C	6,923	30.6
			G.H. Herringshaw	L	1,754*	7.8
			S. Zafar	BCP	117*	0.5
					6,871	30.5

Election	Electors	T'out	Candidate	Party	Votes	%
1950	52,287	77.6	†P.L.E. Shurmer	Lab	24,942	61.5
			P.K. Debenham	C	15,267	37.6
			J.W. Crump	Com	355*	0.9
					9,675	23.9
1951	51,607	76.4	P.L.E. Shurmer	Lab	24,184	61.3
			R.T.H. Lonsdale	C	15,248	38.7
					8,936	22.6
1955	51,057**	72.2	P.L.E. Shurmer	Lab	20,032	54.4
			P.G. Hartley	C	16,821	45.6
					3,211	8.8

[Seat Vacant at Dissolution (Death)]

Election	Electors	T'out	Candidate	Party	Votes	%
1959	47,731	72.5	L.G. Seymour	C	17,751	51.3
			J.T. Webster	Lab	16,865	48.7
					886	2.6
1964	45,877	68.3	R.S.G. Hattersley	Lab	16,287	52.0
			L.G. Seymour	C	15,033	48.0
					1,254	4.0
1966	45,148	66.7	R.S.G. Hattersley	Lab	18,266	60.6
			L.G. Seymour	C	11,868	39.4
					6,398	21.2
1970	43,181	64.9	R.S.G. Hattersley	Lab	14,773	52.7
			A.E.J. Mitton	C	11,427	40.8
			Dr. J.A. Crofton	L	1,813*	6.5
					3,346	11.9

Election	Electors	T'out	Candidate	Party	Votes	%
1950	67,847	83.4	†R.H. Jenkins	Lab	33,077	58.5
			Miss E.M. Pitt	C	20,699	36.6
			S.W. Haslam	L	2,789*	4.9
					12,378	21.9
1951	70,951	81.4	R.H. Jenkins	Lab	34,355	59.5
			Miss E.M. Pitt	C	23,384	40.5
					10,971	19.0
1955	55,004**	72.7	R.H. Jenkins	Lab	23,358	58.4
			J.M. Bailey	C	16,618	41.6
					6,740	16.8
1959	55,674	73.5	R.H. Jenkins	Lab	21,919	53.6
			J.M. Bailey	C	18,996	46.4
					2,923	7.2
1964	55,541	71.0	R.H. Jenkins	Lab	22,421	56.8
			D.L. Knox	C	17,033	43.2
					5,388	13.6
1966	54,505	70.3	Rt. Hon. R.H. Jenkins	Lab	24,598	64.2
			D.L. Knox	C	12,727	33.2
			W.A.J. Dunn	Com	998*	2.6
					11,871	31.0
1970	62,855	63.9	Rt. Hon. R.H. Jenkins	Lab	22,559	56.2
			J.B. Stevens	C	15,848	39.5
			D. Hardy	N Dem P	1,438*	3.6
			S.C. Pegg	Com	298*	0.7
					6,711	16.7

BIRMINGHAM, YARDLEY [75]

Election	Electors	T'out	Candidate	Party	Votes	%
1950	51,792	84.3	†H.C. Usborne	Lab	22,342	51.2
			G.R. Matthews	C	18,431	42.2
			A.S. Ritchie	L	2,553*	5.8
			J. Falconer	Com	347*	0.8
					3,911	9.0
1951	51,994	82.5	H.C. Usborne	Lab	22,800	53.1
			A.E. Shaw	C	20,099	46.9
					2,701	6.2
1955	59,078**	75.0	H.C. Usborne	Lab	23,722	53.5
			P.W. Holland	C	20,598	46.5
					3,124	7.0
1959	59,135	77.1	L.H. Cleaver	C	23,482	51.5
			H.C. Usborne	Lab	22,097	48.5
					1,385	3.0
1964	58,934	77.0	I.L. Evans	Lab/Co-op	22,788	50.2
			L.H. Cleaver	C	22,619	49.8
					169	0.4
1966	58,458	77.6	I.L. Evans	Lab/Co-op	25,568	56.3
			L.H. Cleaver	C	19,809	43.7
					5,759	12.6
1970	62,435	69.7	D.M. Coombs	C	21,827	50.1
			I.L. Evans	Lab/Co-op	21,707	49.9
					120	0.2

BLACKBURN [76]

Election	Electors	T'out	Candidate	Party	Votes	%
1955	62,548	83.1	Mrs. B.A. Castle	Lab	26,241	50.5
			T. Marsden	C	25,752	49.5
					489	1.0
1959	60,362	85.9	Mrs. B.A. Castle	Lab	27,356	52.8
			J.M.A. Yerburgh	C	24,490	47.2
					2,866	5.6
1964	57,034	81.0	Mrs. B.A. Castle	Lab	26,543	57.5
			J.M.A. Yerburgh	C	19,650	42.5
					6,893	15.0
1966	54,911	79.2	Rt. Hon. Barbara A. Castle	Lab	25,381	58.3
			T. Marsden	C	18,133	41.7
					7,248	16.6
1970	55,811	75.6	Rt. Hon. Barbara A. Castle	Lab	22,473	53.2
			Mrs. R.T. Gardner	C	19,737	46.8
					2,736	6.4

BLACKBURN, EAST [77]

Election	Electors	T'out	Candidate	Party	Votes	%
1950	41,377	89.1	†Mrs. B.A. Castle	Lab	19,480	52.8
			J.A. Leavey	C	14,662	39.8
			H. Hague	L	2,743*	7.4
					4,818	13.0
1951	41,310	88.8	Mrs. B.A. Castle	Lab	19,661	53.6
			J.A. Leavey	C	17,029	46.4
					2,632	7.2

This constituency was incorporated into Blackburn in 1955.

Election	Electors	T'out	Candidate	Party	Votes	%
1950	41,068	89.6	†Rt. Hon. R. Assheton	C	19,329	52.6
			†L.J. Edwards	Lab	17,450	47.4
					1,879	5.2
1951	41,285	88.9	Rt. Hon. R. Assheton	C	19,695	53.7
			R.W. Casasola	Lab	16,994	46.3
					2,701	7.4

This constituency was divided in 1955.

Election	Electors	T'out	Candidate	Party	Votes	%
1950	59,117	79.4	†T.A.R.W. Low	C	31,655	67.4
			Mrs. E.B. Muir	Lab	15,308	32.6
					16,347	34.8
1951	58,271	73.2	T.A.R.W. Low	C	29,956	70.2
			S.V. Hyde-Price	Lab	12,727	29.8
					17,229	40.4
1955	56,648	66.7	Rt. Hon. T.A.R.W. Low	C	26,899	71.2
			R. Bushby	Lab	10,869	28.8
					16,030	42.4
1959	58,421*	74.8	Rt. Hon. Sir T.A.R.W. Low	C	25,297	57.8
			W.H. Dugdale	Lab	9,440	21.6
			H. Hague	L	8,990	20.6
					15,857	36.2

[Elevation to the Peerage—Lord Aldington]

Election	Electors	T'out	Candidate	Party	Votes	%
1962 (13/3)	60,242	55.2	N.A. Miscampbell	C	12,711	38.3
			H. Hague	L	11,738	35.3
			Dr. Hon. Shirley C.W. Summerskill	Lab	8,776	26.4
					973	3.0
1964	55,729*	74.7	N.A. Miscampbell	C	19,633	47.2
			H. Hague	L	11,462	27.5
			T. McKellar	Lab	10,543	25.3
					8,171	19.7
1966	55,854	72.9	N.A. Miscampbell	C	19,173	47.1
			G.E. Bingham	Lab	13,863	34.0
			J.H. Hessey	L	7,699	18.9
					5,310	13.1
1970	58,865	68.5	N.A. Miscampbell	C	22,298	55.3
			W. Callon	Lab	13,062	32.4
			B.M. Christon	L	4,946*	12.3
					9,236	22.9

Election	Electors	T'out	Candidate	Party	Votes	%
1950	56,380	82.1	†J.R. Robinson	C	26,800	57.9
			E.A. Machin	Lab	14,190	30.7
			M.H. Woodward	L	5,295*	11.4
					12,610	27.2
1951	55,910	75.0	J.R. Robinson	C	28,171	67.2
			K. Lomas	Lab	13,750	32.8
					14,421	34.4
1955	55,100	67.7	Sir J.R. Robinson	C	24,773	66.4
			A. Davidson	Lab	12,548	33.6
					12,225	32.8
1959	52,927	73.9	Sir J.R. Robinson	C	25,767	65.9
			P.P. Hall	Lab	13,337	34.1
					12,430	31.8

[Seat Vacant at Dissolution (Resignation on appointment as Governor of Bermuda and elevation to the Peerage—Lord Martonmere)]

Election	Electors	T'out	Candidate	Party	Votes	%
1964	57,343*	71.1	P.A.R. Blaker	C	23,769	58.3
			P.P. Hall	Lab	16,986	41.7
					6,783	16.6
1966	56,351	70.5	P.A.R. Blaker	C	21,564	54.3
			E.R. Pearce	Lab	18,166	45.7
					3,398	8.6
1970	58,937	68.3	P.A.R. Blaker	C	21,273	52.9
			P.P. Hall	Lab	13,267	32.9
			D. Chadwick	L	5,730	14.2
					8,006	20.0

Election	Electors	T'out	Candidate	Party	Votes	%
1950	61,984	87.0	†A. Robens	Lab	40,235	74.6
			L.J. Amos	C	13,665	25.4
					26,570	49.2
1951	62,615	86.3	Rt. Hon. A. Robens	Lab	39,823	73.7
			G. Peters	C	14,184	26.3
					25,639	47.4
1955	62,235	80.3	Rt. Hon. A. Robens	Lab	36,522	73.1
			Hon. N. Ridley	C	13,429	26.9
					23,093	46.2
1959	62,599	82.6	Rt. Hon. A. Robens	Lab	38,616	74.6
			D.M. Walters	C	13,122	25.4
					25,494	49.2

[Resignation on appointment as Deputy Chairman of the National Coal Board]

Election	Electors	T'out	Candidate	Party	Votes	%
1960	62,853	54.1	E.J. Milne	Lab	23,438	68.9
(24/11)			D.M. Walters	C	7,366	21.6
			C. Pym	Ind	3,223*	9.5
					16,072	47.3
1964	62,805	78.3	E.J. Milne	Lab	37,336	75.9
			G.P. Davidson	C	11,832	24.1
					25,504	51.8
1966	62,767	74.4	E.J. Milne	Lab	36,493	78.2
			W.J. Prime	C	10,179	21.8
					26,314	56.4
1970	67,911	71.7	E.J. Milne	Lab	36,118	74.2
			A.J. Blackburn	C	12,550	25.8
					23,568	48.4

Note:—

1960: Pym was quoted in the local press as saying that he "liked to think of himself as an Independent Liberal". He claimed that he would not have sought election if the Liberal Party had contested the seat.

BOLTON, EAST [82]

Election	Electors	T'out	Candidate	Party	Votes	%
1950	62,514	87.3	A. Booth	Lab	24,826	45.5
			P.I. Bell	C	21,117	38.7
			A.F. Holt	L	8,647	15.8
					3,709	6.8
1951	63,546	84.8	P.I. Bell	C	27,106	50.3
			A. Booth	Lab	26,751	49.7
					355	0.6
1955	61,601	79.2	P.I. Bell	C	26,145	53.6
			A. Booth	Lab	22,634	46.4
					3,511	7.2
1959	60,580	80.9	P.I. Bell	C	25,885	52.8
			R. Haines	Lab	23,153	47.2
					2,732	5.6

[Resignation on appointment as a County Court Judge]

Election	Electors	T'out	Candidate	Party	Votes	%
1960 (16/11)	60,163	68.2	E. Taylor	C	15,499	37.8
			R.L. Howarth	Lab	14,858	36.2
			C.F. Byers	L	10,173	24.8
			J.E. Dayton	NCP	493*	1.2
					641	1.6
1964	59,227	80.4	R.L. Howarth	Lab	21,937	46.1
			E. Taylor	C	18,785	39.5
			A. Cooper	L	6,873	14.4
					3,152	6.6
1966	58,401	77.0	R.L. Howarth	Lab	26,613	59.2
			E. Taylor	C	18,331	40.8
					8,282	18.4
1970	61,243	73.6	L.D. Reed	C	22,769	50.5
			R.L. Howarth	Lab	22,298	49.5
					471	1.0

Election	Electors	T'out	Candidate	Party	Votes	%
1950	59,476	87.5	†J. Lewis	Lab	23,232	44.6
			W.W. Tong	C	18,184	34.9
			A.L. Tillotson	L	10,653	20.5
					5,048	9.7
1951	58,725	84.8	A.F. Holt	L	26,271	52.8
			J. Lewis	Lab	23,523	47.2
					2,748	5.6
1955	56,724	79.1	A.F. Holt	L	24,827	55.4
			J. Haworth	Lab	20,014	44.6
					4,813	10.8
1959	54,035	79.7	A.F. Holt	L	23,533	54.6
			P.B. Cameron	Lab	19,545	45.4
					3,988	9.2
1964	51,306	78.2	G.J. Oakes	Lab	16,519	41.2
			D. Sisson	C	13,522	33.7
			A.F. Holt	L	10,086	25.1
					2,997	7.5
1966	48,980	78.3	G.J. Oakes	Lab	19,390	50.6
			C.B.S. Dobson	C	14,473	37.7
			R. Glenton	L	4,483*	11.7
					4,917	12.9
1970	50,254	74.0	R.S. Redmond	C	19,225	51.7
			G.J. Oakes	Lab	17,981	48.3
					1,244	3.4

BOOTLE [84]

Election	Electors	T'out	Candidate	Party	Votes	%
1950	58,723	82.1	†J. Kinley	Lab	25,472	52.8
			W. Hill	C	21,673	44.9
			B. McGinnity	AP	1,092*	2.3
					3,799	7.9
1951	62,151*	81.2	J. Kinley	Lab	26,597	52.7
			A.O. Hughes	C	22,535	44.6
			H.J. McHugh	AP	1,340*	2.7
					4,062	8.1
1955	48,381**	75.7	S. Mahon	Lab	19,020	52.0
			H.W. Jones	C	17,582	48.0
					1,438	4.0
1959	50,647	78.3	S. Mahon	Lab	21,294	53.7
			H.O. Cullen	C	18,379	46.3
					2,915	7.4
1964	49,284	70.9	S. Mahon	Lab	21,677	62.0
			G. Halliwell	C	13,285	38.0
					8,392	24.0
1966	47,130	68.2	S. Mahon	Lab	19,412	60.4
			G. Halliwell	C	10,813	33.6
			W.P. Grant	Ind Lab	1,931*	6.0
					8,599	26.8
1970	48,415	65.3	S. Mahon	Lab	20,110	63.6
			G. Halliwell	C	11,496	36.4
					8,614	27.2

Election	Electors	T'out	Candidate	Party	Votes	%
1950	55,378	85.0	†Rt. Hon. B. Bracken	C	27,677	58.8
			Miss D. Lees	Lab	12,790	27.2
			J.C. Holland	L	6,594	14.0
					14,887	31.6
1951	56,936	80.8	Rt. Hon. B. Bracken	C	29,138	63.3
			H.J. Barnes	Lab	11,550	25.1
			J.C. Holland	L	5,338*	11.6
					17,588	38.2

[Elevation to the Peerage—Viscount Bracken]

Election	Electors	T'out	Candidate	Party	Votes	%
1952 (6/2)	56,936	63.8	N. Nicolson	C	22,480	61.8
			R.D. Rees	Lab	8,498	23.4
			J.C. Holland	L	3,673*	10.1
			S. Kermode	Ind	1,693*	4.7
					13,982	38.4
1955	58,092	75.5	N. Nicolson	C	28,757	65.5
			D.J. Buckle	Lab	10,259	23.4
			B.P. Molony	L	4,851*	11.1
					18,498	42.1
1959	60,657	76.7	J.H. Cordle	C	29,014	62.4
			J.D. Rutland	Lab	9,222	19.8
			W.J. Wareham	L	8,308	17.8
					19,792	42.6
1964	63,750*	74.7	J.H. Cordle	C	26,852	56.5
			A.G. Reynard	Lab	10,447	21.9
			Dr. A.C. McLeish	L	10,304	21.6
					16,405	34.6
1966	64,706	74.7	J.H. Cordle	C	27,047	55.9
			C.S. Sabel	Lab	12,598	26.1
			Dr. A.C. McLeish	L	8,698	18.0
					14,449	29.8
1970	70,370	70.9	J.H. Cordle	C	31,104	62.4
			T.C. Bisson	Lab	10,594	21.2
			G.H. Musgrave	L	8,177	16.4
					20,510	41.2

BOURNEMOUTH, WEST [86]

Election	Electors	T'out	Candidate	Party	Votes	%
1950	63,460	83.9	Viscount Cranborne	C	28,548	53.6
			W.A. Boddy	Lab	15,476	29.1
			J. Creasey	L	9,216	17.3
					13,072	24.5
1951	65,369	77.7	Viscount Cranborne	C	33,269	65.5
			Mrs. J.C.M. Hart	Lab	17,532	34.5
					15,737	31.0
[Resignation]						
1954 (18/2)	65,804	45.1	J.B. Eden	C	20,695	69.7
			H. Brinton	Lab	9,006	30.3
					11,689	39.4
1955	65,651	71.7	J.B. Eden	C	31,931	67.8
			C.H. Ford	Lab	15,147	32.2
					16,784	35.6
1959	68,209	72.6	J.B. Eden	C	33,575	67.8
			G.W. Spicer	Lab	15,957	32.2
					17,618	35.6
1964	70,238	73.7	Sir J.B. Eden, Bt.	C	26,114	50.4
			G.W. Spicer	Lab	13,975	27.0
			J.F. Mills	L	11,681	22.6
					12,139	23.4
1966	70,141	73.4	Sir J.B. Eden, Bt.	C	25,740	50.1
			L.F. Bennett	Lab	16,334	31.7
			J.F. Mills	L	9,389	18.2
					9,406	18.4
1970	73,672	69.4	Sir J.B. Eden, Bt.	C	28,714	56.2
			L.F. Bennett	Lab	14,099	27.6
			J.F. Mills	L	8,303	16.2
					14,615	28.6

Election	Electors	T'out	Candidate	Party	Votes	%
1950	49,935	84.6	†M. Webb	Lab	24,822	58.8
			T. Boyce	NL & C	13,375	31.6
			C.F. Sarsby	L	4,063*	9.6
					11,447	27.2
1951	49,625	83.7	Rt. Hon. M. Webb	Lab	25,215	60.7
			A. Tiley	NL & C	16,343	39.3
					8,872	21.4

This constituency was divided in 1955.

BRADFORD, EAST [88]

Election	Electors	T'out	Candidate	Party	Votes	%
1950	54,730	84.7	†F. McLeavy	Lab	27,694	59.8
			G.F. Greenbank	NL & C	12,527	27.0
			J.S. Snowden	L	5,565*	12.0
			H.G. Green	Com	543*	1.2
					15,167	32.8
1951	54,335	84.3	F. McLeavy	Lab	28,796	62.9
			F.W.H. Cook	NL & C	16,999	37.1
					11,797	25.8
1955	51,453**	74.4	F. McLeavy	Lab	23,588	61.6
			G.C. Barber	NL & C	14,713	38.4
					8,875	23.2
1959	47,514	72.8	F. McLeavy	Lab	20,056	58.0
			D.A. Dalgleish	NL & C	14,529	42.0
					5,527	16.0
1964	43,216	67.2	F. McLeavy	Lab	17,945	61.8
			D.T. Lewis	NL & C	11,075	38.2
					6,870	23.6
1966	40,731	65.1	E. Lyons	Lab	18,435	69.5
			H.A. Sissling	NL & C	8,091	30.5
					10,344	39.0
1970	40,485	64.7	E. Lyons	Lab	17,346	66.2
			C.J. Barr	C	8,208	31.3
			G.M. Musa	L	660*	2.5
					9,138	34.9

Election	Electors	T'out	Candidate	Party	Votes	%
1950	51,462	87.7	W.J. Taylor	NL & C	20,628	45.7
			†Mrs. M.E. Nichol	Lab	18,517	41.0
			J. Kitching	L	5,985	13.3
					2,111	4.7
1951	51,836	87.1	W.J. Taylor	NL & C	24,524	54.3
			E.J. Parris	Lab	20,647	45.7
					3,877	8.6
1955	51,472**	81.8	W.J. Taylor	NL & C	21,084	50.1
			Rt. Hon. M. Webb	Lab	21,015	49.9
					69	0.2
1959	51,957*	82.8	W.J. Taylor	NL & C	22,850	53.1
			J. Marshall	Lab	20,179	46.9
					2,671	6.2
1964	51,062	80.4	B.T. Ford	Lab	17,905	43.6
			Sir W.J. Taylor, Bt.	NL & C	16,507	40.2
			E. Robinson	L	6,642	16.2
					1,398	3.4
1966	50,512	77.7	B.T. Ford	Lab	21,727	55.3
			W.H.P. Laycock	C	17,528	44.7
					4,199	10.6
1970	52,290	73.9	B.T. Ford	Lab	20,141	52.1
			W.H.P. Laycock	C	18,511	47.9
					1,630	4.2

Election	Electors	T'out	Candidate	Party	Votes	%
1950	52,135	86.2	†G. Craddock	Lab	21,344	47.5
			J.L. Windle	NL & C	15,998	35.6
			E. Rushworth	L	7,594	16.9
					5,346	11.9
1951	52,544	86.2	G. Craddock	Lab (Ind Lab) (Lab)	21,364	47.2
			G.F. Greenbank	NL & C	17,863	39.4
			E. Rushworth	L	6,072	13.4
					3,501	7.8
1955	53,849**	80.4	G. Craddock	Lab	20,478	47.4
			R.W. Jones	NL & C	16,768	38.7
			A.T. Ellis	L	6,029	13.9
					3,710	8.7
1959	57,018	81.0	G. Craddock	Lab	21,172	45.9
			R.W. Jones	NL & C	18,158	39.3
			H. Womersley	L	6,850	14.8
					3,014	6.6
1964	57,768	78.6	G. Craddock	Lab	21,004	46.2
			J.D.W. Bottomley	NL & C	17,097	37.7
			A. Clegg	L	7,286	16.1
					3,907	8.5
1966	57,456	76.0	G. Craddock	Lab	22,932	52.5
			J.D.W. Bottomley	NL & C	15,435	35.4
			G. Dunkerley	L	5,291*	12.1
					7,497	17.1
1970	63,382	72.1	T.W. Torney	Lab	20,985	45.9
			J.D.W. Bottomley	C	19,009	41.6
			G. Dunkerley	L	5,694*	12.5
					1,976	4.3

BRADFORD, WEST [91]

Election	Electors	T'out	Candidate	Party	Votes	%
1955	50,726	81.7	A. Tiley	NL & C	22,306	53.8
			Mrs. M. Ferguson	Lab/Co-op	19,147	46.2
					3,159	7.6
1959	50,044	81.8	A. Tiley	NL & C	23,012	56.2
			S. Hyam	Lab	17,906	43.8
					5,106	12.4
1964	50,912	76.8	A. Tiley	NL & C	21,121	54.0
			C.N. Haseldine	Lab/Co-op	17,974	46.0
					3,147	8.0
1966	49,440	76.6	C.N. Haseldine	Lab/Co-op	19,704	52.0
			A. Tiley	NL & C	18,170	48.0
					1,534	4.0
1970	53,332	73.9	J.A.D. Wilkinson	C	20,475	52.0
			C.N. Haseldine	Lab/Co-op	18,936	48.0
					1,539	4.0

Election	Electors	T'out	Candidate	Party	Votes	%
1950	43,854	87.7	P.B. Lucas	C	18,408	47.9
			†F.E. Noel-Baker	Lab	17,551	45.7
			D.F. Horne	L	2,086*	5.4
			J.H. Parker	Com	401*	1.0
					857	2.2
1951	43,755	86.2	P.B. Lucas	C	19,612	52.0
			I.L. Lewis	Lab	18,102	48.0
					1,510	4.0
1955	42,528	82.0	P.B. Lucas	C	18,489	53.0
			A.W. Filson	Lab	16,384	47.0
					2,105	6.0
1959	39,881	82.3	D.G. Smith	C	17,869	54.4
			Dr. H.B.O. Cardew	Lab	14,950	45.6
					2,919	8.8
1964	38,467	79.1	D.G. Smith	C	14,019	46.0
			D.W. Chalkley	Lab	13,475	44.3
			M.D. Jones	L	2,951*	9.7
					544	1.7
1966	37,454	82.1	M.C.J. Barnes	Lab	14,638	47.6
			D.G. Smith	C	14,031	45.7
			G.R. King	L	2,063*	6.7
					607	1.9
1970	37,691	73.2	M.C.J. Barnes	Lab	14,051	50.9
			O.C. Wright	C	13,538	49.1
					513	1.8

Election	Electors	T'out	Candidate	Party	Votes	%
1950	55,709	88.0	†F.A. Cobb	Lab	25,588	52.2
			W.E. Woolley	NL & C	23,456	47.8
					2,132	4.4
[Death]						
1950 (4/5)	55,729	85.4	L.J. Edwards	Lab	24,004	50.5
			W.E. Woolley	NL & C	23,567	49.5
					437	1.0
1951	56,300	88.7	L.J. Edwards	Lab	26,105	52.3
			W.E. Woolley	NL & C	23,828	47.7
					2,277	4.6
1955	54,616**	83.7	Rt. Hon. L.J. Edwards	Lab	23,674	51.8
			F.W.H. Cook	NL & C	22,048	48.2
					1,626	3.6
1959	54,422	85.5	Rt. Hon. L.J. Edwards	Lab	23,290	50.1
			M.N. Shaw	NL & C	23,243	49.9
					47	0.2
[Death]						
1960 (17/3)	53,737	82.4	M.N. Shaw	NL & C	22,472	50.8
			G.C. Jackson	Lab	21,806	49.2
					666	1.6
1964	55,063	85.3	G.C. Jackson	Lab	20,734	44.1
			M.N. Shaw	NL & C	19,812	42.2
			J. Pickles	L	6,411	13.7
					922	1.9
1966	55,925	84.0	G.C. Jackson	Lab	25,740	54.8
			C.D. Chapman	C	21,216	45.2
					4,524	9.6
1970	61,560	80.6	G.W. Proudfoot	C	22,953	46.3
			G.C. Jackson	Lab	22,894	46.1
			G.H. Manley	L	3,781*	7.6
					59	0.2

Election	Electors	T'out	Candidate	Party	Votes	%
1950	58,909	78.0	H.S. Johnson	C	22,431	48.8
			J.T. Huddart	Lab	19,430	42.3
			R.M. Buckley	L	4,073*	8.9
					3,001	6.5
1951	60,483	77.1	H.S. Johnson	C	25,923	55.6
			L.C. Cohen	Lab	20,726	44.4
					5,197	11.2
1955	58,622*	70.0	H.S. Johnson	C	23,142	56.4
			L.C. Cohen	Lab	17,885	43.6
					5,257	12.8
1959	61,119	73.8	D.P. James	C	25,411	56.4
			L.C. Cohen	Lab	19,665	43.6
					5,746	12.8
1964	61,820	72.2	D.H. Hobden	Lab	22,308	50.0
			D.P. James	C	22,301	50.0
					7	0.0
1966	61,250	80.1	D.H. Hobden	Lab	24,936	50.8
			A. Bowden	C	24,105	49.2
					831	1.6
1970	65,414	75.1	A. Bowden	C	24,208	49.3
			D.H. Hobden	Lab	21,105	42.9
			O.C.N. Moxon	L	3,833*	7.8
					3,103	6.4

Election	Electors	T'out	Candidate	Party	Votes	%
1950	55,401	78.9	†L.W.B. Teeling	C	26,917	61.6
			L. Knowles	Lab	12,264	28.0
			J.S. Choate	L	4,555*	10.4
					14,653	33.6
1951	56,361	75.5	L.W.B. Teeling	C	29,167	68.5
			Miss E.R. Littlejohn	Lab	13,410	31.5
					15,757	37.0
1955	59,053*	67.5	L.W.B. Teeling	C	27,128	68.0
			L. Knowles	Lab	12,742	32.0
					14,386	36.0
1959	57,238	69.8	L.W.B. Teeling	C	27,972	70.0
			R.G. White	Lab	11,998	30.0
					15,974	40.0
1964	56,391	70.1	Sir L.W.B. Teeling	C	20,998	53.2
			P. Nurse	Lab	11,148	28.2
			D.R. Sinnatt	L	7,362	18.6
					9,850	25.0
1966	55,532	70.3	Sir L.W.B. Teeling	C	22,687	58.1
			J.A. Graham	Lab	16,333	41.9
					6,354	16.2
[Resignation]						
1969 (27/3)	55,385	45.1	Rt. Hon. J. Amery	C	17,636	70.6
			T.C. Skeffington-Lodge	Lab	4,654	18.6
			Miss N. Wyn Ellis	L	2,711*	10.8
					12,982	52.0
1970	59,086	66.6	Rt. Hon. H.J. Amery	C	24,365	61.9
			F. Tonks	Lab	13,771	35.0
			G.E. Thomas	Ind	1,205*	3.1
					10,594	26.9

Election	Electors	T'out	Candidate	Party	Votes	%
1950	51,366	84.5	†S.S. Awbery	Lab	25,889	59.7
			J.W.W. Peyton	C	13,461	31.0
			D.D.O. Jones	L	4,042*	9.3
					12,428	28.7
1951	50,341	83.1	S.S. Awbery	Lab	26,091	62.4
			K.A.P. Dalby	C	15,725	37.6
					10,366	24.8
1955	56,326**	73.8	S.S. Awbery	Lab	25,158	60.5
			K.A.P. Dalby	C	16,406	39.5
					8,752	21.0
1959	49,476	75.0	S.S. Awbery	Lab	19,905	53.6
			L.G. Pine	C	17,209	46.4
					2,696	7.2
1964	41,367	71.9	A.M.F. Palmer	Lab/Co-op	16,207	54.5
			J.R.E. Taylor	C	11,616	39.0
			D.H.R. Burgess	Ind	1,936*	6.5
					4,591	15.5
1966	37,363	69.9	A.M.F. Palmer	Lab/Co-op	15,399	58.9
			J.R.E. Taylor	C	9,410	36.0
			D.H.R. Burgess	Ind	1,322*	5.1
					5,989	22.9
1970	36,120	66.7	A.M.F. Palmer	Lab/Co-op	12,375	51.4
			J.R.E. Taylor	C	9,130	37.9
			A. Rider	L	2,569*	10.7
					3,245	13.5

Election	Electors	T'out	Candidate	Party	Votes	%
1950	49,032	84.4	†W. Coldrick	Lab/Co-op	20,456	49.4
			Lady Apsley	NL & C	16,082	38.9
			Miss I.G. Woodcock	L	4,848*	11.7
					4,374	10.5
1951	49,911	82.8	W. Coldrick	Lab/Co-op	21,910	53.0
			G.M. Nixon-Eckersall	NL & C	19,410	47.0
					2,500	6.0
1955	62,614**	78.0	W. Coldrick	Lab/Co-op	22,740	46.5
			D.W.E. Webster	NL & C	21,864	44.8
			G.W. Stevenson	L	4,236*	8.7
					876	1.7
1959	64,319	79.1	A.C.N. Hopkins	NL & C	24,258	47.7
			W. Coldrick	Lab/Co-op	21,574	42.4
			Mrs. A.M. Pearce	L	5,030*	9.9
					2,684	5.3
1964	62,229	77.1	A.C.N. Hopkins	NL & C	22,423	46.7
			R.F.H. Dobson	Lab	21,212	44.2
			Mrs. A.M. Pearce	Ind L	4,346*	9.1
					1,211	2.5
1966	61,554	77.0	R.F.H. Dobson	Lab	25,699	54.2
			A.C.N. Hopkins	NL & C	21,727	45.8
					3,972	8.4
1970	63,896	72.1	R.J. Adley	C	23,254	50.5
			R.F.H. Dobson	Lab	22,792	49.5
					462	1.0

BRISTOL, NORTH-WEST [98]

Election	Electors	T'out	Candidate	Party	Votes	%
1950	58,800	85.1	†J.G. Braithwaite	C	23,884	47.7
			C. Morris	Lab	21,394	42.7
			Miss F.M. Pugh	L	4,784*	9.6
					2,490	5.0
1951	61,506	86.1	J.G. Braithwaite	C	28,394	53.6
			C. Morris	Lab	24,553	46.4
					3,841	7.2
1955	55,942**	79.1	T.C. Boyd	Lab	22,950	51.9
			Sir J.G. Braithwaite, Bt.	C	21,295	48.1
					1,655	3.8
1959	57,831	82.9	M.J. McLaren	C	24,938	52.0
			T.C. Boyd	Lab	23,019	48.0
					1,919	4.0
1964	59,025	83.1	M.J. McLaren	C	22,129	45.1
			D.J. Watkins	Lab	21,030	42.9
			T.G. Douglas	L	5,883*	12.0
					1,099	2.2
1966	58,894	82.0	J. Ellis	Lab	24,195	50.1
			M.J. McLaren	C	23,526	48.7
			B. Underwood	Com	595*	1.2
					669	1.4
1970	65,003	78.0	M.J. McLaren	C	24,124	47.6
			J. Ellis	Lab	23,075	45.5
			H.J. Stevens	L	3,299*	6.5
			W.E. Williams	Com	227*	0.4
					1,049	2.1

Election	Electors	T'out	Candidate	Party	Votes	%
1950	46,035	85.1	†W.A. Wilkins	Lab	23,456	59.9
			S.L.C. Maydon	C	12,473	31.8
			Dr. H.T. Kay	L	3,259*	8.3
					10,893	28.1
1951	45,697	84.5	W.A. Wilkins	Lab	24,444	63.3
			H.E.P. Buckle	C	14,161	36.7
					10,283	26.6
1955	52,142**	74.7	W.A. Wilkins	Lab	24,954	64.1
			G.E. McWatters	C	13,978	35.9
					10,976	28.2
1959	58,671	75.7	W.A. Wilkins	Lab	27,010	60.8
			G.E. McWatters	C	17,428	39.2
					9,582	21.6
1964	57,449	72.8	W.A. Wilkins	Lab	26,569	63.5
			R.W. Wall	C	15,282	36.5
					11,287	27.0
1966	56,915	69.5	W.A. Wilkins	Lab	26,552	67.1
			R.W. Wall	C	12,998	32.9
					13,554	34.2
1970	61,502	64.9	M.F.L. Cocks	Lab	24,682	61.8
			D.J.F. Hunt	C	15,254	38.2
					9,428	23.6

BRISTOL, SOUTH-EAST [100]

Election	Electors	T'out	Candidate	Party	Votes	%
1950	55,289	85.0	†Rt. Hon. Sir R.S. Cripps	Lab	29,393	62.6
			R.E. Simms	C	12,590	26.8
			F.J. Goudge	L	4,463*	9.5
			J.F. Webb	Com	524*	1.1
					16,803	35.8
[Resignation]						
1950 (30/11)	55,835	61.1	Hon. A.N.W. Benn	Lab	19,367	56.7
			Hon. J.L. Lindsay	C	12,018	35.2
			Mrs. D.M. Gorsky	L	2,752*	8.1
					7,349	21.5
1951	56,493	83.8	Hon. A.N.W. Benn	Lab	30,811	65.0
			Hon. J.L. Lindsay	C	16,555	35.0
					14,256	30.0
1955	54,499**	77.9	Hon. A.N.W. Benn	Lab	25,257	59.5
			R.G. Cooke	C	17,210	40.5
					8,047	19.0
1959	57,416	81.4	Hon. A.N.W. Benn	Lab	26,273	56.2
			M.A.J. St. Clair	C	20,446	43.8
					5,827	12.4
[Succession to the Peerage—Viscount Stansgate]						
1961 (4/5)	59,097	56.7	A.N.W. Benn (Viscount Stansgate)	Lab	23,275	69.5
			M.A.J. St. Clair	C	10,231	30.5
					13,044	39.0
[Resignation]						
1963 (20/8)	60,382	42.2	A.N.W. Benn	Lab	20,313	79.7
			E.D. Martell	Nat FC	4,834	19.0
			Mrs. M.P. Lloyd	Ind	287*	1.1
			G. Pearl	Ind	44*	0.2
					15,479	60.7
1964	62,150	77.9	A.N.W. Benn	Lab	29,117	60.2
			R.S. O'Brien	C	19,282	39.8
					9,835	20.4
1966	66,034	76.2	Rt. Hon. A.N.W. Benn	Lab	30,851	61.4
			C.J.R. Pope	C	19,435	38.6
					11,416	22.8
1970	73,172	72.0	Rt. Hon. A.N.W. Benn	Lab	29,176	55.4
			N.G. Reece	C	23,488	44.6
					5,688	10.8

Notes:—

1961:   Benn succeeded to the Peerage on the death of his father in November 1960. He wished to remain an MP and signed an instrument of renunciation and petitioned the House of Commons to set up a Select Committee to examine his case. The House referred the matter to the Committee of Privileges who confirmed that he was disqualified from remaining in the Commons. A new writ was issued and Benn decided to contest the by-election to draw attention to what he considered to be an unjust law. He was elected, but as the result of an election petition in July 1961, the Court held that Benn was disqualified from being elected a Member of Parliament and that St. Clair had been duly elected. St. Clair then gave an undertaking to vacate the seat if a subsequent change in the law permitted Benn to be re-elected and this he did when the Peerage Act, 1963 made provision for the renunciation of a Peerage.

1963:   Pearl sought election as an 'Anti-Socialist Liberal Conservative' but withdrew on the eve of poll in favour of Martell.

Election	Electors	T'out	Candidate	Party	Votes	%
1950	51,299	82.4	†Rt. Hon. O.F.G. Stanley	C	24,920	58.9
			E.S. Bishop	Lab	12,677	30.0
			Miss H. Nuttall	L	4,688*	11.1
					12,243	28.9
[Death]						
1951	50,894	53.6	Sir W.T. Monckton	C	22,216	81.4
(15/2)			H. Lawrance	Lab	5,072	18.6
					17,144	62.8
1951	50,517	80.5	Sir W.T. Monckton	C	25,858	63.5
			H. Lawrance	Lab	11,716	28.8
			D. Goldblatt	L	3,115*	7.7
					14,142	34.7
1955	58,359**	74.6	Rt. Hon. Sir W.T. Monckton	C	32,767	75.3
			W.H. Johnson	Lab	10,766	24.7
					22,001	50.6
[Elevation to the Peerage—Viscount Monckton of Brenchley]						
1957	57,301	61.1	R.G. Cooke	C	24,585	70.2
(7/3)			W.T. Rodgers	Lab	10,423	29.8
					14,162	40.4
1959	56,080	73.6	R.G. Cooke	C	27,768	67.4
			M.F.L. Cocks	Lab	7,651	18.5
			C.A. Hart-Leverton	L	5,835	14.1
					20,117	48.9
1964	50,052	73.1	R.G. Cooke	C	21,230	58.0
			K.B. Wedmore	L	7,366	20.1
			D. McLaren	Lab	7,306	20.0
			P.M. Kingston	TCP	709*	1.9
					13,864	37.9
1966	48,361	72.2	R.G. Cooke	C	19,783	56.7
			L.W. Bosisto	Lab	8,265	23.7
			R.G.R. Stacey	L	6,850	19.6
					11,518	33.0
1970	50,376	66.3	R.G. Cooke	C	20,110	60.2
			D.J. Blackman	Lab	8,175	24.5
			R.G.R. Stacey	L	5,108	15.3
					11,935	35.7

BROMLEY [102]

Election	Electors	T'out	Candidate	Party	Votes	%
1950	47,369	85.0	†Rt. Hon. M.H. Macmillan	C	23,042	57.3
			Mrs. J.R. Elliott	Lab	12,354	30.7
			P.W. Grafton	L	4,847*	12.0
					10,688	26.6
1951	48,486	81.0	Rt. Hon. M.H. Macmillan	C	25,710	65.4
			T.E.M. McKitterick	Lab	13,585	34.6
					12,125	30.8
1955	47,954	75.2	Rt. Hon. M.H. Macmillan	C	24,612	68.2
			G.B. Kaufman	Lab	11,473	31.8
					13,139	36.4
1959	48,937	79.0	Rt. Hon. M.H. Macmillan	C	27,055	70.0
			A.J. Murray	Lab	11,603	30.0
					15,452	40.0
1964	49,915	77.8	J.L. Hunt	C	20,417	52.5
			J.C. Binns	Lab	9,090	23.4
			W.I. Shipley	L	8,650	22.3
			A.J.W. Haigh	INDEC	461*	1.2
			E.S. Grant	SPGB	234*	0.6
					11,327	29.1
1966	49,533	77.7	J.L. Hunt	C	20,117	52.2
			D. Speakman	Lab	10,290	26.8
			P.H. Billenness	L	8,060	21.0
					9,827	25.4
1970	54,305	69.4	J.L. Hunt	C	22,364	59.3
			J.F. Spellar	Lab	9,328	24.8
			D.E.A. Crowe	L	5,982	15.9
					13,036	34.5

Election	Electors	T'out	Candidate	Party	Votes	%
1950	61,568	89.5	†W.A. Burke	Lab	30,685	55.6
			F.H. Wilson	C	23,626	42.9
			W. Whittaker	Com	526*	1.0
			D. Carradice	ILP	295*	0.5
					7,059	12.7
1951	62,364	88.7	W.A. Burke	Lab	31,261	56.5
			D.P. Dunkley	C	24,034	43.5
					7,227	13.0
1955	60,005	83.5	W.A. Burke	Lab	27,865	55.6
			E. Brooks	C	22,229	44.4
					5,636	11.2
1959	57,990	83.8	D. Jones	Lab	27,675	57.0
			E. Brooks	C	20,902	43.0
					6,773	14.0
1964	54,411	81.7	D. Jones	Lab	25,244	56.8
			T. Mitchell	C	12,365	27.8
			Miss M.R. Mason	L	6,833	15.4
					12,879	29.0
1966	52,947	80.0	D. Jones	Lab	25,583	60.4
			A.S. Royse	C	11,710	27.7
			Miss M.R. Mason	L	5,045*	11.9
					13,873	32.7
1970	56,036	75.8	D. Jones	Lab	24,200	57.0
			J. Birch	C	14,846	34.9
			G. Brownbill	L	3,446*	8.1
					9,354	22.1

BURY and RADCLIFFE [104]

Election	Electors	T'out	Candidate	Party	Votes	%
1950	66,465	87.0	†W. Fletcher	C	26,485	45.8
			J. Owen	Lab	25,705	44.4
			C. Hindley	L	5,662*	9.8
					780	1.4
1951	67,090	86.5	W. Fletcher	C	29,949	51.6
			L.T. Wright	Lab	28,058	48.4
					1,891	3.2
1955	65,379	80.2	J.C. Bidgood	C	28,080	53.6
			T. Brennan	Lab	24,331	46.4
					3,749	7.2
1959	64,897	82.2	J.C. Bidgood	C	28,623	53.7
			R.P. Walsh	Lab	24,715	46.3
					3,908	7.4
1964	65,708	82.3	A.C.D. Ensor	Lab	23,865	44.1
			J.C. Bidgood	C	22,639	41.9
			C.L. Scholes	L	7,589	14.0
					1,226	2.2
1966	66,168	81.2	A.C.D. Ensor	Lab	26,769	49.8
			J.C. Bidgood	C	22,298	41.5
			C.L. Scholes	L	4,694*	8.7
					4,471	8.3
1970	74,545	75.6	M. Fidler	C	29,796	52.8
			D.V. Hunt	Lab	26,592	47.2
					3,204	5.6

Election	Electors	T'out	Candidate	Party	Votes	%
1950	58,742	86.5	H.W. Kerr	C	25,151	49.5
			†A.L. Symonds	Lab	20,297	40.0
			Miss F.L. Josephy	L	5,355*	10.5
					4,854	9.5
1951	60,064	84.4	H.W. Kerr	C	26,570	52.4
			A.L. Symonds	Lab	20,893	41.2
			Miss F.L. Josephy	L	3,257*	6.4
					5,677	11.2
1955	59,868	78.5	H.W. Kerr	C	27,059	57.6
			A.L. Symonds	Lab	19,932	42.4
					7,127	15.2
1959	59,745	79.8	Sir H.W. Kerr, Bt.	C	24,350	51.1
			R.M.D. Davies	Lab	17,543	36.8
			A.G. de Montmorency	L	5,792*	12.1
					6,807	14.3
1964	60,365	79.1	Sir H.W. Kerr, Bt.	C	20,720	43.3
			R.M.D. Davies	Lab	19,331	40.5
			Dr. M.W.B. O'Loughlin	L	7,723	16.2
					1,389	2.8
1966	60,380	80.0	R.M.D. Davies	Lab	21,963	45.5
			D.W.S.S. Lane	C	20,972	43.4
			Dr. M.W.B. O'Loughlin	L	4,928*	10.2
			P.F. King	Ind	439*	0.9
					991	2.1
[Death]						
1967	60,382	65.7	D.W.S.S. Lane	C	20,488	51.6
(21/9)			G.B. Scurfield	Lab	14,510	36.6
			D.R.A. Spreckley	L	4,701*	11.8
					5,978	15.0
1970	65,500	72.4	D.W.S.S. Lane	C	26,252	55.3
			G.B. Scurfield	Lab	21,191	44.7
					5,061	10.6

CARLISLE [106]

Election	Electors	T'out	Candidate	Party	Votes	%
1950	46,247	88.5	A. Hargreaves	Lab	19,031	46.5
			H.E.R. Peers	C	13,850	33.8
			G.W. Iredell	L	8,043	19.7
					5,181	12.7
1951	48,026*	87.4	A. Hargreaves	Lab	19,648	46.8
			N.T. O'Reilly	C	16,456	39.2
			Mrs. D.M. Gorsky	L	5,886	14.0
					3,192	7.6
1955	48,324	82.3	Dr. D.M. Johnson	C	20,071	50.5
			A. Hargreaves	Lab	19,701	49.5
					370	1.0
1959	49,519	84.6	Dr. D.M. Johnson	C (Ind C)	21,948	52.4
			A. Hargreaves	Lab	19,950	47.6
					1,998	4.8
1964	49,121	85.6	R.H. Lewis	Lab	19,169	45.6
			P.T.S. Boydell	C	17,049	40.5
			B.G. Ashmore	L	4,617*	11.0
			Dr. D.M. Johnson	Ind C	1,227*	2.9
					2,120	5.1
1966	48,144	83.5	R.H. Lewis	Lab	22,565	56.1
			G.W. Iredell	C	17,638	43.9
					4,927	12.2
1970	52,294	78.6	R.H. Lewis	Lab	21,866	53.2
			B.A. Marsden	C	19,241	46.8
					2,625	6.4

Election	Electors	T'out	Candidate	Party	Votes	%
1950	48,786	85.0	W.W. Hicks Beach	C	18,009	43.4
			A.G. James	Lab	13,027	31.4
			†D.L. Lipson	Ind	10,449	25.2
					4,982	12.0
1951	49,844	83.2	W.W. Hicks Beach	C	23,674	57.1
			J. Finnigan	Lab	17,777	42.9
					5,897	14.2
1955	51,491	79.4	W.W. Hicks Beach	C	24,259	59.3
			J. Finnigan	Lab	16,638	40.7
					7,621	18.6
1959	52,946	81.5	W.W. Hicks Beach	C	21,997	51.0
			Dr. K.G. Pendse	Lab	12,725	29.5
			G.G. Watson	L	8,428	19.5
					9,272	21.5
1964	54,120	77.5	A.D. Dodds-Parker	C	19,797	47.2
			H. Gray	Lab	14,557	34.7
			J.A. Lemkin	L	7,568	18.1
					5,240	12.5
1966	54,964	77.2	A.D. Dodds-Parker	C	22,683	53.4
			W.J. Wilson	Lab	19,768	46.6
					2,915	6.8
1970	60,141	75.6	A.D. Dodds-Parker	C	22,823	50.2
			L.G. Godwin	Lab	14,213	31.3
			D.G. Aldridge	L	8,431	18.5
					8,610	18.9

Note:—

1950: Lipson advocated a policy of national government.

Election	Electors	T'out	Candidate	Party	Votes	%
1950	64,079	87.0	†G. Benson	Lab	33,914	60.8
			Marquess of Hartington	NL & C	17,231	30.9
			J.W. O'Neill	L	4,052*	7.3
			B. Barker	Com	554*	1.0
					16,683	29.9
1951	64,762	84.2	G. Benson	Lab	34,753	63.7
			J.F. Nash	NL & C	19,776	36.3
					14,977	27.4
1955	64,250	79.9	G. Benson	Lab	29,602	57.6
			F. Hadfield	NL & C	21,748	42.4
					7,854	15.2
1959	65,270	82.7	Sir G. Benson	Lab	30,534	56.6
			J.A. Lemkin	NL & C	17,084	31.6
			G.R.S. Stevenson	L	6,360*	11.8
					13,450	25.0
1964	66,138	78.8	E.G. Varley	Lab	29,452	56.5
			W.G. Blake	C	14,944	28.7
			D.A. McKie	L	7,738	14.8
					14,508	27.8
1966	66,749	76.7	E.G. Varley	Lab	31,542	61.6
			A.T. Hale	C	13,443	26.2
			T.D. Bamford	L	6,227*	12.2
					18,099	35.4
1970	71,051	72.5	E.G. Varley	Lab	30,386	59.0
			J.C. Ramsden	C	16,217	31.5
			T.D. Bamford	L	4,891*	9.5
					14,169	27.5

Election	Electors	T'out	Candidate	Party	Votes	%
1950	58,254	88.2	†R.H.S. Crossman	Lab	30,456	59.3
			T.B. Meek	C	17,003	33.1
			S.H. Davis	L	3,420*	6.7
			W. Alexander	Com	487*	0.9
					13,453	26.2
1951	60,115	85.7	R.H.S. Crossman	Lab	32,108	62.3
			G.B. Welby	C	19,437	37.7
					12,671	24.6
1955	60,769	81.2	R.H.S. Crossman	Lab	27,712	56.2
			Dr. M.A. Hooker	C	21,608	43.8
					6,104	12.4
1959	70,689	81.7	R.H.S. Crossman	Lab	32,744	56.7
			W.J. Biffen	C	24,982	43.3
					7,762	13.4
1964	77,821*	77.9	R.H.S. Crossman	Lab	36,246	59.8
			I.R.E. Gow	C	23,208	38.3
			H. Bourne	Com	1,138*	1.9
					13,038	21.5
1966	78,131	77.3	Rt. Hon. R.H.S. Crossman	Lab	36,757	60.8
			J. Wakeham	C	18,061	29.9
			J.M. Mokrzycki	L	4,235*	7.0
			H. Bourne	Com	1,368*	2.3
					18,696	30.9
1970	86,603	70.6	Rt. Hon. R.H.S. Crossman	Lab	36,275	59.3
			M.E. Jones	C	24,010	39.3
			J. Hosey	Com	841*	1.4
					12,265	20.0

Election	Electors	T'out	Candidate	Party	Votes	%
1950	56,878	87.8	†M. Edelman	Lab	28,924	57.9
			J. Dalley	C	17,807	35.7
			J. Burns	L	3,195*	6.4
					11,117	22.2
1951	57,957	86.4	M. Edelman	Lab	29,826	59.6
			H.S. Clippingdale	C	20,238	40.4
					9,588	19.2
1955	55,845	82.3	M. Edelman	Lab	24,565	53.5
			J. Poole	C	21,392	46.5
					3,173	7.0
1959	53,598	83.6	M. Edelman	Lab	23,035	51.4
			F.C. Maynard	C	21,794	48.6
					1,241	2.8
1964	54,401*	81.4	M. Edelman	Lab	23,355	52.7
			M.R.D. Heseltine	C	19,825	44.8
			R.S. Robinson	Ind	1,112*	2.5
					3,530	7.9
1966	53,768	78.9	M. Edelman	Lab	25,170	59.3
			D.H.J. Martin-Jones	C	17,263	40.7
					7,907	18.6
1970	56,726	74.7	M. Edelman	Lab	24,004	56.7
			F.A. Tuckman	C	18,344	43.3
					5,660	13.4

Election	Electors	T'out	Candidate	Party	Votes	%
1950	60,861	87.2	Miss E.F. Burton	Lab	27,977	52.7
			Rt. Hon. L. Hore-Belisha	C	21,885	41.2
			R.J. Soper	L	3,239*	6.1
					6,092	11.5
1951	61,590	86.2	Miss E.F. Burton	Lab	29,271	55.2
			J.A. Biggs-Davison	C	23,803	44.8
					5,468	10.4
1955	65,404	81.4	Miss E.F. Burton	Lab	27,449	51.6
			Mrs. M.E. Williamson	C	25,761	48.4
					1,688	3.2
1959	67,394	82.1	P.N. Hocking	C	28,584	51.7
			Miss E.F. Burton	Lab	26,754	48.3
					1,830	3.4
1964	70,992*	79.8	W. Wilson	Lab	29,240	51.6
			P.N. Hocking	C	27,407	48.4
					1,833	3.2
1966	70,983	80.2	W. Wilson	Lab	31,237	54.9
			P.N. Hocking	C	25,697	45.1
					5,540	9.8
1970	77,626	74.5	W. Wilson	Lab	30,010	51.9
			G.A. Gardiner	C	27,816	48.1
					2,194	3.8

Election	Electors	T'out	Candidate	Party	Votes	%
1950	43,885	84.5	†M. Bullock	C	22,347	60.2
			R.H. Lewis	Lab	9,403	25.4
			J. Burnie	L	5,336	14.4
					12,944	34.8
1951	44,232	79.8	M. Bullock	C	25,034	70.9
			Mrs. E.M. Edwards	Lab	10,251	29.1
					14,783	41.8
[Resignation]						
1953	43,720	62.5	R.G. Page	C	18,614	68.1
(12/11)			E.J. Adams	Lab	7,545	27.6
			J.A. Freeman	Ind C	1,180*	4.3
					11,069	40.5
1955	58,188**	73.7	R.G. Page	C	29,161	68.0
			E.J. Adams	Lab	13,725	32.0
					15,436	36.0
1959	57,495	77.5	R.G. Page	C	29,801	66.9
			D.E. Brown	Lab	14,745	33.1
					15,056	33.8
1964	57,771*	76.7	R.G. Page	C	21,538	48.6
			R. Hodge	Lab	14,158	32.0
			N. Sellers	L	8,590	19.4
					7,380	16.6
1966	56,318	72.2	R.G. Page	C	21,980	54.1
			A.J. Whipp	Lab	18,674	45.9
					3,306	8.2
1970	59,525	71.2	R.G. Page	C	24,042	56.7
			P.J. Caswell	Lab	18,350	43.3
					5,692	13.4

Election	Electors	T'out	Candidate	Party	Votes	%
1950	63,627	86.9	Sir H.G. Williams	C	29,484	53.4
			Miss M.G. Billson	Lab	20,903	37.8
			G.L. Gray	L	4,882*	8.8
					8,581	15.6
1951	65,204	84.2	Sir H.G. Williams	C	32,282	58.8
			A. Bain	Lab	22,615	41.2
					9,667	17.6
[Death]						
1954	66,483	57.5	J. Hughes-Hallett	C	21,640	56.6
(30/9)			J.W. Wellwood	Lab	13,546	35.4
			J. Walters	L	3,060*	8.0
					8,094	21.2

This constituency was divided in 1955.

CROYDON, NORTH [114]

Election	Electors	T'out	Candidate	Party	Votes	%
1950	63,537	86.8	†F.W. Harris	C	29,420	53.3
			R.E. Prentice	Lab	20,116	36.5
			F.O.H. Rowlands	L	5,600*	10.2
					9,304	16.8
1951	64,522	83.7	F.W. Harris	C	29,984	55.5
			R.E. Prentice	Lab	19,738	36.6
			B.D. Collins	L	4,272*	7.9
					10,246	18.9

This constituency was divided in 1955.

CROYDON, NORTH-EAST [115]

Election	Electors	T'out	Candidate	Party	Votes	%
1955	58,663	77.7	J. Hughes-Hallett	C	25,097	55.1
			G.J. Borrie	Lab	16,616	36.4
			J. Walters	L	3,892*	8.5
					8,481	18.7
1959	57,174	80.3	J. Hughes-Hallett	C	24,345	53.1
			W.J. Wolfgang	Lab	15,440	33.6
			Dr. A.E. Bender	L	6,109	13.3
					8,905	19.5
1964	56,765	75.0	B.B. Weatherill	C	19,930	46.8
			D. Storer	Lab/Co-op	16,099	37.8
			S.R.R. de la Mahotiere	L	6,567	15.4
					3,831	9.0
1966	55,094	76.3	B.B. Weatherill	C	18,302	43.5
			G.F. Elliott	Lab	17,714	42.2
			J.D.O. Henchley	L	6,007	14.3
					588	1.3
1970	58,631	69.8	B.B. Weatherill	C	20,351	49.7
			G.F. Elliott	Lab	16,373	40.0
			R.J. Mayhew	L	4,210*	10.3
					3,978	9.7

CROYDON, NORTH-WEST [116]

Election	Electors	T'out	Candidate	Party	Votes	%
1955	59,575	77.5	F.W. Harris	C	26,297	56.9
			R.W. Huzzard	Lab	15,760	34.1
			Miss I.E. Thurston	L	4,139*	9.0
					10,537	22.8
1959	58,177	78.8	F.W. Harris	C	25,111	54.8
			D.W. Chalkley	Lab	14,658	32.0
			Miss I.E. Thurston	L	6,061	13.2
					10,453	22.8
1964	56,122	74.4	F.W. Harris	C	19,577	46.9
			J.A.P. Palmer	Lab	13,967	33.5
			R.E.J. Banks	L	8,201	19.6
					5,610	13.4
1966	55,042	74.4	F.W. Harris	C	18,578	45.4
			M.J. Stewart	Lab	15,882	38.8
			R.E.J. Banks	L	6,466	15.8
					2,696	6.6
1970	57,064	67.7	R.G. Taylor	C	19,260	49.9
			S.J. Boden	Lab	14,687	38.0
			R.E.J. Banks	L	4,666*	12.1
					4,573	11.9

CROYDON, SOUTH [117]

Election	Electors	T'out	Candidate	Party	Votes	%
1955	62,177	77.2	R.H.M. Thompson	C	27,359	57.0
			A.E. Carr	Lab	20,659	43.0
					6,700	14.0
1959	63,636	79.1	R.H.M. Thompson	C	29,284	58.2
			F.A. Messer	Lab	21,069	41.8
					8,215	16.4
1964	63,443	74.3	Sir R.H.M. Thompson, Bt.	C	24,854	52.7
			T. Burgess	Lab	22,265	47.3
					2,589	5.4
1966	63,146	76.1	D.J. Winnick	Lab	21,496	44.7
			Sir R.H.M. Thompson, Bt.	C	21,415	44.6
			W.E.P. Babbs	L	5,146*	10.7
					81	0.1
1970	73,166	71.4	Sir R.H.M. Thompson, Bt.	C	25,986	49.7
			D.J. Winnick	Lab	22,283	42.7
			M.R. Lane	L	3,673*	7.0
			C.O. Thornton	Ind	303*	0.6
					3,703	7.0

Election	Electors	T'out	Candidate	Party	Votes	%
1950	54,119	83.7	R.H.M. Thompson	C	21,411	47.4
			†D.R. Rees-Williams	Lab	20,424	45.1
			A.R. Mayne	L	3,101*	6.8
			R. Jarvie	Com	336*	0.7
					987	2.3
1951	54,496	82.6	R.H.M. Thompson	C	23,484	52.2
			G.A. Gardiner	Lab	21,534	47.8
					1,950	4.4

This constituency was divided in 1955.

DAGENHAM [119]

Election	Electors	T'out	Candidate	Party	Votes	%
1950	73,477	81.3	†J. Parker	Lab	43,300	72.4
			D. Cook	C	11,565	19.4
			Miss I.E. Thurston	L	3,973*	6.7
			G.T. Bridges	Com	883*	1.5
					31,735	53.0
1951	75,939	77.7	J. Parker	Lab	44,908	76.1
			N.A.F. St. John-Stevas	C	14,112	23.9
					30,796	52.2
1955	76,198	68.9	J. Parker	Lab	38,811	73.9
			R.I. Gray	C	13,718	26.1
					25,093	47.8
1959	73,968	72.5	J. Parker	Lab	37,009	69.0
			F. Waley	C	16,626	31.0
					20,383	38.0
1964	71,424	71.0	J. Parker	Lab	32,851	64.8
			G.E. Currie	C	9,461	18.7
			P.T. Humphrey	L	7,301	14.4
			K. Halpin	Com	1,070*	2.1
					23,390	46.1
1966	69,671	67.4	J. Parker	Lab	35,055	74.7
			G.E. Currie	C	10,530	22.4
			G.C. Wake	Com	1,373*	2.9
					24,525	52.3
1970	74,942	59.1	J. Parker	Lab	31,335	70.8
			H.M. McClancy	C	11,976	27.0
			G.C. Wake	Com	982*	2.2
					19,359	43.8

Election	Electors	T'out	Candidate	Party	Votes	%
1950	59,701	88.0	†D.R. Hardman	Lab	23,528	44.7
			Mrs. G.E.M. Walford	C	17,421	33.2
			G.V. Rogers	L	11,588	22.1
					6,107	11.5
1951	60,728	87.1	Sir F.F. Graham, Bt.	C	26,858	50.8
			D.R. Hardman	Lab	26,045	49.2
					813	1.6
1955	59,448	82.3	Sir F.F. Graham, Bt.	C	25,765	52.6
			A.J. Parkinson	Lab	23,184	47.4
					2,581	5.2
1959	59,342	84.4	A.T. Bourne-Arton	C	24,318	48.6
			R.H. Lewis	Lab	19,901	39.7
			J.P. McQuade	L	5,863*	11.7
					4,417	8.9
1964	58,051	83.0	E.J. Fletcher	Lab	21,751	45.1
			A.T. Bourne-Arton	C	19,841	41.2
			J.G. Pease	L	6,578	13.7
					1,910	3.9
1966	57,557	82.3	E.J. Fletcher	Lab	23,909	50.5
			A.T. Bourne-Arton	C	19,546	41.3
			R.N.W. Oakeshott	L	3,891*	8.2
					4,363	9.2
1970	62,580	76.5	E.J. Fletcher	Lab	23,208	48.5
			A.T. Bourne-Arton	C	19,447	40.6
			S. Newton	L	5,222*	10.9
					3,761	7.9

DARTFORD [121]

Election	Electors	T'out	Candidate	Party	Votes	%
1950	79,087	85.5	†N.N. Dodds	Lab/Co-op	38,128	56.4
			Miss M.H. Roberts	C	24,490	36.2
			H.H. Giles	L	5,011*	7.4
					13,638	20.2
1951	79,620	85.2	N.N. Dodds	Lab/Co-op	40,094	59.1
			Miss M.H. Roberts	C	27,760	40.9
					12,334	18.2

This constituency was divided in 1955.

DERBY, NORTH [122]

Election	Electors	T'out	Candidate	Party	Votes	%
1950	47,462	85.5	†C.A.B. Wilcock	Lab	22,410	55.2
			V.B.J. Seely	C	14,980	36.9
			G.I. Walters	L	3,190*	7.9
					7,430	18.3
1951	47,541	82.5	C.A.B. Wilcock	Lab	22,390	57.1
			V.E. Waldron	C	16,828	42.9
					5,562	14.2
1955	57,201**	75.7	C.A.B. Wilcock	Lab	24,162	55.8
			R.C.P. Rouse	C	19,156	44.2
					5,006	11.6
1959	55,976	76.7	C.A.B. Wilcock	Lab	22,673	52.8
			R.J. Maxwell-Hyslop	C	20,266	47.2
					2,407	5.6
[Death]						
1962 (17/4)	55,105	60.5	N. MacDermot	Lab	16,497	49.4
			L. Irving	L	8,479	25.4
			T.M. Wray	C	7,502	22.5
			T. Lynch	NUSS	886*	2.7
					8,018	24.0
1964	54,318	74.4	N. MacDermot	Lab	21,386	52.9
			D.H. Hene	C	13,991	34.6
			A.L. Smart	L	5,057	12.5
					7,395	18.3
1966	52,601	70.8	N. MacDermot	Lab	23,033	61.8
			D.H. Hene	C	14,215	38.2
					8,818	23.6
1970	57,145	64.3	P. Whitehead	Lab	20,114	54.7
			J.W. Roberts	C	16,635	45.3
					3,479	9.4

Election	Electors	T'out	Candidate	Party	Votes	%
1950	51,318	87.1	†Rt. Hon. P.J. Noel-Baker	Lab	26,887	60.2
			R.C.D. Grimes	C	13,926	31.1
			I. Irving	L	3,900*	8.7
					12,961	29.1
1951	51,681	84.5	Rt. Hon. P.J. Noel-Baker	Lab	27,333	62.6
			R.C.D. Grimes	C	16,344	37.4
					10,989	25.2
1955	54,675**	78.8	Rt. Hon. P.J. Noel-Baker	Lab	23,081	53.6
			M.R. Kimball	C	16,572	38.5
			A.L. Smart	L	3,408*	7.9
					6,509	15.1
1959	54,131	79.2	Rt. Hon. P.J. Noel-Baker	Lab	20,776	48.4
			T.M. Wray	C	17,345	40.5
			A.L. Smart	L	4,746*	11.1
					3,431	7.9
1964	51,944	74.8	Rt. Hon. P.J. Noel-Baker	Lab	22,432	57.7
			T.M. Wray	C	16,420	42.3
					6,012	15.4
1966	51,348	72.6	Rt. Hon. P.J. Noel-Baker	Lab	21,433	57.6
			M.G.C. Fidler	C	11,857	31.8
			A.L. Smart	L	3,967*	10.6
					9,576	25.8
1970	52,938	67.4	W.H. Johnson	Lab	19,407	54.4
			R. Greene	C	16,258	45.6
					3,149	8.8

DEWSBURY [124]

Election	Electors	T'out	Candidate	Party	Votes	%
1950	62,259	87.9	†W.T. Paling	Lab	29,341	53.6
			J.E. Ramsden	NL & C	18,076	33.0
			G.G. Slack	L	7,323	13.4
					11,265	20.6
1951	62,680	85.8	W.T. Paling	Lab	28,650	53.2
			J.E. Ramsden	NL & C	19,562	36.4
			J.S. Snowden	L	5,584*	10.4
					9,088	16.8
1955	55,257**	80.8	W.T. Paling	Lab	23,286	52.2
			M.N. Shaw	C	15,869	35.5
			J.S. Snowden	L	5,516*	12.3
					7,417	16.7
1959	54,894	82.7	D. Ginsburg	Lab	20,870	46.0
			J.M. Fox	C	17,201	37.9
			J.M. McLusky	L	7,321	16.1
					3,669	8.1
1964	55,341	79.5	D. Ginsburg	Lab	21,284	48.4
			Mrs. B.M. Garden	C	15,046	34.2
			A. Allsopp	L	7,679	17.4
					6,238	14.2
1966	55,080	78.0	D. Ginsburg	Lab	23,027	53.5
			D.H. Haynes	C	12,361	28.8
			A. Allsopp	L	7,593	17.7
					10,666	24.7
1970	60,544	74.6	D. Ginsburg	Lab	22,015	48.7
			J.M. Stansfield	C	17,468	38.7
			A. Allsopp	L	5,688	12.6
					4,547	10.0

Election	Electors	T'out	Candidate	Party	Votes	%
1950	56,081	85.6	†R.J. Gunter	Lab	24,449	50.9
			A.P.L. Barber	C	23,571	49.1
					878	1.8
1951	57,581*	86.2	A.P.L. Barber	C	25,005	50.4
			R.J. Gunter	Lab	24,621	49.6
					384	0.8
1955	58,117	81.8	A.P.L. Barber	C	24,598	51.7
			R.J. Gunter	Lab	22,938	48.3
					1,660	3.4
1959	58,505	84.5	A.P.L. Barber	C	26,521	53.6
			W.E. Garrett	Lab	22,935	46.4
					3,586	7.2
1964	57,746	82.7	H. Walker	Lab	23,845	49.9
			Rt. Hon. A.P.L. Barber	C	22,732	47.6
			G.P. Broadhead	Ind	1,201*	2.5
					1,113	2.3
1966	56,013	81.2	H. Walker	Lab	25,777	56.7
			J.M. Whittaker	C	19,689	43.3
					6,088	13.4
1970	59,755	74.9	H. Walker	Lab	22,658	50.7
			P. Davies	C	19,431	43.4
			W.T.W. Blades	L	2,648*	5.9
					3,227	7.3

Note:—

    1964: Broadhead sought election as a 'Radical National Liberal' candidate.

Election	Electors	T'out	Candidate	Party	Votes	%
1950	59,077	87.7	†Rev. G.S. Woods	Lab/Co-op	25,238	48.7
			E.S.T. Johnson	C	21,102	40.7
			H. Kevin-Armitage	L	5,483*	10.6
					4,136	8.0

[Seat Vacant at Dissolution (Death)]

1951	59,772	86.6	W.R. Williams	Lab	26,829	51.8
			W. Howard	C	24,959	48.2
					1,870	3.6

This constituency was divided in 1955.

Election	Electors	T'out	Candidate	Party	Votes	%
1950	69,275	86.8	†G.E.C. Wigg	Lab	32,856	54.6
			R.A. Farran	C	19,825	33.0
			B.S. White	L	7,470*	12.4
					13,031	21.6
1951	70,413	83.7	G.E.C. Wigg	Lab	34,376	58.4
			H.B. Soref	C	24,525	41.6
					9,851	16.8
1955	71,651*	79.8	G.E.C. Wigg	Lab	31,384	54.9
			T.D. Wilson	C	20,333	35.5
			W.L. Lawler	L	5,479*	9.6
					11,051	19.4
1959	72,829	79.5	G.E.C. Wigg	Lab	31,826	54.9
			F.E. Spiller	C	26,101	45.1
					5,725	9.8
1964	74,562	76.5	G.E.C. Wigg	Lab	30,250	53.0
			D.A.R. Howell	C	19,980	35.0
			R.C.S. Fowler	L	6,829*	12.0
					10,270	18.0
1966	74,957	73.9	Rt. Hon. G.E.C. Wigg	Lab	32,693	59.1
			W.D. Williams	C	22,671	40.9
					10,022	18.2

[Resignation on appointment as Chairman of the Horserace Betting Levy Board and elevation to a Life Peerage—Lord Wigg]

Election	Electors	T'out	Candidate	Party	Votes	%
1968 (28/3)	75,935	63.5	W.D. Williams	C	28,016	58.1
			J.W. Gilbert	Lab	16,360	34.0
			D.E. Bird	L	3,809*	7.9
					11,656	24.1
1970	81,481	72.0	J.W. Gilbert	Lab	29,499	50.3
			W.D. Williams	C	29,163	49.7
					336	0.6

Election	Electors	T'out	Candidate	Party	Votes	%
1950	57,671	88.0	†J.H. Hudson	Lab/Co-op	24,157	47.5
			Mrs. E.M.S. Olsen	C	21,753	42.9
			E.A.G. Holloway	L	4,855*	9.6
					2,404	4.6
1951	58,401	87.8	J.H. Hudson	Lab/Co-op	25,698	50.1
			A.M.S. Neave	C	25,578	49.9
					120	0.2
1955	58,245	85.2	J.W. Barter	C	23,040	46.4
			J.H. Hudson	Lab/Co-op	22,794	46.0
			Dr. A.E. Bender	L	3,770*	7.6
					246	0.4
1959	59,768	84.2	J.W. Barter	C	27,312	54.2
			W.S. Hilton	Lab/Co-op	23,036	45.8
					4,276	8.4
1964	59,421	81.0	W.J. Molloy	Lab	20,809	43.2
			J.W. Barter	C	20,782	43.2
			D.F.J. Wood	L	6,532	13.6
					27	0.0
1966	59,315	82.2	W.J. Molloy	Lab	23,730	48.7
			J.W. Barter	C	21,153	43.4
			J.E. Elsom	L	3,858*	7.9
					2,577	5.3
1970	64,092	72.7	W.J. Molloy	Lab	23,459	50.3
			J.W. Barter	C	23,139	49.7
					320	0.6

Election	Electors	T'out	Candidate	Party	Votes	%
1950	58,944	84.7	A.E.U. Maude	C	28,299	56.7
			J. Neary	Lab	17,097	34.2
			Miss B. Corn	L	4,555*	9.1
					11,202	22.5
1951	58,952	82.2	A.E.U. Maude	C	30,261	62.4
			D.G. Allen	Lab	18,204	37.6
					12,057	24.8
1955	56,046	77.9	A.E.U. Maude	C (Ind C)	25,992	59.5
			D.G. Allen	Lab	13,462	30.9
			D.E. Evans	L	4,182*	9.6
					12,530	28.6
[Resignation]						
1958 (12/6)	53,667	64.5	B.C.C. Batsford	C	17,417	50.3
			H.G. Garside	Lab	11,258	32.5
			P. Skelsey	L	5,956	17.2
					6,159	17.8
1959	53,296	78.1	B.C.C. Batsford	C	24,761	59.5
			H.G. Garside	Lab	12,039	28.9
			Sir J.J.A. Mostyn, Bt.	L	4,842*	11.6
					12,722	30.6
1964	51,714	70.1	B.C.C. Batsford	C	22,121	61.0
			J.J. Jaffé	Lab	14,121	39.0
					8,000	22.0
1966	51,283	73.3	B.C.C. Batsford	C	18,968	50.5
			R.L. MacFarquhar	Lab	13,885	36.9
			B.N. Martin-Kaye	L	4,743	12.6
					5,083	13.6
1970	53,763	65.4	B.C.C. Batsford	C	19,326	54.9
			C. Rofe	Lab	12,042	34.3
			G.D. Smith	L	3,784*	10.8
					7,284	20.6

EAST HAM, NORTH [130]

Election	Electors	T'out	Candidate	Party	Votes	%
1950	42,624	84.2	†P. Daines	Lab/Co-op	20,497	57.2
			Sir J. Mayhew	C	11,856	33.0
			J.J. Carroll	L	3,521*	9.8
					8,641	24.2
1951	42,662	83.3	P. Daines	Lab/Co-op	21,444	60.4
			J.D. Hamilton	C	14,085	39.6
					7,359	20.8
1955	40,548	74.9	P. Daines	Lab/Co-op	17,961	59.1
			A. Silverstone	C	12,416	40.9
					5,545	18.2
[Death]						
1957 (30/5)	38,920	57.3	R.E. Prentice	Lab	12,546	56.3
			J.H.S. Bangay	C	6,567	29.4
			E.D. Martell	PL	2,730*	12.2
			W.H. Christopher	ILP	458*	2.1
					5,979	26.9
1959	38,014	74.1	R.E. Prentice	Lab	16,001	56.8
			J.H.S. Bangay	C	12,175	43.2
					3,826	13.6
1964	35,656	67.4	R.E. Prentice	Lab	14,501	60.4
			J.H.S. Bangay	C	9,524	39.6
					4,977	20.8
1966	35,016	64.7	R.E. Prentice	Lab	14,911	65.9
			L. Giovene	C	7,729	34.1
					7,182	31.8
1970	36,695	52.6	Rt. Hon. R.E. Prentice	Lab	11,557	59.9
			D.N. Macfarlane	C	7,735	40.1
					3,822	19.8

Election	Electors	T'out	Candidate	Party	Votes	%
1950	43,857	84.5	†A.J. Barnes	Lab/Co-op	23,002	62.1
			C. Jordan	C	10,956	29.6
			C.A. Borrott	L	2,424*	6.5
			E.C.W. Thomas	Com	401*	1.1
			H. Young	SPGB	256*	0.7
					12,046	32.5
1951	44,274	82.5	A.J. Barnes	Lab/Co-op	23,704	64.9
			J.W. Barter	C	12,813	35.1
					10,891	29.8
1955	42,280	73.1	A.E. Oram	Lab/Co-op	19,808	64.1
			A.J. Pickford	C	11,109	35.9
					8,699	28.2
1959	39,764	74.6	A.E. Oram	Lab/Co-op	18,230	61.5
			R.J. Watts	C	11,422	38.5
					6,808	23.0
1964	38,121	67.9	A.E. Oram	Lab/Co-op	17,069	66.0
			R.J. Watts	C	8,797	34.0
					8,272	32.0
1966	38,197	65.7	A.E. Oram	Lab/Co-op	17,543	69.9
			I.R. Stanbrook	C	7,540	30.1
					10,003	39.8
1970	39,964	55.1	A.E. Oram	Lab/Co-op	13,638	61.9
			C.M. Jackson	C	8,402	38.1
					5,236	23.8

Election	Electors	T'out	Candidate	Party	Votes	%
1950	61,153	88.4	†W.T. Proctor	Lab	27,409	50.7
			H. Sharp	C	22,186	41.0
			Rev. J.H. Jones	L	4,477*	8.3
					5,223	9.7
1951	61,385	86.8	W.T. Proctor	Lab	27,941	52.5
			J. Whiteley	C	25,330	47.5
					2,611	5.0
1955	59,382	81.5	W.T. Proctor	Lab	25,351	52.4
			C.P. Lawson	C	23,025	47.6
					2,326	4.8
1959	59,317*	82.9	W.T. Proctor	Lab	25,566	52.0
			B.R.O. Bell	C	23,580	48.0
					1,986	4.0
1964	58,138*	77.7	L. Carter-Jones	Lab	25,915	57.3
			J.J. Hodgson	C	19,277	42.7
					6,638	14.6
1966	56,714	74.1	L. Carter-Jones	Lab	25,033	59.6
			H.P. Holland	C	15,776	37.5
			M.R. Bennett	Com	1,239*	2.9
					9,257	22.1
1970	59,135	72.7	L. Carter-Jones	Lab	23,913	55.6
			Dr. R. Boyson	C	18,458	42.9
			T.E. Keenan	Com	643*	1.5
					5,455	12.7

Election	Electors	T'out	Candidate	Party	Votes	%
1950	74,988	84.5	†A.H. Albu	Lab	34,897	55.1
			E.P. Hubbard	C	23,325	36.8
			G.E. Thornton	L	5,143*	8.1
					11,572	18.3
1951	74,707	82.5	A.H. Albu	Lab	36,023	58.4
			Mrs. E.M.S. Olsen	C	25,631	41.6
					10,392	16.8
1955	71,739	74.5	A.H. Albu	Lab	30,232	56.6
			Mrs. E.M.S. Olsen	C	23,194	43.4
					7,038	13.2
1959	67,837	75.9	A.H. Albu	Lab	25,958	50.4
			W.H. Bishop	C	25,497	49.6
					461	0.8
1964	64,348	77.0	A.H. Albu	Lab	24,373	49.2
			A.R. McWhirter	C	19,245	38.9
			D.A. Coberman	L	5,917*	11.9
					5,128	10.3
1966	62,520	72.2	A.H. Albu	Lab	26,422	58.6
			E.P. Hubbard	C	18,697	41.4
					7,725	17.2
1970	63,203	66.8	A.H. Albu	Lab	20,626	48.9
			E.P. Hubbard	C	18,481	43.7
			G.E. Longley	L	3,137*	7.4
					2,145	5.2

Election	Electors	T'out	Candidate	Party	Votes	%
1950	47,745	84.8	†E.A.J. Davies	Lab	24,013	59.3
			C.W.C. Turner	C	13,110	32.4
			A.B. Tyler	L	3,368*	8.3
					10,903	26.9
1951	48,309	82.6	E.A.J. Davies	Lab	25,298	63.4
			C.W.C. Turner	C	14,594	36.6
					10,704	26.8
1955	47,197	75.5	E.A.J. Davies	Lab	21,658	60.8
			J.L. Manning	C	13,957	39.2
					7,701	21.6
1959	47,183	77.5	J. Mackie	Lab	20,101	55.0
			F.J.V. Brown	C	16,477	45.0
					3,624	10.0
1964	46,043	76.3	J. Mackie	Lab	17,958	51.1
			F.J.V. Brown	C	11,447	32.6
			J.F. Burnett	L	5,723	16.3
					6,511	18.5
1966	45,487	75.2	J. Mackie	Lab	18,772	54.9
			R.H. Leach	C	11,245	32.9
			J.F. Burnett	L	4,189*	12.2
					7,527	22.0
1970	48,272	66.7	J. Mackie	Lab	16,433	51.0
			Dr. T.E.T. Weston	C	12,403	38.5
			A.A. Stowell	L	3,373*	10.5
					4,030	12.5

Election	Electors	T'out	Candidate	Party	Votes	%
1950	41,222	86.4	I.N. Macleod	C	20,588	57.8
			H.G. Jenkins	Lab	11,395	32.0
			W.P. Campbell	L	3,638*	10.2
					9,193	25.8
1951	41,770	82.5	I.N. Macleod	C	22,351	64.8
			Lady Hendy	Lab	12,126	35.2
					10,225	29.6
1955	41,595	78.2	Rt. Hon. I.N. Macleod	C	22,021	67.7
			W.A. Court	Lab	10,503	32.3
					11,518	35.4
1959	44,983	79.9	Rt. Hon. I.N. Macleod	C	24,861	69.2
			G. Hickman	Lab	11,058	30.8
					13,803	38.4
1964	46,882	81.0	Rt. Hon. I.N. Macleod	C	19,612	51.6
			R. Glenton	L	8,885	23.4
			A.E. Hale	Lab	8,853	23.3
			W.A.C. Mowbray	Ind C	635*	1.7
					10,727	28.2
1966	47,940	80.1	Rt. Hon. I.N. Macleod	C	20,675	53.8
			T.E. Graham	Lab/Co-op	10,518	27.4
			C.T. Ross	L	7,202	18.8
					10,157	26.4
1970	52,982	71.2	Rt. Hon. I.N. Macleod	C	21,858	57.9
			H.C. King	Lab/Co-op	9,896	26.2
			J.F. Burnett	L	4,820	12.8
			K. Taylor	NF	1,175*	3.1
					11,962	31.7
[Death]						
1970 (19/11)	53,239	49.9	C.E. Parkinson	C	15,205	57.3
			H.C. King	Lab/Co-op	6,926	26.0
			A.A. Stowell	L	3,283*	12.3
			K. Taylor	NF	1,176*	4.4
					8,279	31.3

Note:—

1964: Mowbray was opposed to Britain entering the Common Market.

Election	Electors	T'out	Candidate	Party	Votes	%
1955	52,253	79.0	N.N. Dodds	Lab/Co-op	24,957	60.4
			E.L. Gardner	C	16,339	39.6
					8,618	20.8
1959	53,077	81.6	N.N. Dodds	Lab/Co-op	24,523	56.7
			J.J. Davis	C	18,763	43.3
					5,760	13.4
1964	53,967	79.6	N.N. Dodds	Lab/Co-op	22,806	53.1
			B. Black	C	13,951	32.5
			S.W. Vince	L	6,189	14.4
					8,855	20.6
[Death]						
1965 (11/11)	54,776	72.0	A.J. Wellbeloved	Lab	21,835	55.4
			W.D. Madel	C	14,763	37.4
			S.W. Vince	L	2,823*	7.2
					7,072	18.0
1966	53,463	81.7	A.J. Wellbeloved	Lab	24,243	55.5
			W.D. Madel	C	15,033	34.4
			S.W. Vince	L	3,827*	8.8
			L.H. Smith	Com	556*	1.3
					9,210	21.1
1970	57,696	71.4	A.J. Wellbeloved	Lab	23,012	55.9
			H.J. Jackson	C	18,158	44.1
					4,854	11.8

Election	Electors	T'out	Candidate	Party	Votes	%
1950	48,101	85.7	A.F. Brockway	Lab	19,987	48.5
			E.C. Cobb	C	15,594	37.8
			S.C. Wood	L	5,026*	12.2
			P.L.N. Smith	Com	614*	1.5
					4,393	10.7
1951	49,071	84.3	A.F. Brockway	Lab	22,732	54.9
			V.R. Rees	C	18,648	45.1
					4,084	9.8
1955	48,459	79.8	A.F. Brockway	Lab	20,567	53.2
			J. Grant	C	18,124	46.8
					2,443	6.4
1959	52,114	79.9	A.F. Brockway	Lab	20,851	50.1
			A.J. Page	C	20,763	49.9
					88	0.2
1964	56,725	79.9	Sir A.J.C. Meyer, Bt.	C	22,681	50.0
			A.F. Brockway	Lab	22,670	50.0
					11	0.0
1966	56,795	85.3	Miss J. Lestor	Lab	26,553	54.8
			Sir A.J.C. Meyer, Bt.	C	21,890	45.2
					4,663	9.6
1970	62,875	77.8	Miss J. Lestor	Lab	24,103	49.2
			N. Lawson	C	21,436	43.8
			P.G.D. Naylor	L	3,407*	7.0
					2,667	5.4

Election	Electors	T'out	Candidate	Party	Votes	%
1950	52,874	86.0	†J.C. Maude	C	24,339	53.5
			†T.L. Horabin	Lab	21,135	46.5
					3,204	7.0
1951	54,325	84.1	R.D. Williams	C	23,218	50.8
			E.S. Bishop	Lab	18,576	40.6
			Mrs. E.E. Tinkham	L	3,908*	8.6
					4,642	10.2
1955	54,101	79.3	R.D. Williams	C	24,147	56.3
			L.C. Merrion	Lab	18,759	43.7
					5,388	12.6
1959	54,084	82.0	R.D. Williams	C	21,579	48.6
			A.J. Rogers	Lab	15,918	35.9
			G.C. Taylor	L	6,852	15.5
					5,661	12.7
1964	54,176	80.3	Sir R.D. Dudley-Williams, Bt.	C	18,035	41.4
			Mrs. G.P. Dunwoody	Lab	16,673	38.3
			R.C. Thompson	L	8,815	20.3
					1,362	3.1
1966	54,624	83.6	Hon. Mrs. G.P. Dunwoody	Lab	22,199	48.6
			Sir R.D. Dudley-Williams, Bt.	C	18,613	40.7
			R.C. Thompson	L	4,869*	10.7
					3,586	7.9
1970	59,367	81.1	J.G. Hannam	C	21,680	45.0
			Hon. Mrs. G.P. Dunwoody	Lab	20,409	42.4
			D.J. Morrish	L	6,072	12.6
					1,271	2.6

Note:—

1959: Williams changed his surname by Deed Poll to Dudley-Williams in 1964.

Election	Electors	T'out	Candidate	Party	Votes	%
1955	50,650	78.4	A.E. Hunter	Lab	21,521	54.2
			J.A. Erskine-Shaw	C	18,171	45.8
					3,350	8.4
1959	53,417	80.4	A.E. Hunter	Lab	20,320	47.3
			J.B.W. Turner	C	18,070	42.1
			L.A. De Pinna	L	4,533*	10.6
					2,250	5.2
1964	54,147	77.2	A.E. Hunter	Lab	20,733	49.6
			J.B.W. Turner	C	14,927	35.7
			R. Roberts	L	6,141	14.7
					5,806	13.9
1966	53,697	77.3	R.W. Kerr	Lab	22,389	54.0
			Miss B.L. Wallis	C	13,932	33.5
			W.G. Crauford	L	5,206	12.5
					8,457	20.5
1970	60,273	68.2	R.W. Kerr	Lab	21,561	52.5
			Miss B.L. Wallis	C	16,006	38.9
			G.R. King	L	3,536*	8.6
					5,555	13.6

FINCHLEY [140]

Election	Electors	T'out	Candidate	Party	Votes	%
1950	71,887	84.9	†J.F.E. Crowder	C	32,262	52.9
			Mrs. D.M. Pickles	Lab	19,683	32.2
			Sir A. McFadyean	L	9,094	14.9
					12,579	20.7
1951	72,249	84.0	J.F.E. Crowder	C	33,308	54.9
			J. Ashley	Lab	20,520	33.8
			W.J. Done	L	6,853*	11.3
					12,788	21.1
1955	70,757	78.3	Sir J.F.E. Crowder	C	30,233	54.6
			T.R. Lancaster	Lab	17,408	31.4
			Miss A.M.P.H. Sykes	L	7,775	14.0
					12,825	23.2
1959	69,123	80.8	Mrs. M.H. Thatcher	C	29,697	53.2
			E.P. Deakins	Lab	13,437	24.1
			H.I. Spence	L	12,701	22.7
					16,260	29.1
1964	67,522	78.2	Mrs. M.H. Thatcher	C	24,591	46.6
			J.W. Pardoe	L	15,789	29.9
			A.E. Tomlinson	Lab	12,408	23.5
					8,802	16.7
1966	68,422	75.3	Mrs. M.H. Thatcher	C	23,968	46.5
			Mrs. Y. Sieve	Lab	14,504	28.1
			F. Davis	L	13,070	25.4
					9,464	18.4
1970	72,738	65.2	Mrs. M.H. Thatcher	C	25,480	53.7
			M.L. Freeman	Lab	14,295	30.2
			G.D. Mitchell	L	7,614	16.1
					11,185	23.5

Election	Electors	T'out	Candidate	Party	Votes	%
1950	39,368	85.8	†A.S. Moody	Lab	15,249	45.1
			D. Clift	NL & C	13,530	40.1
			†K. Zilliacus	Ind Lab	5,001	14.8
					1,719	5.0
1951	39,536	85.7	A.S. Moody	Lab	19,525	57.6
			D. Clift	NL & C	14,344	42.4
					5,181	15.2
1955	48,692**	78.8	A.S. Moody	Lab	21,653	56.4
			G. Glover	C	16,706	43.6
					4,947	12.8
1959	52,662	81.6	A.S. Moody	Lab	25,319	58.9
			G. Glover	C	17,654	41.1
					7,665	17.8
1964	51,705*	79.9	B. Conlan	Lab	26,633	64.5
			Mrs. O. Sinclair	C	14,654	35.5
					11,979	29.0
1966	52,442	75.7	B. Conlan	Lab	27,628	69.6
			J.H.E. Mendl	C	12,084	30.4
					15,544	39.2
1970	62,011	71.0	B. Conlan	Lab	28,524	64.8
			P.R. Wood	C	15,489	35.2
					13,035	29.6

Note:—

1950:   Zilliacus was a member of the Labour Independent Group.

Election	Electors	T'out	Candidate	Party	Votes	%
1950	38,776	83.9	J.T. Hall	Lab	20,872	64.2
			J.S. Magnay	NL & C	11,660	35.8
					9,212	28.4
1951	38,899	83.8	J.T. Hall	Lab	20,790	63.8
			J.S. Magnay	NL & C	11,811	36.2
					8,979	27.6
1955	46,567**	72.5	J.T. Hall	Lab	22,040	65.3
			J. Quigley	C	11,709	34.7
					10,331	30.6
[Death]						
1955 (7/12)	46,996	42.3	H.E. Randall	Lab	13,196	66.5
			D.A. Wright	C	6,661	33.5
					6,535	33.0
1959	42,643	76.9	H.E. Randall	Lab	21,277	64.9
			D.A. Wright	C	11,509	35.1
					9,768	29.8
1964	41,388*	74.9	H.E. Randall	Lab	21,390	69.0
			D.R. Chapman	C	9,623	31.0
					11,767	38.0
1966	38,878	70.1	H.E. Randall	Lab	20,381	74.8
			E. Greenwood	C	6,878	25.2
					13,503	49.6
1970	34,398	66.7	J.R. Horam	Lab	15,622	68.1
			J.A. O'Sullivan	C	7,328	31.9
					8,294	36.2

GILLINGHAM [143]

Election	Electors	T'out	Candidate	Party	Votes	%
1950	45,866	84.9	F.F.A. Burden	C	20,504	52.7
			†J. Binns	Lab	18,424	47.3
					2,080	5.4
1951	46,731	85.5	F.F.A. Burden	C	21,453	53.7
			E.C. Redhead	Lab	18,489	46.3
					2,964	7.4
1955	47,561	79.5	F.F.A. Burden	C	20,984	55.5
			J.T. Huddart	Lab	16,839	44.5
					4,145	11.0
1959	48,390	80.6	F.F.A. Burden	C	23,142	59.3
			G.B. Kaufman	Lab	15,863	40.7
					7,279	18.6
1964	50,471	78.0	F.F.A. Burden	C	20,228	51.4
			J. Ryman	Lab	14,584	37.0
			G.A. Payne	L	4,052*	10.3
			F. Cotter	Ind	527*	1.3
					5,644	14.4
1966	51,874	78.5	F.F.A. Burden	C	20,158	49.5
			J.C. Binns	Lab	17,018	41.8
			G.A. Payne	L	3,546*	8.7
					3,140	7.7
1970	59,742	73.4	F.F.A. Burden	C	25,813	58.8
			R.E. Bean	Lab	18,057	41.2
					7,756	17.6

Election	Electors	T'out	Candidate	Party	Votes	%
1950	49,005	86.4	†M. Turner-Samuels	Lab	20,202	47.7
			J.A. Kershaw	NL & C	15,708	37.1
			H.A. Guy	L	6,444	15.2
					4,494	10.6
1951	50,554*	85.5	M. Turner-Samuels	Lab	21,097	48.8
			J.A. Kershaw	NL & C	18,836	43.6
			G.E. Payne	L	3,292*	7.6
					2,261	5.2
1955	51,841*	80.9	M. Turner-Samuels	Lab	21,354	50.9
			D. Napley	C	20,606	49.1
					748	1.8
[Death]						
1957 (12/9)	51,815	71.0	J. Diamond	Lab	18,895	51.3
			F.J.V.H. Dashwood	C	10,521	28.6
			P.H. Lort-Phillips	L	7,393	20.1
					8,374	22.7
1959	52,836	82.3	J. Diamond	Lab	19,450	44.7
			H.D.K. Scott	C	16,679	38.4
			P.H. Lort-Phillips	L	7,336	16.9
					2,771	6.3
1964	54,905*	78.5	J. Diamond	Lab	19,631	45.5
			J.H.R. Stokes	C	15,514	36.0
			Mrs. S. Robson	L	7,581	17.6
			R.E. Eckley	Ind	380*	0.9
					4,117	9.5
1966	55,703	77.5	Rt. Hon. J. Diamond	Lab	20,951	48.6
			C.J.J. Balfour	C	15,678	36.3
			Mrs. S. Robson	L	6,540	15.1
					5,273	12.3
1970	61,164	76.1	Mrs. S. Oppenheim	C	21,838	46.9
			Rt. Hon. J. Diamond	Lab	20,777	44.6
			J.P. Heppell	L	3,935*	8.5
					1,061	2.3

Election	Electors	T'out	Candidate	Party	Votes	%
1950	61,644	83.2	Dr. R.F.B. Bennett	C	29,163	56.9
			A.R. Nobes	Lab	18,579	36.2
			E.W. Borrow	L	3,531*	6.9
					10,584	20.7
1951	63,088	80.9	Dr. R.F.B. Bennett	C	30,727	60.2
			N.F. Stogdon	Lab	20,303	39.8
					10,424	20.4
1955	66,475	74.2	Dr. R.F.B. Bennett	C	30,918	62.7
			S.J. Surrey	Lab	18,432	37.3
					12,486	25.4
1959	73,284	75.7	Dr. R.F.B. Bennett	C	35,808	64.6
			A.S. Pratley	Lab	19,654	35.4
					16,154	29.2
1964	82,053	76.0	Dr. R.F.B. Bennett	C	32,369	51.9
			Rev. J.R. Sturges	Lab	18,321	29.4
			E.J. Barber	L	11,684	18.7
					14,048	22.5
1966	85,033	74.5	Dr. R.F.B. Bennett	C	32,752	51.7
			Rev. J.R. Sturges	Lab	21,726	34.3
			B.V. Newman	L	8,849	14.0
					11,026	17.4
1970	100,718	71.7	Dr. R.F.B. Bennett	C	39,234	54.3
			Rev. J.R. Sturges	Lab	21,262	29.4
			P.I. Smith	L	11,754	16.3
					17,972	24.9

Election	Electors	T'out	Candidate	Party	Votes	%
1950	62,140	82.7	†Hon. K.G. Younger	Lab	28,906	56.2
			J. Hall	C	22,494	43.8
					6,412	12.4
1951	63,498	82.0	Hon. K.G. Younger	Lab	29,462	56.6
			C.W. Hewson	NL & C	22,611	43.4
					6,851	13.2
1955	63,176	73.3	Hon. K.G. Younger	Lab	24,926	53.8
			Lord Worsley	C	21,404	46.2
					3,522	7.6
1959	64,350	76.7	C.A.R. Crosland	Lab	24,729	50.1
			W. Pearson	C	24,628	49.9
					101	0.2
1964	62,263*	75.9	C.A.R. Crosland	Lab	25,675	54.3
			W. Pearson	C	21,577	45.7
					4,098	8.6
1966	61,270	74.2	Rt. Hon. C.A.R. Crosland	Lab	26,788	58.9
			P.T. Cormack	C	18,662	41.1
					8,126	17.8
1970	65,581	68.4	Rt. Hon. C.A.R. Crosland	Lab	23,571	52.5
			M.F. Spungin	C	17,460	38.9
			D.J. Hardwidge	L	3,850*	8.6
					6,111	13.6

Election	Electors	T'out	Candidate	Party	Votes	%
1950	70,963	85.1	†D. Brook	Lab	28,800	47.6
			C.H. Lucas	C	20,456	33.9
			A. Pickles	L	9,573	15.9
			R.H. Blackburn	Ind L & C	1,551*	2.6
					8,344	13.7
1951	71,343	84.2	D. Brook	Lab	30,433	50.6
			C.H. Lucas	C	29,670	49.4
					763	1.2
1955	68,714	80.2	M.V. Macmillan	C	28,306	51.4
			D. Brook	Lab	26,771	48.6
					1,535	2.8
1959	67,149	83.3	M.V. Macmillan	C	29,212	52.2
			P.D. Shore	Lab	26,697	47.8
					2,515	4.4
1964	64,455	82.1	Dr. Hon. Shirley C.W. Summerskill	Lab	23,143	43.7
			M.V. Macmillan	C	22,085	41.8
			J.F. Crossley	L	7,664	14.5
					1,058	1.9
1966	62,830	80.4	Dr. Hon. Shirley C.W. Summerskill	Lab	25,391	50.3
			G.A. Turner	C	19,687	39.0
			D.A. Carlin	L	5,423*	10.7
					5,704	11.3
1970	66,222	73.5	Dr. Hon. Shirley C.W. Summerskill	Lab	24,026	49.4
			G.A. Turner	C	23,828	48.9
			A.J.W. Graham	ILP	847*	1.7
					198	0.5

Note:—

1950: Blackburn had been a vice-chairman of Bradford Conservative Association and came forward as a candidate after the Conservative and Liberal Associations had failed to reach agreement on a proposal for a joint anti-Socialist candidate.

Election	Electors	T'out	Candidate	Party	Votes	%
1950	50,786	86.8	F.P. Bishop	C	22,907	52.0
			R.D. Rees	Lab	16,371	37.1
			N.W. Murrell	L	4,827*	10.9
					6,536	14.9
1951	50,688	85.0	F.P. Bishop	C	25,564	59.3
			Mrs. B.J.K. Thompson	Lab	17,540	40.7
					8,024	18.6
1955	50,344**	79.4	F.P. Bishop	C	23,996	60.1
			F.W. Powe	Lab	15,955	39.9
					8,041	20.2
1959	47,635	79.5	F.P. Bishop	C	23,813	62.9
			F.W. Powe	Lab	14,049	37.1
					9,764	25.8
1964	45,512	78.6	J.A. Grant	C	16,534	46.3
			R.V. Spurway	Lab	12,067	33.7
			D.F. Joyner	L	7,168	20.0
					4,467	12.6
1966	44,195	80.2	J.A. Grant	C	15,971	45.1
			A.R. Judge	Lab	14,341	40.5
			A.H.J. Miller	L	5,118	14.4
					1,630	4.6
1970	45,863	71.7	J.A. Grant	C	16,525	50.2
			A.R. Judge	Lab	12,561	38.2
			A.H.J. Miller	L	3,449*	10.5
			S.G. Carter	Ind	358*	1.1
					3,964	12.0

Note:—

1970: Carter was the nominee of the National House Owners' Society.

Election	Electors	T'out	Candidate	Party	Votes	%
1950	60,668	87.2	I.D. Harvey	C	23,680	44.7
			†F.W. Skinnard	Lab	22,216	42.0
			D.A.H. Banks	L	6,393*	12.1
			W.O. Seaman	Com	633*	1.2
					1,464	2.7
1951	61,408	87.9	I.D. Harvey	C	26,896	49.8
			R.D. Rees	Lab	23,725	44.0
			G.J.E. Rhodes	L	3,329*	6.2
					3,171	5.8
1955	49,460**	82.6	I.D. Harvey	C	22,243	54.4
			M. Rees	Lab	18,621	45.6
					3,622	8.8
[Resignation]						
1959	48,820	68.9	A.T. Courtney	C	17,766	52.8
(19/3)			M. Rees	Lab	15,546	46.2
			T. Lynch	NUSS	348*	1.0
					2,220	6.6
1959	49,273	83.5	A.T. Courtney	C	23,554	57.2
			M. Rees	Lab	17,607	42.8
					5,947	14.4
1964	47,954	80.0	A.T. Courtney	C	20,307	52.9
			Miss J. Richardson	Lab	18,048	47.1
					2,259	5.8
1966	47,267	82.8	R.D. Roebuck	Lab	17,374	44.5
			A.T. Courtney	C	16,996	43.4
			M.D. Colne	L	4,749*	12.1
					378	1.1
1970	50,363	76.0	H.J.M. Dykes	C	19,517	51.0
			R.D. Roebuck	Lab	15,496	40.5
			M.D. Colne	L	3,185*	8.3
			G. Cramp	Ind	72*	0.2
					4,021	10.5

Election	Electors	T'out	Candidate	Party	Votes	%
1950	46,781	86.7	†N.A.H. Bower	C	23,744	58.6
			T.L. Littlewood	Lab	11,971	29.5
			P.M. Syrett	L	4,846*	11.9
					11,773	29.1
[Resignation]						
1951	46,599	68.0	Sir A.N. Braithwaite	C	22,826	72.0
(21/4)			T.L. Littlewood	Lab	8,877	28.0
					13,949	44.0
1951	46,979	83.8	Sir A.N. Braithwaite	C	26,549	67.5
			T.L. Littlewood	Lab	12,802	32.5
					13,747	35.0
1955	54,616**	79.4	Sir A.N. Braithwaite	C	30,321	70.0
			R.L. Leonard	Lab	13,024	30.0
					17,297	40.0
1959	54,295	79.2	Sir A.N. Braithwaite	C	30,512	70.9
			P.J. Jenkins	Lab	12,512	29.1
					18,000	41.8
[Death]						
1960	53,905	61.6	A.J. Page	C	18,526	55.7
(17/3)			J.M. Wallbridge	L	7,100	21.4
			P.J. Jenkins	Lab	6,030	18.2
			J.E. Dayton	NCP	1,560*	4.7
					11,426	34.3
1964	53,756	79.8	A.J. Page	C	23,132	53.9
			K.W. Childerhouse	Lab	10,725	25.0
			Dr. A.E. Bender	L	9,055	21.1
					12,407	28.9
1966	53,210	80.2	A.J. Page	C	22,660	53.1
			C.H. Beaumont	Lab	12,313	28.9
			H.C. Seigal	L	7,676	18.0
					10,347	24.2
1970	57,374	72.8	A.J. Page	C	24,867	59.6
			T.P.C. Daniel	Lab	11,462	27.4
			J.F. Smith	L	5,440	13.0
					13,405	32.2

Election	Electors	T'out	Candidate	Party	Votes	%
1950	58,064	87.2	†D.T. Jones	Lab	25,609	50.6
			T.G. Greenwell	C	20,373	40.3
			Dr. F.J. Long	L	4,623*	9.1
					5,236	10.3
1951	59,592	86.6	D.T. Jones	Lab	27,147	52.6
			P.T. Carter	C	24,437	47.4
					2,710	5.2
1955	59,512*	81.8	D.T. Jones	Lab	25,145	51.6
			F.H.G.H. Goodhart	C	23,560	48.4
					1,585	3.2
1959	60,888	83.3	J.S. Kerans	C	25,463	50.2
			D.T. Jones	Lab	25,281	49.8
					182	0.4
1964	59,703	81.9	E. Leadbitter	Lab	25,883	52.9
			G.H. Dodsworth	C	23,016	47.1
					2,867	5.8
1966	59,071	78.5	E. Leadbitter	Lab	27,509	59.3
			H.I. Bransom	C	18,857	40.7
					8,652	18.6
1970	64,320	74.5	E. Leadbitter	Lab	27,704	57.8
			R.M. Marshall	C	20,188	42.2
					7,516	15.6

Election	Electors	T'out	Candidate	Party	Votes	%
1950	69,101	82.1	†E.M. Cooper-Key	C	30,035	52.9
			L.C. Cohen	Lab	17,603	31.0
			P.L.M. Hurd	L	9,122	16.1
					12,432	21.9
1951	69,956	77.4	E.M. Cooper-Key	C	34,495	63.7
			Mrs. C.E. Williamson	Lab	19,621	36.3
					14,874	27.4
1955	48,493**	75.7	E.M. Cooper-Key	C	20,469	55.8
			R.G. White	Lab	11,933	32.5
			J. Montgomerie	L	4,303*	11.7
					8,536	23.3
1959	48,569	74.2	E.M. Cooper-Key	C	22,458	62.3
			J.P. Bryant	Lab	13,576	37.7
					8,882	24.6
1964	49,701	76.3	Sir E.M. Cooper-Key	C	16,902	44.6
			H.A. Fountain	Lab	11,324	29.8
			J.J. Arnold	L	9,716	25.6
					5,578	14.8
1966	49,802	76.4	Sir E.M. Cooper-Key	C	15,324	40.3
			C.B. Kissen	Lab	12,984	34.1
			J.J. Arnold	L	9,744	25.6
					2,340	6.2
1970	55,213	72.9	K.R. Warren	C	20,364	50.6
			C.B. Kissen	Lab	13,549	33.7
			Mrs. P.M. Shields	L	6,324	15.7
					6,815	16.9

Election	Electors	T'out	Candidate	Party	Votes	%
1950	43,893	85.1	†W.H. Ayles	Lab	22,490	60.2
			C.C. Vinson	C	11,218	30.0
			J.W.F. Lett	L	3,093*	8.3
			F.T. Foster	Com	573*	1.5
					11,272	30.2
1951	44,737	82.2	W.H. Ayles	Lab	23,823	64.8
			M.J. Rantzen	C	12,949	35.2
					10,874	29.6
[Resignation]						
1953 (1/4)	44,525	45.0	A.M. Skeffington	Lab	12,797	63.9
			A.J. Sumption	C	7,221	36.1
					5,576	27.8
1955	44,259	76.6	A.M. Skeffington	Lab	19,588	57.8
			A.T. Courtney	C	13,440	39.6
			F.T. Foster	Com	886*	2.6
					6,148	18.2
1959	46,244	80.5	A.M. Skeffington	Lab	18,301	49.2
			J.A. Grant	C	14,149	38.0
			S. Gay	L	4,235*	11.4
			F.T. Foster	Com	527*	1.4
					4,152	11.2
1964	46,512	73.2	A.M. Skeffington	Lab	20,018	58.8
			L.E. Smith	C	13,158	38.6
			F. Stanley	Com	873*	2.6
					6,860	20.2
1966	45,797	72.7	A.M. Skeffington	Lab	20,707	62.2
			L.E. Smith	C	11,883	35.7
			F. Stanley	Com	698*	2.1
					8,824	26.5
1970	49,556	67.2	A.M. Skeffington	Lab	19,192	57.7
			A.W. Potier	C	13,728	41.2
			P. Pink	Com	372*	1.1
					5,464	16.5
[Death]						
1971 (17/6)	50,066	42.3	N.D. Sandelson	Lab	15,827	74.7
			A.W. Potier	C	5,348	25.3
					10,479	49.4

Election	Electors	T'out	Candidate	Party	Votes	%
1950	54,153	86.3	C.I. Orr-Ewing	C	20,755	44.3
			†Mrs. B.A. Gould	Lab	18,500	39.6
			E.D. Martell	L	6,575	14.1
			Mrs. M.E. Pollitt	Com	918*	2.0
					2,255	4.7
1951	54,913	86.3	C.I. Orr-Ewing	C	23,329	49.2
			Hon. F.R. Rea	Lab	20,738	43.8
			K.G. Jupp	L	3,319*	7.0
					2,591	5.4
1955	53,653	80.7	C.I. Orr-Ewing	C	21,934	50.7
			Miss E.M. Monkhouse	Lab	17,874	41.3
			D. Barrington-Hudson	L	3,467*	8.0
					4,060	9.4
1959	52,729	81.7	C.I. Orr-Ewing	C	21,898	50.8
			C.H. Genese	Lab/Co-op	16,566	38.5
			Lady Hills	L	4,598*	10.7
					5,332	12.3
1964	51,137	78.5	Sir C.I. Orr-Ewing, Bt.	C	17,784	44.3
			A.R. Jinkinson	Lab	16,660	41.5
			J.H. Holmes	L	5,719	14.2
					1,124	2.8
1966	49,784	80.0	Sir C.I. Orr-Ewing, Bt.	C	18,468	46.3
			E. Wistrich	Lab	17,868	44.9
			M.G. Cass	L	3,503*	8.8
					600	1.4
1970	51,999	71.0	J.M. Gorst	C	18,192	49.3
			A.A.M. Irvine	Lab	15,013	40.7
			M.G. Cass	L	3,704*	10.0
					3,179	8.6

Election	Electors	T'out	Candidate	Party	Votes	%
1950	57,089	83.6	†Sir H.V.H.D. Lucas-Tooth, Bt.	C	24,917	52.2
			T. Sargant	Lab	15,389	32.2
			C.J.H. Tolley	L	7,436	15.6
					9,528	20.0
1951	57,843	81.7	Sir H.V.H.D. Lucas-Tooth, Bt.	C	26,180	55.4
			Dr. B. Homa	Lab	16,124	34.1
			L. MacLaren	L	4,952*	10.5
					10,056	21.3
1955	54,983	73.2	Sir H.V.H.D. Lucas-Tooth, Bt.	C	25,354	63.0
			Dr. B. Homa	Lab	14,918	37.0
					10,436	26.0
1959	53,545	76.8	Sir H.V.H.D. Lucas-Tooth, Bt.	C	22,971	55.9
			P.K. Archer	Lab	11,016	26.8
			P.H. Billenness	L	7,134	17.3
					11,955	29.1
1964	52,009	73.7	Sir H.V.H.D. Lucas-Tooth, Bt.	C	18,452	48.1
			A.A. Grant	Lab	11,441	29.9
			P.H. Billenness	L	8,430	22.0
					7,011	18.2
1966	51,812	73.2	Sir H.V.H.D. Munro- Lucas-Tooth, Bt.	C	17,176	45.3
			G.J. Samuel	Lab	13,120	34.6
			L. Young	L	7,632	20.1
					4,056	10.7
1970	55,551	65.9	Rt. Hon. P.J.M. Thomas	C	18,901	51.7
			Mrs. G.F. Dimson	Lab	12,712	34.7
			L. Young	L	4,981	13.6
					6,189	17.0

HESTON and ISLEWORTH [156]

Election	Electors	T'out	Candidate	Party	Votes	%
1950	77,262	86.1	R.R. Harris	C	33,292	50.1
			†W.R. Williams	Lab	29,013	43.6
			D.K. Overell	L	4,183*	6.3
					4,279	6.5
1951	78,048	83.8	R.R. Harris	C	35,468	54.2
			P.A.W. Merriton	Lab	29,944	45.8
					5,524	8.4
1955	56,883**	78.9	R.R. Harris	C	25,705	57.3
			Mrs. O.M. Renier	Lab	19,193	42.7
					6,512	14.6
1959	55,121	81.6	R.R. Harris	C	24,486	54.4
			Hon. T.A. Ponsonby	Lab	15,636	34.8
			W.P. Letch	L	4,867*	10.8
					8,850	19.6
1964	52,703	78.3	R.R. Harris	C	19,181	46.5
			J. Dore	Lab	15,651	38.0
			H.C. Seigal	L	6,409	15.5
					3,530	8.5
1966	51,400	79.9	R.R. Harris	C	18,222	44.4
			N.D. Sandelson	Lab	17,296	42.1
			R.L. Afton	L	5,559	13.5
					926	2.3
1970	53,859	71.6	B.J. Hayhoe	C	21,580	56.0
			G.J. Samuel	Lab	16,981	44.0
					4,599	12.0

Election	Electors	T'out	Candidate	Party	Votes	%
1950	72,146	85.7	†G.H.C. Bing	Lab	28,463	46.0
			J.W. Day	C	26,696	43.2
			Miss B.N. Seear	L	6,653*	10.8
					1,767	2.8
1951	73,680	86.1	G.H.C. Bing	Lab	30,010	47.3
			J.W. Day	C	28,976	45.7
			Miss B.N. Seear	L	4,471*	7.0
					1,034	1.6
1955	77,041	82.0	G.W. Lagden	C	29,205	46.2
			G.H.C. Bing	Lab	27,833	44.1
			D.S. Paterson	L	6,117*	9.7
					1,372	2.1
1959	87,544	83.9	G.W. Lagden	C	34,852	47.4
			Miss J. Richardson	Lab	27,530	37.5
			L.H. Jones	L	11,056	15.1
					7,322	9.9
1964	90,828	81.9	G.W. Lagden	C	30,933	41.6
			S.T. Williams	Lab	30,699	41.3
			R.S. Taylor	L	12,725	17.1
					234	0.3
1966	90,969	81.1	A.L. Williams	Lab	38,406	52.1
			G.W. Lagden	C	35,373	47.9
					3,033	4.2
1970	99,643	72.9	J.W. Loveridge	C	36,124	49.7
			A.L. Williams	Lab	30,294	41.7
			B.G. Sell	L	6,227*	8.6
					5,830	8.0

Election	Electors	T'out	Candidate	Party	Votes	%
1950	74,057	85.2	†L.D. Gammans	C	33,927	53.8
			R.A. Pestell	Lab	22,832	36.2
			Miss A.A.E.M. Leevers	L	5,122*	8.1
			G.J. Jones	Com	1,191*	1.9
					11,095	17.6
1951	75,131	82.6	L.D. Gammans	C	36,417	58.7
			R.A. Pestell	Lab	25,643	41.3
					10,774	17.4
1955	72,484	76.3	L.D. Gammans	C	33,294	60.2
			F.E. Mostyn	Lab	20,568	37.2
			G.J. Jones	Com	1,442*	2.6
					12,726	23.0
[Death]						
1957 (30/5)	71,771	63.0	Lady Gammans	C	24,169	53.5
			F.E. Mostyn	Lab	21,038	46.5
					3,131	7.0
1959	71,151	76.7	Lady Gammans	C	30,048	55.0
			F.E. Mostyn	Lab	17,710	32.5
			S. Solomon	L	5,706*	10.5
			G.J. Jones	Com	1,107*	2.0
					12,338	22.5
1964	68,691	70.4	Lady Gammans	C	22,590	46.7
			C.S. Yeo	Lab	18,528	38.3
			S. Solomon	L	6,015*	12.4
			M. Morris	Com	1,258*	2.6
					4,062	8.4
1966	65,739	72.8	H.A.L. Rossi	C	21,116	44.1
			C.S. Yeo	Lab	20,501	42.9
			P.W. Meyer	L	5,026*	10.5
			M. Morris	Com	1,184*	2.5
					615	1.2
1970	64,683	67.4	H.A.L. Rossi	C	21,434	49.1
			P.A.W. Pestell	Lab	17,645	40.5
			L.S. Brass	L	3,755*	8.6
			Mrs. M. Morris	Com	624*	1.4
			E.S. Grant	SPGB	156*	0.4
					3,789	8.6

Election	Electors	T'out	Candidate	Party	Votes	%
1950	61,556	81.9	†A.A.H. Marlowe	C	33,748	66.9
			Hon. F.R. Rea	Lab	11,791	23.4
			J.R. Colclough	L	4,893*	9.7
					21,957	43.5
1951	64,813	77.4	A.A.H. Marlowe	C	37,230	74.2
			A.D. Bermel	Lab	12,934	25.8
					24,296	48.4
1955	65,209	71.0	A.A.H. Marlowe	C	34,314	74.2
			H.F. Parker	Lab	11,961	25.8
					22,353	48.4
1959	67,018	72.2	A.A.H. Marlowe	C	36,150	74.8
			T.J. Marsh	Lab	12,206	25.2
					23,944	49.6
1964	69,143	69.6	A.A.H. Marlowe	C	32,923	68.4
			T.J. Marsh	Lab	15,214	31.6
				–	17,709	36.8
[Resignation]						
1965 (22/7)	69,634	58.5	W.F.M. Maddan	C	25,339	62.2
			T.J. Marsh	Lab	8,387	20.6
			O.C.N. Moxon	L	6,867	16.9
			M. Cossman	Ind	121*	0.3
					16,952	41.6
1966	69,807	72.1	W.F.M. Maddan	C	28,799	57.2
			T. Williams	Lab	12,909	25.7
			O.C.N. Moxon	L	8,037	16.0
			M. Cossman	Ind	574*	1.1
					15,890	31.5
1970	74,789	66.8	W.F.M. Maddan	C	34,287	68.7
			D.G. Nicholas	Lab	15,639	31.3
					18,648	37.4

Election	Electors	T'out	Candidate	Party	Votes	%
1950	45,953	85.7	†J.P.W. Mallalieu	Lab	22,296	56.6
			J.W. Smith	C	17,063	43.4
					5,233	13.2
1951	46,384	86.6	J.P.W. Mallalieu	Lab	22,368	55.7
			J.W. Smith	C	17,799	44.3
					4,569	11.4
1955	51,672**	80.2	J.P.W. Mallalieu	Lab	22,835	55.1
			D. Clift	C	18,611	44.9
					4,224	10.2
1959	51,929	80.6	J.P.W. Mallalieu	Lab	22,474	53.7
			P.M. Beard	C	19,389	46.3
					3,085	7.4
1964	51,193	78.6	J.P.W. Mallalieu	Lab	20,501	51.0
			J.A. Fergusson	C	12,232	30.4
			B. Jennings	L	7,494	18.6
					8,269	20.6
1966	50,509	77.9	J.P.W. Mallalieu	Lab	21,960	55.8
			J.A. Fergusson	C	11,081	28.2
			G.M. Lee	L	6,303	16.0
					10,879	27.6
1970	54,496	75.5	J.P.W. Mallalieu	Lab	20,629	50.2
			J.G. Holt	C	15,632	38.0
			G.M. Lee	L	4,569*	11.1
			Mrs. E. Beresford	Com	308*	0.7
					4,997	12.2

Election	Electors	T'out	Candidate	Party	Votes	%
1950	48,351	86.9	D.W. Wade	L	24,456	58.2
			H.W. Bolt	Lab	17,542	41.8
					6,914	16.4
1951	47,851	85.9	D.W. Wade	L	24,054	58.5
			H.W. Bolt	Lab	17,066	41.5
					6,988	17.0
1955	51,427**	79.3	D.W. Wade	L	24,345	59.7
			J.F. Drabble	Lab	16,418	40.3
					7,927	19.4
1959	51,284	79.7	D.W. Wade	L	25,273	61.8
			J. Marsden	Lab	15,621	38.2
					9,652	23.6
1964	50,748	81.6	K. Lomas	Lab	14,808	35.8
			D.W. Wade	L	13,528	32.7
			J.F.W. Addey	C	13,054	31.5
					1,280	3.1
1966	49,813	82.3	K. Lomas	Lab	17,990	43.9
			J.M. Fox	C	13,514	33.0
			R.H. Hargreaves	L	9,470	23.1
					4,476	10.9
1970	53,107	77.4	K. Lomas	Lab	16,866	41.0
			Hon. R. Storey	C	16,673	40.6
			W.J.L. Wallace	L	6,128	14.9
			R.J. Scott	NF	1,427*	3.5
					193	0.4

Election	Electors	T'out	Candidate	Party	Votes	%
1950	66,720	85.9	G.C. Hutchinson	C	29,950	52.2
			†Mrs. M. Ridealgh	Lab/Co-op	21,385	37.3
			S.W. Alexander	L	6,009*	10.5
					8,565	14.9
1951	67,796	84.8	G.C. Hutchinson	C	31,905	55.5
			Mrs. M. Ridealgh	Lab/Co-op	21,865	38.0
			H.E. Pollard	L	3,709*	6.5
					10,040	17.5

[Resignation on appointment as Chairman of the National Assistance Board]

Election	Electors	T'out	Candidate	Party	Votes	%
1954 (3/2)	67,689	45.4	T.L.I.S.V. Iremonger	C	18,354	59.8
			T.W. Richardson	Lab/Co-op	9,927	32.3
			G.E. Thornton	L	2,430*	7.9
					8,427	27.5
1955	67,496	76.6	T.L.I.S.V. Iremonger	C	28,749	55.6
			R. Groves	Lab	18,248	35.3
			P.L. Rose	L	4,702*	9.1
					10,501	20.3
1959	67,208	79.6	T.L.I.S.V. Iremonger	C	29,609	55.4
			C.F.H. Green	Lab	15,962	29.8
			D.K. Mills	L	7,915	14.8
					13,647	25.6
1964	66,769*	76.9	T.L.I.S.V. Iremonger	C	24,096	46.9
			J.A. Punshon	Lab	16,563	32.3
			D.K. Mills	L	10,692	20.8
					7,533	14.6
1966	66,569	76.7	T.L.I.S.V. Iremonger	C	23,736	46.5
			J.A. Punshon	Lab	20,392	39.9
			J.A. Harris	L	6,953	13.6
					3,344	6.6
1970	69,722	68.7	T.L.I.S.V. Iremonger	C	25,142	52.5
			C.W. Sewell	Lab/Co-op	17,352	36.2
			G.L.P. Wilson	L	5,425*	11.3
					7,790	16.3

Election	Electors	T'out	Candidate	Party	Votes	%
1950	66,450	85.4	A.E. Cooper	C	28,087	49.5
			†J. Ranger	Lab	23,558	41.5
			R.A. Hall	L	4,170*	7.4
			D. Kelly	Com	913*	1.6
					4,529	8.0
1951	66,678	82.7	A.E. Cooper	C	30,177	54.8
			J. Ranger	Lab	24,938	45.2
					5,239	9.6
1955	63,866	75.3	A.E. Cooper	C	27,292	56.7
			J. Ranger	Lab	20,814	43.3
					6,478	13.4
1959	60,678	77.9	A.E. Cooper	C	23,876	50.5
			G.J. Borrie	Lab	16,569	35.0
			R.V. Netherclift	L	6,832	14.5
					7,307	15.5
1964	58,066*	74.7	A.E. Cooper	C	18,152	41.9
			A.J. Shaw	Lab	16,660	38.4
			P. McGregor	L	8,547	19.7
					1,492	3.5
1966	56,302	76.9	A.J. Shaw	Lab	20,613	47.6
			A.E. Cooper	C	18,093	41.8
			Miss I. Watson	L	4,606*	10.6
					2,520	5.8
1970	58,243	68.2	A.E. Cooper	C	18,369	46.3
			A.J. Shaw	Lab	17,087	43.0
			G.L. Wilson	L	3,341*	8.4
			M.E.L. Skeggs	NF	727*	1.8
			M.J. Marks	Ind	190*	0.5
					1,282	3.3

IPSWICH [164]

Election	Electors	T'out	Candidate	Party	Votes	%
1950	72,277	86.8	†R.R. Stokes	Lab	29,386	46.9
			S.W.L. Ripley	C	24,993	39.8
			J.C. Seward	L	8,340	13.3
					4,393	7.1
1951	73,622	85.2	Rt. Hon. R.R. Stokes	Lab	33,463	53.4
			A.E. Holdsworth	C	29,227	46.6
					4,236	6.8
1955	75,792*	80.5	Rt. Hon. R.R. Stokes	Lab	32,306	52.9
			J.C. Cobbold	C	28,724	47.1
					3,582	5.8
[Death]						
1957 (24/10)	77,621	75.6	D.M. Foot	Lab	26,898	45.8
			J.C. Cobbold	C	19,161	32.7
			Miss A.M.P.H. Sykes	L	12,587	21.5
					7,737	13.1
1959	77,633	80.9	D.M. Foot	Lab	25,838	41.1
			J.C. Cobbold	C	22,623	36.0
			Miss A.M.P.H. Sykes	L	14,359	22.9
					3,215	5.1
1964	78,463	79.0	D.M. Foot	Lab	24,648	39.7
			T.A. Hagger	C	22,216	35.9
			Miss A.M.P.H. Sykes	L	14,755	23.8
			Dr. D.R.M. Brown	N Dem P	349*	0.6
					2,432	3.8
1966	78,351	77.5	Sir D.M. Foot	Lab	30,313	49.9
			T.A. Hagger	C	23,440	38.6
			Dr. S. Rundle	L	6,200*	10.2
			Dr. D.R.M. Brown	N Dem P	769*	1.3
					6,873	11.3
1970	86,404	72.8	E.D.D. Money	C	27,704	44.1
			Rt. Hon. Sir D.M. Foot	Lab	27,691	44.0
			N. Lewis	L	5,147*	8.2
			Dr. D.R.M. Brown	N Dem P	2,322*	3.7
					13	0.1

Election	Electors	T'out	Candidate	Party	Votes	%
1955	49,340	79.1	E. Fernyhough	Lab	24,706	63.3
			Miss M. Dickinson	C	14,304	36.7
					10,402	26.6
1959	50,965	80.3	E. Fernyhough	Lab	25,638	62.6
			T.T. Hubble	C	15,286	37.4
					10,352	25.2
1964	50,668	80.0	E. Fernyhough	Lab	26,053	64.2
			T.T. Hubble	C	14,503	35.8
					11,550	28.4
1966	50,158	76.7	E. Fernyhough	Lab	26,006	67.6
			D.J. Robson	C	12,449	32.4
					13,557	35.2
1970	54,652	74.5	E. Fernyhough	Lab	25,861	63.5
			D.J. Robson	C	14,847	36.5
					11,014	27.0

Election	Electors	T'out	Candidate	Party	Votes	%
1950	51,115	88.1	†C.R. Hobson	Lab	21,833	48.4
			K. Hargreaves	C	16,252	36.1
			J.G. Walker	L	6,962	15.5
					5,581	12.3
1951	51,468	87.5	C.R. Hobson	Lab	23,743	52.7
			K. Hargreaves	C	21,295	47.3
					2,448	5.4
1955	49,750	83.9	C.R. Hobson	Lab	19,414	46.5
			W.M.J. Worsley	C	16,011	38.4
			A. Mitchell	L	6,310	15.1
					3,403	8.1
1959	47,981	85.6	W.M.J. Worsley	C	20,626	50.2
			C.R. Hobson	Lab	20,456	49.8
					170	0.4
1964	48,415	85.6	J. Binns	Lab	17,816	42.9
			W.M.J. Worsley	C	15,115	36.5
			W.E. Jones	L	8,529	20.6
					2,701	6.4
1966	48,006	83.5	J. Binns	Lab	22,039	55.0
			J.G. Bellak	C	18,027	45.0
					4,012	10.0
1970	51,140	80.8	Miss J.V. Hall	C	20,957	50.7
			J. Binns	Lab	20,341	49.3
					616	1.4

Election	Electors	T'out	Candidate	Party	Votes	%
1950	61,918	78.2	†M. Hewitson	Lab	27,351	56.5
			R.O. Wilberforce	C	15,951	32.9
			A.R. Hardcastle	L	5,113*	10.6
					11,400	23.6
1951	62,996	76.3	M. Hewitson	Lab	29,674	61.7
			W.R. Bull	C	18,413	38.3
					11,261	23.4

This constituency was divided in 1955.

Election	Electors	T'out	Candidate	Party	Votes	%
1950	56,135	85.3	†H. Pursey	Lab	26,903	56.2
			W.J.C. Heyting	C	13,988	29.2
			T.E. Dalton	L	6,981	14.6
					12,915	27.0
1951	58,028	84.2	H. Pursey	Lab	27,892	57.1
			H. Richman	C	16,368	33.5
			R.W. Sykes	L	4,611*	9.4
					11,524	23.6
1955	69,423**	75.6	H. Pursey	Lab	28,990	55.2
			H. Richman	C	16,284	31.0
			J.J. MacCallum	L	7,242	13.8
					12,706	24.2
1959	73,826*	79.0	H. Pursey	Lab	30,667	52.6
			Mrs. M. Heath	C	17,648	30.2
			J.J. MacCallum	L	10,043	17.2
					13,019	22.4
1964	73,151	74.8	H. Pursey	Lab	30,634	56.0
			Mrs. M. Heath	C	14,284	26.1
			N.W. Turner	L	9,781	17.9
					16,350	29.9
1966	71,694	73.4	H. Pursey	Lab	34,457	65.5
			Mrs. M. Heath	C	11,385	21.6
			N.W. Turner	L	6,795	12.9
					23,072	43.9
1970	75,597	68.3	J.L. Prescott	Lab	36,859	71.4
			N.S.H. Lamont	C	14,736	28.6
					22,123	42.8

Election	Electors	T'out	Candidate	Party	Votes	%
1950	55,640	85.1	†Rt. Hon. R.K. Law	C	23,482	49.6
			T.L.A. Taylor	Lab	18,156	38.3
			A. Burrell	L	5,723*	12.1
					5,326	11.3
1951	56,485	82.8	Rt. Hon. R.K. Law	C	27,168	58.1
			C.W. Bridges	Lab	19,584	41.9
					7,584	16.2

[Elevation to the Peerage—Lord Coleraine]

Election	Electors	T'out	Candidate	Party	Votes	%
1954 (11/2)	57,036	45.7	P.H.B. Wall	C	16,107	61.8
			C.W. Bridges	Lab	9,974	38.2
					6,133	23.6

This constituency was divided in 1955.

KINGSTON UPON HULL, NORTH [170]

Election	Electors	T'out	Candidate	Party	Votes	%
1950	48,808	86.3	W.R.A. Hudson	C	18,811	44.7
			C.F.C. Lawson	Lab	18,041	42.8
			G.S. Atkinson	L	5,268	12.5
					770	1.9
1951	50,262	84.7	W.R.A. Hudson	C	22,545	53.0
			J.H. Foord	Lab	20,025	47.0
					2,520	6.0
1955	65,880**	77.4	W.R.A. Hudson	C	25,780	50.6
			J.H. Foord	Lab	25,190	49.4
					590	1.2
1959	63,918	81.6	J.M. Coulson	C	23,612	45.2
			J.H. Foord	Lab	22,910	44.0
			A. Butcher	L	5,604*	10.8
					702	1.2
1964	61,783	77.2	H. Solomons	Lab	20,664	43.3
			J.M. Coulson	C	19,483	40.8
			Mrs. L.S. Millward	L	7,570	15.9
					1,181	2.5
[Death]						
1966 (27/1)	61,418	76.3	J.K. McNamara	Lab	24,479	52.2
			T.F.H. Jessel	C	19,128	40.8
			Mrs. L.S. Millward	L	2,945*	6.3
			R.W. Gott	RA	253*	0.5
			R.E. Eckley	Ind	35*	0.1
			K.R. Woodburne	Ind	33*	0.1
					5,351	11.4
1966	61,112	79.0	J.K. McNamara	Lab	26,640	55.2
			T.F.H. Jessel	C	17,871	37.0
			Mrs. L.S. Millward	L	3,747*	7.8
					8,769	18.2
1970	65,618	70.1	J.K. McNamara	Lab	26,302	57.2
			J.E. Townend	C	17,912	38.9
			W.A.C. Harvey	Ind	1,808*	3.9
					8,390	18.3

Note:—

1970: Harvey was opposed to Britain entering the Common Market.

KINGSTON UPON HULL, WEST [171]

Election	Electors	T'out	Candidate	Party	Votes	%
1955	65,670	70.1	M. Hewitson	Lab	25,785	56.0
			R. Northam	C	20,262	44.0
					5,523	12.0
1959	64,100	75.6	M. Hewitson	Lab	25,446	52.5
			T.H.F. Farrell	C	23,011	47.5
					2,435	5.0
1964	61,577	70.9	J. Johnson	Lab	24,855	56.9
			J.G. Bellak	C	18,825	43.1
					6,030	13.8
1966	58,743	70.4	J. Johnson	Lab	26,816	64.8
			J.G.D. Shaw	C	14,551	35.2
					12,265	29.6
1970	59,511	64.8	J. Johnson	Lab	24,050	62.3
			T.E. Forrow	C	14,537	37.7
					9,513	24.6

KINGSTON UPON THAMES [172]

Election	Electors	T'out	Candidate	Party	Votes	%
1950	73,375	85.2	†J.A. Boyd-Carpenter	C	36,886	59.0
			Dr. Nora M. Johns	Lab	21,229	33.9
			D.G. Maskrey	L	4,429*	7.1
					15,657	25.1
1951	74,803	81.1	J.A. Boyd-Carpenter	C	38,516	63.5
			R. Hesketh	Lab	22,117	36.5
					16,399	27.0
1955	61,762**	76.4	Rt. Hon. J.A. Boyd-Carpenter	C	31,069	65.9
			G.H. Loman	Lab	16,104	34.1
					14,965	31.8
1959	60,403	77.9	Rt. Hon. J.A. Boyd-Carpenter	C	31,649	67.3
			T. Braddock	Lab	15,408	32.7
					16,241	34.6
1964	58,884*	77.1	Rt. Hon. J.A. Boyd-Carpenter	C	23,973	52.8
			T. Braddock	Lab	13,611	30.0
			Dr. S. Rundle	L	7,827	17.2
					10,362	22.8
1966	57,705	77.0	Rt. Hon. J.A. Boyd-Carpenter	C	22,781	51.3
			J.S. Cook	Lab	14,915	33.6
			M.F. Burns	L	6,722	15.1
					7,866	17.7
1970	59,737	69.2	Rt. Hon. J.A. Boyd-Carpenter	C	23,426	56.6
			R.H. Crockett	Lab	13,090	31.7
			S.J.E. Wells	L	4,822*	11.7
					10,336	24.9

Election	Electors	T'out	Candidate	Party	Votes	%
1950	50,544	78.3	†G. Porter	Lab	24,030	60.7
			W. Barford	C	13,351	33.8
			V.L.R. Delepine	L	2,176*	5.5
					10,679	26.9
1951	49,858*	77.1	G. Porter	Lab	23,967	62.3
			W. Barford	C	14,475	37.7
					9,492	24.6

This constituency was divided in 1955.

LEEDS, EAST [174]

Election	Electors	T'out	Candidate	Party	Votes	%
1955	61,944	76.2	D.W. Healey	Lab	26,083	55.2
			C.D. Chapman	C	21,144	44.8
					4,939	10.4
1959	66,074	79.7	D.W. Healey	Lab	28,707	54.5
			J.A. Fawcett	C	23,922	45.5
					4,785	9.0
1964	66,944*	76.1	D.W. Healey	Lab	29,480	57.9
			J.A. Fawcett	C	21,474	42.1
					8,006	15.8
1966	67,189	72.7	Rt. Hon. D.W. Healey	Lab	30,073	61.5
			A.R.M. Graham	C	18,796	38.5
					11,277	23.0
1970	76,532	65.9	Rt. Hon. D.W. Healey	Lab	28,827	57.2
			P. Crotty	C	21,112	41.8
			Mrs. J. Bellamy	Com	513*	1.0
					7,715	15.4

Election	Electors	T'out	Candidate	Party	Votes	%
1950	56,075	84.2	†Rt. Hon. O. Peake	C	27,766	58.8
			R.J. Hurst	Lab	15,018	31.8
			Mrs. W.F. Underhill	L	4,446*	9.4
					12,748	27.0
1951	58,219*	81.7	Rt. Hon. O. Peake	C	30,290	63.7
			P. Taylor	Lab	17,249	36.3
					13,041	27.4

This constituency was divided in 1955.

Election	Electors	T'out	Candidate	Party	Votes	%
1950	48,131	82.3	†Miss A.M. Bacon	Lab	21,599	54.6
			J.C. Bidgood	C	14,780	37.3
			W.G.V. Jones	L	2,612*	6.6
			B. Ramelson	Com	612*	1.5
					6,819	17.3
1951	47,461*	80.9	Miss A.M. Bacon	Lab	22,402	58.3
			J.C. Bidgood	C	15,991	41.7
					6,411	16.6
1955	55,441**	73.1	Rt. Hon. O. Peake	C	24,902	61.4
			H.M. Waterman	Lab	15,623	38.6
					9,279	22.8

[Elevation to the Peerage—Viscount Ingleby]

Election	Electors	T'out	Candidate	Party	Votes	%
1956 (9/2)	55,876	39.9	Sir K.S. Joseph, Bt.	C	14,081	63.2
			H.M. Waterman	Lab	8,212	36.8
					5,869	26.4
1959	54,594	75.0	Sir K.S. Joseph, Bt.	C	26,240	64.1
			H.M. Waterman	Lab	14,709	35.9
					11,531	28.2
1964	54,740*	71.1	Rt. Hon. Sir K.S. Joseph, Bt.	C	23,613	60.7
			K. Gould	Lab	15,288	39.3
					8,325	21.4
1966	53,824	68.1	Rt. Hon. Sir K.S. Joseph, Bt.	C	20,813	56.8
			D.A. Mallen	Lab	15,851	43.2
					4,962	13.6
1970	55,597	65.4	Rt. Hon. Sir K.S. Joseph, Bt.	C	20,720	57.0
			A.J. Patient	Lab	15,653	43.0
					5,067	14.0

Election	Electors	T'out	Candidate	Party	Votes	%
1950	48,876	85.5	D. Kaberry	C	24,161	57.8
			V. Mishcon	Lab	14,562	34.8
			J.O. Hogley	L	3,078*	7.4
					9,599	23.0
1951	50,184*	82.4	D. Kaberry	C	25,873	62.6
			Miss M. Veitch	Lab	15,490	37.4
					10,383	25.2
1955	64,142**	75.6	D. Kaberry	C	31,923	65.8
			D.B. Matthews	Lab	16,594	34.2
					15,329	31.6
1959	69,243	77.6	D. Kaberry	C	35,210	65.5
			D.B. Matthews	Lab	18,508	34.5
					16,702	31.0
1964	74,417	77.2	Sir D. Kaberry, Bt.	C	29,859	52.0
			D.B. Matthews	Lab	18,862	32.8
			R.H.J. Rhodes	L	8,728	15.2
					10,997	19.2
1966	74,191	73.1	Sir D. Kaberry, Bt.	C	30,168	55.6
			C.J. Morgan	Lab	24,044	44.4
					6,124	11.2
1970	80,249	69.9	Sir D. Kaberry, Bt.	C	29,227	52.1
			K.J. Woolmer	Lab	20,795	37.1
			J.R. Worrall	L	6,048*	10.8
					8,432	15.0

Election	Electors	T'out	Candidate	Party	Votes	%
1950	57,625	84.6	†Rt. Hon. H.T.N. Gaitskell	Lab	29,795	61.1
			B.H. Wood	C	14,436	29.6
			E. Meeks	L	4,525*	9.3
					15,359	31.5
1951	57,436*	82.2	Rt. Hon. H.T.N. Gaitskell	Lab	30,712	65.1
			Miss W.D. Brown	C	16,493	34.9
					14,219	30.2
1955	54,424**	72.9	Rt. Hon. H.T.N. Gaitskell	Lab	25,833	65.2
			Miss W.D. Brown	C	13,817	34.8
					12,016	30.4
1959	52,822	79.0	Rt. Hon. H.T.N. Gaitskell	Lab	24,442	58.6
			J.F.W. Addey	C	12,956	31.0
			J.B. Meeks	L	4,340*	10.4
					11,486	27.6
[Death]						
1963	49,313	60.5	M. Rees	Lab	18,785	63.0
(20/6)			J.O. Udal	C	5,996	20.1
			B. Walsh	L	4,399	14.7
			B. Ramelson	Com	670*	2.2
					12,789	42.9
1964	49,151	72.0	M. Rees	Lab	22,339	63.1
			P.A. Woodward	C	12,123	34.3
			B. Ramelson	Com	928*	2.6
					10,216	28.8
1966	49,474	68.1	M. Rees	Lab	23,171	68.8
			P.A. Woodward	C	9,813	29.1
			B. Ramelson	Com	714*	2.1
					13,358	39.7
1970	49,490	66.0	M. Rees	Lab	19,536	59.8
			G.K. MacPherson	C	9,311	28.5
			S.J. Cooksey	L	3,810*	11.7
					10,225	31.3

Election	Electors	T'out	Candidate	Party	Votes	%
1950	48,621	85.3	†Rt. Hon. J. Milner	Lab	23,994	57.8
			C.E. Kirwin	C	15,262	36.8
			A. Hope	L	2,234*	5.4
					8,732	21.0
1951	48,826*	84.4	Rt. Hon. J. Milner	Lab	24,929	60.5
			C.E. Kirwin	C	16,277	39.5
					8,652	21.0

[Elevation to the Peerage—Lord Milner of Leeds]

Election	Electors	T'out	Candidate	Party	Votes	%
1952 (7/2)	48,826	55.7	D.W. Healey	Lab	17,194	63.2
			C.E. Kirwin	C	9,995	36.8
					7,199	26.4
1955	57,211**	67.9	Miss A.M. Bacon	Lab	25,714	66.2
			W.W.J. Dunn	C	13,142	33.8
					12,572	32.4
1959	48,457	70.0	Miss A.M. Bacon	Lab	21,795	64.2
			J.B. Womersley	C	12,146	35.8
					9,649	28.4
1964	38,326	64.3	Miss A.M. Bacon	Lab	16,672	67.7
			J.E. Macdonald	C	7,964	32.3
					8,708	35.4
1966	33,199	61.4	Rt. Hon. Alice M. Bacon	Lab	14,633	71.8
			Mrs. J.G. Todd	C	5,743	28.2
					8,890	43.6
1970	29,865	58.4	S. Cohen	Lab	10,930	62.7
			Mrs. M. Sexton	C	5,182	29.7
			E.A. Britten	L	1,135*	6.5
			B. Scott	Com	199*	1.1
					5,748	33.0

Election	Electors	T'out	Candidate	Party	Votes	%
1950	47,873	86.4	†T.C. Pannell	Lab	21,339	51.5
			B. Mather	C	16,824	40.7
			C. Rhodes	L	3,209*	7.8
					4,515	10.8
1951	48,082*	85.9	T.C. Pannell	Lab	22,357	54.1
			B. Mather	C	18,957	45.9
					3,400	8.2
1955	60,202**	77.4	T.C. Pannell	Lab	24,576	52.8
			J. Hiley	C	18,312	39.3
			H. Hudson	L	3,699*	7.9
					6,264	13.5
1959	60,269	78.3	T.C. Pannell	Lab	25,878	54.9
			D.L. Crouch	C	21,285	45.1
					4,593	9.8
1964	60,973	74.5	T.C. Pannell	Lab	22,968	50.6
			I.M. Glover	C	15,697	34.5
			D. Pedder	L	6,787	14.9
					7,271	16.1
1966	60,176	72.0	Rt. Hon. T.C. Pannell	Lab	24,391	56.3
			I.M. Glover	C	13,883	32.0
			D. Pedder	L	5,062*	11.7
					10,508	24.3
1970	63,442	65.7	Rt. Hon. T.C. Pannell	Lab	21,618	51.8
			A. Leitch	C	14,749	35.4
			Mrs. P.A. Armitage	L	5,341	12.8
					6,869	16.4

Election	Electors	T'out	Candidate	Party	Votes	%
1950	52,183	85.8	†T.N. Donovan	Lab	25,303	56.5
			H.A. Taylor	C	14,908	33.3
			M.J. Moroney	L	4,257*	9.5
			F.C. Westacott	Com	327*	0.7
					10,395	23.2

[Resignation on appointment as a High Court Judge]

Election	Electors	T'out	Candidate	Party	Votes	%
1950	51,482	63.0	A.L. Ungoed-Thomas	Lab	18,777	57.9
(28/9)			H.A. Taylor	C	13,642	42.1
					5,135	15.8
1951	51,771	84.4	Sir A.L. Ungoed-Thomas	Lab	26,209	60.0
			W. Browne	C	17,478	40.0
					8,731	20.0
1955	50,121	78.5	Sir A.L. Ungoed-Thomas	Lab	22,264	56.6
			Mrs. T.I. Street	C	17,094	43.4
					5,170	13.2
1959	47,733	78.4	Sir A.L. Ungoed-Thomas	Lab	19,421	51.9
			Miss A.H. Spokes	C	17,990	48.1
					1,431	3.8

[Resignation on appointment as a High Court Judge]

Election	Electors	T'out	Candidate	Party	Votes	%
1962	44,667	60.8	T.G. Bradley	Lab	11,274	41.5
(12/7)			D. Bond	L	9,326	34.3
			R.G. Marlar	C	6,578	24.2
					1,948	7.2
1964	43,107	77.5	T.G. Bradley	Lab	15,494	46.4
			R.D.G. Williams	C	12,195	36.5
			F.I. Glenton	L	5,712	17.1
					3,299	9.9
1966	41,772	75.4	T.G. Bradley	Lab	17,007	54.0
			R.D.G. Williams	C	10,769	34.2
			F.I. Glenton	L	3,703*	11.8
					6,238	19.8
1970	43,343	71.0	T.G. Bradley	Lab	15,016	48.8
			P.E.F. Heneage	C	14,125	45.9
			D.J. Taylor	Ind	1,616*	5.3
					891	2.9

Note:—

1970: Taylor was the chairman and nominee of the Leicester branch of the Anti-Immigration Society which was formed in Leicester in March 1968.

Election	Electors	T'out	Candidate	Party	Votes	%
1950	51,740	85.9	†B. Janner	Lab	23,505	52.9
			N. Nicolson	C	15,912	35.8
			R.A. Burrows	L	5,036*	11.3
					7,593	17.1
1951	52,532	84.3	B. Janner	Lab	25,184	56.8
			W.J.C. Heyting	C	19,125	43.2
					6,059	13.6
1955	53,472	78.7	B. Janner	Lab	22,807	54.2
			F.A. Tomlinson	C	19,297	45.8
					3,510	8.4
1959	51,922	79.5	B. Janner	Lab	21,515	52.1
			F.A. Tomlinson	C	19,742	47.9
					1,773	4.2
1964	49,707	76.2	Sir B. Janner	Lab	21,134	55.8
			E.G.A. Farnham	C	16,740	44.2
					4,394	11.6
1966	48,605	73.7	Sir B. Janner	Lab	21,822	60.9
			D.C.M. Mather	C	14,015	39.1
					7,807	21.8
1970	53,064	70.9	G.E. Janner	Lab	18,226	48.5
			S.J. Symington	C	15,584	41.4
			R.J. Rogers	L	2,862*	7.6
			R.E. Welford	N Dem P	935*	2.5
					2,642	7.1

Election	Electors	T'out	Candidate	Party	Votes	%
1950	47,497	85.9	Rt. Hon. C. Waterhouse	C	20,964	51.4
			S.K. Lewis	Lab	14,823	36.3
			C.A. Newport	L	5,024*	12.3
					6,141	15.1
1951	47,841	83.8	Rt. Hon. C. Waterhouse	C	23,853	59.5
			E. Taylor	Lab/Co-op	16,225	40.5
					7,628	19.0
1955	51,747**	78.5	Rt. Hon. C. Waterhouse	C	26,070	64.2
			E.J. Masters	Lab	14,529	35.8
					11,541	28.4
[Resignation]						
1957 (28/11)	52,452	56.4	W.J. Peel	C	18,023	61.0
			Miss B. Boothroyd	Lab	11,541	39.0
					6,482	22.0
1959	53,810	78.3	W.J. Peel	C	28,390	67.4
			D.J. Williams	Lab	13,760	32.6
					14,630	34.8
1964	54,143	76.7	W.J. Peel	C	23,236	56.0
			W.B. Chambers	Lab	11,090	26.7
			C.J. Beech	L	7,205	17.3
					12,146	29.3
1966	53,803	73.3	W.J. Peel	C	23,615	59.9
			C. Grundy	Lab	15,819	40.1
					7,796	19.8
1970	58,813	71.9	W.J. Peel	C	26,483	62.7
			W. Hilbourne	Lab	15,788	37.3
					10,695	25.4

Election	Electors	T'out	Candidate	Party	Votes	%
1950	51,134	83.8	†H.W. Bowden	Lab	23,399	54.6
			Mrs. D. Russell	C	14,727	34.4
			T.A. Pratt	L	4,720*	11.0
					8,672	20.2
1951	50,507	82.5	H.W. Bowden	Lab	24,340	58.4
			E.H. Wall	C	17,347	41.6
					6,993	16.8
1955	50,602	76.1	H.W. Bowden	Lab	21,487	55.8
			Mrs. D. Russell	C	16,998	44.2
					4,489	11.6
1959	47,762	78.5	H.W. Bowden	Lab	17,395	46.4
			A.D. Walder	C	14,652	39.1
			J.W. Ward	L	5,438	14.5
					2,743	7.3
1964	44,311	77.5	Rt. Hon. H.W. Bowden	Lab	16,957	49.4
			T.G. Boardman	C	12,851	37.4
			T.A. Pratt	L	4,533	13.2
					4,106	12.0
1966	43,373	74.0	Rt. Hon. H.W. Bowden	Lab	18,822	58.7
			T.G. Boardman	C	13,268	41.3
					5,554	17.4

[Resignation on appointment as Chairman of the Independent Television Authority and elevation to a Life Peerage—Lord Aylestone]

Election	Electors	T'out	Candidate	Party	Votes	%
1967 (2/11)	43,476	57.5	T.G. Boardman	C	12,897	51.6
			N.D. Sandelson	Lab	8,958	35.9
			C.J. Beech	L	3,125	12.5
					3,939	15.7
1970	44,863	71.3	T.G. Boardman	C	14,611	45.8
			C. Grundy	Lab	14,505	45.3
			J.T. Roper	L	2,124*	6.6
			J.E. Kyneston	NF	749*	2.3
					106	0.5

Election	Electors	T'out	Candidate	Party	Votes	%
1950	61,804	87.4	†H. Boardman	Lab	34,320	63.5
			J. Whiteley	C	19,720	36.5
					14,600	27.0
1951	62,182	86.0	H. Boardman	Lab	33,881	63.4
			H.D. Moore	C	19,585	36.6
					14,296	26.8
1955	60,256	80.1	H. Boardman	Lab	30,098	62.4
			J.B. Leck	C	18,142	37.6
					11,956	24.8
1959	58,911	82.4	H. Boardman	Lab	31,672	65.2
			W. Cameron	C	16,897	34.8
					14,775	30.4
1964	57,470	77.6	H. Boardman	Lab	30,102	67.5
			N.M.B. Brown	C	14,478	32.5
					15,624	35.0
1966	57,930	74.3	H. Boardman	Lab	29,552	68.7
			R.R. Hipkiss	C	13,490	31.3
					16,062	37.4
1970	64,149	71.3	H. Boardman	Lab	26,625	58.2
			J.P. McGuire	C	15,314	33.5
			J. Knowles	Ind	3,776*	8.3
					11,311	24.7

Election	Electors	T'out	Candidate	Party	Votes	%
1950	78,491	83.3	†Rev. R.W. Sorensen	Lab	35,702	54.6
			P.J. Williams	C	24,052	36.8
			C.O. Appleton	L	5,650*	8.6
					11,650	17.8
1951	79,445	82.2	Rev. R.W. Sorensen	Lab	37,728	57.8
			P.J. Williams	C	27,563	42.2
					10,165	15.6
1955	74,944	74.3	Rev. R.W. Sorensen	Lab	29,747	53.4
			R.C. Buxton	C	21,543	38.7
			E.L.F. Richards	L	4,421*	7.9
					8,204	14.7
1959	70,996	74.4	Rev. R.W. Sorensen	Lab	28,367	53.7
			R.C. Buxton	C	24,448	46.3
					3,919	7.4
1964	66,905	70.2	Rev. R.W. Sorensen	Lab	23,640	50.3
			R.C. Buxton	C	15,714	33.5
			A.H. Mackay	L	7,598	16.2
					7,926	16.8

[Elevation to a Life Peerage—Lord Sorensen]

Election	Electors	T'out	Candidate	Party	Votes	%
1965 (21/1)	66,905	57.7	R.C. Buxton	C	16,544	42.8
			Rt. Hon. P.C. Gordon Walker	Lab	16,339	42.4
			A.H. Mackay	L	5,382	14.0
			J. Lynch	UK & DP	157*	0.4
			T.N.M. Delf	Ind	156*	0.4
					205	0.4
1966	64,727	76.1	Rt. Hon. P.C. Gordon Walker	Lab	26,803	54.4
			R.C. Buxton	C	18,157	36.9
			A.H. Mackay	L	3,851*	7.8
			W.R. Hanley	ILP	441*	0.9
					8,646	17.5
1970	66,540	62.1	Rt. Hon. P.C. Gordon Walker	Lab	23,386	56.6
			R.C. Buxton	C	17,906	43.4
					5,480	13.2

Notes:—

1965: Gordon Walker was Secretary of State for Foreign Affairs. He subsequently resigned.

Delf sought election as a 'Disarmament' candidate.

Election	Electors	T'out	Candidate	Party	Votes	%
1950	48,582	88.7	†G.S. de Freitas	Lab	21,537	50.0
			J.W.F. Hill	NL & C	17,784	41.2
			Miss J.M. Henderson	L	3,753*	8.2
					3,753	8.2
1951	49,279	87.7	G.S. de Freitas	Lab	23,400	54.
			M.V. Macmillan	C	19,840	45.9
					3,560	8.2
1955	49,729	85.1	G.S. de Freitas	Lab	23,773	56.2
			P.F.H. Emery	C	18,551	43.8
					5,222	12.4
1959	50,933	84.2	G.S. de Freitas	Lab	23,629	55.
			L.H. Priestley	C	19,240	44.9
					4,389	10.2

[Resignation on appointment as United Kingdom High Commissioner in Ghana]

Election	Electors	T'out	Candidate	Party	Votes	%
1962 (8/3)	50,262	75.0	D. Taverne	Lab	19,038	50.5
			W.P. Grieve	C	11,386	30.2
			P.A.T. Furnell	L	6,856	18.2
			A. Taylor	Ind	412*	1.1
					7,652	20.3
1964	51,420*	80.3	D. Taverne	Lab	19,737	47.8
			R.M.C. McNair-Wilson	C	15,015	36.4
			P.A.T. Furnell	L	6,519	15.8
					4,722	11.4
1966	50,165	78.7	D. Taverne	Lab	23,006	58.3
			R.T. Alexander	C	16,469	41.2
					6,537	16.6
1970	52,827	74.5	D. Taverne	Lab	20,090	51.0
			R.T. Alexander	C	15,340	39.0
			G.T. Blades	Ind	3,937*	10.0
					4,750	12.0

Note:—

1962: Taylor advocated the re-introduction of a period of compulsory service in H.M. Forces.

lection	Electors	T'out	Candidate	Party	Votes	%
950	54,806	78.3	†A.J. Irvine	Lab	21,834	50.9
			E. Errington	C	18,830	43.9
			J. Bowen	L	2,247*	5.2
					3,004	7.0
951	55,570	76.4	A.J. Irvine	Lab	22,906	53.9
			H.M. Steward	C	19,569	46.1
					3,337	7.8
955	57,391**	68.0	A.J. Irvine	Lab	20,060	51.4
			H.S.L. Rigg	C	18,940	48.6
					1,120	2.8
959	54,824	70.7	A.J. Irvine	Lab	19,725	50.9
			J. Norton	C	19,026	49.1
					699	1.8
964	49,657	65.6	A.J. Irvine	Lab	19,221	59.0
			N.S. Jamieson	C	13,335	41.0
					5,886	18.0
966	47,704	60.5	A.J. Irvine	Lab	18,203	63.1
			M. Howard	C	10,662	36.9
					7,541	26.2
970	43,520	58.7	Rt. Hon. Sir A.J. Irvine	Lab	14,752	57.7
			M. Howard	C	10,804	42.3
					3,948	15.4

Election	Electors	T'out	Candidate	Party	Votes	%
1950	46,756	72.8	†Mrs. E.M. Braddock	Lab	19,492	57.
			Sir J.F.R. Reynolds, Bt.	C	14,150	41.
			A.G. Cleather	Ind Lab	381*	1.
					5,342	15.
1951	47,612	69.2	Mrs. E.M. Braddock	Lab	19,887	60.
			J.O. Tiernan	C	13,052	39.
					6,835	20.
1955	55,458**	62.5	Mrs. E.M. Braddock	Lab	19,457	56.
			Mrs. A.E. Papworth	C	12,271	35.
			L. Murphy	Ind Lab	2,928*	8.
					7,186	20.
1959	51,052	60.5	Mrs. E.M. Braddock	Lab	18,916	61.
			T. Beattie-Edwards	C	11,945	38.
					6,971	22.
1964	44,542	54.4	Mrs. E.M. Braddock	Lab	16,985	70.
			V. Burke	C	7,239	29.
					9,746	40.
1966	40,319	50.7	Mrs. E.M. Braddock	Lab	15,089	73.
			B.V. Groombridge	C	5,372	26.
					9,717	47.
1970	34,362	53.6	R. Parry	Lab	12,995	70.
			A.G. Phillips	C	4,638	25.
			R. O'Hara	Com	775*	4.
					8,357	45.

LIVERPOOL, GARSTON [190]

lection	Electors	T'out	Candidate	Party	Votes	%
950	65,001	84.9	†H.V.A.M. Raikes	C	31,750	57.6
			E. Hewitt	Lab	17,447	31.6
			Prof. W.L. Blease	L	5,966*	10.8
					14,303	26.0
951	68,336	80.0	H.V.A.M. Raikes	C	35,650	65.2
			A. Morris	Lab	19,025	34.8
					16,625	30.4
955	62,373**	71.0	Sir H.V.A.M. Raikes	C (Ind C)	28,130	63.5
			T.E. Nixon	Lab	16,161	36.5
					11,969	27.0

Resignation]

957 (5/12)	63,445	49.7	R.M. Bingham	C	15,521	49.2
			I.I. Levin	Lab	11,217	35.6
			A.D. Dennis	L	4,807	15.2
					4,304	13.6
959	65,506	74.4	R.M. Bingham	C	31,441	64.5
			B. Crookes	Lab	17,284	35.5
					14,157	29.0
964	66,464	72.9	R.M. Bingham	C	24,100	49.8
			J.D. Hamilton	Lab	17,626	36.4
			F. Kirk	L	6,708	13.8
					6,474	13.4
966	66,678	68.2	T.V.N. Fortescue	C	24,716	54.4
			W.H. Waldron	Lab	20,746	45.6
					3,970	8.8
970	75,674	65.9	T.V.N. Fortescue	C	28,381	56.9
			C.J. Smith	Lab	21,456	43.1
					6,925	13.8

LIVERPOOL, KIRKDALE [191]

Election	Electors	T'out	Candidate	Party	Votes	%
1950	49,495	79.7	†W. Keenan	Lab	19,219	48.7
			D.J. Lewis	C	18,591	47.1
			Miss J.S. Pritchard	L	1,648*	4.2
					628	1.6
1951	49,466	77.9	W. Keenan	Lab	19,637	51.0
			D.J. Lewis	C	18,879	49.0
					758	2.0
1955	60,738**	70.6	N.A. Pannell	C	22,356	52.1
			W. Keenan	Lab	20,542	47.9
					1,814	4.2
1959	57,102	73.7	N.A. Pannell	C	22,416	53.3
			T.H. Hockton	Lab/Co-op	19,669	46.7
					2,747	6.6
1964	52,426	69.1	J.A. Dunn	Lab	20,128	55.5
			N.A. Pannell	C	16,120	44.5
					4,008	11.0
1966	49,429	65.7	J.A. Dunn	Lab	19,233	59.3
			N.A. Pannell	C	13,219	40.7
					6,014	18.6
1970	49,066	63.8	J.A. Dunn	Lab	17,678	56.5
			M.P. Tinné	C	13,615	43.5
					4,063	13.0

ection	Electors	T'out	Candidate	Party	Votes	%
▶50	57,393	74.8	†D.G. Logan	Lab	28,087	65.4
			J.V. Woollam	C	14,240	33.2
			J. Coward	Com	615*	1.4
					13,847	32.2
▶51	58,929	71.1	D.G. Logan	Lab	28,558	68.2
			N.A. Pannell	C	13,344	31.8
					15,214	36.4
▶55	56,176*	60.1	D.G. Logan	Lab	21,928	65.0
			G.F. Allanson	C	11,821	35.0
					10,107	30.0
▶59	51,914	62.5	D.G. Logan	Lab	20,051	61.8
			J.F. Bradley	C	12,384	38.2
					7,667	23.6

[Death]

▶64 (1/6)	43,440	42.0	W.H. Alldritt	Lab	13,558	74.3
			B.M. Keefe	C	4,684	25.7
					8,874	48.6
▶64	43,830	59.6	W.H. Alldritt	Lab	17,984	68.9
			B.M. Keefe	C	7,393	28.3
			T.E. Cassin	Com	725*	2.8
					10,591	40.6
▶66	38,176	51.7	W.H. Alldritt	Lab	14,244	72.2
			R.H. Morris	C	4,730	23.9
			T.E. Cassin	Com	779*	3.9
					9,514	48.3
▶70	29,239	50.7	W.H. Alldritt	Lab	11,074	74.8
			R.H. Morris	C	3,740	25.2
					7,334	49.6

[Resignation]

▶71 (1/4)	25,257	37.7	F. Marsden	Lab	6,795	71.3
			G.B. Porter	C	1,751	18.4
			P. Mahon	Ind Lab	981*	10.3
					5,044	52.9

Note:—

1971: Mahon sought election as a 'Labour and against abortion' candidate.

Election	Electors	T'out	Candidate	Party	Votes	%
1950	54,393	80.4	J.R. Bevins	C	21,658	49
			†J. Gibbins	Lab	19,038	43
			Miss A.D. Holt	L	3,030*	6
					2,620	6
1951	55,336	77.5	J.R. Bevins	C	23,254	54
			W.E. Lawn	Lab/Co-op	19,620	45
					3,634	8
1955	52,575*	69.6	J.R. Bevins	C	20,576	56
			W.E. Lawn	Lab/Co-op	16,037	43
					4,539	12
1959	49,686	70.9	J.R. Bevins	C	19,575	55
			W.H. Sefton	Lab	15,660	44
					3,915	11
1964	46,451	67.5	R. Crawshaw	Lab	17,080	54
			Rt. Hon. J.R. Bevins	C	14,296	45
					2,784	8
1966	44,261	65.8	R. Crawshaw	Lab	16,488	56
			B.M. Keefe	C	12,643	43
					3,845	13
1970	45,080	62.3	R. Crawshaw	Lab	15,276	54
			B.M. Keefe	C	12,820	45
					2,456	8

Election	Electors	T'out	Candidate	Party	Votes	%
1950	63,962	83.1	K.P. Thompson	C	26,250	49.4
			†J. Haworth	Lab	21,983	41.4
			E. Heywood	L	4,901*	9.2
					4,267	8.0
1951	64,502*	81.0	K.P. Thompson	C	28,014	53.6
			I.I. Levin	Lab	24,262	46.4
					3,752	7.2
1955	59,522**	75.3	K.P. Thompson	C	23,851	53.2
			J.J. Cleary	Lab	20,989	46.8
					2,862	6.4
1959	57,312	77.7	K.P. Thompson	C	24,288	54.5
			G. McCartney	Lab	20,254	45.5
					4,034	9.0
1964	52,892	75.6	E.S. Heffer	Lab	21,452	53.6
			Sir K.P. Thompson, Bt.	C	18,546	46.4
					2,906	7.2
1966	51,373	71.2	E.S. Heffer	Lab	20,950	57.3
			Sir K.P. Thompson, Bt.	C	15,617	42.7
					5,333	14.6
1970	53,824	68.1	E.S. Heffer	Lab	20,530	56.0
			J. Norton	C	16,124	44.0
					4,406	12.0

Election	Electors	T'out	Candidate	Party	Votes	%
1950	60,950	82.4	J.D.R.T. Tilney	C	26,164	52.1
			W. Hamling	Lab	18,559	36.9
			T.J.V. Parry	L	5,512*	11.0
					7,605	15.2
1951	61,133	78.3	J.D.R.T. Tilney	C	28,179	58.9
			W. Hamling	Lab	19,702	41.1
					8,477	17.8
1955	57,489**	70.8	J.D.R.T. Tilney	C	28,172	69.2
			Mrs. M. Aspin	Lab	12,552	30.8
					15,620	38.4
1959	55,679	75.8	J.D.R.T. Tilney	C	26,624	63.2
			Mrs. M. Aspin	Lab	10,392	24.6
			T.S. Rothwell	L	5,161*	12.2
					16,232	38.6
1964	56,490	73.7	J.D.R.T. Tilney	C	20,598	49.5
			S.G. Thorne	Lab	12,338	29.6
			C.E. Carr	L	8,719	20.9
					8,260	19.9
1966	55,631	71.0	J.D.R.T. Tilney	C	19,179	48.5
			R. Ashcroft	Lab	13,529	34.3
			C.E. Carr	L	6,771	17.2
					5,650	14.2
1970	59,131	69.4	J.D.R.T. Tilney	C	19,127	46.6
			C.E. Carr	L	11,650	28.4
			G. Woodburn	Lab	10,253	25.0
					7,477	18.2

Election	Electors	T'out	Candidate	Party	Votes	%
1950	64,762	81.6	†Rt. Hon. Sir D.P.M. Fyfe	C	27,449	51.9
			†B.V. Kirby	Lab	25,417	48.1
					2,032	3.8
1951	66,208	80.3	Rt. Hon. Sir D.P.M. Fyfe	C	27,441	51.6
			L.C. Edwards	Lab	25,734	48.4
					1,707	3.2

[Resignation on appointment as Lord Chancellor and elevation to the Peerage—Viscount Kilmuir]

Election	Electors	T'out	Candidate	Party	Votes	%
1954 (18/11)	67,570	58.9	J.V. Woollam	C	21,158	53.2
			C.R. Fenton	Lab/Co-op	18,650	46.8
					2,508	6.4
1955	54,100**	73.3	J.V. Woollam	C	21,124	53.3
			C.R. Fenton	Lab/Co-op	18,540	46.7
					2,584	6.6
1959	54,804	76.8	J.V. Woollam	C	22,719	54.0
			A.D.G. Paxton	Lab	19,386	46.0
					3,333	8.0
1964	52,650*	73.4	E. Ogden	Lab	21,134	54.7
			J.V. Woollam	C	17,519	45.3
					3,615	9.4
1966	51,948	67.6	E. Ogden	Lab	19,988	56.9
			P.W.I. Rees	C	15,150	43.1
					4,838	13.8
1970	60,484	64.4	E. Ogden	Lab	22,324	57.3
			M.A. Latham	C	16,619	42.7
					5,705	14.6

Election	Electors	T'out	Candidate	Party	Votes	%
1950	56,569	87.1	Dr. C. Hill	NL & C	22,946	46.6
			†W.N. Warbey	Lab	21,860	44.4
			W.G. Matthews	L	4,447*	9.0
					1,086	2.2
1951	57,535	87.6	Dr. C. Hill	NL & C	26,554	52.7
			W.N. Warbey	Lab	23,842	47.3
					2,712	5.4
1955	57,932	83.1	Dr. Rt. Hon. C. Hill	NL & C	24,722	51.3
			M. Janis	Lab	20,304	42.2
			Miss J.M. Henderson	L	3,140*	6.5
					4,418	9.1
1959	59,769	82.5	Dr. Rt. Hon. C. Hill	NL & C	27,153	55.1
			C.R. Fenton	Lab/Co-op	22,134	44.9
					5,019	10.2

[Elevation to a Life Peerage—Lord Hill of Luton]

Election	Electors	T'out	Candidate	Party	Votes	%
1963	59,395	74.0	W. Howie	Lab	21,108	48.0
(7/11)			Sir J. Fletcher-Cooke	C	17,359	39.5
			M.A. Benjamin	L	5,001*	11.4
			Dr. A.P.J. Chater	Com	490*	1.1
					3,749	8.5
1964	59,299	79.8	W. Howie	Lab	23,751	50.2
			C.F.C. Simeons	C	23,028	48.6
			Dr. A.P.J. Chater	Com	567*	1.2
					723	1.6
1966	59,725	79.2	W. Howie	Lab	23,069	48.8
			C.F.C. Simeons	C	20,605	43.6
			T.H. Daniels	L	3,049*	6.4
			Dr. A.P.J. Chater	Com	586*	1.2
					2,464	5.2
1970	62,429	73.2	C.F.C. Simeons	C	23,308	51.0
			W. Howie	Lab	21,959	48.0
			Dr. A.P.J. Chater	Com	447*	1.0
					1,349	3.0

Election	Electors	T'out	Candidate	Party	Votes	%
1950	49,732	81.5	L.M. Lever	Lab	22,628	55.8
			E. Hodson	C	17,895	44.2
					4,733	11.6
1951	50,821	78.5	L.M. Lever	Lab	22,150	55.5
			E. Hodson	C	17,732	44.5
					4,418	11.0
1955	60,737**	71.7	L.M. Lever	Lab	22,822	52.4
			G. Hampson	C	20,740	47.6
					2,082	4.8
1959	57,166	72.6	L.M. Lever	Lab	24,134	58.1
			H. Sharp	C	17,392	41.9
					6,742	16.2
1964	52,228	63.3	L.M. Lever	Lab	20,248	61.2
			W.A.P. Manser	C	12,834	38.8
					7,414	22.4
1966	46,208	59.1	L.M. Lever	Lab	17,274	63.2
			J.G. Cluff	C	9,251	33.9
			F.J. Hamley	UM	796*	2.9
					8,023	29.3
1970	40,817	59.9	G.B. Kaufman	Lab	13,728	56.1
			I.K. Paley	C	10,726	43.9
					3,002	12.2

Election	Electors	T'out	Candidate	Party	Votes	%
1950	59,096	85.7	†J. Diamond	Lab	21,392	42.
			R. Jamieson	C	21,350	42.
			H.D. Moore	L	7,317	14.
			B. Ainley	Com	562*	1.
					42	0.
1951	60,180	85.0	E.S.T. Johnson	C	25,076	49.
			J. Diamond	Lab	22,804	44.
			F. Smith	L	3,287*	6.
					2,272	4.
1955	58,653	77.3	E.S.T. Johnson	C	25,395	56.
			J. Diamond	Lab	19,959	44.
					5,436	12.
1959	57,851	81.5	E.S.T. Johnson	C	22,163	47.
			R.B. Chrimes	Lab	17,790	37.
			R.M. Hammond	L	7,223	15.
					4,373	9.
1964	56,481	79.5	P.B. Rose	Lab	19,570	43.
			E.S.T. Johnson	C	18,348	40.
			R.M. Hammond	L	7,002	15.
					1,222	2.
1966	54,498	75.5	P.B. Rose	Lab	21,571	52.
			D.C. Stanley	C	15,271	37.
			L.G. Bayley	L	4,297*	10.
					6,300	15.
1970	57,917	69.5	P.B. Rose	Lab	21,437	53.
			A.M. Maguire	C	18,838	46.
					2,599	6.

Election	Electors	T'out	Candidate	Party	Votes	%
1950	47,786	79.5	†N.H. Lever	Lab	22,012	57.9
			K.A. Quas-Cohen	C	12,181	32.1
			B. McManus	L	3,794*	10.0
					9,831	25.8
1951	48,652	75.3	N.H. Lever	Lab	22,810	62.3
			G.W. Singleton	C	13,802	37.7
					9,008	24.6
1955	53,169**	65.7	N.H. Lever	Lab	21,721	62.2
			J.M. Eayrs	C	13,190	37.8
					8,531	24.4
1959	47,156	69.0	N.H. Lever	Lab	20,941	64.3
			Miss M.P. O'Gara	C	11,605	35.7
					9,336	28.6
1964	40,276	60.1	N.H. Lever	Lab	16,046	66.3
			J.H. Tresman	C	8,163	33.7
					7,883	32.6
1966	35,201	57.0	N.H. Lever	Lab	14,206	70.9
			A.A. O'Connor	C	5,844	29.1
					8,362	41.8
1970	30,464	55.9	Rt. Hon. N.H. Lever	Lab	10,912	64.1
			T.R. Arnold	C	6,110	35.9
					4,802	28.2

MANCHESTER, CLAYTON [201]

Election	Electors	T'out	Candidate	Party	Votes	%
1950	55,859	82.7	†H. Thorneycroft	Lab	29,128	63.0
			D.H. Broome	C	14,800	32.0
			H. Walls	L	2,295*	5.0
					14,328	31.0
1951	56,126	78.6	H. Thorneycroft	Lab	27,985	63.4
			Miss M.S. Grant	C	16,122	36.6
					11,863	26.8

This constituency was divided in 1955.

MANCHESTER, EXCHANGE [202]

Election	Electors	T'out	Candidate	Party	Votes	%
1950	45,285	74.8	†W. Griffiths	Lab	18,335	54.1
			R.S. Harper	C	13,716	40.5
			J. Cooper	L	1,812*	5.4
					4,619	13.6
1951	46,448	71.8	W. Griffiths	Lab	18,475	55.4
			I.W. Owen	C	14,881	44.6
					3,594	10.8
1955	52,376**	63.2	W. Griffiths	Lab	20,203	61.0
			B.R.V.Z. de Ferranti	C	12,922	39.0
					7,281	22.0
1959	46,072	65.0	W. Griffiths	Lab	19,328	64.6
			L. Smith	C	10,604	35.4
					8,724	29.2
1964	36,175	55.8	W. Griffiths	Lab	13,952	69.1
			Miss B.A. Brookes	C	6,242	30.9
					7,710	38.2
1966	26,400	53.7	W. Griffiths	Lab	10,425	73.5
			J. Stuart-Mills	C	3,761	26.5
					6,664	47.0
1970	21,080	57.0	W. Griffiths	Lab	8,234	68.5
			W.J. Loftus	C	3,341	27.8
			G.E. Spencer	Ind	440*	3.7
					4,893	40.7

Election	Electors	T'out	Candidate	Party	Votes	%
1950	59,541	85.5	†W.H. Oldfield	Lab	28,088	55.2
			J. Watts	C	18,564	36.5
			A.M. Caplin	L	3,377*	6.6
			S. Abbott	Com	873*	1.7
					9,524	18.7
1951	60,722	81.6	W.H. Oldfield	Lab	28,763	58.0
			S.H. Garlick	C	20,815	42.0
					7,948	16.0
1955	54,824**	76.5	K. Zilliacus	Lab	21,102	50.3
			K.B. Campbell	C	20,833	49.7
					269	0.6
1959	55,846	82.0	K. Zilliacus	Lab (Ind Lab) (Lab)	23,337	50.9
			H.D. Moore	C	22,480	49.1
					857	1.8
1964	56,721	76.4	K. Zilliacus	Lab	23,895	55.1
			E. Hodson	C	19,465	44.9
					4,430	10.2
1966	56,706	72.6	K. Zilliacus	Lab	24,726	60.1
			I.K. Paley	C	16,418	39.9
					8,308	20.2
[Death]						
1967 (2/11)	57,980	72.4	K. Marks	Lab	19,259	45.9
			W.S. Churchill	C	18,682	44.5
			T.J. Lacey	L	2,471*	5.9
			J. Creasey	APA	1,123*	2.7
			V.T. Eddisford	Com	437*	1.0
					577	1.4
1970	61,563	71.9	K. Marks	Lab	23,679	53.5
			J.A. Kevill	C	17,594	39.7
			J.M. Ashley	L	3,013*	6.8
					6,085	13.8

MANCHESTER, MOSS SIDE [204]

Election	Electors	T'out	Candidate	Party	Votes	%
1950	56,849	78.7	Rt. Hon. Florence Horsbrugh	C	25,347	56.7
			R.W. Casasola	Lab	16,769	37.5
			E.P. Atkin	L	2,607*	5.8
					8,578	19.2
1951	57,794	77.0	Rt. Hon. Florence Horsbrugh	C	27,697	62.2
			F. Allaun	Lab	16,819	37.8
					10,878	24.4
1955	53,194	69.1	Rt. Hon. Dame Florence Horsbrugh	C	23,631	64.3
			K. Marks	Lab	13,103	35.7
					10,528	28.6
1959	51,271	69.2	J. Watts	C	22,090	62.3
			N. Morris	Lab	13,371	37.7
					8,719	24.6
[Death]						
1961 (7/11)	49,580	46.7	F.H. Taylor	C	9,533	41.2
			R.H. Hargreaves	L	6,447	27.8
			G.J. Oakes	Lab	5,980	25.8
			W. Hesketh	UM	1,212*	5.2
					3,086	13.4
1964	50,142	65.5	F.H. Taylor	C	14,875	45.4
			P.W. Michelson	Lab	10,647	32.4
			R.H. Hargreaves	L	7,297	22.2
					4,228	13.0
1966	45,243	65.4	F.H. Taylor	C	13,436	45.5
			G.R. Church	Lab	12,353	41.7
			D.F. Prusmann	L	3,801	12.8
					1,083	3.8
1970	45,620	64.4	F.H. Taylor	C	15,546	52.9
			F. Hatton	Lab	13,833	47.1
					1,713	5.8

Note:—

1950: Polling was delayed until March 9 owing to the death, after nomination, of the Conservative candidate and former Member of Parliament, E.L. Fleming.

Election	Electors	T'out	Candidate	Party	Votes	%
1955	56,720	72.7	W.R. Williams	Lab	24,638	59.8
			H. Day	C	16,596	40.2
					8,042	19.6
1959	54,610	76.0	W.R. Williams	Lab	24,975	60.2
			M.B. Scholfield	C	16,537	39.8
					8,438	20.4
[Death]						
1963	52,940	46.1	C.R. Morris	Lab	16,101	65.9
(5/12)			G.W.G. Fitzsimons	C	7,139	29.2
			E. Marsden	Com	1,185*	4.9
					8,962	36.7
1964	53,195	71.3	C.R. Morris	Lab	22,589	59.6
			G.W.G. Fitzsimons	C	13,387	35.3
			E. Marsden	Com	1,947*	5.1
					9,202	24.3
1966	51,682	65.9	C.R. Morris	Lab	22,103	65.0
			R.J. Chronnell	C	10,465	30.7
			E. Marsden	Com	1,479*	4.3
					11,638	34.3
1970	50,401	64.0	C.R. Morris	Lab	19,397	60.2
			B.M. Allanson	C	12,296	38.1
			B. Panter	Com	552*	1.7
					7,101	22.1

MANCHESTER, WITHINGTON [206]

Election	Electors	T'out	Candidate	Party	Votes	%
1950	51,124	85.3	F.W. Cundiff	C	22,817	52.3
			L.T. Wright	Lab	14,206	32.6
			L.F. Behrens	L	6,591	15.1
					8,611	19.7
1951	52,017	79.6	Sir R.A. Cary	C	26,804	64.7
			J. Clough	Lab	14,604	35.3
					12,200	29.4
1955	60,941**	71.9	Sir R.A. Cary	C	25,707	58.6
			J.B. Hayes	Lab	13,054	29.8
			G.V. Davies	L	5,077*	11.6
					12,653	28.8
1959	59,457	74.5	Sir R.A. Cary, Bt.	C	23,170	52.3
			R.E. Sheldon	Lab	13,476	30.4
			G.V. Davies	L	7,675	17.3
					9,694	21.9
1964	56,996	72.3	Sir R.A. Cary, Bt.	C	18,259	44.3
			K. Openshaw	Lab	13,117	31.8
			G.V. Davies	L	9,860	23.9
					5,142	12.5
1966	54,585	71.2	Sir R.A. Cary, Bt.	C	16,676	42.9
			D.G. Clark	Lab	16,029	41.3
			G.V. Davies	L	6,150	15.8
					647	1.6
1970	57,088	67.9	Sir R.A. Cary, Bt.	C	18,854	48.7
			M.A. Noble	Lab	15,365	39.6
			J. Clarney	L	4,540*	11.7
					3,489	9.1

Election	Electors	T'out	Candidate	Party	Votes	%
1950	54,851	84.2	Mrs. E. Hill	C	22,775	49.4
			C.W. Bridges	Lab	17,191	37.2
			E. Noble	L	5,607*	12.1
			Miss F. Dean	Com	588*	1.3
					5,584	12.2
1951	63,017	80.4	Mrs. E. Hill	C	28,611	56.5
			L.L. Hanbidge	Lab	22,045	43.5
					6,566	13.0
1955	64,968**	76.3	Mrs. E. Hill	C	26,200	52.8
			N. Atkinson	Lab	23,378	47.2
					2,822	5.6
1959	69,925	80.9	Mrs. E. Hill	C	28,934	51.2
			A. Morris	Lab/Co-op	27,625	48.8
					1,309	2.4
1964	70,704	79.6	A. Morris	Lab/Co-op	26,870	47.8
			Mrs. E. Hill	C	22,093	39.2
			T.N. Armstrong	L	7,336	13.0
					4,777	8.6
1966	69,229	74.8	A. Morris	Lab/Co-op	27,485	53.2
			F. Lofthouse	C	18,548	35.8
			T.N. Armstrong	L	5,717*	11.0
					8,937	17.4
1970	78,036	70.2	A. Morris	Lab/Co-op	30,260	55.3
			H.D. Moore	C	24,505	44.7
					5,755	10.6

Election	Electors	T'out	Candidate	Party	Votes	%
1950	55,749	88.1	R.E.D. Ryder	C	23,938	48.7
			†A.M.F. Palmer	Lab	21,135	43.0
			R.I. Douglas	L	4,055*	8.3
					2,803	5.7
1951	56,049	86.7	R.E.D. Ryder	C	26,488	54.5
			A.M.F. Palmer	Lab/Co-op	22,086	45.5
					4,402	9.0
1955	54,332	81.6	H.E. Atkins	C	25,373	57.2
			R.J. Edwards	Lab	18,983	42.8
					6,390	14.4
1959	52,178	82.5	H.E. Atkins	C	25,603	59.5
			R.W. Kerr	Lab	17,444	40.5
					8,159	19.0
1964	49,854	82.3	H.E. Atkins	C	19,032	46.4
			K.W. May	Lab	16,234	39.5
			N.D.M. McGeorge	L	5,781	14.1
					2,798	6.9
1966	48,807	81.2	H.E. Atkins	C	20,028	50.5
			K.W. May	Lab	19,608	49.5
					420	1.0
1970	50,504	73.0	Miss J.E. Fookes	C	18,727	50.8
			K.W. May	Lab	15,244	41.4
			R.H. Insoll	L	2,876*	7.8
					3,483	9.4

Election	Electors	T'out	Candidate	Party	Votes	%
1950	56,086	82.9	†Rt. Hon. H.A. Marquand	Lab	29,185	62.7
			†A. Edwards	C	12,405	26.7
			Dr. W.S.R. Thomas	L	4,540*	9.8
			Dr. N. Levy	Com	367*	0.8
					16,780	36.0
1951	58,110	80.9	Rt. Hon. H.A. Marquand	Lab	31,277	66.5
			R.M. Turton	C	15,749	33.5
					15,528	33.0
1955	59,563	72.7	Rt. Hon. H.A. Marquand	Lab	27,036	62.4
			B.A. Connelly	C	16,278	37.6
					10,758	24.8
1959	62,666	76.2	Rt. Hon. H.A. Marquand	Lab	29,391	61.5
			D.R. Chapman	C	18,365	38.5
					11,026	23.0

[Resignation on appointment as Director of the International Institute for Labour Studies]

Election	Electors	T'out	Candidate	Party	Votes	%
1962 (14/3)	59,880	52.2	Rt. Hon. A.G. Bottomley	Lab	18,928	60.5
			G.E. Scott	L	7,145	22.9
			F.A.S. Wood	C	4,613	14.8
			E.J. Hamm	UM	550*	1.8
					11,783	37.6
1964	58,062*	72.9	Rt. Hon. A.G. Bottomley	Lab	29,432	69.5
			F.A.S. Wood	C	12,917	30.5
					16,515	39.0
1966	55,407	68.3	Rt. Hon. A.G. Bottomley	Lab	28,404	75.1
			P. Darby	C	9,420	24.9
					18,984	50.2
1970	54,899	60.5	Rt. Hon. A.G. Bottomley	Lab	23,581	71.0
			N.N. Laville	C	9,623	29.0
					13,958	42.0

Election	Electors	T'out	Candidate	Party	Votes	%
1950	53,951	86.4	†G. Cooper	Lab	21,593	46.3
			L.F. Wright	C	17,760	38.1
			C.P. Fothergill	L	7,273	15.6
					3,833	8.2
1951	54,640	86.3	J.E.S. Simon	C	24,622	52.2
			D. Dunwoodie	Lab/Co-op	22,525	47.8
					2,097	4.4
1955	52,916	82.4	J.E.S. Simon	C	25,495	58.4
			Mrs. R.A. Smythe	Lab/Co-op	18,134	41.6
					7,361	16.8
1959	53,059	84.5	J.E.S. Simon	C	24,602	54.9
			E.J. Fletcher	Lab	15,892	35.4
			G.W.I. Hodgson	L	4,336*	9.7
					8,710	19.5

[Resignation on appointment as President of the Probate, Divorce and Admiralty Division of the High Court of Justice]

Election	Electors	T'out	Candidate	Party	Votes	%
1962 (6/6)	52,740	72.2	Dr. J.W. Bray	Lab	15,095	39.7
			B.A. Connelly	C	12,825	33.7
			G.E. Scott	L	9,829	25.8
			R.E. Eckley	Ind	189*	0.5
			M. Thompson	Ind Ser	117*	0.3
					2,270	6.0
1964	52,905*	84.1	Dr. J.W. Bray	Lab	19,904	44.7
			A.J. Sumption	C	18,759	42.2
			J.C.A. Rettie	L	5,816	13.1
					1,145	2.5
1966	53,276	81.5	Dr. J.W. Bray	Lab	23,649	54.5
			J.H.V. Sutcliffe	C	19,756	45.5
					3,893	9.0
1970	59,037	75.1	J.H.V. Sutcliffe	C	22,374	50.4
			Dr. J.W. Bray	Lab	21,986	49.6
					388	0.8

Election	Electors	T'out	Candidate	Party	Votes	%
1950	73,160	85.8	L.R. Carr	C	31,881	50.7
			†T. Braddock	Lab	27,055	43.1
			Mrs. D.L. Page	L	3,864*	6.2
					4,826	7.6
1951	73,575	84.6	L.R. Carr	C	34,056	54.7
			H.E. Randall	Lab	28,187	45.3
					5,869	9.4
1955	72,028	80.5	L.R. Carr	C	32,798	56.5
			H.G. Jenkins	Lab	25,208	43.5
					7,590	13.0
1959	70,463	81.6	L.R. Carr	C	33,661	58.5
			E.J.C. Smythe	Lab/Co-op	23,845	41.5
					9,816	17.0
1964	67,967	79.2	Rt. Hon. L.R. Carr	C	25,087	46.7
			R.C. Mackay	Lab	21,175	39.3
			W.A. Heath	L	6,902	12.8
			S.E. French	Com	657*	1.2
					3,912	7.4
1966	66,709	79.4	Rt. Hon. L.R. Carr	C	24,234	45.8
			T.J. Higgs	Lab	23,706	44.7
			R.C. Burgess	L	4,470*	8.4
			S.E. French	Com	580*	1.1
					528	1.1
1970	72,513	68.9	Rt. Hon. L.R. Carr	C	27,257	54.6
			R.C. Vincent	Lab	22,047	44.1
			S.E. French	Com	638*	1.3
					5,210	10.5

Election	Electors	T'out	Candidate	Party	Votes	%
1950	52,450	88.6	†S.S. Silverman	Lab	25,358	54.6
			A. Green	C	21,116	45.4
					4,242	9.2
1951	52,614	89.0	S.S. Silverman	Lab (Ind Lab) (Lab)	25,611	54.7
			A. Green	C	21,211	45.3
					4,400	9.4
1955	50,355	83.4	S.S. Silverman	Lab	22,135	52.7
			Mrs. M.E. Kellett	C	19,844	47.3
					2,291	5.4
1959	48,472	85.5	S.S. Silverman	Lab (Ind Lab) (Lab)	20,407	49.2
			J. Crabtree	C	19,143	46.2
			T.C. Emmott	Lan P	1,889*	4.6
					1,264	3.0
1964	46,718	80.8	S.S. Silverman	Lab	20,205	53.5
			D.C. Waddington	C	17,561	46.5
					2,644	7.0
1966	46,144	80.9	S.S. Silverman	Lab	18,406	49.3
			P. Davies	C	13,829	37.0
			P.J. Downey	Ind	5,117	13.7
					4,577	12.3
[Death]						
1968 (27/6)	45,420	74.2	D.C. Waddington	C	16,466	48.9
			Miss B. Boothroyd	Lab	12,944	38.4
			D. Chadwick	L	3,016*	9.0
			M.B.P. Tattersall	Ind	1,255*	3.7
					3,522	10.5
1970	49,051	78.2	D.C. Waddington	C	19,881	51.8
			E.D.H. Hoyle	Lab	18,471	48.2
					1,410	3.6

Notes:—

1966: Downey was the nominee of the 1965 Committee for the Return of Capital Punishment. The committee had been formed by a group of Manchester businessmen.

1968: Tattersall sought election as an 'English Nationalist' candidate.

Election	Electors	T'out	Candidate	Party	Votes	%
1950	59,776	87.6	†J.D. Mack	Lab	30,249	57.7
			J.A. Friend	C	22,132	42.3
					8,117	15.4
1951	60,649	87.5	S.T. Swingler	Lab	30,814	58.0
			J.A. Friend	C	22,278	42.0
					8,536	16.0
1955	61,776	80.7	S.T. Swingler	Lab	28,314	56.8
			F.H. Taylor	C	21,569	43.2
					6,745	13.6
1959	63,623	84.4	S.T. Swingler	Lab	29,840	55.6
			T. Prendergast	C	23,838	44.4
					6,002	11.2
1964	63,934	82.2	S.T. Swingler	Lab	30,470	58.0
			J. Lovering	C	22,073	42.0
					8,397	16.0
1966	63,872	79.9	S.T. Swingler	Lab	31,548	61.8
			Mrs. P.E. Fenner	C	19,497	38.2
					12,051	23.6
[Death]						
1969 (30/10)	65,344	72.3	J. Golding	Lab	21,786	46.1
			N.R. Winterton	C	20,744	43.9
			D.R.A. Spreckley	L	2,999*	6.4
			D. Parker	DP	1,699*	3.6
					1,042	2.2
1970	69,811	65.5	J. Golding	Lab	22,329	48.8
			N.R. Winterton	C	20,223	44.3
			F.D. Wright	L	1,954*	4.3
			Dr. P.H. Boyle	DP	1,194*	2.6
					2,106	4.5

Election	Electors	T'out	Candidate	Party	Votes	%
1950	49,696	79.6	†L. Wilkes	Lab	25,190	63.6
			G.C. White	C	13,567	34.3
			F.G. Barton	ILP	812*	2.1
					11,623	29.3
1951	49,505	80.9	E.W. Short	Lab	25,637	64.0
			F.T. Webster	C	13,325	33.3
			F.G. Barton	ILP	1,066*	2.7
					12,312	30.7
1955	55,309**	70.9	E.W. Short	Lab	26,102	66.6
			G. Peters	C	13,099	33.4
					13,003	33.2
1959	49,929	73.2	E.W. Short	Lab	24,051	65.8
			W.D. Rutter	C	12,485	34.2
					11,566	31.6
1964	41,913	69.1	E.W. Short	Lab	20,547	70.9
			W.D. Rutter	C	7,896	27.3
			T.G. Welch	Com	532*	1.8
					12,651	43.6
1966	38,209	65.9	Rt. Hon. E.W. Short	Lab	19,291	76.7
			J.J. Walker-Smith	C	5,474	21.7
			T.G. Welch	Com	404*	1.6
					13,817	55.0
1970	31,494	61.5	Rt. Hon. E.W. Short	Lab	13,671	70.6
			M.St.J. Way	C	4,256	22.0
			D. Lesser	L	1,433*	7.4
					9,415	48.6

Election	Electors	T'out	Candidate	Party	Votes	%
1950	56,055	85.6	†A. Blenkinsop	Lab	24,694	51.4
			P.G. Williams	C	18,866	39.3
			W. McKeag	L	4,446*	9.3
					5,828	12.1
1951	55,965	86.6	A. Blenkinsop	Lab	25,621	52.9
			A. Edwards	C	22,850	47.1
					2,771	5.8
1955	53,907	81.3	A. Blenkinsop	Lab	22,816	52.1
			G.F.H. Walker	C	20,994	47.9
					1,822	4.2
1959	50,616	84.6	W.F. Montgomery	C	21,457	50.1
			A. Blenkinsop	Lab	21,359	49.9
					98	0.2
1964	48,886	83.4	G.W. Rhodes	Lab/Co-op	21,200	52.0
			W.F. Montgomery	C	19,556	48.0
					1,644	4.0
1966	46,663	80.3	G.W. Rhodes	Lab/Co-op	22,408	59.8
			T.T. Hubble	C	15,082	40.2
					7,326	19.6
1970	47,090	75.3	G.W. Rhodes	Lab/Co-op	20,612	58.2
			P.E. Heselton	C	14,832	41.8
					5,780	16.4

Election	Electors	T'out	Candidate	Party	Votes	%
1950	56,205	83.7	†Rt. Hon. Sir C.M. Headlam, Bt.	C	25,325	53.8
			W.H. Shackleton	Lab	16,860	35.9
			A. Herbert	L	4,839*	10.3
					8,465	17.9
1951	55,370	84.6	Rt. Hon. G. Lloyd George	NL & C	23,930	51.1
			I.E. Geffen	Lab	17,005	36.3
			C. Gray	Ind C	5,904	12.6
					6,925	14.8
1955	50,955	77.6	Rt. Hon. G. Lloyd George	NL & C	25,236	63.8
			B. Chisholm	Lab	14,303	36.2
					10,933	27.6

[Elevation to the Peerage—Viscount Tenby]

Election	Electors	T'out	Candidate	Party	Votes	%
1957 (21/3)	49,240	64.1	R.W. Elliott	C	19,017	60.2
			T.L. MacDonald	Lab	12,555	39.8
					6,462	20.4
1959	47,930	79.1	R.W. Elliott	C	24,588	64.9
			Dr. Muriel F. Lloyd-Prichard	Lab	13,316	35.1
					11,272	29.8
1964	42,331	75.6	R.W. Elliott	C	19,502	60.9
			S. Lee	Lab	12,515	39.1
					6,987	21.8
1966	40,900	75.0	R.W. Elliott	C	15,243	49.6
			F.R. Griffin	Lab	12,550	40.9
			A. Share	L	2,902*	9.5
					2,693	8.7
1970	42,053	67.8	R.W. Elliott	C	15,978	56.1
			R.G. Eccles	Lab	12,518	43.9
					3,460	12.2

Note:—

1951: A split in the local Conservative Association resulted in a breakaway association being formed in May 1951. In July 1951 the new association was officially recognised by the National Union of Conservative and Unionist Associations and the former official Conservative Association was disaffiliated. Gray was the nominee of the disaffiliated association.

Election	Electors	T'out	Candidate	Party	Votes	%
1950	61,556	87.2	†E. Popplewell	Lab	31,230	58.2
			A.E. Pain	C	21,949	40.9
			R. McNair	Com	492*	0.9
					9,281	17.3
1951	62,916	87.2	E. Popplewell	Lab	31,765	57.9
			J.M. Bazin	C	23,081	42.1
					8,684	15.8
1955	57,142**	79.8	E. Popplewell	Lab	25,401	55.7
			A. Grey	C	20,217	44.3
					5,184	11.4
1959	64,509	82.0	E. Popplewell	Lab	28,956	54.7
			C.D. Larrow	C	23,933	45.3
					5,023	9.4
1964	63,943	79.4	E. Popplewell	Lab	29,603	58.3
			H.I. Bransom	C	21,149	41.7
					8,454	16.6
1966	63,628	75.8	R.C. Brown	Lab	30,219	62.7
			D.A. Orde	C	18,002	37.3
					12,217	25.4
1970	74,154	70.7	R.C. Brown	Lab	30,805	58.7
			Dr. C. Lipman	C	21,644	41.3
					9,161	17.4

Election	Electors	T'out	Candidate	Party	Votes	%
1950	74,502	87.6	†R.T. Paget	Lab	31,946	49.0
			R.L. Agnew	C	24,664	37.8
			S.H. Alloway	L	8,619	13.2
					7,282	11.2
1951	75,551	86.4	R.T. Paget	Lab	35,038	53.7
			J.V. Collier	C	30,244	46.3
					4,794	7.4
1955	73,712	82.6	R.T. Paget	Lab	32,119	52.7
			W.G. Clark	C	28,771	47.3
					3,348	5.4
1959	72,521	82.9	R.T. Paget	Lab	27,823	46.3
			Mrs. J.C.J. Knight	C	25,106	41.8
			A.T. Smith	L	7,170*	11.9
					2,717	4.5
1964	73,129	79.7	R.T. Paget	Lab	28,568	49.1
			Mrs. J.C.J. Knight	C	24,128	41.4
			Miss I. Watson	L	5,557*	9.5
					4,440	7.7
1966	72,781	76.4	R.T. Paget	Lab (Ind Lab) (Lab)	31,541	56.7
			O.C. Wright	C	24,052	43.3
					7,489	13.4
1970	74,502	72.0	R.T. Paget	Lab	27,424	51.2
			C.E. Parkinson	C	26,183	48.8
					1,241	2.4

Election	Electors	T'out	Candidate	Party	Votes	%
1950	42,887	86.2	†J. Paton	Lab	21,898	59.3
			V.R. Rees	C	8,704	23.5
			D.C.T. Bennett	L	6,376	17.2
					13,194	35.8
1951	43,363*	84.1	J. Paton	Lab	22,880	62.7
			T.C. Eaton	C	13,587	37.3
					9,293	25.4
1955	40,843	75.3	J. Paton	Lab	18,682	60.7
			T.C. Eaton	C	12,087	39.3
					6,595	21.4
1959	41,221	76.9	J. Paton	Lab	19,092	60.2
			D.R. Chance	C	12,609	39.8
					6,483	20.4
1964	39,886	74.5	G.D. Wallace	Lab	18,111	60.9
			A.E. Turner	C	11,620	39.1
					6,491	21.8
1966	38,580	74.2	G.D. Wallace	Lab	18,777	65.6
			A.E. Turner	C	9,851	34.4
					8,926	31.2
1970	43,562	71.4	G.D. Wallace	Lab	18,564	59.7
			A.E. Turner	C	11,868	38.2
			C.C. Fairhead	IPP	658*	2.1
					6,696	21.5

Election	Electors	T'out	Candidate	Party	Votes	%
1950	41,273	84.9	†H.G. Strauss	C	18,693	53.3
			Dr. Mabel P. Tylecote	Lab	16,368	46.7
					2,325	6.6
1951	43,103	84.3	H.G. Strauss	C	19,082	52.5
			Dr. Mabel P. Tylecote	Lab	17,234	47.5
					1,848	5.0

[Seat Vacant at Dissolution (Elevation to the Peerage—Lord Conesford)]

Election	Electors	T'out	Candidate	Party	Votes	%
1955	45,402	78.3	A.G.F. Rippon	C	18,659	52.5
			Dr. Mabel P. Tylecote	Lab	16,901	47.5
					1,758	5.0
1959	43,789	82.2	A.G.F. Rippon	C	19,128	53.1
			G.D. Wallace	Lab	16,884	46.9
					2,244	6.2
1964	42,744	82.7	C.B.B. Norwood	Lab	17,973	50.9
			Rt. Hon. A.G.F. Rippon	C	17,362	49.1
					611	1.8
1966	42,045	83.2	C.B.B. Norwood	Lab	19,163	54.8
			A.R. Gurney	C	15,808	45.2
					3,355	9.6
1970	46,402	78.3	Dr. I.T. Stuttaford	C	17,067	47.0
			C.F. Ascher	Lab	16,241	44.7
			Mrs. L. Parker	L	3,031*	8.3
					826	2.3

Election	Electors	T'out	Candidate	Party	Votes	%
1950	50,130	82.9	I. Winterbottom	Lab	19,237	46.3
			Sir R.A. Cary	C	17,487	42.1
			J.M. Glyn-Barton	L	4,814*	11.6
					1,750	4.2
1951	50,260	81.4	I. Winterbottom	Lab	20,517	50.2
			J.A. Crean	C	20,378	49.8
					139	0.4
1955	56,463**	72.7	J.K. Cordeaux	C	20,903	50.9
			I. Winterbottom	Lab	20,145	49.1
					758	1.8
1959	62,475*	73.4	J.K. Cordeaux	C	24,004	52.3
			I. Winterbottom	Lab	21,869	47.7
					2,135	4.6
1964	55,988	71.4	J. Dunnett	Lab	21,040	52.7
			J.K. Cordeaux	C	18,912	47.3
					2,128	5.4
1966	53,542	67.7	J. Dunnett	Lab	21,348	58.9
			A.E.J. Mitton	C	14,922	41.1
					6,426	17.8
1970	52,438	60.5	J. Dunnett	Lab	17,638	55.6
			B. Brook-Partridge	C	14,079	44.4
					3,559	11.2

Election	Electors	T'out	Candidate	Party	Votes	%
1950	52,042	84.3	†J. Harrison	Lab	20,404	46.6
			L.H. Gluckstein	C	18,079	41.2
			E.A.B. Fletcher	L	5,368*	12.2
					2,325	5.4
1951	52,406	83.3	J. Harrison	Lab	20,865	47.7
			S. Shephard	C	20,601	47.2
			Lady Abrahams	L	2,209*	5.1
					264	0.5

This constituency was divided in 1955.

Election	Electors	T'out	Candidate	Party	Votes	%
1955	60,234	79.6	J. Harrison	Lab	26,552	55.4
			I.G. Colvin	C	20,462	42.7
			J.H. Peck	Com	916*	1.9
					6,090	12.7

[Seat Vacant at Dissolution (Death)]

Election	Electors	T'out	Candidate	Party	Votes	%
1959	63,163*	80.5	W.C. Whitlock	Lab	24,005	47.2
			A.G. Blake	C	18,952	37.3
			S. Thomas	L	6,581	12.9
			J.H. Peck	Com	1,331*	2.6
					5,053	9.9
1964	66,477	77.8	W.C. Whitlock	Lab	29,535	57.1
			P.D. Fry	C	20,578	39.8
			J.H. Peck	Com	1,579*	3.1
					8,957	17.3
1966	67,321	74.0	W.C. Whitlock	Lab	30,260	60.8
			J.N.L. Tillett	C	18,509	37.1
			J.H. Peck	Com	1,070*	2.1
					11,751	23.7
1970	70,634	69.4	W.C. Whitlock	Lab	25,898	52.8
			W. Derbyshire	C	18,616	38.0
			Mrs. M.V. Edwards	L	3,763*	7.7
			J.H. Peck	Com	741*	1.5
					7,282	14.8

lection	Electors	T'out	Candidate	Party	Votes	%
950	57,365	86.1	†T. O'Brien	Lab	30,223	61.1
			T. Gardner	C	13,016	26.4
			T.H. Whalley	L	5,432*	11.0
			A. West	Com	719*	1.5
					17,207	34.7
951	60,392	83.4	T. O'Brien	Lab	32,694	64.9
			T. Gardner	C	17,650	35.1
					15,044	29.8

This constituency was divided in 1955.

Election	Electors	T'out	Candidate	Party	Votes	%
1950	45,864	85.4	†H.N. Smith	Lab/Co-op	18,806	48.
			W.R. Rees-Davies	C	17,165	43.8
			E.G. Watkins	L	3,182*	8.
					1,641	4.
1951	46,413	84.5	H.N. Smith	Lab/Co-op	19,844	50.
			W.R. Rees-Davies	C	19,362	49.
					482	1.
1955	65,449**	78.3	D.M. Keegan	C	29,145	56.
			H.N. Smith	Lab/Co-op	22,092	43.
					7,053	13.
1959	65,459*	79.2	W.G. Clark	C	29,607	57.
			Hon. J.E. Silkin	Lab	22,235	42.
					7,372	14.
1964	65,663	78.2	W.G. Clark	C	23,594	46.
			W.F. Back	Lab	21,046	41.
			B.S. Stratford	L	6,690	13.
					2,548	5.
1966	64,597	75.6	G.H. Perry	Lab	24,580	50.
			W.G. Clark	C	24,264	49.
					316	0.
1970	71,295	69.8	P.N. Fowler	C	26,762	53.7
			G.H. Perry	Lab	23,031	46.
					3,731	7.

lection	Electors	T'out	Candidate	Party	Votes	%
955	61,969	76.1	T. O'Brien	Lab	25,539	54.1
			F.M. Richardson	C	21,631	45.9
					3,908	8.2
959	54,582*	80.5	P.H.B. Tapsell	C	22,052	50.2
			Sir T. O'Brien	Lab	21,888	49.8
					164	0.4
964	53,542	81.8	M. English	Lab	23,055	52.6
			P.H.B. Tapsell	C	20,763	47.4
					2,292	5.2
966	52,561	78.3	M. English	Lab	23,859	58.0
			D. Penfold	C	17,311	42.0
					6,548	16.0
970	56,723	71.0	M. English	Lab	21,255	52.8
			M.W. Suthers	C	19,003	47.2
					2,252	5.6

Election	Electors	T'out	Candidate	Party	Votes	%
1950	65,230	86.3	†A. Moyle	Lab	28,379	50.
			L.C. Baxter	C	17,281	30.
			R.K. Brown	L	10,620	18.
					11,098	19.
1951	65,975	83.3	A. Moyle	Lab	30,610	55.
			W.L.O. Somers	C	24,338	44.
					6,272	11.
1955	66,622	78.6	A. Moyle	Lab	24,123	46.
			P.A. Bridger	C	19,068	36.
			D. Mirfin	L	9,171	17.
					5,055	9.
1959	68,892	80.8	A. Moyle	Lab	23,861	42.
			J.F. Vernon	C	21,478	38.
			D. Mirfin	L	10,343	18.
					2,383	4.
1964	69,109	78.8	F.J. Horner	Lab	22,099	40.
			P.H. Lugg	C	21,182	38.
			C. Floris	L	11,210	20.
					917	1.
1966	69,780	76.7	F.J. Horner	Lab	28,490	53.
			P.H. Lugg	C	25,020	46.
					3,470	6.
1970	77,342	72.3	J.H.R. Stokes	C	29,403	52.
			F.J. Horner	Lab	26,499	47.
					2,904	5.

OLDHAM, EAST [228]

lection	Electors	T'out	Candidate	Party	Votes	%
950	56,895	84.1	†F. Fairhurst	Lab	21,510	45.0
			W.H.L. Richmond	C	21,117	44.1
			Miss W.C. Kirkman	L	5,206*	10.9
					393	0.9
951	56,967*	82.8	I.M. Horobin	C	24,621	52.2
			J.A. Joyce	Lab	22,564	47.8
					2,057	4.4
955	55,980*	77.7	Sir I.M. Horobin	C	19,185	44.1
			C. Mapp	Lab	18,805	43.2
			R.F. Leslie	L	5,506	12.7
					380	0.9
959	54,520	79.8	C. Mapp	Lab	19,329	44.5
			Sir I.M. Horobin	C	17,499	40.2
			D.I. Wrigley	L	6,660	15.3
					1,830	4.3
964	51,898	76.8	C. Mapp	Lab	18,112	45.4
			Rt. Hon. H.A. Nutting	C	14,181	35.6
			Miss M.E. Burton	L	7,574	19.0
					3,931	9.8
966	50,167	72.7	C. Mapp	Lab	18,431	50.5
			P.M. Beard	C	12,796	35.1
			D.E. Mann	L	5,262	14.4
					5,635	15.4
970	51,012	65.2	J.A. Lamond	Lab	17,020	51.1
			H.P. Holland	C	16,260	48.9
					760	2.2

Election	Electors	T'out	Candidate	Party	Votes	%
1950	55,657	85.1	†C.L. Hale	Lab	22,533	47.
			I.M. Horobin	C	17,740	37.
			J.T. Middleton	L	6,635	14.
			W. Mawdsley	Com	438*	0.
					4,793	10.
1951	56,324*	83.5	C.L. Hale	Lab	23,712	50.
			Hon. J.E.P. Grigg	C	19,517	41.
			C.P. Fothergill	L	3,823*	8.
					4,195	8.
1955	54,352*	78.1	C.L. Hale	Lab	23,164	54.
			Hon. J.E.P. Grigg	C	19,265	45.
					3,899	9.
1959	51,845	79.3	C.L. Hale	Lab	22,624	55.
			J.H.V. Sutcliffe	C	18,505	45.
					4,119	10.
1964	48,933	75.1	C.L. Hale	Lab	21,588	58.
			W.A. Bromley-Davenport	C	15,152	41.
					6,436	17.
1966	47,584	70.9	C.L. Hale	Lab	20,648	61.
			K.B. Campbell	C	13,076	38.
					7,572	22.
[Resignation]						
1968 (13/6)	46,807	54.7	K.B. Campbell	C	11,904	46.
			M.H. Meacher	Lab	8,593	33.
			J. Creasey	APA	3,389	13.
			D.A.R. Green	L	1,707*	6.
					3,311	12.
1970	49,823	67.0	M.H. Meacher	Lab	16,062	48.
			K.B. Campbell	C	14,387	43.
			B.M. Lomax	L	2,944*	8.
					1,675	5.

Election	Electors	T'out	Candidate	Party	Votes	%
1950	69,161	84.9	†Hon. Q.M. Hogg	C	27,508	46.9
			Lady Pakenham	Lab	23,902	40.7
			D.W. Tweddle	L	6,807*	11.6
			E. Keeling	Com	494*	0.8
					3,606	6.2

[Succession to the Peerage—Viscount Hailsham]

Election	Electors	T'out	Candidate	Party	Votes	%
1950 (2/11)	69,249	69.3	H.F.L. Turner	C	27,583	57.5
			S.K. Lewis	Lab	20,385	42.5
					7,198	15.0
1951	70,494	82.0	H.F.L. Turner	C	32,367	56.0
			G.H. Elvin	Lab	25,427	44.0
					6,940	12.0
1955	67,721	78.2	H.F.L. Turner	C (Ind C) (C)	27,708	52.3
			G.H. Elvin	Lab	19,930	37.6
			I.R.M. Davies	L	5,336*	10.1
					7,778	14.7
1959	66,655	78.9	Hon. C.M. Woodhouse	C	26,798	51.0
			L.N. Anderton	Lab	18,310	34.8
			I.R.M. Davies	L	7,491	14.2
					8,488	16.2
1964	67,011*	77.3	Hon. C.M. Woodhouse	C	22,212	42.9
			D.E.T. Luard	Lab	20,783	40.1
			I.R.M. Davies	L	8,797	17.0
					1,429	2.8
1966	66,303	79.3	D.E.T. Luard	Lab	24,412	46.5
			Hon. C.M. Woodhouse	C	21,987	41.8
			A.D.C. Peterson	L	6,152*	11.7
					2,425	4.7
1970	70,986	74.6	Hon. C.M. Woodhouse	C	24,873	47.0
			D.E.T. Luard	Lab	22,989	43.4
			P.H. Reeves	L	5,103*	9.6
					1,884	3.6

Election	Electors	T'out	Candidate	Party	Votes	%
1950	69,881	87.2	†M.M. Foot	Lab	30,812	50.6
			R.F.E.S. Churchill	NL & C	27,329	44.9
			A.C. Cann	L	2,766*	4.5
					3,483	5.7
1951	72,611*	85.3	M.M. Foot	Lab	32,158	51.9
			R.F.E.S. Churchill	NL & C	29,768	48.1
					2,390	3.8
1955	68,235**	77.1	Miss J.H. Vickers	NL & C	24,821	47.1
			M.M. Foot	Lab	24,721	47.0
			A.R. Mayne	L	3,100*	5.9
					100	0.1
1959	64,236	78.6	Miss J.H. Vickers	NL & C (C)	28,481	56.4
			M.M. Foot	Lab	22,027	43.6
					6,454	12.8
1964	60,959	73.6	Miss J.H. Vickers	C	24,241	54.0
			R.E. Crabb	Lab	20,615	46.0
					3,626	8.0
1966	59,313	76.2	Dame Joan Vickers	C	22,760	50.4
			R.E. Crabb	Lab	22,441	49.6
					319	0.8
1970	59,597	71.0	Dame Joan Vickers	C	21,843	51.6
			F.K. Taylor	Lab	20,471	48.4
					1,372	3.2

PLYMOUTH, SUTTON [232]

Election	Electors	T'out	Candidate	Party	Votes	%
1950	66,711	86.4	†Mrs. L.A. Middleton	Lab	27,512	47.8
			Hon. J.J. Astor	C	26,588	46.1
			K.H.B. Major	L	3,541*	6.1
					924	1.7
1951	66,894*	85.4	Hon. J.J. Astor	C	28,908	50.6
			Mrs. L.A. Middleton	Lab	28,198	49.4
					710	1.2
1955	71,367**	78.9	Hon. J.J. Astor	C	30,051	53.4
			Mrs. L.A. Middleton	Lab	26,241	46.6
					3,810	6.8
1959	74,078	79.3	I.M. Fraser	C	32,752	55.8
			J.D. Richards	Lab	25,991	44.2
					6,761	11.6
1964	73,591	76.7	I.M. Fraser	C	24,722	43.8
			Dr. J.E.O. Dunwoody	Lab	24,312	43.1
			C.E.G. Cocks	L	7,383	13.1
					410	0.7
1966	73,398	78.9	Dr. D.A.L. Owen	Lab	31,567	54.5
			I.M. Fraser	C	26,345	45.5
					5,222	9.0
1970	80,223	72.3	Dr. D.A.L. Owen	Lab	29,383	50.6
			J. Goss	C	28,636	49.4
					747	1.2

Election	Electors	T'out	Candidate	Party	Votes	%
1950	53,681	87.3	†G.O. Sylvester	Lab	35,432	75.6
			M. Grant	NL & C	11,431	24.4
					24,001	51.2
1951	53,856	86.0	G.O. Sylvester	Lab	35,280	76.2
			Miss I.M.P. Pike	NL & C	11,043	23.8
					24,237	52.4
1955	53,877	79.5	G.O. Sylvester	Lab	32,646	76.2
			A.G. Blake	NL & C	10,183	23.8
					22,463	52.4
1959	54,677	84.3	G.O. Sylvester	Lab	35,194	76.4
			E.T. Bowman	NL & C	10,884	23.6
					24,310	52.8
[Death]						
1962 (22/3)	54,126	63.3	J. Harper	Lab	26,461	77.3
			A.P. Dean	C	6,633	19.4
			R.E. Eckley	Ind	1,146*	3.3
					19,828	57.9
1964	54,774	77.6	J. Harper	Lab	32,357	76.2
			J.F. Whitfield	C	10,128	23.8
					22,229	52.4
1966	54,551	75.6	J. Harper	Lab	32,328	78.4
			A.F. Wigram	C	8,927	21.6
					23,401	56.8
1970	60,146	70.6	J. Harper	Lab	31,774	74.8
			I. Deslandes	C	10,687	25.2
					21,087	49.6

Election	Electors	T'out	Candidate	Party	Votes	%
1950	56,606	87.1	†M.J. Wheatley	C	24,344	49.3
			†E.M. King	Lab	17,831	36.2
			W. Ridgway	L	7,130	14.5
					6,513	13.1
1951	59,286	85.0	R.A. Pilkington	C	26,998	53.6
			L.J. Matchan	Lab	18,346	36.4
			W. Ridgway	L	5,029*	10.0
					8,652	17.2
1955	61,004	80.9	R.A. Pilkington	C	26,594	53.9
			F.C. Reeves	Lab	17,032	34.5
			J.C. Holland	L	5,750*	11.6
					9,562	19.4
1959	63,554	80.3	R.A. Pilkington	C	26,956	52.9
			A.J. Williams	Lab	15,325	30.0
			J.C. Holland	L	8,735	17.1
					11,631	22.9
1964	66,000	80.0	H.O. Murton	C	24,440	46.2
			H. Toch	Lab	16,158	30.6
			H.C.R. Ballam	L	12,234	23.2
					8,282	15.6
1966	67,687	79.0	H.O. Murton	C	25,451	47.6
			D.A. Sutton	Lab	19,630	36.7
			B.S. Sherriff	L	8,394	15.7
					5,821	10.9
1970	77,927	75.1	H.O. Murton	C	31,100	53.1
			I.S. Campbell	Lab	17,610	30.1
			G.M. Goode	L	9,846	16.8
					13,490	23.0

Election	Electors	T'out	Candidate	Party	Votes	%
1950	59,711	83.7	G.P. Stevens	C	29,477	59.0
			P. Knight	Lab	17,691	35.4
			A.E. Jones	L	2,821*	5.6
					11,786	23.6
1951	61,641	81.7	G.P. Stevens	C	31,702	63.0
			J.O'N. Ryan	Lab	18,647	37.0
					13,055	26.0
1955	68,299*	73.0	G.P. Stevens	C	32,014	64.2
			S.C. Davis	Lab	17,859	35.8
					14,155	28.4
1959	79,885	74.3	G.P. Stevens	C	38,834	65.4
			D.G. Reynolds	Lab	20,553	34.6
					18,281	30.8
1964	91,491*	75.2	I.S. Lloyd	C	33,208	48.2
			T.A. Molloy	Lab	23,365	34.0
			G.R. Collings	L	12,212	17.8
					9,843	14.2
1966	96,166	74.0	I.S. Lloyd	C	34,446	48.4
			T.A. Molloy	Lab	26,197	36.8
			D.J.H. Griffiths	L	10,540	14.8
					8,249	11.6
1970	112,593	71.5	I.S. Lloyd	C	43,733	54.4
			R.R. Kenward	Lab/Co-op	26,492	32.9
			R.H. Anstey	L	10,226	12.7
					17,241	21.5

Election	Electors	T'out	Candidate	Party	Votes	%
1950	58,288	83.5	†Sir J.M. Lucas, Bt.	C	31,124	64.0
			L.C. Merrion	Lab	17,545	36.0
					13,579	28.0
1951	59,306	80.8	Sir J.M. Lucas, Bt.	C	30,548	63.8
			D.S. Wallace	Lab	17,350	36.2
					13,198	27.6
1955	57,311*	72.4	Sir J.M. Lucas, Bt.	C	27,887	67.2
			L.W. Carroll	Lab	13,600	32.8
					14,287	34.4
1959	55,121	72.3	Sir J.M. Lucas, Bt.	C	27,892	70.0
			F. Towell	Lab	11,979	30.0
					15,913	40.0
1964	53,915	71.0	Sir J.M. Lucas, Bt.	C	24,387	63.7
			R.W.S. Pryke	Lab	13,904	36.3
					10,483	27.4
1966	52,941	70.7	R.B. Pink	C	22,713	60.6
			P.B. Smith	Lab	14,738	39.4
					7,975	21.2
1970	56,093	67.4	R.B. Pink	C	23,962	63.4
			A.F.W. White	Lab	13,847	36.6
					10,115	26.8

Election	Electors	T'out	Candidate	Party	Votes	%
1950	58,892	83.5	T.H. Clarke	C	24,924	50.7
			†D.W.T. Bruce	Lab	23,979	48.8
			G.H. Swanton	Com	257*	0.5
					945	1.9
1951	59,262	83.5	T.H. Clarke	C	25,363	51.3
			Mrs. A.L. Birk	Lab	24,115	48.7
					1,248	2.6
1955	56,597*	77.4	T.H. Clarke	C	23,729	54.2
			Mrs. A.L. Birk	Lab	20,060	45.8
					3,669	8.4
1959	53,206	76.9	T.H. Clarke	C	23,600	57.7
			Dr. M. Bresler	Lab	17,334	42.3
					6,266	15.4
1964	49,517	74.8	T.H. Clarke	C	18,762	50.7
			F.A. Judd	Lab	18,265	49.3
					497	1.4
1966	47,247	76.5	F.A. Judd	Lab	18,685	51.7
			T.H. Clarke	C	17,458	48.3
					1,227	3.4
1970	46,953	72.3	F.A. Judd	Lab	17,169	50.6
			T.H. Clarke	C	16,214	47.7
			L.B. Gauntlett	Ind	579*	1.7
					955	2.9

Election	Electors	T'out	Candidate	Party	Votes	%
1950	52,086	86.8	J. Amery	C	21,888	48.5
			†Dr. S. Segal	Lab	20,950	46.3
			C.J. Hemelryk	L	2,012*	4.4
			P.J. Devine	Com	366*	0.8
					938	2.2
1951	52,647	87.5	J. Amery	C	23,598	51.2
			T. Hourigan	Lab	22,490	48.8
					1,108	2.4
1955	51,220	81.4	J. Amery	C	22,310	53.5
			E. Hewitt	Lab	19,407	46.5
					2,903	7.0
1959	52,212	83.4	J. Amery	C	23,990	55.1
			A. Davidson	Lab	19,529	44.9
					4,461	10.2
1964	52,233	78.7	Rt. Hon. J. Amery	C	20,566	50.0
			R.W. Kerr	Lab	20,552	50.0
					14	0.0
1966	50,140	81.1	R.H. Atkins	Lab	21,539	53.0
			Rt. Hon. J. Amery	C	19,121	47.0
					2,418	6.0
1970	51,746	76.7	Miss M. Holt	C	20,102	50.6
			R.H. Atkins	Lab	17,140	43.2
			D.T. Jones	L	2,458*	6.2
					2,962	7.4

PRESTON, SOUTH [239]

Election	Electors	T'out	Candidate	Party	Votes	%
1950	52,835	85.7	†E.A.A. Shackleton	Lab	22,716	50.2
			N.L.D. McLean	C	22,567	49.8
					149	0.4
1951	52,610	86.5	E.A.A. Shackleton	Lab	22,760	50.0
			N.L.D. McLean	C	22,744	50.0
					16	0.0
1955	51,933*	81.9	A. Green	C	21,497	50.6
			E.A.A. Shackleton	Lab	21,023	49.4
					474	1.2
1959	49,809	82.1	A. Green	C	21,954	53.7
			T.G. Bradley	Lab	18,935	46.3
					3,019	7.4
1964	48,685*	78.8	P. Mahon	Lab	19,352	50.5
			A. Green	C	19,004	49.5
					348	1.0
1966	48,345	79.9	P. Mahon	Lab	20,720	53.6
			A. Green	C	17,931	46.4
					2,789	7.2
1970	52,181	75.9	A. Green	C	20,480	51.7
			P. Mahon	Lab	19,149	48.3
					1,331	3.4

Election	Electors	T'out	Candidate	Party	Votes	%
1950	49,729	88.9	C. Banks	C	18,269	41.3
			A.G. Collings	Lab	18,205	41.2
			R.S. Wainwright	L	7,731	17.5
					64	0.1
1951	50,521	88.9	C. Banks	C	24,138	53.7
			A.G. Collings	Lab	20,782	46.3
					3,356	7.4
1955	50,175	85.4	C. Banks	C (Ind C) (C)	20,445	47.7
			B.A. Payton	Lab	15,881	37.1
			R.S. Wainwright	L	6,526	15.2
					4,564	10.6
1959	52,285	86.9	J. Hiley	C	22,752	50.0
			V.P. Richardson	Lab	16,241	35.8
			J.S. Snowden	L	6,429	14.2
					6,511	14.2
1964	54,939	84.5	J. Hiley	C	21,581	46.5
			B.P. Atha	Lab	16,100	34.7
			J.T. Wilson	L	8,732	18.8
					5,481	11.8
1966	55,860	83.3	J. Hiley	C	20,782	44.6
			E. Brierley	Lab	18,410	39.6
			R.H.J. Rhodes	L	7,353	15.8
					2,372	5.0
1970	62,335	79.2	J. Hiley	C	24,308	49.2
			J. Mann	Lab	18,313	37.1
			G.V.J. Pratt	L	6,754	13.7
					5,995	12.1

Election	Electors	T'out	Candidate	Party	Votes	%
1955	59,678	84.1	I. Mikardo	Lab	25,228	50.2
			F.M. Bennett	C	24,990	49.8
					238	0.4
1959	58,772	82.8	P.F.H. Emery	C	26,314	54.0
			I. Mikardo	Lab	22,372	46.0
					3,942	8.0
1964	59,371*	79.8	P.F.H. Emery	C	20,815	43.9
			J.M.H. Lee	Lab	20,805	43.9
			M.F. Burns	L	5,759*	12.2
					10	0.0
1966	59,132	84.0	J.M.H. Lee	Lab	25,338	51.0
			P.F.H. Emery	C	21,205	42.7
			E.H. Palfrey	L	3,127*	6.3
					4,133	8.3
1970	63,313	74.1	Dr. G.F. Vaughan	C	23,598	50.4
			J.M.H. Lee	Lab	22,444	47.8
			A. Boothroyd	DP	867*	1.8
					1,154	2.6

Election	Electors	T'out	Candidate	Party	Votes	%
1950	39,261	86.8	†R.W.G. Mackay	Lab	15,681	46.0
			Sir J.S.V. Marling, Bt.	C	15,154	44.5
			J.M. Derrick	L	3,238*	9.5
					527	1.5
1951	39,681	86.8	F.M. Bennett	C	17,378	50.4
			R.W.G. Mackay	Lab	17,076	49.6
					302	0.8

This constituency was divided in 1955.

Election	Electors	T'out	Candidate	Party	Votes	%
1950	41,307	88.1	†I. Mikardo	Lab	17,704	48.6
			D.C. Rissik	C	15,450	42.5
			G.L. Opperman	L	3,225*	8.9
					2,254	6.1
1951	41,694	86.7	I. Mikardo	Lab	18,570	51.4
			H. Pryce	C	17,561	48.6
					1,009	2.8

This constituency was divided in 1955.

Election	Electors	T'out	Candidate	Party	Votes	%
1950	62,367	86.2	†Sir G.S. Harvie-Watt, Bt.	C	30,907	57.4
			K.T. Westwood	Lab	17,238	32.1
			D.H. Ennals	L	5,634*	10.5
					13,669	25.3
1951	63,267	82.8	Sir G.S. Harvie-Watt, Bt.	C	30,743	58.7
			Miss F. White	Lab	16,707	31.9
			D.H. Ennals	L	4,933*	9.4
					14,036	26.8
1955	61,365	77.5	Sir G.S. Harvie-Watt, Bt.	C	27,628	58.1
			J.S. Barr	Lab	14,673	30.8
			Miss E.M. Haynes	L	5,266*	11.1
					12,955	27.3
1959	59,852	79.4	A.H.F. Royle	C	27,161	57.2
			C.H. Archibald	Lab	12,975	27.3
			J.A. Baker	L	7,359	15.5
					14,186	29.9
1964	57,622*	76.5	A.H.F. Royle	C	22,203	50.4
			A.C. Brownjohn	Lab	14,053	31.9
			J.A. Baker	L	7,800	17.7
					8,150	18.5
1966	55,534	79.4	A.H.F. Royle	C	21,831	49.5
			D.G. Boulton	Lab	15,608	35.4
			P.M.T. Sheldon-Williams	L	6,661	15.1
					6,223	14.1
1970	57,031	71.7	A.H.F. Royle	C	20,979	51.3
			A.R. Palmer	Lab	12,981	31.7
			Dr. S. Rundle	L	6,934	17.0
					7,998	19.6

Election	Electors	T'out	Candidate	Party	Votes	%
1950	64,544	88.0	J. Hale	Lab	25,484	44.8
			W. Schofield	C	21,280	37.5
			R.T.B. Fulford	L	10,042	17.7
					4,204	7.3
1951	64,373	85.7	W. Schofield	C	27,797	50.4
			J. Hale	Lab	27,343	49.6
					454	0.8
1955	62,126	82.8	W. Schofield	C	26,518	51.5
			J. McCann	Lab	24,928	48.5
					1,590	3.0
[Death]						
1958 (12/2)	61,809	80.2	J. McCann	Lab	22,133	44.7
			L.H.C. Kennedy	L	17,603	35.5
			J.E. Parkinson	C	9,827	19.8
					4,530	9.2
1959	61,091	85.6	J. McCann	Lab	21,689	41.5
			L.H.C. Kennedy	L	18,949	36.2
			T. Normanton	C	11,665	22.3
					2,740	5.3
1964	59,695	82.3	J. McCann	Lab	22,927	46.7
			Dr. T.L. Hobday	L	14,212	28.9
			T. Normanton	C	11,968	24.4
					8,715	17.8
1966	59,175	79.0	J. McCann	Lab	24,481	52.4
			E.G.L. Collins	C	13,239	28.3
			Miss B.N. Seear	L	9,004	19.3
					11,242	24.1
1970	63,629	72.8	J. McCann	Lab	19,247	41.6
			C. Smith	L	14,076	30.4
			M. Andrew	C	12,978	28.0
					5,171	11.2

Election	Electors	T'out	Candidate	Party	Votes	%
1950	58,492	84.2	†A.G. Bottomley	Lab	24,855	50.5
			R. Mathew	C	24,378	49.5
					477	1.0
1951	60,724	85.5	A.G. Bottomley	Lab	26,390	50.8
			R. Mathew	C	25,543	49.2
					847	1.6
1955	61,819*	82.2	Rt. Hon. A.G. Bottomley	Lab	26,645	52.4
			J.D. Campbell	C	24,198	47.6
					2,447	4.8
1959	64,386	80.8	J.M.G. Critchley	C	26,510	51.0
			Rt. Hon. A.G. Bottomley	Lab	25,487	49.0
					1,023	2.0
1964	67,139*	76.4	Mrs. A.P. Kerr	Lab	26,161	51.0
			J.M.G. Critchley	C	25,148	49.0
					1,013	2.0
1966	68,661	78.1	Mrs. A.P. Kerr	Lab	27,938	52.1
			J.M.G. Critchley	C	25,692	47.9
					2,246	4.2
1970	77,190	71.5	Mrs. P.E. Fenner	C	30,263	54.8
			Mrs. A.P. Kerr	Lab	24,922	45.2
					5,341	9.6

ROMFORD [247]

Election	Electors	T'out	Candidate	Party	Votes	%
1950	70,114	85.7	J.C. Lockwood	C	27,656	46.1
			†T. Macpherson.	Lab	26,387	43.9
			N. Clarke	L	6,014*	10.0
					1,269	2.2
1951	77,483	83.8	J.C. Lockwood	C	33,120	51.0
			Rt. Hon. A.C. Jones	Lab	31,822	49.0
					1,298	2.0
1955	68,942**	75.5	R.J. Ledger	Lab/Co-op	27,326	52.5
			R.J.S. Harvey	C	24,701	47.5
					2,625	5.0
1959	73,082	80.4	R.J. Ledger	Lab/Co-op	25,558	43.5
			R.J.S. Harvey	C	24,951	42.5
			D. Geary	L	8,228	14.0
					607	1.0
1964	73,473	77.8	R.J. Ledger	Lab/Co-op	27,143	47.6
			A.T.R. Fletcher	C	21,046	36.8
			D. Geary	L	8,133	14.2
			E. Bates	Ind	811*	1.4
					6,097	10.8
1966	72,089	75.4	R.J. Ledger	Lab/Co-op	31,221	57.4
			B.J. Higgs	C	23,160	42.6
					8,061	14.8
1970	79,289	66.9	R.L. Leonard	Lab	27,899	52.6
			M.J. Neubert	C	25,139	47.4
					2,760	5.2

Note:—

1964: Bates was founder and chairman of the National Ratepayers' and Tenants' Protection Association and was the nominee of the Romford branch.

Election	Electors	T'out	Candidate	Party	Votes	%
1950	53,785	88.9	†A.W.J. Greenwood	Lab	21,596	45.2
			T.M. Backhouse	C	19,483	40.7
			Mrs. L.M. Tomlinson	L	6,757	14.1
					2,113	4.5
1951	54,134	88.6	A.W.J. Greenwood	Lab	24,814	51.7
			T.M. Backhouse	C	23,144	48.3
					1,670	3.4
1955	52,288	84.2	A.W.J. Greenwood	Lab	23,472	53.3
			J.E. Parkinson	C	20,561	46.7
					2,911	6.6
1959	50,577	86.3	A.W.J. Greenwood	Lab	20,743	47.5
			J.R.T. Holt	C	18,152	41.6
			A. Cooper	L	4,752*	10.9
					2,591	5.9
1964	48,392	81.8	A.W.J. Greenwood	Lab	21,371	54.0
			C.C. Baillieu	C	18,230	46.0
					3,141	8.0
1966	47,357	80.4	Rt. Hon. A.W.J. Greenwood	Lab	21,093	55.4
			C.C. Baillieu	C	16,984	44.6
					4,109	10.8
1970	49,900	78.2	R.W.T. Bray	C	20,448	52.4
			Miss B. Boothroyd	Lab	18,568	47.6
					1,880	4.8

Election	Electors	T'out	Candidate	Party	Votes	%
1950	55,469	87.3	†J.H. Jones	Lab	31,211	64.4
			R.B.F.S. Body	C	14,744	30.5
			Mrs. M. Foster	L	2,458*	5.1
					16,467	33.9
1951	56,337	84.2	J.H. Jones	Lab	31,124	65.6
			W.G. Blake	C	16,317	34.4
					14,807	31.2
1955	55,971	77.4	J.H. Jones	Lab	27,423	63.3
			W.G. Blake	C	15,882	36.7
					11,541	26.6
1959	57,080	78.9	J.H. Jones	Lab	28,298	62.8
			R. Hall	C	16,759	37.2
					11,539	25.6
[Death]						
1963 (28/3)	57,541	56.3	B.K. O'Malley	Lab	22,441	69.3
			J.M. Barrass	C	9,209	28.4
			R.E. Eckley	Ind	742*	2.3
					13,232	40.9
1964	57,937	71.6	B.K. O'Malley	Lab	27,585	66.5
			J.M. Barrass	C	13,907	33.5
					13,678	33.0
1966	57,229	68.7	B.K. O'Malley	Lab	27,402	69.7
			E.R. Cooke	C	11,925	30.3
					15,477	39.4
1970	60,460	62.9	B.K. O'Malley	Lab	25,246	66.4
			E.R. Cooke	C	12,770	33.6
					12,476	32.8

Election	Electors	T'out	Candidate	Party	Votes	%
1950	59,552	83.6	†Rt. Hon. A. Henderson	Lab	31,988	64.3
			R.B.J. Barnes	C	13,092	26.3
			A. Yates	L	4,692*	9.4
					18,896	38.0
1951	60,462	80.8	Rt. Hon. A. Henderson	Lab	32,579	66.7
			D. Napley	C	16,263	33.3
					16,316	33.4
1955	59,908*	72.1	Rt. Hon. A. Henderson	Lab	28,166	65.3
			A.A. Hill	C	14,998	34.7
					13,168	30.6
1959	59,895	74.0	Rt. Hon. A. Henderson	Lab	27,151	61.3
			A. Taylor	C	17,174	38.7
					9,977	22.6
1964	59,842	70.4	Rt. Hon. A. Henderson	Lab	25,352	60.2
			G.R. Anstee	C	16,751	39.8
					8,601	20.4
1966	59,881	69.2	P.K. Archer	Lab	27,269	65.8
			D.S. Adams	C	14,175	34.2
					13,094	31.6
1970	63,837	63.5	P.K. Archer	Lab	25,001	61.7
			P.M. Smith	C	15,537	38.3
					9,464	23.4

Election	Electors	T'out	Candidate	Party	Votes	%
1950	45,574	88.0	F.P. Crowder	C	23,077	57.5
			Mrs. A.L. Birk	Lab	13,568	33.8
			Mrs. G.R. Wood	L	3,482*	8.7
					9,509	23.7
1951	47,016	84.6	F.P. Crowder	C	25,295	63.6
			T.J. Parker	Lab/Co-op	14,491	36.4
					10,804	27.2
1955	47,698	79.8	F.P. Crowder	C	24,806	65.2
			G.S. Burden	Lab	13,251	34.8
					11,555	30.4
1959	49,198	83.7	F.P. Crowder	C	23,480	57.0
			J.L. King	Lab	10,424	25.3
			R.A. Walker	L	7,295	17.7
					13,056	31.7
1964	49,358	81.4	F.P. Crowder	C	21,036	52.4
			P.T.A. Marlowe	Lab	11,331	28.2
			R.A. Walker	L	7,806	19.4
					9,705	24.2
1966	49,334	81.7	F.P. Crowder	C	20,731	51.4
			P.L.N. Smith	Lab	13,455	33.4
			R.A. Walker	L	6,128	15.2
					7,276	18.0
1970	54,702	73.1	F.P. Crowder	C	24,247	60.6
			B.H. Silverman	Lab	11,541	28.9
			Miss J.M. Arram	L	4,188*	10.5
					12,706	31.7

ST. HELENS [252]

Election	Electors	T'out	Candidate	Party	Votes	%
1950	73,640	84.9	†Rt. Hon. Sir H.W. Shawcross	Lab	39,514	63.2
			A.G.F. Hall-Davis	C	20,741	33.2
			J.H. Winskill	L	2,263*	3.6
					18,773	30.0
1951	74,659	79.7	Rt. Hon. Sir H.W. Shawcross	Lab	37,688	63.3
			M.H.C. Hughes-Young	C	21,830	36.7
					15,858	26.6
1955	75,588*	73.5	Rt. Hon. Sir H.W. Shawcross	Lab	35,737	64.3
			A.M. Caplin	C	19,854	35.7
					15,883	28.6

[Resignation]

Election	Electors	T'out	Candidate	Party	Votes	%
1958 (12/6)	74,695	54.6	L. Spriggs	Lab	26,405	64.7
			M. Carlisle	C	14,411	35.3
					11,994	29.4
1959	75,280	76.9	L. Spriggs	Lab	35,961	62.1
			M. Carlisle	C	21,956	37.9
					14,005	24.2
1964	70,465	72.3	L. Spriggs	Lab	34,137	67.0
			H.K. Speed	C	16,826	33.0
					17,311	34.0
1966	68,675	68.6	L. Spriggs	Lab	33,325	70.8
			C.C. Fielden	C	13,776	29.2
					19,549	41.6
1970	74,448	64.6	L. Spriggs	Lab	31,587	65.7
			I.D. McGaw	C	16,509	34.3
					15,078	31.4

Election	Electors	T'out	Candidate	Party	Votes	%
1950	60,973	81.3	†E.A. Hardy	Lab	26,873	54.2
			W.G. Sinclair	C	18,625	37.6
			S. Needoff	L	4,057*	8.2
					8,248	16.6
1951	61,114	79.7	E.A. Hardy	Lab	27,729	57.0
			J.E. Parkinson	C	20,951	43.0
					6,778	14.0
1955	55,853	69.8	F. Allaun	Lab	20,351	52.2
			J. Whiteley	C	18,623	47.8
					1,728	4.4
1959	51,231	73.8	F. Allaun	Lab	20,639	54.6
			J.H. Franks	C	17,171	45.4
					3,468	9.2
1964	48,109	66.8	F. Allaun	Lab	19,641	61.1
			J.H. Franks	C	12,498	38.9
					7,143	22.2
1966	44,841	61.1	F. Allaun	Lab	18,409	67.2
			G.W.G. Fitzsimons	C	9,000	32.8
					9,409	34.4
1970	45,701	62.2	F. Allaun	Lab	15,853	55.7
			J.B. Leck	C	9,583	33.7
			A.S. Bell	L	3,000*	10.6
					6,270	22.0

SALFORD, WEST [254]

Election	Electors	T'out	Candidate	Party	Votes	%
1950	61,913	85.0	†C. Royle	Lab	26,885	51.1
			S. Bell	C	21,593	41.0
			L.H. Storey	L	4,174*	7.9
					5,292	10.1
1951	62,144	83.0	C. Royle	Lab	27,542	53.4
			W.G. Sinclair	C	24,055	46.6
					3,487	6.8
1955	58,701	74.9	C. Royle	Lab	22,413	51.0
			H.D. Moore	C	21,554	49.0
					859	2.0
1959	56,490	77.0	C. Royle	Lab	23,167	53.3
			H.H. Davies	C	20,306	46.7
					2,861	6.6

[Seat Vacant at Dissolution (Elevation to a Life Peerage—Lord Royle)]

Election	Electors	T'out	Candidate	Party	Votes	%
1964	50,514*	73.1	S. Orme	Lab	20,490	55.5
			A.E. Clark	C	16,446	44.5
					4,044	11.0
1966	48,390	67.2	S. Orme	Lab	19,237	59.2
			A.E. Clark	C	13,257	40.8
					5,980	18.4
1970	47,733	65.6	S. Orme	Lab	16,986	54.3
			A.E. Clark	C	14,310	45.7
					2,676	8.6

Election	Electors	T'out	Candidate	Party	Votes	%
1950	49,650	86.4	†J.B. Hynd	Lab	30,726	71.6
			L.S.E. Farris	NL & C	12,185	28.4
					18,541	43.2
1951	50,907	82.7	J.B. Hynd	Lab	29,958	71.1
			H.L. Lambert	NL & C	12,161	28.9
					17,797	42.2
1955	64,601**	72.1	J.B. Hynd	Lab	33,071	71.0
			H.L. Lambert	NL & C	13,503	29.0
					19,568	42.0
1959	65,024	75.3	J.B. Hynd	Lab	33,676	68.8
			H.L. Lambert	NL & C	15,304	31.2
					18,372	37.6
1964	63,046	72.0	J.B. Hynd	Lab	30,318	66.9
			H.L. Lambert	C	10,223	22.5
			C. Wood	L	4,831*	10.6
					20,095	44.4
1966	61,889	67.6	J.B. Hynd	Lab	32,336	77.3
			B.A. Marsden	C	9,511	22.7
					22,825	54.6
1970	59,949	63.5	A.E.P. Duffy	Lab	26,482	69.6
			Miss P.M. Santhouse	C	10,986	28.9
			P.H. Sims	Ind	581*	1.5
					15,496	40.7

SHEFFIELD, BRIGHTSIDE [256]

Election	Electors	T'out	Candidate	Party	Votes	%
1950	55,298	84.6	R.E. Winterbottom	Lab	32,542	69.6
			H.S.V. Smith	NL & C	13,136	28.1
			H. Hill	Com	1,081*	2.3
					19,406	41.5
1951	55,364	81.4	R.E. Winterbottom	Lab	31,519	69.9
			A.L. Wood	NL & C	12,433	27.6
			H. Hill	Com	1,116*	2.5
					19,086	42.3
1955	58,156**	71.1	R.E. Winterbottom	Lab	27,643	66.9
			E.W. Flynn	NL & C	12,239	29.6
			H. Hill	Com	1,461*	3.5
					15,404	37.3
1959	57,090	73.5	R.E. Winterbottom	Lab	28,302	67.4
			H.C. Holmes	NL & C	12,269	29.3
			H. Hill	Com	1,373*	3.3
					16,033	38.1
1964	54,927	70.3	R.E. Winterbottom	Lab	27,317	70.7
			A. Leitch	C	9,963	25.8
			H. Hill	Com	1,356*	3.5
					17,354	44.9
1966	53,015	66.2	R.E. Winterbottom	Lab	26,653	75.9
			R.W. Hadfield	C	7,476	21.3
			H. Hill	Com	989*	2.8
					19,177	54.6
[Death]						
1968 (13/6)	51,582	49.8	E. Griffiths	Lab	14,179	55.1
			Dr. A.C. Renfrew	C	8,931	34.8
			R.R. Wilkinson	Com	1,069*	4.2
			R. Guest	Ind	918*	3.6
			H.L. Lambert	Nat Ind	586*	2.3
					5,248	20.3
1970	53,499	62.0	E. Griffiths	Lab	23,941	72.2
			A.H. Newton	C	8,572	25.8
			G. Ashberry	Com	665*	2.0
					15,369	46.4

SHEFFIELD, HALLAM [257]

Election	Electors	T'out	Candidate	Party	Votes	%
1950	50,051	86.4	†R. Jennings	NL & C	28,159	65.1
			H.C. Spears	Lab	11,444	26.5
			A.E. Jones	L	3,641*	8.4
					16,715	38.6
1951	49,989	82.0	R. Jennings	NL & C	29,016	70.8
			F.W. Beaton	Lab	11,988	29.2
					17,028	41.6
1955	61,231**	74.1	Sir R. Jennings	NL & C	30,069	66.2
			J. Marsden	Lab	15,330	33.8
					14,739	32.4
1959	60,225	76.1	J.H. Osborn	NL & C (C)	28,747	62.7
			E.S. Sachs	Lab	11,938	26.1
			B. Roseby	L	5,119*	11.2
					16,809	36.6
1964	58,226	74.1	J.H. Osborn	C	23,719	54.9
			A.G. Kingscott	Lab	11,635	27.0
			G.H. Manley	L	7,807	18.1
					12,084	27.9
1966	56,078	75.0	J.H. Osborn	C	21,593	51.3
			P. Hardy	Lab	13,663	32.5
			D.T. Lloyd	L	6,799	16.2
					7,930	18.8
1970	58,735	69.8	J.H. Osborn	C	25,134	61.3
			A.H. Broadley	Lab	12,884	31.4
			P. Singh	L	2,972*	7.3
					12,250	29.9

Note:—

1964: Osborn joined the Liberal-Unionist Group in the House of Commons as an associate member.

Election	Electors	T'out	Candidate	Party	Votes	%
950	53,596	88.1	†P.G. Roberts	NL & C	26,560	56.3
			A.H. Jennings	Lab	17,856	37.8
			P. Beckerlegge	L	2,779*	5.9
					8,704	18.5
951	53,807	84.6	P.G. Roberts	NL & C	27,776	61.0
			A.H. Jennings	Lab	17,729	39.0
					10,047	22.0
955	65,667**	77.0	P.G. Roberts	NL & C	30,798	60.9
			J. Sewell	Lab	19,747	39.1
					11,051	21.8
959	72,648	77.6	Sir P.G. Roberts, Bt.	NL & C (C)	33,236	59.0
			Miss J. Mellors	Lab	23,109	41.0
					10,127	18.0
964	75,582	76.0	Sir P.G. Roberts, Bt.	C	29,587	51.5
			F.O. Hooley	Lab	27,883	48.5
					1,704	3.0
966	75,345	78.7	F.O. Hooley	Lab	31,996	54.0
			J.D. Spence	C	27,267	46.0
					4,729	8.0
970	80,943	73.4	J.D. Spence	C	27,950	47.1
			F.O. Hooley	Lab	27,237	45.8
			A.J. Singleton	L	4,220*	7.1
					713	1.3

Note:—

1964: Roberts joined the Liberal-Unionist Group in the House of Commons as an associate member.

SHEFFIELD, HILLSBOROUGH [259]

Election	Electors	T'out	Candidate	Party	Votes	%
1950	56,581	87.1	G. Darling	Lab/Co-op	28,925	58.7
			Sir K. Edge, Bt.	NL & C	19,613	39.8
			M. Bennett	Com	759*	1.5
					9,312	18.9
1951	56,415	84.9	G. Darling	Lab/Co-op	28,274	59.0
			G. Wadsworth	NL & C	19,617	41.0
					8,657	18.0
1955	54,643**	73.0	G. Darling	Lab/Co-op	23,438	58.8
			S.K. Arnold	NL & C	16,428	41.2
					7,010	17.6
1959	51,023	75.9	G. Darling	Lab/Co-op	21,888	56.5
			S.K. Arnold	NL & C	16,845	43.5
					5,043	13.0
1964	47,478	74.5	G. Darling	Lab/Co-op	22,071	62.4
			R.J. Lawther	C	13,278	37.6
					8,793	24.8
1966	47,788	70.3	G. Darling	Lab/Co-op	22,799	67.9
			M.J. Mallett	C	10,774	32.1
					12,025	35.8
1970	46,483	65.0	Rt. Hon. G. Darling	Lab/Co-op	18,775	62.1
			C.I. Patnick	C	11,445	37.9
					7,330	24.2

Election	Electors	T'out	Candidate	Party	Votes	%
1950	49,685	83.8	†H. Morris	Lab	30,317	72.8
			A.M. Cook	NL & C	11,311	27.2
					19,006	45.6
[Resignation]						
1950	49,586	62.9	Rt. Hon. Sir F. Soskice	Lab	22,080	70.9
(5/4)			J.P. Hunt	NL & C	8,365	26.8
			E.L. Moore	Com	729*	2.3
					13,715	44.1
1951	49,708	79.5	Rt. Hon. Sir F. Soskice	Lab	28,880	73.0
			T.A. Stobbs	NL & C	10,655	27.0
					18,225	46.0

This constituency was divided in 1955.

Note:—

1950:   Soskice was Solicitor-General.
(5/4)

Election	Electors	T'out	Candidate	Party	Votes	%
1950	53,006	85.2	F.W. Mulley	Lab	30,558	67.7
			H. Pryce	NL & C	13,678	30.3
			A. Fullard	Com	909*	2.0
					16,880	37.4
1951	54,058	82.5	F.W. Mulley	Lab	30,842	69.2
			S.B. Rippon	NL & C	13,743	30.8
					17,099	38.4
1955	55,373**	71.3	F.W. Mulley	Lab	28,904	73.2
			S.B. Rippon	NL & C	10,565	26.8
					18,339	46.4
1959	51,533	71.2	F.W. Mulley	Lab	26,078	71.1
			J. Neill	NL & C	10,598	28.9
					15,480	42.2
1964	46,633	68.6	F.W. Mulley	Lab	24,196	75.6
			F.W. Adams	C	7,816	24.4
					16,380	51.2
1966	47,165	64.8	Rt. Hon. F.W. Mulley	Lab	24,550	80.3
			R.A. Burns	C	5,017	16.4
			C. Morton	Com	1,002*	3.3
					19,533	63.9
1970	52,935	58.5	Rt. Hon. F.W. Mulley	Lab	23,302	75.2
			R.T. Renton	C	7,024	22.7
			C. Morton	Com	637*	2.1
					16,278	52.5

Election	Electors	T'out	Candidate	Party	Votes	%
1950	54,307	85.3	†P.C. Gordon Walker	Lab	28,750	62.1
			J.T. Fallon	C	17,553	37.9
					11,197	24.2
1951	54,793	83.5	Rt. Hon. P.C. Gordon Walker	Lab	27,739	60.6
			A.N. Giles	C	18,012	39.4
					9,727	21.2
1955	52,748	75.5	Rt. Hon. P.C. Gordon Walker	Lab	23,151	58.2
			J.J. Wells	C	16,656	41.8
					6,495	16.4
1959	49,794	75.9	Rt. Hon. P.C. Gordon Walker	Lab	20,670	54.7
			P.H.S. Griffiths	C	17,126	45.3
					3,544	9.4
1964	47,305	74.1	P.H.S. Griffiths	C	16,690	47.6
			Rt. Hon. P.C. Gordon Walker	Lab	14,916	42.6
			D. Hugill	L	3,172*	9.1
			D.T. Davies	Ind	262*	0.7
					1,774	5.0
1966	44,960	75.4	A.M.W. Faulds	Lab	18,440	54.4
			P.H.S. Griffiths	C	14,950	44.1
			R. Stanley	BNP	508*	1.5
					3,490	10.3
1970	45,164	68.2	A.M.W. Faulds	Lab	16,077	52.2
			B.B. Rathbone	C	13,968	45.4
			M. Gupta	L	747*	2.4
					2,109	6.8

Note:—

1964: Davies was opposed to coloured immigration.

SOUTHALL [263]

Election	Electors	T'out	Candidate	Party	Votes	%
1950	60,752	82.7	†G.A. Pargiter	Lab	27,107	53.9
			N.J. Cole	C	18,392	36.6
			W.T. Andrews	L	3,917*	7.8
			J.A. Purton	Com	839*	1.7
					8,715	17.3
1951	59,885	84.0	G.A. Pargiter	Lab	29,123	57.9
			H.J. Berkeley	C	21,169	42.1
					7,954	15.8
1955	57,633	76.5	G.A. Pargiter	Lab	25,207	57.2
			A. Tickler	C	18,872	42.8
					6,335	14.4
1959	55,290	76.4	G.A. Pargiter	Lab	22,285	52.7
			M.T.B. Underhill	C	19,966	47.3
					2,319	5.4
1964	53,558	70.2	G.A. Pargiter	Lab	18,041	48.0
			Miss B. Maddin	C	16,144	42.9
			J.E. Bean	BNP	3,410*	9.1
					1,897	5.1
1966	52,811	70.8	S.J. Bidwell	Lab	19,989	53.4
			Miss B. Maddin	C	14,642	39.2
			J.E. Bean	BNP	2,768*	7.4
					5,347	14.2
1970	55,980	64.5	S.J. Bidwell	Lab	19,389	53.6
			K.G. Reeves	C	15,166	42.0
			J.S. Shaw	NF	1,572*	4.4
					4,223	11.6

lection	Electors	T'out	Candidate	Party	Votes	%
950	66,254	84.0	†R. Morley	Lab	29,749	53.4
			Sir R.H. Hobart, Bt.	NL & C	24,536	44.1
			W. Craven-Ellis	Nat	1,380*	2.5
					5,213	9.3
951	67,038	83.6	R. Morley	Lab	30,330	54.1
			R.J. Stranger	NL & C	25,708	45.9
					4,622	8.2
955	67,098**	78.3	Dr. H.M. King	Lab	29,149	55.5
			L.T. Loader	C	23,378	44.5
					5,771	11.0
959	69,886	78.0	Dr. H.M. King	Lab	29,123	53.4
			E.M. King	C	25,390	46.6
					3,733	6.8
964	72,170	76.1	Dr. H.M. King	Lab	28,949	52.7
			G.G. Olson	C	18,974	34.5
			J. Cherryson	L	7,007	12.8
					9,975	18.2
966	72,846	49.0	Dr. Rt. Hon. H.M. King	Lab	30,463	85.4
			K.D. Hunt	Ind	5,217	14.6
					25,246	70.8
970	80,737	54.2	Dr. Rt. Hon. H.M. King	Lab	29,417	67.2
			E.N.I. Bray	N Dem P	9,581	21.9
			B.H. Phillips	Ind	4,794*	10.9
					19,836	45.3
Resignation]						
971 (7/5)	81,371	50.1	R.C. Mitchell	Lab	22,575	55.4
			J.W. Spicer	C	12,900	31.6
			E.N.I. Bray	N Dem P	3,090*	7.6
			J. Cherryson	L	2,214*	5.4
					9,675	23.8

otes:—

1964-1970: King was the Speaker of the House of Commons from October 1965 until December 1970.

1966: Hunt sought election as a 'Non-Party Democratic Nationalist' and was opposed to coloured immigration.

1970: Phillips advocated that the Speaker should not represent a constituency but become an ex-officio member of the House of Commons.

Election	Electors	T'out	Candidate	Party	Votes	%
1950	62,106	84.4	Dr. H.M. King	Lab	25,052	47.
			P.A.R. Bremridge	NL & C	23,663	45.
			S. Fry	L	3,697*	7.
					1,389	2.
1951	62,733	83.5	Dr. H.M. King	Lab	26,430	50.
			J.A. Paul	NL & C	25,965	49.
					465	0.
1955	66,256**	78.7	J.M. Howard	C	26,707	51.
			C.A.R. Crosland	Lab	22,865	43.
			T.C. Stanley-Little	L	2,583*	5.
					3,842	7.
1959	67,087	79.9	J.M. Howard	C	30,176	56.
			Mrs. S.V.T.B. Williams	Lab	23,410	43.
					6,766	12.
1964	66,572	76.7	Sir J. Fletcher-Cooke	C	25,700	50.
			R.C. Mitchell	Lab	25,352	49.
					348	0.
1966	65,174	78.1	R.C. Mitchell	Lab	24,628	48.
			Sir J. Fletcher-Cooke	C	22,188	43.
			G.A.W. Cleverley	L	4,102*	8.
					2,440	4.
1970	70,614	73.5	S.J.A. Hill	C	24,660	47.
			R.C. Mitchell	Lab	22,858	44.
			J.R. Wallis	L	4,349*	8.
					1,802	3.

SOUTHEND, EAST [266]

Election	Electors	T'out	Candidate	Party	Votes	%
1950	52,393	82.5	S.J. McAdden	C	20,395	47.1
			R.J. Minney	Lab	18,230	42.2
			J.G. Runciman	L	4,616*	10.7
					2,165	4.9
1951	54,020	80.6	S.J. McAdden	C	24,088	55.3
			L.C. Merrion	Lab	19,478	44.7
					4,610	10.6
1955	55,635**	74.0	S.J. McAdden	C	23,958	58.2
			W.H. Clough	Lab	17,200	41.8
					6,758	16.4
1959	55,265	75.5	S.J. McAdden	C	24,712	59.3
			E.J. Trevett	Lab	16,987	40.7
					7,725	18.6
1964	55,763	76.2	Sir S.J. McAdden	C	19,775	46.6
			E.J. Trevett	Lab	16,408	38.6
			D.E. Evans	L	6,296	14.8
					3,367	8.0
1966	54,878	76.9	Sir S.J. McAdden	C	19,125	45.3
			P.R. Clyne	Lab	18,608	44.1
			K.W. Baynes	L	4,495*	10.6
					517	1.2
1970	57,663	71.3	Sir S.J. McAdden	C	24,025	58.5
			P.R. Clyne	Lab	17,065	41.5
					6,960	17.0

SOUTHEND, WEST   [267]

Election	Electors	T'out	Candidate	Party	Votes	%
1950	71,392	83.0	†H. Channon	C	34,100	57.6
			E.C. Hutchison	Lab/Co-op	15,254	25.7
			J.H.M. Scott	L	9,907	16.7
					18,846	31.9
1951	71,957	79.0	H. Channon	C	39,287	69.1
			H.N. Lyall	Lab	17,532	30.9
					21,755	38.2
1955	57,424**	74.1	H. Channon	C	27,326	64.2
			V.G. Marchesi	Lab	8,866	20.8
			Miss H.J. Harvey	L	6,375	15.0
					18,460	43.4
[Death]						
1959	60,773	42.9	H.P.G. Channon	C	14,493	55.6
(29/1)			Miss H.J. Harvey	L	6,314	24.2
			A. Pearson-Clarke	Lab	5,280	20.2
					8,179	31.4
1959	60,999	77.7	H.P.G. Channon	C	27,612	58.3
			Miss H.J. Harvey	L	10,577	22.3
			A. Pearson-Clarke	Lab	9,219	19.4
					17,035	36.0
1964	64,132	78.8	H.P.G. Channon	C	25,555	50.6
			G.C. Hoyer-Millar	L	14,548	28.8
			M.R. Winsbury	Lab	10,423	20.6
					11,007	21.8
1966	64,487	78.4	H.P.G. Channon	C	25,713	50.9
			M. Burstin	Lab	13,856	27.4
			G.C. Hoyer-Millar	L	10,958	21.7
					11,857	23.5
1970	68,940	70.8	H.P.G. Channon	C	29,304	60.1
			M. Burstin	Lab	12,419	25.4
			J.H. Barnett	L	7,077	14.5
					16,885	34.7

lection	Electors	T'out	Candidate	Party	Votes	%
950	57,447	86.4	†A.B. Baxter	C	30,302	61.1
			Miss V. Dart	Lab	11,023	22.2
			G. Ellenbogen	L	8,286	16.7
					19,279	38.9
951	57,462	84.1	A.B. Baxter	C	30,044	62.2
			Miss V. Dart	Lab	10,889	22.5
			E.T. Malindine	L	7,402	15.3
					19,155	39.7
955	55,745	77.1	Sir A.B. Baxter	C	26,794	62.3
			G.L. Caunt	Lab	8,584	20.0
			G.J. Bridge	L	7,614	17.7
					18,210	42.3
959	54,869	77.1	Sir A.B. Baxter	C	25,704	60.8
			G.J. Bridge	L	8,968	21.2
			S.J. Chapman	Lab	7,613	18.0
					16,736	39.6

[Seat Vacant at Dissolution (Death)]

lection	Electors	T'out	Candidate	Party	Votes	%
964	53,198	76.4	Hon. A.G. Berry	C	22,251	54.8
			G.J. Bridge	L	9,600	23.6
			S.J. Chapman	Lab	8,787	21.6
					12,651	31.2
966	52,705	75.1	Hon. A.G. Berry	C	21,171	53.5
			P.S. Gourgey	Lab	9,743	24.6
			G.J. Bridge	L	8,679	21.9
					11,428	28.9
970	55,875	67.7	Hon. A.G. Berry	C	22,963	60.8
			R.B. Bastin	Lab/Co-op	9,389	24.8
			G.J. Bridge	L	5,451	14.4
					13,574	36.0

Election	Electors	T'out	Candidate	Party	Votes	%
1950	64,590	81.8	†Rt. Hon. R.S. Hudson	C	29,766	56
			J.P. Bonney	Lab	14,159	26
			H. Ellington	L	8,933	16.
					15,607	29
1951	65,018	77.7	Rt. Hon. R.S. Hudson	C	30,388	60.
			H.O. Ellis	Lab	12,535	24.
			H.D. Bentliff	L	7,576	15.
					17,853	35.

[Elevation to the Peerage—Viscount Hudson]

Election	Electors	T'out	Candidate	Party	Votes	%
1952 (6/2)	65,018	61.0	R.F. Fleetwood-Hesketh	C	24,589	62
			A.L. Tillotson	Lab	11,310	28.
			H.D. Bentliff	L	3,776*	9.
					13,279	33.
1955	62,618	68.8	R.F. Fleetwood-Hesketh	C	30,268	70.
			P.B. Cameron	Lab	12,827	29.
					17,441	40.
1959	62,466	76.8	W.I. Percival	C	26,905	56.
			S. Goldberg	L	11,292	23.
			C.W. Hadfield	Lab	9,805	20.
					15,613	32.
1964	60,288	76.5	W.I. Percival	C	23,917	51.
			L. Goldwater	Lab	11,572	25.
			C.J. Coleman	L	10,609	23.
					12,345	26.
1966	60,218	72.7	W.I. Percival	C	22,324	51.
			J.L. Prescott	Lab	12,798	29.
			C.J. Coleman	L	8,630	19.
					9,526	21.
1970	64,772	70.6	W.I. Percival	C	22,958	50.
			R.C. Fearn	L	13,809	30.
			B.T. George	Lab	8,950	19.
					9,149	20.

Election	Electors	T'out	Candidate	Party	Votes	%
1950	72,463	81.7	†Rt. Hon. J.C. Ede	Lab	33,452	56.5
			J. Chalmers	C	15,897	26.8
			J. George	L	9,446	16.0
			F.O. Smith	Com	415*	0.7
					17,555	29.7
1951	74,657*	80.5	Rt. Hon. J.C. Ede	Lab	33,633	56.0
			J. Chalmers	C	20,208	33.6
			C.J. Kitchell	L	6,270*	10.4
					13,425	22.4
1955	74,340	71.6	Rt. Hon. J.C. Ede	Lab	31,734	59.6
			J. Chalmers	C	21,482	40.4
					10,252	19.2
1959	75,538	74.4	Rt. Hon. J.C. Ede	Lab	32,577	58.0
			J. Chalmers	C	23,638	42.0
					8,939	16.0
1964	72,697	74.1	A. Blenkinsop	Lab	29,694	55.2
			J. Chalmers	C	16,344	30.3
			T.H.C. Wardlaw	L	7,837	14.5
					13,350	24.9
1966	71,578	68.7	A. Blenkinsop	Lab	31,829	64.7
			C.M. Dallas	C	17,340	35.3
					14,489	29.4
1970	75,032	66.8	A. Blenkinsop	Lab	30,191	60.2
			Dr. J. McKee	C	19,960	39.8
					10,231	20.4

Election	Electors	T'out	Candidate	Party	Votes	%
1950	53,686	88.5	†N.J. Hulbert	C	22,762	47.8
			A.M. Watson	Lab	19,134	40.3
			W.H. Evans	L	5,638*	11.9
					3,628	7.5
1951	54,576	85.4	N.J. Hulbert	C	25,691	55.1
			J. Owen	Lab	20,893	44.9
					4,798	10.2
1955	53,271	79.8	N.J. Hulbert	C	23,547	55.4
			Mrs. M.E. Nichol	Lab	18,980	44.6
					4,567	10.8
1959	53,287	82.1	Sir N.J. Hulbert	C	23,487	53.7
			M.E.J. Swain	Lab	20,265	46.3
					3,222	7.4
1964	52,283	81.5	A. Gregory	Lab	18,969	44.5
			Sir N.J. Hulbert	C	17,067	40.1
			B. Downs	L	6,560	15.4
					1,902	4.4
1966	50,370	79.1	A. Gregory	Lab	21,598	54.2
			I.W. Owen	C	18,262	45.8
					3,336	8.4
1970	52,647	74.9	I.W. Owen	C	18,132	46.0
			A. Gregory	Lab	17,261	43.8
			S. Collier	L	4,022*	10.2
					871	2.2

Election	Electors	T'out	Candidate	Party	Votes	%
1950	48,032	86.9	†Sir A.B. Gridley	C	19,079	45.7
			H. Ponsonby	Lab	16,897	40.5
			R. Hewitt	L	5,778	13.8
					2,182	5.2
1951	48,413	84.2	Sir A.B. Gridley	C	22,075	54.2
			F. Bibby	Lab	18,675	45.8
					3,400	8.4

[Elevation to the Peerage—Lord Gridley]

1955 (3/2)	46,559	64.6	H.M. Steward	C	16,321	54.3
			H. Davies	Lab	13,758	45.7
					2,563	8.6
1955	47,251*	79.0	H.M. Steward	C	20,698	55.5
			E.A.C. Roberts	Lab	16,612	44.5
					4,086	11.0
1959	47,265	81.5	H.M. Steward	C	20,522	53.3
			S. Orme	Lab	17,982	46.7
					2,540	6.6
1964	45,955	81.8	M. Orbach	Lab	16,755	44.6
			H.M. Steward	C	13,718	36.5
			Dr. D.F. Kerr	L	7,107	18.9
					3,037	8.1
1966	45,406	76.7	M. Orbach	Lab	19,456	55.8
			C. Howson	C	15,387	44.2
					4,069	11.6
1970	49,142	73.3	M. Orbach	Lab	16,747	46.5
			C. Howson	C	14,679	40.7
			T.G. Jones	L	4,613	12.8
					2,068	5.8

Election	Electors	T'out	Candidate	Party	Votes	%
1950	48,573	89.4	†G.R. Chetwynd	Lab	23,475	54.(
			R.A. Lamb	C	16,495	38.(
			A.G. Gamble	L	3,475*	8.(
					6,980	16.(
1951	50,104	88.0	G.R. Chetwynd	Lab	24,558	55.:
			H.C.R. Laslett	C	19,511	44.:
					5,047	11.4
1955	51,366*	83.8	G.R. Chetwynd	Lab	23,422	54.4
			C.B. Longbottom	C	19,607	45.6
					3,815	8.8
1959	53,224	83.9	G.R. Chetwynd	Lab	23,961	53.7
			G.J.K. Coles	C	20,684	46.3
					3,277	7.4

[Resignation on appointment as Director of the North-East Development Council]

Election	Electors	T'out	Candidate	Party	Votes	%
1962 (5/4)	53,390	81.5	W.T. Rodgers	Lab	19,694	45.3
			G.J.K. Coles	C	12,112	27.8
			J.H. Mulholland	L	11,722	26.9
					7,582	17.5
1964	53,263	81.8	W.T. Rodgers	Lab	22,011	50.5
			R.W.T. Bray	C	15,424	35.4
			J.H. Mulholland	L	6,130	14.1
					6,587	15.1
1966	52,345	77.4	W.T. Rodgers	Lab	24,248	59.8
			P.V. Radford	C	15,547	38.4
			E. Jones	Com	710*	1.8
					8,701	21.4
1970	55,494	73.2	W.T. Rodgers	Lab	22,283	54.9
			P.V. Radford	C	17,960	44.2
			E. Jones	Com	369*	0.9
					4,323	10.7

lection	Electors	T'out	Candidate	Party	Votes	%
)50	64,035	83.2	†Dr. B. Stross	Lab	34,908	65.5
			W. Hancock	C	18,361	34.5
					16,547	31.0
)51	64,519	82.2	Dr. B. Stross	Lab	34,260	64.6
			H.R. Fleck	C	18,770	35.4
					15,490	29.2
)55	62,444*	71.3	Dr. B. Stross	Lab	28,452	63.9
			G.B. Price	C	16,097	36.1
					12,355	27.8
)59	62,220	75.3	Dr. B. Stross	Lab	28,630	61.1
			J.P.H. Harrison	C	18,205	38.9
					10,425	22.2
)64	59,140	72.3	Sir B. Stross	Lab	27,424	64.2
			J.P.H. Harrison	C	15,322	35.8
					12,102	28.4
)66	57,379	68.3	R.B. Cant	Lab	26,653	68.0
			K.G. Reeves	C	12,515	32.0
					14,138	36.0
)70	59,818	50.1	R.B. Cant	Lab	18,758	62.6
			Mrs. E. Ashley	C	11,227	37.4
					7,531	25.2

Election	Electors	T'out	Candidate	Party	Votes	%
1950	60,629	85.0	†A.E. Davies	Lab	36,896	71.(
			P.W. Hodgens	C	14,647	28.∙
					22,249	43.∶
1951	61,282	83.8	A.E. Davies	Lab	36,692	71.∙
			J.B. Coventry	NL & C	14,668	28.(
					22,024	42.∶
[Death]						
1953 (31/3)	60,638	50.5	Mrs. H. Slater	Lab/Co-op	23,103	75.∙
			S.F. Middup	C	7,502	24.∙
					15,601	51.(
1955	58,518*	75.3	Mrs. H. Slater	Lab/Co-op	29,473	66.∙
			S.F. Middup	C	14,599	33.
					14,874	33.∶
1959	58,336	78.6	Mrs. H. Slater	Lab/Co-op	29,336	64.(
			S.F. Middup	C	16,522	36.(
					12,814	28.(
1964	55,886	76.2	Mrs. H. Slater	Lab/Co-op	27,584	64.∙
			B.D. Barton	C	15,025	35.∶
					12,559	29.∙
1966	54,978	72.4	J.S. Forrester	Lab	28,481	71.∙
			L.C.N. Bury	C	11,335	28.∙
					17,146	43.(
1970	58,780	53.1	J.S. Forrester	Lab	20,642	66.∙
			J.S. Heath	C	10,542	33.∶
					10,100	32.∙

STOKE-ON-TRENT, SOUTH [276]

Election	Electors	T'out	Candidate	Party	Votes	%
1950	62,485	85.3	†E. Smith	Lab	34,339	64.4
			L. Orridge	C	14,637	27.5
			W.H. Kemp	L	4,302*	8.1
					19,702	36.9
1951	63,667	84.2	E. Smith	Lab	35,261	65.8
			B.G.C. Webb	C	18,355	34.2
					16,906	31.6
1955	66,212*	73.6	E. Smith	Lab	31,003	63.6
			B.G.C. Webb	C	17,739	36.4
					13,264	27.2
1959	63,777	78.2	E. Smith	Lab	29,578	59.3
			G.S. Tucker	C	20,318	40.7
					9,260	18.6
1964	63,138	75.7	E. Smith	Lab	28,928	60.6
			C. Howson	C	18,839	39.4
					10,089	21.2
1966	62,530	71.0	J. Ashley	Lab	27,380	61.6
			F.W. Thornton	C	14,769	33.3
			S.J. Lomas	Com	2,262*	5.1
					12,611	28.3
1970	67,953	50.7	J. Ashley	Lab	20,770	60.2
			R.J. Apps	C	13,341	38.7
			S.J. Lomas	Com	364*	1.1
					7,429	21.5

Election	Electors	T'out	Candidate	Party	Votes	%
1950	72,732	86.9	S. Storey	C	30,678	48.5
			†H.L. Austin	Lab	25,075	39.7
			Hon. S.R. Cawley	L	7,467*	11.8
					5,603	8.8
1951	73,318	83.4	S. Storey	C	35,419	58.0
			C. Mapp	Lab	25,694	42.0
					9,725	16.0
1955	71,410	76.1	S. Storey	C	33,101	60.9
			F.G. Barton	Lab	21,267	39.1
					11,834	21.8
1959	71,304	79.1	S. Storey	C	32,888	58.3
			E. Reid	Lab	23,538	41.7
					9,350	16.6
1964	69,369	79.2	Sir S. Storey, Bt.	C	22,004	40.1
			E. Cavanagh	Lab	20,080	36.5
			Dr. M.P. Winstanley	L	12,884	23.4
					1,924	3.6
1966	68,093	77.1	E.A. Davies	Lab	24,739	47.1
			Sir S. Storey, Bt.	C	21,374	40.7
			C.L. Jones	L	6,382*	12.2
					3,365	6.4
1970	71,006	75.0	W.S. Churchill	C	28,629	53.8
			E.A. Davies	Lab	24,614	46.2
					4,015	7.6

Election	Electors	T'out	Candidate	Party	Votes	%
1950	54,416	84.3	†F.T. Willey	Lab	24,810	54.0
			S. Hudson	C	17,469	38.1
			J.L. Hurst	L	3,614*	7.9
					7,341	15.9
1951	52,652	83.7	F.T. Willey	Lab	23,792	54.0
			R. Kendall	C	20,302	46.0
					3,490	8.0
1955	60,255*	75.7	F.T. Willey	Lab	24,237	53.1
			A.M.H.Y.M. Herbert	C	21,401	46.9
					2,836	6.2
1959	57,763	80.5	F.T. Willey	Lab	24,341	52.4
			P.E. Heselton	C	22,133	47.6
					2,208	4.8
1964	56,856	76.3	F.T. Willey	Lab	24,024	55.4
			P.E. Heselton	C	18,195	41.9
			R.C. Middlewood	Ind C	1,157*	2.7
					5,829	13.5
1966	56,197	74.5	Rt. Hon. F.T. Willey	Lab	25,438	60.8
			P.L. Rost	C	16,423	39.2
					9,015	21.6
1970	60,921	69.8	Rt. Hon. F.T. Willey	Lab	25,779	60.6
			J.M. Reay-Smith	C	16,738	39.4
					9,041	21.2

Note:—

1964: Middlewood was opposed to the nationalization of industry.

Election	Electors	T'out	Candidate	Party	Votes	%
1950	65,833	83.3	†R. Ewart	Lab	27,192	49.6
			H. Wilkinson	C	22,012	40.2
			C.J. Kitchell	L	5,604*	10.2
					5,180	9.4
1951	65,928	82.2	R. Ewart	Lab	27,257	50.3
			P.G. Williams	C	26,951	49.7
					306	0.6
[Death]						
1953	65,453	72.7	P.G. Williams	C	23,114	48.6
(13/5)			A.G.S. Whipp	Lab	21,939	46.1
			R.F. Leslie	L	2,524*	5.3
					1,175	2.5
1955	61,615*	77.4	P.G. Williams	C (Ind C) (C)	24,727	51.9
			E. Armstrong	Lab	22,953	48.1
					1,774	3.8
1959	68,014	80.4	P.G. Williams	C	27,825	50.9
			E. Armstrong	Lab	26,835	49.1
					990	1.8
1964	66,239	75.8	G.A.T. Bagier	Lab	25,900	51.6
			P.G. Williams	C	24,334	48.4
					1,566	3.2
1966	63,554	75.5	G.A.T. Bagier	Lab	27,567	57.5
			P.E. Heselton	C	20,398	42.5
					7,169	15.0
1970	67,751	70.2	G.A.T. Bagier	Lab	26,840	56.4
			D.A. Orde	C	20,722	43.6
					6,118	12.8

Election	Electors	T'out	Candidate	Party	Votes	%
1955	44,331	79.5	N.T.L. Fisher	C	22,863	64.9
			S.G. Richards	Lab	12,380	35.1
					10,483	29.8
1959	45,165	79.0	N.T.L. Fisher	C	24,058	67.4
			A. Imisson	Lab	11,633	32.6
					12,425	34.8
1964	44,846	75.4	N.T.L. Fisher	C	20,499	60.6
			D.E. Heather	Lab	13,337	39.4
					7,162	21.2
1966	44,894	77.0	N.T.L. Fisher	C	19,989	57.9
			D.E. Heather	Lab	14,561	42.1
					5,428	15.8
1970	47,661	70.4	N.T.L. Fisher	C	17,359	51.7
			R.D. Kerr-Waller	Lab	10,469	31.2
			C.F. Green	L	4,027*	12.0
			E. Scruby	Ind C	1,706*	5.1
					6,890	20.5

Note:—

1970: Scruby sought election as an 'Independent Enoch Powell Conservative' and advocated drastic curbs on immigration and also opposed Britain entering the Common Market.

Election	Electors	T'out	Candidate	Party	Votes	%
1950	59,141	86.7	†S.H. Marshall	C	29,200	56.9
			Mrs. H.O. Judd	Lab	17,706	34.5
			H.J. Wheeler	L	4,389*	8.6
					11,494	22.4
1951	59,848	81.7	S.H. Marshall	C	30,684	62.8
			E.K.I. Hurst	Lab	18,202	37.2
					12,482	25.6
[Resignation]						
1954	59,292	55.6	R.C. Sharples	C	21,930	66.5
(4/11)			N.T. Poulter	Lab	11,023	33.5
					10,907	33.0
1955	58,529	76.4	R.C. Sharples	C	29,538	66.0
			R.M. Lewis	Lab	15,205	34.0
					14,333	32.0
1959	58,898	79.6	R.C. Sharples	C	27,344	58.3
			F.A. Judd	Lab	11,946	25.5
			J. Montgomerie	L	7,600	16.2
					15,398	32.8
1964	58,763	74.3	R.C. Sharples	C	22,975	52.7
			P. Derrick	Lab	11,839	27.1
			J. Montgomerie	L	8,827	20.2
					11,136	25.6
1966	57,227	76.4	R.C. Sharples	C	22,331	51.1
			F.J. Ward	Lab	13,235	30.3
			N.D.M. McGeorge	L	8,134	18.6
					9,096	20.8
1970	60,991	67.6	R.C. Sharples	C	23,957	58.1
			J. Dowsett	Lab	11,261	27.3
			N.D.M. McGeorge	L	6,023	14.6
					12,696	30.8

Election	Electors	T'out	Candidate	Party	Votes	%
955	58,839	76.7	Rt. Hon. G.W. Lloyd	C	31,552	69.9
			C.B.B. Norwood	Lab	13,565	30.1
					17,987	39.8
959	65,347	79.4	Rt. Hon. G.W. Lloyd	C	33,064	63.7
			R.S.G. Hattersley	Lab	11,310	21.8
			K.J. Hovers	L	7,543	14.5
					21,754	41.9
964	73,933	78.3	Rt. Hon. G.W. Lloyd	C	31,772	54.8
			M.H. Whincup	L	14,745	25.5
			P.E. Tombs	Lab	11,399	19.7
					17,027	29.3
966	75,779	76.3	Rt. Hon. G.W. Lloyd	C	30,350	52.5
			D.A. Finnigan	Lab	14,257	24.6
			M.H. Whincup	L	13,237	22.9
					16,093	27.9
970	92,727	69.1	Rt. Hon. G.W. Lloyd	C	36,774	57.4
			P.M. Tebbutt	Lab	18,134	28.3
			L.A. King	L	9,163	14.3
					18,640	29.1

Election	Electors	T'out	Candidate	Party	Votes	%
1950	48,966	87.2	†T. Reid	Lab	21,976	51.
			Sir G.E. Tritton, Bt.	C	13,697	32.
			Mrs. D.M. Gorsky	L	6,726	15.
			I. Gradwell	Com	295*	0.
					8,279	19.
1951	49,598	84.8	T. Reid	Lab	23,980	57
			Sir G.E. Tritton, Bt.	C	18,072	43.
					5,908	14.
1955	49,879*	80.0	F.E. Noel-Baker	Lab	21,926	54.
			P.W. Medd	C	17,987	45.
					3,939	9.
1959	55,339	80.0	F.E. Noel-Baker	Lab	24,087	54.
			G.L. Pears	C	20,178	45.
					3,909	8.
1964	58,923	74.8	F.E. Noel-Baker	Lab	26,464	60.
			N.G. Reece	C	16,651	37.
			I. Gradwell	Com	944*	2.
					9,813	22.
1966	57,582	73.5	F.E. Noel-Baker	Lab	25,966	61.
			N.G. Reece	C	15,523	36.
			I. Gradwell	Com	838*	2.
					10,443	24.

[Resignation]

Election	Electors	T'out	Candidate	Party	Votes	%
1969 (30/10)	57,851	69.8	C.J.F. Ward	C	16,843	41.
			D.L. Stoddart	Lab	16,365	40.
			Hon. C.W. Layton	L	6,193	15.
			Miss J. Gradwell	Com	518*	1.
			F. Willis	Ind	446*	1.
					478	1.
1970	61,305	75.6	D.L. Stoddart	Lab	25,731	55.
			C.J.F. Ward	C	20,155	43.
			Miss J. Gradwell	Com	456*	1.
					5,576	12.

Note:—

1969: Willis sought election as a 'Young Socialist'. He was a member of the Socialist Labour League.

lection	Electors	T'out	Candidate	Party	Votes	%
950	65,708	82.8	†C. Williams	C	29,153	53.6
			R. Briscoe	Lab	14,287	26.2
			H.S. Townend	L	10,987	20.2
					14,866	27.4
951	66,456	80.0	C. Williams	C	31,441	59.2
			R. Briscoe	Lab	14,801	27.8
			D.R.E. Abel	L	6,904	13.0
					16,640	31.4
955	65,353	75.5	C. Williams	C	29,777	60.4
			R. Briscoe	Lab	12,547	25.4
			P.J. Bessell	L	7,012	14.2
					17,230	35.0
Death]						
955 (15/12)	65,702	62.6	F.M. Bennett	C	20,964	51.0
			W. Hamling	Lab	10,383	25.2
			P.J. Bessell	L	9,775	23.8
					10,581	25.8
959	67,608	76.9	F.M. Bennett	C	29,527	56.8
			W.V. Cooper	Lab	11,784	22.7
			T.O. Kellock	L	10,685	20.5
					17,743	34.1
964	73,276	75.0	F.M. Bennett	C	28,801	52.4
			H.L.J. Brunner	L	13,652	24.8
			Mrs. T.W. Thompson	Lab	12,530	22.8
					15,149	27.6
966	74,985	77.4	Sir F.M. Bennett	C	28,693	49.4
			R.S. Dash	Lab	16,594	28.6
			H.L.J. Brunner	L	12,750	22.0
					12,099	20.8
970	82,837	73.8	Sir F.M. Bennett	C	33,996	55.6
			P.S.T. Bryers	Lab	15,948	26.1
			K.P. Jenkins	L	11,163	18.3
					18,048	29.5

Election	Electors	T'out	Candidate	Party	Votes	%
1950	66,943	81.0	†F. Messer	Lab/Co-op	30,901	57.0
			P.J. Faulkner	C	16,862	31.1
			R. Allen	L	5,665*	10.4
			G.R. Cross	Com	802*	1.5
					14,039	25.9
1951	66,866	79.8	F. Messer	Lab/Co-op	33,312	62.4
			P.J. Faulkner	C	20,061	37.6
					13,251	24.8
1955	63,242	70.2	Sir F. Messer	Lab/Co-op	26,636	60.0
			I.M. Fraser	C	17,753	40.0
					8,883	20.0
1959	59,794	72.0	A.G. Brown	Lab (Ind) (C)	22,325	51.9
			Hon. D.J.G. Hennessy	C	15,688	36.4
			L.G. Lepley	L	5,030*	11.7
					6,637	15.5
1964	55,644	63.9	N. Atkinson	Lab	19,458	54.7
			A.G. Brown	C	11,577	32.6
			L.G. Lepley	L	4,526	12.7
					7,881	22.1
1966	54,079	59.8	N. Atkinson	Lab	21,111	65.3
			H.J.M. Dykes	C	11,222	34.7
					9,889	30.6
1970	51,258	55.3	N. Atkinson	Lab	17,367	61.3
			L.T. Simmonds	C	10,975	38.7
					6,392	22.6

TWICKENHAM [286]

lection	Electors	T'out	Candidate	Party	Votes	%
950	76,810	85.7	†E.H. Keeling	C	36,757	55.9
			J.T. Stonehouse	Lab	23,088	35.1
			D.A. Forwood	L	5,950*	9.0
					13,669	20.8
951	77,444	81.3	E.H. Keeling	C	39,080	62.1
			Miss E.E.B. Chipchase	Lab	23,871	37.9
					15,209	24.2
Death]						
955 (5/1)	76,147	47.3	R.G. Cooke	C	23,075	64.0
			R.P. Pitman	Lab	12,953	36.0
					10,122	28.0
955	75,106	77.0	R.G. Cooke	C	33,726	58.3
			P. O'Gorman	Lab	17,450	30.2
			Miss M. Neilson	L	6,626*	11.5
					16,276	28.1
959	73,852	79.8	R.G. Cooke	C	33,677	57.2
			Mrs. A.P. Clark	Lab	16,638	28.2
			K.A. Powell	L	8,589	14.6
					17,039	29.0
964	72,154	77.7	R.G. Cooke	C	27,427	48.9
			W.E. Wolff	Lab	15,231	27.2
			J. Woolfe	L	12,306	22.0
			M.H. Craft	INDEC	1,073*	1.9
					12,196	21.7
966	70,675	78.6	R.G. Cooke	C	26,512	47.7
			D. Carlton	Lab	18,884	34.0
			S. Goldblatt	L	10,160	18.3
					7,628	13.7
Seat Vacant at Dissolution (Death)]						
970	73,974	71.0	T.F.H. Jessel	C	28,571	54.4
			J.H.W. Grant	Lab	16,950	32.3
			D.K. Rebak	L	6,516*	12.4
			R. Franklin	Ind	462*	0.9
					11,621	22.1

Note:—

1970: Franklin sought election as a 'Peoples Representative' candidate.

Election	Electors	T'out	Candidate	Party	Votes	%
1950	69,501	84.0	Miss I.M.B. Ward	C	28,785	49.3
			†Miss G.M. Colman	Lab.	23,148	39.6
			Dr. E.B. Slack	L	6,452*	11.1
					5,637	9.7
1951	70,904	84.5	Miss I.M.B. Ward	C	33,800	56.4
			Miss G.M. Colman	Lab	26,144	43.6
					7,656	12.8
1955	70,758	79.3	Miss I.M.B. Ward	C	30,949	55.1
			J. Finegan	Lab	20,113	35.8
			R. Cairncross	L	5,082*	9.1
					10,836	19.3
1959	72,273	80.5	Dame Irene Ward	C	32,810	56.4
			W.H. Hutchison	Lab	18,866	32.4
			D.N. Thompson	L	6,525*	11.2
					13,944	24.0
1964	75,017	79.0	Dame Irene Ward	C	33,342	56.3
			A.E. Booth	Lab	25,894	43.7
					7,448	12.6
1966	75,044	78.4	Dame Irene Ward	C	29,210	49.7
			G.J. Adam	Lab	25,814	43.8
			Dr. J.C. Edwards	Ind L	3,846*	6.5
					3,396	5.9
1970	78,913	75.9	Dame Irene Ward	C	30,773	51.4
			J.H. Beecham	Lab	23,927	39.9
			R.S. Turner	L	5,221*	8.7
					6,846	11.5

Election	Electors	T'out	Candidate	Party	Votes	%
1950	53,763	87.3	†Rt. Hon. A. Greenwood	Lab	25,996	55.4
			H. Watson	C	15,925	33.9
			S.J. Berwin	L	5,022*	10.7
					10,071	21.5
1951	54,529	85.3	Rt. Hon. A. Greenwood	Lab	27,100	58.3
			M. Grant	C	19,398	41.7
					7,702	16.6
[Death]						
1954 (21/10)	54,733	68.6	Rt. Hon. A.C. Jones	Lab	21,822	58.1
			M.V. Macmillan	C	15,714	41.9
					6,108	16.2
1955	59,828**	77.9	Rt. Hon. A.C. Jones	Lab	28,180	60.5
			D. Hinchcliffe	C	18,435	39.5
					9,745	21.0
1959	60,791	82.0	Rt. Hon. A.C. Jones	Lab	29,705	59.6
			T.M. Jopling	C	20,114	40.4
					9,591	19.2
1964	60,863*	78.0	W. Harrison	Lab	26,315	55.5
			J.D. Spence	C	14,385	30.3
			J.M. Collins	L	6,753	14.2
					11,930	25.2
1966	60,245	73.4	W. Harrison	Lab	28,907	65.4
			R. Benson	C	15,299	34.6
					13,608	30.8
1970	64,705	72.8	W. Harrison	Lab	27,352	58.1
			D. Smith	C	15,668	33.3
			Miss B.N. Seear	L	4,071*	8.6
					11,684	24.8

Election	Electors	T'out	Candidate	Party	Votes	%
1950	72,029	82.5	†A.E. Marples	C	33,904	57.0
			J.L. Hindle	Lab	18,989	32.0
			A.W. Jones	L	6,507*	11.0
					14,915	25.0
1951	74,190	79.7	A.E. Marples	C	37,423	63.3
			F.F. Jarvis	Lab	21,718	36.7
					15,705	26.6
1955	73,149	72.3	A.E. Marples	C	33,537	63.4
			W.T. Clements	Lab	19,319	36.6
					14,218	26.8
1959	72,660	77.2	Rt. Hon. A.E. Marples	C	35,567	63.4
			G. Woodburn	Lab	20,501	36.6
					15,066	26.8
1964	70,311	76.6	Rt. Hon. A.E. Marples	C	24,784	46.0
			I.I. Levin	Lab	18,663	34.6
			D.T.G. Evans	L	10,432	19.4
					6,121	11.4
1966	68,919	76.1	Rt. Hon. A.E. Marples	C	22,901	43.7
			R.G. Truman	Lab	22,312	42.6
			D.T.G. Evans	L	7,207	13.7
					589	1.1
1970	72,024	74.9	Rt. Hon. A.E. Marples	C	24,283	45.0
			C.J. Wells	Lab	21,172	39.2
			D.J. Evans	L	5,577*	10.3
			J.D. Hill	Ind	2,946*	5.5
					3,111	5.8

Note:—

1970: Hill was opposed to Britain entering the Common Market.

lection	Electors	T'out	Candidate	Party	Votes	%
1950	68,496	87.5	†J. McKay	Lab	33,790	56.3
			D.F-M. Appleby	C	21,643	36.1
			J.W. Craggs	L	4,532*	7.6
					12,147	20.2
1951	69,715	87.2	J. McKay	Lab	35,678	58.7
			G.C. Crangle	C	25,099	41.3
					10,579	17.4
1955	73,928	81.0	J. McKay	Lab	34,625	57.8
			R.B. Baird	C	25,275	42.2
					9,350	15.6
1959	80,235	83.5	J. McKay	Lab	37,862	56.5
			R.B. Baird	C	29,096	43.5
					8,766	13.0
1964	80,863	81.5	W.E. Garrett	Lab	39,841	60.4
			R.B. Baird	C	26,096	39.6
					13,745	20.8
1966	78,666	77.5	W.E. Garrett	Lab	39,744	65.2
			Dr. P.C. Price	C	21,205	34.8
					18,539	30.4
1970	85,556	74.5	W.E. Garrett	Lab	39,065	61.3
			E.M. White	C	24,650	38.7
					14,415	22.6

Election	Electors	T'out	Candidate	Party	Votes	%
1950	75,594	86.2	†W.T. Wells	Lab	36,483	56.(
			†Sir J.D. Barlow, Bt.	NL & C	28,700	44.(
					7,783	12.(
1951	77,195	83.1	W.T.Wells	Lab	33,556	52.:
			F. Roper	C	23,083	36.(
			Mrs. B.E. Lewis	L	7,517*	11.`
					10,473	16.:

This constituency was divided in 1955.

election	Electors	T'out	Candidate	Party	Votes	%
955	55,357	77.0	W.T. Wells	Lab	26,665	62.5
			Dr. F.R. Roberts	NL & C	15,970	37.5
					10,695	25.0
959	59,257	76.7	W.T. Wells	Lab	27,693	61.0
			J.G. Ackers	C	17,741	39.0
					9,952	22.0
964	63,061*	71.9	W.T. Wells	Lab	27,842	61.4
			A.J.L. Barnes	C	17,518	38.6
					10,324	22.8
966	64,449	70.9	W.T. Wells	Lab	29,710	65.1
			A.J.L. Barnes	C	15,953	34.9
					13,757	30.2
970	72,273	66.8	W.T. Wells	Lab	27,543	57.1
			A.J.L. Barnes	C	20,128	41.7
			D.J. Brayford	Com	597*	1.2
					7,415	15.4

WALSALL, SOUTH [293]

Election	Electors	T'out	Candidate	Party	Votes	%
1955	56,990	80.2	Sir H.J. d'Avigdor-Goldsmid, Bt.	C	24,077	52.7
			J.A.F. Ennals	Lab	21,651	47.3
					2,426	5.4
1959	62,804	83.1	Sir H.J. d'Avigdor-Goldsmid, Bt.	C	30,471	58.4
			J.A.F. Ennals	Lab	21,689	41.6
					8,782	16.8
1964	72,216*	79.1	Sir H.J. d'Avigdor-Goldsmid, Bt.	C	32,602	57.1
			B.C. Stanley	Lab	24,532	42.9
					8,070	14.2
1966	73,083	77.2	Sir H.J. d'Avigdor-Goldsmid, Bt.	C	30,161	53.4
			R.G. Drake	Lab	26,280	46.6
					3,881	6.8
1970	81,965	72.9	Sir H.J. d'Avigdor-Goldsmid, Bt.	C	35,545	59.5
			G.S. Rea	Lab	24,196	40.5
					11,349	19.0

Election	Electors	T'out	Candidate	Party	Votes	%
1950	46,603	84.4	†H.W. Wallace	Lab	18,478	46.9
			D.H. Barber	C	15,206	38.7
			I.F. Drower	L	5,654	14.4
					3,272	8.2
1951	46,683	85.8	H.W. Wallace	Lab	19,036	47.6
			J.E. Harvey	C	18,016	45.0
			G.E. Thornton	L	2,815*	7.0
			W.G. Boaks	Ind	174*	0.4
					1,020	2.6
1955	45,169	80.8	J.E. Harvey	C	16,873	46.3
			H.W. Wallace	Lab	15,744	43.1
			N.H. Cork	L	3,882*	10.6
					1,129	3.2
1959	43,892	80.9	J.E. Harvey	C	16,622	46.8
			Mrs. M. McKay	Lab	13,721	38.7
			N.H. Cork	L	4,974	14.0
			W.H. Christopher	ILP	183*	0.5
					2,901	8.1
1964	41,504	79.3	J.E. Harvey	C	14,140	43.0
			W.O.J. Robinson	Lab	13,745	41.7
			J.P.J. Ellis	L	5,042	15.3
					395	1.3
1966	40,981	80.1	W.O.J. Robinson	Lab	15,703	47.9
			J.E. Harvey	C	13,896	42.3
			J.P.J. Ellis	L	3,229*	9.8
					1,807	5.6
[Death]						
1969	40,694	51.2	R.M.C. McNair-Wilson	C	13,158	63.1
(27/3)			Dr. C. Phipps	Lab	7,679	36.9
					5,479	26.2
1970	43,043	71.0	R.M.C. McNair-Wilson	C	14,260	46.7
			J.E. Tomlinson	Lab	13,733	45.0
			D.G. Kirkland	L	2,547*	8.3
					527	1.7

Election	Electors	T'out	Candidate	Party	Votes	%
1950	42,684	81.7	†Rt. Hon. C.R. Attlee	Lab	21,095	60.
			J.A. Paul	C	8,988	25.
			A.W. Pim	L	4,102*	11.
			†H.L. Hutchinson	Ind Lab	704*	2
					12,107	34.
1951	42,063	81.9	Rt. Hon. C.R. Attlee	Lab	23,021	66.
			E.D.L. du Cann	C	11,447	33.
					11,574	33.
1955	40,570	72.5	Rt. Hon. C.R. Attlee	Lab	19,327	65.
			R.P. Hornby	C	10,077	34.
					9,250	31.

[Elevation to the Peerage—Earl Attlee]

Election	Electors	T'out	Candidate	Party	Votes	%
1956	39,839	52.0	E.C. Redhead	Lab	13,388	64.
(1/3)			R.P. Hornby	C	4,184	20.
			W.O. Smedley	L	3,037	14.
			W.G. Boaks	Ind	89*	0.
					9,204	44.
1959	38,226	76.1	E.C. Redhead	Lab	15,980	54.
			H. Midgley	C	7,872	27.
			W.O. Smedley	L	5,229	18.
					8,108	27.
1964	35,512	72.2	E.C. Redhead	Lab	14,405	56.
			E.M. Ogden	C	6,780	26.
			C.A. Hart-Leverton	L	4,437	17.
					7,625	29.
1966	33,751	71.0	E.C. Redhead	Lab	14,665	61.
			F.J. Silvester	C	5,940	24.
			D.W. Bramley	L	3,370	14.
					8,725	36.

[Death]

Election	Electors	T'out	Candidate	Party	Votes	%
1967	33,262	54.0	F.J. Silvester	C	6,652	37.
(21/9)			E.P. Deakins	Lab	6,590	36.
			Mrs. M.E. Wingfield	L	4,105	22.
			W.O. Smedley	Ind	542*	3.
			R.G. Allen	Ind	63*	0.
					62	0.
1970	35,125	65.2	E.P. Deakins	Lab	12,472	54.
			F.J. Silvester	C	7,870	34.
			Prof. I.W. Roxburgh	L	2,564*	11.
					4,602	20.

Notes:—

  1950: Hutchinson was a member of the Labour Independent Group.

  1967: Smedley was opposed to Britain entering the Common Market.

  Allen advocated the introduction of commercial radio.

Election	Electors	T'out	Candidate	Party	Votes	%
1964	44,612*	79.3	C.P.F. Jenkin	C	19,580	55.4
			J.E. Lockwood	L	8,901	25.1
			J.G. Morrell	Lab	6,917	19.5
					10,679	30.3
1966	44,256	76.8	C.P.F. Jenkin	C	19,063	56.1
			D.E. de Saxe	Lab	8,785	25.8
			J.C. Griffiths	L	6,150	18.1
					10,278	30.3
1970	48,417	67.8	C.P.F. Jenkin	C	20,065	61.1
			A.P. Barker	Lab	8,522	26.0
			R.H. Hoskins	L	4,224	12.9
					11,543	35.1

From 1950 until 1964 this constituency was named Woodford, *q.v.*

Election	Electors	T'out	Candidate	Party	Votes	%
1950	54,166	86.0	†Dr. H.B.W. Morgan	Lab	26,482	56.8
			F.L. Neep	C	17,730	38.0
			J.C. Park	L	1,899*	4.1
			J.J. Grady	Com	496*	1.1
					8,752	18.8
1951	54,848	82.7	Dr. H.B.W. Morgan	Lab	26,225	57.8
			Miss J.F. Crowther	C	17,623	38.8
			J.C. Park	L	1,537*	3.4
					8,602	19.0
1955	53,826*	73.9	Dr. Rt. Hon. Edith Summerskill	Lab	22,721	57.1
			H.H. Davies	C	17,075	42.9
					5,646	14.2
1959	52,884	76.9	Dr. Rt. Hon. Edith Summerskill	Lab	22,890	56.3
			F.O. Stansfield	C	17,791	43.7
					5,099	12.6

[Elevation to a Life Peerage—Baroness Summerskill]

Election	Electors	T'out	Candidate	Party	Votes	%
1961	50,972	56.7	W.T. Williams	Lab/Co-op	16,149	55.9
(20/4)			Miss B.A. Brookes	C	9,149	31.6
			F.R. Tetlow	L	3,623	12.5
					7,000	24.3
1964	50,368	71.4	W.T. Williams	Lab/Co-op	20,551	57.1
			W.A. Lowe	C	11,297	31.4
			M.F. Pitts	L	4,119*	11.5
					9,254	25.7
1966	49,207	68.9	W.T. Williams	Lab/Co-op	21,930	64.6
			W.P. Adshead	C	8,918	26.3
			E.J. Woods	L	3,070*	9.1
					13,012	38.3
1970	50,012	65.2	W.T. Williams	Lab/Co-op	20,970	64.3
			A.B. Gooch	C	11,647	35.7
					9,323	28.6

Election	Electors	T'out	Candidate	Party	Votes	%
1950	52,651	87.3	†J. Freeman	Lab	21,759	47.4
			J.M. Bemrose	C	20,302	44.2
			H.B. Bush	L	3,879*	8.4
					1,457	3.2
1951	53,568	87.2	J. Freeman	Lab	22,370	47.9
			S.W.L. Ripley	C	21,862	46.8
			H.B. Bush	L	2,469*	5.3
					508	1.1
1955	52,662	82.4	F.W. Farey-Jones	C	22,546	52.0
			E.A. Bramall	Lab	20,829	48.0
					1,717	4.0
1959	53,388	84.8	F.W. Farey-Jones	C	21,216	46.9
			Mrs. R. Short	Lab	18,315	40.4
			I.S. Steers	L	5,753	12.7
					2,901	6.5
1964	53,543	83.6	R.H. Tuck	Lab	20,224	45.2
			F.W. Farey-Jones	C	18,744	41.9
			Miss M. Neilson	L	5,797	12.9
					1,480	3.3
1966	52,888	82.9	R.H. Tuck	Lab	23,832	54.4
			D.W. Clarke	C	19,996	45.6
					3,836	8.8
1970	56,523	76.2	R.H. Tuck	Lab	19,698	45.7
			D.W. Clarke	C	19,622	45.5
			C.G. Watkins	L	3,778*	8.8
					76	0.2

Election	Electors	T'out	Candidate	Party	Votes	%
1950	68,899	86.3	†S.N. Evans	Lab	33,215	55.
			H.R. Wilkins	C	17,761	29.
			R.J. Bowker	L	8,494	14.
					15,454	25.
1951	70,710	82.3	S.N. Evans	Lab	35,196	60.
			H.R. Wilkins	C	22,971	39.
					12,225	21.
1955	59,260**	72.9	S.N. Evans	Lab	26,064	60.
			R.E. Hall	C	17,120	39.
					8,944	20.
[Resignation]						
1957 (28/2)	59,602	60.0	J.T. Stonehouse	Lab/Co-op	22,235	62.
			P.H.B. Tapsell	C	9,999	28.
			M.J. Wade	Ind	3,529*	9.
					12,236	34.
1959	60,297	76.9	J.T. Stonehouse	Lab/Co-op	24,147	52.
			E. Knight	C	17,464	37.
			F.B. Willmott	L	4,780*	10.
					6,683	14.
1964	61,395	71.2	J.T. Stonehouse	Lab/Co-op	23,473	53.
			D.M. Harman	C	20,251	46.
					3,222	7.
1966	61,481	72.0	J.T. Stonehouse	Lab/Co-op	26,041	58.
			D.M. Harman	C	18,213	41.
					7,828	17.
1970	65,528	68.1	Rt. Hon. J.T. Stonehouse	Lab/Co-op	23,998	53.
			D.M. Harman	C	20,627	46.
					3,371	7.

Note:—

1957: Wade fought the election entirely on the issue of the rising cost of living. The local Liberal Association issued a statement of qualified approval of his candidature.

WEMBLEY, NORTH [300]

Election	Electors	T'out	Candidate	Party	Votes	%
1950	48,817	88.5	E.E. Bullus	C	22,430	51.9
			B. Lewis	Lab/Co-op	14,987	34.7
			A.B. Dann	L	5,770	13.4
					7,443	17.2
1951	49,481	87.1	E.E. Bullus	C	24,112	55.9
			B. Lewis	Lab/Co-op	15,394	35.7
			R.A. Winch	L	3,607*	8.4
					8,718	20.2
1955	48,874	82.3	E.E. Bullus	C	22,701	56.5
			Mrs. J. Phillips	Lab	12,592	31.3
			Lady Abrahams	L	4,916*	12.2
					10,109	25.2
1959	47,554	83.1	E.E. Bullus	C	22,211	56.2
			R.M. Lewis	Lab	11,131	28.2
			D.G. Valentine	L	6,171	15.6
					11,080	28.0
1964	46,037	80.6	E.E. Bullus	C	18,325	49.5
			I. Harrington	Lab	11,960	32.2
			W.G. Crauford	L	6,805	18.3
					6,365	17.3
1966	44,944	80.9	Sir E.E. Bullus	C	17,497	48.1
			K.W. Childerhouse	Lab	13,290	36.5
			P.M.R. Cowen	L	5,587	15.4
					4,207	11.6
1970	47,632	72.1	Sir E.E. Bullus	C	18,345	53.4
			K.W. Childerhouse	Lab	11,916	34.7
			J.R. Kingsbury	L	4,083*	11.9
					6,429	18.7

Election	Electors	T'out	Candidate	Party	Votes	%
1950	48,678	88.3	R.S. Russell	C	20,920	48.7
			†C. Barton	Lab	17,251	40.1
			C.F. Jackson	L	4,366*	10.2
			N.W.H. Gill	Com	430*	1.0
					3,669	8.6
1951	48,769	86.0	R.S. Russell	C	23,380	55.8
			D. Clark	Lab	18,546	44.2
					4,834	11.6
1955	46,650	80.7	R.S. Russell	C	22,052	58.6
			E.C. Hutchison	Lab/Co-op	15,596	41.4
					6,456	17.2
1959	45,150	82.6	R.S. Russell	C	19,733	52.9
			E. MacKenzie	Lab	12,166	32.6
			J.E.C. Perry	L	5,403	14.5
					7,567	20.3
1964	43,899	78.4	Sir R.S. Russell	C	16,512	48.0
			M.N. Elliott	Lab	12,199	35.4
			J.E.C. Perry	L	5,713	16.6
					4,313	12.6
1966	42,843	79.3	Sir R.S. Russell	C	15,377	45.3
			M.N. Elliott	Lab	14,194	41.8
			D. Conyers	L	4,386	12.9
					1,183	3.5
1970	44,797	69.0	Sir R.S. Russell	C	16,578	53.6
			M.N. Elliott	Lab	14,336	46.4
					2,242	7.2

Election	Electors	T'out	Candidate	Party	Votes	%
1950	58,260	82.8	†Rt. Hon. J. Dugdale	Lab	31,564	65.4
			Viscount Ednam	C	16,697	34.6
					14,867	30.8
1951	59,656	80.5	Rt. Hon. J. Dugdale	Lab	30,845	64.2
			G.D. Johnstone	C	17,186	35.8
					13,659	28.4
1955	60,485	70.2	Rt. Hon. J. Dugdale	Lab	26,242	61.8
			F.J.V.H. Dashwood	C	16,222	38.2
					10,020	23.6
1959	64,111	72.5	Rt. Hon. J. Dugdale	Lab	26,702	57.4
			A.H. Windrum	C	19,809	42.6
					6,893	14.8
[Death]						
1963	63,304	55.2	M.A. Foley	Lab	20,510	58.8
(4/7)			G. Hawkins	C	8,246	23.6
			N.R.W. Mawle	L	6,161	17.6
					12,264	35.2
1964	64,289	64.7	M.A. Foley	Lab	22,942	55.1
			G. Hawkins	C	18,664	44.9
					4,278	10.2
1966	63,489	68.8	M.A. Foley	Lab	25,287	57.9
			G. Hawkins	C	18,413	42.1
					6,874	15.8
1970	68,159	62.2	M.A. Foley	Lab	23,412	55.2
			G. Hawkins	C	18,976	44.8
					4,436	10.4

Election	Electors	T'out	Candidate	Party	Votes	%
1950	63,288	77.8	†A.W.J. Lewis	Lab	33,782	68.6
			R.M. Prior	C	12,623	25.6
			R.L. Phillips	L	2,349*	4.8
			Miss G.W. Dickinson	Ind	503*	1.0
					21,159	43.0
1951	63,318	76.6	A.W.J. Lewis	Lab	34,156	70.4
			J.A. Erskine-Shaw	C	14,328	29.6
					19,828	40.8
1955	61,346	67.4	A.W.J. Lewis	Lab	27,249	65.9
			Miss M.C. Bowen	C	10,712	25.9
			D.J.H. Penwarden	L	3,393*	8.2
					16,537	40.0
1959	57,828	70.4	A.W.J. Lewis	Lab	24,096	59.2
			J.G. Jones	C	9,318	22.9
			D.A.S. Brooke	L	7,271	17.9
					14,778	36.3
1964	55,824	62.8	A.W.J. Lewis	Lab	21,228	60.5
			Miss A.J. Pilkington	L	7,005	20.0
			C. Brocklebank-Fowler	C	6,844	19.5
					14,223	40.5
1966	53,672	61.8	A.W.J. Lewis	Lab	21,778	65.6
			Miss A.J. Pilkington	L	5,882	17.7
			W.J. Shearman	C	5,527	16.7
					15,896	47.9
1970	55,490	50.4	A.W.J. Lewis	Lab	17,664	63.2
			W.J. Shearman	C	7,130	25.5
			B.G. McCarthy	L	3,167*	11.3
					10,534	37.7

Note:—

1950: Miss Dickinson sought election as a 'Christian Democrat' candidate.

Election	Electors	T'out	Candidate	Party	Votes	%
1950	56,790	78.5	†F.E. Jones	Lab	36,754	82.4
			Mrs. M.L. de la Motte	C	5,422*	12.2
			G.G. Young	L	1,686*	3.8
			W.J.F. Norris	Com	730*	1.6
					31,332	70.2
1951	56,627	77.3	F.E. Jones	Lab	37,195	85.0
			Mrs. M.L. de la Motte	C	6,586	15.0
					30,609	70.0
1955	53,862	65.8	F.E. Jones	Lab	29,451	83.1
			E.J. Emden	C	5,997	16.9
					23,454	66.2
1959	52,341	71.1	F.E. Jones	Lab	28,017	75.3
			P. Goldman	C	5,188	13.9
			O.P. French	L	4,020*	10.8
					22,829	61.4
1964	49,574	63.9	F.E. Jones	Lab	23,599	74.4
			E. Johnson	L	4,264	13.5
			R. Mitchell	C	3,835*	12.1
					19,335	60.9
1966	47,990	61.8	Rt. Hon. Sir F.E. Jones	Lab	22,902	77.2
			R. Mitchell	C	3,410*	11.5
			E. Johnson	L	3,367*	11.3
					19,492	65.7
1970	49,751	48.9	Rt. Hon. Sir F.E. Jones	Lab	18,899	77.7
			B.C. Balcomb	C	5,422	22.3
					13,477	55.4

Election	Electors	T'out	Candidate	Party	Votes	%
1950	58,667	89.3	†R.W. Williams	Lab	32,746	62.5
			H. Dowling	C	15,733	30.0
			I.S. Webster	L	2,651*	5.1
			T. Rowlandson	Com	1,243*	2.4
					17,013	32.5
1951	59,318	87.0	R.W. Williams	Lab	34,530	66.9
			D.C. Walls	C	17,078	33.1
					17,452	33.8
1955	57,575	80.3	R.W. Williams	Lab	29,755	64.4
			H.D. Lowe	C	14,883	32.2
			T. Rowlandson	Com	1,567*	3.4
					14,872	32.2
[Death]						
1958 (12/6)	54,956	70.3	E.A. Fitch	Lab	27,415	71.0
			J.J. Hodgson	C	10,248	26.5
			M. Weaver	Com	972*	2.5
					17,167	44.5
1959	55,155	83.8	E.A. Fitch	Lab	30,664	66.4
			J.J. Hodgson	C	14,615	31.6
			M. Weaver	Com	945*	2.0
					16,049	34.8
1964	51,986	79.4	E.A. Fitch	Lab	28,640	69.4
			I.K. Paley	C	11,648	28.2
			M. Weaver	Com	988*	2.4
					16,992	41.2
1966	51,967	76.0	E.A. Fitch	Lab	28,754	72.8
			M. Kingston	C	9,876	25.0
			M. Weaver	Com	858*	2.2
					18,878	47.8
1970	57,616	72.3	E.A. Fitch	Lab	28,102	67.5
			A. Daniels	C	12,882	30.9
			J. Kay	Com	672*	1.6
					15,220	36.6

WILLESDEN, EAST [306]

Election	Electors	T'out	Candidate	Party	Votes	%
1950	62,601	82.5	†M. Orbach	Lab	24,345	47.1
			S.S. Hammersley	C	21,004	40.7
			W.J. Done	L	6,310*	12.2
					3,341	6.4
1951	62,962	81.8	M. Orbach	Lab	26,695	51.8
			R.E. Simms	C	24,827	48.2
					1,868	3.6
1955	60,604	76.1	M. Orbach	Lab	23,397	50.7
			R.E. Simms	C	22,738	49.3
					659	1.4
1959	58,865	73.4	T.H.H. Skeet	C	22,709	52.6
			M. Orbach	Lab	20,499	47.4
					2,210	5.2
1964	57,153	68.8	R. Freeson	Lab	20,543	52.3
			T.H.H. Skeet	C	18,755	47.7
					1,788	4.6
1966	56,085	71.1	R. Freeson	Lab	21,767	54.7
			P.D. Fry	C	14,761	37.0
			M. Brahams	L	2,765*	6.9
			Mrs. O.E.M. Bysouth	Ind	556*	1.4
					7,006	17.7
1970	57,109	62.4	R. Freeson	Lab	20,073	56.3
			H.W. Cutler	C	15,564	43.7
					4,509	12.6

Note:—

1966: Mrs. Bysouth sought election as a 'New Deal' candidate.

WILLESDEN, WEST [307]

Election	Electors	T'out	Candidate	Party	Votes	%
1950	66,808	83.2	†S.P. Viant	Lab	33,963	61.1
			Dr. A. Genevieve Rewcastle	C	17,848	32.1
			K.S.B. Ahluwalia	L	2,853*	5.1
			D.A. Michaelson	Com	938*	1.7
					16,115	29.0
1951	66,417	82.7	S.P. Viant	Lab	35,296	64.3
			J.L. Bott	C	19,632	35.7
					15,664	28.6
1955	63,559	74.4	S.P. Viant	Lab	29,185	61.8
			P.B. Kenyon	C	18,074	38.2
					11,111	23.6
1959	61,534	73.0	L.A. Pavitt	Lab/Co-op	25,680	57.2
			Mrs. P.S. Brookes	C	17,946	39.9
			L.G. Burt	Com	1,324*	2.9
					7,734	17.3
1964	59,800	63.5	L.A. Pavitt	Lab/Co-op	23,862	62.8
			J.S. Grose	C	12,961	34.2
			L.G. Burt	Com	1,130*	3.0
					10,901	28.6
1966	57,276	63.6	L.A. Pavitt	Lab/Co-op	24,944	68.5
			Miss A.P. Thomas	C	10,362	28.4
			L.G. Burt	Com	1,140*	3.1
					14,582	40.1
1970	54,983	59.3	L.A. Pavitt	Lab/Co-op	21,918	67.2
			R.F. Dyason	C	10,163	31.2
			L.G. Burt	Com	515*	1.6
					11,755	36.0

Election	Electors	T'out	Candidate	Party	Votes	%
1950	76,728	85.7	C.W. Black	C	40,339	61.3
			G.L. Deacon	Lab	20,296	30.9
			I.F. Gibson	L	5,136*	7.8
					20,043	30.4
1951	77,067	82.6	C.W. Black	C	42,218	66.3
			C.H. Ford	Lab	21,424	33.7
					20,794	32.6
1955	43,099**	78.3	C.W. Black	C	22,112	65.5
			G.E. Janner	Lab	11,622	34.5
					10,490	31.0
1959	42,151	76.4	Sir C.W. Black	C	21,538	66.9
			L.M. Kershaw	Lab	10,678	33.1
					10,860	33.8
1964	40,947	74.9	Sir C.W. Black	C	15,952	52.0
			Dr. J.R. Daly	Lab	8,891	29.0
			G.E. Scott	L	5,817	19.0
					7,061	23.0
1966	40,248	75.0	Sir C.W. Black	C	15,191	50.4
			T. Braddock	Lab	9,517	31.5
			J.R. Macdonald	L	5,475	18.1
					5,674	18.9
1970	42,742	66.9	R.M.O. Havers	C	15,285	53.5
			R. Holmes	Lab	8,554	29.9
			J.R. Macdonald	L	4,749	16.6
					6,731	23.6

Election	Electors	T'out	Candidate	Party	Votes	%
1950	59,338	83.1	†J. Baird	Lab	29,235	59.3
			A.W.G. Holland	C	14,592	29.6
			Dr. A. Brown	L	5,482*	11.1
					14,643	29.7
1951	60,808	80.9	J. Baird	Lab	30,643	62.3
			J.P.J. Ellis	NL & C	18,563	37.7
					12,080	24.6
1955	53,171**	71.4	J. Baird	Lab	23,596	62.1
			F. Hardman	C	14,387	37.9
					9,209	24.2
1959	51,217	72.4	J. Baird	Lab	20,436	55.1
			O.A. Pomeroy	C	16,639	44.9
					3,797	10.2
1964	49,843	68.0	Mrs. R. Short	Lab	18,997	56.0
			Mrs. M.M.M. Greenaway	C	14,914	44.0
					4,083	12.0
1966	49,109	69.3	Mrs. R. Short	Lab	21,067	61.9
			G.I. Wright	C	12,965	38.1
					8,102	23.8
1970	51,290	66.7	Mrs. R. Short	Lab	17,251	50.4
			G.I. Wright	C	15,358	44.9
			Mrs. S.M. Wright	NF	1,592*	4.7
					1,893	5.5

Election	Electors	T'out	Candidate	Party	Votes	%
1950	50,460	87.2	J.E. Powell	C	20,239	46.0
			†H.D. Hughes	Lab	19,548	44.4
			W.F.H. Rollason	L	4,229*	9.6
					691	1.6
1951	51,124	86.3	J.E. Powell	C	23,660	53.6
			Mrs. A.P. Llewelyn Davies	Lab	20,464	46.4
					3,196	7.2
1955	54,303**	77.7	J.E. Powell	C	25,318	60.0
			L.H. Burgess	Lab/Co-op	16,898	40.0
					8,420	20.0
1959	51,293	78.4	J.E. Powell	C	25,696	63.9
			E.L.J. Thorne	Lab	14,529	36.1
					11,167	27.8
1964	50,244	75.3	Rt. Hon. J.E. Powell	C	21,736	57.4
			A.J. Gardner	Lab	11,880	31.4
			J.N.G. Lloyd	L	4,233*	11.2
					9,856	26.0
1966	49,390	73.6	Rt. Hon. J.E. Powell	C	21,466	59.1
			A.S. Collier	Lab	14,881	40.9
					6,585	18.2
1970	53,484	76.2	Rt. Hon. J.E. Powell	C	26,220	64.4
			J.A.N. Bamfield	Lab	11,753	28.8
			E. Robinson	L	2,459*	6.0
			P.E. Carter	Com	189*	0.5
			R.G.P. Menzies	Ind	77*	0.2
			D.P. Dass	Ind	52*	0.1
					14,467	35.6

Notes:—

1970: Menzies advocated a pro-immigration policy.

Dass sought election as a 'Human Rights Coalition' candidate and advocated a policy of racial harmony. He retired on the eve of poll in favour of Bamfield.

Election	Electors	T'out	Candidate	Party	Votes	%
1950	72,592	86.1	†Rt. Hon. W.L.S. Churchill	C	37,239	59.(
			S.H. Hills	Lab	18,740	30.(
			H.V. Davies	L	5,664*	9.⁺
			W.G.P. Brooks	Com	827*	1.:
					18,499	29.{
1951	77,975	83.4	Rt. Hon. W.L.S. Churchill	C	40,938	63.(
			W.A. Archer	Lab	22,359	34.4
			J.R. Campbell	Com	871*	1.3
			A. Hancock	Ind	851*	1.3
					18,579	28.6
1955	45,193**	76.0	Rt. Hon. Sir W.L.S. Churchill	C	25,069	73.0
			A.K.M. Milner	Lab	9,261	27.0
					15,808	46.0
1959	45,070	77.3	Rt. Hon. Sir W.L.S. Churchill	C	24,815	71.2
			A.C. Latham	Lab	10,018	28.8
					14,797	42.4

The name of this constituency was changed in 1964 to Wanstead and Woodford, *q.v.*

WOOD GREEN [312]

Election	Electors	T'out	Candidate	Party	Votes	%
1950	66,564	81.7	†W.J. Irving	Lab/Co-op	28,480	52.4
			J.D. McEwen	C	20,013	36.8
			J.P.J. Ellis	L	5,875*	10.8
					8,467	15.6
1951	66,586	81.7	W.J. Irving	Lab/Co-op	30,360	55.8
			B.G. Irvine	C	24,060	44.2
					6,300	11.6
1955	63,015	75.1	Mrs. J.S. Butler	Lab/Co-op	25,523	53.9
			G. Cathles	C	21,811	46.1
					3,712	7.8
1959	59,380	75.1	Mrs. J.S. Butler	Lab/Co-op	22,869	51.3
			R.G. Shillingford	C	21,735	48.7
					1,134	2.6
1964	55,593	70.3	Mrs. J.S. Butler	Lab/Co-op	22,131	56.6
			G. Cathles	C	16,939	43.4
					5,192	13.2
1966	53,559	67.3	Mrs. J.S. Butler	Lab/Co-op	21,922	60.8
			L.J. Goldman	C	14,133	39.2
					7,789	21.6
1970	53,653	60.9	Mrs. J.S. Butler	Lab/Co-op	18,666	57.1
			M.P.R. Malynn	C	14,022	42.9
					4,644	14.2

Election	Electors	T'out	Candidate	Party	Votes	%
1950	56,622	86.1	†Hon. G.R. Ward	C	24,147	49.(
			J. Evans	Lab/Co-op	19,807	40.(
			W.H. Gardiner	L	4,786*	9.(
					4,340	9.(
1951	57,192	82.1	Hon. G.R. Ward	C	26,060	55.(
			L.V. Pike	Lab	20,909	44.(
					5,151	11.(
1955	58,012*	77.8	Hon. G.R. Ward	C	25,610	56.8
			L.V. Pike	Lab	19,508	43.2
					6,102	13.6
1959	59,117	79.3	Rt. Hon. G.R. Ward	C	27,024	57.7
			B.C. Stanley	Lab	19,832	42.3
					7,192	15.4

[Elevation to the Peerage—Viscount Ward of Witley]

Election	Electors	T'out	Candidate	Party	Votes	%
1961 (16/3)	59,219	64.2	P.E. Walker	C	15,087	39.7
			B.C. Stanley	Lab	11,490	30.2
			R. Glenton	L	11,435	30.1
					3,597	9.5
1964	60,287	79.3	P.E. Walker	C	24,345	50.9
			J. Martin	Lab	17,038	35.6
			J.G. Parry	L	6,448	13.5
					7,307	15.3
1966	60,925	77.9	P.E. Walker	C	25,398	53.5
			F. Barrington-Ward	Lab	22,057	46.5
					3,341	7.0
1970	69,895	73.0	P.E. Walker	C	29,717	58.3
			P. Jones	Lab	21,275	41.7
					8,442	16.6

Election	Electors	T'out	Candidate	Party	Votes	%
1950	52,572	84.0	†O.L. Prior-Palmer	C	29,475	66.8
			E. Duchin	Lab	10,028	22.7
			W.A.J.H. Horne	L	4,647*	10.5
					19,447	44.1
1951	54,122	80.0	O.L. Prior-Palmer	C	32,302	74.6
			G.W. Reynolds	Lab	10,978	25.4
					21,324	49.2
1955	55,456	72.7	O.L. Prior-Palmer	C	31,106	77.1
			B.R. Stevens	Lab	9,231	22.9
					21,875	54.2
1959	60,505	76.1	Sir O.L. Prior-Palmer	C	31,396	68.2
			F.R. Mason	Lab	7,618	16.5
			D.R.E. Abel	L	7,045	15.3
					23,778	51.7
1964	64,931	76.2	T.L. Higgins	C	30,203	61.0
			P.L. Rose	L	11,320	22.9
			R.L. Butler	Lab	7,976	16.1
					18,883	38.1
1966	66,279	75.7	T.L. Higgins	C	29,903	59.6
			A.P. Lester	Lab	10,281	20.5
			R. Roberts	L	8,955	17.8
			E.W.J. Moloney	Ind C	1,044*	2.1
					19,622	39.1
1970	71,935	70.0	T.L. Higgins	C	33,051	65.7
			Mrs. S.M. Bartlet	Lab	8,989	17.8
			M.J. Rooke	L	8,336	16.5
					24,062	47.9

YORK [315]

Election	Electors	T'out	Candidate	Party	Votes	%
1950	72,527	87.6	H.B.H. Hylton-Foster	C	29,421	46.3
			†H. Davies	Lab	29,344	46.2
			H.S. Clay	L	4,760*	7.5
					77	0.1
1951	74,829	86.4	H.B.H. Hylton-Foster	C	32,777	50.7
			T.C. Skeffington-Lodge	Lab	31,856	49.3
					921	1.4
1955	73,849	83.5	Sir H.B.H. Hylton-Foster	C	31,402	50.9
			T.E.M. McKitterick	Lab	30,298	49.1
					1,104	1.8
1959	73,717	84.3	C.B. Longbottom	C	33,099	53.3
			Dr. D.R.L.M. Poirier	Lab	29,025	46.7
					4,074	6.6
1964	71,719*	83.0	C.B. Longbottom	C	26,521	44.6
			A.W. Lyon	Lab	25,428	42.7
			D.T. Lloyd	L	7,565	12.7
					1,093	1.9
1966	70,431	82.7	A.W. Lyon	Lab	32,167	55.2
			C.B. Longbottom	C	26,067	44.8
					6,100	10.4
1970	74,769	76.3	A.W. Lyon	Lab	29,619	51.9
			B. Askew	C	27,422	48.1
					2,197	3.8

ENGLAND —— COUNTIES

BEDFORDSHIRE, BEDFORD [316]

Election	Electors	T'out	Candidate	Party	Votes	%
1950	52,592	87.5	A.C.J. Soames	C	21,942	47.7
			†T.C. Skeffington-Lodge	Lab	19,834	43.1
			L.J. Humphrey	L	4,060*	8.8
			Mrs. E.L. Matthews	Com	207*	0.4
					2,108	4.6
1951	54,047	87.1	A.C.J. Soames	C	23,278	49.4
			P. Parker	Lab	20,492	43.5
			F.H. Philpott	L	3,323*	7.1
					2,786	5.9
1955	54,439*	81.8	A.C.J. Soames	C	24,733	55.5
			H.J. Aldridge	Lab	19,792	44.5
					4,941	11.0
1959	55,278	83.6	Rt. Hon. A.C.J. Soames	C	23,495	50.9
			M.A. Foley	Lab	16,728	36.2
			M.L. Rowlandson	L	5,966	12.9
					6,767	14.7
1964	58,912	80.4	Rt. Hon. A.C.J. Soames	C	21,404	45.2
			B.S. Parkyn	Lab	18,256	38.5
			W.E. Norton	L	7,712	16.3
					3,148	6.7
1966	60,352	81.5	B.S. Parkyn	Lab	22,257	45.2
			Rt. Hon. A.C.J. Soames	C	21,879	44.5
			J.E. Burrell	L	5,080*	10.3
					378	0.7
1970	67,317	77.4	T.H.H. Skeet	C	26,330	50.5
			B.S. Parkyn	Lab	21,051	40.4
			A.W. Butcher	L	4,740*	9.1
					5,279	10.1

Election	Electors	T'out	Candidate	Party	Votes	%
1950	49,519	86.2	†A.T. Lennox-Boyd	C	17,671	41.4
			W. Howell	Lab	15,512	36.3
			E.K. Martell	L	9,511	22.3
					2,159	5.1
1951	50,813	85.3	A.T. Lennox-Boyd	C	19,681	45.4
			T.L.A. Taylor	Lab	17,818	41.1
			D.W. Tweddle	L	5,863	13.5
					1,863	4.3
1955	51,699*	81.4	Rt. Hon. A.T. Lennox-Boyd	C	23,012	54.7
			T.C. Skeffington-Lodge	Lab	19,048	45.3
					3,964	9.4
1959	53,889	84.5	Rt. Hon. A.T. Lennox-Boyd	C	21,301	46.8
			B.E. Magee	Lab	16,127	35.4
			W.G. Matthews	L	8,099	17.8
					5,174	11.4

[Elevation to the Peerage—Viscount Boyd of Merton]

Election	Electors	T'out	Candidate	Party	Votes	%
1960 (16/11)	54,276	71.1	S.L.E. Hastings	C	17,503	45.4
			B.E. Magee	Lab	11,281	29.2
			W.G. Matthews	L	9,550	24.8
			C.F.H. Gilliard	NCP	235*	0.6
					6,222	16.2
1964	58,640	83.0	S.L.E. Hastings	C	22,414	46.1
			C.T. Bell	Lab	17,096	35.
			W.G. Matthews	L	9,184	18.9
					5,318	10.9
1966	61,923	82.3	S.L.E. Hastings	C	23,447	46.1
			C.T. Bell	Lab	20,369	40.1
			P.L. Rose	L	7,138	14.1
					3,078	6.1
1970	73,030	77.4	S.L.E. Hastings	C	29,670	52.
			D.F. Harrowell	Lab	19,035	33.
			J.P. Christian	L	7,799	13.
					10,635	18.

ction	Electors	T'out	Candidate	Party	Votes	%
50	51,039	86.9	E.W. Moeran	Lab	20,070	45.3
			W.A. Fearnley-Whittingstall	NL & C	18,546	41.8
			J.S. Knight	L	5,725	12.9
					1,524	3.5
51	51,887	86.7	N.J. Cole	NL & C	22,917	50.9
			E.W. Moeran	Lab	22,068	49.1
					849	1.8
55	54,050	81.9	N.J. Cole	NL & C	23,365	52.8
			E.W. Moeran	Lab	20,897	47.2
					2,468	5.6
59	65,416	83.9	N.J. Cole	NL & C	25,861	47.1
			W.H. Johnson	Lab	21,102	38.5
			Mrs. R.R. Soskin	L	7,912	14.4
					4,759	8.6
64	83,307	80.8	N.J. Cole	C	33,838	50.3
			D.J. Nisbet	Lab	33,499	49.7
					339	0.6
66	86,403	83.7	G.E. Roberts	Lab	34,549	47.8
			N.J. Cole	C	30,319	41.9
			H. Simonds-Gooding	L	7,484*	10.3
					4,230	5.9
70	101,164	77.2	W.D. Madel	C	38,085	48.7
			G.E. Roberts	Lab	33,107	42.4
			G.S. Shocket	L	6,956*	8.9
					4,978	6.3

Election	Electors	T'out	Candidate	Party	Votes	%
1950	54,004	82.1	†Sir R.G.C. Glyn, Bt.	C	20,595	4
			R.J. McCullagh	Lab	16,733	3
			E.D.T. Vane	L	6,612	1
			J.C.D. Dunman	Com	396*	
					3,862	
1951	55,856	80.0	Sir R.G.C. Glyn, Bt.	C	24,774	5
			J.E.G. Curthoys	Lab	19,891	4
					4,883	1

[Elevation to the Peerage—Lord Glyn]

Election	Electors	T'out	Candidate	Party	Votes	%
1953 (30/6)	56,851	75.9	A.M.S. Neave	C	22,986	5
			E.C. Castle	Lab	17,126	3
			G.R. Allen	L	3,060*	1
					5,860	1
1955	58,487	80.1	A.M.S. Neave	C	25,613	5
			Mrs. M. Reid	Lab	16,979	3
			G.R. Allen	L	4,270*	
					8,634	1
1959	63,844	80.8	A.M.S. Neave	C	27,943	5
			P. Picard	Lab	16,971	3
			Mrs. V. Perl	L	6,651	1
					10,972	2
1964	69,102	80.6	A.M.S. Neave	C	26,707	4
			F.J. Riddell	Lab	20,334	3
			Mrs. V. Perl	L	8,627	1
					6,373	1
1966	72,575	82.5	A.M.S. Neave	C	27,749	4
			A.H.S. Matterson	Lab	24,447	4
			D.H.V. Case	L	7,703	1
					3,302	
1970	85,838	77.5	A.M.S. Neave	C	36,209	54
			N.H. Price	Lab	23,136	34
			S.R.C. Evans	L	7,198*	10
					13,073	19

ection	Electors	T'out	Candidate	Party	Votes	%
50	42,374	81.1	†A.R. Hurd	C	18,150	52.8
			G.C. Jackson	Lab	11,914	34.7
			E. Burrows	L	4,284*	12.5
					6,236	18.1
51	42,728	78.7	A.R. Hurd	C	20,102	59.8
			G.C. Jackson	Lab	13,507	40.2
					6,595	19.6
55	57,404**	78.3	A.R. Hurd	C	26,080	58.1
			J.A.A. Evans	Lab	18,843	41.9
					7,237	16.2
59	62,854	78.7	Sir A.R. Hurd	C	29,703	60.0
			D.L. Stoddart	Lab	19,787	40.0
					9,916	20.0

eat Vacant at Dissolution (Elevation to a Life Peerage—Lord Hurd]

64	69,338*	79.3	Hon. J. Astor	C	24,936	45.4
			D.L. Stoddart	Lab	18,943	34.4
			D. Egginton	L	11,124	20.2
					5,993	11.0
66	72,348	79.1	Hon. J. Astor	C	25,908	45.3
			R.L. Spiller	Lab	21,762	38.0
			S.C. Davies	L	9,571	16.7
					4,146	7.3
70	85,933	72.5	Hon. J. Astor	C	30,380	48.8
			T.J.K. Sims	Lab	18,647	29.9
			D.S.C. Clouston	L	13,279	21.3
					11,733	18.9

Election	Electors	T'out	Candidate	Party	Votes	%
1950	51,580	82.0	†C.E. Mott-Radclyffe	C	23,512	5!
			Miss M. Nicholson	Lab	14,300	33
			A.C.G. Mars	L	4,495*	1(
					9,212	2†
1951	52,640	79.0	C.E. Mott-Radclyffe	C	25,612	6†
			Miss M. Nicholson	Lab	15,977	3£
					9,635	23
1955	54,649	73.3	C.E. Mott-Radclyffe	C	25,390	63
			W.O.J. Robinson	Lab	14,666	3€
					10,724	2€
1959	60,673	75.5	Sir C.E. Mott-Radclyffe	C	29,942	6£
			W.E. Robinson	Lab	15,864	34
					14,078	3(
1964	65,770	76.4	Sir C.E. Mott-Radclyffe	C	25,274	5(
			P.A. Fletcher	Lab	13,632	27
			P.G.N. Badge	L	11,336	22
					11,642	23
1966	67,694	76.3	Sir C.E. Mott-Radclyffe	C	25,630	49
			R.R. Brown	Lab	17,300	33
			S.R. Jakobi	L	8,744	16
					8,330	16
1970	77,743	70.5	Dr. A. Glyn	C	32,264	58
			T.D. Sullivan	Lab	16,214	29
			R.J. Trevallion	L	6,343*	11
					16,050	29

ection	Electors	T'out	Candidate	Party	Votes	%
50	44,101	81.0	Hon. P.F. Remnant	C	20,612	57.8
			E.A. Hubble	Lab	10,296	28.8
			J.P. McQuade	L	4,793	13.4
					10,316	29.0
51	45,239	78.5	Hon. P.F. Remnant	C	21,652	61.0
			E.A. Hubble	Lab	10,606	29.9
			J.P. McQuade	L	3,233*	9.1
					11,046	31.1
55	56,657**	76.6	Hon. P.F. Remnant	C	25,843	59.5
			T.G. Boston	Lab	12,895	29.7
			J.P. McQuade	L	4,679*	10.8
					12,948	29.8
59	67,144	80.0	W.R. van Straubenzee	C	30,896	57.5
			T.G. Boston	Lab	14,905	27.8
			C.W.J. Rout	L	7,899	14.7
					15,991	29.7
64	82,375*	79.2	W.R. van Straubenzee	C	32,777	50.2
			J. Ellis	Lab	17,954	27.5
			Mrs. M.E. Wingfield	L	13,875	21.3
			C. Ford	Ind C	645*	1.0
					14,823	22.7
66	89,629	79.1	W.R. van Straubenzee	C	34,011	47.9
			R.J. Carter	Lab	24,437	34.5
			Mrs. M.E. Wingfield	L	12,464	17.6
					9,574	13.4
70	108,870	72.1	W.R. van Straubenzee	C	43,183	55.0
			C.A.R. Helm	Lab	22,630	28.8
			D.H.V. Case	L	12,704	16.2
					20,553	26.2

Election	Electors	T'out	Candidate	Party	Votes	%
1950	47,261	83.4	G.S. Summers	C	17,623	44
			A.S. Harman	Lab	14,262	3(
			G.G. Moir	L	7,547	1S
					3,361	8
1951	48,181	83.1	G.S. Summers	C	22,455	5(
			A.S. Harman	Lab	17,605	43
					4,850	12
1955	49,833	81.8	G.S. Summers	C	20,330	49
			A.S. Harman	Lab	14,569	35
			H.L. Fry	L	5,869	14
					5,761	14
1959	54,089	81.3	Sir G.S. Summers	C	22,504	51
			H. Gray	Lab	13,549	30
			H.L. Fry	L	7,897	18
					8,955	20
1964	63,262	80.0	Sir G.S. Summers	C	23,856	47
			G.D. Western	Lab	16,467	32
			T. Joyce	L	10,301	20
					7,389	14
1966	65,968	79.9	Sir G.S. Summers	C	23,673	44
			P. Allison	Lab	19,766	37
			T. Joyce	L	9,272	17
					3,907	7
1970	77,193	75.6	T.H.F. Raison	C	31,084	53
			J.E. Mitchell	Lab	20,441	35
			P.S. Kinsey	L	6,849*	11
					10,643	18

lection	Electors	T'out	Candidate	Party	Votes	%
950	51,181	86.2	†A.M. Crawley	Lab	20,782	47.1
			S.F. Markham	C	19,128	43.4
			J.D.G. Kellock	L	4,196*	9.5
					1,654	3.7
951	52,310	86.6	S.F. Markham	C	22,688	50.1
			A.M. Crawley	Lab	22,634	49.9
					54	0.2
955	53,298	85.1	Sir S.F. Markham	C	23,250	51.3
			Dr. D.G. Evans	Lab	22,110	48.7
					1,140	2.6
959	54,905	86.4	Sir S.F. Markham	C	22,304	47.1
			I.R. Maxwell	Lab	20,558	43.3
			E.L.F. Richards	L	4,577*	9.6
					1,746	3.8
964	58,109	86.5	I.R. Maxwell	Lab	23,085	45.9
			Mrs. M.E. Kellett	C	21,604	43.0
			J.R. Wallis	L	5,578*	11.1
					1,481	2.9
966	60,966	85.9	I.R. Maxwell	Lab	24,854	47.4
			Mrs. M.E. Kellett	C	22,600	43.2
			J.M. Cornwall	L	4,914*	9.4
					2,254	4.2
970	72,248	81.8	W.R. Benyon	C	28,088	47.5
			I.R. Maxwell	Lab	25,567	43.2
			J.M. Cornwall	L	5,475*	9.3
					2,521	4.3

Election	Electors	T'out	Candidate	Party	Votes	%
1950	53,482	85.7	R.M. Bell	C	26,865	58.
			C.A. Dee	Lab	11,389	24.
			B.H. Belfrage	L	7,559	16.
					15,476	33.
1951	56,373	80.1	R.M. Bell	C	30,976	68.
			C.A. Dee	Lab	14,170	31.
					16,806	37.
1955	60,501	78.1	R.M. Bell	C	29,165	61.
			W.E. Robinson	Lab	11,184	23.
			P. Brunner	L	6,885	14.
					17,981	38.
1959	72,466	79.8	R.M. Bell	C	34,154	59.
			R. Sankey	Lab	13,050	22.
			R.K. Brown	L	10,589	18.
					21,104	36.
1964	81,466	78.9	R.M. Bell	C	33,905	52.
			R.K. Brown	L	16,151	25.
			J. Ryan	Lab	14,216	22.
					17,754	27.
1966	82,678	80.3	R.M. Bell	C	33,997	51.
			F.E. Field	Lab	17,005	25.
			H.T. Cowie	L	15,348	23.
					16,992	25.
1970	93,692	72.8	R.M. Bell	C	40,039	58.
			K. Davison	Lab	16,465	24.
			I.M. Fowler	L	11,750	17.
					23,574	34.

Election	Electors	T'out	Candidate	Party	Votes	%
1950	59,500	85.8	†J.E. Haire	Lab	21,491	42.0
			Hon. W.W. Astor	C	21,015	41.2
			B.A. Law	L	8,354	16.4
			Mrs. E.R. Leigh	Com	199*	0.4
					476	0.8
1951	60,799	86.2	Hon. W.W. Astor	C	27,084	51.7
			J.E. Haire	Lab	25,331	48.3
					1,753	3.4

[Succession to the Peerage—Viscount Astor]

Election	Electors	T'out	Candidate	Party	Votes	%
1952 (4/11)	61,273	83.9	J. Hall	C	26,750	52.0
			J.E. Haire	Lab	24,650	48.0
					2,100	4.0
1955	63,094	82.0	J. Hall	C	29,845	57.7
			R. Fletcher	Lab	21,905	42.3
					7,940	15.4
1959	68,199	84.7	J. Hall	C	30,774	53.3
			W.G. Fordham	Lab	19,904	34.5
			A.D. Dennis	L	7,068*	12.2
					10,870	18.8
1964	75,902	81.3	J. Hall	C	30,877	50.0
			M.C.J. Barnes	Lab	21,534	34.9
			A.D. Dennis	L	9,330	15.1
					9,343	15.1
1966	79,422	80.7	J. Hall	C	31,577	49.3
			J. Holland	Lab	24,498	38.2
			M. Janis	L	8,037	12.5
					7,079	11.1
1970	95,634	75.1	J. Hall	C	40,151	55.9
			B.S. Jones	Lab	23,341	32.5
			E.H. Palfrey	L	8,297*	11.6
					16,810	23.4

Election	Electors	T'out	Candidate	Party	Votes	%
1950	56,622	83.4	S.G. Howard	C	21,846	46.3
			†A.E. Stubbs	Lab	19,046	40.3
			R.T. Howlett	L	6,348	13.4
					2,800	6.0
1951	57,430	81.2	S.G. Howard	C	25,095	53.8
			H.D.L.G. Walston	Lab	21,558	46.2
					3,537	7.6
1955	58,425	78.9	S.G. Howard	C	25,025	54.3
			H.D.L.G. Walston	Lab	21,051	45.7
					3,974	8.6
1959	60,698	78.0	S.G. Howard	C	27,407	57.9
			W. Royle	Lab	19,928	42.1
					7,479	15.8

[Resignation on appointment as a High Court Judge]

Election	Electors	T'out	Candidate	Party	Votes	%
1961 (16/3)	61,593	62.4	F.L. Pym	C	17,643	45.9
			R.M.D. Davies	Lab	11,566	30.1
			R.G. Moore	L	9,219	24.0
					6,077	15.8
1964	65,015	79.8	F.L. Pym	C	24,883	48.0
			E.L. Rutherford	Lab	17,636	34.0
			R.G. Moore	L	9,347	18.0
					7,247	14.0
1966	67,869	79.2	F.L. Pym	C	25,600	47.7
			J.N. Hughes	Lab	20,433	38.0
			J.R.C. Beale	L	7,698	14.3
					5,167	9.7
1970	78,271	75.5	F.L. Pym	C	32,264	54.6
			J.N. Hughes	Lab	19,993	33.8
			Mrs. M.M. Brown	L	6,861*	11.6
					12,271	20.8

lection	Electors	T'out	Candidate	Party	Votes	%
950	59,554	88.9	†W.S. Shepherd	C	30,740	58.1
			Rev. G.H. Jones	Lab	13,389	25.3
			G.E. Samways	L	8,801	16.6
					17,351	32.8
951	60,266	85.7	W.S. Shepherd	C	32,369	62.6
			Rev. G.H. Jones	Lab	12,910	25.0
			G.E. Samways	L	6,388*	12.4
					19,459	37.6
955	61,626*	80.6	W.S. Shepherd	C	30,940	62.3
			H.V. Stone	Lab	10,966	22.1
			R.A. Palmer	L	7,756	15.6
					19,974	40.2
959	71,205	83.7	W.S. Shepherd	C	32,787	55.0
			R.N. Cuss	L	15,468	25.9
			C.R. Morris	Lab	11,373	19.1
					17,319	29.1
964	86,743	83.6	W.S. Shepherd	C	33,911	46.7
			R.N. Cuss	L	25,220	34.8
			S.N.M. Moxley	Lab	13,379	18.5
					8,691	11.9
966	91,893	82.4	Dr. M.P. Winstanley	L	32,071	42.3
			W.S. Shepherd	C	31,416	41.5
			S.N.M. Moxley	Lab	12,244	16.2
					655	0.8
970	107,225	80.0	T. Normanton	C	39,728	46.3
			Dr. M.P. Winstanley	L	37,974	44.3
			R. Stott	Lab	8,062*	9.4
					1,754	2.0

Election	Electors	T'out	Candidate	Party	Votes	%
1950	54,869	83.9	†B.E. Nield	C	23,660	51.4
			Rev. C. McKinnon	Lab	16,021	34.8
			A.H. Willitt	L	6,342	13.8
					7,639	16.6
1951	55,348	82.6	B.E. Nield	C	26,743	58.5
			J.G. Hughes	Lab	18,958	41.5
					7,785	17.0
1955	56,452	77.9	B.E. Nield	C	24,905	56.
			J.M. Forrester	Lab	13,903	31.6
			J.D.S. Llewellyn	L	5,145*	11.
					11,002	25.

[Resignation on appointment as Judge of the Crown Court and Recorder of Manchester]

Election	Electors	T'out	Candidate	Party	Votes	%
1956 (15/11)	57,137	71.5	J.M. Temple	C	21,137	51.7
			L. Carter-Jones	Lab	14,789	36.3
			J.D.S. Llewellyn	L	4,942*	12.
					6,348	15.5
1959	57,617	78.7	J.M. Temple	C	27,847	61.4
			L. Carter-Jones	Lab	17,492	38.6
					10,355	22.8
1964	59,654	79.6	J.M. Temple	C	23,172	48.8
			A.B. Blond	Lab	16,708	35.2
			P.J. Samuel	L	7,583	16.0
					6,464	13.6
1966	60,295	78.0	J.M. Temple	C	21,673	46.
			J. Crawford	Lab	18,870	40.
			P.J. Samuel	L	6,516	13.8
					2,803	6.0
1970	68,069	73.1	J.M. Temple	C	25,877	52.0
			J. Crawford	Lab	18,872	38.0
			M.J.G. Tompkins	L	4,978*	10.0
					7,005	14.0

ection	Electors	T'out	Candidate	Party	Votes	%
50	62,688	86.7	†S.S. Allen	Lab	28,981	53.3
			Dr. J.R.T. Turner	C	25,355	46.7
					3,626	6.6
51	63,011	86.5	S.S. Allen	Lab	28,488	52.2
			Dr. J.R.T. Turner	C	26,045	47.8
					2,443	4.4
55	50,577**	81.5	S.S. Allen	Lab	21,629	52.5
			G.F. Boston	C	15,273	37.1
			T.S. Rothwell	L	4,306*	10.4
					6,356	15.4
59	50,971	82.1	S.S. Allen	Lab	22,811	54.5
			G.L. Beaman	C	19,030	45.5
					3,781	9.0
64	52,175	79.0	S.S. Allen	Lab	23,579	57.2
			A.G. Barbour	C	17,657	42.8
					5,922	14.4
66	52,370	75.6	S.S. Allen	Lab	24,140	61.0
			A.G. Barbour	C	15,430	39.0
					8,710	22.0
70	57,515	71.0	S.S. Allen	Lab	22,160	54.3
			A.R. Goodlad	C	18,678	45.7
					3,482	8.6

Election	Electors	T'out	Candidate	Party	Votes	%
1950	57,617	87.1	†W.H. Bromley-Davenport	C	29,707	59.
			C. Hamnett	Lab	12,794	25.
			L.L. Maitland	L	7,703	15.
					16,913	33.
1951	58,725	83.0	W.H. Bromley-Davenport	C	34,114	70.
			C. Hamnett	Lab	14,640	30.
					19,474	40.
1955	49,756**	77.7	W.H. Bromley-Davenport	C	29,074	75.
			C. Hamnett	Lab	9,588	24.
					19,486	50.
1959	52,999	81.8	W.H. Bromley-Davenport	C	27,270	63.
			F.R. Tetlow	L	8,117	18.
			N. Selwyn	Lab	7,945	18.
					19,153	44.
1964	62,495	80.3	Sir W.H. Bromley-Davenport	C	26,826	53.
			M. Hunkin	L	12,499	24.
			D. Dollimore	Lab	10,882	21.
					14,327	28.
1966	65,160	79.1	Sir W.H. Bromley-Davenport	C	26,550	51.
			G.J. Tordoff	L	12,839	24.
			K.J. Hill	Lab	12,174	23.
					13,711	26.
1970	74,169	74.8	J.E.H. Davies	C	33,194	59.8
			A.F. Bennett	Lab	11,612	20.
			G.J. Tordoff	L	10,684	19.
					21,582	38.

Election	Electors	T'out	Candidate	Party	Votes	%
1950	56,609	89.4	†A.V. Harvey	C	25,781	50.9
			F. Blackburn	Lab	19,219	38.0
			C.F. Doncaster	L	5,621*	11.1
					6,562	12.9
1951	57,134	87.3	A.V. Harvey	C	29,434	59.0
			Mrs. A.E. Taylor	Lab	20,428	41.0
					9,006	18.0
1955	56,991	80.6	A.V. Harvey	C	27,551	60.0
			K. Lomas	Lab	18,362	40.0
					9,189	20.0
1959	58,892	82.6	Sir A.V. Harvey	C	28,978	59.6
			J.F. Bex	Lab	19,652	40.4
					9,326	19.2
1964	62,175	84.1	Sir A.V. Harvey	C	24,824	47.5
			D.W. Coe	Lab	18,464	35.3
			G. Hewlett-Johnson	L	8,975	17.2
					6,360	12.2
1966	64,639	81.7	Sir A.V. Harvey	C	24,736	46.8
			A.G. Read	Lab	20,533	38.9
			D.F. Burden	L	7,545	14.3
					4,203	7.9
1970	72,900	76.4	Sir A.V. Harvey	C	29,023	52.1
			B.S. Jeuda	Lab	18,571	33.3
			R.M. Hammond	L	8,124	14.6
					10,452	18.8

Election	Electors	T'out	Candidate	Party	Votes	%
1955	42,679	77.6	R.G. Grant-Ferris	C	20,250	61.1
			L. Knight	Lab	12,884	38.9
					7,366	22.2
1959	43,655	83.5	R.G. Grant-Ferris	C	17,613	48.3
			L. Knight	Lab	10,876	29.8
			G.M. Harvey	L	7,983	21.9
					6,737	18.5
1964	45,423	81.5	R.G. Grant-Ferris	C	17,171	46.3
			J. Golding	Lab	11,254	30.4
			D.A.R. Green	L	8,613	23.3
					5,917	15.9
1966	47,685	79.3	R.G. Grant-Ferris	C	16,543	43.7
			D.A. Kean	Lab	14,310	37.9
			D.A.R. Green	L	6,950	18.4
					2,233	5.8
1970	56,880	77.6	Sir R.G. Grant-Ferris	C	20,397	46.2
			D. Beetham	Lab	15,124	34.3
			R.N. Cuss	L	8,595	19.5
					5,273	11.9

CHESHIRE, NORTHWICH [334]

Election	Electors	T'out	Candidate	Party	Votes	%
1950	59,346	87.7	†J.G. Foster	C	25,144	48.4
			C. Mapp	Lab	19,886	38.2
			Dr. W.N. Leak	L	6,989	13.4
					5,258	10.2
1951	61,750	83.7	J.G. Foster	C	29,375	56.8
			R.P. Walsh	Lab	22,300	43.2
					7,075	13.6
1955	43,691**	79.7	J.G. Foster	C	20,697	59.4
			J.D. Page	Lab	14,142	40.6
					6,555	18.8
1959	44,305	84.5	J.G. Foster	C	20,396	54.5
			J. Crawford	Lab	12,426	33.2
			R.E. Lewis	L	4,602*	12.3
					7,970	21.3
1964	44,001	83.0	Sir J.G. Foster	C	17,277	47.4
			J. Crawford	Lab	12,892	35.3
			G.J. Tordoff	L	6,331	17.3
					4,385	12.1
1966	44,413	82.3	Sir J.G. Foster	C	16,483	45.1
			S.B. Jones	Lab	15,780	43.1
			D.B. Taylor	L	4,310*	11.8
					703	2.0
1970	50,608	78.5	Sir J.G. Foster	C	20,366	51.3
			A. Bates	Lab	15,746	39.6
			T.N. Armstrong	L	3,604*	9.1
					4,620	11.7

Election	Electors	T'out	Candidate	Party	Votes	%
1950	46,253	88.6	D.F. Vosper	C	22,145	54.1
			H.L. Wharrad	Lab	14,063	34.3
			P.H. Griffiths	L	4,768*	11.6
					8,082	19.8
1951	46,699	85.2	D.F. Vosper	C	24,821	62.4
			J.L. Hindle	Lab	14,980	37.6
					9,841	24.8
1955	47,487	81.1	D.F. Vosper	C	24,682	64.1
			D. Barker	Lab	13,852	35.9
					10,830	28.2
1959	49,584	81.6	Rt. Hon. D.F. Vosper	C	26,615	65.8
			J. Barnett	Lab	13,837	34.2
					12,778	31.6

[Seat Vacant at Dissolution (Resignation on appointment as Chairman of the National Assistance Board and elevation to a Life Peerage—Lord Runcorn]

Election	Electors	T'out	Candidate	Party	Votes	%
1964	52,664	83.7	M. Carlisle	C	21,586	49.0
			P.L. Jackson	Lab	14,127	32.1
			R.W. Jordan	L	8,343	18.9
					7,459	16.9
1966	54,036	82.1	M. Carlisle	C	21,472	48.4
			M.J.E. Taylor	Lab	16,290	36.7
			T.A. Maher	L	6,606	14.9
					5,182	11.7
1970	61,331	77.0	M. Carlisle	C	25,272	53.5
			M.J.E. Taylor	Lab	16,204	34.3
			C.K. Sumner	L	5,741*	12.2
					9,068	19.2

Election	Electors	T'out	Candidate	Party	Votes	%
1950	57,456	87.7	†Rev. G. Lang	Lab	23,462	46.5
			D. Glover	C	21,619	42.9
			D.F. Burden	L	4,930*	9.8
			D.P. Herrick	Com	389*	0.8
					1,843	3.6
1951	57,759	87.4	F. Blackburn	Lab	25,402	50.3
			D. Glover	C	25,104	49.7
					298	0.6
1955	56,359	83.5	F. Blackburn	Lab	23,617	50.2
			I.W. Owen	C	23,462	49.8
					155	0.4
1959	55,183	83.4	F. Blackburn	Lab	23,732	51.5
			E.J. Brown	C	22,309	48.5
					1,423	3.0
1964	54,496	78.7	F. Blackburn	Lab	23,164	54.0
			S.B. Chapman	C	19,739	46.0
					3,425	8.0
1966	57,249	73.6	F. Blackburn	Lab	23,974	56.9
			J.E. Rogerson	C	18,153	43.1
					5,821	13.8
1970	63,823	73.5	T. Pendry	Lab	22,226	47.4
			J.E. Rogerson	C	19,377	41.3
			R.N. Cooke	L	5,303*	11.3
					2,849	6.1

Election	Electors	T'out	Candidate	Party	Votes	%
1950	59,642	85.9	†J.S.B. Lloyd	C	29,232	57.1
			H.A. Kelly	Lab	15,993	31.2
			T.M. Banks	L	6,018*	11.7
					13,239	25.9
1951	61,197	81.7	J.S.B. Lloyd	C	32,631	65.2
			R.B. Chrimes	Lab	17,392	34.8
					15,239	30.4
1955	64,082	76.5	Rt. Hon. J.S.B. Lloyd	C	33,027	67.4
			R.B. Chrimes	Lab	15,976	32.6
					17,051	34.8
1959	71,025	82.5	Rt. Hon. J.S.B. Lloyd	C	39,807	67.9
			F.W. Venables	Lab	18,805	32.1
					21,002	35.8
1964	78,856	81.3	Rt. Hon. J.S.B. Lloyd	C	32,084	50.1
			Mrs. M. Aspin	Lab	17,445	27.2
			P.H. Williams	L	14,574	22.7
					14,639	22.9
1966	82,056	79.7	Rt. Hon. J.S.B. Lloyd	C	31,477	48.1
			D.V. Hunt	Lab	21,624	33.1
			P.H. Williams	L	12,313	18.8
					9,853	15.0
1970	94,443	74.3	Rt. Hon. J.S.B. Lloyd	C	38,655	55.1
			R.G. Paterson	Lab	22,197	31.7
			Miss G. Jones	L	9,276	13.2
					16,458	23.4

Note:—

1970:   Lloyd was the Speaker of the House of Commons from January 1971.

Election	Electors	T'out	Candidate	Party	Votes	%
1950	46,881	84.3	†D. Marshall	C	19,441	49.2
			J.M. Foot	L	11,649	29.5
			W. Royle	Lab	8,434	21.3
					7,792	19.7
1951	46,617	84.6	D. Marshall	C	20,086	50.9
			T.S. Roseveare	L	10,088	25.6
			W. Royle	Lab	9,244	23.5
					9,998	25.3
1955	45,715	79.5	D. Marshall	C	17,858	49.2
			T.S. Roseveare	L	10,199	28.0
			E.F. Wilde	Lab	8,304	22.8
					7,659	21.2
1959	45,000	81.5	D. Marshall	C	16,853	46.0
			P.J. Bessell	L	14,052	38.3
			T.F. Mitchell	Lab	5,769	15.7
					2,801	7.7
1964	44,906	82.7	P.J. Bessell	L	18,046	48.6
			Sir D. Marshall	C	14,910	40.2
			T.F. Mitchell	Lab	4,172*	11.2
					3,136	8.4
1966	46,115	84.4	P.J. Bessell	L	18,144	46.6
			J.M. Gorst	C	16,121	41.4
			R. Blank	Lab	4,674*	12.0
					2,023	5.2
1970	51,803	80.7	R.A. Hicks	C	20,187	48.3
			P.A. Tyler	L	16,267	38.9
			A.F. Long	Lab	5,350	12.8
					3,920	9.4

Election	Electors	T'out	Candidate	Party	Votes	%
1950	53,248	82.6	F.H. Hayman	Lab	18,958	43.1
			†P.G. Agnew	C	16,997	38.7
			G.G. Sharp	L	8,013	18.2
					1,961	4.4
1951	53,870	83.6	F.H. Hayman	Lab	20,850	46.3
			N. Nicolson	C	19,847	44.1
			H.S. Townend	L	4,343*	9.6
					1,003	2.2
1955	53,791	78.3	F.H. Hayman	Lab	21,587	51.2
			P.P. King	C	20,540	48.8
					1,047	2.4
1959	53,763	81.6	F.H. Hayman	Lab	20,083	45.8
			Miss A.M. Tennant	C	15,886	36.2
			N.A.S. Gibson	L	7,890	18.0
					4,197	9.6
1964	54,569	77.6	F.H. Hayman	Lab	18,847	44.5
			Hon. R.T. Boscawen	C	15,921	37.6
			E.H. Hambly	L	7,559	17.9
					2,926	6.9

[Seat Vacant at Dissolution (Death)]

Election	Electors	T'out	Candidate	Party	Votes	%
1966	55,323	82.5	Dr. J.E.O. Dunwoody	Lab	21,394	46.8
			Hon. R.T. Boscawen	C	18,131	39.7
			Miss A.M.P.H. Sykes	L	6,144	13.5
					3,263	7.1
1970	62,001	77.8	W.D. Mudd	C	21,477	44.5
			Dr. J.E.O. Dunwoody	Lab	19,954	41.4
			A.G.S.T. Davey	L	5,843*	12.1
			R.G. Jenkin	MK	960*	2.0
					1,523	3.1

Election	Electors	T'out	Candidate	Party	Votes	%
1950	42,550	85.9	Sir H. Roper	C	17,059	46.6
			D.M. Foot	L	13,987	38.3
			H.L. Richardson	Lab	5,521	15.1
					3,072	8.3
1951	43,084	85.7	Sir H. Roper	C	18,009	48.8
			D.M. Foot	L	12,869	34.8
			W.C. Ferman	Lab	6,049	16.4
					5,140	14.0
1955	43,145	82.3	Sir H. Roper	C	16,824	47.3
			E.T. Malindine	L	15,220	42.9
			V.E. Cornford	Lab	3,465*	9.8
					1,604	4.4
1959	42,764	83.7	J.S.R. Scott-Hopkins	C	16,701	46.6
			E.T. Malindine	L	15,712	43.9
			W.C. Ferman	Lab	3,389*	9.5
					989	2.7
1964	43,076	83.1	J.S.R. Scott-Hopkins	C	16,352	45.7
			C.M.K. Bruton	L	15,683	43.8
			R.S. Dash	Lab	3,497*	9.8
			E.G.C. Voullaire	Ind	265*	0.7
					669	1.9
1966	43,480	87.5	J.W. Pardoe	L	18,460	48.5
			J.S.R. Scott-Hopkins	C	16,952	44.5
			R.S. Wills	Lab	2,647*	7.0
					1,508	4.0
1970	47,905	85.2	J.W. Pardoe	L	19,863	48.6
			S.J. Day	C	19,233	47.1
			E.W.J. Hill	Lab	1,741*	4.3
					630	1.5

Note:—

1964: Voullaire was opposed to Britain entering the Common Market.

Election	Electors	T'out	Candidate	Party	Votes	%
1950	44,342	81.6	Hon. G.R. Howard	NL & C	16,653	46.0
			P.D. Shore	Lab	11,118	30.7
			E.F. Allison	L	8,421	23.3
					5,535	15.3
1951	44,885	78.7	Hon. G.R. Howard	NL & C	18,828	53.3
			A. Maddison	Lab/Co-op	11,216	31.8
			J.D.G. Kellock	L	5,273	14.9
					7,612	21.5
1955	44,374	73.9	Hon. G.R. Howard	NL & C	17,063	52.1
			L.S. Pawley	Lab	9,728	29.6
			D.A.H. Banks	L	6,020	18.3
					7,335	22.5
1959	44,010	74.4	Hon. G.R. Howard	NL & C	15,700	47.9
			D. Longden	Lab	8,802	26.9
			G.E.L. Whitmarsh	L	8,258	25.2
					6,898	21.0
1964	43,890	75.1	Hon. G.R. Howard	NL & C	14,040	42.6
			G.E.L. Whitmarsh	L	9,641	29.3
			T.F.G. Jones	Lab	9,265	28.1
					4,399	13.3
1966	44,419	77.9	J.W.F. Nott	NL & C (C)	14,312	41.4
			T.F.G. Jones	Lab	10,713	30.9
			J.C.T. Trewin	L	9,593	27.7
					3,599	10.5
1970	48,567	75.1	J.W.F. Nott	C	18,581	50.9
			Dr. Maureen E. Castle	Lab	9,913	27.2
			H.L. Fry	L	7,981	21.9
					8,668	23.7

Election	Electors	T'out	Candidate	Party	Votes	%
1950	54,374	83.3	H.G.B. Wilson	C	18,910	41.8
			H. Brinton	Lab	15,617	34.5
			G.E.L. Whitmarsh	L	10,747	23.7
					3,293	7.3
1951	54,935	81.3	H.G.B. Wilson	C	24,883	55.7
			J.N. Newby	Lab	19,752	44.3
					5,131	11.4
1955	54,798	78.7	H.G.B. Wilson	C	19,900	46.1
			J.N. Newby	Lab	15,183	35.2
			Miss B.N. Seear	L	8,056	18.7
					4,717	10.9
1959	55,185	80.2	H.G.B. Wilson	C	19,544	44.2
			R.J.R. Blindell	Lab	15,057	34.0
			Miss B.N. Seear	L	9,637	21.8
					4,487	10.2
1964	56,980	79.2	H.G.B. Wilson	C	18,328	40.6
			D.W.J. Grazier	Lab	14,224	31.5
			W.R. Hosking	L	12,575	27.9
					4,104	9.1
1966	58,362	79.2	H.G.B. Wilson	C	18,701	40.4
			R.C.J. Scott	Lab	17,093	37.0
			W.R. Hosking	L	10,450	22.6
					1,608	3.4
1970	65,963	76.6	P.J.S. Dixon	C	24,894	49.3
			R.C. Cuss	Lab	16,684	33.0
			M. Steed	L	8,923	17.7
					8,210	16.3

Election	Electors	T'out	Candidate	Party	Votes	%
1950	51,594	85.3	R.D. Scott	C	21,214	48.:
			†W.H.W. Roberts	L	12,333	28.(
			C.J. Taylor	Lab	10,441	23.:
					8,881	20.:
1951	51,575*	83.5	R.D. Scott	C	23,274	54.(
			J. Rafferty	Lab	10,759	25.(
			S.V.S. Howard	L	8,857	20.(
			W. Brownrigg	Ind	158*	0.4
					12,515	29.(
1955	50,875	77.9	W.S.I. Whitelaw	C	22,791	57.6
			T.L. MacDonald	Lab	9,119	23.0
			F.J. Sleath	L	7,342	18.5
			W. Brownrigg	Ind	368*	0.9
					13,672	34.6
1959	51,190	79.1	W.S.I. Whitelaw	C	23,551	58.1
			B.P. Atha	Lab	9,342	23.1
			B.G. Ashmore	L	7,602	18.8
					14,209	35.0
1964	50,840	80.6	W.S.I. Whitelaw	C	21,228	51.8
			Mrs. K.M.A. Roberts	Lab	10,490	25.6
			W. Jackson	L	9,279	22.6
					10,738	26.2
1966	50,621	78.7	W.S.I. Whitelaw	C	20,982	52.7
			Mrs. K.M.A. Roberts	Lab	12,081	30.3
			J.R. Howe	L	6,757	17.0
					8,901	22.4
1970	54,251	74.4	Rt. Hon. W.S.I. Whitelaw	C	23,800	59.0
			R. Longworth	Lab	10,256	25.4
			W. Jackson	L	6,316	15.6
					13,544	33.6

CUMBERLAND, WHITEHAVEN [344]

Election	Electorate	T'out	Candidate	Party	Votes	%
1950	43,751	87.0	†F. Anderson	Lab	22,850	60.0
			W. Nunn	C	15,233	40.0
					7,617	20.0
1951	45,963	85.2	F. Anderson	Lab	23,190	59.2
			G.W. Iredell	C	15,990	40.8
					7,200	18.4
1955	45,957	83.8	F. Anderson	Lab	22,348	58.0
			G.W. Iredell	C	16,154	42.0
					6,194	16.0
[Death]						
1959 (18/6)	46,246	79.2	J.B. Symonds	Lab	21,475	58.6
			G.W. Iredell	C	15,151	41.4
					6,324	17.2
1959	46,650	84.5	J.B. Symonds	Lab	22,783	57.8
			H.J. Pedraza	C	16,653	42.2
					6,130	15.6
1964	47,193	82.0	J.B. Symonds	Lab	23,267	60.1
			E.C.S.J.G. Brudenell	C	15,440	39.9
					7,827	20.2
1966	46,532	78.8	J.B. Symonds	Lab	22,726	62.0
			J.A. Kevill	C	13,935	38.0
					8,791	24.0
1970	50,289	78.3	J.A. Cunningham	Lab	22,974	58.3
			Dr. W.G. McKay	C	16,418	41.7
					6,556	16.6

Election	Electors	T'out	Candidate	Party	Votes	%
1950	48,716	89.4	†T.F. Peart	Lab	25,104	57.6
			Mrs. H. Fox	C	14,009	32.2
			D.C.G. Sibley	L	4,460*	10.2
					11,095	25.4
1951	49,291	87.5	T.F. Peart	Lab	25,893	60.0
			Mrs. H. Fox	C	17,249	40.0
					8,644	20.0
1955	49,094	86.1	T.F. Peart	Lab	25,110	59.4
			T.M. Brannan	C	17,182	40.6
					7,928	18.8
1959	49,401	85.9	T.F. Peart	Lab	25,537	60.2
			T.M. Brannan	C	16,894	39.8
					8,643	20.4
1964	49,220	83.5	T.F. Peart	Lab	25,522	62.1
			H. Denman	C	15,565	37.9
					9,957	24.2
1966	49,078	80.4	Rt. Hon. T.F. Peart	Lab	24,981	63.3
			M.F. Turner-Bridger	C	14,475	36.7
					10,506	26.6
1970	52,280	77.5	Rt. Hon. T.F. Peart	Lab	24,975	61.7
			M.F. Turner-Bridger	C	15,532	38.3
					9,443	23.4

DERBYSHIRE, BELPER [346]

Election	Electors	T'out	Candidate	Party	Votes	%
1950	65,480	88.8	†G.A. Brown	Lab	30,904	53.2
			M.V. Argyle	C	21,581	37.1
			Dr. J.P. Lawrie	L	5,650*	9.7
					9,323	16.1
1951	66,325	86.8	Rt. Hon. G.A. Brown	Lab	32,875	57.1
			S.F. Middup	C	24,678	42.9
					8,197	14.2
1955	66,585	81.6	Rt. Hon. G.A. Brown	Lab	30,214	55.6
			J. Twells	C	24,115	44.4
					6,099	11.2
1959	69,336	84.2	Rt. Hon. G.A. Brown	Lab	31,344	53.7
			Mrs. J. Ratcliffe	C	27,007	46.3
					4,337	7.4
1964	74,891	86.1	Rt. Hon. G.A. Brown	Lab	30,481	47.3
			J.L. Lowther	C	24,169	37.5
			N. Heathcote	L	9,807	15.2
					6,312	9.8
1966	76,914	84.1	Rt. Hon. G.A. Brown	Lab	34,495	53.3
			J.L. Lowther	C	30,221	46.7
					4,274	6.6
1970	86,608	80.1	D.G. Stewart-Smith	C	35,757	51.5
			Rt. Hon. G.A. Brown	Lab	33,633	48.5
					2,124	3.0

Election	Electors	T'out	Candidate	Party	Votes	%
1950	48,935	86.2	†H. Neal	Lab	34,017	80.6
			J.K. Cordeaux	C	8,184	19.4
					25,833	61.2
1951	49,362	85.4	H. Neal	Lab	33,661	79.9
			J.K. Cordeaux	C	8,472	20.1
					25,189	59.8
1955	49,144	77.6	H. Neal	Lab	30,074	78.9
			B.R.O. Bell	C	8,055	21.1
					22,019	57.8
1959	50,455	82.5	H. Neal	Lab	32,536	78.2
			R.G. Marlar	C	9,076	21.8
					23,460	56.4
1964	49,900	78.9	H. Neal	Lab	31,234	79.3
			P.T. Cormack	C	8,131	20.7
					23,103	58.6
1966	49,491	76.6	H. Neal	Lab	31,114	82.0
			P.C. Coleman	C	6,815	18.0
					24,299	64.0
1970	52,552	70.8	D.E. Skinner	Lab	28,830	77.5
			I.J. Humphrey	C	8,371	22.5
					20,459	55.0

ction	Electors	T'out	Candidate	Party	Votes	%
0	50,351	85.8	†A.H.E. Molson	C	19,740	45.7
			W.M. Halsall	Lab	16,933	39.2
			T.S. Rothwell	L	6,539	15.1
					2,807	6.5
1	50,624	85.9	A.H.E. Molson	C	21,305	48.9
			W.M. Halsall	Lab	18,127	41.7
			Hon. S.R. Cawley	L	4,070*	9.4
					3,178	7.2
5	49,612	79.5	A.H.E. Molson	C	19,094	48.4
			N. McBride	Lab	13,652	34.6
			Hon. S.R. Cawley	L	6,712	17.0
					5,442	13.8
9	49,196	82.7	Rt. Hon. A.H.E. Molson	C	18,738	46.0
			B. Conlan	Lab	13,827	34.0
			Hon. S.R. Cawley	L	8,138	20.0
					4,911	12.0

evation to a Life Peerage—Lord Molson]

1	48,183	72.5	A.D. Walder	C	13,069	37.4
/3)			W.M. Halsall	Lab	11,201	32.1
			D.I. Wrigley	L	10,674	30.5
					1,868	5.3
4	48,445	85.3	A.D. Walder	C	15,753	38.1
			J.F.H. Roper	Lab	14,416	34.9
			D.I. Wrigley	L	11,147	27.0
					1,337	3.2
6	48,747	84.2	P.M. Jackson	Lab	16,938	41.2
			A.D. Walder	C	16,124	39.3
			D.I. Wrigley	L	7,990	19.5
					814	1.9
70	55,308	80.9	S. Le Marchant	C	19,558	43.7
			P.M. Jackson	Lab	18,054	40.4
			D.I. Wrigley	L	7,119	15.9
					1,504	3.3

Election	Electors	T'out	Candidate	Party	Votes	%
1950	68,769	88.5	†G.H. Oliver	Lab	39,495	6
			G.E. Macpherson	L	11,262	1
			D.F.R. Evans	C	10,113	1
					28,233	4
1951	69,773	86.5	G.H. Oliver	Lab	40,671	6
			C.F. Baker	C	10,273	1
			G.E. Macpherson	L	9,387	1
					30,398	5
1955	69,967	80.4	G.H. Oliver	Lab	38,961	6
			J.A. Farr	C	17,268	3
					21,693	3
1959	69,719	83.5	G.H. Oliver	Lab	39,930	6
			G.I. Walters	C	18,286	3
					21,644	3
1964	68,796	82.0	R. Fletcher	Lab	33,924	6
			J.N.L. Tillett	C	13,542	24
			Mrs. M.V. Edwards	L	8,930	1
					20,382	3
1966	68,478	76.1	R. Fletcher	Lab	36,522	7
			B.J. Eales	C	15,582	29
					20,940	4
1970	74,080	74.2	R. Fletcher	Lab	32,961	59
			R.D. Beardsley	C	15,870	28
			W. Smit	L	6,157*	1
					17,091	3

ction	Electors	T'out	Candidate	Party	Votes	%
50	58,397	86.5	†H. White	Lab	33,472	66.3
			G.R. Shaw	C	17,021	33.7
					16,451	32.6
51	59,284	84.4	H. White	Lab	33,376	66.7
			P. Hughes	C	16,655	33.3
					16,721	33.4
55	68,537	76.7	H. White	Lab	34,965	66.5
			G.R. Shaw	C	17,621	33.5
					17,344	33.0
59	73,678	80.8	T.H. Swain	Lab	37,444	62.9
			R.A. Ward	C	22,112	37.1
					15,332	25.8
64	77,285	77.9	T.H. Swain	Lab	38,657	64.2
			M.F. Spungin	C	21,564	35.8
					17,093	28.4
66	78,331	73.8	T.H. Swain	Lab	38,723	66.9
			M.F. Spungin	C	19,123	33.1
					19,600	33.8
70	89,849	69.8	T.H. Swain	Lab	38,181	60.9
			J.P. Pashley	C	24,550	39.1
					13,631	21.8

Election	Electors	T'out	Candidate	Party	Votes	%
1950	70,423	86.9	†A.J. Champion	Lab	30,039	49.
			J.C. Jennings	C	24,789	40
			M. James	L	6,396*	10.
					5,250	8.
1951	72,538	86.4	A.J. Champion	Lab	33,020	52.
			J.C. Jennings	C	29,663	47.
					3,357	5.
1955	60,476**	82.1	A.J. Champion	Lab	25,620	51.
			F.L.J. Jackson	C	24,039	48.
					1,581	3.
1959	65,457	85.1	F.L.J. Jackson	C	25,374	45.
			A.J. Champion	Lab	25,362	45.
			T. Lynch	L	4,980*	8.
					12	0.
1964	70,245	82.8	J.T. Park	Lab	29,528	50.
			P.C.H.E. Myers	C	28,655	49.
					873	1.
1966	72,551	81.8	J.T. Park	Lab	32,407	54.
			P.C.H.E. Myers	C	26,911	45.
					5,496	9.
1970	81,665	75.5	P.L. Rost	C	32,185	52.
			J. Ryman	Lab	29,461	47.
					2,724	4.

DERBYSHIRE, WEST [352]

Election	Electors	T'out	Candidate	Party	Votes	%
1950	44,069	87.5	E.B. Wakefield	C	20,015	51.9
			N. Gratton	Lab	13,478	35.0
			G.F. Strange	L	5,070	13.1
					6,537	16.9
1951	44,786	84.4	E.B. Wakefield	C	22,223	58.8
			R.H. Lewis	Lab	15,578	41.2
					6,645	17.6
1955	44,170	80.0	E.B. Wakefield	C	21,052	59.6
			R.B. Stirling	Lab	14,296	40.4
					6,756	19.2
1959	43,881	81.9	E.B. Wakefield	C	22,034	61.3
			A.E. Kitts	Lab	13,925	38.7
					8,109	22.6

[Resignation on appointment as United Kingdom High Commissioner in Malta]

1962 (5/6)	43,506	79.4	A.M. Crawley	C	12,455	36.1
			R.L. Gardner-Thorpe	L	11,235	32.5
			J. Dilks	Lab	9,431	27.3
			R. Gregory	Ind	1,433*	4.1
					1,220	3.6
1964	44,344	85.8	A.M. Crawley	C	16,825	44.2
			R.L. Gardner-Thorpe	L	11,559	30.4
			J. Dilks	Lab	9,669	25.4
					5,266	13.8
1966	44,414	83.4	A.M. Crawley	C	18,383	49.6
			P. Whitehead	Lab	13,791	37.2
			Mrs. M.V. Edwards	L	4,874	13.2
					4,592	12.4

[Resignation]

1967 (3/11)	44,611	64.5	J.S.R. Scott-Hopkins	C	16,319	56.6
			M.A. Pinney	L	5,696	19.8
			R. Corbett	Lab	5,284	18.4
			R. Goodall	Ind	1,496*	5.2
					10,623	36.8
1970	47,811	76.7	J.S.R. Scott-Hopkins	C	22,692	61.9
			F.C. Inglis	Lab	13,976	38.1
					8,716	23.8

Note:—

1962: Gregory was opposed to Britain entering the Common Market.

Election	Electors	T'out	Candidate	Party	Votes	%
1950	54,869	84.4	†C. Drewe	C	26,767	5
			G.R. Sargeant	Lab	10,816	2
			G.L.G. Barrington	L	8,742	1
					15,951	3
1951	56,022	82.5	C. Drewe	C	27,015	5
			J.B. Halse	L	9,858	2
			N.L. Stevens	Lab	9,369	2
					17,157	3
1955	56,203	79.7	R. Mathew	C	25,808	5
			J.B. Halse	L	11,067	2
			F.W. Thornton	Lab	7,907	1
					14,741	3
1959	57,172	80.1	R. Mathew	C	25,959	5
			J.B. Halse	L	12,906	2
			F.W. Morgan	Lab	6,928	1
					13,053	2
1964	61,067	78.8	R. Mathew	C	26,475	5
			W. Deal	L	12,354	2
			Mrs. M. Clark	Lab	9,273	1
					14,121	2
1966	63,044	78.6	R. Mathew	C	26,966	5
			Mrs. M. Clark	Lab	13,257	2
			R. Hicks	L	9,342	1
					13,709	2
[Death]						
1967 (16/3)	64,025	72.6	P.F.H. Emery	C	26,501	5
			Mrs. B.V. Trethewey	L	10,509	2
			Mrs. M. Clark	Lab	9,501	2
					15,992	3
1970	72,072	76.7	P.F.H. Emery	C	32,885	5
			Mrs. B.V. Trethewey	L	11,330	2
			M.D.D. Newitt	Lab	11,072	2
					21,555	3

tion	Electors	T'out	Candidate	Party	Votes	%
0	44,316	86.3	†C.H.M. Peto	C	17,724	46.4
			G.D. Naylor	L	11,640	30.4
			W.A. Baker	Lab	8,892	23.2
					6,084	16.0
1	44,975	83.9	C.H.M. Peto	C	19,780	52.4
			W.H. Wilkey	Lab	10,632	28.2
			G.A. Halse	L	7,326	19.4
					9,148	24.2
5	43,906	81.1	Hon. J.L. Lindsay	C	16,784	47.1
			J.J. Thorpe	L	11,558	32.5
			H. Heslop	Lab	7,272	20.4
					5,226	14.6
9	43,486	84.8	J.J. Thorpe	L	15,831	42.9
			Hon. J.L. Lindsay	C	15,469	42.0
			G.W. Pitt	Lab	5,567	15.1
					362	0.9
4	44,510	84.3	J.J. Thorpe	L	19,031	50.7
			M.H.B. Peto	C	13,895	37.0
			A.F. Paton	Lab	4,603*	12.3
					5,136	13.7
6	45,192	85.3	J.J. Thorpe	L	16,797	43.6
			T.C. Keigwin	C	15,631	40.5
			J.H. Rayner	Lab	6,127	15.9
					1,166	3.1
0	50,453	85.0	Rt. Hon. J.J. Thorpe	L	18,893	44.1
			T.C. Keigwin	C	18,524	43.2
			C.J. Mullin	Lab	5,268*	12.3
			B.G. Morris	DP	175*	0.4
					369	0.9

Election	Electors	T'out	Candidate	Party	Votes	%
1950	43,863	84.7	†H.G. Studholme	C	18,682	5
			F.W. Harcourt-Munning	Lab	10,189	2
			J.D. Wyatt	L	8,281	2
					8,493	2
1951	45,053*	78.8	H.G. Studholme	C	22,683	6
			F.W. Harcourt-Munning	Lab	12,833	3
					9,850	2
1955	45,096	76.9	H.G. Studholme	C	18,991	5
			H. Lawrance	Lab	8,755	2
			R.G. Moore	L	6,939	2
					10,236	2
1959	46,908	78.5	Sir H.G. Studholme, Bt.	C	19,778	5
			R.G. Moore	L	9,008	2
			B.R. Weston	Lab	8,022	2
					10,770	2
1964	52,124	78.3	Sir H.G. Studholme, Bt.	C	19,493	4
			T.G. Jones	L	14,093	3
			J.A. Elswood	Lab	7,226	1
					5,400	1
1966	54,045	81.4	M.R.D. Heseltine	C	21,644	4
			C. Trethewey	L	13,461	3
			Mrs. P.A. Middleton	Lab	8,902	2
					8,183	1
1970	58,594	77.2	M.R.D. Heseltine	C	25,846	5
			M.E.B. Banks	L	10,397	2
			H.M. Luscombe	Lab	8,982	1
					15,449	3

Election	Electors	T'out	Candidate	Party	Votes	%
950	46,536	85.0	†D. Heathcoat-Amory	C	20,606	52.1
			A.E.P. Duffy	Lab	12,055	30.5
			C.H. Blackburn	L	6,885	17.4
					8,551	21.6
951	47,522	81.3	D. Heathcoat-Amory	C	24,532	63.5
			A.E.P. Duffy	Lab	14,084	36.5
					10,448	27.0
955	47,858	76.3	D. Heathcoat-Amory	C	23,475	64.3
			A.E.P. Duffy	Lab	13,051	35.7
					10,424	28.6
959	48,416	80.7	Rt. Hon. D. Heathcoat-Amory	C	21,714	55.6
			Dr. J.E.O. Dunwoody	Lab	9,836	25.2
			J.J. Collier	L	7,504	19.2
					11,878	30.4

[Elevation to the Peerage—Viscount Amory]

Election	Electors	T'out	Candidate	Party	Votes	%
960 (16/11)	48,956	68.4	R.J. Maxwell-Hyslop	C	15,308	45.7
			J.J. Collier	L	12,268	36.7
			R.F.H. Dobson	Lab	5,895	17.6
					3,040	9.0
964	50,854	80.1	R.J. Maxwell-Hyslop	C	19,280	47.3
			J.J. Collier	L	14,053	34.5
			J.T. Mitchard	Lab	7,397	18.2
					5,227	12.8
966	51,907	80.7	R.J. Maxwell-Hyslop	C	20,351	48.6
			F.K. Taylor	Lab	11,325	27.0
			F.J. Suter	L	10,225	24.4
					9,026	21.6
970	58,081	77.0	R.J. Maxwell-Hyslop	C	24,689	55.2
			R. Hewetson	Lab	10,823	24.2
			F.J. Suter	L	9,229	20.6
					13,866	31.0

Election	Electors	T'out	Candidate	Party	Votes	%
1950	45,036	83.2	†Hon. G. Lambert	NL & C	19,128	51.1
			Mrs. E. Rashleigh	L	9,589	25.6
			T.B.H. Chappell	Lab	8,735	23.3
					9,539	25.5
1951	45,770*	76.4	Hon. G. Lambert	NL & C	23,162	66.2
			G.R. Sargeant	Lab	11,812	33.8
					11,350	32.4
1955	44,712	69.2	Hon. G. Lambert	NL & C	20,124	65.1
			L. Lamb	Lab	10,812	34.9
					9,312	30.2

[Succession to the Peerage—Viscount Lambert]

Election	Electors	T'out	Candidate	Party	Votes	%
1958	43,790	80.6	M.R. Bonham Carter	L	13,408	38.0
(27/3)			A.H.F. Royle	NL & C	13,189	37.4
			L. Lamb	Lab	8,697	24.6
					219	0.6
1959	44,029	86.2	P.B. Browne	C	17,283	45.6
			M.R. Bonham Carter	L	15,018	39.6
			R.F.H. Dobson	Lab	5,633	14.8
					2,265	6.0
1964	44,176	85.1	P.M. Mills	C	16,899	45.0
			M.R. Bonham Carter	L	14,831	39.4
			Dr. D.A.L. Owen	Lab	5,867	15.6
					2,068	5.6
1966	44,375	85.8	P.M. Mills	C	17,912	47.0
			L.A. Lacey	L	14,260	37.5
			A.F. Paton	Lab	5,891	15.5
					3,652	9.5
1970	48,706	81.1	P.M. Mills	C	21,328	54.0
			L.A. Lacey	L	11,455	29.0
			T.K. Marston	Lab	6,695	17.0
					9,873	25.0

DEVON, TOTNES [358]

lection	Electors	T'out	Candidate	Party	Votes	%
950	62,972	84.6	†R.H. Rayner	C	26,104	49.0
			D.G. Widdicombe	Lab	15,767	29.6
			Dr. H.E. Desch	L	10,974	20.6
			E.P. Tapscott	Com	423*	0.8
					10,337	19.4
951	63,066	82.8	R.H. Rayner	C	28,005	53.6
			C.A. O'Donnell	Lab	16,409	31.4
			Dr. H.E. Desch	L	7,835	15.0
					11,596	22.2
955	62,710	80.8	R.L. Mawby	C	26,381	52.1
			D.J.P. Mann	Lab	14,787	29.2
			A.C. Shobbrook	L	9,471	18.7
					11,594	22.9
959	63,071	80.5	R.L. Mawby	C	26,925	53.1
			T.J.B. Heelas	Lab	13,116	25.8
			T.C. Jones	L	10,719	21.1
					13,809	27.3
964	66,292	78.8	R.L. Mawby	C	25,417	48.7
			R.C.J. Scott	Lab	14,542	27.8
			E.B. Taylor	L	12,297	23.5
					10,875	20.9
966	67,466	79.4	R.L. Mawby	C	25,623	47.9
			B. Smethurst	Lab	16,900	31.5
			P.A. Tyler	L	11,066	20.6
					8,723	16.4
970	74,644	77.0	R.L. Mawby	C	31,519	54.8
			R. Blank	Lab	16,429	28.6
			D.C. Penhaligon	L	9,515	16.6
					15,090	26.2

Election	Electors	T'out	Candidate	Party	Votes	%
1950	41,591	85.0	R.F. Crouch	C	15,324	43.:
			†C.F. Byers	L	15,227	43.
			J.R.T. Griffith	Lab	4,807	13.(
					97	0.:
1951	42,815	86.4	R.F. Crouch	C	17,392	47.(
			C.F. Byers	L	16,645	45.(
			J.R.T. Griffith	Lab	2,946*	8.(
					747	2.(
1955	44,142	82.2	R.F. Crouch	C	18,906	52.
			Hon. M. Portman	L	11,747	32.(
			H.J. Dutfield	Lab	5,633	15.(
					7,159	19.(
[Death]						
1957 (27/6)	45,346	75.8	R.H. Glyn	C	15,513	45.
			J.A. Emlyn-Jones	L	12,411	36.
			H.J. Dutfield	Lab	6,278	18.:
			H.C. Wright	Ind	170*	0.(
					3,102	9.(
1959	46,844	82.0	R.H. Glyn	C	20,255	52.(
			J.A. Emlyn-Jones	L	11,604	30.:
			H.J. Dutfield	Lab	6,548	17.(
					8,651	22.(
1964	50,065	81.7	Sir R.H. Glyn, Bt.	C	19,898	48.(
			R.A. Lamb	L	14,768	36.(
			J.F. Armstrong	Lab	6,253	15.:
					5,130	12.(
1966	51,885	82.1	Sir R.H. Glyn, Bt.	C	20,520	48.:
			R.A. Lamb	L	15,005	35.:
			J.D. Rutland	Lab	7,090	16.(
					5,515	13.(
1970	62,614	78.6	D.P. James	C	28,471	57.(
			P.G. Watkins	L	12,095	24.(
			H.R. White	Lab	8,626	17.(
					16,376	33.:

lection	Electors	T'out	Candidate	Party	Votes	%
950	52,117	84.4	†Viscount Hinchingbrooke	C	20,014	45.5
			F.N. Stacey	Lab	17,471	39.7
			W.T.R. Rawson	L	6,489	14.8
					2,543	5.8
951	53,501	84.0	Viscount Hinchingbrooke	C	21,679	48.3
			F.N. Stacey	Lab	18,244	40.6
			W.E. Ward	L	5,005*	11.1
					3,435	7.7
955	55,039	79.3	Viscount Hinchingbrooke	C (Ind C) (C)	22,119	50.7
			F.N. Stacey	Lab	16,702	38.3
			G.M. Goode	L	4,798*	11.0
					5,417	12.4
959	56,196	78.8	Viscount Hinchingbrooke	C	22,050	49.8
			C.F. Ascher	Lab	15,357	34.7
			L.I. Norbury-Williams	L	6,887	15.5
					6,693	15.1

[Succession to the Peerage—Earl of Sandwich]

962	58,574	70.2	N.G. Barnett	Lab	13,783	33.5
22/11)			A.E.U. Maude	C	13,079	31.8
			L.I. Norbury-Williams	L	8,910	21.7
			Sir P.K. Debenham, Bt.	Ind C	5,057*	12.3
			P.O. Burn	Ind Ser	181*	0.4
			M. Fudge	Ind Ser	82*	0.2
			J.C. O'Connor	Ind Ser	45*	0.1
					704	1.7
964	59,963	81.0	E.M. King	C	21,209	43.7
			N.G. Barnett	Lab	20,274	41.7
			Earl of Mayo	L	7,100	14.6
					935	2.0
966	60,593	82.5	E.M. King	C	22,997	46.0
			F.W. Morgan	Lab	21,120	42.3
			G.M. Goode	L	5,862*	11.7
					1,877	3.7
970	66,953	79.1	E.M. King	C	27,580	52.1
			R.G. May	Lab	20,716	39.1
			K.N. Searby	L	4,680*	8.8
					6,864	13.0

Note:—

1962: Debenham was opposed to Britain entering the Common Market and he was supported by the Earl of Sandwich and the Beaverbrook press.

Election	Electors	T'out	Candidate	Party	Votes	%
1950	43,202	84.0	†K.S.D.W. Digby	C	18,771	51.8
			C.J. Kane	Lab	11,967	33.0
			C.J.G. Cameron	L	5,531	15.2
					6,804	18.8
1951	43,900	82.1	K.S.D.W. Digby	C	21,739	60.3
			C.J. Kane	Lab	14,308	39.7
					7,431	20.6
1955	44,026	80.1	K.S.D.W. Digby	C	21,007	59.6
			L.W. King	Lab	14,244	40.4
					6,763	19.2
1959	44,109	81.9	K.S.D.W. Digby	C	19,747	54.7
			L.W. King	Lab	11,536	31.9
			J.H. Goodden	L	4,850	13.4
					8,211	22.8
1964	44,951	81.7	K.S.D.W. Digby	C	17,841	48.6
			L.W. King	Lab	10,631	29.0
			M.A. Pinney	L	8,242	22.4
					7,210	19.6
1966	45,452	81.7	K.S.D.W. Digby	C	17,709	47.6
			F.D. Shirreff	Lab	11,757	31.7
			M.A. Pinney	L	7,676	20.7
					5,952	15.9
1970	50,651	76.8	K.S.D.W. Digby	C	21,081	54.2
			G. Sakwa	Lab	10,526	27.0
			A.N.W. Percival	L	7,314	18.8
					10,555	27.2

Election	Electors	T'out	Candidate	Party	Votes	%
1950	50,011	86.5	†Rt. Hon. E.H.J.N. Dalton	Lab	25,039	57.9
			Viscount Lambton	C	13,669	31.6
			L.W. Malby	L	4,527*	10.5
					11,370	26.3
1951	50,280	85.1	Rt. Hon. E.H.J.N. Dalton	Lab	25,881	60.5
			B.L. Butcher	C	16,895	39.5
					8,986	21.0
1955	49,051*	77.0	Rt. Hon. E.H.J.N. Dalton	Lab	21,804	57.7
			R.D.M. Youngson	C	15,959	42.3
					5,845	15.4
1959	48,865	80.8	H.J. Boyden	Lab	21,706	55.0
			N.W. Murray	C	13,377	33.9
			J.G. Pease	L	4,377*	11.1
					8,329	21.1
1964	47,338	76.2	H.J. Boyden	Lab	22,310	61.8
			J.V. Ropner	C	13,782	38.2
					8,528	23.6
1966	46,256	73.4	H.J. Boyden	Lab	22,015	64.8
			J.V. Ropner	C	11,936	35.2
					10,079	29.6
1970	49,291	71.1	H.J. Boyden	Lab	21,257	60.7
			T.J. Wiseman	C	13,769	39.3
					7,488	21.4

DURHAM, BLAYDON [363]

Election	Electors	T'out	Candidate	Party	Votes	%
1950	47,010	87.5	†Rt. Hon. W. Whiteley	Lab	28,343	68.9
			L.F. Lawson	C	12,772	31.1
					15,571	37.8
1951	47,445	87.6	Rt. Hon. W. Whiteley	Lab	28,337	68.2
			C.P.L. Satchwell	C	13,223	31.8
					15,114	36.4
1955	47,138	80.7	Rt. Hon. W. Whiteley	Lab	25,273	66.5
			J.M. Reay-Smith	C	12,750	33.5
					12,523	33.0
[Death]						
1956	47,581	56.5	R.E. Woof	Lab	18,791	69.9
(2/2)			J.M. Reay-Smith	C	8,077	30.1
					10,714	39.8
1959	47,854	82.9	R.E. Woof	Lab	25,969	65.4
			G.W. Iredell	C	13,719	34.6
					12,250	30.8
1964	48,566	80.0	R.E. Woof	Lab	25,926	66.7
			N.C. Bailey	C	12,932	33.3
					12,994	33.4
1966	49,682	77.4	R.E. Woof	Lab	26,629	69.2
			B. Bligh	C	11,849	30.8
					14,780	38.4
1970	54,804	72.3	R.E. Woof	Lab	25,724	64.9
			N.H. D'Aguiar	C	13,926	35.1
					11,798	29.8

Election	Electors	T'out	Candidate	Party	Votes	%
1950	52,393	87.3	P. Bartley	Lab	35,348	77.3
			H.J.M. Millican	C	10,379	22.7
					24,969	54.6
1951	53,260	86.6	P. Bartley	Lab	35,511	77.0
			H.J.M. Millican	C	10,632	23.0
					24,879	54.0
1955	53,247	79.6	P. Bartley	Lab	32,323	76.3
			D.A. Wright	C	10,047	23.7
					22,276	52.6
[Death]						
1956 (27/9)	53,191	64.9	N. Pentland	Lab	27,912	80.8
			W. Rees-Mogg	C	6,625	19.2
					21,287	61.6
1959	53,884	83.0	N. Pentland	Lab	33,901	75.8
			W. Rees-Mogg	C	10,838	24.2
					23,063	51.6
1964	55,076	79.4	N. Pentland	Lab	32,895	75.2
			J.M. Gorst	C	10,851	24.8
					22,044	50.4
1966	56,345	74.9	N. Pentland	Lab	32,467	77.0
			C.M.K. Taylor	C	9,720	23.0
					22,747	54.0
1970	63,829	73.7	N. Pentland	Lab	33,694	71.6
			D. Ramshaw	C	13,363	28.4
					20,331	43.2

Election	Electors	T'out	Candidate	Party	Votes	%
1950	60,181	86.8	†J.E. Glanville	Lab	34,907	66.8
			P.C. Goodhart	C	12,634	24.2
			N. Dees	L	4,721*	9.0
					22,273	42.6
1951	60,622	85.1	J.E. Glanville	Lab	35,705	69.2
			G.F.H. Walker	C	15,861	30.8
					19,844	38.4
1955	59,607	77.5	W. Stones	Lab	30,979	67.0
			W.F. Montgomery	C	15,224	33.0
					15,755	34.0
1959	59,206	81.7	W. Stones	Lab	32,307	66.8
			D.A. Orde	C	16,037	33.2
					16,270	33.6
1964	56,792	76.7	W. Stones	Lab	29,676	68.1
			D.W. Stokoe	C	13,901	31.9
					15,775	36.2
1966	55,246	73.5	D.J. Watkins	Lab	29,753	73.3
			R.W.G. Sanderson	C	10,858	26.7
					18,895	46.6
1970	58,246	70.2	D.J. Watkins	Lab	28,985	70.9
			N.G. Trotter	C	11,914	29.1
					17,071	41.8

DURHAM, DURHAM [366]

Election	Electors	T'out	Candidate	Party	Votes	%
1950	60,814	87.0	†C.F. Grey	Lab	36,024	68.1
			H.C.R. Laslett	C	16,903	31.9
					19,121	36.2
1951	61,611	86.1	C.F. Grey	Lab	35,597	67.1
			R.J. Fisher	C	17,447	32.9
					18,150	34.2
1955	61,729	79.5	C.F. Grey	Lab	32,412	66.1
			C.P. MacCarthy	C	16,640	33.9
					15,772	32.2
1959	62,192	81.8	C.F. Grey	Lab	33,795	66.4
			C.P. MacCarthy	C	17,106	33.6
					16,689	32.8
1964	60,984	78.8	C.F. Grey	Lab	32,818	68.3
			J.M. Whittaker	C	15,209	31.7
					17,609	36.6
1966	61,021	74.7	C.F. Grey	Lab	32,200	70.6
			R.M. Yorke	C	13,383	29.4
					18,817	41.2
1970	68,816	73.3	W.M. Hughes	Lab	33,766	66.9
			E. Greenwood	C	16,707	33.1
					17,059	33.8

Election	Electors	T'out	Candidate	Party	Votes	%
1950	53,984	87.7	†Rt. Hon. E. Shinwell	Lab	38,367	81.0
			C.A. Macfarlane	C	8,972	19.0
					29,395	62.0
1951	54,096	86.7	Rt. Hon. E. Shinwell	Lab	37,899	80.8
			G.W. Rossiter	C	9,025	19.2
					28,874	61.6
1955	54,748	79.4	Rt. Hon. E. Shinwell	Lab	34,352	79.1
			G.W. Rossiter	C	9,095	20.9
					25,257	58.2
1959	56,690	80.8	Rt. Hon. E. Shinwell	Lab	36,552	79.8
			G.W. Rossiter	C	9,259	20.2
					27,293	59.6
1964	56,229	75.2	Rt. Hon. E. Shinwell	Lab	34,028	80.4
			G.W. Rossiter	C	8,270	19.6
					25,758	60.8
1966	55,923	70.5	Rt. Hon. E. Shinwell	Lab	32,097	81.4
			W.M. Spicer	C	7,350	18.6
					24,747	62.8
1970	60,290	69.5	J.D. Dormand	Lab	33,418	79.8
			W.M. Spicer	C	8,457	20.2
					24,961	59.6

Election	Electors	T'out	Candidate	Party	Votes	%
1950	53,571	87.2	†W.R. Blyton	Lab	36,044	77.1
			Mrs. B. Bolam	C	10,682	22.9
					25,362	54.2
1951	57,454	86.6	W.R. Blyton	Lab	37,718	75.8
			Mrs. B. Bolam	C	12,042	24.2
					25,676	51.6
1955	55,166*	79.5	W.R. Blyton	Lab	33,375	76.1
			T.E.S. Egerton	C	10,476	23.9
					22,899	52.2
1959	56,780	83.4	W.R. Blyton	Lab	35,960	75.9
			A.R.C. Arbuthnot	C	11,398	24.1
					24,562	51.8
1964	55,897	78.7	T.W. Urwin	Lab	32,914	74.8
			Dr. P.C. Price	C	11,076	25.2
					21,838	49.6
1966	56,001	73.9	T.W. Urwin	Lab	32,067	77.5
			F.H.M. Craig-Cooper	C	9,304	22.5
					22,763	55.0
1970	62,501	71.7	T.W. Urwin	Lab	32,888	73.4
			F.H.M. Craig-Cooper	C	11,914	26.6
					20,974	46.8

Election	Electors	T'out	Candidate	Party	Votes	%
1950	64,700	82.8	†E. Fernyhough	Lab	33,751	63.0
			J.L. Cox	C	16,895	31.5
			E.G.S. Chalkley	L	2,940*	5.5
					16,856	31.5
1951	65,252*	84.6	E. Fernyhough	Lab (Ind Lab) (Lab)	35,963	65.2
			J.L. Cox	C	19,217	34.8
					16,746	30.4

This constituency was divided in 1955.

Election	Electors	T'out	Candidate	Party	Votes	%
950	51,563	86.5	†J.D. Murray	Lab	31,084	69.7
			J. Quigley	C	13,530	30.3
					17,554	39.4
951	52,084	85.1	J.D. Murray	Lab	30,417	68.7
			J. Quigley	C	13,885	31.3
					16,532	37.4
955	50,885	79.1	J.W. Ainsley	Lab	27,116	67.4
			T.T. Hubble	C	13,110	32.6
					14,006	34.8
959	50,629	81.4	J.W. Ainsley	Lab	28,064	68.1
			Mrs. O. Sinclair	C	13,172	31.9
					14,892	36.2
964	47,812	78.0	E. Armstrong	Lab	26,006	69.7
			K.L. Ellis	C	11,280	30.3
					14,726	39.4
966	46,789	73.4	E. Armstrong	Lab	25,260	73.6
			Hon. C.N.G. MacAndrew	C	9,070	26.4
					16,190	47.2
970	47,771	72.9	E. Armstrong	Lab	24,245	69.6
			A.E. Page	C	10,590	30.4
					13,655	39.2

Election	Electors	T'out	Candidate	Party	Votes	%
1950	51,441	87.0	J. Slater	Lab	27,946	62.5
			J.E.S. Walford	C	16,782	37.5
					11,164	25.0
1951	52,426	86.4	J. Slater	Lab	28,219	62.3
			E.H. Harrison	C	17,095	37.7
					11,124	24.6
1955	57,031*	79.9	J. Slater	Lab	27,221	59.7
			D.F-M. Appleby	C	18,368	40.3
					8,853	19.4
1959	63,535	82.5	J. Slater	Lab	30,642	58.5
			D.F-M. Appleby	C	21,771	41.5
					8,871	17.0
1964	66,886	79.5	J. Slater	Lab	32,273	60.7
			C.F. Thring	C	20,931	39.3
					11,342	21.4
1966	69,287	76.0	J. Slater	Lab	34,058	64.7
			C.F. Thring	C	18,620	35.3
					15,438	29.4
1970	83,771	72.7	D. Reed	Lab	36,867	60.5
			A.A. Beck	C	24,036	39.5
					12,831	21.0

Election	Electors	T'out	Candidate	Party	Votes	%
1950	59,209	79.6	B.R. Braine	C	23,803	50.5
			A.E. Oram	Lab/Co-op	19,437	41.3
			S. Hayden	L	3,872*	8.2
					4,366	9.2
1951	61,652	77.1	B.R. Braine	C	26,936	56.6
			B.R. Clapham	Lab/Co-op	20,613	43.4
					6,323	13.2
1955	58,872**	75.5	R.B.F.S. Body	C	24,327	54.7
			B.R. Clapham	Lab/Co-op	20,121	45.3
					4,206	9.4
1959	78,328	80.4	E.L. Gardner	C	29,224	46.5
			Mrs. R.A. Smythe	Lab/Co-op	24,402	38.7
			P.M.T. Sheldon-Williams	L	9,347	14.8
					4,822	7.8
1964	96,762	82.5	E.L. Gardner	C	35,347	44.3
			Mrs. R.A. Smythe	Lab/Co-op	33,755	42.3
			P.M.T. Sheldon-Williams	L	10,706	13.4
					1,592	2.0
1966	102,198	84.1	E. Moonman	Lab	40,013	46.6
			E.L. Gardner	C	38,371	44.6
			L.R. Wernick	L	7,587*	8.8
					1,642	2.0
1970	123,121	74.3	R.A. McCrindle	C	47,719	52.2
			E. Moonman	Lab	43,765	47.8
					3,954	4.4

Election	Electors	T'out	Candidate	Party	Votes	%
1950	61,930	84.3	H. Ashton	C	28,541	54.7
			†E.R. Millington	Lab	23,682	45.3
					4,859	9.4
1951	63,433	83.3	H. Ashton	C	29,069	55.0
			J. Haworth	Lab	23,775	45.0
					5,294	10.0
1955	55,920**	81.8	H. Ashton	C	25,450	55.6
			B.F.C. Floud	Lab	20,301	44.4
					5,149	11.2
1959	61,630	81.3	Sir H. Ashton	C	29,992	59.8
			B.R. Clapham	Lab	20,124	40.2
					9,868	19.6
1964	70,158	82.8	N.A.F. St. John-Stevas	C	27,849	48.0
			E.G. Lawrence	Lab	20,816	35.8
			W.P. Longhurst	L	9,414	16.2
					7,033	12.2
1966	73,535	82.5	N.A.F. St. John-Stevas	C	28,600	47.1
			C. George	Lab	23,625	39.0
			W.P. Longhurst	L	8,419	13.9
					4,975	8.1
1970	88,227	75.7	N.A.F. St. John-Stevas	C	36,821	55.2
			G. Kennedy	Lab	23,780	35.6
			Miss J. Hunt	L	5,811*	8.7
			J.D. Steel	Ind	355*	0.5
					13,041	19.6

Note:—

1970: Steel sought election as an 'Independent and Animal Dignity' candidate. He opposed factory farming and advocated free-range farming.

Election	Electors	T'out	Candidate	Party	Votes	%
1955	46,583	79.7	J.A. Biggs-Davison	C (Ind C) (C)	19,503	52.5
			D. Clark	Lab/Co-op	17,628	47.5
					1,875	5.0
1959	50,213	82.2	J.A. Biggs-Davison	C	23,422	56.7
			A.S. Harman	Lab	17,860	43.3
					5,562	13.4
1964	53,398	81.9	J.A. Biggs-Davison	C	20,699	47.3
			E. Moonman	Lab	16,978	38.8
			Miss G.C.Z. Collis	L	6,058	13.9
					3,721	8.5
1966	54,443	81.3	J.A. Biggs-Davison	C	20,906	47.3
			E.P. Deakins	Lab	18,338	41.4
			Miss G.C.Z. Collis	L	5,007*	11.3
					2,568	5.9
1970	60,976	72.9	J.A. Biggs-Davison	C	26,454	59.5
			W.J. Sheaff	Lab	17,972	40.5
					8,482	19.0

Election	Electors	T'out	Candidate	Party	Votes	%
1950	53,048	86.8	C.J.M. Alport	C	21,403	46.5
			†C.G.P. Smith	Lab	20,472	44.5
			D. Goldblatt	L	4,157*	9.0
					931	2.0
1951	54,551	84.8	C.J.M. Alport	C	25,063	54.2
			Mrs. X.N. Field	Lab	21,217	45.8
					3,846	8.4
1955	55,527	80.5	C.J.M. Alport	C	24,796	55.5
			N.R. Thomas	Lab/Co-op	19,898	44.5
					4,898	11.0
1959	57,776*	82.4	C.J.M. Alport	C	24,592	51.6
			Mrs. J.I. Edmondson	Lab	17,096	35.9
			P.M. Linfoot	L	5,942*	12.5
					7,496	15.7

[Resignation on appointment as United Kingdom High Commissioner in the Federation of Rhodesia and Nyasaland and elevation to a Life Peerage—Lord Alport]

Election	Electors	T'out	Candidate	Party	Votes	%
1961 (16/3)	58,448	64.9	P.A.F. Buck	C	17,891	47.2
			J.W. Fear	Lab	12,547	33.1
			H.L. Fry	L	7,487	19.7
					5,344	14.1
1964	61,742	82.1	P.A.F. Buck	C	23,319	46.1
			C.C.P. Williams	Lab	19,780	39.0
			E.W. Rodnight	L	7,566	14.9
					3,539	7.1
1966	64,843	82.3	P.A.F. Buck	C	24,320	45.6
			M.H. Meacher	Lab	23,305	43.7
			P.S. Watts	L	5,714*	10.7
					1,015	1.9
1970	74,991	77.5	P.A.F. Buck	C	30,562	52.5
			J.G. Bartlett	Lab	20,325	35.0
			P.S. Watts	L	7,248*	12.5
					10,237	17.5

election	Electors	T'out	Candidate	Party	Votes	%
950	57,102	86.6	C.N.B. Davies	C	24,292	49.2
			†Mrs. E.L. Manning	Lab	20,385	41.2
			P.E. Lewis	L	4,755*	9.6
					3,907	8.0
951	58,764	85.1	G.B. Finlay	C	27,392	54.8
			Mrs. E.L. Manning	Lab	22,598	45.2
					4,794	9.6
955	68,184	82.3	G.B. Finlay	C	26,065	46.4
			Mrs. E.L. Manning	Lab	22,542	40.2
			L.T.J. Arlott	L	7,528	13.4
					3,523	6.2
959	83,647	84.3	G.B. Finlay	C	31,507	44.7
			D.F.W. Ford	Lab/Co-op	27,114	38.4
			L.T.J. Arlott	L	11,913	16.9
					4,393	6.3
964	94,655	83.3	A.S. Newens	Lab	34,991	44.4
			G.B. Finlay	C	31,753	40.3
			Miss B.N. Seear	L	12,093	15.3
					3,238	4.1
966	97,645	82.4	A.S. Newens	Lab	38,914	48.4
			E.M. Ogden	C	31,406	39.0
			D.A. McKie	L	10,162	12.6
					7,508	9.4
970	115,409	73.4	N.B. Tebbit	C	43,615	51.5
			A.S. Newens	Lab	41,040	48.5
					2,575	3.0

Election	Electors	T'out	Candidate	Party	Votes	%
1950	55,052	81.9	†Sir J.S. Holmes	NL & C	22,814	50.
			M. Janis	Lab	16,756	37.
			L. Train	L	5,536*	12.
					6,058	13.
1951	56,381	78.8	Sir J.S. Holmes	NL & C	26,169	58.
			M. Janis	Lab	18,244	41.
					7,925	17.

[Elevation to the Peerage—Lord Dovercourt]

Election	Electors	T'out	Candidate	Party	Votes	%
1954 (11/2)	56,225	58.8	J.E. Ridsdale	NL & C	19,532	59.
			Miss S.V.T.B. Catlin	Lab	13,535	40.
					5,997	18.
1955	56,003	75.6	J.E. Ridsdale	NL & C	23,889	56.
			Miss S.V.T.B. Catlin	Lab	14,425	34.
			W.I. Akst	L	4,010*	9.
					9,464	22.
1959	58,194	76.5	J.E. Ridsdale	NL & C	23,653	53.
			W.O.J. Robinson	Lab	11,588	26.
			T.E. Dale	L	5,507*	12.
			L.F. Rose	Ind	3,744*	8.
					12,065	27.
1964	66,350	75.1	J.E. Ridsdale	NL & C	25,102	50.
			D.J. Winnick	Lab	14,877	29.
			T.E. Dale	L	9,824	19.
					10,225	20.
1966	70,599	74.4	J.E. Ridsdale	NL & C (C)	24,975	47.
			S.R. Hatch	Lab	18,335	34.
			T.E. Dale	L	9,219	17.
					6,640	12.
1970	82,117	74.5	J.E. Ridsdale	C	32,754	53.
			A.W. Phillips	Lab	19,923	32.
			T.E. Dale	L	8,519	13.
					12,831	20.

ection	Electors	T'out	Candidate	Party	Votes	%
50	50,220	86.2	†T.E.N. Driberg	Lab	20,567	47.6
			A.R. Moody	C	18,843	43.5
			W.D. Abernethy	L	3,859*	8.9
					1,724	4.1
51	51,282	87.4	T.E.N. Driberg	Lab	22,756	50.8
			A.R. Moody	C	22,052	49.2
					704	1.6
55	52,027	83.5	A.B.C. Harrison	C	22,002	50.6
			L. Scutts	Lab	21,452	49.4
					550	1.2
59	54,378*	83.1	A.B.C. Harrison	C	21,772	48.3
			S.G. Richards	Lab	19,532	43.2
			L.C.M. Walsh	L	3,860*	8.5
					2,240	5.1
64	57,020	83.3	A.B.C. Harrison	C	21,547	45.3
			S.G. Richards	Lab	20,016	42.2
			W.H. Jacks	L	5,924*	12.5
					1,531	3.1
66	59,616	83.3	A.B.C. Harrison	C	22,572	45.5
			B.L.H. Douglas-Mann	Lab	22,066	44.4
			W.H. Jacks	L	5,015*	10.1
					506	1.1
70	72,364	79.8	A.B.C. Harrison	C	29,229	50.6
			S.M.A. Haseler	Lab	22,957	39.7
			J.R.C. Beale	L	5,574*	9.7
					6,272	10.9

Election	Electors	T'out	Candidate	Party	Votes	%
1950	46,998	84.4	†Rt. Hon. R.A. Butler	C	19,797	49.9
			S.S. Wilson	Lab	14,908	37.6
			W.O. Smedley	L	4,963	12.5
					4,889	12.3
1951	47,836	83.1	Rt. Hon. R.A. Butler	C	20,564	51.7
			R. Groves	Lab	15,425	38.8
			W.O. Smedley	L	3,774*	9.5
					5,139	12.9
1955	47,922	79.6	Rt. Hon. R.A. Butler	C	20,671	54.2
			Rev. H.N. Horne	Lab	14,253	37.4
			Miss H.G. Carson	L	3,209*	8.4
					6,418	16.8
1959	48,477*	81.2	Rt. Hon. R.A. Butler	C	20,955	53.2
			Rev. H.N. Horne	Lab	14,173	36.0
			D.J. Ridley	L	4,245*	10.8
					6,782	17.2
1964	50,724	82.4	Rt. Hon. R.A. Butler	C	20,610	49.4
			M.D. Cornish	Lab	15,655	37.4
			F.P.D. Moore	L	5,539	13.2
					4,955	12.0

[Resignation on appointment as Master of Trinity College, Cambridge, and elevation to a Life Peerage—Lord Butler of Saffron Walden]

Election	Electors	T'out	Candidate	Party	Votes	%
1965 (23/3)	51,029	76.1	P.M. Kirk	C	18,851	48.6
			M.D. Cornish	Lab	15,358	39.5
			F.P.D. Moore	L	4,626*	11.9
					3,493	9.
1966	52,221	82.5	P.M. Kirk	C	20,441	47.5
			S.M.A. Haseler	Lab	17,176	39.8
			F.P.D. Moore	L	5,487	12.7
					3,265	7.
1970	60,019	77.3	P.M. Kirk	C	24,549	52.9
			K.T. Weetch	Lab	14,885	32.
			F.P.D. Moore	L	6,959	15.0
					9,664	20.8

lection	Electors	T'out	Candidate	Party	Votes	%
955	47,132	72.9	B.R. Braine	C	20,531	59.7
			E.W. Harby	Lab/Co-op	13,841	40.3
					6,690	19.4
959	60,316	76.5	B.R. Braine	C	28,124	61.0
			R.M. Fryer	Lab	17,991	39.0
					10,133	22.0
964	78,364	75.0	B.R. Braine	C	33,494	57.0
			A. Pearson-Clarke	Lab	25,293	43.0
					8,201	14.0
966	85,151	77.3	B.R. Braine	C	31,942	48.5
			D.W. Edwards	Lab	26,208	39.8
			Miss J.M. Arram	L	7,706*	11.7
					5,734	8.7
970	100,167	72.0	B.R. Braine	C	41,589	57.7
			D.W. Edwards	Lab	23,684	32.9
			C.H. Bohling	L	6,811*	9.4
					17,905	24.8

Election	Electors	T'out	Candidate	Party	Votes	%
1950	50,962	85.3	†H.J. Delargy	Lab	22,893	52.
			A.M.S. Neave	C	13,306	30.
			†L.J. Solley	Ind Lab	4,250*	9.8
			W.H.H. Siddons	L	3,010*	6.9
					9,587	22.
1951	53,157	82.8	H.J. Delargy	Lab	28,851	65.8
			G.W. Lagden	C	15,166	34.9
					13,685	31.0
1955	63,030	75.2	H.J. Delargy	Lab	31,375	66.2
			G.A. Petty	C	16,046	33.8
					15,329	32.4
1959	67,054	78.2	H.J. Delargy	Lab	32,270	61.8
			W.E. McNamara	C	20,188	38.8
					12,082	23.0
1964	71,519	74.2	H.J. Delargy	Lab	30,372	57.3
			R.A. McCrindle	C	14,615	27.5
			A.N.H. Blackburn	L	8,094	15.2
					15,757	29.8
1966	72,502	72.7	H.J. Delargy	Lab	31,998	60.7
			C.J. Hodgson	C	14,094	26.7
			J.C. Moran	L	6,648	12.6
					17,904	34.0
1970	84,259	65.7	H.J. Delargy	Lab	30,874	55.7
			G.F.J. Bright	C	19,486	35.2
			Miss K.J. Fleetwood	L	5,024*	9.1
					11,388	20.5

Note:—

1950: Solley was a member of the Labour Independent Group.

lection	Electors	T'out	Candidate	Party	Votes	%
950	56,763	81.3	†Rt. Hon. W.S. Morrison	C	23,942	52.0
			R.M. Bennett	Lab	15,660	33.9
			N.W. Gillett	L	6,102	13.2
			Hon. W. Philipps	Com	423*	0.9
					8,282	18.1
951	58,103	78.0	Rt. Hon. W.S. Morrison	C	26,978	59.5
			A.E. Sumbler	Lab	18,353	40.5
					8,625	19.0
955	55,305**	68.3	Rt. Hon. W.S. Morrison	C	25,372	67.2
			D.C. Cox	Ind Lab	12,394	32.8
					12,978	34.4
959	58,099	76.6	Hon. N. Ridley	C	28,169	63.3
			J.M. Bowyer	Lab	16,314	36.7
					11,855	26.6
964	61,626	78.0	Hon. N. Ridley	C	24,786	51.5
			J.M. Bowyer	Lab	15,518	32.3
			A.G. de Montmorency	L	7,790	16.2
					9,268	19.2
966	63,568	74.9	Hon. N. Ridley	C	27,690	58.2
			M.G. Dalling	Lab	19,919	41.8
					7,771	16.4
970	72,980	73.9	Hon. N. Ridley	C	30,217	56.0
			H.G. Lovell	Lab	16,131	29.9
			D. Robinson	L	7,593	14.1
					14,086	26.1

ote:—

1951-   Morrison was the Speaker of the House of Commons from October 31, 1951.
1955:

Election	Electors	T'out	Candidate	Party	Votes	%
1950	57,689	86.9	C.A.R. Crosland	Lab	24,458	48.8
			B. Davidson	C	18,320	36.6
			S.V.S. Howard-Stepney	L	7,342	14.6
					6,138	12.2
1951	58,296	86.2	C.A.R. Crosland	Lab	27,808	55.3
			Mrs. M. Hickling	C	22,470	44.7
					5,338	10.6
1955	51,166**	81.7	F.V. Corfield	C	21,760	52.1
			E.S. Bishop	Lab	20,034	47.9
					1,726	4.2
1959	57,026	83.7	F.V. Corfield	C	26,168	54.8
			J. Holland	Lab	21,567	45.2
					4,601	9.6
1964	68,781	84.2	F.V. Corfield	C	26,504	45.7
			M.F.L. Cocks	Lab	22,790	39.4
			B.S. Sherriff	L	8,611	14.9
					3,714	6.3
1966	74,023	84.4	F.V. Corfield	C	28,224	45.2
			M.F.L. Cocks	Lab	26,800	42.9
			E.C. Hart	L	7,421*	11.9
					1,424	2.3
1970	87,503	78.6	F.V. Corfield	C	35,045	50.9
			M.G. Dalling	Lab	26,067	37.9
			A. Lambert	L	7,680*	11.2
					8,978	13.0

Election	Electors	T'out	Candidate	Party	Votes	%
1955	55,962	84.3	J.A. Kershaw	C	23,318	49.4
			R.W. Evely	Lab	19,375	41.1
			E.B. Ayliffe	L	4,489*	9.5
					3,943	8.3
1959	57,220	85.2	J.A. Kershaw	C	23,448	48.1
			A.T. Evans	Lab	18,336	37.6
			C.J. McNair	L	6,988	14.3
					5,112	10.5
1964	57,906*	85.4	J.A. Kershaw	C	21,802	44.1
			D.V. Hunt	Lab	18,889	38.2
			I.P. Crawford	L	8,747	17.7
					2,913	5.9
1966	58,779	85.8	J.A. Kershaw	C	21,804	43.3
			T.M. Cox	Lab	20,259	40.1
			J.V. Smith	L	8,397	16.6
					1,545	3.2
1970	66,072	80.3	J.A. Kershaw	C	27,089	51.1
			R.D. Wheatley	Lab	19,158	36.1
			D.M. Davies	L	6,799	12.8
					7,931	15.0

Election	Electors	T'out	Candidate	Party	Votes	%
1950	67,010	85.4	W.R.D. Perkins	C	24,874	43.
			†B.T. Parkin	Lab	24,846	43.
			Mrs. M. MacAlpine	L	7,518	13.
					28	0.
1951	68,287*	86.0	W.R.D. Perkins	C	30,140	51.
			B.T. Parkin	Lab	28,558	48.
					1,582	2.

This constituency was divided in 1955.

lection	Electors	T'out	Candidate	Party	Votes	%
950	50,513	82.3	†M.P. Price	Lab	22,765	54.8
			G.F. Boston	C	13,664	32.9
			Dr. H.B. Houldsworth	L	5,125*	12.3
					9,101	21.9
951	51,020*	82.3	M.P. Price	Lab	24,334	58.0
			A. Russell	C	17,655	42.0
					6,679	16.0
955	51,772	78.6	M.P. Price	Lab	22,366	54.9
			B.J.Y. Williams	C	18,346	45.1
					4,020	9.8
959	54,202	80.8	C.W. Loughlin	Lab	21,634	49.4
			Miss O.K.L. Lloyd-Baker	C	16,223	37.1
			E.J. Radley	L	5,921	13.5
					5,411	12.3
964	56,407	79.6	C.W. Loughlin	Lab	22,420	49.9
			D. St. P. Barnard	C	15,300	34.1
			R.A. Cook	L	7,191	16.0
					7,120	15.8
966	57,443	78.0	C.W. Loughlin	Lab	23,181	51.8
			S.H.A.F. Hopkins	C	15,476	34.5
			K.G. Harvey	L	6,137	13.7
					7,705	17.3
970	63,599	77.2	C.W. Loughlin	Lab	22,637	46.1
			S.H.A.F. Hopkins	C	21,530	43.9
			Dr. J.A. Svendsen	L	4,932*	10.0
					1,107	2.2

Election	Electors	T'out	Candidate	Party	Votes	%
1950	50,991	79.7	†Rt. Hon. O. Lyttelton	C	21,238	52.2
			N.F. Hidden	Lab	15,066	37.1
			J.H. Goodden	L	4,355*	10.7
					6,172	15.1
1951	53,123	77.8	Rt. Hon. O. Lyttelton	C	24,951	60.3
			R.N. Hales	Lab	16,402	39.7
					8,549	20.6

[Elevation to the Peerage—Viscount Chandos]

Election	Electors	T'out	Candidate	Party	Votes	%
1954	54,231	58.7	Sir E. Errington	C	19,108	60.1
(28/10)			W. Cuthbertson	Lab	12,701	39.9
					6,407	20.2
1955	54,209	73.9	Sir E. Errington	C	22,701	56.6
			J.D. Richards	Lab	13,129	32.8
			Miss E. Lakeman	L	4,232*	10.6
					9,572	23.8
1959	56,820	75.9	Sir E. Errington	C	25,161	58.3
			R.E. Brooks	Lab	12,270	28.8
			Miss E. Lakeman	L	5,679	13.2
					12,891	29.8
1964	66,120	75.0	Sir E. Errington, Bt.	C	25,797	52.0
			Mrs. E.K. Collard	Lab	13,718	27.7
			G.E. Owen	L	10,066	20.3
					12,079	24.3
1966	69,612	75.4	Sir E. Errington, Bt.	C	25,672	48.8
			D.H. Silvester	Lab	16,776	32.0
			G.E. Owen	L	10,025	19.
					8,896	16.9
1970	84,252	71.1	J.M.G. Critchley	C	33,447	55.8
			R.T. Bogg	Lab	18,916	31.0
			P. Gibbons	L	7,551	12.0
					14,531	24.3

Election	Electors	T'out	Candidate	Party	Votes	%
1950	57,099	79.5	†P.W. Donner	C	25,151	55.4
			Mrs. M. Clark	Lab	20,257	44.6
					4,894	10.8
1951	58,385	79.9	P.W. Donner	C	26,045	55.9
			A.E. Carr	Lab	20,580	44.1
					5,465	11.8
1955	57,025**	76.6	D.K. Freeth	C	24,973	57.2
			W. Royle	Lab	18,683	42.8
					6,290	14.4
1959	60,979	79.6	D.K. Freeth	C	25,314	52.2
			S.G. Conbeer	Lab	14,070	29.0
			Dr. L.G. Housden	L	9,126	18.8
					11,244	23.2
1964	68,698	78.1	D.B. Mitchell	C	26,466	49.3
			B. Tilley	Lab	18,490	34.5
			B.E. Goldstone	L	8,708	16.2
					7,976	14.8
1966	72,397	78.6	D.B. Mitchell	C	26,076	45.9
			A.J. Kazantzis	Lab	22,417	39.4
			J.W. Matthew	L	8,379	14.7
					3,659	6.5
1970	91,948	75.0	D.B. Mitchell	C	35,138	50.9
			D.V. Carter	Lab	25,664	37.2
			R.A. Musselwhite	L	8,183*	11.9
					9,474	13.7

Election	Electors	T'out	Candidate	Party	Votes	%
1955	48,929	81.5	D.E.C. Price	C	20,215	50
			J.E. Haire	Lab	19,670	49
					545	1
1959	55,215	84.5	D.E.C. Price	C	24,949	53
			C.J.S. Rowland	Lab	21,693	46
					3,256	7
1964	61,334	83.9	D.E.C. Price	C	23,429	45
			J.S. Boswell	Lab	21,341	41
			J.F. Rice	L	6,685	13
					2,088	4
1966	63,992	83.7	D.E.C. Price	C	24,337	45
			J.A.A. Evans	Lab	23,636	44
			J.F. Rice	L	5,617*	10
					701	1
1970	75,586	78.6	D.E.C. Price	C	30,300	51
			R.T.F. Flach	Lab	22,248	37
			C.J. Clayton	L	6,825*	11
					8,052	13

HAMPSHIRE, NEW FOREST [390]

ction	Electors	T'out	Candidate	Party	Votes	%
50	62,258	81.6	†O.E. Crosthwaite-Eyre	C	28,427	55.9
			A.W. White	Lab	15,986	31.5
			H.L. Fry	L	6,380	12.6
					12,441	24.4
51	63,545	77.3	O.E. Crosthwaite-Eyre	C	31,574	64.3
			A.W. White	Lab	17,537	35.7
					14,037	28.6
55	53,724**	73.2	O.E. Crosthwaite-Eyre	C	27,027	68.7
			H.J. Barnes	Lab	12,285	31.3
					14,742	37.4
59	58,958	74.0	O.E. Crosthwaite-Eyre	C	29,949	68.7
			R.C. Mitchell	Lab	13,667	31.3
					16,282	37.4
54	68,955*	75.9	Sir O.E. Crosthwaite-Eyre	C	27,884	53.3
			C.B. Kissen	Lab	12,924	24.7
			G.N.D. Locock	L	11,497	22.0
					14,960	28.6
56	71,884	74.2	Sir O.E. Crosthwaite-Eyre	C	27,292	51.2
			M.H. Jones	Lab	14,260	26.7
			G.N.D. Locock	L	11,757	22.1
					13,032	24.5

[esignation]

68 '11)	75,610	55.9	P.M.E.D. McNair-Wilson	C	28,025	66.3
			G.N.D. Locock	L	8,430	19.9
			A.G. Reynard	Lab	5,836	13.8
					19,595	46.4
70	83,356	71.9	P.M.E.D. McNair-Wilson	C	36,041	60.2
			D.M. Offenbach	Lab	13,576	22.6
			P.W.S. Johnson	L	10,322	17.2
					22,465	37.6

Election	Electors	T'out	Candidate	Party	Votes	%
1950	63,409	78.0	†Sir G.D. Jeffreys	C	27,201	54.
			Mrs. I.F. Candy	Lab.	15,472	31.
			H.H.L. Dickson	L	6,813	13.
					11,729	23.
1951	65,259	77.8	Hon. P.R. Legh	C	29,845	58.
			E.E. Preidel	Lab	15,770	31.
			H.H.L. Dickson	L	5,182*	10.
					14,075	27.
1955	50,994**	69.7	Hon. P.R. Legh	C	24,826	69.
			F.R. Mason	Lab	10,736	30.
					14,090	39.
1959	52,796	73.6	Hon. P.R. Legh	C	23,687	60.
			J.S.P. Davey	Lab	8,278	21.
			R.M. Digby	L	6,912	17.
					15,409	39.

[Succession to the Peerage—Lord Newton]

Election	Electors	T'out	Candidate	Party	Votes	%
1960 (16/11)	53,547	53.6	Miss J.M. Quennell	C	15,613	54.
			R.M. Digby	L	8,310	29.
			W. Royle	Lab	4,777	16.
					7,303	25.
1964	57,983*	75.4	Miss J.M. Quennell	C	23,603	54.
			R.M. Digby	L	11,338	25.
			Lady Wilson	Lab	8,477	19.
			Miss R.M. de Bounevialle	Loyalist	292*	0.
					12,265	28.
1966	60,404	75.7	Miss J.M. Quennell	C	23,933	52.
			R.M. Digby	L	10,931	23.
			Lady Wilson	Lab	10,874	23.
					13,002	28.
1970	69,608	72.2	Miss J.M. Quennell	C	30,414	60.
			K. Horrocks	Lab	10,307	20.
			Mrs. P. Jessel	L	7,783	15.
			R.M. Digby	Ind	1,766*	3.
					20,107	40.

Note:—

1970: Digby was the nominee of the Petersfield Independent Political Association which was formed in May 1969 by a number of former members of the local Liberal Association.

lection	Electors	T'out	Candidate	Party	Votes	%
950	65,960	84.0	P.H.B.O. Smithers	C	31,462	56.8
			L.F.S. Cornillie	Lab/Co-op	23,955	43.2
					7,507	13.6
951	67,080	83.7	P.H.B.O. Smithers	C	31,700	56.5
			E.C. Neate	Lab	24,418	43.5
					7,282	13.0
955	47,464**	76.7	P.H.B.O. Smithers	C	23,827	65.4
			J.G. Ridley	Lab	12,591	34.6
					11,236	30.8
959	48,321	76.7	P.H.B.O. Smithers	C	24,924	67.3
			Mrs. M.J. Manning	Lab	12,132	32.7
					12,792	34.6

Resignation on appointment as Secretary-General of the Council of Europe]

lection	Electors	T'out	Candidate	Party	Votes	%
964	50,313	68.7	M.C. Morgan-Giles	C	18,032	52.2
(4/5)			C.P. Seyd	Lab	11,968	34.6
			J.B.S. Edwards	L	4,567	13.2
					6,064	17.6
964	50,786	79.8	M.C. Morgan-Giles	C	21,502	53.1
			C.P. Seyd	Lab	12,495	30.8
			E.T.S. Read	L	6,510	16.1
					9,007	22.3
966	52,695	77.9	M.C. Morgan-Giles	C	21,162	51.6
			S.E. Spicer	Lab	12,485	30.4
			E.T.S. Read	L	7,390	18.0
					8,677	21.2
970	61,476	74.6	M.C. Morgan-Giles	C	25,249	55.0
			C. Perry	Lab	11,773	25.7
			J.W. Matthew	L	8,867	19.3
					13,476	29.3

Election	Electors	T'out	Candidate	Party	Votes	%
1950	44,059	80.5	†J.P.L. Thomas	C	18,314	51.
			W. Pigott	Lab	11,185	31.
			A.E. Farr	L	5,965	16.
					7,129	20.
1951	44,579	77.6	J.P.L. Thomas	C	21,204	61.
			W. Pigott	Lab	13,396	38.
					7,808	22.
1955	44,242	78.8	Rt. Hon. J.P.L. Thomas	C	18,058	51.
			H.F. Owen	L	8,658	24.
			Mrs. E.L.P. Seers	Lab	8,154	23.
					9,400	27.

[Elevation to the Peerage—Viscount Cilcennin]

Election	Electors	T'out	Candidate	Party	Votes	%
1956 (14/2)	44,529	61.5	J.D. Gibson-Watt	C	12,129	44.
			H.F. Owen	L	9,979	36.
			B.C. Stanley	Lab	5,277	19.
					2,150	7.
1959	45,340	79.5	J.D. Gibson-Watt	C	17,763	49.
			R. Day	L	10,185	28.
			J.W. Wardle	Lab	8,097	22.
					7,578	20.
1964	49,462	79.1	J.D. Gibson-Watt	C	17,780	45.
			T.J.H. Bishop	Lab	12,020	30.
			K.S. Vaus	L	9,322	23.
					5,760	14.
1966	50,853	77.3	J.D. Gibson-Watt	C	17,529	44.
			M.K. Prendergast	Lab	14,782	37.
			K.S. Vaus	L	6,996	17.
					2,747	7.
1970	56,363	73.4	J.D. Gibson-Watt	C	22,011	53.
			G.D. Purnell	Lab	14,410	34.
			T.R. Crowther	L	4,953*	12.
					7,601	18.

ection	Electors	T'out	Candidate	Party	Votes	%
50	39,935	80.9	†A.E. Baldwin	C	18,036	55.9
			E.J.M. Jones	Lab	8,402	26.0
			G. Morgan-Harris	L	5,850	18.1
					9,634	29.9
51	40,306	74.2	A.E. Baldwin	C	19,952	66.7
			E.J.M. Jones	Lab	9,939	33.3
					10,013	33.4
55	40,098	70.4	A.E. Baldwin	C	18,487	65.5
			A.T. Evans	Lab	9,740	34.5
					8,747	31.0
59	39,306	76.4	C. Bossom	C	16,642	55.4
			T.G. Jones	L	6,905	23.0
			F.W. Bowerman	Lab	6,475	21.6
					9,737	32.4
64	38,805	77.1	Hon. C. Bossom	C	15,238	50.9
			Dr. E.P. Cadbury	L	8,941	29.9
			K.A. Gulleford	Lab	5,750	19.2
					6,297	21.0
66	38,880	75.2	Hon. Sir C. Bossom, Bt.	C	15,045	51.4
			Dr. E.P. Cadbury	L	7,647	26.2
			K.R. Simmons	Lab	6,536	22.4
					7,398	25.2
970	41,719	72.9	Hon. Sir C. Bossom, Bt.	C	17,630	58.0
			R.J. Pincham	L	6,462	21.2
			M.G.M. Sloman	Lab	6,321	20.8
					11,168	36.8

Election	Electors	T'out	Candidate	Party	Votes	%
1950	70,687	87.4	R. Maudling	C	32,953	53
			†Dr. S.J.L. Taylor	Lab	22,419	36
			W.H. Jones	L	6,441*	10
					10,534	17
1951	72,408	86.1	R. Maudling	C	35,527	56,
			C.R. Fenton	Lab/Co-op	22,375	35
			W.H. Jones	L	4,463*	7,
					13,152	21,
1955	61,255**	81.4	Rt. Hon. R. Maudling	C	30,299	60,
			S. Hyam	Lab	19,570	39,
					10,729	21,
1959	64,739	81.7	Rt. Hon. R. Maudling	C	33,136	62,
			R.M. Prideaux	Lab	19,737	37,
					13,399	25,
1964	65,493	81.6	Rt. Hon. R. Maudling	C	25,537	47,
			D.H.P. Levy	Lab	17,024	31,
			H.R. Tinker	L	10,172	19,
			Rev. P.H. Figgis	Ind	706*	1,
					8,513	15,
1966	65,487	80.5	Rt. Hon. R. Maudling	C	24,833	47,
			G. Hickman	Lab	19,347	36,
			H.R. Tinker	L	8,539	16,
					5,486	10,
1970	71,988	71.3	Rt. Hon. R. Maudling	C	26,845	52,
			Mrs. J.E.M. Baker	Lab/Co-op	18,166	35,
			J.D.O. Henchley	L	6,329*	12,
					8,679	16,

Note:—

1964: Figgis sought election as a 'Pacifist' candidate.

Election	Electors	T'out	Candidate	Party	Votes	%
1955	59,857	79.1	D.C. Walker-Smith	C	26,936	56.9
			W.S. Hilton	Lab/Co-op	20,418	43.1
					6,518	13.8
1959	66,913	82.0	Rt. Hon. D.C. Walker-Smith	C	28,201	51.4
			S.J. Bidwell	Lab	18,020	32.8
			K.J.W. Spargo	L	8,656	15.8
					10,181	18.6
1964	76,186	81.0	Rt. Hon. Sir D.C. Walker-Smith, Bt.	C	29,749	48.2
			D.C.G. Potter	Lab	21,887	35.5
			E.W. Morgan	L	10,088	16.3
					7,862	12.7
1966	79,322	80.1	Rt. Hon. Sir D.C. Walker-Smith, Bt.	C	29,618	46.6
			B.C.S. Murphy	Lab	24,412	38.4
			E.W. Morgan	L	9,501	15.0
					5,206	8.2
1970	93,489	73.6	Rt. Hon. Sir D.C. Walker-Smith, Bt.	C	37,668	54.7
			M.S. Thomas	Lab/Co-op	23,601	34.3
			D. Walsh	L	7,538*	11.0
					14,067	20.4

Election	Electors	T'out	Candidate	Party	Votes	%
1950	51,608	85.0	†Viscountess Davidson	C	22,022	50.1
			R. Moss	Lab	15,165	34.6
			P.A. Stevens	L	6,696	15.3
					6,857	15.5
1951	52,313	83.8	Viscountess Davidson	C	25,620	58.4
			N.I. Mackenzie	Lab	18,220	41.6
					7,400	16.8
1955	60,013	83.8	Viscountess Davidson	C	25,648	51.0
			N.I. Mackenzie	Lab	19,512	38.8
			E.C. Saich	L	5,111*	10.2
					6,136	12.2
1959	70,962	85.3	J.H. Allason	C	30,189	49.9
			B.F.C. Floud	Lab	21,954	36.3
			Miss M. Neilson	L	8,358	13.8
					8,235	13.6
1964	82,087	84.5	J.H. Allason	C	31,119	44.8
			G.D. Hitchcock	Lab	26,273	37.9
			A.J. Whiteside	L	11,986	17.3
					4,846	6.9
1966	84,410	84.6	J.H. Allason	C	31,742	44.4
			R. Corbett	Lab	29,704	41.6
			A.J. Whiteside	L	9,970	14.0
					2,038	2.8
1970	99,254	78.3	J.H. Allason	C	40,417	52.0
			P.A. Fletcher	Lab	28,067	36.1
			A.J. Wilson	L	9,274*	11.9
					12,350	15.9

Election	Electors	T'out	Candidate	Party	Votes	%
1950	65,687	83.2	†D.C. Walker-Smith	C	25,074	45.9
			L. Scutts	Lab	19,324	35.4
			T.P. Hughes	L	10,234	18.7
					5,750	10.5
1951	67,110	80.8	D.C. Walker-Smith	C	30,519	56.3
			R.W. Marsh	Lab/Co-op	23,708	43.7
					6,811	12.6
1955	53,556**	82.2	Lord Balniel	C	25,014	56.8
			J. McKnight	Lab	19,030	43.2
					5,984	13.6
1959	64,106	84.3	Lord Balniel	C	31,418	58.2
			G.D. Southgate	Lab	22,597	41.8
					8,821	16.4
1964	74,450	84.6	Lord Balniel	C	29,134	46.3
			T.A. Deacon	Lab	25,161	39.9
			Mrs. A.C.M. Harman	L	8,722	13.8
					3,973	6.4
1966	76,234	83.7	Lord Balniel	C	32,302	50.6
			P. Nurse	Lab	31,508	49.4
					794	1.2
1970	88,147	78.7	Lord Balniel	C	36,494	52.6
			Mrs. Y. Sieve	Lab	26,924	38.8
			J.M. Melling	L	5,994*	8.6
					9,570	13.8

Election	Electors	T'out	Candidate	Party	Votes	%
1950	60,941	85.8	N.T.L. Fisher	C	23,580	45.1
			†P.A. Jones	Lab	21,829	41.8
			F.S. Haigh	L	6,863	13.1
					1,751	3.3
1951	61,967	85.0	N.T.L. Fisher	C	27,719	52.6
			P.J.H. Benenson	Lab	24,941	47.4
					2,778	5.2
1955	62,258**	83.2	W.F.M. Maddan	C	26,371	50.9
			P.J.H. Benenson	Lab	25,406	49.1
					965	1.8
1959	75,493	85.4	W.F.M. Maddan	C	30,193	46.8
			P.J.H. Benenson	Lab	25,818	40.0
			R. Glenton	L	8,481	13.2
					4,375	6.8
1964	87,825	84.5	Mrs. S.V.T.B. Williams	Lab	34,034	45.8
			W.F.M. Maddan	C	30,649	41.3
			Mrs. E.T. Dangerfield	L	9,564	12.9
					3,385	4.5
1966	90,840	82.3	Mrs. S.V.T.B. Williams	Lab	42,233	56.5
			J.H.R. Stokes	C	32,483	43.5
					9,750	13.0
1970	108,668	77.6	Mrs. S.V.T.B. Williams	Lab	40,932	48.5
			R.N. Luce	C	37,258	44.2
			T.N. Willis	L	6,148*	7.3
					3,674	4.3

Election	Electors	T'out	Candidate	Party	Votes	%
1950	61,644	84.9	Hon. J. Grimston	C	24,733	47.2
			†C.W. Dumpleton	Lab	22,351	42.7
			D.R.E. Abel	L	5,280*	10.1
					2,382	4.5
1951	62,431	84.1	Hon. J. Grimston	C	28,602	54.5
			J. McKnight	Lab	23,911	45.5
					4,691	9.0
1955	47,827**	79.3	Hon. J. Grimston	C	21,828	57.5
			Mrs. R. Short	Lab	16,107	42.5
					5,721	15.0
1959	52,823	82.8	V.H. Goodhew	C	23,157	52.9
			L.W. Carroll	Lab	14,650	33.5
			W.A.N. Jones	L	5,948	13.6
					8,507	19.4
1964	55,658	82.6	V.H. Goodhew	C	22,063	48.0
			B.L.H. Douglas-Mann	Lab	16,672	36.3
			W.G. Brown	L	7,231	15.7
					5,391	11.7
1966	56,248	83.0	V.H. Goodhew	C	22,260	47.7
			J.K. Kyle	Lab	19,428	41.6
			J.J. Wates	L	4,977*	10.7
					2,832	6.1
1970	62,373	76.3	V.H. Goodhew	C	24,503	51.5
			C.H. Beaumont	Lab	16,629	35.0
			C.A. Shaw	L	6,439	13.5
					7,874	16.5

Election	Electors	T'out	Candidate	Party	Votes	%
1950	49,520	86.1	G.J.M. Longden	C	23,608	55.4
			L. Allaker	Lab	14,913	35.0
			G.C. Middleton	L	4,114*	9.6
					8,695	20.4
1951	54,150	85.0	G.J.M. Longden	C	27,049	58.8
			L. Allaker	Lab	18,991	41.2
					8,058	17.6
1955	62,383	81.3	G.J.M. Longden	C	28,847	56.9
			W. Thomas	Lab	21,878	43.1
					6,969	13.8
1959	69,291	84.4	G.J.M. Longden	C	29,724	50.8
			A.J. Whiteside	Lab	19,487	33.3
			D.A.H. Banks	L	9,278	15.9
					10,237	17.5
1964	74,502	83.0	G.J.M. Longden	C	28,308	45.7
			S.J. Bidwell	Lab	22,237	36.0
			D. Brown	L	11,301	18.3
					6,071	9.7
1966	74,777	83.1	G.J.M. Longden	C	28,378	45.7
			S.J. Chapman	Lab	25,186	40.5
			P.A.S. Benton	L	8,596	13.8
					3,192	5.2
1970	85,654	75.8	G.J.M. Longden	C	32,661	50.4
			B.J. Grocott	Lab	24,214	37.3
			J.E.S. Jarrett	L	7,489*	11.5
			R.W. Skilton	Ind	542*	0.8
					8,447	13.1

Election	Electors	T'out	Candidate	Party	Votes	%
1950	43,699	82.6	†D.L-M. Renton	NL & C	18,551	51.4
			F.R. MacDonald	Lab	13,096	36.3
			W.G.F. Thompson	L	4,442*	12.3
					5,455	15.1
1951	44,982	80.8	D.L-M. Renton	NL & C	20,845	57.4
			F.R. MacDonald	Lab	15,487	42.6
					5,358	14.8
1955	45,757	77.1	D.L-M. Renton	NL & C	20,609	58.4
			J.A. Franks	Lab	14,670	41.6
					5,939	16.8
1959	46,794	80.4	D.L-M. Renton	NL & C	20,254	53.9
			J.W. Fear	Lab	11,983	31.8
			R.E.W. Vanderplank	L	5,389	14.3
					8,271	22.1
1964	50,483	78.8	Rt. Hon. D.L-M. Renton	NL & C	20,320	51.1
			L.J. Potter	Lab	12,456	31.3
			P.G.H. Thorold	L	6,992	17.6
					7,864	19.8
1966	53,745	77.6	Rt. Hon. Sir D.L-M. Renton	NL & C (C)	20,504	49.1
			M. Lawn	Lab	15,276	36.7
			D.R.A. Spreckley	L	5,900	14.2
					5,228	12.4
1970	66,505	75.3	Rt. Hon. Sir D.L-M. Renton	C	27,398	54.7
			J.P.P. Curran	Lab	17,588	35.1
			Dr. M.W.B. O'Loughlin	L	5,082*	10.2
					9,810	19.6

Election	Electors	T'out	Candidate	Party	Votes	%
1950	60,070	79.6	†E.A.H. Legge-Bourke	C	21,528	45.0
			A.F. Gray	Lab	16,565	34.6
			T.G. Jones	L	9,733	20.4
					4,963	10.4
1951	60,918	75.9	E.A.H. Legge-Bourke	C (Ind C) (C)	26,319	56.9
			A.F. Gray	Lab	19,915	43.1
					6,404	13.8
1955	61,188	70.7	E.A.H. Legge-Bourke	C	24,862	57.4
			A.F. Gray	Lab	18,416	42.6
					6,446	14.8
1959	61,387	74.7	E.A.H. Legge-Bourke	C	26,173	57.0
			J.D. Page	Lab	19,705	43.0
					6,468	14.0
1964	61,004	73.8	Sir E.A.H. Legge-Bourke	C	25,317	56.2
			C. Shaw	Lab	19,692	43.8
					5,625	12.4
1966	60,758	75.9	Sir E.A.H. Legge-Bourke	C	21,320	46.2
			G. Nurse	Lab	19,566	42.4
			D.M. Rigby	L	5,250*	11.4
					1,754	3.8
1970	67,226	71.9	Sir E.A.H. Legge-Bourke	C	28,972	59.9
			R.E. O'Hare	Lab	19,366	40.1
					9,606	19.8

ction	Electors	T'out	Candidate	Party	Votes	%
50	67,581	80.6	†Sir P.D. Macdonald	C	32,984	60.5
			S.G. Conbeer	Lab	21,496	39.5
					11,488	21.0
51	67,501	80.3	Sir P.D. Macdonald	C	33,501	61.8
			S.G. Conbeer	Lab	20,712	38.2
					12,789	23.6
55	67,297	74.3	Sir P.D. Macdonald	C	31,335	62.6
			S.G. Conbeer	Lab	18,698	37.4
					12,637	25.2
59	66,939	74.1	H.F.M. Woodnutt	C	31,228	62.9
			E.C. Amey	Lab	18,396	′37.1
					12,832	25.8
64	69,215	74.3	H.F.M. Woodnutt	C	27,497	53.5
			W.H.J. Mann	Lab	16,244	31.6
			Miss B.E.M.S. Bliss	L	7,666	14.9
					11,253	21.9
66	70,877	75.0	H.F.M. Woodnutt	C	25,862	48.6
			P. Stephenson	Lab	15,411	29.0
			S.S. Ross	L	11,915	22.4
					10,451	19.6
70	80,537	72.1	H.F.M. Woodnutt	C	30,437	52.4
			K.W. Boulton	Lab	13,111	22.6
			S.S. Ross	L	12,883	22.2
			R.W.J. Cawdell	VNP	1,607*	2.8
					17,326	29.8

411

Election	Electors	T'out	Candidate	Party	Votes	%
1950	48,607	84.1	W.F. Deedes	C	21,095	51
			N.D. Sandelson	Lab	14,948	36.
			H.C. Shirley	L	4,828*	11.
					6,147	15
1951	49,715	81.9	W.F. Deedes	C	24,093	59.
			N.D. Sandelson	Lab	16,645	40.
					7,448	18
1955	50,821	78.1	W.F. Deedes	C	23,992	60.
			N.D. Sandelson	Lab	15,685	39.
					8,307	21.
1959	52,097	77.5	W.F. Deedes	C	25,383	62.
			R.G. Ward	Lab	14,983	37.
					10,400	25.
1964	54,879	77.5	Rt. Hon. W.F. Deedes	C	21,026	49.
			C.A. Thomas	Lab	11,989	28.
			J.G.W. Peck	L	9,531	22.
					9,037	21.
1966	56,727	75.3	Rt. Hon. W.F. Deedes	C	21,362	50.
			C.A. Thomas	Lab	13,249	31.
			J.G.W. Peck	L	8,121	19.
					8,113	19.
1970	66,909	72.6	Rt. Hon. W.F. Deedes	C	26,649	54.
			J.M. Bowyer	Lab	14,037	28.
			F.C. Truman	L	7,902	16.
					12,612	25.

ection	Electors	T'out	Candidate	Party	Votes	%
950	57,407	82.5	†J.B. White	C	26,491	55.9
			J. Newman	Lab	14,563	30.8
			K.G. Jupp	L	6,296	13.3
					11,928	25.1
951	58,546	80.1	J.B. White	C	28,632	61.1
			J.A.E. Jones	Lab	14,543	31.0
			T.H. Payne	L	3,695*	7.9
					14,089	30.1
Resignation]						
953	59,009	49.2	L.M. Thomas	C	19,490	67.1
(2/2)			J.A.E. Jones	Lab	9,560	32.9
					9,930	34.2
955	59,431	72.7	L.M. Thomas	C	28,739	66.6
			R.G. Ward	Lab	14,444	33.4
					14,295	33.2
959	62,011	75.1	L.M. Thomas	C	30,846	66.2
			G.E. Peters	Lab	15,746	33.8
					15,100	32.4
964	67,639	76.3	Sir L.M. Thomas	C	26,827	51.9
			G.S. Cobbett	Lab	15,211	29.5
			E.W. Moss	L	9,582	18.6
					11,616	22.4
966	71,604	76.1	D.L. Crouch	C	27,160	49.8
			B. Sawbridge	Lab	15,372	28.2
			E.W. Moss	L	11,962	22.0
					11,788	21.6
970	80,373	74.6	D.L. Crouch	C	33,222	55.4
			H.G.N. Clother	Lab	15,172	25.3
			D.C.P. Gracie	L	11,553	19.3
					18,050	30.1

Election	Electors	T'out	Candidate	Party	Votes	%
1950	65,231	86.3	Miss M.P. Hornsby-Smith	C	25,215	44.
			†G.D. Wallace	Lab	25,048	44.
			D.A. Hughes	L	6,039*	10.
					167	0.
1951	70,906	88.0	Miss M.P. Hornsby-Smith	C	31,679	50.
			G.D. Wallace	Lab	30,699	49.
					980	1.
1955	58,063**	84.9	Miss M.P. Hornsby-Smith	C	24,514	49.
			G.D. Wallace	Lab	20,644	41.!
			D.C. Blackburn	L	4,120*	8.‹
					3,870	7.!
1959	59,646	85.8	Miss M.P. Hornsby-Smith	C	25,748	50.:
			Mrs. M. Reid	Lab	19,069	37.:
			D.C. Blackburn	L	6,366*	12.‹
					6,679	13.(
1964	60,678	82.9	Rt. Hon. Dame Patricia Hornsby-Smith	C	22,251	44.:
			R.W. Huzzard	Lab	20,736	41.:
			Mrs. S. Hobday	L	7,291	14.!
					1,515	3.
1966	59,898	84.3	A.H. Macdonald	Lab	22,757	45.‹
			Rt. Hon. Dame Patricia Hornsby-Smith	C	21,947	43.!
			P. Hayden	L	5,761*	11.‹
					810	1.(
1970	66,483	75.5	Rt. Hon. Dame Patricia Hornsby-Smith	C	24,650	49.1
			A.H. Macdonald	Lab	21,287	42.‹
			R.L. Coverson	L	4,268*	8.!
					3,363	6.:

Election	Electors	T'out	Candidate	Party	Votes	%
1955	58,854	81.0	S. Irving	Lab/Co-op	25,928	54.4
			P.E. Walker	C	21,730	45.6
					4,198	8.8
1959	66,599	83.0	S. Irving	Lab/Co-op	25,323	45.9
			P.E. Walker	C	24,047	43.5
			B.C. Davis	L	5,881*	10.6
					1,276	2.4
1964	72,305	81.5	S. Irving	Lab/Co-op	27,371	46.4
			J.J. Davis	C	22,496	38.2
			M. Janis	L	9,047	15.4
					4,875	8.2
1966	73,359	80.8	S. Irving	Lab/Co-op	29,547	49.8
			P.J.E. Trew	C	22,638	38.2
			P. Loftus	L	7,094*	12.0
					6,909	11.6
1970	81,704	74.1	P.J.E. Trew	C	27,822	46.0
			Rt. Hon. S. Irving	Lab/Co-op	27,262	45.0
			J.P. Johnson	L	5,453*	9.0
					560	1.0

Election	Electors	T'out	Candidate	Party	Votes	%
1950	60,999	85.8	J.S-W. Arbuthnot	C	25,640	49.0
			W.J. Owen	Lab/Co-op	23,331	44.0
			B.E. Goldstone	L	2,873*	5.5
			R.T. Morrison	Com	474*	0.9
					2,309	4.4
1951	62,402	85.7	J.S-W. Arbuthnot	C	28,511	53.3
			W.J. Owen	Lab/Co-op	24,995	46.7
					3,516	6.6
1955	63,064	81.8	J.S-W. Arbuthnot	C	27,316	52.9
			H.W. Lee	Lab	24,298	47.1
					3,018	5.8
1959	63,512	82.9	J.S-W. Arbuthnot	C	27,939	53.1
			H.W. Lee	Lab	24,698	46.9
					3,241	6.2
1964	64,876	82.7	D.H. Ennals	Lab	24,115	44.9
			Sir J.S-W. Arbuthnot, Bt.	C	23,697	44.2
			B.W. Budd	L	5,843*	10.9
					418	0.7
1966	65,664	84.2	D.H. Ennals	Lab	27,256	49.3
			T.C.G. Stacey	C	24,040	43.5
			B.W. Budd	L	3,981*	7.2
					3,216	5.8
1970	72,580	80.7	P.W.I. Rees	C	30,103	51.4
			D.H. Ennals	Lab	28,454	48.6
					1,649	2.8

Election	Electors	T'out	Candidate	Party	Votes	%
1950	56,162	86.3	†P.L. Wells	Lab	23,620	48.7
			J.E. Brooks	C	21,381	44.1
			Miss E.M. Graham	L	3,486*	7.2
					2,239	4.6
1951	57,193	86.0	P.L. Wells	Lab	24,884	50.6
			C. Bossom	C	24,322	49.4
					562	1.2
1955	57,543	83.2	P.L. Wells	Lab	23,981	50.1
			C. Bossom	C	23,922	49.9
					59	0.2
1959	57,760	83.8	P.L. Wells	Lab	24,327	50.3
			Mrs. E.M.S. Olsen	C	24,074	49.7
					253	0.6
[Death]						
1964 (4/6)	60,049	74.8	T.G. Boston	Lab	24,749	55.1
			Mrs. E.M.S. Olsen	C	19,808	44.1
			R.E. Eckley	Ind	352*	0.8
					4,941	11.0
1964	60,500	81.7	T.G. Boston	Lab	24,243	49.1
			Mrs. E.M.S. Olsen	C	20,279	41.0
			P. Hayden	L	4,882*	9.9
					3,964	8.1
1966	62,896	79.9	T.G. Boston	Lab	26,375	52.5
			R.D. Moate	C	23,886	47.5
					2,489	5.0
1970	71,677	78.2	R.D. Moate	C	29,914	53.4
			T.G. Boston	Lab	26,103	46.6
					3,811	6.8

Election	Electors	T'out	Candidate	Party	Votes	%
1950	49,038	83.2	†H.R. Mackeson	C	23,767	58.2
			M. Murray	Lab	13,885	34.0
			Mrs. R.W. Bateson	L	3,168*	7.8
					9,882	24.2
1951	50,358	79.0	H.R. Mackeson	C	25,792	64.9
			I.R. Jones	Lab	13,968	35.1
					11,824	29.8
1955	50,392	72.8	Sir H.R. Mackeson, Bt.	C	23,851	65.0
			L.L. Reeves	Lab	12,849	35.0
					11,002	30.0
1959	50,825	75.6	A.P. Costain	C	21,726	56.6
			W.E. Simpkins	Lab	9,346	24.3
			R.D. Emerson	L	7,351	19.1
					12,380	32.3
1964	53,388	71.0	A.P. Costain	C	23,587	62.2
			M.J. Stewart	Lab	14,314	37.8
					9,273	24.4
1966	54,059	71.3	A.P. Costain	C	22,964	59.6
			J.R. Horam	Lab	15,562	40.4
					7,402	19.2
1970	61,067	68.8	A.P. Costain	C	27,031	64.3
			N.A. Hyman	Lab	13,772	32.8
			H.W. Button	Ind	1,219*	2.9
					13,259	31.5

lection	Electors	T'out	Candidate	Party	Votes	%
)50	61,792	86.3	†Sir R.T.D. Acland, Bt.	Lab	28,297	53.1
			J.G. Lowe	C	22,726	42.6
			Mrs. M.D. Ayliffe	L	2,298*	4.3
					5,571	10.5
)51	63,393	85.7	Sir R.T.D. Acland, Bt.	Lab	30,055	55.3
			C.P.T. Burke	C	24,300	44.7
					5,755	10.6
ieat Vacant at Dissolution (Seeks re-election on leaving the Labour Party)]						
)55	59,099**	80.7	P.M. Kirk	C	22,058	46.2
			V. Mishcon	Lab	19,149	40.1
			Sir R.T.D. Acland, Bt.	Ind	6,514	13.7
					2,909	6.1
)59	63,299	82.3	P.M. Kirk	C	27,124	52.1
			V. Mishcon	Lab	24,962	47.9
					2,162	4.2
)64	71,408*	80.4	A.J. Murray	Lab	26,074	45.4
			P.M. Kirk	C	25,326	44.1
			J.H. Barnett	L	6,015*	10.5
					748	1.3
)66	74,175	82.0	A.J. Murray	Lab	30,276	49.7
			R.L. White	C	25,484	41.9
			J.H. Barnett	L	5,092*	8.4
					4,792	7.8
)70	84,046	76.0	R.L. White	C	29,924	46.8
			A.J. Murray	Lab	28,711	45.0
			M.J. Dunn	L	5,234*	8.2
					1,213	1.8

)te:—

1955: Acland was opposed to the manufacture of the hydrogen bomb.

Election	Electors	T'out	Candidate	Party	Votes	%
1950	68,022	83.0	†Hon. E. Carson	C	31,345	5
			T.C. Boyd	Lab	20,522	3
			C.J.V. Wrong	L	4,561*	8
					10,823	1
1951	69,782	78.0	Hon. E. Carson	C	33,551	6
			O.L. Shaw	Lab	20,892	3
					12,659	2
[Resignation]						
1953 (12/3)	70,177	58.7	W.R. Rees-Davies	C	25,261	6
			F.E. Woodbridge	Lab	15,935	3
					9,326	2
1955	69,910	71.9	W.R. Rees-Davies	C	31,270	6
			K. Jones	Lab	18,981	3
					12,289	2
1959	71,952	75.1	W.R. Rees-Davies	C	29,453	54
			H.A. Fountain	Lab	17,555	3
			G.E. MacDonald-Jones	L	6,998	13
					11,898	2
1964	78,664	74.2	W.R. Rees-Davies	C	27,870	47
			E. Wistrich	Lab	20,520	35
			D.B. Norrington	L	9,979	17
					7,350	12
1966	81,453	75.7	W.R. Rees-Davies	C	29,302	47
			L.J.A. Bishop	Lab	24,416	39
			F.G. Redman	L	7,952	12
					4,886	7
1970	89,093	72.3	W.R. Rees-Davies	C	33,434	51
			L.J.A. Bishop	Lab	21,709	33
			T.D. Gates	L	7,176*	11
			I.R.P. Josephs	Ind C	2,136*	3
					11,725	18

Note:—

1970: Josephs sought election as a 'Conservative and Consult the People' candidate.

ection	Electors	T'out	Candidate	Party	Votes	%
50	59,835	81.8	†A.C. Bossom	C	25,008	51.1
			H.A. White	Lab	18,377	37.6
			T.F. Rice	L	5,546*	11.3
					6,631	13.5
51	60,549	80.5	A.C. Bossom	C	27,606	56.6
			H.A. White	Lab	21,159	43.4
					6,447	13.2
55	61,144	77.1	Sir A.C. Bossom, Bt.	C	27,267	57.9
			O.L. Shaw	Lab	19,861	42.1
					7,406	15.8
959	63,311	78.6	J.J. Wells	C	30,115	60.5
			A.B.S. Soper	Lab	19,652	39.5
					10,463	21.0
964	68,539	78.0	J.J. Wells	C	25,079	46.9
			J. Daly	Lab	17,143	32.1
			S. Blow	L	11,244	21.0
					7,936	14.8
966	71,882	74.3	J.J. Wells	C	29,208	54.7
			M.J. O'Flaherty	Lab	24,214	45.3
					4,994	9.4
970	84,440	72.2	J.J. Wells	C	31,316	51.4
			K.M. Graham	Lab	18,473	30.3
			S. Blow	L	11,167	18.3
					12,843	21.1

Election	Electors	T'out	Candidate	Party	Votes	%
1950	50,704	85.1	†Sir W. Smithers	C	24,450	56.7
			G.H.C. Vaughan	Lab	14,161	32.8
			Lady Abrahams	L	4,523*	10.5
					10,289	23.9
1951	53,023	82.0	Sir W. Smithers	C	27,244	62.7
			R.D.V. Williams	Lab	16,241	37.3
					11,003	25.4
[Death]						
1955 (20/1)	55,069	55.4	W.D.M. Sumner	C	20,082	65.8
			R.D.V. Williams	Lab	10,426	34.2
					9,656	31.6
1955	46,581**	79.4	W.D.M. Sumner	C	22,166	59.9
			N.J. Hart	Lab	10,230	27.6
			A.B. Howard	L	4,610*	12.5
					11,936	32.3
1959	51,872	82.8	W.D.M. Sumner	C	24,303	56.6
			N.J. Hart	Lab	9,543	22.2
			J.O. Galloway	L	9,092	21.2
					14,760	34.4
[Resignation on appointment as a County Court Judge]						
1962 (14/3)	53,779	80.3	E.R. Lubbock	L	22,846	52.9
			P. Goldman	C	14,991	34.7
			A.R. Jinkinson	Lab	5,350*	12.4
					7,855	18.2
1964	54,846	85.3	E.R. Lubbock	L	22,637	48.4
			N.D. McWhirter	C	19,565	41.8
			P.A.W. Merriton	Lab	4,609*	9.8
					3,072	6.6
1966	55,776	86.9	E.R. Lubbock	L	22,615	46.7
			N.D. McWhirter	C	20,993	43.3
			D.J. Sleigh	Lab	4,870*	10.0
					1,622	3.4
1970	65,112	79.2	I.R. Stanbrook	C	24,385	47.3
			E.R. Lubbock	L	23,063	44.7
			D.I. Grant	Lab	4,098*	8.0
					1,322	2.6

ection	Electors	T'out	Candidate	Party	Votes	%
50	57,563	84.9	J.C. Rodgers	C	25,292	51.8
			J. Spencer	Lab	17,610	36.0
			E.R. Moulton-Barrett	L	5,969*	12.2
					7,682	15.8
51	58,299	81.5	J.C. Rodgers	C	28,668	60.4
			J.N. Powrie	Lab	18,823	39.6
					9,845	20.8
55	59,937	78.1	J.C. Rodgers	C	28,936	61.8
			J.N. Powrie	Lab	17,858	38.2
					11,078	23.6
59	62,701	80.2	J.C. Rodgers	C	28,186	56.0
			R.C. Ogley	Lab	14,265	28.4
			Mrs. N. Penman	L	7,819	15.6
					13,921	27.6
64	68,820	80.1	Sir J.C. Rodgers, Bt.	C	28,678	52.1
			P.B.M. Pearce	Lab	14,958	27.1
			Mrs. N. Penman	L	11,480	20.8
					13,720	25.0
66	71,644	79.2	Sir J.C. Rodgers, Bt.	C	28,651	50.5
			P.B.M. Pearce	Lab	18,338	32.3
			A.N.H. Blackburn	L	9,746	17.2
					10,313	18.2
70	81,583	73.9	Sir J.C. Rodgers, Bt.	C	32,654	54.1
			J.F. Ovenden	Lab	15,376	25.5
			R.F. Webster	L	12,290	20.4
					17,278	28.6

Election	Electors	T'out	Candidate	Party	Votes	%
1950	64,397	83.5	†G.W. Williams	C	27,893	51.
			B.R. Clapham	Lab	19,525	36.
			L.A. Willard	L	5,634*	10.
			Dr. E.F.St.J. Lyburn	Ind C	739*	1
					8,368	15.
1951	65,097	80.6	G.W. Williams	C	31,377	59.
			B. Bagnari	Lab	21,109	40.
					10,268	19
1955	64,709	75.5	G.W. Williams	C	29,521	60.
			R.L. Fagg	Lab	19,325	39.
					10,196	20.
[Resignation]						
1956 (7/6)	65,100	60.6	R.P. Hornby	C	20,515	52.
			R.L. Fagg	Lab	18,913	48.
					1,602	4.
1959	67,320	78.5	R.P. Hornby	C	31,687	59.
			K.W. May	Lab	21,181	40.
					10,506	19.
1964	71,789	78.7	R.P. Hornby	C	27,802	49
			D. Savage	Lab	19,037	33.
			W.E.P. Babbs	L	9,682	17
					8,765	15
1966	74,464	77.3	R.P. Hornby	C	26,896	46.
			W.E. Wolff	Lab	20,068	34
			C.H. Bloy	L	10,586	18.
					6,828	11.
1970	83,300	72.0	R.P. Hornby	C	31,890	53
			Mrs. M.M. Colquhoun	Lab	17,897	29
			H.E. Hill	L	10,167	17
					13,993	23

ction	Electors	T'out	Candidate	Party	Votes	%
50	55,218	88.4	†C. Kenyon	Lab	23,233	47.6
			A. Fountaine	Ind C	22,872	46.9
			Miss F.E. Adams	L	2,706*	5.5
					361	0.7
51	55,603	88.1	C. Kenyon	Lab	24,771	50.6
			A.G.F. Hall-Davies	C	24,188	49.4
					583	1.2
55	57,700**	84.3	C. Kenyon	Lab	24,994	51.4
			A.G.F. Hall-Davies	C	23,656	48.6
					1,338	2.8
59	59,086	85.6	C. Kenyon	Lab	25,641	50.7
			F.H. Taylor	C	24,965	49.3
					676	1.4
64	60,330	84.6	C. Kenyon	Lab	24,710	48.5
			J.H.V. Sutcliffe	C	20,997	41.1
			A.W. Bell	L	5,331*	10.4
					3,713	7.4
66	61,551	81.1	C. Kenyon	Lab	27,319	54.8
			Mrs. C.M. Monks	C	22,575	45.2
					4,744	9.6
70	71,220	79.0	Mrs. C.M. Monks	C	26,577	47.2
			D.A. Forwood	Lab	24,900	44.3
			G. Payne	L	4,428*	7.9
			B.J.A. Elder	Ind	334*	0.6
					1,677	2.9

te:-

1950: Fountaine was the nominee of the local Conservative Association but his candidature was not approved by the Conservative Party's Standing Advisory Committee on Candidates.

Election	Electors	T'out	Candidate	Party	Votes	%
1950	45,758	91.7	R. Fort	C	20,814	49
			†H.E. Randall	Lab	18,359	43
			J.W. Wyers	L	2,765*	6
					2,455	5
1951	46,150	90.1	R. Fort	C	23,007	55
			H. Bradley	Lab	18,582	44
					4,425	10
1955	44,893	85.3	R. Fort	C	21,615	56
			W. Rutter	Lab	16,671	43
					4,944	13

[Seat Vacant at Dissolution (Death)]

Election	Electors	T'out	Candidate	Party	Votes	%
1959	44,350	86.6	F.F. Pearson	C	22,314	58
			W. Rutter	Lab	16,103	41
					6,211	16
1964	44,594	85.3	F.F. Pearson	C	18,559	48
			E.D.H. Hoyle	Lab	14,278	37
			M. Strange	L	5,209	13
					4,281	11
1966	44,822	83.5	Sir F.F. Pearson, Bt.	C	17,244	46
			R. Hodge	Lab	15,014	40
			Mrs. V.I. MacMillan	L	5,168	13
					2,230	6
1970	49,753	79.5	A.D. Walder	C	20,430	51
			K.C. Bodfish	Lab	14,158	35
			Mrs. V.I. MacMillan	L	4,965	12
					6,272	15

Election	Electors	T'out	Candidate	Party	Votes	%
1950	41,161	89.6	†W.R.S. Prescott	C	17,903	48.6
			R. Haines	Lab	13,334	36.1
			J. Booth	L	5,656	15.3
					4,569	12.5
1951	41,321	88.6	C.F. Fletcher-Cooke	C	17,785	48.5
			R. Haines	Lab	14,605	39.9
			R.F. Leslie	L	4,236*	11.6
					3,180	8.6
1955	55,322**	82.3	C.F. Fletcher-Cooke	C	26,729	58.7
			R. Haines	Lab	18,813	41.3
					7,916	17.4
1959	55,461	84.1	C.F. Fletcher-Cooke	C	·27,483	58.9
			J.T. Park	Lab	19,141	41.1
					8,342	17.8
1964	58,014	83.7	C.F. Fletcher-Cooke	C	20,343	41.9
			G.R. Cryer	Lab	15,559	32.1
			S.C. Holt	L	12,641	26.0
					4,784	9.8
1966	59,066	82.6	C.F. Fletcher-Cooke	C	20,598	42.2
			B. Whittam	Lab	18,863	38.7
			S.C. Holt	L	9,339	19.1
					1,735	3.5
1970	66,494	76.7	C.F. Fletcher-Cooke	C	26,728	52.3
			B. Whittam	Lab	17,634	34.6
			A. Cooper	L	6,663	13.1
					9,094	17.7

Election	Electors	T'out	Candidate	Party	Votes	%
1950	50,863	88.1	†Rt. Hon. G. Tomlinson	Lab	25,375	56.6
			F. Kay	C	14,266	31.8
			A. Lomax	L	5,189*	11.6
					11,109	24.8
1951	51,189	86.8	Rt. Hon. G. Tomlinson	Lab	26,297	59.2
			J. Seddon	C	18,112	40.8
					8,185	18.4
[Death]						
1952 (27/11)	51,340	71.0	E. Thornton	Lab	21,834	59.9
			H.D. Moore	C	14,615	40.1
					7,219	19.8
1955	52,818	81.5	E. Thornton	Lab	24,829	57.7
			D.C. Waddington	C	18,231	42.3
					6,598	15.4
1959	56,092*	83.3	E. Thornton	Lab	27,393	58.6
			A.S. Royse	C	19,356	41.4
					8,037	17.2
1964	58,275	78.8	E. Thornton	Lab	28,493	62.1
			A.S. Royse	C	17,421	37.9
					11,072	24.2
1966	60,634	74.8	E. Thornton	Lab	30,015	66.2
			M. Andrew	C	15,329	33.8
					14,686	32.4
1970	69,494	72.3	J.F.H. Roper	Lab/Co-op	29,392	58.5
			I.A. Johnston	C	20,867	41.5
					8,525	17.0

Election	Electors	T'out	Candidate	Party	Votes	%
1950	60,703	88.0	†H. Sutcliffe	C	23,518	44.1
			C.J. Hurley	Lab	21,482	40.2
			W.H. Watkinson	L	8,404	15.7
					2,036	3.9
1951	61,320	85.1	H. Sutcliffe	C	28,086	53.8
			C.J. Hurley	Lab	24,083	46.2
					4,003	7.6
1955	59,203	81.8	J.A. Leavey	C	25,824	53.3
			A.L. Tillotson	Lab	22,614	46.7
					3,210	6.6
1959	57,868	84.7	J.A. Leavey	C	19,742	40.2
			H. Nevin	Lab	17,588	35.9
			G.E. Macpherson	L	11,713	23.9
					2,154	4.3
1964	59,733	82.8	J. Barnett	Lab	20,174	40.8
			J.A. Leavey	C	19,358	39.1
			W.E. Critchley	L	9,914	20.1
					816	1.7
1966	63,438	79.6	J. Barnett	Lab	24,701	49.0
			D.C. Waddington	C	19,048	37.7
			J. Clarney	L	6,732	13.3
					5,653	11.3
1970	72,048	76.2	J. Barnett	Lab	25,081	45.7
			I. MacGregor	C	24,178	44.1
			F.J. Beetham	L	5,620*	10.2
					903	1.6

Election	Electors	T'out	Candidate	Party	Votes	%
1950	52,363	85.0	†Rt. Hon. J.H. Wilson	Lab	21,536	48.:
			S. Smart	C	20,702	46.!
			H.G. Edwards	L	1,905*	4.:
			L.J. McGree	Com	387*	0.!
					834	1.!
1951	54,230	84.8	Rt. Hon. J.H. Wilson	Lab	23,582	51.:
			F.L. Neep	C	22,389	48.:
					1,193	2.!
1955	60,036*	78.5	Rt. Hon. J.H. Wilson	Lab	24,858	52.
			W.G.O. Morgan	C	22,300	47.:
					2,558	5.!
1959	77,371	77.9	Rt. Hon. J.H. Wilson	Lab	33,111	54.!
			G.B. Woolfenden	C	27,184	45.
					5,927	9.!
1964	86,129*	76.7	Rt. Hon. J.H. Wilson	Lab	42,213	63.!
			H. Tucker	C	22,940	34.
			M.C.W. Baker	Ind Com	899*	1.!
					19,273	29.:
1966	88,288	70.1	Rt. Hon. J.H. Wilson	Lab	41,132	66.!
			Dr. T.L. Hobday	C	20,182	32.!
			D.E. Sutch	NTP	585*	0.!
					20,950	33.!
1970	106,896	67.6	Rt. Hon. J.H. Wilson	Lab	45,583	63..
			J.N.M. Entwistle	C	24,509	33.!
			J.W.G. Sparrow	DP	1,232*	1.
			J.I. Kenny	Com	890*	1.:
					21,074	29.:

Note:—

1964: Baker was the nominee of the North of England Communist Association, a breakaway organisation formed by former members of the Communist Party.

Election	Electors	T'out	Candidate	Party	Votes	%
950	50,476	88.7	†T.J. Brown	Lab	32,145	71.8
			J.G. Scott	C	12,612	28.2
					19,533	43.6
951	51,121	87.0	T.J. Brown	Lab	32,148	72.3
			J.A. Porter	C	12,305	27.7
					19,843	44.6
955	50,614	81.0	T.J. Brown	Lab	29,830	72.7
			G.L. Beaman	C	11,183	27.3
					18,647	45.4
959	51,273	83.0	T.J. Brown	Lab	30,752	72.3
			W. Clegg	C	11,795	27.7
					18,957	44.6
964	54,140	79.6	M.T.F. McGuire	Lab	31,042	72.0
			F.H.G.H. Goodhart	C	12,077	28.0
					18,965	44.0
966	55,703	75.4	M.T.F. McGuire	Lab	30,915	73.6
			J. Birch	C	11,075	26.4
					19,840	47.2
970	66,723	70.7	M.T.F. McGuire	Lab	32,295	68.5
			A.R. Coupe	C	14,877	31.5
					17,418	37.0

Election	Electors	T'out	Candidate	Party	Votes	%
1950	44,881	85.1	†F.H.R. Maclean	C	18,437	48.2
			A.E.V.A. Farrer	Lab	15,341	40.2
			H. Rogerson	L	4,416*	11.6
					3,096	8.0
1951	44,917	86.1	F.H.R. Maclean	C	20,555	53.2
			Miss D. Lees	Lab	18,099	46.8
					2,456	6.4
1955	43,811	80.3	F.H.R. Maclean	C	19,873	56.5
			C.S.B. Attlee	Lab	15,324	43.5
					4,549	13.0
1959	43,714	82.4	H.J. Berkeley	C	20,783	57.7
			E. Gardner	Lab	15,255	42.3
					5,528	15.4
1964	44,068	79.7	H.J. Berkeley	C	18,811	53.5
			E. Gardner	Lab	16,330	46.5
					2,481	7.0
1966	43,611	79.2	S. Henig	Lab	18,168	52.6
			H.J. Berkeley	C	16,357	47.4
					1,811	5.2
1970	47,576	79.6	Mrs. M.E. Kellett	C	18,584	49.1
			S. Henig	Lab	16,843	44.5
			A.R.C. Paton	L	2,436*	6.4
					1,741	4.6

Note:—

1970: Mrs. Kellett became Mrs. Kellett-Bowman upon her marriage in 1971.

Election	Electors	T'out	Candidate	Party	Votes	%
1950	56,175	86.9	†E.E. Gates	C	24,521	50.2
			C.S. Hilditch	Lab	16,716	34.3
			E. Harrison	L	7,564	15.5
					7,805	15.9
1951	56,657	85.0	Sir J.D. Barlow, Bt.	C	26,073	54.1
			A. Knight	Lab	16,323	33.9
			E. Harrison	L	5,757*	12.0
					9,750	20.2
1955	58,416	75.5	Sir J.D. Barlow, Bt.	C	27,096	61.5
			E.E. Dell	Lab	16,989	38.5
					10,107	23.0
1959	65,855	80.0	Sir J.D. Barlow, Bt.	C	31,416	59.7
			F.G. Barton	Lab	21,248	40.3
					10,168	19.4
1964	69,658	79.4	Sir J.D. Barlow, Bt.	C	22,192	40.1
			R. Leighton	Lab	20,066	36.3
			S. Crilly	L	13,064	23.6
					2,126	3.8
1966	68,602	78.0	D.W. Coe	Lab	23,938	44.7
			Sir J.D. Barlow, Bt.	C	20,121	37.6
			S. Crilly	L	9,457	17.7
					3,817	7.1
1970	76,750	74.5	A.G.B. Haselhurst	C	25,030	43.8
			D.W. Coe	Lab	23,988	41.9
			S. Crilly	L	8,175	14.3
					1,042	1.9

Election	Electors	T'out	Candidate	Party	Votes	%
1950	55,279	84.2	†Sir W.J.I. Fraser	C	28,041	60.3
			A. Gaskell	Lab	12,768	27.4
			G.De P. Leeming	L	5,723*	12.3
					15,273	32.9
1951	55,913	80.4	Sir W.J.I. Fraser	C	31,211	69.4
			E. Gardner	Lab	13,732	30.6
					17,479	38.8
1955	56,089	74.4	Sir W.J.I. Fraser	C	29,706	71.2
			W.F. Fielding	Lab	12,005	28.8
					17,701	42.4

[Elevation to a Life Peerage—Lord Fraser of Lonsdale]

Election	Electors	T'out	Candidate	Party	Votes	%
1958	57,349	63.8	B.R.V.Z. de Ferranti	C	23,923	65.3
(6/11)			F.R. McManus	Lab	12,692	34.7
					11,231	30.6
1959	57,654	77.2	B.R.V.Z. de Ferranti	C	30,228	68.0
			F.R. McManus	Lab	14,253	32.0
					15,975	36.0
1964	59,626	77.1	A.G.F. Hall-Davis	C	24,756	53.8
			F.R. McManus	Lab	12,392	27.0
			J.R. Smallwood	Ind L	8,818	19.2
					12,364	26.8
1966	60,764	76.5	A.G.F. Hall-Davis	C	24,138	51.9
			I. Limmer	Lab	13,838	29.8
			D.M. Clark	L	8,526	18.3
					10,300	22.1
1970	66,305	72.6	A.G.F. Hall-Davis	C	27,442	57.0
			E. Garbutt	Lab	13,916	28.9
			A.W. Drury	L	6,792	14.1
					13,526	28.1

Election	Electors	T'out	Candidate	Party	Votes	%
1950	61,246	88.0	†F. Lee	Lab	31,832	59.1
			K. Lewis	C	22,068	40.9
					9,764	18.2
1951	61,727	87.2	F. Lee	Lab	31,374	58.3
			H.W. Jones	C	22,476	41.7
					8,898	16.6
1955	61,885*	81.8	F. Lee	Lab	29,299	57.9
			N.A. Miscampbell	C	21,344	42.1
					7,955	15.8
1959	65,124	83.1	F. Lee	Lab	31,041	57.4
			N.A. Miscampbell	C	23,065	42.6
					7,976	14.8
1964	71,734	82.0	F. Lee	Lab	32,932	55.9
			D.C. Stanley	C	17,980	30.6
			C.L. Jones	L	7,919	13.5
					14,952	25.3
1966	75,328	78.0	Rt. Hon. F. Lee	Lab	36,901	62.8
			P.H. Craig	C	21,845	37.2
					15,056	25.6
1970	89,413	74.3	Rt. Hon. F. Lee	Lab	34,873	52.6
			J.P. Stanley	C	25,863	38.9
			R.E. Magee	L	5,678*	8.5
					9,010	13.7

Election	Electors	T'out	Candidate	Party	Votes	%
1950	46,743	82.8	Hon. R.O. Stanley	C	23,538	60
			P.H.W. Couldry	Lab	10,515	27
			J.W. Robinson	L	4,631*	12
					13,023	33
1951	47,309	77.6	Hon. R.O. Stanley	C	25,419	69.
			J.B. Morris	Lab	11,284	30.
					14,135	38.
1955	48,081	68.6	Hon. R.O. Stanley	C	23,812	72.
			L. Spriggs	Lab	9,152	27.
					14,660	44.
1959	52,521*	73.0	Hon. R.O. Stanley	C	27,045	70.
			J. Myerscough	Lab	11,307	29.
					15,738	41.
1964	59,008	72.2	Hon. R.O. Stanley	C	27,801	65.
			R.G. Truman	Lab	14,777	34.
					13,024	30.(
1966	61,526	73.4	W. Clegg	C	24,217	53.
			K. Bell	Lab	14,045	31.
			J.R. Smallwood	L	6,058	13.
			P.A. Lowe	Ind	826*	1.
					10,172	22.(
1970	71,558	68.3	W. Clegg	C	33,667	68.8
			R.W. Hill	Lab	15,235	31.2
					18,432	37.(

Note:—

1966: Lowe sought election as a 'Coalition Unity' candidate.

Election	Electors	T'out	Candidate	Party	Votes	%
1950	51,535	83.9	Rt. Hon. Sir R.H. Cross, Bt.	C	28,654	66.3
			L.C. Edwards	Lab	14,583	33.7
					14,071	32.6

[Resignation on appointment as Governor of Tasmania]

1951	52,311	64.7	Rt. Hon. Sir J.A. Salter	C	24,190	71.5
(5/4)			H.A. Kelly	Lab	8,969	26.5
			F.G. Barton	ILP	686*	2.0
					15,221	45.0

1951	50,379*	78.7	Rt. Hon. Sir J.A. Salter	C	26,729	67.4
			E. Kavanagh	Lab	12,908	32.6
					13,821	34.8

[Elevation to the Peerage—Lord Salter]

1953	50,784	54.1	D. Glover	C	17,984	65.4
(2/11)			Mrs. M. Ferguson	Lab	9,512	34.6
					8,472	30.8

1955	54,198**	73.1	D. Glover	C	27,066	68.4
			T.W. Henry	Lab	12,527	31.6
					14,539	36.8

1959	61,420	77.6	D. Glover	C	32,952	69.1
			G.E. Roberts	Lab	14,701	30.9
					18,251	38.2

1964	71,050*	75.8	Sir D. Glover	C	33,704	62.6
			J. Harold	Lab	20,156	37.4
					13,548	25.2

1966	75,464	73.9	Sir D. Glover	C	32,763	58.8
			W.J. Quinn	Lab	22,983	41.2
					9,780	17.6

1970	90,946	72.6	H.B. Soref	C	40,517	61.4
			R.M. Kilroy-Silk	Lab	25,486	38.6
					15,031	22.8

Election	Electors	T'out	Candidate	Party	Votes	%
1950	60,242	83.6	†C.G. Lancaster	C	33,619	66.8
			J.B. O'Hara	Lab	11,341	22.5
			J.E. Gouldbourn	L	5,402*	10.7
					22,278	44.3
1951	60,206	79.9	C.G. Lancaster	C	35,726	74.2
			L.H. Burgess	Lab	12,408	25.8
					23,318	48.4
1955	60,623*	72.6	C.G. Lancaster	C	33,204	75.4
			R.C. Jelley	Lab	10,809	24.6
					22,395	50.8
1959	65,310	75.8	C.G. Lancaster	C	36,988	74.7
			N. Holding	Lab	12,521	25.3
					24,467	49.4
1964	71,011*	77.0	C.G. Lancaster	C	31,824	58.2
			J.D. Lees	L	11,885	21.7
			B. Stevenson	Lab	10,971	20.1
					19,939	36.5
1966	73,462	74.6	C.G. Lancaster	C	29,779	54.3
			D. Owen	Lab	13,455	24.6
			J.D. Lees	L	11,532	21.1
					16,324	29.7
1970	85,186	72.8	E.L. Gardner	C	39,459	63.6
			D.L. Mahon	Lab	13,354	21.5
			A. Thomson	L	9,214	14.9
					26,105	42.1

lection	Electors	T'out	Candidate	Party	Votes	%
950	54,833	88.2	†R.J. Davies	Lab	30,117	62.3
			Miss J.F. Crowther	C	18,259	37.7
					11,858	24.6
Resignation]						
951	54,909	76.5	J.T. Price	Lab	25,368	60.4
21/6)			F.J. Land	C	16,614	39.6
					8,754	20.8
951	55,375	86.6	J.T. Price	Lab	29,319	61.1
			F.J. Land	C	18,644	38.9
					10,675	22.2
955	55,151	83.0	J.T. Price	Lab	27,900	61.0
			E. Dunnett	C	17,848	39.0
					10,052	22.0
959	56,948	84.3	J.T. Price	Lab	29,359	61.2
			J.E. Gouldbourn	C	18,634	38.8
					10,725	22.4
964	59,797	81.9	J.T. Price	Lab	30,249	61.7
			J. Hanrahan	C	18,738	38.3
					11,511	23.4
966	61,349	78.8	J.T. Price	Lab	31,387	65.0
			J. Hanrahan	C	16,927	35.0
					14,460	30.0
970	69,564	76.9	J.T. Price	Lab	29,674	55.4
			Dr. C.A. Unsworth	C	23,847	44.6
					5,827	10.8

Election	Electors	T'out	Candidate	Party	Votes	%
1950	44,528	88.2	J.E. MacColl	Lab	21,253	54.
			R.A. Pilkington	C	18,033	45.
					3,220	8.
1951	45,761	87.4	J.E. MacColl	Lab	21,688	54.
			F.H. Wilson	C	18,315	45.
					3,373	8.
1955	45,990*	83.1	J.E. MacColl	Lab	19,823	51.
			Miss B.A. Brookes	C	18,374	48.
					1,449	3.
1959	48,966	83.4	J.E. MacColl	Lab	21,218	52.
			B.L. Butcher	C	19,620	48.
					1,598	4.
1964	55,242	77.9	J.E. MacColl	Lab	24,446	56.
			A. Pickering	C	18,572	43.
					5,874	13.
1966	60,269	72.8	J.E. MacColl	Lab	26,613	60.7
			A. Pickering	C	17,235	39.
					9,378	21.
1970	71,598	68.8	J.E. MacColl	Lab	28,384	57.7
			G.H. Pierce	C	20,841	42.3
					7,543	15.4

LEICESTERSHIRE, BOSWORTH [434]

ction	Electors	T'out	Candidate	Party	Votes	%
50	61,979	88.1	†A.C. Allen	Lab	29,282	53.6
			M.A.L. Cripps	C	15,988	29.3
			L.W. Harvey	L	9,315	17.1
					13,294	24.3
51	63,084	85.4	A.C. Allen	Lab	30,767	57.1
			D.C. Bray	C	23,122	42.9
					7,645	14.2
55	63,360*	80.7	A.C. Allen	Lab	27,626	54.0
			D.C. Bray	C	23,526	46.0
					4,100	8.0
59	65,115	83.0	W.L. Wyatt	Lab	27,734	51.3
			P.L. Braithwaite	C	26,341	48.7
					1,393	2.6
64	67,114	82.8	W.L. Wyatt	Lab	25,334	45.6
			P.L. Braithwaite	C	19,583	35.2
			J. David	L	10,652	19.2
					5,751	10.4
66	68,462	79.8	W.L. Wyatt	Lab	27,427	50.2
			C.J.P. Wood	C	19,654	36.0
			A.H. Extance	L	7,526	13.8
					7,773	14.2
70	78,192	77.3	Hon. A.C. Butler	C	30,732	50.9
			W.L. Wyatt	Lab	29,677	49.1
					1,055	1.8

Election	Electors	T'out	Candidate	Party	Votes	%
1950	62,874	89.0	J.M. Baldock	C	27,842	49.
			†H.C. Attewell	Lab	21,381	38.
			H.C. Bazeley	L	6,467*	11.
			N.H. Symington	Ind	273*	0.
					6,461	11.
1951	64,285	87.6	J.M. Baldock	C	29,395	52.
			T.C. Boyd	Lab	21,648	38.
			H.C. Bazeley	L	5,258*	9.
					7,747	13.
1955	61,019**	83.3	J.M. Baldock	C	27,257	53.
			R.N. Hales	Lab	17,073	33.
			E. Rushworth	L	6,524	12.
					10,184	20.
1959	67,790	84.6	J.A. Farr	C	29,281	51.
			J.R. Mably	Lab	16,767	29.
			E. Rushworth	L	11,333	19.
					12,514	21.
1964	80,122	83.4	J.A. Farr	C	32,905	49.
			G.H. Perry	Lab	20,389	30.
			E. Rushworth	L	13,533	20.
					12,516	18.
1966	86,198	81.6	J.A. Farr	C	32,450	46.
			W.F. Higgins	Lab	25,453	36.
			J.O. Galloway	L	12,475	17.
					6,997	9.
1970	103,125	77.3	J.A. Farr	C	44,933	56.
			J. Marshall	Lab	25,728	32.
			W.E.H. Pickard	L	9,079*	11.
					19,205	24.

Election	Electors	T'out	Candidate	Party	Votes	%
1950	51,873	87.0	†Dr. M. Follick	Lab	25,921	57.5
			S.F. Middup	C	19,196	42.5
					6,725	15.0
1951	52,914	85.9	Dr. M. Follick	Lab	25,894	57.0
			Mrs. P.E. Gordon-Spencer	C	19,571	43.0
					6,323	14.0
1955	53,183*	82.4	J.D. Cronin	Lab	24,044	54.9
			M.V. Argyle	C	19,781	45.1
					4,263	9.8
1959	54,225	84.0	J.D. Cronin	Lab	21,496	47.2
			C.G. Waite	C	17,749	39.0
			R.E. Hancock	L	6,303	13.8
					3,747	8.2
1964	55,193	83.9	J.D. Cronin	Lab	22,081	47.6
			J.L. Leatham	C	17,671	38.2
			G.R.S. Stevenson	L	6,558	14.2
					4,410	9.4
1966	55,583	82.3	J.D. Cronin	Lab	22,935	50.2
			Hon. R. Elton	C	16,911	37.0
			B.S. Stratford	L	5,875	12.8
					6,024	13.2
1970	63,564	79.1	J.D. Cronin	Lab	22,806	45.4
			Hon. R. Elton	C	22,272	44.3
			J. Mokrzycki	L	5,185*	10.3
					534	1.1

Election	Electors	T'out	Candidate	Party	Votes	%
1950	58,676	87.5	†H.A. Nutting	C	26,177	51.0
			A. Crawford	Lab	19,621	38.2
			W.H. Kirby	L	5,518*	10.8
					6,556	12.8
1951	59,671	85.5	H.A. Nutting	C	28,689	56.3
			K.F. Urwin	Lab	22,308	43.7
					6,381	12.6
1955	60,986	80.9	Rt. Hon. H.A. Nutting	C	30,074	60.9
			K.F. Urwin	Lab	19,294	39.1
					10,780	21.8
[Resignation]						
1956 (19/12)	63,516	56.5	Miss I.M.P. Pike	C	19,133	53.3
			E.J. Masters	Lab	16,771	46.7
					2,362	6.6
1959	70,233	81.4	Miss I.M.P. Pike	C	34,997	61.2
			C.W. Shepherd	Lab	22,176	38.8
					12,821	22.4
1964	77,285	82.6	Miss I.M.P. Pike	C	32,842	51.4
			D.J. Williams	Lab	19,578	30.7
			G.V.J. Pratt	L	11,392	17.9
					13,264	20.7
1966	79,616	80.5	Miss I.M.P. Pike	C	30,776	48.0
			J.R. Frears	Lab	23,181	36.2
			G.V.J. Pratt	L	10,108	15.8
					7,595	11.8
1970	90,971	76.0	Miss I.M.P. Pike	C	38,782	56.1
			K. Wood	Lab	20,907	30.2
			J.B. Pick	L	9,465	13.7
					17,875	25.9

Election	Electors	T'out	Candidate	Party	Votes	%
1950	68,411	82.2	†H.W. Butcher	NL & C	30,336	54.0
			H.W. Lee	Lab	22,374	39.8
			R.D. Blankley	L	3,500*	6.2
					7,962	14.2
1951	69,453	78.7	H.W. Butcher	NL & C	31,683	57.9
			Miss J.A. Walters	Lab	22,994	42.1
					8,689	15.8
1955	70,040	76.1	Sir H.W. Butcher	NL & C	28,412	53.3
			W.A. Rippon	Lab	19,329	36.2
			C. Valentine	L	5,581*	10.5
					9,083	17.1
1959	70,588	76.8	Sir H.W. Butcher	NL & C	29,013	53.6
			J.D.T. Williamson	Lab	17,839	32.9
			C. Valentine	L	7,334	13.5
					11,174	20.7
1964	71,064	73.9	Sir H.W. Butcher, Bt.	NL & C	29,082	55.4
			W. Long	Lab	23,451	44.6
					5,631	10.8
1966	70,765	75.0	R.B.F.S. Body	C	26,683	50.3
			R.H. Hickman	Lab	26,367	49.7
					316	0.6
1970	77,184	74.9	R.B.F.S. Body	C	33,580	58.1
			R.N.H. Sackur	Lab	24,241	41.9
					9,339	16.2

Election	Electors	T'out	Candidate	Party	Votes	%
1950	54,877	84.6	E.M. Smith	C	19,195	41.4
			A.E. Millett	Lab	14,457	31.1
			†W.D. Kendall	Ind	12,792	27.5
					4,738	10.3

[Seat Vacant at Dissolution (Death)]

1951	56,671	84.1	J.B. Godber	C	20,712	43.5
			A.E. Millett	Lab	18,540	38.9
			W.D. Kendall	L	8,396	17.6
					2,172	4.6
1955	57,546	82.8	J.B. Godber	C	24,188	50.8
			W.L. Wyatt	Lab	21,813	45.8
			Rev. R.C. Gaul	L	1,624*	3.4
					2,375	5.0
1959	59,026	81.9	J.B. Godber	C	27,482	56.8
			T.C. Skeffington-Lodge	Lab	20,867	43.2
					6,615	13.6
1964	62,677*	78.8	Rt. Hon. J.B. Godber	C	27,634	55.9
			P. Horton	Lab	21,770	44.1
					5,864	11.8
1966	64,323	80.6	Rt. Hon. J.B. Godber	C	24,748	47.7
			Mrs. M. Large	Lab	22,590	43.6
			D.C. Howie	L	4,503*	8.7
					2,158	4.1
1970	73,626	76.6	Rt. Hon. J.B. Godber	C	33,070	58.7
			W.F. Higgins	Lab	23,296	41.3
					9,774	17.4

ection	Electors	T'out	Candidate	Party	Votes	%
50	39,665	83.8	†R.J.E. Conant	C	16,498	49.6
			T.G. Bradley	Lab	13,712	41.3
			C. Valentine	L	3,024*	9.1
					2,786	8.3
51	40,116	82.2	R.J.E. Conant	C	17,850	54.1
			T.G. Bradley	Lab	15,127	45.9
					2,723	8.2
55	40,818	79.7	Sir R.J.E. Conant, Bt.	C	17,675	54.3
			T.G. Bradley	Lab	14,856	45.7
					2,819	8.6
59	41,061	80.9	K. Lewis	C	19,078	57.4
			C.S.B. Attlee	Lab	14,137	42.6
					4,941	14.8
64	42,514	79.3	K. Lewis	C	18,720	55.5
			V. Butler	Lab/Co-op	14,990	44.5
					3,730	11.0
66	43,419	77.6	K. Lewis	C	17,991	53.4
			V. Butler	Lab/Co-op	15,704	46.6
					2,287	6.8
70	50,287	75.4	K. Lewis	C	22,803	60.1
			H. Toch	Lab	15,136	39.9
					7,667	20.2

Election	Electors	T'out	Candidate	Party	Votes	%
1950	64,068	85.7	†E.L. Mallalieu	Lab	28,934	52
			M.F. Staniland	C	18,521	33.
			D.M. Cowley	L	7,438	13
					10,413	19.
1951	65,775	82.4	E.L. Mallalieu	Lab	31,151	57.
			C.P. Lawson	C	23,062	42.
					8,089	15.
1955	67,808	74.7	E.L. Mallalieu	Lab	27,847	55.
			D.S.B. Hopkins	C	22,826	45.
					5,021	10
1959	71,138	78.6	E.L. Mallalieu	Lab	28,997	51.
			R.C. Baker	C	26,893	48.
					2,104	3.
1964	76,420	77.5	E.L. Mallalieu	Lab	29,480	49.
			R.C. Baker	C	22,674	38.
			K.W. Baynes	L	7,088*	12.
					6,806	11.
1966	77,484	72.4	E.L. Mallalieu	Lab	33,699	60.
			Miss A.H. Spokes	C	22,391	39.
					11,308	20.
1970	87,058	67.6	E.L. Mallalieu	Lab	31,434	53.
			Miss A.H. Spokes	C	27,449	46.
					3,985	6.

ction	Electors	T'out	Candidate	Party	Votes	%
0	49,402	83.5	†Rt. Hon. H.F.C. Crookshank	C	17,066	41.4
			G.S. Saville	Lab	14,890	36.1
			H.I. Spence	L	9,279	22.5
					2,176	5.3
1	50,672	80.1	Rt. Hon. H.F.C. Crookshank	C	19,915	49.1
			G.R.S. Hawkins	Lab	16,074	39.6
			J.W.L. Gregory	L	4,580*	11.3
					3,841	9.5
5	50,399	76.8	Rt. Hon. H.F.C. Crookshank	C	21,576	55.8
			G.R.S. Hawkins	Lab	17,107	44.2
					4,469	11.6

evation to the Peerage—Viscount Crookshank]

6 /2)	50,806	61.9	M.R. Kimball	C	12,836	40.8
			H.D.L.G. Walston	Lab	11,830	37.6
			H.I. Spence	L	6,806	21.6
					1,006	3.2
9	50,051	80.8	M.R. Kimball	C	20,056	49.6
			H.D.L.G. Walston	Lab	13,247	32.7
			Dr. R.I. Douglas	L	7,147	17.7
					6,809	16.9
4	51,499	78.2	M.R. Kimball	C	19,235	47.7
			Dr. D.R.L.M. Poirier	Lab	12,126	30.1
			Dr. R.I. Douglas	L	8,930	22.2
					7,109	17.6
6	52,432	75.8	M.R. Kimball	C	18,770	47.2
			A. Day	Lab	14,904	37.5
			G.R.S. Stevenson	L	6,064	15.3
					3,866	9.7
0	59,099	74.7	M.R. Kimball	C	22,163	50.2
			M.P. Tracy	Lab	14,454	32.7
			R.B. Blackmore	L	7,543	17.1
					7,709	17.5

Election	Electors	T'out	Candidate	Party	Votes	%
1950	43,183	78.7	†J.F.W. Maitland	C	22,329	65
			F.H. Clark	Lab	11,671	34
					10,658	31
1951	43,285	76.7	J.F.W. Maitland	C	22,043	66
			F.H. Clark	Lab	11,143	33
					10,900	32
1955	42,967	71.0	J.F.W. Maitland	C	20,392	66
			W. Pashby	Lab	10,122	33
					10,270	33
1959	42,262	70.3	J.F.W. Maitland	C	19,799	66
			H.W. Peck	Lab	9,928	33
					9,871	33
1964	42,778	74.7	Sir J.F.W. Maitland	C	15,854	49
			T.F. Smith	L	8,069	25
			R. Brumby	Lab	8,044	25
					7,785	24
1966	42,625	75.9	P.H.B. Tapsell	C	15,090	46
			R.N.H. Sackur	Lab	9,715	30
			T.F. Smith	L	7,552	23
					5,375	16
1970	46,959	74.2	P.H.B. Tapsell	C	19,299	55
			E.A. Skinns	Lab	8,860	25
			R.S. Miller	L	6,707	19
					10,439	30

Election	Electors	T'out	Candidate	Party	Votes	%
1950	49,207	82.4	†C. Osborne	C	19,647	48.4
			H.J.H. Dyer	Lab	15,063	37.2
			A.W. Cox	L	5,817	14.4
					4,584	11.2
1951	49,995	80.5	C. Osborne	C	21,587	53.7
			H.J.H. Dyer	Lab	15,819	39.3
			Rev. R.C. Gaul	L	2,822*	7.0
					5,768	14.4
1955	50,329	73.7	C. Osborne	C	21,796	58.8
			Dr. D.R.L.M. Poirier	Lab	15,276	41.2
					6,520	17.6
1959	51,773	76.5	C. Osborne	C	24,211	61.1
			F.R. MacDonald	Lab	15,408	38.9
					8,803	22.2
1964	55,677*	77.9	Sir C. Osborne	C	21,227	49.0
			F.R. MacDonald	Lab	14,188	32.7
			E.I. Marshall	L	7,949	18.3
					7,039	16.3
1966	57,430	75.0	Sir C. Osborne	C	19,977	46.3
			R. Brumby	Lab	15,885	36.9
			Dr. E.I. Marshall	L	7,222	16.8
					4,092	9.4
[Death]						
1969 (4/12)	62,911	44.7	J.H. Archer	C	16,317	57.9
			B. Briggs	Lab	5,590	19.9
			J. Adams	L	5,003	17.8
			Sir G.P.M. FitzGerald, Bt.	DP	1,225*	4.4
					10,727	38.0
1970	67,443	71.7	J.H. Archer	C	25,659	53.1
			J. Murray	Lab	16,403	33.9
			J. Adams	L	6,279	13.0
					9,256	19.2

Election	Electors	T'out	Candidate	Party	Votes	%
1950	70,161	81.8	G.B. Craddock	C	26,177	45.6
			F.W. Temple	Lab	26,146	45.6
			F.J. Halpin	L	5,048*	8.8
					31	0.0
1951	72,599	83.9	G.B. Craddock	C	31,031	50.9
			A.E. Hunter	Lab	29,908	49.1
					1,123	1.8
1955	46,050**	77.7	G.B. Craddock	C	20,888	58.4
			J.P. Carruthers	Lab	14,906	41.6
					5,982	16.8
1959	52,115	81.3	G.B. Craddock	C	25,221	59.6
			J.P. Carruthers	Lab	17,128	40.4
					8,093	19.2
1964	59,000	80.1	Sir G.B. Craddock	C	22,230	47.0
			R.S. Stokes	Lab	16,797	35.5
			M.J. Hayes	L	8,252	17.5
					5,433	11.5
1966	60,676	80.9	Sir G.B. Craddock	C	22,473	45.8
			R.G. Wallace	Lab	19,986	40.7
			Miss N. Wyn Ellis	L	6,624	13.5
					2,487	5.1
1970	68,579	73.3	H.E. Atkins	C	27,266	54.2
			P.L. Cheney	Lab	18,239	36.3
			R.H. Longland	L	4,792*	9.5
					9,027	17.9

Election	Electors	T'out	Candidate	Party	Votes	%
950	49,446	84.6	†F. Beswick	Lab/Co-op	20,139	48.2
			C.B. Thorne	C	17,741	42.4
			J.E. Aylett	L	3,933*	9.4
					2,398	5.8
1951	51,022	84.7	F. Beswick	Lab/Co-op	21,249	49.1
			L.C. Curran	C	19,701	45.6
			L. Fior	L	2,289*	5.3
					1,548	3.5
1955	53,372	81.7	F. Beswick	Lab/Co-op	22,244	51.0
			L.C. Curran	C	21,368	49.0
					876	2.0
1959	56,997	84.3	L.C. Curran	C	22,360	46.5
			F. Beswick	Lab/Co-op	20,970	43.6
			G.R. Goodall	L	4,746*	9.9
					1,390	2.9
1964	58,226	80.8	L.C. Curran	C	20,519	43.7
			T.J. Parker	Lab	19,866	42.2
			G.R. Goodall	L	6,644	14.1
					653	1.5
1966	58,070	82.6	J. Ryan	Lab	21,793	45.5
			L.C. Curran	C	20,903	43.6
			G.R. Goodall	L	5,241*	10.9
					890	1.9
1970	63,362	74.9	L.C. Curran	C	23,414	49.3
			J. Ryan	Lab	19,768	41.7
			G.R. Goodall	L	4,265*	9.0
					3,646	7.6

Election	Electors	T'out	Candidate	Party	Votes	%
1950	47,199	84.3	†F. Medlicott	NL & C	20,407	51.
			G.W. Holderness	Lab	16,516	41
			P.V.B. Jebb	L	2,859*	7.
					3,891	9.
1951	47,923*	81.8	F. Medlicott	NL & C	21,909	55.
			J.R. Lambley	Lab	17,270	44.
					4,639	11.
1955	49,268	77.4	Sir F. Medlicott	NL & C (Ind) (NL & C)	21,851	57.
			Miss E.R. Littlejohn	Lab	16,288	42.
					5,563	14.
1959	54,436	79.9	R.C.M. Collard	NL & C	21,918	50.
			F.H. Stone	Lab	15,131	34.
			G.M. Goode	L	6,465	14.
					6,787	15.
[Death]						
1962 (22/11)	58,483	60.2	I.H.J.L. Gilmour	NL & C (C)	13,268	37.
			G.B.L. Bennett	Lab	13,048	37.
			G.M. Goode	L	7,915	22.
			A.S.K. Colman	Ind L	909*	2.
			J. Andrews	Ind Ser	79*	0.
					220	0.
1964	61,254	81.5	I.H.J.L. Gilmour	C	24,486	49.
			G.B.L. Bennett	Lab	18,481	37.
			G.M. Goode	L	6,961	13.
					6,005	12.
1966	64,492	79.8	I.H.J.L. Gilmour	C	27,935	54.
			B. Davies	Lab	23,529	45.
					4,406	8.
1970	75,695	76.8	I.H.J.L. Gilmour	C	32,921	56.7
			C.R. Coyne	Lab	19,030	32.7
			R. Drew	L	6,172*	10.6
					13,891	24.0

Note:—

1962: Colman was opposed to Britain entering the Common Market.

,ection	Electors	T'out	Candidate	Party	Votes	%
)50	51,040	83.8	†F.J. Wise	Lab	19,399	45.3
			R. Scott-Miller	C	19,129	44.7
			R.A. Winch	L	4,266*	10.0
					270	0.6
)51	51,914	82.8	R. Scott-Miller	C	21,954	51.1
			F.J. Wise	Lab	21,017	48.9
					937	2.2
)55	51,867	78.2	R. Scott-Miller	C	20,949	51.6
			H.M. Lawson	Lab	19,611	48.4
					1,338	3.2
)59	52,125	79.8	D.G. Bullard	C	21,671	52.1
			G.C. Jackson	Lab	19,906	47.9
					1,765	4.2
)64	53,186	80.5	J.D. Page	Lab	21,460	50.1
			D.G. Bullard	C	21,356	49.9
					104	0.2
)66	53,833	82.9	J.D. Page	Lab	23,324	52.3
			D.G. Bullard	C	21,305	47.7
					2,019	4.6
)70	60,800	78.3	C. Brocklebank-Fowler	C	23,822	50.0
			J.D. Page	Lab	23,789	50.0
					33	0.0

Election	Electors	T'out	Candidate	Party	Votes	%
1950	48,906	84.3	†E.G. Gooch	Lab	19,790	48.0
			D.M. Reid	NL & C	17,741	43.0
			A.H. Jones	L	3,703*	9.0
					2,049	5.0
1951	50,032	83.7	E.G. Gooch	Lab	21,067	50.3
			D.M. Reid	NL & C	20,788	49.7
					279	0.6
1955	49,674	81.6	E.G. Gooch	Lab	20,899	51.5
			Sir W.S. Jameson	NL & C	19,657	48.5
					1,242	3.0
1959	48,756	79.8	E.G. Gooch	Lab	19,784	50.8
			F.H. Easton	NL & C	19,126	49.2
					658	1.6

[Seat Vacant at Dissolution (Death)]

Election	Electors	T'out	Candidate	Party	Votes	%
1964	48,488	79.7	B. Hazell	Lab	19,360	50.1
			F.H. Easton	C	19,307	49.9
					53	0.2
1966	49,106	83.2	B. Hazell	Lab	20,796	50.9
			R.F. Howell	C	20,059	49.1
					737	1.8
1970	55,349	80.4	R.F. Howell	C	24,587	55.3
			B. Hazell	Lab	19,903	44.7
					4,684	10.6

NORFOLK, SOUTH [450]

Election	Electors	T'out	Candidate	Party	Votes	%
1950	42,870	83.9	P.A.D. Baker	C	18,143	50.5
			†C.P. Mayhew	Lab	15,714	43.7
			G.Q. Bryant	L	2,097*	5.8
					2,429	6.8
1951	43,668	82.4	P.A.D. Baker	C	19,610	54.5
			L. Scutts	Lab	16,371	45.5
					3,239	9.0

Expulsion from the House of Commons]

1955	44,092	66.6	J.E.B. Hill	C	15,119	51.5
(13/1)			J.M. Stewart	Lab	14,254	48.5
					865	3.0
1955	43,887	81.8	J.E.B. Hill	C	18,690	52.1
			J.M. Stewart	Lab	17,215	47.9
					1,475	4.2
1959	43,458	82.4	J.E.B. Hill	C	19,275	53.8
			J.M. Stewart	Lab	16,542	46.2
					2,733	7.6
1964	44,774	82.7	J.E.B. Hill	C	17,178	46.4
			F.R. Thompson	Lab	15,012	40.6
			B.H.P. Turner	L	4,819	13.0
					2,166	5.8
1966	46,557	81.4	J.E.B. Hill	C	16,968	44.7
			G.B.L. Bennett	Lab	16,849	44.5
			R.L. Crouch	L	4,079*	10.8
					119	0.2
1970	55,476	78.6	J.E.B. Hill	C	22,614	51.9
			C. Shaw	Lab	17,172	39.4
			B.E. Goldstone	L	3,811*	8.7
					5,442	12.5

Note:—

1951: Baker was expelled from the House of Commons on December 16, 1954, as a result of being convicted at the Central Criminal Court on November 30, 1954. He was sentenced to seven years imprisonment for uttering forged documents. See House of Commons Papers, 1954-55 (11) x, 535.

Election	Electors	T'out	Candidate	Party	Votes	%
1950	39,620	83.4	†S. Dye	Lab	15,649	47.
			D.G. Bullard	C	15,389	46.
			G.J.S. Dennis	L	2,009*	6.
					260	0.
1951	40,552	82.6	D.G. Bullard	C	16,970	50.
			S. Dye	Lab	16,528	49.
					442	1.
1955	40,396	82.6	S. Dye	Lab	16,781	50.
			D.G. Bullard	C	16,588	49.
					193	0.
[Death]						
1959 (25/3)	39,971	75.2	A.V. Hilton	Lab	15,314	51.
			Mrs. M.E. Kellett	C	13,960	46.
			A. Fountaine	Nat	785*	2.
					1,354	4.
1959	40,283	83.5	A.V. Hilton	Lab	16,858	50.
			Mrs. M.E. Kellett	C	16,780	49.
					78	0.
1964	41,192	82.0	P.L. Hawkins	C	16,728	49.
			A.V. Hilton	Lab	16,605	49.
			V.E. Welch	Ind	427*	1.
					123	0.
1966	41,651	84.0	P.L. Hawkins	C	17,880	51.
			N.J. Insley	Lab	17,105	48.
					775	2.
1970	48,145	80.6	P.L. Hawkins	C	22,220	57
			L.J. Potter	Lab	16,572	42
					5,648	14.

Notes:—

1959: Fountaine advocated a nationalist policy and received some support from the
(25/3) National Labour Party of which he became President shortly after the election.

1964: Welch was opposed to Britain entering the Common Market.

ection	Electors	T'out	Candidate	Party	Votes	%
50	51,093	84.1	†E. Kinghorn	Lab	19,131	44.6
			E.C. Baker	C	17,969	41.8
			R.T.A. Cornwell	L	5,854	13.6
					1,162	2.8
51	52,060	83.3	A. Fell	C	22,180	51.2
			E. Kinghorn	Lab	21,165	48.8
					1,015	2.4
55	52,350	79.7	A. Fell	C (Ind C) (C)	21,317	51.1
			E. Kinghorn	Lab	20,400	48.9
					917	2.2
59	52,847	79.6	A. Fell	C	22,827	54.3
			S.C. Davis	Lab	19,248	45.7
					3,579	8.6
64	54,000	80.3	A. Fell	C	20,310	46.8
			S.C. Davis	Lab	18,381	42.4
			D.R.A. Spreckley	L	4,680*	10.8
					1,929	4.4
66	54,836	79.9	H. Gray	Lab	22,296	50.9
			A. Fell	C	21,499	49.1
					797	1.8
70	60,159	77.4	A. Fell	C	23,088	49.6
			H. Gray	Lab	19,931	42.8
			Mrs. J.R. Knott	L	3,523*	7.6
					3,157	6.8

Election	Electors	T'out	Candidate	Party	Votes	%
1950	65,236	88.4	†G.R. Mitchison	Lab	30,423	52
			Sir G. Isham	C	22,169	38
			I.T. Morrow	L	4,692*	8
			L.P. O'Connor	Com	368*	0
					8,254	14
1951	66,985	87.2	G.R. Mitchison	Lab	32,604	56
			C.P.B. Bailey	C	25,777	44
					6,827	11
1955	69,764	81.6	G.R. Mitchison	Lab	31,398	56
			J.F. Nash	C	25,495	44
					5,903	10
1959	74,696	83.5	G.R. Mitchison	Lab	32,933	52
			J.H. Lewis	C	29,448	47
					3,485	5

[Seat Vacant at Dissolution (Elevation to a Life Peerage—Lord Mitchison)]

Election	Electors	T'out	Candidate	Party	Votes	%
1964	80,469	81.5	Sir G.S. de Freitas	Lab	36,210	55
			J.H. Lewis	C	29,405	44
					6,805	10
1966	82,509	81.3	Sir G.S. de Freitas	Lab	35,337	52
			Dr. T.E.T. Weston	C	23,877	35
			A.T. Smith	L	7,903*	11
					11,460	17
1970	94,882	76.0	Rt. Hon. Sir G.S. de Freitas	Lab	34,803	48
			J.C. Taylor	C	30,613	42
			A.J.W. Haigh	L	6,695*	9
					4,190	5

ection	Electors	T'out	Candidate	Party	Votes	%
50	57,502	86.4	H. Nicholls	C	22,815	46.0
			†S. Tiffany	Lab/Co-op	22,671	45.6
			W.I. Akst	L	4,180*	8.4
					144	0.4
51	58,831	86.8	H. Nicholls	C	24,536	48.1
			A.E.V.A. Farrer	Lab	24,163	47.3
			W.I. Akst	L	2,367*	4.6
					373	0.8
55	59,513	83.0	H. Nicholls	C	26,319	53.3
			A.E.V.A. Farrer	Lab	23,081	46.7
					3,238	6.6
59	60,545	83.0	H. Nicholls	C	27,414	54.6
			Miss B. Boothroyd	Lab	22,830	45.4
					4,584	9.2
64	63,181	81.8	Sir H. Nicholls, Bt.	C	24,045	46.5
			D.A. Saunders	Lab	21,428	41.5
			L. Young	L	6,181*	12.0
					2,617	5.0
66	63,839	81.4	Sir H. Nicholls, Bt.	C	23,944	46.1
			M.J. Ward	Lab	23,941	46.0
			B.E. Goldstone	L	4,093*	7.9
					3	0.1
70	71,493	78.2	Sir H. Nicholls, Bt.	C	30,227	54.1
			M.J. Ward	Lab	25,662	45.9
					4,565	8.2

Election	Electors	T'out	Candidate	Party	Votes	%
1950	44,873	87.1	†R.E. Manningham-Buller	C	18,612	47.
			D.G. Webb	Lab	16,852	43.
			L. Evans	L	3,620*	9.
					1,760	4.
1951	46,234	85.9	R.E. Manningham-Buller	C	21,282	53.
			D.G. Webb	Lab	18,434	46.
					2,848	7.
1955	47,614	81.6	Rt. Hon. Sir R.E. Manningham-Buller	C	21,497	55.
			R.H. Lewis	Lab	17,339	44.
					4,158	10.
1959	51,403	82.7	Rt. Hon. Sir R.E. Manningham-Buller, Bt.	C	24,226	57.
			A. Richardson	Lab	18,292	43.
					5,934	14.

[Resignation on appointment as Lord Chancellor and elevation to the Peerage—Lord Dilhorne]

Election	Electors	T'out	Candidate	Party	Votes	%
1962 (22/11)	52,575	69.0	A.A. Jones	C	14,921	41.
			I. Wilde	Lab	14,004	38.
			N. Picarda	L	7,002	19.
			P.B. Buchan	Ind Ser	332*	0.
					917	2.
1964	55,080	83.0	A.A. Jones	C	24,823	54.
			I. Wilde	Lab	20,916	45.
					3,907	8.
1966	57,626	82.2	A.A. Jones	C	25,023	52.
			G.T. Ridge	Lab	22,332	47.
					2,691	5.
1970	73,005	77.8	A.A. Jones	C	29,070	51.
			G.J. Roberts	Lab	21,131	37.
			C.A.P. Smout	L	6,626*	11.
					7,939	13.

Election	Electors	T'out	Candidate	Party	Votes	%
950	51,326	89.5	†G.S. Lindgren	Lab	21,640	47.1
			J.C. Sayer	C	13,075	28.5
			E.T. Malindine	L	11,229	24.4
					8,565	18.6
1951	52,077	88.4	G.S. Lindgren	Lab	24,113	52.4
			F.R. Parsons	C	21,912	47.6
					2,201	4.8
1955	51,811	86.0	G.S. Lindgren	Lab	22,745	51.0
			A.A. Jones	C	21,819	49.0
					926	2.0
1959	52,261	86.7	M.A. Hamilton	C	22,964	50.7
			G.S. Lindgren	Lab	22,358	49.3
					606	1.4
1964	53,224	87.1	H. Howarth	Lab	19,592	42.2
			M.A. Hamilton	C	19,545	42.2
			P.A.J. Pettit	L	7,227	15.6
					47	0.0
1966	54,566	86.5	H. Howarth	Lab	24,705	52.4
			J.L. Leatham	C	22,472	47.6
					2,233	4.8
[Death]						
1969 (4/12)	59,540	69.6	P.D. Fry	C	22,548	54.4
			J.H. Mann	Lab	16,499	39.8
			M.P. Coney	Ind	2,421*	5.8
					6,049	14.6
1970	64,563	81.4	P.D. Fry	C	27,459	52.2
			J.H. Mann	Lab	25,107	47.8
					2,352	4.4

Note:—

1969: Coney was opposed to Britain entering the Common Market and also to coloured immigration.

Election	Electors	T'out	Candidate	Party	Votes	%
1950	42,075	80.1	†R.A.F. Thorp	C	14,804	43.9
			Sir A.S. Comyns Carr	L	10,260	30.4
			J. Davis	Lab	8,651	25.7
					4,544	13.5
1951	42,438	78.8	Viscount Lambton	C	17,632	52.7
			T.H. Jones	Lab/Co-op	11,069	33.1
			J.B. Frankenburg	L	4,759	14.2
					6,563	19.6
1955	41,664	72.8	Viscount Lambton	C	18,301	60.3
			J. Frater	Lab	12,024	39.7
					6,277	20.6
1959	40,951	77.0	Viscount Lambton	C	19,904	63.1
			R.C. Jelley	Lab	11,637	36.9
					8,267	26.2
1964	39,915	79.5	Viscount Lambton	C	15,851	49.9
			R.C. Jelley	Lab	8,218	25.9
			N.B. Madison	L	7,681	24.2
					7,633	24.0
1966	39,155	76.6	Viscount Lambton	C	14,281	47.7
			J.W. Conway	Lab	9,908	33.0
			A. Herbert	L	5,796	19.3
					4,373	14.7
1970	41,669	73.7	A.C.F. Lambton	C	15,558	50.7
			R.N. Wareing	Lab/Co-op	8,413	27.4
			A.J. Beith	L	6,741	21.9
					7,145	23.3

Note:—

1966: Lambton succeeded to the Peerage (Earl of Durham) in February 1970 but he disclaimed it for life.

Election	Electors	T'out	Candidate	Party	Votes	%
1950	46,635	61.9	†Rt. Hon. D. Clifton Brown	C	24,703	85.6
			A. Hancock	Ind L	4,154	14.4
					20,549	71.2
1951	47,363	82.4	R.M. Speir	C	23,267	59.6
			T.L. MacDonald	Lab	15,768	40.4
					7,499	19.2
1955	47,438	77.3	R.M. Speir	C	23,462	64.0
			W.E. Garrett	Lab	13,198	36.0
					10,264	28.0
1959	49,906	81.1	R.M. Speir	C	25,500	63.0
			W.H.W. Roberts	Lab	14,980	37.0
					10,520	26.0
1964	54,122	81.9	R.M. Speir	C	22,468	50.7
			J. Alderson	Lab	14,127	31.9
			D.A. Robson	L	7,722	17.4
					8,341	18.8
1966	55,320	78.5	Rt. Hon. A.G.F. Rippon	C	20,889	48.1
			J.B. Lamb	Lab/Co-op	16,105	37.1
			D.A. Robson	L	6,434	14.8
					4,784	11.0
1970	62,564	75.4	Rt. Hon. A.G.F. Rippon	C	24,516	51.9
			J.E. Miller	Lab	16,645	35.3
			D.V. Cogan	L	6,021	12.8
					7,871	16.6

Note:—

1950: Clifton Brown was the Speaker of the House of Commons.

Election	Electors	T'out	Candidate	Party	Votes	%
1950	44,507	86.6	†R.J. Taylor	Lab	27,548	71.!
			T. Turnbull	C	10,973	28.!
					16,575	43.(
1951	45,117	85.5	R.J. Taylor	Lab	27,718	71.!
			P.M. Colvin-Smith	C	10,843	28.
[Death]					16,875	43.!
1954 (4/11)	45,177	73.0	W.J. Owen	Lab/Co-op	23,491	71.:
			R.W. Elliott	C	9,469	28.:
					14,022	42.(
1955	44,866	80.4	W.J. Owen	Lab/Co-op	25,452	70.(
			R.W. Elliott	C	10,619	29.4
					14,833	41.:
1959	45,361	84.1	W.J. Owen	Lab/Co-op	27,435	71.!
			D. Bloom	C	10,716	28.1
					16,719	43.!
1964	44,451	80.8	W.J. Owen	Lab/Co-op	26,114	72.7
			D. Bloom	C	9,805	27.3
					16,309	45.4
1966	44,096	76.9	W.J. Owen	Lab/Co-op	25,223	74.4
			N.D.S. Porter	C	8,698	25.6
					16,525	48.8

[Seat Vacant at Dissolution (Resignation)]

Election	Electors	T'out	Candidate	Party	Votes	%
1970	47,556	76.0	G. Grant	Lab	21,826	60.4
			K.I. Tunnicliffe	C	9,515	26.3
			R. McClure	L	4,825	13.3
					12,311	34.1

Election	Electors	T'out	Candidate	Party	Votes	%
1955	59,820	76.5	W.N. Warbey	Lab	32,905	71.9
			A.S. Plane	C	12,836	28.1
					20,069	43.8
1959	61,139	82.0	W.N. Warbey	Lab	35,432	70.7
			J.G.W. Sandys	C	14,690	29.3
					20,742	41.4
1964	61,960	77.2	W.N. Warbey	Lab	34,841	72.8
			T.L. Wright	C	12,989	27.2
					21,852	45.6
1966	62,019	73.3	D.I. Marquand	Lab	33,477	73.6
			E.T. Gibbons	C	11,991	26.4
					21,486	47.2
1970	67,623	70.2	D.I. Marquand	Lab	32,372	68.2
			R.N. Kemm	C	15,089	31.8
					17,283	36.4

Election	Electors	T'out	Candidate	Party	Votes	%
1950	62,879	87.2	†Rt. Hon. F.J. Bellenger	Lab	31,589	57.6
			J.J.C. Irving	C	17,622	32.2
			W.G.E. Dyer	L	5,590*	10.2
					13,967	25.4
1951	64,139	84.4	Rt. Hon. F.J. Bellenger	Lab	32,850	60.7
			W.A. Sime	C	21,257	39.3
					11,593	21.4
1955	58,203**	79.5	Rt. Hon. F.J. Bellenger	Lab	26,873	58.1
			Mrs. K.V. Maiden	C	19,375	41.9
					7,498	16.2
1959	59,907	80.2	Rt. Hon. F.J. Bellenger	Lab	27,875	58.0
			M.J. Cowling	C	20,162	42.0
					7,713	16.0
1964	60,752	77.0	Rt. Hon. F.J. Bellenger	Lab	27,612	59.0
			R.W.M. Orme	C	19,167	41.0
					8,445	18.0
1966	61,047	73.4	Rt. Hon. F.J. Bellenger	Lab	27,623	61.6
			R.W.M. Orme	C	17,195	38.4
					10,428	23.2
[Death]						
1968 (31/10)	63,364	68.0	J.W. Ashton	Lab	21,394	49.7
			J.T. Lester	C	20,654	47.9
			T. Lynch	NUSS	1,053*	2.4
					740	1.8
1970	68,942	76.6	J.W. Ashton	Lab	28,959	54.9
			J.T. Lester	C	20,698	39.2
			M. Hayden-Baillie	L	3,125*	5.9
					8,261	15.7

ction	Electors	T'out	Candidate	Party	Votes	%
50	56,815	86.1	†F.S. Cocks	Lab	35,471	72.5
			C.P.B. Bailey	C	13,445	27.5
					22,026	45.0
51	57,785	84.1	F.S. Cocks	Lab	35,317	72.7
			A.J. Gorman	C	13,274	27.3
					22,043	45.4
eath]						
53	58,175	63.5	W.N. Warbey	Lab	27,356	74.1
7/9)			A.J. Gorman	C	9,559	25.9
					17,797	48.2

This constituency was divided in 1955.

Election	Electors	T'out	Candidate	Party	Votes	%
1950	55,008	87.2	†K.W.M. Pickthorn	C	19,585	40.9
			†Mrs. F.B. Paton	Lab	19,190	40.0
			C.C. Kirk	L	9,176	19.1
					395	0.9
1951	56,362	87.0	K.W.M. Pickthorn	C	24,429	49.8
			Mrs. F.B. Paton	Lab	20,685	42.2
			G.W.H. Parker	L	3,930*	8.0
					3,744	7.6
1955	59,479	81.0	K.W.M. Pickthorn	C	27,521	57.1
			Mrs. F.B. Paton	Lab	20,664	42.9
					6,857	14.2
1959	64,554	82.7	Sir K.W.M. Pickthorn, Bt.	C	30,722	57.6
			P. Myers	Lab	22,645	42.4
					8,077	15.2
1964	71,285	83.4	Sir K.W.M. Pickthorn, Bt.	C	27,896	46.9
			R.B. Mellor	Lab	21,546	36.2
			M.G. Payne	L	10,034	16.9
					6,350	10.7
1966	75,931	82.7	P.W. Holland	C	28,635	45.6
			A.L. Ramsden	Lab	24,589	39.2
			M.G. Payne	L	9,570	15.2
					4,046	6.4
1970	89,446	74.8	P.W. Holland	C	39,840	59.6
			C. Bennett	Lab	27,043	40.4
					12,797	19.2

lection	Electors	T'out	Candidate	Party	Votes	%
)50	63,315	85.8	†H.B. Taylor	Lab	36,224	66.6
			H.L. Milliard	C	12,495	23.0
			C.H.P. Robinson	L	5,145*	9.5
			W.L. Ellis	Com	482*	0.9
					23,729	43.6
)51	63,662	83.3	H.B. Taylor	Lab	37,097	69.9
			Mrs. M.E. Williamson	C	15,961	30.1
					21,136	39.8
)55	55,215**	78.3	H.B. Taylor	Lab	29,643	68.5
			I.B. Church	C	13,610	31.5
					16,033	37.0
)59	56,674	80.8	H.B. Taylor	Lab	31,066	67.9
			Hon. M.R.V. Eliot	C	14,700	32.1
					16,366	35.8
)64	58,698	77.9	H.B. Taylor	Lab	29,055	63.6
			K.H. Clarke	C	10,021	21.9
			R. Strauther	L	6,628	14.5
					19,034	41.7
)66	59,868	75.0	J.D. Concannon	Lab	28,849	64.3
			K.H. Clarke	C	9,987	22.2
			R. Strauther	L	5,483*	12.2
			F.C. Westacott	Com	590*	1.3
					18,862	42.1
)70	67,233	68.7	J.D. Concannon	Lab	30,554	66.1
			C.W.H. Morton	C	15,027	32.5
			F.C. Westacott	Com	628*	1.4
					15,527	33.6

NOTTINGHAMSHIRE, NEWARK [465]

Election	Electors	T'out	Candidate	Party	Votes	%
1950	60,660	88.1	†G. Deer	Lab	28,959	54.
			†S. Shephard	C	21,522	40.
			E.H. Pickering	L	2,950*	5.
					7,437	13.
1951	62,353	85.5	G. Deer	Lab	30,476	57.
			R.H. Watson	C	22,817	42
					7,659	14.
1955	52,655**	83.5	G. Deer	Lab	23,057	52.
			R.H. Watson	C	20,916	47.
					2,141	4.
1959	54,597	84.9	G. Deer	Lab	24,072	51.
			P. Jenkin-Jones	C	22,300	48.
					1,772	3.
1964	57,906	83.1	E.S. Bishop	Lab	26,171	54.
			P. Jenkin-Jones	C	21,975	45.
					4,196	8.
1966	59,492	81.2	E.S. Bishop	Lab	27,402	56.
			P. Jenkin-Jones	C	20,913	43.
					6,489	13.
1970	67,947	76.1	E.S. Bishop	Lab	26,455	51.
			D.G. Allen	C	25,235	48.
					1,220	2.

ection	Electors	T'out	Candidate	Party	Votes	%
50	60,868	87.8	M. Redmayne	C	27,497	51.5
			H.M. Lawson	Lab	20,860	39.0
			Mrs. E.F. Stallabrass	L	5,065*	9.5
					6,637	12.5
51	62,218	86.0	M. Redmayne	C	30,972	57.9
			R.J. Ledger	Lab	22,506	42.1
					8,466	15.8
55	54,760**	82.9	M. Redmayne	C	23,509	51.8
			D.R. Hardman	Lab	21,866	48.2
					1,643	3.6
59	58,971	85.4	M. Redmayne	C	27,392	54.4
			N.D. Sandelson	Lab	22,952	45.6
					4,440	8.8
64	63,606	83.4	Rt. Hon. M. Redmayne	C	27,936	52.6
			A.C. Latham	Lab	25,137	47.4
					2,799	5.2
66	65,436	85.5	A.J. Gardner	Lab	25,623	45.8
			Rt. Hon. Sir M. Redmayne, Bt.	C	25,243	45.1
			M.J. Smith	L	5,085*	9.1
					380	0.7
70	75,183	79.7	K.H. Clarke	C	30,966	51.6
			A.J. Gardner	Lab	24,798	41.4
			P.M. Browne	L	4,180*	7.0
					6,168	10.2

Election	Electors	T'out	Candidate	Party	Votes	%
1950	58,809	83.6	†A.D. Dodds-Parker	C	21,365	43.4
			C.R. Fenton	Lab/Co-op	19,408	39.5
			L.W. Robson	L	8,392	17.1
					1,957	3.9
1951	59,897	82.8	A.D. Dodds-Parker	C	23,246	46.9
			W.J. Bird	Lab	19,672	39.6
			L.W. Robson	L	6,706	13.5
					3,574	7.3
1955	61,019	77.1	A.D. Dodds-Parker	C	25,598	54.4
			N.F. Stogdon	Lab	21,473	45.6
					4,125	8.8
1959	64,414	81.0	H.N. Marten	C	26,413	50.7
			D.J. Buckle	Lab	19,699	37.7
			A.S.K. Colman	L	6,074*	11.6
					6,714	13.0
1964	70,178	82.4	H.N. Marten	C	27,281	47.2
			G.T. Fowler	Lab	22,159	38.3
			F.J. Ware	L	7,851	13.6
			J.C. Hayward	Agric	534*	0.9
					5,122	8.9
1966	74,279	81.9	H.N. Marten	C	28,932	47.5
			D.W. Young	Lab	24,529	40.3
			Mrs. P. Jessel	L	7,407*	12.2
					4,403	7.2
1970	88,919	77.3	H.N. Marten	C	36,712	53.4
			A.C. Booth	Lab	25,166	36.6
			G.J. Fisher	L	6,859*	10.0
					11,546	16.8

lection	Electors	T'out	Candidate	Party	Votes	%
950	50,749	81.7	J.A. Hay	C	20,488	49.4
			A.E.G. Hawkins	Lab	14,709	35.5
			P.W.V. Minoprio	L	6,255	15.1
					5,779	13.9
951	51,997	78.3	J.A. Hay	C	23,621	58.0
			C. Gallop	Lab	17,090	42.0
					6,531	16.0
955	54,459	75.4	J.A. Hay	C	24,061	58.6
			Miss N.J.T. Wiles	Lab	16,980	41.4
					7,081	17.2
959	58,319	78.3	J.A. Hay	C	24,417	53.4
			A. Ledger	Lab/Co-op	15,014	32.9
			F.C. Truman	L	6,261	13.7
					9,403	20.5
964	64,617*	78.3	J.A. Hay	C	24,898	49.3
			A. Ledger	Lab/Co-op	16,614	32.8
			A.W. Giles	L	9,081	17.9
					8,284	16.5
966	69,584	75.2	J.A. Hay	C	28,994	55.4
			G. Cunningham	Lab	23,320	44.6
					5,674	10.8
970	84,669	74.0	J.A. Hay	C	33,452	53.5
			Miss M.J. Denby	Lab	19,310	30.8
			A.W. Giles	L	8,907	14.2
			D.F.B. Brunner	Ind	960*	1.5
					14,142	22.7

Note:—

1970: Brunner was opposed to Britain entering the Common Market.

Election	Electors	T'out	Candidate	Party	Votes	%
1950	46,189	79.9	†U. Corbett	C	22,340	60.5
			I.A.J. Williams	Lab	14,573	39.5
					7,767	21.0
1951	47,168	77.7	C.J. Holland-Martin	C	22,073	60.2
			R.J. Barker	Lab	14,596	39.8
					7,477	20.4
1955	47,040	71.8	C.J. Holland-Martin	C	20,816	61.7
			R.J. Barker	Lab	12,937	38.3
					7,879	23.4
1959	46,735	76.2	C.J. Holland-Martin	C	21,464	60.3
			J. Garwell	Lab	14,138	39.7
					7,326	20.6
[Death]						
1960 (16/11)	46,699	63.6	J. More	C	13,777	46.4
			D.G. Rees	L	8,127	27.3
			J. Garwell	Lab	7,812	26.3
					5,650	19.1
1964	47,482	77.5	J. More	C	17,290	47.0
			M.K. Prendergast	Lab	10,763	29.2
			J.C. Griffiths	L	8,768	23.8
					6,527	17.8
1966	48,370	73.9	J. More	C	19,603	54.9
			J.W. Gilbert	Lab	16,123	45.1
					3,480	9.8
1970	55,084	73.2	J. More	C	22,104	54.8
			D. Nagington	Lab	12,800	31.7
			C.R. Oddie	L	5,444	13.5
					9,304	23.1

Election	Electors	T'out	Candidate	Party	Votes	%
1950	48,700	78.3	Hon. W.D. Ormsby-Gore	C	23,562	61.8
			A.G. Wait	Lab	14,556	38.2
					9,006	23.6
1951	49,830	76.9	Hon. W.D. Ormsby-Gore	C	23,843	62.2
			A.G. Wait	Lab	14,471	37.8
					9,372	24.4
1955	50,289	70.2	Hon. W.D. Ormsby-Gore	C	22,859	64.8
			M.E. Boggin	Lab	12,434	35.2
					10,425	29.6
1959	50,772	74.2	Rt. Hon. W.D. Ormsby-Gore	C	21,055	55.9
			G. Thomas	Lab	10,531	28.0
			D.G. Rees	L	6,068	16.1
					10,524	27.9

[Resignation on appointment as United Kingdom Ambassador to the United States]

Election	Electors	T'out	Candidate	Party	Votes	%
1961 (8/11)	50,057	60.8	W.J. Biffen	C	12,428	40.8
			J.R. Buchanan	L	8,647	28.4
			A.B. Walden	Lab	8,519	28.0
			J.E. Dayton	PF	839*	2.8
					3,781	12.4
1964	50,066	76.6	W.J. Biffen	C	18,184	47.4
			G.J. Costley	Lab	11,407	29.8
			T.R. Crowther	L	8,745	22.8
					6,777	17.6
1966	50,102	73.3	W.J. Biffen	C	17,727	48.2
			G.J. Costley	Lab	13,011	35.4
			T.R. Crowther	L	6,010	16.4
					4,716	12.8
1970	55,575	72.2	W.J. Biffen	C	20,361	50.8
			N. Turner	Lab	10,801	26.9
			Dr. E.P. Cadbury	L	8,963	22.3
					9,560	23.9

Election	Electors	T'out	Candidate	Party	Votes	%
1950	44,249	83.9	†J.A. Langford-Holt	C	18,470	49.7
			R.B. Cant	Lab	12,542	33.8
			N.W. Elliott	L	6,126	16.5
					5,928	15.9
1951	44,891	80.7	J.A. Langford-Holt	C	21,503	59.3
			R.B. Cant	Lab	14,735	40.7
					6,768	18.6
1955	45,239	77.5	J.A. Langford-Holt	C	21,319	60.8
			D.G. Allen	Lab	13,726	39.2
					7,593	21.6
1959	46,846	80.5	J.A. Langford-Holt	C	19,970	53.0
			K.V. Russell	Lab	11,338	30.1
			H. Shaw	L	6,387	16.9
					8,632	22.9
1964	49,025	78.2	Sir J.A. Langford-Holt	C	18,517	48.3
			J.O. Murphy	Lab	12,658	33.0
			G.K. Roberts	L	7,180	18.7
					5,859	15.3
1966	50,484	76.9	Sir J.A. Langford-Holt	C	17,569	45.2
			T.S. Pritchard	Lab	14,603	37.6
			W. Marsh	L	6,660	17.2
					2,966	7.6
1970	57,419	73.1	Sir J.A. Langford-Holt	C	22,619	53.9
			P.A. Kent	Lab	13,413	31.9
			I. Brodie	L	5,960	14.2
					9,206	22.0

lection	Electors	T'out	Candidate	Party	Votes	%
950	45,209	81.3	†I.O. Thomas	Lab	19,730	53.7
			F.G. Bibbings	C	17,039	46.3
					2,691	7.4
951	46,254	83.1	I.O. Thomas	Lab	20,109	52.3
			J.H. Cordle	C	18,305	47.7
					1,804	4.6
955	46,897	80.1	W. Yates	C	19,019	50.6
			I.O. Thomas	Lab	18,541	49.4
					478	1.2
959	48,789	84.2	W. Yates	C	22,030	53.6
			D.W.T. Bruce	Lab	19,052	46.4
					2,978	7.2
964	54,519	82.0	W. Yates	C	21,765	48.7
			D.W.T. Bruce	Lab	19,078	42.7
			J.N. Davies	L	3,839*	8.6
					2,687	6.0
966	57,265	81.3	G.T. Fowler	Lab	23,692	50.9
			W. Yates	C	22,846	49.1
					846	1.8
1970	65,973	78.9	Dr. J.A.P. Trafford	C	26,282	50.5
			G.T. Fowler	Lab	25,764	49.5
					518	1.0

Election	Electors	T'out	Candidate	Party	Votes	%
1950	51,884	85.8	G. Wills	C	21,732	48.8
			N.E. Carr	Lab/Co-op	16,053	36.1
			W.S.R. King-Hall	Ind	6,708	15.1
					5,679	12.7
1951	53,198	84.6	G. Wills	C	25,365	56.3
			N.E. Carr	Lab/Co-op	19,656	43.7
					5,709	12.6
1955	53,920	78.0	G. Wills	C	24,887	59.2
			A.E. Sumbler	Lab	17,170	40.8
					7,717	18.4
1959	55,770	81.8	Sir G. Wills	C	23,002	50.5
			J. Finnigan	Lab	14,706	32.2
			P.G. Watkins	L	7,893	17.3
					8,296	18.3
1964	57,941	80.3	Sir G. Wills	C	20,822	44.7
			N.J. Hart	Lab	14,645	31.5
			P.G. Watkins	L	9,009	19.4
			M.L. de V. Hart	Ind	2,038*	4.4
					6,177	13.2
1966	58,515	80.2	Sir G. Wills	C	20,850	44.4
			R. Mayer	Lab	17,864	38.1
			P.G. Watkins	L	8,205	17.5
					2,986	6.3
[Death]						
1970 (12/3)	65,836	70.3	T.J. King	C	25,687	55.5
			R. Mayer	Lab	14,772	31.9
			P.M. O'Loughlin	L	5,832	12.6
					10,915	23.6
1970	66,067	77.2	T.J. King	C	26,685	52.3
			R.J. Billington	Lab	18,224	35.8
			P.M. O'Loughlin	L	6,066*	11.9
					8,461	16.5

Note:—

1964: Hart was opposed to Britain entering the Common Market and the nominee of the Bridgwater Independent Parliamentary Association.

Election	Electors	T'out	Candidate	Party	Votes	%
1950	59,919	87.7	E.H.C. Leather	C	23,953	45.6
			Mrs. X.N. Field	Lab	23,050	43.8
			A.E. Whitcher	L	5,573*	10.6
					903	1.8
1951	59,167*	88.5	E.H.C. Leather	C	27,465	52.4
			R.J. Hurst	Lab	24,917	47.6
					2,548	4.8
1955	58,282*	85.4	E.H.C. Leather	C	26,985	54.2
			D.R. Llewellyn	Lab	22,802	45.8
					4,183	8.4
1959	63,231	85.5	E.H.C. Leather	C	30,432	56.3
			E.F. Wilde	Lab	23,649	43.7
					6,783	12.6
1964	70,186*	85.4	A.P. Dean	C	27,814	46.3
			D.T. White	Lab	23,896	39.9
			M.E. Willies	L	8,253	13.8
					3,918	6.4
1966	72,803	85.3	A.P. Dean	C	28,824	46.4
			B. Tilley	Lab	26,526	42.7
			M.E. Willies	L	6,745*	10.9
					2,298	3.7
1970	84,808	79.1	A.P. Dean	C	38,975	58.1
			J.T. Mitchard	Lab	28,121	41.9
					10,854	16.2

Election	Electors	T'out	Candidate	Party	Votes	%
1950	50,261	88.8	H.L.d'A. Hopkinson	C	20,724	46.4
			†V.J. Collins	Lab	19,352	43.4
			J.R. Phillipson	L	4,561*	10.2
					1,372	3.0
1951	51,313	89.0	H.L.d'A. Hopkinson	C	24,826	54.4
			V.J. Collins	Lab	20,845	45.6
					3,981	8.8
1955	51,564	85.5	Rt. Hon. H.L.d'A. Hopkinson	C	22,962	52.1
			R.A. Pestell	Lab	17,420	39.5
			G.L.G. Barrington	L	3,684*	8.4
					5,542	12.6

[Elevation to the Peerage—Lord Colyton]

Election	Electors	T'out	Candidate	Party	Votes	%
1956 (14/2)	51,978	75.0	E.D.L. du Cann	C	19,820	50.8
			R.A. Pestell	Lab	19,163	49.2
					657	1.6
1959	52,675	87.1	E.D.L. du Cann	C	22,680	49.4
			L.V. Pike	Lab	16,182	35.3
			C.M.K. Bruton	L	7,031	15.3
					6,498	14.1
1964	54,202	84.7	E.D.L. du Cann	C	21,367	46.5
			L.V. Pike	Lab	16,619	36.2
			Hon. Mrs. M.I.G. Heathcoat-Amory	L	7,944	17.3
					4,748	10.3
1966	55,108	85.4	E.D.L. du Cann	C	22,369	47.6
			R.J. Bradbury	Lab	19,216	40.8
			Hon. Mrs. M.I.G. Heathcoat-Amory	L	5,460*	11.6
					3,153	6.8
1970	61,805	79.0	Rt. Hon. E.D.L. du Cann	C	26,158	53.5
			S. Mama	Lab	17,823	36.5
			G.L. O'Donnell	L	4,871*	10.0
					8,335	17.0

Election	Electors	T'out	Candidate	Party	Votes	%
1950	56,058	86.3	†D.C. Boles	C	20,613	42.6
			Lady Archibald	Lab	17,987	37.2
			A. Marreco	L	9,771	20.2
					2,626	5.4
1951	57,028	84.2	S.L.C. Maydon	C	26,524	55.3
			D.R. Llewellyn	Lab	21,481	44.7
					5,043	10.6
1955	57,057	79.5	S.L.C. Maydon	C	25,624	56.5
			Dr. M. Bresler	Lab	19,745	43.5
					5,879	13.0
1959	57,455	83.6	S.L.C. Maydon	C	23,357	48.6
			J.A.A. Evans	Lab	16,452	34.3
			P.R. Hobhouse	L	8,220	17.1
					6,905	14.3
1964	58,588*	81.7	S.L.C. Maydon	C	20,663	43.2
			R.G. White	Lab	15,080	31.5
			H.L. Fry	L	12,132	25.3
					5,583	11.7
1966	58,609	81.5	S.L.C. Maydon	C	20,528	43.0
			J.G. Cousins	Lab	16,989	35.6
			H.L. Fry	L	10,224	21.4
					3,539	7.4
1970	65,381	77.4	Hon. R.T. Boscawen	C	25,106	49.6
			F.R. Thompson	Lab	16,335	32.3
			W.F.J. Pinching	L	9,174	18.1
					8,771	17.3

Election	Electors	T'out	Candidate	Party	Votes	%
1950	57,098	83.1	†I.L. Orr-Ewing	C	26,767	56.4
			M.H. Hill	Lab	13,294	28.0
			F.A. Kew	L	7,394	15.6
					13,473	28.4
1951	58,241	79.7	I.L. Orr-Ewing	C	30,485	65.7
			R.G. Andrews	Lab	15,942	34.3
					14,543	31.4
1955	59,135*	73.8	Sir I.L. Orr-Ewing	C	27,357	62.7
			R.G. Andrews	Lab	16,275	37.3
					11,082	25.4
[Death]						
1958 (12/6)	59,758	72.2	D.W.E. Webster	C	21,271	49.3
			S.E. Hampton	Lab	11,295	26.2
			E.B. Taylor	L	10,588	24.5
					9,976	23.1
1959	60,795	79.7	D.W.E. Webster	C	27,881	57.6
			S.E. Hampton	Lab	10,977	22.6
			E.B. Taylor	L	9,609	19.8
					16,904	35.0
1964	64,762	79.0	D.W.E. Webster	C	27,143	53.1
			Miss J. Stephen	Lab/Co-op	12,248	23.9
			I.D. McDonald	L	11,771	23.0
					14,895	29.2
1966	67,871	78.5	D.W.E. Webster	C	27,733	52.1
			M.E. Butcher	Lab/Co-op	15,340	28.8
			I.D. McDonald	L	10,173	19.1
					12,393	23.3
[Death]						
1969 (27/3)	73,077	60.8	A.W. Wiggin	C	29,211	65.7
			E.R.F. Deal	L	8,739	19.7
			N. Bosanquet	Lab	6,504	14.6
					20,472	46.0
1970	79,263	73.7	A.W. Wiggin	C	33,816	57.9
			Miss S.R. Palmer	Lab/Co-op	14,473	24.8
			E.R.F. Deal	L	10,120	17.3
					19,343	33.1

lection	Electors	T'out	Candidate	Party	Votes	%
950	56,790	87.5	†W.H. Kingsmill	C	21,145	42.6
			M. Shinwell	Lab	19,532	39.3
			L. MacLaren	L	8,990	18.1
					1,613	3.3
951	57,525	88.0	J.W.W. Peyton	C	23,701	46.8
			M. Murray	Lab	20,780	41.1
			Miss M.L. Winsor	L	6,118*	12.1
					2,921	5.7
955	58,714	85.1	J.W.W. Peyton	C	24,059	48.2
			M. Murray	Lab	19,793	39.6
			G.F. Taylor	L	6,089*	12.2
					4,266	8.6
959	59,737	85.2	J.W.W. Peyton	C	23,771	46.7
			W.A. Baker	Lab	17,638	34.7
			G.F. Taylor	L	9,484	18.6
					6,133	12.0
964	61,838	83.3	J.W.W. Peyton	C	21,919	42.6
			A.C. Reed	Lab	17,171	33.3
			G.F. Taylor	L	12,426	24.1
					4,748	9.3
966	62,755	83.7	J.W.W. Peyton	C	22,664	43.2
			J.A. Elswood	Lab	20,584	39.2
			D.E. Evans	L	9,248	17.6
					2,080	4.0
970	70,178	79.4	J.W.W. Peyton	C	27,689	49.7
			J.A. Elswood	Lab	20,621	37.0
			D.E. Evans	L	7,418	13.3
					7,068	12.7

Election	Electors	T'out	Candidate	Party	Votes	%
1950	56,520	85.4	†C.J. Simmons	Lab	24,302	50.3
			R.D. Williams	C	19,665	40.7
			T.P. Hanley	L	4,329*	9.0
					4,637	9.6
1951	57,322	85.0	C.J. Simmons	Lab	25,510	52.4
			J. Dalley	C	23,212	47.6
					2,298	4.8
1955	62,179*	78.9	C.J. Simmons	Lab	25,013	51.0
			W.H. Green	C	24,064	49.0
					949	2.0
1959	71,161	81.9	J.E. Talbot	C	31,202	53.5
			C.J. Simmons	Lab	27,069	46.5
					4,133	7.0
1964	80,218	80.0	J.E. Talbot	C	33,370	52.0
			P.K. Archer	Lab	28,968	45.2
			W.H. Brown	Ind	1,820*	2.8
					4,402	6.8
1966	84,210	79.0	J.E. Talbot	C	34,026	51.2
			Dr. Katharine C. Rogers	Lab	32,459	48.8
					1,567	2.4
[Death]						
1967 (27/4)	85,845	68.0	W.F. Montgomery	C	31,371	53.8
			D.A. Forwood	Lab	21,151	36.2
			M. Steed	L	4,536*	7.8
			J. Creasey	APA	1,305*	2.2
					10,220	17.6
1970	97,680	73.3	W.F. Montgomery	C	43,440	60.6
			T.S. Pritchard	Lab	28,203	39.4
					15,237	21.2

Note:—

1964: Brown was opposed to Britain entering the Common Market.

Election	Electors	T'out	Candidate	Party	Votes	%
1950	56,152	86.1	W.A. Colegate	C	24,903	51.5
			†A.W. Lyne	Lab	23,418	48.5
					1,485	3.0
1951	56,813	86.3	W.A. Colegate	C	24,884	50.7
			J.T. Stonehouse	Lab	24,151	49.3
					733	1.4
1955	57,025	80.8	J.C. Jennings	C	24,519	53.2
			E. Taylor	Lab/Co-op	21,546	46.8
					2,973	6.4
1959	58,229	82.4	J.C. Jennings	C	26,926	56.1
			E. McGarry	Lab	21,032	43.9
					5,894	12.2
1964	59,083	80.2	J.C. Jennings	C	25,236	53.2
			T.S. Pritchard	Lab	22,161	46.8
					3,075	6.4
1966	60,034	78.7	J.C. Jennings	C	23,773	50.3
			C.W. Shepherd	Lab	23,496	49.7
					277	0.6
1970	66,725	75.7	J.C. Jennings	C	27,428	54.3
			R.G. Truman	Lab	23,063	45.7
					4,365	8.6

STAFFORDSHIRE, CANNOCK [481]

Election	Electors	T'out	Candidate	Party	Votes	%
1950	57,520	85.7	†Miss J. Lee	Lab	33,476	67.9
			Mrs. M. Hickling	NL & C	15,818	32.1
					17,658	35.8
1951	58,254	83.1	Miss J. Lee	Lab	32,379	66.9
			A.C. Farrington	NL & C	16,041	33.1
					16,338	33.8
1955	58,553**	76.9	Miss J. Lee	Lab	26,677	59.2
			J.H.R. Newey	NL & C	18,379	40.8
					8,298	18.4
1959	65,472	79.6	Miss J. Lee	Lab	29,624	56.9
			P.H. Lugg	NL & C	22,485	43.1
					7,139	13.8
1964	72,149	76.2	Miss J. Lee	Lab	31,608	57.5
			C.J.P. Vereker	C	23,334	42.5
					8,274	15.0
1966	76,299	73.7	Miss J. Lee	Lab	33,621	59.8
			H.R. Elliston	C	22,594	40.2
					11,027	19.6
1970	89,982	70.9	P.T. Cormack	C	32,665	51.2
			Rt. Hon. Jennie Lee	Lab	31,136	48.8
					1,529	2.4

lection	Electors	T'out	Candidate	Party	Votes	%
950	64,921	86.0	†H. Davies	Lab	30,044	53.8
			R.M. Speir	C	25,820	46.2
					4,224	7.6
951	66,253	86.2	H. Davies	Lab	29,502	51.7
			R.B.F.S. Body	C	27,592	48.3
					1,910	3.4
955	68,062	81.5	H. Davies	Lab	28,273	51.0
			Miss I.M.P. Pike	C	27,214	49.0
					1,059	2.0
959	72,777	83.9	H. Davies	Lab	31,096	50.9
			Sir J.H. Wedgwood, Bt.	C	29,947	49.1
					1,149	1.8
964	77,497	81.3	H. Davies	Lab	33,558	53.3
			H. Goodwin	C	29,409	46.7
					4,149	6.6
966	79,880	78.8	H. Davies	Lab	35,334	56.2
			F.A. Swinnerton	C	27,573	43.8
					7,761	12.4
970	89,617	67.5	D.L. Knox	C	27,899	46.1
			Rt. Hon. H. Davies	Lab	26,359	43.6
			R.M. Burman	L	6,219*	10.3
					1,540	2.5

Election	Electors	T'out	Candidate	Party	Votes	%
1950	62,452	86.3	†J.W. Snow	Lab	29,199	54.2
			Mrs. S.A. Ward	C	24,681	45.8
					4,518	8.4
1951	64,045	85.5	J.W. Snow	Lab	28,826	52.6
			G. Hampson	C	25,941	47.4
					2,885	5.2
1955	48,250**	80.9	J.W. Snow	Lab	21,071	54.0
			J.O.T. Blow	C	17,966	46.0
					3,105	8.0
1959	50,240	81.9	J.W. Snow	Lab	21,341	51.9
			Dr. F.R. Roberts	C	19,791	48.1
					1,550	3.8
1964	57,679	80.9	J.W. Snow	Lab	22,644	48.5
			K. Dunkley	C	18,828	40.3
			A.H. Extance	L	5,206*	11.2
					3,816	8.2
1966	65,728	78.8	J.W. Snow	Lab	27,971	54.0
			B.A. Webb	C	23,837	46.0
					4,134	8.0
1970	82,180	73.7	J.A. d'Avigdor-Goldsmid	C	31,274	51.6
			T.J. Pitt	Lab	29,298	48.4
					1,976	3.2

Election	Electors	T'out	Candidate	Party	Votes	%
1950	53,120	86.0	†Hon. H.C.P.J. Fraser	C	24,046	52.7
			†S.T. Swingler	Lab	19,008	41.6
			Rev. W.J. Eldowney	L	2,617*	5.7
					5,038	11.1
1951	54,123	84.1	Hon. H.C.P.J. Fraser	C	25,795	56.6
			G.P. Grant	Lab	19,749	43.4
					6,046	13.2
1955	55,395	79.0	Hon. H.C.P.J. Fraser	C	26,206	59.9
			K.E. Richardson	Lab	17,550	40.1
					8,656	19.8
1959	57,078	80.8	Hon. H.C.P.J. Fraser	C	28,107	60.9
			A. Gregory	Lab	18,034	39.1
					10,073	21.8
1964	62,417	81.0	Rt. Hon. H.C.P.J. Fraser	C	25,373	50.2
			A.L. Ballham	Lab	18,587	36.8
			B.D. King	L	6,593	13.0
					6,786	13.4
1966	64,319	79.4	Rt. Hon. H.C.P.J. Fraser	C	25,259	49.4
			G.S. Rea	Lab	20,218	39.6
			E. Furniss	L	5,623*	11.0
					5,041	9.8
1970	74,639	73.4	Rt. Hon. H.C.P.J. Fraser	C	30,056	54.8
			M.J.K. Stanworth	Lab	20,380	37.2
			W. Williams	L	4,370*	8.0
					9,676	17.6

Election	Electors	T'out	Candidate	Party	Votes	%
1950	55,495	82.5	W.T. Aitken	C	22,559	49.
			Miss C.A.W. McCall	Lab	18,430	40.
			H.W. Sparham	L	4,780*	10.
					4,129	9.
1951	56,851	79.8	W.T. Aitken	C	24,679	54.
			N. Stanley	Lab	20,690	45.
					3,989	8.
1955	56,854	78.3	W.T. Aitken	C	24,532	55.
			N. Stanley	Lab	19,962	44.
					4,570	10.
1959	57,908	78.6	W.T. Aitken	C	26,730	58.
			Mrs. A.M.A. Walter	Lab	18,768	41.
					7,962	17.
[Death]						
1964	60,587	74.6	E.W. Griffiths	C	22,141	49.
(14/5)			N.J. Insley	Lab	19,682	43.
			R.L. Afton	L	3,387*	7.
					2,459	5.
1964	61,143	82.2	E.W. Griffiths	C	25,206	50.
			N.J. Insley	Lab	20,216	40.
			R.L. Afton	L	4,840*	9.
					4,990	10.
1966	64,549	78.9	E.W. Griffiths	C	27,782	54.
			C.J.V. Seager	Lab	23,140	45.
					4,642	9.
1970	77,519	77.4	E.W. Griffiths	C	36,688	61.
			C.J.V. Seager	Lab	23,286	38.
					13,402	22.

Election	Electors	T'out	Candidate	Party	Votes	%
950	56,855	83.8	†E.L. Granville	L	17,755	37.2
			J.H. Harrison	C	17,128	36.0
			L.G. Emsden	Lab	12,474	26.2
			Mrs. D.P. Chadwick	Com	271*	0.6
					627	1.2
951	58,518	83.3	J.H. Harrison	C	19,791	40.6
			E.L. Granville	L	17,608	36.1
			H.E.J. Falconer	Lab	11,340	23.3
					2,183	4.5
955	57,092*	82.9	J.H. Harrison	C	21,317	45.0
			E.L. Granville	Lab	20,428	43.2
			Mrs. S. Robson	L	5,582*	11.8
					889	1.8
959	56,395	84.0	J.H. Harrison	C	22,333	47.1
			E.L. Granville	Lab	19,849	41.9
			Mrs. S. Robson	L	5,215*	11.0
					2,484	5.2
964	57,087	82.5	Sir J.H. Harrison, Bt.	C	21,555	45.8
			J.W. Fear	Lab	16,129	34.2
			D.J. Newby	L	9,437	20.0
					5,426	11.6
966	57,851	81.5	Sir J.H. Harrison, Bt.	C	21,044	44.6
			R.W.S. Pryke	Lab	17,431	37.0
			D.J. Newby	L	8,661	18.4
					3,613	7.6
70	63,623	78.3	Sir J.H. Harrison, Bt.	C	26,099	52.4
			R.E. Manley	Lab	17,735	35.6
			I.S.T. Senior	L	5,962*	12.0
					8,364	16.8

Election	Electors	T'out	Candidate	Party	Votes	%
1950	55,456	83.8	†E. Evans	Lab	20,838	44.
			P.G. Whitefoord	C	17,516	37.
			Miss R.C. English	L	8,132	17.
					3,322	7.
1951	56,582	81.9	E. Evans	Lab	23,591	50.
			A.H. Willetts	C	22,744	49.
					847	1.
1955	56,850	79.6	E. Evans	Lab	23,587	52.
			J.T. Griffiths	C	21,672	47.
					1,915	4.
1959	57,814	81.6	J.M.L. Prior	C	24,324	51.
			E. Evans	Lab	22,835	48.
					1,489	3.
1964	60,775	82.5	J.M.L. Prior	C	23,976	47.
			R.H. Atkins	Lab	21,272	42.
			C.G.A. Steele	L	4,911*	9.
					2,704	5.
1966	62,881	83.1	J.M.L. Prior	C	24,063	46.
			M.D. Cornish	Lab	23,705	45.
			D.R. Crome	L	4,513*	8.
					358	0.
1970	72,458	78.5	J.M.L. Prior	C	28,842	50.
			D.A. Baker	Lab	23,319	41.
			D.R. Crome	L	4,737*	8.
					5,523	9.

lection	Electors	T'out	Candidate	Party	Votes	%
950	57,846	84.5	†Hon. J.H. Hare	C	23,599	48.3
			†R. Hamilton	Lab	19,062	39.0
			Sir F.E. James	L	6,219	12.7
					4,537	9.3
951	59,163	82.1	Hon. J.H. Hare	C	27,262	56.1
			R.J. Lewis	Lab/Co-op	21,310	43.9
					5,952	12.2
955	58,890*	79.7	Hon. J.H. Hare	C	25,185	53.7
			R.J. Lewis	Lab/Co-op	17,995	38.3
			Mrs. A.H. Scott	L	3,760*	8.0
					7,190	15.4
959	60,756	81.1	Rt. Hon. J.H. Hare	C	26,130	53.0
			R.B. Stirling	Lab	16,248	33.0
			A. Herbert	L	6,914	14.0
					9,882	20.0

[Elevation to the Peerage—Viscount Blakenham]

963	62,893	70.5	K.M. Stainton	C	22,005	49.6
5/12)			F.E. Woodbridge	Lab	16,416	37.0
			A. Herbert	L	5,935	13.4
					5,589	12.6
964	63,785	81.8	K.M. Stainton	C	26,370	50.5
			F.E. Woodbridge	Lab	17,778	34.1
			E.M. Wheeler	L	8,044	15.4
					8,592	16.4
966	66,329	80.2	K.M. Stainton	C	26,689	50.1
			M.F. Madden	Lab	19,680	37.0
			E.M. Wheeler	L	6,839	12.9
					7,009	13.1
970	78,109	76.0	K.M. Stainton	C	32,393	54.6
			B. Orriss	Lab	19,829	33.4
			E.M. Wheeler	L	7,136*	12.0
					12,564	21.2

Election	Electors	T'out	Candidate	Party	Votes	%
1950	63,720	88.1	†A.H. Head	C	29,493	52.
			Dr. S. Sharman	Lab	21,536	38.
			D.W. Clarke	L	5,132*	9.
					7,957	14.
1951	65,313	85.1	A.H. Head	C	32,634	58.
			C.H. Davies	Lab	22,928	41.
					9,706	17.
1955	67,655	80.7	Rt. Hon. A.H. Head	C	30,429	55.
			H.R. Cole	Lab	18,924	34.
			J.H.G. Browne	L	5,277*	9.
					11,505	21.
1959	68,391	82.5	Rt. Hon. A.H. Head	C	30,454	54.
			J.H. Powell	Lab	17,210	30.
			J.H.G. Browne	L	8,744	15.
					13,244	23.

[Resignation on appointment as United Kingdom High Commissioner in the Federation of Nigeria and elevation to the Peerage—Viscount Head]

Election	Electors	T'out	Candidate	Party	Votes	%
1960 (16/11)	68,469	54.2	W. Elliot	C	19,175	51.
			J.H.G. Browne	L	10,250	27.
			B. Thomas	Lab	7,696	20.
					8,925	24.
1964	66,637	80.2	W. Elliot	C	26,118	48.
			B. Thomas	Lab	16,105	30.
			J.H.G. Browne	L	11,207	21.
					10,013	18.
1966	65,971	79.4	W. Elliot	C	24,615	47.0
			P.J. Bassett	Lab	18,746	35.
			J.H.G. Browne	L	8,988	17.
					5,869	11.
1970	71,119	71.2	W. Elliot	C	27,342	53.
			G.S. Baker	Lab	16,896	33.4
			J.H.G. Browne	L	6,411	12.
					10,446	20.

Election	Electors	T'out	Candidate	Party	Votes	%
1950	45,182	82.7	L.F. Heald	C	19,326	51.7
			D. Gordon	Lab	14,090	37.7
			G.E. Owen	L	3,969*	10.6
					5,236	14.0
1951	47,307	81.1	L.F. Heald	C	20,539	53.6
			D. Gordon	Lab/Co-op	14,849	38.7
			G.E. Owen	L	2,961*	7.7
					5,690	14.9
1955	48,812	77.2	Sir L.F. Heald	C	23,021	61.1
			R.H. Edwards	Lab	14,656	38.9
					8,365	22.2
1959	55,609	79.4	Rt. Hon. Sir L.F. Heald	C	24,836	56.2
			J.S. Barr	Lab	14,150	32.1
			A.R. Mayne	L	5,146*	11.7
					10,686	24.1
1964	58,960	77.8	Rt. Hon. Sir L.F. Heald	C	22,497	49.0
			A.J. Edwards	Lab	14,513	31.7
			F.M.J. Lee	L	8,844	19.3
					7,984	17.3
1966	59,844	78.0	Rt. Hon. Sir L.F. Heald	C	22,584	48.4
			A.J. Edwards	Lab	16,231	34.8
			F.M.J. Lee	L	7,852	16.8
					6,353	13.6
1970	67,724	71.1	W.M.J. Grylls	C	27,239	56.6
			C.P. Slater	Lab	15,653	32.5
			A.F. Cook	L	5,239*	10.9
					11,586	24.1

SURREY, DORKING [491]

Election	Electors	T'out	Candidate	Party	Votes	%
1950	44,774	83.4	†G.C. Touche	C	22,096	59.1
			J.D. Richards	Lab	11,114	29.8
			G.G.G. Francis	L	4,128*	11.1
					10,982	29.3
1951	45,969	80.7	G.C. Touche	C	24,416	65.8
			J.D. Richards	Lab	12,664	34.2
					11,752	31.6
1955	47,328	76.9	Sir G.C. Touche	C	24,451	67.2
			R.P. Walsh	Lab	11,942	32.8
					12,509	34.4
1959	51,092	79.8	Rt. Hon. Sir G.C. Touche	C	24,564	60.2
			S.R. Mills	Lab	9,605	23.6
			W.S. Watson	L	6,582	16.2
					14,959	36.6
1964	54,032	79.4	Sir G.E. Sinclair	C	23,862	55.7
			D.S. Tilbé	Lab	9,806	22.8
			W.S. Watson	L	8,773	20.4
			Mrs. B. Davies	Pat P	476*	1.1
					14,056	32.9
1966	54,296	79.0	Sir G.E. Sinclair	C	23,087	53.8
			Mrs. B. Dunmore	Lab	12,201	28.4
			G.H. Kahan	L	7,629	17.8
					10,886	25.4
1970	58,889	73.1	Sir G.E. Sinclair	C	25,393	59.0
			W.J. Fahy	Lab	10,523	24.5
			J.A. Baker	L	7,103	16.5
					14,870	34.5

SURREY, EAST [492]

Election	Electors	T'out	Candidate	Party	Votes	%
1950	61,598	87.2	†Hon. M.L. Astor	C	32,711	60.9
			N. Whine	Lab	12,499	23.3
			Mrs. W. Wills	L	8,484	15.8
					20,212	37.6
1951	63,986	81.3	C.J.A. Doughty	C	37,966	73.0
			N. Whine	Lab	14,056	27.0
					23,910	46.0
1955	65,179	76.5	C.J.A. Doughty	C	37,276	74.8
			Miss J.G. Hall	Lab	12,567	25.2
					24,709	49.6
1959	69,996	81.1	C.J.A. Doughty	C	36,310	63.9
			K.S. Vaus	L	10,376	18.3
			J.C. Hunt	Lab	10,102	17.8
					25,934	45.6
1964	71,818	79.2	C.J.A. Doughty	C	31,827	55.9
			M.R. Lane	L	16,049	28.2
			J.S. Cook	Lab	9,020	15.9
					15,778	27.7
1966	71,417	79.3	C.J.A. Doughty	C	30,900	54.5
			M.R. Lane	L	16,407	29.0
			C. Shaw	Lab	9,347	16.5
					14,493	25.5
1970	78,904	73.1	W.G. Clark	C	35,773	61.9
			P.W. Meyer	L	11,749	20.4
			M.D. Simmons	Lab	10,186	17.7
					24,024	41.5

Election	Electors	T'out	Candidate	Party	Votes	%
1950	63,254	86.2	†Rt. Hon. M.S. McCorquodale	C	33,103	60.1
			F.M. Hardie	Lab	15,256	28.0
			N.G. Hudson	L	6,153*	11.3
					17,847	32.1
1951	64,594	81.9	Rt. Hon. M.S. McCorquodale	C	36,333	68.7
			F.M. Hardie	Lab	16,584	31.3
					19,749	37.4
1955	66,379	77.6	P.A.G. Rawlinson	C	36,779	71.4
			A.B.S. Soper	Lab	14,706	28.6
					22,073	42.8
1959	69,592	81.1	P.A.G. Rawlinson	C	35,484	62.8
			D.E. Heather	Lab	11,039	19.6
			R.W.M. Walsh	L	9,910	17.6
					24,445	43.2
1964	72,626	79.9	Rt. Hon. Sir P.A.G. Rawlinson	C	31,959	55.0
			R.W.M. Walsh	L	13,968	24.1
			A.L. Williams	Lab	12,131	20.9
					17,991	30.9
1966	72,684	79.2	Rt. Hon. Sir P.A.G. Rawlinson	C	31,434	54.6
			C. Carter	Lab	13,841	24.0
			R.W.M. Walsh	L	12,305	21.4
					17,593	30.6
1970	79,874	72.5	Rt. Hon. Sir P.A.G. Rawlinson	C	35,541	61.4
			E.G. Wilson	Lab	12,767	22.1
			P.H. Billenness	L	9,563	16.5
					22,774	39.3

Election	Electors	T'out	Candidate	Party	Votes	%
1950	63,438	85.6	W. Robson Brown	C	33,094	60.9
			Miss E.E.B. Chipchase	Lab	15,514	28.6
			Miss H.J. Harvey	L	5,704*	10.5
					17,580	32.3
1951	64,479	83.3	W. Robson Brown	C	33,755	62.8
			P.C. McNally	Lab	15,334	28.6
			Miss H.J. Harvey	L	4,612*	8.6
					18,421	34.2
1955	66,925	79.3	W. Robson Brown	C	33,774	63.6
			F.A. Messer	Lab	13,132	24.8
			G.E. Owen	L	6,146*	11.6
					20,642	38.8
1959	72,183	81.5	Sir W. Robson Brown	C	37,155	63.2
			P.E. Vanson	Lab	12,934	22.0
			G.E. Owen	L	8,730	14.8
					24,221	41.2
1964	74,669	79.2	Sir W. Robson Brown	C	33,226	56.2
			P.E. Vanson	Lab	13,644	23.1
			Hon. S.R. Cawley	L	12,259	20.7
					19,582	33.1
1966	75,593	78.0	Sir W. Robson Brown	C	32,649	55.3
			C. Rofe	Lab	15,023	25.5
			Hon. S.R. Cawley	L	11,310	19.2
					17,626	29.8
1970	84,668	72.1	D.C.M. Mather	C	37,727	61.8
			Prof. R.S. Scorer	Lab	14,449	23.7
			G.H. Kahan	L	8,845	14.5
					23,278	38.1

Election	Electors	T'out	Candidate	Party	Votes	%
1950	46,807	83.0	†G. Nicholson	C	21,665	55.8
			E.C. Neate	Lab	12,972	33.4
			F.P. Shannon	L	4,202*	10.8
					8,693	22.4
1951	47,586	80.4	G. Nicholson	C	24,239	63.3
			C.L. James	Lab	14,041	36.7
					10,198	26.6
1955	47,861	76.3	G. Nicholson	C	23,717	64.9
			J.S.P. Davey	Lab	12,811	35.1
					10,906	29.8
1959	50,249	79.4	Sir G. Nicholson, Bt.	C	23,538	59.0
			Dr. J.G. Turner	Lab	9,800	24.6
			D.W. Saunders	L	6,538	16.4
					13,738	34.4
1964	53,054	78.7	Sir G. Nicholson, Bt.	C	21,382	51.2
			D.W. Saunders	L	11,876	28.4
			K.F. Urwin	Lab	8,500	20.4
					9,506	22.8
1966	53,815	80.0	M.V. Macmillan	C	21,028	48.8
			D.W. Saunders	L	12,036	28.0
			L.G.R. Pinchen	Lab	9,988	23.2
					8,992	20.8
1970	60,120	73.4	M.V. Macmillan	C	25,113	56.9
			P.M.O. Stonham	L	10,178	23.1
			L.G.R. Pinchen	Lab	8,817	20.0
					14,935	33.8

Election	Electors	T'out	Candidate	Party	Votes	%
1950	53,499	84.1	G.R.H. Nugent	C	24,983	55.6
			V.G. Wilkinson	Lab	15,443	34.3
			F.H. Philpott	L	4,552*	10.1
					9,540	21.3
1951	54,858	79.6	G.R.H. Nugent	C	27,604	63.2
			V.G. Wilkinson	Lab	16,068	36.8
					11,536	26.4
1955	56,118	76.4	G.R.H. Nugent	C	27,113	63.2
			G.R. Bellerby	Lab	15,785	36.8
					11,328	26.4
1959	58,963	80.2	G.R.H. Nugent	C	27,198	57.5
			G.R. Bellerby	Lab	13,756	29.1
			A.R. Braybrooke	L	6,318	13.4
					13,442	28.4
1964	60,714*	78.6	Rt. Hon. Sir G.R.H. Nugent, Bt.	C	24,277	50.9
			G.E.H. Griffith	Lab	13,365	28.0
			C.J.N. Martin	L	10,052	21.1
					10,912	22.9
1966	60,815	78.7	D.A.R. Howell	C	24,116	50.4
			C.H.R. Thornberry	Lab	15,771	32.9
			J.R. Buchanan	L	7,992	16.7
					8,345	17.5
1970	68,154	72.1	D.A.R. Howell	C	27,203	55.3
			P.B. Smith	Lab	13,108	26.7
			M.J. Walton	L	8,822	18.0
					14,095	28.6

Note:—

1950-1959:	Nugent joined the Liberal-Unionist Group in the House of Commons as an associate member.

Election	Electors	T'out	Candidate	Party	Votes	%
1950	50,415	85.1	J.K. Vaughan-Morgan	C	23,027	53.6
			C.J. Garnsworthy	Lab/Co-op	13,931	32.5
			A.S. Batham	L	5,953	13.9
					9,096	21.1
1951	51,790	83.3	J.K. Vaughan-Morgan	C	24,137	55.9
			C.J. Garnsworthy	Lab/Co-op	14,287	33.1
			A.S. Batham	L	4,740*	11.0
					9,850	22.8
1955	56,013	78.8	J.K. Vaughan-Morgan	C	27,210	61.7
			C.J. Garnsworthy	Lab	16,903	38.3
					10,307	23.4
1959	60,266	82.4	J.K. Vaughan-Morgan	C	26,966	54.4
			C.J. Garnsworthy	Lab	14,465	29.1
			Mrs. A.H. Scott	L	8,205	16.5
					12,501	25.3
1964	63,240	79.7	Rt. Hon. Sir J.K. Vaughan-Morgan, Bt.	C	24,380	48.4
			C.J. Garnsworthy	Lab	14,991	29.7
			A.A. Stowell	L	11,058	21.9
					9,389	18.7
1966	63,687	80.1	Rt. Hon. Sir J.K. Vaughan-Morgan, Bt.	C	24,163	47.4
			J.E.A. Samuels	Lab	16,649	32.6
			A.A. Stowell	L	10,197	20.0
					7,514	14.8
1970	71,449	74.0	Sir R.E.G. Howe	C	28,462	53.9
			M.P. Farley	Lab	15,433	29.2
			K.S. Vaus	L	8,952	16.9
					13,029	24.7

Election	Electors	T'out	Candidate	Party	Votes	%
1950	50,672	83.2	H.A. Watkinson	C	24,454	58.0
			T. Davies	Lab	13,157	31.2
			M.F. Turner-Bridger	L	4,567*	10.8
					11,297	26.8
1951	51,867	78.7	H.A. Watkinson	C	26,522	64.9
			W.E. Wolff	Lab	14,313	35.1
					12,209	29.8
1955	57,119	75.7	H.A. Watkinson	C	27,860	64.4
			R.D.V. Williams	Lab	15,393	35.6
					12,467	28.8
1959	64,295	77.3	Rt. Hon. H.A. Watkinson	C	33,521	67.4
			R.D.V. Williams	Lab	16,210	32.6
					17,311	34.8

[Seat Vacant at Dissolution (Elevation to the Peerage—Viscount Watkinson)]

Election	Electors	T'out	Candidate	Party	Votes	%
1964	77,207*	78.1	C.G.D. Onslow	C	31,170	51.7
			H.G.N. Clother	Lab	17,834	29.6
			Mrs. A.H. Scott	L	11,285	18.7
					13,336	22.1
1966	80,880	77.1	C.G.D. Onslow	C	32,057	51.4
			M. Downing	Lab	19,210	30.8
			Mrs. A.H. Scott	L	11,104	17.8
					12,847	20.6
1970	93,579	70.1	C.G.D. Onslow	C	37,220	56.7
			R.M. Taylor	Lab	18,652	28.4
			P. Wade	L	9,763	14.9
					18,568	28.3

Election	Electors	T'out	Candidate	Party	Votes	%
1950	69,932	85.1	†C.S. Taylor	C	35,425	59.5
			R. Groves	Lab	18,304	30.8
			C.L.H. Douglas-Bate	L	5,766*	9.1
					17,121	28.1
1951	71,398	81.9	C.S. Taylor	C	39,278	67.1
			C.S.B. Attlee	Lab	19,217	32.9
					20,061	34.2
1955	59,810**	75.8	Sir C.S. Taylor	C	29,779	65.7
			J.A. Lewis	Lab	15,561	34.3
					14,218	31.4
1959	62,971	77.3	Sir C.S. Taylor	C	27,874	57.3
			A.A. Dumont	Lab	11,837	24.3
			R.L. Gardner-Thorpe	L	8,955	18.4
					16,037	33.0
1964	70,251	76.7	Sir C.S. Taylor	C	26,410	49.0
			S. Terrell	L	15,441	28.7
			Mrs. J.E.M. Baker	Lab/Co-op	12,034	22.3
					10,969	20.3
1966	72,870	77.2	Sir C.S. Taylor	C	26,039	46.2
			S. Terrell	L	16,746	29.8
			J.H. High	Lab	12,620	22.4
			V.H. Petty	Ind C	883*	1.6
					9,293	16.4
1970	84,207	73.7	Sir C.S. Taylor	C	30,296	48.8
			S. Terrell	L	23,308	37.5
			C.G. Abley	Lab	8,475	13.7
					6,988	11.3

Election	Electors	T'out	Candidate	Party	Votes	%
1950	66,243	81.7	†R.S. Clarke	C	29,786	55.1
			Mrs. C.E. Williamson	Lab	12,983	24.0
			J.C. McLaughlin	L	11,329	20.9
					16,803	31.1
1951	67,771	80.3	R.S. Clarke	C	32,803	60.3
			H. Atkinson	Lab	14,271	26.2
			J.C. McLaughlin	L	7,375	13.5
					18,532	34.1
1955	61,567**	75.1	Hon. Mrs. E.V.E. Emmet	C	28,450	61.5
			M. Mason	Lab	11,750	25.4
			Mrs. J.St. John Thornton	L	6,034	13.1
					16,700	36.1
1959	65,437	77.9	Hon. Mrs. E.V.E. Emmet	C	31,759	62.3
			R.W.G. Humphreys	Lab	10,104	19.8
			P.A.T. Furnell	L	9,100	17.9
					21,655	42.5
1964	70,172	78.0	Hon. Mrs. E.V.E. Emmet	C	29,094	53.2
			R.G. Holme	L	14,753	27.0
			W.H. Hill	Lab	10,859	19.8
					14,341	26.2

[Elevation to a Life Peerage—Baroness Emmet of Amberley]

Election	Electors	T'out	Candidate	Party	Votes	%
1965 (4/2)	70,172	64.5	G. Johnson Smith	C	24,896	55.0
			R.G. Holme	L	14,279	31.5
			J.A.A. Evans	Lab	6,101	13.5
					10,617	23.5
1966	74,383	76.8	G. Johnson Smith	C	31,595	55.3
			J.H. Downie	L	13,611	23.8
			A.H. Roberts	Lab	11,938	20.9
					17,984	31.5
1970	86,448	72.5	G. Johnson Smith	C	38,359	61.1
			D. Smithers	L	12,343	19.7
			A.L. Banks	Lab	12,014	19.2
					26,016	41.4

Election	Electors	T'out	Candidate	Party	Votes	%
1950	64,231	81.0	†T.V.H. Beamish	C	30,430	58.5
			A.W. Briggs	Lab	15,023	28.9
			Mrs. F. Kingdon-Ward	L	6,565	12.6
					15,407	29.6
1951	65,712	78.3	T.V.H. Beamish	C	34,345	66.8
			A.W. Briggs	Lab	17,082	33.2
					17,263	33.6
1955	49,885**	74.8	T.V.H. Beamish	C	24,938	66.8
			J.L. Eley	Lab	12,392	33.2
					12,546	33.6
1959	56,338	75.8	T.V.H. Beamish	C	29,642	69.4
			W. Reay	Lab	13,065	30.6
					16,577	38.8
1964	63,452	76.4	Sir T.V.H. Beamish	C	26,818	55.3
			R.E. Fitch	Lab	12,757	26.3
			G.A. Dowden	L	8,924	18.4
					14,061	29.0
1966	67,413	76.3	Sir T.V.H. Beamish	C	27,529	53.6
			R.E. Manley	Lab	14,561	28.3
			G.A. Dowden	L	9,328	18.1
					12,968	25.3
1970	79,154	72.7	Sir T.V.H. Beamish	C	33,592	58.3
			Q. Barry	Lab	14,904	25.9
			M. Holt	L	9,083	15.8
					18,688	32.4

SUSSEX (EAST), RYE [502]

lection	Electors	T'out	Candidate	Party	Votes	%
955	53,223	73.4	B.G. Irvine	C	28,500	73.0
			T.I. Payne	Lab	10,560	27.0
					17,940	46.0
959	54,599	77.6	B.G. Irvine	C	27,465	64.8
			J.R. Murray	L	7,549	17.8
			D.S. Tilbé	Lab	7,359	17.4
					19,916	47.0
964	58,777	77.4	B.G. Irvine	C	27,240	59.9
			K.G. Wellings	L	10,264	22.5
			A.E. Arblaster	Lab	8,014	17.6
					16,976	37.4
966	60,965	75.7	B.G. Irvine	C	27,056	58.6
			K.G. Wellings	L	9,957	21.6
			D.R. Collins	Lab	9,155	19.8
					17,099	37.0
970	68,013	73.9	B.G. Irvine	C	32,300	64.2
			H.A. Fountain	Lab	9,031	18.0
			R.K.J.F. Young	L	8,947	17.8
					23,269	46.2

Election	Electors	T'out	Candidate	Party	Votes	%
1950	63,794	82.9	†W.N. Cuthbert	C	30,774	58.2
			W.T. Parsons	Lab	15,220	28.8
			H.S. Beardmore	L	6,879	13.0
					15,554	29.4
1951	66,515	78.0	W.N. Cuthbert	C	34,946	67.4
			Mrs. M. Reid	Lab	16,923	32.6
					18,023	34.8
[Resignation]						
1954 (9/3)	66,991	54.2	H.B. Kerby	C	24,857	68.5
			Mrs. M. Reid	Lab	11,420	31.5
					13,437	37.0
1955	69,034	73.0	H.B. Kerby	C	35,180	69.8
			F.W. Banfield	Lab	15,188	30.2
					19,992	39.6
1959	75,601	76.5	H.B. Kerby	C	37,034	64.0
			A.L. Bell	Lab	12,745	22.0
			A.L. Ford	L	8,081	14.0
					24,289	42.0
1964	84,026	76.5	H.B. Kerby	C	36,943	57.5
			A.A.R. Thompson	Lab	15,624	24.3
			P.M. Bulwer	L	11,671	18.2
					21,319	33.2
1966	87,743	75.8	H.B. Kerby	C	36,913	55.4
			R.R. Kenward	Lab	18,817	28.3
			P.M. Bulwer	L	10,816	16.3
					18,096	27.1
1970	100,360	72.0	H.B. Kerby	C	43,917	60.8
			B.M. Lyne	Lab	16,531	22.9
			P.F. Bartram	L	11,769	16.3
					27,386	37.9
[Death]						
1971 (1/4)	101,356	53.1	R.N. Luce	C	34,482	64.1
			R.R. Kenward	Lab	11,228	20.9
			P.F. Bartram	L	7,917	14.7
			G.E. Thomas	Ind	191*	0.3
					23,254	43.2

ection	Electors	T'out	Candidate	Party	Votes	%
‣50	57,946	80.5	†Hon. L.W. Joynson-Hicks	C	29,106	62.4
			D.G. Packham	Lab	12,614	27.1
			R.V. Gibson	L	4,911*	10.5
					16,492	35.3
‣51	59,667	77.3	Hon. L.W. Joynson-Hicks	C	32,166	69.7
			D.G. Packham	Lab	13,971	30.3
					18,195	39.4
‣55	60,712	71.8	Hon. L.W. Joynson-Hicks	C	30,857	70.8
			M. Jones	Lab	12,735	29.2
					18,122	41.6

uccession to the Peerage—Viscount Brentford]

‣58	63,119	51.7	W.H. Loveys	C	23,158	70.9
/11)			W.E. Simpkins	Lab	9,504	29.1
					13,654	41.8
‣59	63,958	73.8	W.H. Loveys	C	30,755	65.2
			J.S. Spooner	Lab	9,546	20.2
			J. Newman	L	6,913	14.6
					21,209	45.0
‣64	70,637	74.0	W.H. Loveys	C	30,222	57.8
			D.G. Kinsella	L	11,912	22.8
			A.J. Cohen	Lab	10,155	19.4
					18,310	35.0
‣66	74,951	73.2	W.H. Loveys	C	31,358	57.2
			D.J. Burnett	Lab	13,784	25.1
			P.J. Collins	L	9,714	17.7
					17,574	32.1

Death]

‣69	80,681	53.4	C.J. Chataway	C	31,966	74.2
‣2/5)			D.G. Kinsella	L	5,879	13.6
			A.F.W. White	Lab	5,257*	12.2
					26,087	60.6
‣70	86,966	70.0	C.J. Chataway	C	38,120	62.6
			N.D. Sandelson	Lab	12,574	20.6
			D.G. Kinsella	L	10,205	16.8
					25,546	42.0

Election	Electors	T'out	Candidate	Party	Votes	%
1950	47,992	80.0	†Rt. Hon. Earl Winterton	C	21,627	56.
			H.R. Nicholls	Lab	11,204	29.
			Miss E.M. Marchant	L	5,539	14.
					10,423	27.
1951	48,910	77.7	C.F.H. Gough	C	25,204	66.
			R.W. Kerr	Lab	12,803	33.
					12,401	32.
1955	59,776*	76.4	C.F.H. Gough	C	28,598	62.
			W.A. Baker	Lab	17,088	37.
					11,510	25.
1959	76,618	80.0	C.F.H. Gough	C	37,275	60.
			A.E. Pegler	Lab	24,012	39.
					13,263	21.
1964	85,816	79.5	P.M. Hordern	C	32,318	47.
			A.E. Pegler	Lab	22,450	32.
			O.G.N. Burne	L	12,570	18.
			J. Lee	Ind	865*	1.
					9,868	14.
1966	88,872	79.0	P.M. Hordern	C	32,139	45.
			J.M. Bowyer	Lab	26,098	37.
			O.G.N. Burne	L	11,930	17.
					6,041	8.
1970	105,532	74.2	P.M. Hordern	C	41,994	53.
			A.J. Edwards	Lab	27,706	35.
			H.C.A. Gill	L	8,574*	11.
					14,288	18.

Note:—

1964: Lee sought election as a 'Christian Progressive' candidate.

ection	Electors	T'out	Candidate	Party	Votes	%
55	54,596	81.5	R. Moss	Lab	22,796	51.2
			W.J. Peel	C	21,691	48.8
					1,105	2.4
59	62,449	84.4	G.R. Matthews	C	26,498	50.2
			R. Moss	Lab	26,235	49.8
					263	0.4
64	70,085*	83.5	C.J.S. Rowland	Lab	29,425	50.3
			G.R. Matthews	C	29,062	49.7
					363	0.6
66	73,621	85.7	C.J.S. Rowland	Lab	33,831	53.6
			J.W.P. Aitken	C	29,250	46.4
					4,581	7.2
Death]						
68 (28/3)	77,889	66.0	H.K. Speed	C	33,344	64.8
			R.L. MacFarquhar	Lab	18,081	35.2
					15,263	29.6
970	99,666	75.7	H.K. Speed	C	40,077	53.1
			N.P. Lister	Lab	35,353	46.9
					4,724	6.2

Election	Electors	T'out	Candidate	Party	Votes	%
1950	68,485	87.3	†F.G. Bowles	Lab	35,129	58.7
			Mrs. P.E. Gordon-Spencer	C	16,488	27.6
			J. Harris	L	8,177	13.7
					18,641	31.1
1951	69,861	85.0	F.G. Bowles	Lab	35,651	60.1
			J.E. Tippett	C	17,356	29.1
			G.C. Middleton	L	6,383*	10.7
					18,295	30.9
1955	56,452**	79.7	F.G. Bowles	Lab	25,112	55.8
			R.D.D. Griffith	C	14,828	33.0
			J.B. Frankenburg	L	5,048*	11.2
					10,284	22.8
1959	58,038	81.8	F.G. Bowles	Lab	24,894	52.5
			C.G. Miller	C	15,354	32.3
			J. Campbell	L	7,227	15.2
					9,540	20.2
1964	61,627	80.1	F.G. Bowles	Lab	26,059	52.8
			D.S. Marland	C	14,357	29.1
			J. Campbell	L	8,953	18.1
					11,702	23.7

[Elevation to a Life Peerage—Lord Bowles]

Election	Electors	T'out	Candidate	Party	Votes	%
1965 (21/1)	61,627	60.8	Rt. Hon. F. Cousins	Lab	18,325	49.0
			D.S. Marland	C	13,084	34.9
			J. Campbell	L	6,047	16.1
					5,241	14.1
1966	63,826	79.7	Rt. Hon. F. Cousins	Lab	27,452	53.9
			D.S. Marland	C	16,049	31.6
			A. Meredith	L	7,356	14.5
					11,403	22.3

[Resignation]

Election	Electors	T'out	Candidate	Party	Votes	%
1967 (9/3)	65,562	66.1	L.J. Huckfield	Lab	18,239	42.1
			D.L. Knox	C	14,185	32.7
			A. Meredith	L	7,644	17.6
			J. Creasey	APA	2,755*	6.4
			D.C.T. Bennett	Nat Party	517*	1.2
					4,054	9.4
1970	75,048	76.3	L.J. Huckfield	Lab	32,877	57.4
			Miss S. Lewis-Smith	C	18,767	32.8
			A.D.N. Harrison	L	5,602*	9.8
					14,110	24.6

Note:—

1965: Cousins was Minister of Technology.

WARWICKSHIRE, RUGBY [508]

ection	Electors	T'out	Candidate	Party	Votes	%
50	44,228	88.2	J. Johnson	Lab	15,983	41.0
			J.C.G. Dance	C	14,947	38.3
			†W.J. Brown	Ind	8,080	20.7
					1,036	2.7
51	45,392	87.7	J. Johnson	Lab	19,995	50.3
			J.C.G. Dance	C	19,796	49.7
					199	0.6
55	46,011	85.4	J. Johnson	Lab	19,709	50.2
			H.B. Soref	C	18,331	46.6
			E.H. Shafer	Ind	1,274*	3.2
					1,378	3.6
59	47,809	85.6	A.R. Wise	C	17,429	42.6
			J. Johnson	Lab	16,959	41.4
			S. Goldblatt	L	6,413	15.7
			A.S. Frost	Ind	142*	0.3
					470	1.2
64	50,332*	84.6	A.R. Wise	C	19,221	45.1
			D.H. Childs	Lab	17,532	41.2
			S. Goldblatt	L	5,522	13.0
			A.S. Frost	Ind	304*	0.7
					1,689	3.9
66	51,330	84.9	W.G. Price	Lab	21,797	50.0
			A.R. Wise	C	21,388	49.1
			A.S. Frost	Ind	397*	0.9
					409	0.9
70	57,813	82.0	W.G. Price	Lab	25,041	52.9
			J.H.P. Griffith	C	22,086	46.6
			A.S. Frost	Ind	254*	0.5
					2,955	6.3

otes:—

1955: Shafer was opposed to the manufacture of the hydrogen bomb.

1959- Frost sought election as a 'Social Credit' candidate and received support from the
1970: Social Credit Political League (re-named the Social Credit Party in 1964).

Election	Electors	T'out	Candidate	Party	Votes	%
1950	46,831	86.9	†M.A. Lindsay	C	25,758	63
			W.N.A. Camp	Lab	11,741	28
			Mrs. A.L.C. Hayes	L	3,206*	7
					14,017	34
1951	47,627	83.2	M.A. Lindsay	C	27,871	70
			J. Johnson	Lab	11,747	29
					16,124	40
1955	51,897	78.3	M.A. Lindsay	C	29,323	72
			Miss M. Large	Lab	11,300	27
					18,023	44
1959	60,227	80.6	M.A. Lindsay	C	35,862	73
			E.J. Bowen	Lab	12,682	26
					23,180	47
1964	67,639	80.5	W.P. Grieve	C	32,355	59
			T.W.K. Scott	Lab	11,969	22
			L. Farrell	L	10,097	18
					20,386	37
1966	69,211	74.8	W.P. Grieve	C	34,008	65
			D.A. Forwood	Lab	17,760	34
					16,248	31
1970	80,279	73.2	W.P. Grieve	C	37,756	64
			D. Gray	Lab	13,181	22
			R.A. Davis	L	7,795	13
					24,575	41

WARWICKSHIRE, STRATFORD [510]

ection	Electors	T'out	Candidate	Party	Votes	%
50	45,661	83.1	J.D. Profumo	C	21,492	56.6
			R.G.M. Brown	Lab	12,143	32.0
			H.S. Seaborne	L	4,318*	11.4
					9,349	24.6
51	46,666	79.9	J.D. Profumo	C	24,041	64.5
			H. Hilditch	Lab	13,246	35.5
					10,795	29.0
55	47,451	75.6	J.D. Profumo	C	24,587	68.6
			T.L.K. Locksley	Lab	11,275	31.4
					13,312	37.2
59	49,660	76.8	J.D. Profumo	C	26,146	68.5
			J. Stretton	Lab	12,017	31.5
					14,129	37.0

[esignation]

63	52,357	69.4	A.E.U. Maude	C	15,846	43.5
(5/8)			A.M.W. Faulds	Lab	12,376	34.1
			D. Mirfin	L	7,622	21.0
			M.S. Blair	B & CP	281*	0.8
			D.E. Sutch	NTP	209*	0.6
					3,470	9.4
64	53,989	80.0	A.E.U. Maude	C	23,236	53.8
			A.M.W. Faulds	Lab	12,646	29.3
			D. Mirfin	L	7,307	16.9
					10,590	24.5
66	55,907	78.0	A.E.U. Maude	C	22,381	51.3
			V.G. Hale	Lab	12,954	29.7
			G.H. Herringshaw	L	6,556	15.0
			C.G. Clayton-Wright	Ind C	1,733*	4.0
					9,427	21.6
70	65,255	74.2	A.E.U. Maude	C	28,106	58.1
			P.E. Tombs	Lab	11,393	23.5
			D.R. Bruce	L	8,895	18.4
					16,713	34.6

Election	Electors	T'out	Candidate	Party	Votes	%
1950	69,000	83.2	†Sir J.S.P. Mellor, Bt.	C	36,017	62
			Miss A.A.M. Wilson	Lab	21,364	37
					14,653	25
1951	70,518	81.6	Sir J.S.P. Mellor, Bt.	C (Ind C) (C)	36,628	63
			D.G. Allen	Lab	20,893	36
					15,735	27

This constituency was divided in 1955.

¦ction	Electors	T'out	Candidate	Party	Votes	%
50	55,218	82.9	†Rt. Hon. R.A. Eden	C	27,353	59.8
			H. Bithell	Lab	18,400	40.2
					8,953	19.6
51	56,766	82.4	Rt. Hon. R.A. Eden	C	28,282	60.5
			W. Wilson	Lab	18,479	39.5
					9,803	21.0
55	59,019	78.8	Rt. Hon. Sir R.A. Eden	C	29,979	64.5
			W. Wilson	Lab	16,513	35.5
					13,466	29.0
esignation]						
57	61,315	77.9	J.G.S. Hobson	C	24,948	52.3
/3)			W. Wilson	Lab	22,791	47.7
					2,157	4.6
59	62,849	82.7	J.G.S. Hobson	C	32,513	62.6
			W. Wilson	Lab	19,434	37.4
					13,079	25.2
64	68,803*	80.4	Rt. Hon. Sir J.G.S. Hobson	C	29,749	53.8
			N.J. Spearing	Lab	18,865	34.1
			P.S. Gibson	L	6,676*	12.1
					10,884	19.7
66	71,022	78.9	Rt. Hon. Sir J.G.S. Hobson	C	28,918	51.6
			L.J. Huckfield	Lab	20,221	36.1
			A. Butcher	L	6,912*	12.3
					8,697	15.5
)eath]						
68	72,366	58.5	D.G. Smith	C	28,914	68.3
8/3)			R.J. Carter	Lab	6,992	16.5
			A. Butcher	L	6,415	15.2
					21,922	51.8
70	80,284	72.7	D.G. Smith	C	36,994	63.4
			J.T. Watkinson	Lab	21,355	36.6
					15,639	26.8

Election	Electors	T'out	Candidate	Party	Votes	%
1950	47,130	85.5	†W.M.F. Vane	C	22,228	5£
			A.G.D. Acland	L	9,054	2:
			P.N. Wilson	Lab	9,031	2:
					13,174	3:
1951	47,697	83.5	W.M.F. Vane	C	23,227	58
			P.N. Wilson	Lab	9,119	22
			A.G.D. Acland	L	7,493	18
					14,108	3£
1955	47,222	77.6	W.M.F. Vane	C	21,048	57
			I.R. Million	Lab	7,901	21
			A.G.D. Acland	L	7,688	2
					13,147	35
1959	46,991	78.8	W.M.F. Vane	C	20,676	55
			A.G.D. Acland	L	8,984	24
			C. Hughes-Stanton	Lab	7,359	19
					11,692	31

[Seat Vacant at Dissolution (Elevation to the Peerage—Lord Inglewood)]

Election	Electors	T'out	Candidate	Party	Votes	%
1964	46,888	78.8	T.M. Jopling	C	19,125	51
			A. Herbert	L	11,078	30
			N. Plamping	Lab	6,752	18
					8,047	21
1966	46,944	75.5	T.M. Jopling	C	17,907	50.
			A.W. Bell	L	9,052	25
			J.E. Dayton	Lab	8,465	23.
					8,855	24.
1970	53,365	72.0	T.M. Jopling	C	21,253	55.
			J.G. Pease	L	9,426	24
			R.S. Ward	Lab	7,757	20.
					11,827	30.

ection	Electors	T'out	Candidate	Party	Votes	%
50	48,497	83.0	†D.M. Eccles	C	17,845	44.3
			G.A. Drain	Lab	13,748	34.2
			W.G. Collins	L	8,661	21.5
					4,097	10.1
51	49,494	81.5	D.M. Eccles	C	22,601	56.0
			D.R. Evans	Lab	17,723	44.0
					4,878	12.0
55	50,278	80.0	Sir D.M. Eccles	C	20,847	51.8
			W.J. Smith	Lab	14,152	35.2
			A.R. Braybrooke	L	5,208	13.0
					6,695	16.6
59	51,923	80.2	Rt. Hon. Sir D.M. Eccles	C	21,696	52.1
			R.W. Portus	Lab	12,911	31.0
			J.C. Hall	L	7,059	16.9
					8,785	21.1

[Elevation to the Peerage—Viscount Eccles]

62	53,657	68.0	D.E. Awdry	C	13,439	36.9
(2/11)			Hon. C.W. Layton	L	11,851	32.5
			R.W. Portus	Lab	10,633	29.1
			K. Jerrome	Ind Ser	260*	0.7
			J.P. Naylor	Ind Ser	237*	0.6
			M.J.A. Smith	Ind Ser	88*	0.2
					1,588	4.4
64	55,071	81.2	D.E. Awdry	C	18,089	40.4
			Hon. C.W. Layton	L	16,546	37.0
			G.H. Radice	Lab	10,086	22.6
					1,543	3.4
66	55,717	82.8	D.E. Awdry	C	18,275	39.7
			Hon. C.W. Layton	L	17,581	38.1
			G.H. Radice	Lab	10,257	22.2
					694	1.6
70	63,055	77.7	D.E. Awdry	C	24,371	49.7
			Mrs. M.E. Wingfield	L	13,833	28.2
			J. Eddie	Lab	10,807	22.1
					10,538	21.5

Election	Electors	T'out	Candidate	Party	Votes	%
1950	46,833	82.1	†M.C. Hollis	C	17,401	45
			W.E. Cave	Lab	16,216	42
			R.W.T. Aston	L	4,832	12
					1,185	3
1951	47,981	81.4	M.C. Hollis	C	20,319	52
			W.E. Cave	Lab	18,742	48
					1,577	4
1955	49,047*	78.6	H.P. Pott	C	20,317	52
			W.E. Cave	Lab	18,242	47
					2,075	5
1959	50,779	79.2	H.P. Pott	C	20,682	51
			W.E. Cave	Lab	16,844	41
			J. Norton	Ind L	2,707*	6
					3,838	9
[Death]						
1964 (14/5)	55,019	75.8	C.A. Morrison	C	19,554	46
			I.H.H. Rogers	Lab	17,884	42
			Prof. M.P. Fogarty	L	4,281*	10
					1,670	3
1964	55,514	81.4	C.A. Morrison	C	21,118	46
			I.H.H. Rogers	Lab	17,170	38
			Prof. M.P. Fogarty	L	6,881	15
					3,948	8
1966	59,237	81.0	Hon. C.A. Morrison	C	21,429	44
			I. Hamilton	Lab	18,832	39
			Prof. M.P. Fogarty	L	7,730	16
					2,597	5
1970	72,116	76.4	Hon. C.A. Morrison	C	28,475	51
			R.O. Faulkner	Lab	20,442	37
			J.D.H. Jones	L	6,210*	11
					8,033	14

ction	Electors	T'out	Candidate	Party	Votes	%
50	45,958	83.7	†J.G. Morrison	C	17,301	45.0
			W.A.J. Case	Lab	12,319	32.0
			A. Campbell-Johnson	L	8,847	23.0
					4,982	13.0
51	47,585	80.2	J.G. Morrison	C	21,798	57.1
			R.R. Thomas	Lab	16,386	42.9
					5,412	14.2
55	48,823	77.7	J.G. Morrison	C	20,271	53.4
			J. Papworth	Lab	12,632	33.3
			J.M. Booker	L	5,037	13.3
					7,639	20.1
59	49,997	78.2	J.G. Morrison	C	20,641	52.8
			Dr. J.A. Cannon	Lab	12,932	33.1
			J.M. Booker	L	5,516	14.1
					7,709	19.7
64	52,865	78.6	J.G. Morrison	C	20,071	48.3
			L.A. Mills	Lab	14,311	34.4
			H. Capstick	L	7,176	17.3
					5,760	13.9

[ievation to the Peerage—Lord Margadale]

65	52,865	69.1	M.A. Hamilton	C	17,599	48.2
/2)			L.A. Mills	Lab	13,660	37.4
			H. Capstick	L	4,699	12.9
			H.B.T. Cox	Ind C	553*	1.5
					3,939	10.8
66	53,895	76.2	M.A. Hamilton	C	22,601	55.0
			R.C. Smith	Lab	18,462	45.0
					4,139	10.0
70	61,104	72.1	M.A. Hamilton	C	26,549	60.3
			A. Waugh	Lab	17,493	39.7
					9,056	20.6

Election	Electors	T'out	Candidate	Party	Votes	%
1950	51,252	86.3	†R.V. Grimston	C	17,445	39
			R.J. Travess	Lab	15,766	35
			H.B. Richardson	L	11,031	24
					1,679	3
1951	52,129	86.2	R.V. Grimston	C	19,654	43
			R.J. Travess	Lab	17,623	39
			H.B. Richardson	L	7,666	17
					2,031	4
1955	52,334	82.4	Sir R.V. Grimston, Bt.	C	19,684	45
			R.J. Travess	Lab	16,295	37
			P.L.M. Hurd	L	7,165	16
					3,389	7
1959	53,238	84.1	Sir R.V. Grimston, Bt.	C	20,396	45
			J.G. Ridley	Lab	14,570	32
			B.T. Wigoder	L	9,816	21
					5,826	13
1964	55,847	82.8	D.M. Walters	C	19,950	43
			P.W. Hopkins	Lab	15,049	32
			B.T. Wigoder	L	11,232	24
					4,901	10
1966	58,341	82.5	D.M. Walters	C	20,989	43
			P.W. Hopkins	Lab	18,192	37
			I.M. Fowler	L	8,962	18
					2,797	5
1970	67,454	78.2	D.M. Walters	C	26,524	50
			J. McLaren	Lab	17,413	33
			R.G. Otter	L	8,781	16
					9,111	17

ection	Electors	T'out	Candidate	Party	Votes	%
950	57,462	85.8	J.M.C. Higgs	C	21,674	43.9
			D.P. Chesworth	Lab	21,484	43.6
			R.W.T. Hill	L	6,145*	12.5
					190	0.3
951	58,765	86.5	J.M.C. Higgs	C	26,736	52.6
			D.P. Chesworth	Lab	24,083	47.4
					2,653	5.2
955	60,898	81.7	J.C.G. Dance	C	27,461	55.2
			L.J. George	Lab	22,287	44.8
					5,174	10.4
959	66,924	83.5	J.C.G. Dance	C	32,473	58.1
			C.B.B. Norwood	Lab	23,433	41.9
					9,040	16.2
964	73,272	82.9	J.C.G. Dance	C	29,616	48.7
			N.P. Lister	Lab	22,673	37.3
			S.L. Stockdale	L	8,485	14.0
					6,943	11.4
966	76,220	80.2	J.C.G. Dance	C	32,400	53.0
			N.P. Lister	Lab	28,704	47.0
					3,696	6.0
970	83,877	76.6	J.C.G. Dance	C	37,544	58.5
			T.A.G. Davis	Lab	26,670	41.5
					10,874	17.0
Death]						
971 (7/5)	86,243	67.0	T.A.G. Davis	Lab	29,809	51.6
			H.D. Miller	C	27,941	48.4
					1,868	3.2

Election	Electors	T'out	Candidate	Party	Votes	%
1950	54,640	84.1	G.D.N. Nabarro	C	22,950	49
			†L. Tolley	Lab	19,145	41
			J.M. Eccles	L	3,844*	8
					3,805	8
1951	55,179	83.0	G.D.N. Nabarro	C	25,483	55
			I.A.J. Williams	Lab	20,325	44
					5,158	11
1955	56,216	78.4	G.D.N. Nabarro	C	26,142	59
			I.A.J. Williams	Lab	17,918	40
					8,224	18
1959	58,223	79.1	G.D.N. Nabarro	C	27,699	60
			Mrs. J. Tomlinson	Lab	18,356	39
					9,343	20
1964	60,606	79.4	Sir E.T.C. Brinton	C	24,425	50
			G.W. Jones	Lab	17,571	36
			L.A. King	L	5,824*	12
			M.S. Blair	B & CP	310*	0
					6,854	14
1966	62,445	75.9	Sir E.T.C. Brinton	C	24,628	52
			J.W. Wardle	Lab	21,451	45
			R. Smith	Ind	1,292*	2
					3,177	6
1970	72,360	73.9	Sir E.T.C. Brinton	C	27,667	51
			G.F. Smith	Lab	18,297	34
			Dr. H.H.B. Lamb	L	7,502	14
					9,370	17

lection	Electors	T'out	Candidate	Party	Votes	%
950	53,148	80.2	†R. De la Bère	C	26,948	63.2
			J.P.T. Hopwood	Lab	15,668	36.8
					11,280	26.4
951	54,883	75.9	R. De la Bère	C	27,229	65.4
			J.P.T. Hopwood	Lab	14,434	34.6
					12,795	30.8
955	55,730*	72.9	P.G. Agnew	C	26,811	66.0
			E.L.J. Thorne	Lab	13,831	34.0
					12,980	32.0
959	57,687	75.6	Sir P.G. Agnew, Bt.	C	25,824	59.2
			D.W. Young	Lab	10,884	25.0
			Dr. E.H.L. Harries	L	6,890	15.8
					14,940	34.2
964	60,030	77.3	Sir P.G. Agnew, Bt.	C	23,740	51.2
			A.J. Batchelor	L	11,503	24.8
			S.P.W. Drewer	Lab	11,137	24.0
					12,237	26.4
966	61,518	76.1	Sir G.D.N. Nabarro	C	24,198	51.7
			K.A. Gulleford	Lab	13,114	28.0
			R.G. Otter	L	9,476	20.3
					11,084	23.7
970	70,375	72.1	Sir G.D.N. Nabarro	C	30,648	60.4
			A.E. Bailey	Lab	12,839	25.3
			J.C. Hall	L	7,262	14.3
					17,809	35.1

Election	Electors	T'out	Candidate	Party	Votes	%
1950	57,782	83.0	†G.W. Odey	C	26,699	55.
			A.W. Gray	Lab	12,399	25.
			H.S. Freemantle	L	7,719	16.
			G. Thorley	Ind C	1,121*	2.
					14,300	29.
1951	59,067	80.0	G.W. Odey	C	27,937	59.
			T. Brennan	Lab	12,778	27.
			H.S. Freemantle	L	6,522	13.
					15,159	32.

This constituency was divided in 1955.

ection	Electors	T'out	Candidate	Party	Votes	%
150	62,602	81.9	Hon. R.F. Wood	C	26,124	50.9
			†G. Wadsworth	L	16,158	31.5
			W. Pashby	Lab	9,013	17.6
					9,966	19.4
151	63,860	78.4	Hon. R.F. Wood	C	30,576	61.1
			G. McQuade	Lab	12,931	25.8
			D.E. Moore	L	6,546	13.1
					17,645	35.3
155	52,583**	69.4	Hon. R.F. Wood	C	25,880	70.9
			Mrs. K.M. Roberts	Lab	10,614	29.1
					15,266	41.8
159	53,621*	69.9	Hon. R.F. Wood	C	27,438	73.2
			H. Moor	Lab	10,047	26.8
					17,391	46.4
164	55,268	72.8	Rt. Hon. R.F. Wood	C	22,729	56.5
			J.K. McNamara	Lab	9,002	22.4
			J.J. MacCallum	L	8,494	21.1
					13,727	34.1
166	56,333	71.5	Rt. Hon. R.F. Wood	C	21,976	54.5
			J.E. Tomlinson	Lab/Co-op	11,939	29.7
			T. Silverwood	L	6,349	15.8
					10,037	24.8
170	61,716	69.8	Rt. Hon. R.F. Wood	C	25,053	58.1
			H.A. Clarke	Lab	11,546	26.8
			T. Silverwood	L	6,497	15.1
					13,507	31.3

Election	Electors	T'out	Candidate	Party	Votes	%
1955	50,790	74.8	P.H.B. Wall	C	26,162	68.!
			H. Roberts	Lab	11,820	31.
					14,342	37.!
1959	53,906	80.5	P.H.B. Wall	C	26,102	60.
			D.N. Bancroft	Lab	9,750	22.!
			W.I. Cooper	L	7,562	17.‹
					16,352	37.!
1964	58,501	79.4	P.H.B. Wall	C	26,131	56.:
			P. Allison	Lab	10,360	22.:
			S. Burnley	L	9,986	21.!
					15,771	33.!
1966	61,232	76.5	P.H.B. Wall	C	25,566	54.!
			Mrs. P. Clarke	Lab	13,017	27.!
			S. Burnley	L	8,277	17.`
					12,549	26.
1970	74,813	74.9	P.H.B. Wall	C	30,042	53.!
			C.M. Denton	Lab	15,862	28.:
			S.C. Haywood	L	10,129	18.
					14,180	25.:

lection	Electors	T'out	Candidate	Party	Votes	%
955	47,676	73.7	P.E.O. Bryan	C	20,486	58.2
			R.W. Bowes	Lab	9,088	25.9
			W.D. Ramsdale	L	5,575	15.9
					11,398	32.3
959	47,310	75.8	P.E.O. Bryan	C	20,681	57.6
			J. Rhodes	Lab	7,809	21.8
			R.H. Hargreaves	L	7,384	20.6
					12,872	35.8
964	47,973	75.9	P.E.O. Bryan	C	19,367	53.2
			J.O.K. Crawford	L	9,067	24.9
			A. Day	Lab	7,974	21.9
					10,300	28.3
966	48,768	71.8	P.E.O. Bryan	C	17,701	50.6
			G. McNamara	Lab	9,421	26.9
			J.J. MacCallum	L	7,885	22.5
					8,280	23.7
970	54,592	71.0	P.E.O. Bryan	C	22,102	57.0
			J.W.R. Graham	Lab	9,567	24.7
			J.F. Crossley	L	6,951	17.9
			T.S.J. Makoni	Ind	154*	0.4
					12,535	32.3

Note:—

1970: Makoni advocated a policy of non-racism and anti-racialism.

Election	Electors	T'out	Candidate	Party	Votes	%
1950	65,589	85.8	†O.G. Willey	Lab	28,940	51.4
			E.C. Peake	C	21,332	37.9
			A.L.B. Childe	L	5,996*	10.7
					7,608	13.5
1951	66,963	85.1	O.G. Willey	Lab	31,237	54.8
			P.H.B. Wall	C	25,756	45.2
					5,481	9.6
[Death]						
1952	67,296	71.4	A.M.F. Palmer	Lab/Co-op	25,985	54.1
(23/10)			P.H.B. Wall	C	22,064	45.9
					3,921	8.2
1955	68,208	80.8	A.M.F. Palmer	Lab/Co-op	27,649	50.2
			G.W. Proudfoot	C	27,468	49.8
					181	0.4
1959	71,281	83.1	G.W. Proudfoot	C	30,445	51.4
			A.M.F. Palmer	Lab/Co-op	28,790	48.6
					1,655	2.8
1964	76,693	83.6	J. Tinn	Lab	28,596	44.6
			G.W. Proudfoot	C	24,124	37.6
			J.W. Stevens	L	11,387	17.8
					4,472	7.0
1966	78,832	81.1	J. Tinn	Lab	34,303	53.6
			G.W. Proudfoot	C	22,423	35.1
			M.F. Pitts	L	7,229*	11.3
					11,880	18.5
1970	92,328	72.9	J. Tinn	Lab	36,213	53.8
			Dr. P.C. Price	C	31,130	46.2
					5,083	7.6

Election	Electors	T'out	Candidate	Party	Votes	%
1950	48,723	79.7	†Sir T.L. Dugdale, Bt.	C	22,999	59.2
			F.W. Beaton	Lab	8,694	22.4
			D.E. Moore	L	7,157	18.4
					14,305	36.8
1951	49,954	74.4	Sir T.L. Dugdale, Bt.	C	26,231	70.6
			R. Hoyle	Lab	10,915	29.4
					15,316	41.2
1955	50,490	67.2	Sir T.L. Dugdale, Bt.	C	24,979	73.6
			R. Hoyle	Lab	8,974	26.4
					16,005	47.2

[Seat Vacant at Dissolution (Elevation to the Peerage—Lord Crathorne)]

Election	Electors	T'out	Candidate	Party	Votes	%
1959	52,416	71.5	T.P.G. Kitson	C	28,270	75.4
			Mrs. M. McMillan	Lab	9,203	24.6
					19,067	50.8
1964	56,926	75.6	T.P.G. Kitson	C	25,345	58.9
			G.A. Knott	Lab	8,908	20.7
			K. Schellenberg	L	8,787	20.4
					16,437	38.2
1966	58,315	71.3	T.P.G. Kitson	C	23,541	56.6
			W.P. Lisle	Lab	10,210	24.6
			K. Schellenberg	L	7,824	18.8
					13,331	32.0
1970	70,908	68.4	T.P.G. Kitson	C	30,471	62.8
			M.J. Aldrich	Lab	12,702	26.2
			J.R. Smithson	L	5,354*	11.0
					17,769	36.6

Election	Electors	T'out	Candidate	Party	Votes	%
1950	64,762	80.8	†A.C.M. Spearman	C	28,896	55.
			P. Taylor	Lab	14,421	27.
			R.W. Sykes	L	8,989	17.
					14,475	27.
1951	65,351	75.9	A.C.M. Spearman	C	32,988	66.
			H. Brinton	Lab	16,621	33.
					16,367	33.
1955	64,531	72.6	A.C.M. Spearman	C	27,133	57.
			J. Archer	Lab	10,488	22.
			G. Gray	L	9,215	19.
					16,645	35.
1959	63,938	72.7	Sir A.C.M. Spearman	C	25,276	54.
			G. Gray	L	10,759	23.
			N.G. Barnett	Lab	10,468	22.
					14,517	31.
1964	65,611	74.9	Sir A.C.M. Spearman	C	22,632	46.
			R.S. Rowntree	L	14,725	29.
			P. Hardy	Lab	11,818	24.
					7,907	16.
1966	66,143	74.1	M.N. Shaw	C	21,141	43.
			R.S. Rowntree	L	15,599	31.8
			J. Goodhand	Lab	11,848	24.
			Dr. M. Jane Ellis	Ind C	429*	0.
					5,542	11.
1970	73,400	71.5	M.N. Shaw	C	26,154	49.8
			M.F. Pitts	L	16,517	31.8
			Miss J.G. Hewitson	Lab	9,802	18.
					9,637	18.

Election	Electors	T'out	Candidate	Party	Votes	%
1950	49,373	81.5	†R.H. Turton	C	26,324	65.4
			I.E. Geffen	Lab	11,480	28.5
			H. Aldam	L	2,441*	6.1
					14,844	36.9
1951	49,797	77.4	R.H. Turton	C	27,854	72.3
			A.J. Parkinson	Lab	10,692	27.7
					17,162	44.6
1955	50,212	73.4	R.H. Turton	C	25,467	69.1
			G.R. Mitton	Lab	11,382	30.9
					14,085	38.2
1959	52,517	75.7	Rt. Hon. R.H. Turton	C	27,413	69.0
			Dr. J.W. Bray	Lab	12,318	31.0
					15,095	38.0
1964	57,697	73.8	Rt. Hon. R.H. Turton	C	28,272	66.4
			D.L. Hussey	Lab	14,315	33.6
					13,957	32.8
1966	57,967	70.3	Rt. Hon. R.H. Turton	C	25,089	61.6
			R.A. Wilson	Lab	15,647	38.4
					9,442	23.2
1970	63,864	72.3	Rt. Hon. R.H. Turton	C	30,892	66.9
			J.R. Bradshaw	Lab	15,309	33.1
					15,583	33.8

Election	Electors	T'out	Candidate	Party	Votes	%
1950	50,180	87.3	†L. Ropner	C	25,199	57.5
			B. Hazell	Lab	18,626	42.5
					6,573	15.0
1951	51,372	85.1	L. Ropner	C	25,155	57.6
			H.V. Wiseman	Lab	18,537	42.4
					6,618	15.2
1955	52,066	81.1	Sir L. Ropner, Bt.	C	24,194	57.3
			G.W. Rhodes	Lab	18,027	42.7
					6,167	14.6
1959	54,448	82.4	Sir L. Ropner, Bt.	C	26,200	58.4
			R.W. Bowes	Lab	18,647	41.6
					7,553	16.8
1964	58,246*	81.4	M.J.H. Alison	C	27,897	58.8
			N. Holding	Lab	19,533	41.2
					8,364	17.6
1966	62,650	79.8	M.J.H. Alison	C	28,183	56.3
			S. Cohen	Lab	21,841	43.7
					6,342	12.6
1970	78,047	75.7	M.J.H. Alison	C	35,198	59.6
			E.K. Grime	Lab	23,861	40.4
					11,337	19.2

Election	Electors	T'out	Candidate	Party	Votes	%
1950	58,265	86.5	†Rt. Hon. W.G. Hall	Lab	24,910	49.4
			Mrs. E.E. Smith	C	15,826	31.4
			R.F. Leslie	L	9,654	19.2
					9,084	18.0
1951	58,243	87.1	Rt. Hon. W.G. Hall	Lab	26,455	52.2
			Lady Violet Bonham Carter	L	24,266	47.8
					2,189	4.4
1955	52,540**	81.1	Rt. Hon. W.G. Hall	Lab	23,108	54.2
			S. Cheetham	C	19,512	45.8
					3,596	8.4
1959	51,777	84.1	Rt. Hon. W.G. Hall	Lab	19,284	44.3
			C.J. Barr	C	13,030	29.9
			R.S. Wainwright	L	11,254	25.8
					6,254	14.4
[Death]						
1963 (21/3)	51,397	78.9	A.E.P. Duffy	Lab	18,033	44.4
			R.S. Wainwright	L	15,994	39.5
			A.C. Alexander	C	6,238	15.4
			A. Fox	Ind	266*	0.7
					2,039	4.9
1964	52,006	84.8	A.E.P. Duffy	Lab	18,537	42.1
			R.S. Wainwright	L	18,350	41.6
			A.C. Alexander	C	7,207	16.3
					187	0.5
1966	52,555	86.2	R.S. Wainwright	L	22,006	48.5
			A.E.P. Duffy	Lab	19,507	43.1
			Dr. R.D. Hall	C	3,786*	8.4
					2,499	5.4
1970	58,604	80.8	D.G. Clark	Lab	18,896	39.9
			R.S. Wainwright	L	18,040	38.1
			K.E. Davy	C	10,417	22.0
					856	1.8

Note:—

1963: Fox was opposed to the laws governing public entertainment and licensing.

Election	Electors	T'out	Candidate	Party	Votes	%
1950	57,736	88.0	†Rt. Hon. W. Paling	Lab	40,420	79.6
			Mrs. A.L.G. Dower	NL & C	10,365	20.4
					30,055	59.2
1951	58,204	85.9	Rt. Hon. W. Paling	Lab	39,782	79.6
			J. Sizer	C	10,197	20.4
					29,585	59.2
1955	58,473	80.6	Rt. Hon. W. Paling	Lab	36,718	77.9
			Hon. R.D.G. Winn	C	10,402	22.1
					26,316	55.8
1959	59,444	84.6	E. Wainwright	Lab	39,088	77.7
			D.S.W. Blacker	C	11,205	22.3
					27,883	55.4
1964	59,617	79.1	E. Wainwright	Lab	38,101	80.8
			B. Bligh	C	9,069	19.2
					29,032	61.6
1966	58,739	76.7	E. Wainwright	Lab	36,735	81.6
			J.W. Roberts	C	6,121	13.6
			P. Hargreaves	Ind	2,170*	4.8
					30,614	68.0
1970	62,935	71.9	E. Wainwright	Lab	33,966	75.1
			A.B. Cowl	C	6,848	15.1
			P. Hargreaves	L	4,426*	9.8
					27,118	60.0

Election	Electors	T'out	Candidate	Party	Votes	%
1950	61,312	87.7	†Rt. Hon. T. Williams	Lab	39,789	74.0
			D. Graham	C	12,982	24.1
			S. Taylor	Com	1,007*	1.9
					26,807	49.9
1951	62,345*	85.9	Rt. Hon. T. Williams	Lab	39,687	74.1
			D.S.B. Hopkins	C	13,862	25.9
					25,825	48.2
1955	64,210	81.2	Rt. Hon. T. Williams	Lab	38,433	73.7
			J.V. Thornton	C	13,701	26.3
					24,732	47.4
1959	68,876	83.8	R. Kelley	Lab	40,935	70.9
			G.H. Dodsworth	C	16,787	29.1
					24,148	41.8
1964	73,120	80.8	R. Kelley	Lab	42,452	71.9
			D. Jeffcock	C	16,593	28.1
					25,859	43.8
1966	74,946	78.3	R. Kelley	Lab	43,973	74.9
			R. Storey	C	14,738	25.1
					29,235	49.8
1970	83,618	73.2	R. Kelley	Lab	42,496	69.5
			T.W.G. Jackson	C	18,673	30.5
					23,823	39.0

Election	Electors	T'out	Candidate	Party	Votes	%
1950	49,719	85.5	†G. Jeger	Lab	25,635	60
			F.W. Farey-Jones	C	16,853	39
					8,782	20
1951	51,280	84.2	G. Jeger	Lab	26,088	60
			A. Marreco	NL & C	17,073	39
					9,015	20
1955	52,190	78.3	G. Jeger	Lab	25,420	62
			G.B. Welby	NL & C	15,456	37
					9,964	24
1959	53,191	80.7	G. Jeger	Lab	26,352	61
			D. Sisson	NL & C	16,581	38
					9,771	22
1964	54,050	77.4	G. Jeger	Lab	25,256	60
			C.D. Chapman	NL & C	15,435	36
			W. Carr	Com	1,165*	2
					9,821	23
1966	55,842	73.5	G. Jeger	Lab	26,117	63
			R.M. Whitfield	NL & C	13,969	34
			W. Carr	Com	952*	2
					12,148	29
1970	63,111	69.5	G. Jeger	Lab	26,424	60
			I.R. Bloomer	C	17,457	39
					8,967	20
[Death]						
1971 (27/5)	63,484	55.6	Dr. E.I. Marshall	Lab	24,323	68
			I.R. Bloomer	C	10,990	31
					13,333	37

Election	Electors	T'out	Candidate	Party	Votes	%
1950	51,323	81.2	†C. York	C	28,582	68.5
			E.J. Parris	Lab	13,114	31.5
					15,468	37.0
1951	51,852	78.7	C. York	C	28,806	70.6
			C.W. Sewell	Lab	12,021	29.4
					16,785	41.2
[Resignation]						
1954	51,743	55.3	J.E. Ramsden	C	20,263	70.8
(11/3)			E. Kavanagh	Lab	8,367	29.2
					11,896	41.6
1955	51,570	71.9	J.E. Ramsden	C	26,799	72.3
			T. Evers	Lab	10,258	27.7
					16,541	44.6
1959	53,248	74.5	J.E. Ramsden	C	29,466	74.3
			F.B. Singleton	Lab	10,196	25.7
					19,270	48.6
1964	55,141	77.0	Rt. Hon. J.E. Ramsden	C	24,474	57.6
			B.M. Black	L	9,332	22.0
			E. Lyons	Lab	8,655	20.4
					15,142	35.6
1966	56,021	74.5	Rt. Hon. J.E. Ramsden	C	22,932	55.0
			W. Greaves	L	9,518	22.8
			R.E. Holmes	Lab	9,267	22.2
					13,414	32.2
1970	62,570	70.0	Rt. Hon. J.E. Ramsden	C	26,167	59.7
			W. Greaves	L	8,825	20.2
			B. Hellowell	Lab	8,797	20.1
					17,342	39.5

Election	Electors	T'out	Candidate	Party	Votes	%
1950	65,968	88.2	†H.E. Holmes	Lab	47,934	82.4
			Miss J.P. Asquith	NL & C	10,254	17.6
					37,680	64.8
1951	67,370	85.1	H.E. Holmes	Lab	47,402	82.7
			G.W. Proudfoot	C	9,911	17.3
					37,491	65.4
1955	64,060**	79.9	H.E. Holmes	Lab	42,603	83.3
			W.H. Leay	C	8,561	16.7
					34,042	66.6
1959	65,705	83.6	A. Beaney	Lab	45,153	82.2
			W.H. Leay	C	9,788	17.8
					35,365	64.4
1964	64,957	78.8	A. Beaney	Lab	42,528	83.1
			J.R.M. Keatley	C	8,668	16.9
					33,860	66.2
1966	64,521	76.0	A. Beaney	Lab	41,887	85.4
			C.W.R. Pickthorn	C	7,165	14.6
					34,722	70.8
1970	69,059	71.7	A. Beaney	Lab	40,013	80.8
			M.C. Tucker	C	9,534	19.2
					30,479	61.6

Election	Electors	T'out	Candidate	Party	Votes	%
1950	49,026	87.5	†T.J. Brooks	Lab	31,986	74.5
			T. Heseltine	NL & C	10,929	25.5
					21,057	49.0
1951	49,426	85.5	A. Roberts	Lab	31,052	73.5
			T. Heseltine	NL & C	11,199	26.5
					19,853	47.0
1955	48,514	78.1	A. Roberts	Lab	27,846	73.5
			J. Bird	C	10,040	26.5
					17,806	47.0
1959	49,139	83.1	A. Roberts	Lab	29,672	72.7
			J.A.C. Briggs	C	11,169	27.3
					18,503	45.4
1964	50,655	77.5	A. Roberts	Lab	28,477	72.5
			F.K. Roberts	C	10,785	27.5
					17,692	45.0
1966	51,807	74.3	A. Roberts	Lab	29,416	76.4
			J.E.R. Wauchope	C	9,084	23.6
					20,332	52.8
1970	58,047	71.6	A. Roberts	Lab	28,421	68.4
			D.H. Cargill	C	13,132	31.6
					15,289	36.8

Election	Electors	T'out	Candidate	Party	Votes	%
1950	64,333	87.7	†H.G. McGhee	Lab	34,979	62.0
			D. Hinchcliffe	C	16,128	28.6
			A.F. Smith	L	5,316*	9.4
					18,851	33.4
1951	66,156	85.1	H.G. McGhee	Lab	36,169	64.2
			D. Hinchcliffe	C	20,145	35.8
					16,024	28.4
1955	59,029**	80.0	H.G. McGhee	Lab	29,432	62.3
			L.B. Fulton	C	17,796	37.7
					11,636	24.6
[Death]						
1959 (11/6)	60,800	65.0	J.J. Mendelson	Lab	25,315	64.1
			J.B. Deby	C	14,196	35.9
					11,119	28.2
1959	61,397	82.9	J.J. Mendelson	Lab	31,117	61.1
			J.B. Deby	C	19,809	38.9
					11,308	22.2
1964	63,196	81.1	J.J. Mendelson	Lab	29,784	58.1
			B. Askew	C	13,095	25.6
			R. Swinden	L	8,372	16.3
					16,689	32.5
1966	63,943	78.9	J.J. Mendelson	Lab	31,419	62.3
			B. Askew	C	11,817	23.4
			R. Swinden	L	7,191	14.3
					19,602	38.9
1970	72,850	73.9	J.J. Mendelson	Lab	31,615	58.7
			A. Pickup	C	14,897	27.7
			D. Mirfin	L	7,347	13.6
					16,718	31.0

Election	Electors	T'out	Candidate	Party	Votes	%
1950	40,000	84.0	†M. Stoddart-Scott	C	22,292	66.3
			W.S. Hill	Lab	11,317	33.7
					10,975	32.6
1951	40,499	83.1	M. Stoddart-Scott	C	23,047	68.4
			S.J. Andrews	Lab	10,627	31.6
					12,420	36.8
1955	40,451	78.8	M. Stoddart-Scott	C	21,977	68.9
			E. Brierley	Lab	9,912	31.1
					12,065	37.8
1959	41,184	79.0	Sir M. Stoddart-Scott	C	22,757	69.9
			J.H. Swann	Lab	9,791	30.1
					12,966	39.8
1964	41,773	80.6	Sir M. Stoddart-Scott	C	18,503	55.0
			R.H.H. Duncan	L	7,814	23.2
			P.A. O'Grady	Lab	7,341	21.8
					10,689	31.8
1966	42,141	78.9	Sir M. Stoddart-Scott	C	17,352	52.1
			M. McGowan	Lab	8,607	25.9
			R.H.H. Duncan	L	7,301	22.0
					8,745	26.2
1970	47,395	73.7	Sir M. Stoddart-Scott	C	21,211	60.7
			D. Daniel	Lab	9,147	26.2
			Miss V.S. Craven	L	4,583	13.1
					12,064	34.5

Election	Electors	T'out	Candidate	Party	Votes	%
1950	63,057	87.4	†D. Griffiths	Lab	42,222	76.6
			W.R.A. Breare	C	12,887	23.4
					29,335	53.2
1951	64,243	86.3	D. Griffiths	Lab	41,990	75.7
			R. Hall	C	13,470	24.3
					28,520	51.4
1955	67,132	78.8	D. Griffiths	Lab	39,968	75.6
			W.A.V. Hoskins	C	12,916	24.4
					27,052	51.2
1959	71,652	82.8	D. Griffiths	Lab	43,962	74.1
			W.A.V. Hoskins	C	15,369	25.9
					28,593	48.2
1964	74,833	77.4	D. Griffiths	Lab	43,101	74.4
			R.W. Hadfield	C	14,813	25.6
					28,288	48.8
1966	76,420	74.3	D. Griffiths	Lab	43,634	76.8
			J.M. Clarke	C	13,167	23.2
					30,467	53.6
1970	87,331	70.7	P. Hardy	Lab	44,322	71.8
			R.A.B. Durant	C	17,418	28.2
					26,904	43.6

YORKSHIRE (West Riding), SHIPLEY [540]

ection	Electors	T'out	Candidate	Party	Votes	%
)50	46,981	89.4	G.A.N. Hirst	C	18,390	43.7
			†Rt. Hon. A.C. Jones	Lab	18,309	43.6
			W.A. Lupton	L	5,021*	12.0
			L.T. Robb	Com	273*	0.7
					81	0.1
)51	47,178	90.5	G.A.N. Hirst	C	20,396	47.7
			T.J. Roberts	Lab	18,893	44.3
			S.J. Berwin	L	3,399*	8.0
					1,503	3.4
)55	46,205	86.2	G.A.N. Hirst	C	22,582	56.7
			E. Gardner	Lab	17,251	43.3
					5,331	13.4
)59	45,460*	87.0	G.A.N. Hirst	C	22,536	57.0
			M. English	Lab	17,025	43.0
					5,511	14.0
)64	45,905	86.7	G.A.N. Hirst	C	19,076	47.9
			C. Price	Lab	15,545	39.1
			J.P. Heppell	L	5,165	13.0
					3,531	8.8
)66	45,895	86.6	G.A.N. Hirst	C (Ind C)	18,466	46.5
			J. Collins	Lab	16,966	42.7
			J.P. Heppell	L	4,304*	10.8
					1,500	3.8
)70	50,385	82.5	J.M. Fox	C	20,938	50.4
			N. Free	Lab	16,161	38.9
			A.M. Micklem	L	4,468*	10.7
					4,777	11.5

Election	Electors	T'out	Candidate	Party	Votes	%
1950	50,901	88.9	†G.B. Drayson	C	22,254	49
			T.J. Roberts	Lab	16,290	36
			E.A. Greenwood	L	6,689	14
					5,964	13
1951	51,207	86.1	G.B. Drayson	C	26,024	59
			E. Hewitt	Lab	18,064	41
					7,960	18
1955	49,710	82.5	G.B. Drayson	C	25,101	61
			V.P. Richardson	Lab	15,919	38
					9,182	22
1959	49,037	85.6	G.B. Drayson	C	20,278	48
			F.O. Hooley	Lab	11,178	26
			Miss K.C. Graham	L	10,543	25
					9,100	21
1964	47,827	84.0	G.B. Drayson	C	18,561	46
			R. MacSween	Lab	11,715	29
			W.E.H. Pickard	L	9,886	24
					6,846	17
1966	47,448	82.0	G.B. Drayson	C	17,532	45
			G.A. Knott	Lab	13,276	34
			W.E.H. Pickard	L	8,104	20
					4,256	11
1970	51,555	78.7	G.B. Drayson	C	20,817	51
			K. Targett	Lab	12,011	29
			Mrs. J.Y.L. Burns	L	7,733	19
					8,806	21

Election	Electors	T'out	Candidate	Party	Votes	%
1950	56,980	88.3	†A.L.N.D. Houghton	Lab	22,846	45.4
			P.E.O. Bryan	C	19,181	38.1
			A.J. Liddell Hart	L	8,306	16.5
					3,665	7.3
1951	56,921	86.9	A.L.N.D. Houghton	Lab	22,766	46.0
			P.E.O. Bryan	C	21,118	42.7
			J.G. Walker	L	5,573*	11.3
					1,648	3.3
1955	54,631	81.4	A.L.N.D. Houghton	Lab	20,092	45.2
			Miss M.B. Harvie Anderson	C	17,309	38.9
			J.G. Walker	L	7,046	15.9
					2,783	6.3
1959	52,560	82.9	A.L.N.D. Houghton	Lab	18,949	43.4
			R.K. McKim	C	16,993	39.0
			J.G. Walker	L	7,654	17.6
					1,956	4.4
1964	50,065	79.5	A.L.N.D. Houghton	Lab	21,582	54.2
			R.K. McKim	C	18,220	45.8
					3,362	8.4
1966	48,832	77.7	Rt. Hon. A.L.N.D. Houghton	Lab	21,591	56.9
			W.G. Burman	C	16,361	43.1
					5,230	13.8
1970	50,037	75.6	Rt. Hon. A.L.N.D. Houghton	Lab	16,583	43.8
			W.G. Burman	C	16,114	42.6
			D.T. Shutt	L	5,137	13.6
					469	1.2

WALES and MONMOUTHSHIRE ——— BOROUGHS

ABERDARE [543]

ection	Electors	T'out	Candidate	Party	Votes	%
50	51,437	86.9	†D.E. Thomas	Lab	33,930	75.9
			R.N.E. Hinton	C	6,098	13.6
			W.I. Samuel	PC	3,310*	7.4
			Dr. A.T.M. Wilson	Com	1,382*	3.1
					27,832	62.3
51	51,423	86.1	D.E. Thomas	Lab	34,783	78.5
			J. Lewis	C	6,810	15.4
			W.I. Samuel	PC	2,691*	6.1
					27,973	63.1
Death]						
54 (8/10)	50,916	69.7	A.R. Probert	Lab	24,658	69.5
			G.R. Evans	PC	5,671	16.0
			M.H.A. Roberts	C	5,158	14.5
					18,987	53.5
55	50,333	78.3	A.R. Probert	Lab	29,528	75.0
			W.J.A. Bain	C	6,162	15.6
			T. Beasley	PC	3,703*	9.4
					23,366	59.4
59	49,124	83.1	A.R. Probert	Lab	30,889	75.7
			B. McGlynn	C	6,584	16.1
			K.P. Thomas	PC	3,367*	8.2
					24,305	59.6
64	47,519	79.1	A.R. Probert	Lab	29,106	77.4
			P.N. Price	C	5,780	15.4
			D.W.H. Thomas	PC	2,723*	7.2
					23,326	62.0
66	46,618	77.0	A.R. Probert	Lab	26,322	73.3
			P.N. Price	C	4,204*	11.7
			J.E.W. Williams	PC	3,073*	8.6
			Dr. A.T.M. Wilson	Com	2,305*	6.4
					22,118	61.6
70	48,771	78.0	A.R. Probert	Lab	22,817	60.0
			Dr. G.M. Jones	PC	11,431	30.0
			D.C. Purnell	C	2,484*	6.5
			Dr. A.T.M. Wilson	Com	1,317*	3.5
					11,386	30.0

CARDIFF, NORTH [544]

Election	Electors	T'out	Candidate	Party	Votes	%
1950	60,543	84.4	D.T. Llewellyn	C	23,988	46.
			W. Howlett	Lab	21,081	41
			D.A. Jones	L	6,017*	11
					2,907	5.
1951	60,767*	85.6	D.T. Llewellyn	C	29,408	56.
			J. Evans	Lab/Co-op	22,600	43.
					6,808	13.
1955	61,352	80.9	D.T. Llewellyn	C	29,409	59.
			L. Abse	Lab	20,224	40.
					9,185	18
1959	59,986	82.9	D.S. Box	C	28,737	57.
			G.S. Viner	Lab	18,054	36.
			E.P. Roberts	PC	2,553*	5.
			S.G. Worth	Ind	408*	0.
					10,683	21.
1964	60,632	80.7	D.S. Box	C	21,837	44
			J.A. Reynolds	Lab	18,215	37.
			D.G. Rees	L	7,806	16
			E.P. Roberts	PC	1,058*	2.
					3,622	7.
1966	59,092	79.0	E. Rowlands	Lab	23,669	50.
			D.S. Box	C	22,997	49.
					672	1.
1970	61,057	76.7	M.H.A. Roberts	C	21,983	46.
			E. Rowlands	Lab	20,207	43.
			H.J. O'Brien	L	2,701*	5.
			B.M. Edwards	PC	1,927*	4.
					1,776	3.

Note:—

1959: Worth advocated a policy of disarmament.

lection	Electors	T'out	Candidate	Party	Votes	%
950	60,825	83.3	†L.J. Callaghan	Lab	26,254	51.8
			Dr. J.J. Hayward	C	20,359	40.2
			P.A.T. Furnell	L	4,080*	8.0
					5,895	11.6
951	60,902*	84.9	L.J. Callaghan	Lab	28,112	54.3
			H. West	C	23,613	45.7
					4,499	8.6
955	60,767	79.3	L.J. Callaghan	Lab	25,722	53.4
			M.H.A. Roberts	C	22,482	46.6
					3,240	6.8
959	64,574	82.0	L.J. Callaghan	Lab	26,915	50.8
			M.H.A. Roberts	C	26,047	49.2
					868	1.6
964	65,632	79.9	L.J. Callaghan	Lab	30,129	57.5
			E.R. Dexter	C	22,288	42.5
					7,841	15.0
966	65,394	78.9	Rt. Hon. L.J. Callaghan	Lab	29,313	56.8
			N. Lloyd-Edwards	C	18,476	35.8
			G.W. Parsons	L	3,829*	7.4
					10,837	21.0
970	69,067	73.2	Rt. Hon. L.J. Callaghan	Lab	26,226	51.9
			N. Lloyd-Edwards	C	20,771	41.1
			R.B. Davies	PC	2,585*	5.1
			G.W. Parsons	NF	982*	1.9
					5,455	10.8

CARDIFF, WEST [546]

Election	Electors	T'out	Candidate	Party	Votes	%
1950	60,918	82.2	†T.G. Thomas	Lab	27,200	54.3
			C.S. Hallinan	C	22,893	45.7
					4,307	8.6
1951	62,528*	84.1	T.G. Thomas	Lab	28,995	55.1
			A.L. Hallinan	C	23,595	44.9
					5,400	10.2
1955	61,446	76.7	T.G. Thomas	Lab	26,042	55.3
			E. Simons	C	21,080	44.7
					4,962	10.6
1959	59,524	80.0	T.G. Thomas	Lab	25,390	53.3
			A.L. Hallinan	C	22,258	46.7
					3,132	6.6
1964	57,511	76.4	T.G. Thomas	Lab	25,998	59.2
			K.T. Flynn	C	17,941	40.8
					8,057	18.4
1966	57,088	75.1	T.G. Thomas	Lab	26,139	61.0
			S.W. Doxsey	C	16,714	39.0
					9,425	22.0
1970	61,253	71.0	Rt. Hon. T.G. Thomas	Lab	21,655	49.7
			R.C. Williams	C	15,878	36.5
			Dr. D. Hughes	PC	4,378*	10.1
			S.R.C. Wanhill	L	1,594*	3.7
					5,777	13.2

Election	Electors	T'out	Candidate	Party	Votes	%
1950	43,156	85.9	†S.O. Davies	Lab	29,210	78.8
			L.F. Haddrill	C	6,294	17.0
			T.R. Morgan	Ind	1,571*	4.2
					22,916	61.8
1951	42,937	84.4	S.O. Davies	Lab	28,841	79.6
				(Ind Lab)		
				(Lab)		
			J.F. Lynam	C	7,405	20.4
					21,436	59.2
1955	42,933	77.3	S.O. Davies	Lab	25,630	77.2
			A.D. Arnold	C	7,548	22.8
					18,082	54.4
1959	42,153	81.8	S.O. Davies	Lab	26,608	77.1
				(Ind Lab)		
				(Lab)		
			Mrs. M.M.M. Greenaway	C	7,885	22.9
					18,723	54.2
1964	40,542	76.3	S.O. Davies	Lab	23,275	75.3
			S.W. Doxsey	C	4,767	15.4
			I.B. Rees	PC	2,878*	9.3
					18,508	59.9
1966	39,474	73.9	S.O. Davies	Lab	21,737	74.5
			G.L. Preece	C	4,082	14.0
			M. Stephens	PC	3,361*	11.5
					17,655	60.5
1970	41,291	77.9	S.O. Davies	Ind Lab	16,701	51.9
			T.J. Lloyd	Lab	9,234	28.7
			E. Jones	C	3,169*	9.8
			E.C. Rees	PC	3,076*	9.6
					7,467	23.2

Notes: —

1950: Morgan advocated a policy of Welsh nationalism.

1970: Davies had indicated his willingness to contest the election but his name was not submitted to the Labour Party selection conference which chose Lloyd as their prospective candidate.

As a result of Davies contesting the election he was expelled from the Labour Party in July 1970.

Election	Electors	T'out	Candidate	Party	Votes	%
1950	71,066	87.9	†P. Freeman	Lab	31,858	51.
			†I. Thomas	C	21,866	35.
			W.J. Owen	L	8,761	14.
					9,992	16.
1951	72,185	86.3	P. Freeman	Lab	32,883	52.
			T.E.R. Rhys-Roberts	C	24,166	38.
			W.J. Owen	L	5,247*	8.
					8,717	14.
1955	71,989*	81.6	P. Freeman	Lab	31,537	53.
			D.S. Box	C	27,177	46.
					4,360	7.
[Death]						
1956	71,943	72.1	Rt. Hon. Sir F. Soskice	Lab	29,205	56.
(6/7)			D.S. Box	C	20,720	39.
			E.P. Roberts	PC	1,978*	3.
					8,485	16.
1959	71,342	82.1	Rt. Hon. Sir F. Soskice	Lab	31,125	53.
			A.D. Arnold	C	27,477	46.
					3,648	6.
1964	70,387	79.0	Rt. Hon. Sir F. Soskice	Lab	31,962	57.
			P. Temple-Morris	C	23,649	42.
					8,313	15.
1966	68,131	78.8	R.J. Hughes	Lab	32,098	59.
			P. Temple-Morris	C	21,599	40.
					10,499	19.
1970	71,520	75.7	R.J. Hughes	Lab	30,132	55.
			A.D. Arnold	C	22,005	40.
			A.R. Vickery	PC	1,997*	3.
					8,127	15.

RHONDDA, EAST [549]

ection	Electors	T'out	Candidate	Party	Votes	%
)50	40,124	87.5	†W.H. Mainwaring	Lab	26,645	75.9
			H. Pollitt	Com	4,463	12.7
			G. Nicholls	C	2,634*	7.5
			D. Davies	PC	1,357*	3.9
					22,182	63.2
)51	40,270	85.5	W.H. Mainwaring	Lab	27,958	81.2
			O.P. Stutchbury	C	3,522*	10.2
			I. Cox	Com	2,948*	8.6
					24,436	71.0
)55	39,059	77.1	W.H. Mainwaring	Lab	21,859	72.6
			Mrs. A. Powell	Com	4,544	15.1
			H.R. Rowlands	C	3,711*	12.3
					17,315	57.5
)59	37,908	83.2	G.E. Davies	Lab	20,565	65.2
			Mrs. A. Powell	Com	4,580	14.5
			D.H. Peace	C	3,629*	11.5
			N.O. Williams	PC	2,776*	8.8
					15,985	50.7
)64	36,228	79.5	G.E. Davies	Lab	20,510	71.2
			Mrs. A. Powell	Com	3,385*	11.8
			D.C. Purnell	C	2,548*	8.8
			G.P. James	PC	2,361*	8.2
					17,125	59.4
)66	35,509	78.5	G.E. Davies	Lab	21,567	77.4
			Mrs. A. Powell	Com	2,349*	8.4
			G.P. James	PC	2,088*	7.5
			W.K.R. Ricketts	C	1,857*	6.7
					19,218	69.0
)70	36,836	77.5	G.E. Davies	Lab	19,602	68.6
			G.P. James	PC	6,931	24.3
			R.C. Mullett	C	1,359*	4.8
			A.L. Jones	Com	659*	2.3
					12,671	44.3

Election	Electors	T'out	Candidate	Party	Votes	%
1950	37,484	87.9	I.R. Thomas	Lab	27,150	82.
			J.P. Driscoll	C	3,632*	11.
			J.K. Davies	PC	2,183*	6.
					23,518	71.
1951	37,315	86.4	I.R. Thomas	Lab	26,123	81.
			E. Simons	C	3,635*	11.
			J.K. Davies	PC	2,467*	7.
					22,488	69.
1955	35,943	80.3	I.R. Thomas	Lab	21,288	73.
			G.P. James	PC	4,424	15.
			C.P.T. Burke	C	3,134*	10.
					16,864	58.
1959	34,450	85.2	I.R. Thomas	Lab	21,130	72.
			G.P. James	PC	4,978	17.
			F.L. Pym	C	3,242*	11.
					16,152	55.
1964	32,401	80.7	I.R. Thomas	Lab	20,713	79.
			N. Lloyd-Edwards	C	2,754*	10.
			H.V. Davies	PC	2,668*	10.
					17,959	68.
1966	31,189	80.3	I.R. Thomas	Lab	19,060	76.
			H.V. Davies	PC	2,172*	8.
			Dr. B. Sandford-Hill	C	1,955*	7.
			A. True	Com	1,853*	7.
					16,888	67.
[Death]						
1967 (9/3)	30,692	82.2	T.A. Jones	Lab	12,373	49.
			H.V. Davies	PC	10,067	39.9
			A. True	Com	1,723*	6.
			G.J.J. Neale	C	1,075*	4.
					2,306	9.
1970	30,811	81.5	T.A. Jones	Lab	18,779	74.
			H.V. Davies	PC	3,528	14.0
			J.D. Morgan	C	1,610*	6.
			A. True	Com	1,201*	4.
					15,251	60.

Election	Electors	T'out	Candidate	Party	Votes	%
1950	53,014	81.9	†D.L. Mort	Lab	32,680	75.3
			J.F. Lynam	C	10,712	24.7
					21,968	50.6
1951	53,790	82.8	D.L. Mort	Lab	32,790	73.6
			J.C. Hope	C	11,768	26.4
					21,022	47.2
1955	54,010*	72.1	D.L. Mort	Lab	28,198	72.4
			Miss R.S. Guest	C	10,726	27.6
					17,472	44.8
1959	55,301	80.1	D.L. Mort	Lab	29,884	67.5
			H.J.F. Crum Ewing	C	9,754	22.0
			E.C. Rees	PC	4,651*	10.5
					20,130	45.5
[Death]						
1963	55,328	55.9	N. McBride	Lab	18,909	61.2
(28/3)			R. Owens	L	4,895	15.8
			Rev. L. Atkin	PP	2,462*	8.0
			Miss A.P. Thomas	C	2,272*	7.3
			E.C. Rees	PC	1,620*	5.2
			H. Pearce	Com	773*	2.5
					14,014	45.4
1964	55,505	76.3	N. McBride	Lab	30,904	73.0
			O.C. Wright	C	7,863	18.6
			E.C. Rees	PC	3,556*	8.4
					23,041	54.4
1966	54,459	73.8	N. McBride	Lab	30,290	75.5
			T. Knowles	C	6,241	15.5
			E.C. Rees	PC	2,749*	6.8
			W.R. Jones	Com	902*	2.2
					24,049	60.0
1970	58,603	70.2	N. McBride	Lab	28,183	68.5
			M.J. Murphy	C	8,191	19.9
			D.R. Evans	PC	4,188*	10.2
			W.R. Jones	Com	563*	1.4
					19,992	48.6

Election	Electors	T'out	Candidate	Party	Votes	%
1950	58,362	83.8	†P. Morris	Lab	26,273	53.7
			Sir L. Jones	NL & C	22,608	46.3
					3,665	7.4
1951	59,051	84.6	P. Morris	Lab	26,061	52.2
			H.B. Kerby	C	23,901	47.8
					2,160	4.4
1955	58,923*	75.1	P. Morris	Lab	22,647	51.2
			B. McGlynn	C	21,626	48.8
					1,021	2.4
1959	58,045	82.1	J.E.H. Rees	C	24,043	50.4
			P. Morris	Lab	23,640	49.6
					403	0.8
1964	59,091	81.4	A.J. Williams	Lab	23,019	47.9
			J.E.H. Rees	C	20,382	42.4
			O.G. Williams	L	4,672*	9.7
					2,637	5.5
1966	58,889	80.4	A.J. Williams	Lab	26,703	56.4
			J.E.H. Rees	C	20,650	43.6
					6,053	12.8
1970	64,686	75.8	A.J. Williams	Lab	24,622	50.2
			J.E.H. Rees	C	21,384	43.6
			G. ap Gwent	PC	3,033*	6.2
					3,238	6.6

WALES and MONMOUTHSHIRE ––– COUNTIES

Election	Electors	T'out	Candidate	Party	Votes	%
1950	35,490	82.7	†Lady Megan Lloyd George	L	13,688	46.7
			C. Hughes	Lab	11,759	40.0
			J.O. Jones	C	3,919	13.3
					1,929	6.7
1951	36,117	81.4	C. Hughes	Lab	11,814	40.1
			Lady Megan Lloyd George	L	11,219	38.2
			O.M. Roberts	C	6,366	21.7
					595	1.9
1955	35,980	80.4	C. Hughes	Lab	13,986	48.4
			J.W. Hughes	L	9,413	32.6
			O.H. Hughes	C	3,333*	11.5
			J.R. Jones	PC	2,183*	7.5
					4,573	15.8
1959	36,281	77.6	C. Hughes	Lab	13,249	47.0
			O.M. Roberts	C	7,005	24.9
			Dr. R.T. Jones	PC	4,121	14.6
			R.G. Lloyd	L	3,796	13.5
					6,244	22.1
1964	35,793	78.6	C. Hughes	Lab	13,553	48.1
			J.E. Jones	C	7,016	25.0
			E.G. Jones	L	5,730	20.4
			Dr. R.T. Jones	PC	1,817*	6.5
					6,537	23.1
1966	36,950	73.2	C. Hughes	Lab	14,874	55.0
			J.E. Jones	C	9,576	35.4
			J.W. Meredith	PC	2,596*	9.6
					5,298	19.6
1970	41,334	78.2	Rt. Hon. C. Hughes	Lab	13,966	43.2
			J.E. Jones	C	9,220	28.5
			J.L. Williams	PC	7,140	22.1
			G.W. Roddick	L	2,013*	6.2
					4,746	14.7

BRECONSHIRE and RADNORSHIRE [554]

Election	Electors	T'out	Candidate	Party	Votes	%
1950	51,951	88.8	†T.E. Watkins	Lab	22,519	48.8
			J.D. Gibson-Watt	C	19,690	42.7
			R.M.R. Paton	L	3,903*	8.5
					2,829	6.1
1951	52,728	89.3	T.E. Watkins	Lab	24,572	52.2
			J.D. Gibson-Watt	C	22,489	47.8
					2,083	4.4
1955	51,969	86.8	T.E. Watkins	Lab	23,953	53.1
			H.G. Partridge	C	16,412	36.4
			Dr. W.S.R. Thomas	L	4,745*	10.5
					7,541	16.7
1959	51,357	86.4	T.E. Watkins	Lab	25,411	57.3
			J.H. Davies	C	18,939	42.7
					6,472	14.6
1964	50,159	82.8	T.E. Watkins	Lab	23,967	57.7
			F.T. Stevens	C	15,415	37.1
			T.R. Morgan	PC	2,165*	5.2
					8,552	20.6
1966	49,464	80.5	T.E. Watkins	Lab	22,902	57.5
			F.T. Stevens	C	14,523	36.5
			T.R. Morgan	PC	2,410*	6.0
					8,379	21.0
1970	52,629	82.0	C.E. Roderick	Lab	18,736	43.5
			G.J.J. Neale	C	13,892	32.2
			G.W. Howells	L	8,169	18.9
			W.G. Jenkins	PC	2,349*	5.4
					4,844	11.3

Election	Electors	T'out	Candidate	Party	Votes	%
1950	43,483	85.9	†G.O. Roberts	Lab	18,369	49.1
			E.R. Thomas	L	7,791	20.9
			G.W. Williams	C	6,315	16.9
			J.E. Jones	PC	4,882	13.1
					10,578	28.2
1951	43,453	82.5	G.O. Roberts	Lab	22,375	62.4
			J.E.B. Davies	C	13,479	37.6
					8,896	24.8
1955	42,753	82.4	G.O. Roberts	Lab	17,682	50.2
			O.M. Roberts	C	8,461	24.0
			R.E. Jones	PC	5,815	16.5
			D.G. Williams	L	3,277*	9.3
					9,221	26.2
1959	41,202	83.4	G.O. Roberts	Lab	17,506	51.0
			T.E. Hooson	C	9,564	27.8
			D.O. Jones	PC	7,293	21.2
					7,942	23.2
1964	40,671	80.4	G.O. Roberts	Lab	17,777	54.4
			Miss S. Roberts	C	7,915	24.2
			R.E. Jones	PC	6,998	21.4
					9,862	30.2
1966	40,121	78.4	G.O. Roberts	Lab	17,650	56.1
			G.R. Prys	C	6,972	22.2
			H. Roberts	PC	6,834	21.7
					10,678	33.9
1970	41,560	81.7	Rt. Hon. G.O. Roberts	Lab	13,627	40.0
			J.R.J. Lewis	PC	11,331	33.4
			Miss K.J. Smith	C	6,812	20.1
			Dr. J.A. Williams	L	2,195*	6.5
					2,296	6.6

Election	Electors	T'out	Candidate	Party	Votes	%
1950	46,669	84.6	W.E.E. Jones	Lab	15,176	38.4
			†D.A. Price-White	C	14,373	36.4
			H.E. Hooson	L	9,937	25.2
					803	2.0
1951	46,425	84.9	P.J.M. Thomas	C	17,115	43.4
			W.E.E. Jones	Lab	16,532	41.9
			H.E. Hooson	L	5,791	14.7
					583	1.5
1955	45,846	84.7	P.J.M. Thomas	C	18,705	48.1
			W.E.E. Jones	Lab	13,881	35.8
			Dr. H.M. Lewis	L	3,217*	8.3
			I.B. Rees	PC	3,019*	7.8
					4,824	12.3
1959	45,660	82.7	P.J.M. Thomas	C	17,795	47.1
			S. Jones	Lab	13,260	35.1
			J.H. Bellis	L	3,845*	10.2
			I.B. Rees	PC	2,852*	7.6
					4,535	12.0
1964	46,151	80.3	Rt. Hon. P.J.M. Thomas	C	18,753	50.6
			G.E. Roberts	Lab	15,234	41.1
			G. Hughes	PC	3,058*	8.3
					3,519	9.5
1966	45,825	83.7	G.E.H. Davies	Lab	18,203	47.5
			Rt. Hon. P.J.M. Thomas	C	17,622	45.9
			R.E. Jones	PC	2,552*	6.6
					581	1.6
1970	48,662	82.0	I.W.P. Roberts	C	16,927	42.4
			G.E.H. Davies	Lab	16,024	40.2
			D.E. Thomas	PC	4,311*	10.8
			E.L. Morris	L	2,626*	6.6
					903	2.2

Election	Electors	T'out	Candidate	Party	Votes	%
1950	44,627	73.6	†E.R. Bowen	L	17,093	52.1
			I.J. Morgan	Lab	9,055	27.6
			Dr. G.S.R. Little	C	6,680	20.3
					8,038	24.5
1951	41,977	70.6	E.R. Bowen	L	19,954	67.3
			Rev. B. Williams	Lab	9,697	32.7
					10,257	34.6
1955	39,902	72.7	E.R. Bowen	L	18,907	65.2
			D. Jones-Davies	Lab	10,090	34.8
					8,817	30.4
1959	38,878	78.0	E.R. Bowen	L	17,868	59.0
			Mrs. L.R. Hughes	Lab	8,559	28.2
			G.W. Evans	PC	3,880	12.8
					9,309	30.8
1964	37,964	78.9	E.R. Bowen	L	11,500	38.4
			D.J. Davies	Lab	9,281	31.0
			A.J. Ryder	C	5,897	19.7
			G.W. Evans	PC	3,262*	10.9
					2,219	7.4
1966	37,553	81.1	D.E. Morgan	Lab	11,302	37.1
			E.R. Bowen	L	10,779	35.4
			J.S. Thomas	C	5,893	19.4
			E.G. Millward	PC	2,469*	8.1
					523	1.7
1970	40,302	82.1	D.E. Morgan	Lab	11,063	33.5
			H.C. Lloyd Williams	L	9,800	29.6
			H.W.J. ap Robert	PC	6,498	19.6
			D.F.R. George	C	5,715	17.3
					1,263	3.9

Election	Electors	T'out	Candidate	Party	Votes	%
1950	58,444	83.4	†R.H. Morris	L	24,472	50.2
			†A.L. Ungoed-Thomas	Lab	24,285	49.8
					187	0.4
1951	58,709	86.5	R.H. Morris	L	25,632	50.5
			D. Owen	Lab	25,165	49.5
					467	1.0
1955	57,956*	85.1	Sir R.H. Morris	L	24,410	49.5
			J. Evans	Lab	21,077	42.7
			Mrs. J.E. Davies	PC	3,835*	7.8
					3,333	6.8
[Death]						
1957 (28/2)	57,183	87.5	Lady Megan Lloyd George	Lab	23,679	47.3
			J.M. Davies	L	20,610	41.2
			Mrs. J.E. Davies	PC	5,741*	11.5
					3,069	6.1
1959	57,195	85.4	Lady Megan Lloyd George	Lab	23,399	47.9
			A.T. Davies	L	16,766	34.3
			J.B. Evans	C	6,147	12.6
			H.H. Roberts	PC	2,545*	5.2
					6,633	13.6
1964	55,786	84.5	Lady Megan Lloyd George	Lab	21,424	45.4
			A.T. Davies	L	15,210	32.3
			G.R. Evans	PC	5,495*	11.7
			Mrs. H.E. Protheroe-Beynon	C	4,996*	10.6
					6,214	13.1
1966	55,407	83.0	Lady Megan Lloyd George	Lab	21,221	46.2
			D.H. Davies	L	11,988	26.1
			G.R. Evans	PC	7,416	16.1
			S.J. Day	C	5,338*	11.6
					9,233	20.1
[Death]						
1966 (14/7)	55,407	74.9	G.R. Evans	PC	16,179	39.0
			G.P. Davies	Lab	13,743	33.1
			D.H. Davies	L	8,650	20.8
			S.J. Day	C	2,934*	7.1
					2,436	5.9
1970	58,823	83.7	G.G. Jones	Lab	18,719	38.0
			G.R. Evans	PC	14,812	30.1
			H.G.E. Thomas	L	10,707	21.8
			L.H. Davies	C	4,975*	10.1
					3,907	7.9

lection	Electors	T'out	Candidate	Party	Votes	%
950	68,655	80.9	†Rt. Hon. J. Griffiths	Lab	39,326	70.8
			H.G.E. Thomas	L	7,700	13.9
			D.P. Owen	C	6,362*	11.5
			Rev. D.E. Morgan	PC	2,134*	3.8
					31,626	56.9
951	67,157	81.6	Rt. Hon. J. Griffiths	Lab	39,731	72.5
			H. Gardner	C	11,315	20.6
			Rev. D.E. Morgan	PC	3,765*	6.9
					28,416	51.9
955	64,858*	78.7	Rt. Hon. J. Griffiths	Lab	34,021	66.7
			T.H.H. Skeet	C	10,640	20.8
			Rev. D.E. Morgan	PC	6,398	12.5
					23,381	45.9
959	64,048	81.1	Rt. Hon. J. Griffiths	Lab	34,625	66.7
			H. Gardner	C	10,128	19.5
			Rev. D.E. Morgan	PC	7,176	13.8
					24,497	47.2
964	62,235	79.4	Rt. Hon. J. Griffiths	Lab	32,546	65.9
			P.A. Maybury	C	6,300	12.8
			E. Lewis	L	6,031*	12.2
			Dr. W.T.P. Davies	PC	3,469*	7.0
			R.E. Hitchon	Com	1,061*	2.1
					26,246	53.1
1966	61,621	76.5	Rt. Hon. J. Griffiths	Lab	33,674	71.4
			J.C. Peel	C	7,143	15.1
			Dr. W.T.P. Davies	PC	5,132*	10.9
			R.E. Hitchon	Com	1,211*	2.6
					26,531	56.3
1970	64,616	77.4	D.J.D. Davies	Lab	31,398	62.7
			C.R. James	PC	8,387	16.8
			Miss M.A. Jones	C	5,777*	11.6
			D.J. Lewis	L	3,834*	7.7
			R.E. Hitchon	Com	603*	1.2
					23,011	45.9

Election	Electors	T'out	Candidate	Party	Votes	%
1950	54,614	82.3	E.H.G. Evans	NL & C	17,473	38.9
			G.T. Hughes	L	16,264	36.2
			J.G. Hughes	Lab	11,205	24.9
					1,209	2.7
1951	54,011	82.2	E.H.G. Evans	NL & C	20,269	45.7
			J.I. Jones	Lab	12,354	27.8
			H.E.P. Roberts	L	11,758	26.5
					7,915	17.9
1955	53,589	79.1	E.H.G. Evans	NL & C	18,312	43.2
			Dr. G.T. Hughes	L	13,671	32.2
			J.R.J. Lewis	Lab	10,421	24.6
					4,641	11.0
1959	53,000	80.9	W.G.O. Morgan	NL & C (C)	17,893	41.7
			Dr. G.T. Hughes	L	13,268	31.0
			S. Williams	Lab	8,620	20.1
			Dr. D.A. Jones	PC	3,077*	7.2
					4,625	10.7
1964	54,032	80.5	W.G.O. Morgan	C	17,970	41.4
			Dr. W.B.E. Ellis-Jones	L	13,331	30.6
			S. Williams	Lab	8,754	20.1
			Dr. D.A. Jones	PC	3,444*	7.9
					4,639	10.8
1966	54,715	80.6	W.G.O. Morgan	C	17,382	39.4
			A.T. Davies	L	12,725	28.9
			E. Griffiths	Lab	11,305	25.6
			W.M. Edwards	PC	2,695*	6.1
					4,657	10.5
1970	60,732	78.5	W.G.O. Morgan	C	21,246	44.6
			Mrs. A.C. Roberts	Lab	12,537	26.3
			I. Hughes-Evans	L	8,636	18.1
			E.G. Matthews	PC	5,254*	11.0
					8,709	18.3

Election	Electors	T'out	Candidate	Party	Votes	%
1950	63,455	87.3	†R. Richards	Lab	32,042	57.8
			W.G. Cooper	NL & C	14,117	25.5
			Dr. H.M. Lewis	L	8,287	15.0
			G. Bowen	PC	960*	1.7
					17,925	32.3
1951	64,736	84.8	R. Richards	Lab	33,759	61.6
			W.G. Cooper	NL & C	19,124	34.8
			A.D. Thomas	PC	1,997*	3.6
					14,635	26.8
[Death]						
1955 (17/3)	64,788	62.4	J.I. Jones	Lab	23,402	57.9
			G.W.G. Jones	NL & C	12,476	30.8
			D.E. Morgan	PC	4,572*	11.3
					10,926	27.1
1955	64,788	76.2	J.I. Jones	Lab	27,945	56.6
			G.W.G. Jones	NL & C	16,286	33.0
			D.E. Morgan	PC	5,139*	10.4
					11,659	23.6
1959	66,150	81.4	J.I. Jones	Lab	30,101	55.9
			G.H. Pierce	NL & C	17,144	31.9
			D.E. Morgan	PC	6,579*	12.2
					12,957	24.0
1964	66,530	78.7	J.I. Jones	Lab	30,478	58.2
			G.H. Pierce	NL & C	17,240	32.9
			J.R. Thomas	PC	4,673*	8.9
					13,238	25.3
1966	66,441	77.2	J.I. Jones	Lab	30,039	58.5
			G.H. Pierce	NL & C	12,596	24.6
			W. McBriar	L	6,351*	12.4
			J.R. Thomas	PC	2,297*	4.5
					17,443	33.9
1970	72,744	75.2	R.T. Ellis	Lab	31,089	56.8
			G.B. Patterson	C	15,649	28.6
			W. McBriar	L	5,067*	9.3
			C. Golding	PC	2,894*	5.3
					15,440	28.2

Election	Electors	T'out	Candidate	Party	Votes	%
1950	50,411	88.0	Mrs. E.L. White	Lab	21,529	48.
			G.B.H. Currie	C	14,832	33.
			S.G. Waterhouse	L	8,010	18.
					6,697	15.
1951	51,575	86.4	Mrs. E.L. White	Lab	23,959	53.8
			G.B.H. Currie	C	20,580	46.
					3,379	7.6
1955	51,560	84.1	Mrs. E.L. White	Lab	22,828	52.6
			K.G. Knee	C	20,554	47.4
					2,274	5.2
1959	52,635	86.4	Mrs. E.L. White	Lab	22,776	50.1
			F. Hardman	C	22,701	49.9
					75	0.2
1964	54,076	86.9	Mrs. E.L. White	Lab	25,469	54.2
			F. Hardman	C	21,513	45.8
					3,956	8.4
1966	55,119	86.5	Mrs. E.L. White	Lab	24,442	51.3
			F. Hardman	C	15,960	33.5
			D.O. Diamond	L	6,348	13.3
			G. Hughes	PC	902*	1.9
					8,482	17.8
1970	64,793	81.2	S.B. Jones	Lab	24,227	46.1
			R.M. Amyes	C	20,145	38.3
			D.O. Diamond	L	5,888*	11.2
			G. Hughes	PC	2,332*	4.4
					4,082	7.8

lection	Electors	T'out	Candidate	Party	Votes	%
950	45,599	86.6	†E.N.C. Birch	C	19,088	48.4
			D.V. Leadbeater	Lab	12,369	31.3
			W.A. Ellis	L	8,036	20.3
					6,719	17.1
951	46,322	83.2	E.N.C. Birch	C	23,433	60.8
			D.V. Leadbeater	Lab	15,118	39.2
					8,315	21.6
955	46,529	81.0	E.N.C. Birch	C	20,980	55.7
			H.G. Jones	Lab	12,628	33.5
			G. Owen	L	4,060*	10.8
					8,352	22.2
959	47,490	82.7	Rt. Hon. E.N.C. Birch	C	20,446	52.0
			R.G. Waterhouse	Lab	12,925	32.9
			L.E. Roberts	L	4,319*	11.0
			E.N.C. Williams	PC	1,594*	4.1
					7,521	19.1
964	50,147	80.7	Rt. Hon. E.N.C. Birch	C	18,515	45.7
			W.H. Edwards	Lab	13,298	32.8
			D.M. Thomas	L	7,482	18.5
			E.N.C. Williams	PC	1,195*	3.0
					5,217	12.9
966	51,346	81.9	Rt. Hon. E.N.C. Birch	C	18,179	43.2
			R.T. Ellis	Lab	15,137	36.0
			D.M. Thomas	L	7,137	17.0
			D.A. Lloyd	PC	1,585*	3.8
					3,042	7.2
970	58,115	77.8	Sir A.J.C. Meyer, Bt.	C	20,999	46.4
			J.G. Evans	Lab	13,655	30.2
			D.M. Thomas	L	7,437	16.5
			Dr. A.O. Jones	PC	3,108*	6.9
					7,344	16.2

Election	Electors	T'out	Candidate	Party	Votes	%
1950	49,667	85.8	†W.G. Cove	Lab	29,278	68.
			A.M.H.Y.M. Herbert	NL & C	8,091	19
			J.M. Thomas	L	5,263*	12.
					21,187	49.
1951	50,071	84.6	W.G. Cove	Lab	30,498	72
			J.W. Loveridge	C	11,878	28.
					18,620	44.
1955	52,616	79.3	W.G. Cove	Lab	29,003	69.
			R.E.G. Howe	C	12,706	30.
					16,297	39.
1959	56,316	82.1	J. Morris	Lab	30,397	65.
			R.E.G. Howe	C	12,759	27
			I.M. Lewis	PC	3,066*	6.
					17,638	38.
1964	56,777	80.9	J. Morris	Lab	33,103	72.
			J.S. Thomas	C	9,424	20.
			G. John	PC	2,118*	4.
			Dr. J.T. Hart	Com	1,260*	2.
					23,679	51.
1966	57,179	78.3	J. Morris	Lab	33,763	75.
			R.A. Hicks	C	9,369	20.
			Dr. J.T. Hart	Com	1,620*	3.
					24,394	54.
1970	62,481	74.8	Rt. Hon. J. Morris	Lab	31,314	66.
			I. Grist	C	10,419	22.
			G. Farmer	PC	3,912*	8.
			Dr. J.T. Hart	Com	1,102*	2.
					20,895	44.

GLAMORGANSHIRE, BARRY [565]

ection	Electors	T'out	Candidate	Party	Votes	%
50	54,298	86.0	Mrs. D.M. Rees	Lab	20,770	44.5
			D.M. Evans	C	19,745	42.3
			J.A. Emlyn-Jones	L	6,180	13.2
					1,025	2.2
51	55,022*	86.8	H.R. Gower	C	24,715	51.7
			Mrs. D.M. Rees	Lab	23,066	48.3
					1,649	3.4
55	56,003	83.6	H.R. Gower	C	27,085	57.9
			D. Jones	Lab	19,722	42.1
					7,363	15.8
59	60,206	84.9	H.R. Gower	C	30,313	59.3
			D.R. Evans	Lab	20,790	40.7
					9,523	18.6
64	64,319	82.3	H.R. Gower	C	28,600	54.0
			D.I. Marquand	Lab	24,334	46.0
					4,266	8.0
66	65,194	83.6	H.R. Gower	C	27,957	51.3
			J. Thomas	Lab	26,563	48.7
					1,394	2.6
970	74,958	79.3	H.R. Gower	C	31,957	53.7
			J. Allison	Lab	23,286	39.2
			E.O. Williams	PC	4,200*	7.1
					8,671	14.5

Election	Electors	T'out	Candidate	Party	Votes	%
1950	46,321	84.3	†Rt. Hon. N. Edwards	Lab	30,270	77.
			K.J. Lloyd	C	8,771	22.
					21,499	55.
1951	46,893	84.4	Rt. Hon. N. Edwards	Lab	30,523	77.
			K.G. Knee	C	9,041	22.
					21,482	54.
1955	47,131	78.6	Rt. Hon. N. Edwards	Lab	27,852	75.
			J.H. Davies	C	9,180	24.
					18,672	50.
1959	46,671	83.0	Rt. Hon. N. Edwards	Lab	28,154	72.
			W.R. Lewis	C	7,181	18.
			J.D.A. Howell	PC	3,420*	8.
					20,973	54.
1964	45,969	78.4	Rt. Hon. N. Edwards	Lab	26,011	72.
			R.J. Maddocks	C	6,086	16.
			P.J.S. Williams	PC	3,956*	11.
					19,925	55.
1966	46,240	76.7	Rt. Hon. N. Edwards	Lab	26,330	74.
			R.J. Maddocks	C	5,182	14.
			J.D.A. Howell	PC	3,949*	11.
					21,148	59.
[Death]						
1968 (18/7)	46,578	75.9	A.T. Evans	Lab	16,148	45.
			Dr. P.J.S. Williams	PC	14,274	40.
			R. Williams	C	3,687*	10.
			P.G. Sadler	L	1,257*	3.
					1,874	5.
1970	51,703	78.1	A.T. Evans	Lab	24,972	61.
			Dr. P.J.S. Williams	PC	11,505	28.
			P.N. Price	C	3,917*	9.
					13,467	33.

ction	Electors	T'out	Candidate	Party	Votes	%
50	50,603	84.5	†D.R. Grenfell	Lab	32,564	76.1
			R. Harding	NL & C	10,208	23.9
					22,356	52.2
51	51,016	84.3	D.R. Grenfell	Lab	32,661	75.9
			R. Harding	NL & C	10,351	24.1
					22,310	51.8
55	50,193	76.8	D.R. Grenfell	Lab	26,304	68.3
			B.G. Jones	NL & C	8,135	21.1
			E.C. Rees	PC	4,101*	10.6
					18,169	47.2
59	49,480	82.9	I. Davies	Lab	27,441	66.9
			M.R.D. Heseltine	NL & C	9,837	24.0
			Dr. J.G. Griffiths	PC	3,744*	9.1
					17,604	42.9
54	49,219	79.8	I. Davies	Lab	27,895	71.0
			J.H.P. Griffith	NL & C	8,822	22.5
			Dr. J.G. Griffiths	PC	2,562*	6.5
					19,073	48.5
66	49,731	77.9	I. Davies	Lab	29,910	77.2
			D.R.O. Lewis	C	8,852	22.8
					21,058	54.4
70	54,246	77.0	I. Davies	Lab	26,485	63.4
			M.J. Carter	C	9,435	22.6
			C.G. Davies	PC	5,869	14.0
					17,050	40.8

Election	Electors	T'out	Candidate	Party	Votes	%
1950	51,720	87.5	†D.J. Williams	Lab	33,034	72
			J.C. Hope	C	6,225	13
			Dr. O.V. Jones	L	4,425*	9
			A.C. Thomas	Com	1,584*	3
					26,809	59
1951	52,203	85.9	D.J. Williams	Lab	34,496	76
			D.G. Jennings	C	10,367	23
					24,129	53
1955	51,422	77.9	D.J. Williams	Lab	30,581	76
			J.C. Hope	C	9,467	23
					21,114	52
1959	51,711	82.6	D.J. Williams	Lab	30,469	71
			D.N.I. Pearce	C	10,263	24
			J.J. David	Com	1,962*	4
					20,206	47
1964	50,318	80.2	D.R. Coleman	Lab	29,692	73
			M.N. Scrogie	C	8,342	20
			J.J. David	Com	2,342*	5
					21,350	52
1966	49,694	78.7	D.R. Coleman	Lab	31,183	79
			P.H. Valerio	C	6,312	16
			J.J. David	Com	1,632*	4
					24,871	63
1970	52,667	75.4	D.R. Coleman	Lab	28,378	71
			D.H.J. Martin-Jones	C	6,765	17
			G. John	PC	4,012*	10
			H. Pearce	Com	579*	1
					21,613	54

ection	Electors	T'out	Candidate	Party	Votes	%
50	56,184	85.2	W.E. Padley	Lab	35,836	74.8
			H.R. Gower	C	9,791	20.5
			Miss M. Llewellyn	Com	1,619*	3.4
			I. Davies	MGC	613*	1.3
					26,045	54.3
51	56,726	84.9	W.E. Padley	Lab	37,022	76.9
			P.L. Powell	C	9,504	19.7
			T. David	BEP	1,643*	3.4
					27,518	57.2
55	55,976	78.7	W.E. Padley	Lab	33,275	75.6
			D.G. Jennings	C	10,751	24.4
					22,524	51.2
59	57,192	82.3	W.E. Padley	Lab	35,170	74.7
			T.O. Ewart-James	C	11,905	25.3
					23,265	49.4
64	58,848	79.7	W.E. Padley	Lab	34,178	72.8
			R.M. Thomas	C	10,250	21.9
			Mrs. M. Tucker	PC	2,470*	5.3
					23,928	50.9
66	59,523	79.0	W.E. Padley	Lab	33,545	71.3
			R.M. Thomas	C	6,872	14.6
			Mrs. J.T. Gibbs	L	6,632	14.1
					26,673	56.7
70	65,666	75.7	W.E. Padley	Lab	33,436	67.3
			A.F. Gardner	C	10,415	21.0
			E.J. Merriman	PC	5,828*	11.7
					23,021	46.3

Election	Electors	T'out	Candidate	Party	Votes	%
1950	53,275	84.3	†A. Pearson	Lab	30,945	68.
			T.E.R. Rhys-Roberts	C	9,049	20.
			D.I.C. Lewis	L	4,895*	10.
					21,896	48.
1951	54,126	83.3	A. Pearson	Lab	32,586	72.
			J.L. Manning	C	12,511	27.
					20,075	44.
1955	54,214	74.9	A. Pearson	Lab	28,881	71.
			T.R.V. Tyrrell	C	11,718	28.
					17,163	42.
1959	53,903	81.2	A. Pearson	Lab	29,853	68.
			Sir B.M. Rhys Williams, Bt.	C	13,896	31.
					15,957	36.
1964	53,859	76.9	A. Pearson	Lab	29,533	71.
			Hon. J.R. Warrender	C	11,859	28.
					17,674	42.
1966	55,088	74.7	A. Pearson	Lab	30,840	74.
			K. Green-Wanstall	C	10,325	25.
					20,515	49.
1970	65,191	74.5	B.T. John	Lab	28,414	58.
			M.C. Withers	C	8,205	16.
			Mrs. M.G. Murphy	L	6,871	14.
			D.E. Jones	PC	5,059*	10.
					20,209	41.

ection	Electors	T'out	Candidate	Party	Votes	%
50	27,941	88.8	†E.O. Roberts	L	9,647	38.8
			O. Parry	Lab	8,577	34.6
			J.F. Williams-Wynne	C	3,846	15.5
			G.R. Evans	PC	2,754*	11.1
					1,070	4.2
51	28,019	87.3	T.W. Jones	Lab	10,505	42.9
			E.O. Roberts	L	9,457	38.7
			W.G.O. Morgan	C	4,505	18.4
					1,048	4.2
55	27,472	86.2	T.W. Jones	Lab	9,056	38.3
			H.E. Jones	L	6,374	26.9
			G.R. Evans	PC	5,243	22.1
			J.V. Jenkins	NL & C	3,001	12.7
					2,682	11.4
59	26,435	84.5	T.W. Jones	Lab	9,095	40.8
			B.G. Jones	L	8,119	36.3
			G.R. Evans	PC	5,127	22.9
					976	4.5
64	26,392	83.1	T.W. Jones	Lab	8,420	38.4
			R.O. Jones	L	7,171	32.7
			D.E. Morgan	PC	3,697	16.8
			A.E.C.L. Jones-Lloyd	C	2,656*	12.1
					1,249	5.7
66	25,395	85.8	W.H. Edwards	Lab	9,628	44.2
			E.G. Jones	L	7,733	35.5
			I.L. Jenkins	PC	2,490*	11.4
			A.E.C.L. Jones-Lloyd	C	1,948*	8.9
					1,895	8.7
970	26,434	84.3	W.H. Edwards	Lab	8,861	39.8
			D.W. Wigley	PC	5,425	24.3
			I.E. Thomas	L	5,034	22.6
			D.E.H. Edwards	C	2,965	13.3
					3,436	15.5

Election	Electors	T'out	Candidate	Party	Votes	%
1950	40,211	84.6	†G. Daggar	Lab	29,609	87.1
			O.J. Lewis	C	4,403	12.9
					25,206	74.2
[Death]						
1950 (30/11)	40,011	71.1	Rev. L. Williams	Lab	24,622	86.5
			R.B.F.S. Body	C	3,839	13.5
					20,783	73.0
1951	40,128	84.0	Rev. L. Williams	Lab	29,321	86.9
			J. Radcliff	C	4,404	13.1
					24,917	73.8
1955	39,111	79.1	Rev. L. Williams	Lab	25,599	82.7
			A.G. Davies	C	4,081	13.2
			T.R. Morgan	PC	1,259*	4.1
					21,518	69.5
1959	38,674	81.9	Rev. L. Williams	Lab	26,934	85.0
			R.J. Maddocks	C	4,740	15.0
					22,194	70.0
1964	37,310	75.5	Rev. L. Williams	Lab	24,204	85.9
			P.W.I. Rees	C	3,973	14.1
					20,231	71.8
[Death]						
1965 (1/4)	36,567	63.2	A.C. Williams	Lab	18,256	79.0
			P.W.I. Rees	C	3,309	14.3
			E.J. Merriman	PC	1,551*	6.7
					14,947	64.7
1966	36,122	73.4	A.C. Williams	Lab	23,353	88.1
			A.P. Wallis	C	3,151*	11.9
					20,202	76.2
1970	37,350	75.1	J. Thomas	Lab	22,819	81.4
			J.E. Rendle	C	3,478*	12.4
			D.B. Harries	PC	1,751*	6.2
					19,341	69.0

ection	Electors	T'out	Candidate	Party	Votes	%
50	43,954	85.5	H.J. Finch	Lab	31,329	83.4
			R.C. Pitman	C	6,247	16.6
					25,082	66.8
51	44,417	85.4	H.J. Finch	Lab	31,582	83.3
			J. Smith	C	6,339	16.7
					25,243	66.6
55	44,753	81.6	H.J. Finch	Lab	30,104	82.4
			J.S.R. Scott-Hopkins	C	6,412	17.6
					23,692	64.8
59	44,890	83.6	H.J. Finch	Lab	30,697	81.8
			C.J. Cox	C	6,817	18.2
					23,880	63.6
64	44,538	79.1	H.J. Finch	Lab	29,425	83.5
			C.J. Cox	C	5,810	16.5
					23,615	67.0
66	44,944	76.7	H.J. Finch	Lab	29,723	86.2
			J.N. Williams	C	4,739	13.8
					24,984	72.4
70	49,096	76.7	N.G. Kinnock	Lab	28,078	74.6
			P. Marland	C	5,799	15.4
			C.M. Davey	PC	3,780*	10.0
					22,279	59.2

Election	Electors	T'out	Candidate	Party	Votes	%
1950	40,370	86.7	†Rt. Hon. A. Bevan	Lab	28,245	80.
			G.B. Finlay	C	6,745	19.
					21,500	61.
1951	40,293	87.0	Rt. Hon. A. Bevan	Lab (Ind Lab) (Lab)	28,283	80.
			J.E. Bowen	C	6,754	19.
					21,529	61.
1955	39,305	83.7	Rt. Hon. A. Bevan	Lab	26,058	79.
			J.E. Bowen	C	6,822	20.
					19,236	58.
1959	39,299	85.8	Rt. Hon. A. Bevan	Lab	27,326	81.
			A.G. Davies	C	6,404	19.
					20,922	62.
[Death]						
1960 (17/11)	39,234	76.1	M.M. Foot	Lab (Ind Lab) (Lab)	20,528	68.
			Sir B.M. Rhys Williams, Bt.	C	3,799	12.
			P.H. Lort-Phillips	L	3,449*	11.
			E.P. Roberts	PC	2,091*	7.
					16,729	56.
1964	37,936	79.5	M.M. Foot	Lab	25,220	83.
			Sir B.M. Rhys Williams, Bt.	C	4,949	16.
					20,271	67.
1966	36,953	79.3	M.M. Foot	Lab	24,936	85.
			J.R. Lovill	C	4,352	14.
					20,584	70.
1970	38,461	78.4	M.M. Foot	Lab	21,817	72.
			A. Donaldson	L	4,371	14.
			E.S. Jenkins	C	2,146*	7.
			D.J. Baskerville	PC	1,805*	6.
					17,446	57.

MONMOUTHSHIRE, MONMOUTH [575]

ection	Electors	T'out	Candidate	Party	Votes	%
50	47,709	83.2	†G.E.P. Thorneycroft	C	21,956	55.3
			G.F. Thomas	Lab	17,725	44.7
					4,231	10.6
51	48,314*	83.7	G.E.P. Thorneycroft	C	22,475	55.6
			Miss J. Richardson	Lab	17,952	44.4
					4,523	11.2
55	49,252*	81.5	Rt. Hon. G.E.P. Thorneycroft	C	22,970	57.2
			Miss J. Richardson	Lab	17,173	42.8
					5,797	14.4
59	53,628	83.1	Rt. Hon. G.E.P. Thorneycroft	C	25,422	57.0
			G.S.D. Parry	Lab	19,165	43.0
					6,257	14.0
64	60,603	84.7	Rt. Hon. G.E.P. Thorneycroft	C	22,635	44.1
			A.C. Kerr	Lab	21,921	42.7
			D.H. Davies	L	6,764	13.2
					714	1.4
66	64,356	84.3	D. Anderson	Lab	28,619	52.7
			Rt. Hon. G.E.P. Thorneycroft	C	25,654	47.3
					2,965	5.4
70	75,546	80.5	J.S. Thomas	C	28,312	46.5
			D. Anderson	Lab	26,957	44.3
			D.M. Hando	L	4,061*	6.7
			S.K. Neale	PC	1,501*	2.5
					1,355	2.2

Election	Electors	T'out	Candidate	Party	Votes	%
1950	46,151	84.8	†D.G. West	Lab	28,267	72
			A. Russell	C	6,616	16
			E.A.R. Mathias	L	4,240*	10
					21,651	55
1951	46,290	84.3	D.G. West	Lab	29,553	75
			A.O. Hewitt	C	9,464	24
					20,089	51
1955	46,920	77.1	D.G. West	Lab	26,372	72
			A.O. Hewitt	C	9,800	27
					16,572	45

[Elevation to a Life Peerage—Lord Granville-West]

Election	Electors	T'out	Candidate	Party	Votes	%
1958 (10/11)	47,332	61.7	L. Abse	Lab	20,000	68
			P.S. Thomas	C	6,273	21
			B.C.L. Morgan	PC	2,927*	10
					13,727	47
1959	47,452	80.5	L. Abse	Lab	26,755	70
			P.S. Thomas	C	8,903	23
			B.C.L. Morgan	PC	2,519*	6
					17,852	46
1964	48,024	77.8	L. Abse	Lab	27,852	74
			P.D. Mendel	C	8,169	21
			W.E. Jones	Com	1,329*	3
					19,683	52
1966	48,040	75.4	L. Abse	Lab	27,909	77
			P.T. James	C	7,418	20
			W.E. Jones	Com	897*	2
					20,491	56
1970	53,821	72.0	L. Abse	Lab	27,402	70
			W.M. Bell	C	8,869	22
			H. Webb	PC	2,053*	5
			B. Wilkinson	Com	435*	1
					18,533	47

ection	Electors	T'out	Candidate	Party	Votes	%
▮50	32,372	86.8	†Rt. Hon. E.C. Davies	L	14,401	51.3
			H. West	C	7,621	27.1
			J.D. Williams	Lab	6,070	21.6
					6,780	24.2
▮51	32,387	76.1	Rt. Hon. E.C. Davies	L	17,075	69.2
			D.C. Jones	Lab	7,584	30.8
					9,491	38.4
▮55	31,983	73.6	Rt. Hon. E.C. Davies	L	16,021	68.1
			D.C. Jones	Lab	7,521	31.9
					8,500	36.2
▮59	31,154	83.8	Rt. Hon. E.C. Davies	L	10,970	42.1
			F.L. Morgan	C	8,176	31.3
			D.C. Jones	Lab	6,950	26.6
					2,794	10.8
▮eath]						
▮62	30,202	85.1	H.E. Hooson	L	13,181	51.3
▮5/5)			R.H. Dawson	C	5,632	21.9
			T. Davies	Lab	5,299	20.6
			Rev. I.F. Elis	PC	1,594*	6.2
					7,549	29.4
▮64	30,154	84.1	H.E. Hooson	L	10,738	42.3
			A.W. Wiggin	C	6,768	26.7
			G.M. Evans	Lab	5,696	22.5
			Rev. I.F. Elis	PC	2,167*	8.5
					3,970	15.6
▮66	29,951	82.8	H.E. Hooson	L	10,278	41.4
			A.W. Wiggin	C	6,784	27.4
			G.M. Evans	Lab	5,891	23.8
			T. Edwards	PC	1,841*	7.4
					3,494	14.0
▮70	32,304	82.3	H.E. Hooson	L	10,202	38.4
			D.J.D. Williams	C	7,891	29.7
			D.W. Thomas	Lab	5,335	20.1
			E.G. Millward	PC	3,145*	11.8
					2,311	8.7

Election	Electors	T'out	Candidate	Party	Votes	%
1950	61,253	83.2	D.L. Donnelly	Lab	25,550	50.1
			†Rt. Hon. G. Lloyd George	NL & C	25,421	49.9
					129	0.2
1951	62,381	86.0	D.L. Donnelly	Lab	25,994	48.5
			F.W. Farey-Jones	C	16,968	31.6
			Dr. D.H. Pennant	L	10,688	19.9
					9,026	16.9
1955	62,381	84.0	D.L. Donnelly	Lab	27,002	51.5
			W.L. Davies	Ind	25,410	48.5
					1,592	3.0
1959	62,372	83.7	D.L. Donnelly	Lab	27,623	53.0
			H.G. Partridge	C	22,301	42.7
			W.G. Williams	PC	2,253*	4.3
					5,322	10.2
1964	62,196	81.5	D.L. Donnelly	Lab	23,926	47.2
			H.G. Partridge	C	15,340	30.3
			A. Coulthard	L	9,679	19.1
			D. Thomas	PC	1,717*	3.4
					8,586	16.9
1966	62,110	79.8	D.L. Donnelly	Lab (Ind Lab) (DP)	23,852	48.1
			F.M. Fisher	C	17,921	36.2
			O.G. Williams	L	5,308*	10.7
			J. Sheppard	PC	2,460*	5.0
					5,931	11.9
1970	70,649	77.9	R.N. Edwards	C	19,120	34.
			G.S.D. Parry	Lab	17,889	32.5
			D.L. Donnelly	DP	11,824	21.5
			W.I. Samuel	PC	3,681*	6.
			D.W. Thomas	L	2,541*	4.6
					1,231	2.2

Note:—

1955: Davies was supported by the local Conservative and Liberal Associations.

SCOTLAND —— BURGHS

Election	Electors	T'out	Candidate	Party	Votes	%
1950	63,047	82.9	†H.S.J. Hughes	Lab	31,594	60.5
			A. Tennant	C	15,705	30.0
			J.G. Wilson	L	3,574*	6.8
			R.H. Cooney	Com	1,391*	2.7
					15,889	30.5
1951	62,817	82.9	H.S.J. Hughes	Lab	33,711	64.7
			F. Magee	C	18,365	35.3
					15,346	29.4
1955	66,385*	74.6	H.S.J. Hughes	Lab	33,153	67.0
			C.A.B. Malden	C	16,357	33.0
					16,796	34.0
1959	66,351	76.7	H.S.J. Hughes	Lab	32,793	64.5
			J. Stewart-Clark	C	15,137	29.7
			W.A. Milne	SNP	2,964*	5.8
					17,656	34.8
1964	61,785	74.8	H.S.J. Hughes	Lab	31,844	68.9
			J.C. McInnes	C	14,366	31.1
					17,478	37.8
1966	59,157	72.1	H.S.J. Hughes	Lab	28,799	67.5
			J.M.M. Humphrey	C	8,768	20.6
			Mrs. D.W. MacPherson	L	4,350*	10.2
			Mrs. M. Rose	Com	719*	1.7
					20,031	46.9
1970	63,833	69.9	R. Hughes	Lab	27,707	62.0
			D.J. Williams	C	9,807	22.0
			J. McKenna	SNP	3,756*	8.4
			F. McCallum	L	2,835*	6.4
			A.J. Ingram	Com	521*	1.2
					17,900	40.0

Election	Electors	T'out	Candidate	Party	Votes	%
1950	57,340	84.9	†Lady Tweedsmuir	C	26,128	53.7
			Mrs. O.R. Cruchley	Lab	17,302	35.5
			R.T. Pirie	L	5,248*	10.8
					8,826	18.2
1951	59,589	82.7	Lady Tweedsmuir	C	28,947	58.7
			S. Shaw	Lab	20,325	41.3
					8,622	17.4
1955	57,921*	80.2	Lady Tweedsmuir	C	26,817	57.7
			Mrs. J.C.M. Hart	Lab	19,627	42.3
					7,190	15.4
1959	58,086	81.6	Lady Tweedsmuir	C	25,471	53.8
			P.M. Doig	Lab	17,349	36.6
			Mrs. E.T. Dangerfield	L	4,558*	9.6
					8,122	17.2
1964	61,639	81.0	Lady Tweedsmuir	C	25,824	51.7
			D.C. Dewar	Lab	21,926	43.9
			J.B. Reid	SNP	2,197*	4.4
					3,898	7.8
1966	62,206	81.3	D.C. Dewar	Lab	23,291	46.0
			Lady Tweedsmuir	C	21,492	42.5
			N.W. King	L	5,797*	11.5
					1,799	3.5
1970	68,020	77.2	I.M. Sproat	C	23,843	45.4
			D.C. Dewar	Lab	22,754	43.3
			K.J.B.S. MacLeod	L	3,135*	6.0
			B.M. Cockie	SNP	2,777*	5.3
					1,089	2.1

Election	Electors	T'out	Candidate	Party	Votes	%
950	47,837	86.1	†Mrs. J. Mann	Lab	23,339	56.6
			J.R. McMillan	C	16,552	40.2
			T.P. O'Callaghan	AP	1,315*	3.2
					6,787	16.4
951	49,254	85.5	Mrs. J. Mann	Lab	24,159	57.4
			J.R. McMillan	C	17,952	42.6
					6,207	14.8
955	50,220*	79.4	Mrs. J. Mann	Lab	22,269	55.8
			D.C. Anderson	C	17,605	44.2
					4,664	11.6
959	53,223	84.0	J. Dempsey	Lab	22,747	50.9
			Mrs. C.S. Morton	C	21,953	49.1
					794	1.8
964	53,863	81.2	J. Dempsey	Lab	27,178	62.1
			A.W. Thomson	C	16,580	37.9
					10,598	24.2
966	53,422	77.2	J. Dempsey	Lab	26,491	64.2
			W.C. Raeburn	C	14,777	35.8
					11,714	28.4
970	57,984	76.5	J. Dempsey	Lab	26,117	58.9
			W.J. Rennie	C	15,574	35.1
			W. Brown	SNP	2,667*	6.0
					10,543	23.8

DUNDEE, EAST [582]

Election	Electors	T'out	Candidate	Party	Votes	%
1950	55,032	88.6	†T.F. Cook	Lab	26,005	53.
			J. Henderson	NL & C	21,658	44.
			D.P. Bowman	Com	1,093*	2.
					4,347	9.
1951	56,784	87.2	T.F. Cook	Lab	26,668	53.
			Miss J.S. Murray	NL & C	22,863	46.
					3,805	7.
[Death]						
1952 (17/7)	55,149	71.5	G.M. Thomson	Lab	22,161	56.
			P.T. Cowcher	NL & C	14,035	35.
			D. Stewart	SNP	2,931*	7.
			E.G. Macfarlane	WPP	290*	0.
					8,126	20.
1955	57,403	82.3	G.M. Thomson	Lab	25,646	54.
			R.R. Taylor	NL & C	21,606	45.
					4,040	8.
1959	58,537	82.6	G.M. Thomson	Lab	26,263	54.
			R.A. McCrindle	NL & C	22,082	45.
					4,181	8.
1964	59,451	80.0	G.M. Thomson	Lab	26,062	54.
			J.L. Marshall	NL & C	21,499	45.
					4,563	9.
1966	57,502	78.8	Rt. Hon. G.M. Thomson	Lab	25,530	56.
			J.L. Marshall	C	19,804	43.
					5,726	12.
1970	61,553	76.1	Rt. Hon. G.M. Thomson	Lab	22,630	48.
			J.A. Stewart	C	19,832	42.
			I. Macaulay	SNP	4,181*	8.
			E.G. Macfarlane	WGP	176*	0.
					2,798	5.

lection	Electors	T'out	Candidate	Party	Votes	%
950	60,235	88.1	†Rt. Hon. E.J.St.L. Strachey	Lab	28,386	53.5
			H.J. Scrymgeour-Wedderburn	NL & C	23,685	44.6
			C.J. Canning	L	986*	1.9
					4,701	8.9
951	64,797	86.8	Rt. Hon. E.J.St.L. Strachey	Lab	29,020	51.6
			J.D.B. Junor	L	25,714	45.7
			D.P. Bowman	Com	1,508*	2.7
					3,306	5.9
955	62,415	82.7	Rt. Hon. E.J.St.L. Strachey	Lab	26,082	50.5
			G.H.M. Pirie	NL & C	24,208	46.9
			D.P. Bowman	Com	1,335*	2.6
					1,874	3.6
959	62,804	82.9	Rt. Hon. E.J.St.L. Strachey	Lab	25,857	49.6
			Dr. R.R. Taylor	NL & C	25,143	48.3
			D.P. Bowman	Com	1,086*	2.1
					714	1.3
Death]						
963	62,004	71.6	P.M. Doig	Lab	22,449	50.6
21/11)			Dr. R.R. Taylor	NL & C	17,494	39.4
			Dr. J.C. Lees	SNP	3,285*	7.4
			D.P. Bowman	Com	1,170*	2.6
					4,955	11.2
964	62,325	81.5	P.M. Doig	Lab	27,090	53.4
			H.C. Scarlett	NL & C	22,473	44.2
			D.P. Bowman	Com	1,228*	2.4
					4,617	9.2
966	62,230	79.9	P.M. Doig	Lab	26,705	53.8
			C.A. McNab	C	18,345	36.9
			J.W. Cruddas	L	3,454*	6.9
			D.P. Bowman	Com	1,217*	2.4
					8,360	16.9
970	66,767	76.3	P.M. Doig	Lab	26,271	51.5
			J.B.A. Payne	C	19,449	38.2
			J.A. Shepherd	SNP	4,441*	8.7
			H. McLevy	Com	809*	1.6
					6,822	13.3

DUNFERMLINE BURGHS [584]

Election	Electors	T'out	Candidate	Party	Votes	%
1950	46,037	83.9	J. Clunie	Lab	23,641	61.2
			J.S. Kerr	NL & C	14,967	38.8
					8,674	22.4
1951	46,999	85.5	J. Clunie	Lab	24,547	61.1
			J.S. Kerr	NL & C	15,657	38.9
					8,890	22.2
1955	46,827	77.6	J. Clunie	Lab	22,146	61.0
			Mrs. C.R. McNee	NL & C	14,170	39.0
					7,976	22.0
1959	47,737	80.1	Dr. A.E. Thompson	Lab	23,478	61.4
			W.A. Elliott	NL & C	14,744	38.6
					8,734	22.8
1964	47,288*	77.2	A. Hunter	Lab	22,468	61.6
			I.C. Kirkwood	NL & C	14,033	38.4
					8,435	23.2
1966	46,472	76.3	A. Hunter	Lab	20,709	58.4
			I.C. Kirkwood	C	9,446	26.6
			J.A. Cook	SNP	5,304	15.0
					11,263	31.8
1970	50,935	74.1	A. Hunter	Lab	21,532	57.1
			I.C. Kirkwood	C	12,086	32.0
			J.A. Cook	SNP	3,657*	9.7
			J. Neilson	Com	462*	1.2
					9,446	25.1

Election	Electors	T'out	Candidate	Party	Votes	%
1950	46,513	74.3	†A. Gilzean	Lab	16,568	47.9
			F.C. Watt	C	13,631	39.4
			L. Gellatly	L	3,446*	10.0
			D.F. Renton	Com	646*	1.9
			H. Sleigh	Ind	282*	0.8
					2,937	8.5
1951	45,993	76.7	T. Oswald	Lab	18,429	52.2
			W.J.M. Kean	C	16,847	47.8
					1,582	4.4
1955	47,251**	68.8	T. Oswald	Lab	16,735	51.4
			R. Harris	C	15,796	48.6
					939	2.8
1959	42,781	72.7	T. Oswald	Lab	15,849	51.0
			N.R. Wylie	C	15,232	49.0
					617	2.0
1964	36,588	71.8	T. Oswald	Lab	14,174	54.0
			N.H. Fairbairn	C	12,082	46.0
					2,092	8.0
1966	33,910	69.4	T. Oswald	Lab	13,862	58.9
			N.H Fairbairn	C	9,667	41.1
					4,195	17.8
1970	31,364	66.0	T. Oswald	Lab	9,561	46.2
			M.L. Rifkind	C	8,000	38.6
			Mrs. C.M. Moore	SNP	1,666*	8.0
			Dr. A.D. Oliver	L	1,486*	7.2
					1,561	7.6

Note:—

1950: Sleigh advocated a policy of Scottish nationalism.

Election	Electors	T'out	Candidate	Party	Votes	%
1950	54,379	83.2	†Rt. Hon. J.T. Wheatley	Lab	24,072	53.
			C.E.M. Donaldson	C	17,531	38.
			J. Hope	L	3,632*	8.
					6,541	14.
1951	55,595	83.8	Rt. Hon. J.T. Wheatley	Lab	25,201	54.
			W. Grant	C	21,400	45.
					3,801	8.

[Resignation on appointment as a Senator of the College of Justice—Lord Wheatley]

Election	Electors	T'out	Candidate	Party	Votes	%
1954	53,159	61.8	E.G. Willis	Lab	18,950	57.
(8/4)			W. Grant	C	13,922	42.
					5,028	15.
1955	53,655*	75.4	E.G. Willis	Lab	21,240	52.
			W.I.R. Fraser	C	19,198	47.
					2,042	5.
1959	54,756	80.7	E.G. Willis	Lab	22,244	50.
			Earl of Dalkeith	C	21,932	49.
					312	0.
1964	54,581*	81.0	E.G. Willis	Lab	24,808	56.
			R.L. McEwen	C	19,376	43.
					5,432	12.
1966	54,311	77.4	E.G. Willis	Lab	25,423	60.
			J.S.B. Henderson	C	16,614	39.
					8,809	21.
1970	57,350	74.5	G.S. Strang	Lab	22,171	51.
			N. Gow	C	16,657	39.
			Mrs. H.B. Davidson	SNP	3,502*	8.
			Mrs. I. Swan	Com	413*	1.
					5,514	12.

Election	Electors	T'out	Candidate	Party	Votes	%
1950	45,594	80.7	†J.H. Hoy	Lab	18,111	49.3
			E.C. Mekie	NL & C	15,841	43.0
			T.M. Frew	L	2,846*	7.7
					2,270	6.3
1951	45,859	84.0	J.H. Hoy	Lab	19,308	50.1
			E.C. Mekie	NL & C	19,236	49.9
					72	0.2
1955	42,531	77.8	J.H. Hoy	Lab	16,337	49.4
			Mrs. J.S. Shearer	NL & C	10,693	32.3
			Sir A.H.A. Murray	Ind	6,055	18.3
					5,644	17.1
1959	39,750	79.5	J.H. Hoy	Lab	15,092	47.8
			G. Stewart	NL & C	12,018	38.0
			Sir A.H.A. Murray	L	4,475	14.2
					3,074	9.8
1964	36,877	77.9	J.H. Hoy	Lab	15,934	55.5
			G. Stewart	NL & C	12,777	44.5
					3,157	11.0
1966	35,652	76.1	J.H. Hoy	Lab	15,407	56.8
			W.A. Elliott	C	11,443	42.2
			Miss H.M. Arundel	Com	279*	1.0
					3,964	14.6
1970	35,614	73.2	R.K. Murray	Lab	12,066	46.3
			W.A. Elliott	C	10,682	41.0
			Miss M.G. Thomson	SNP	1,827*	7.0
			Mrs. J. Shein	L	1,490*	5.7
					1,384	5.3

Note:—

1955: Murray was a former Lord Provost of Edinburgh and had failed to secure nomination as the National Liberal and Conservative candidate for the constituency.

Election	Electors	T'out	Candidate	Party	Votes	%
1950	44,226	78.7	J.L. Clyde	C	17,826	51.2
			†E.G. Willis	Lab	13,683	39.3
			I.P. Crawford	L	3,302*	9.5
					4,143	11.9
1951	44,294	80.0	J.L. Clyde	C	20,836	58.8
			E.G. Willis	Lab	14,604	41.2
					6,232	17.6

[Resignation on appointment as Lord Justice General and Lord President of the Court of Session—Lord Clyde]

Election	Electors	T'out	Candidate	Party	Votes	%
1955 (27/1)	41,446	46.4	Rt. Hon. W.R. Milligan	C	11,413	59.4
			G. Scott	Lab	7,799	40.6
					3,614	18.8
1955	45,952**	72.0	Rt. Hon. W.R. Milligan	C	20,425	61.7
			G. Scott	Lab	12,664	38.3
					7,761	23.4
1959	42,270	73.9	Rt. Hon. W.R. Milligan	C	19,991	64.0
			G.G. Stott	Lab	11,235	36.0
					8,756	28.0

[Resignation on appointment as a Senator of the College of Justice—Lord Milligan]

Election	Electors	T'out	Candidate	Party	Votes	%
1960 (19/5)	41,546	53.8	Earl of Dalkeith	C	12,109	54.2
			R.K. Murray	Lab	6,775	30.3
			R.T. McPake	L	3,458	15.5
					5,334	23.9
1964	39,888	73.6	Earl of Dalkeith	C	17,094	58.2
			A.D. Reid	Lab	12,264	41.8
					4,830	16.4
1966	37,056	73.9	Earl of Dalkeith	C	13,765	50.3
			W.S. Dalgleish	Lab	10,730	39.2
			L.W. Oliver	L	2,871*	10.5
					3,035	11.1
1970	35,099	70.1	Earl of Dalkeith	C	13,005	52.8
			R.F. Cook	Lab	9,127	37.1
			C.A. Dow	L	2,475*	10.1
					3,878	15.7

Note:—

1955: Milligan was Lord Advocate.
(27/1)

lection	Electors	T'out	Candidate	Party	Votes	%
950	55,754	82.0	†Lord John Hope	C	23,107	50.5
			T.A. MacNair	Lab	17,912	39.2
			Mrs. C.R. McNee	L	4,703*	10.3
					5,195	11.3
951	57,843	83.3	Lord John Hope	C	27,804	57.7
			D. Connell	Lab	20,405	42.3
					7,399	15.4
955	51,119**	77.3	Lord John Hope	C	23,496	59.5
			D. Connell	Lab	16,011	40.5
					7,485	19.0
959	53,178	80.3	Lord John Hope	C	25,742	60.3
			J.P. Mackintosh	Lab	16,950	39.7
					8,792	20.6

[Seat Vacant at Dissolution (Elevation to the Peerage—Lord Glendevon)]

lection	Electors	T'out	Candidate	Party	Votes	%
964	53,743*	81.6	N.R. Wylie	C	20,181	46.0
			M.J. Williamson	Lab	17,794	40.6
			C.L. Abernethy	L	5,862	13.4
					2,387	5.4
966	53,020	80.5	N.R. Wylie	C	19,176	45.0
			W. Wallace	Lab	19,132	44.8
			Dr. D. Clarke	L	4,363*	10.2
					44	0.2
970	61,498	77.0	N.R. Wylie	C	21,829	46.1
			E.G.F. Stewart	Lab	18,646	39.4
			Dr. D. Clarke	L	4,055*	8.6
			A.W.S. Rae	SNP	2,814*	5.9
					3,183	6.7

Election	Electors	T'out	Candidate	Party	Votes	%
1950	43,224	82.1	†Sir W.Y. Darling	C	23,081	65.0
			W.P. Earsman	Lab	8,725	24.6
			L.H. Diaches	L	3,699*	10.4
					14,356	40.4
1951	44,914	81.4	Sir W.Y. Darling	C	26,545	72.6
			J.A. Forsyth	Lab	10,030	27.4
					16,515	45.2
1955	47,626	77.2	Sir W.Y. Darling	C	24,836	67.5
			J.A. Forsyth	Lab	11,949	32.5
					12,887	35.0
[Resignation]						
1957	48,071	65.8	A.M.C. Hutchison	C	14,421	45.6
(29/5)			J.A. Forsyth	Lab	9,781	30.9
			Hon. W. Douglas-Home	L	7,439	23.5
					4,640	14.7
1959	48,767	81.2	A.M.C. Hutchison	C	22,799	57.6
			A.D. Reid	Lab	11,285	28.5
			Hon. W. Douglas-Home	L	5,505	13.9
					11,514	29.1
1964	50,055*	80.3	A.M.C. Hutchison	C	21,375	53.2
			J.W. Kerr	Lab	13,555	33.7
			R.H. Guild	L	5,272	13.1
					7,820	19.5
1966	50,450	77.6	A.M.C. Hutchison	C	20,820	53.2
			J.W. Kerr	Lab	15,487	39.5
			H.M. Robertson	SNP	2,856*	7.3
					5,333	13.7
1970	55,675	74.1	A.M.C. Hutchison	C	19,851	48.2
			J.T. Henderson	Lab	15,071	36.5
			R.H. Guild	L	3,469*	8.4
			Dr. D.J.D. Stevenson	SNP	2,861*	6.9
					4,780	11.7

Election	Electors	T'out	Candidate	Party	Votes	%
1950	54,281	82.8	†G.I.C. Hutchison	C	26,978	60.0
			C. Morgan	Lab/Co-op	14,377	32.0
			Mrs. M.R. Walker	L	3,586*	8.0
					12,601	28.0
1951	55,147	83.1	G.I.C. Hutchison	C	30,232	66.0
			H.S. Wilson	Lab	15,607	34.0
					14,625	32.0
1955	51,256**	75.7	Sir G.I.C. Hutchison	C	26,000	67.0
			J.A.C. Thomson	Lab	12,784	33.0
					13,216	34.0
1959	57,293	80.3	J.A. Stodart	C	25,976	56.5
			J.K. Stocks	Lab	14,044	30.5
			D.F. Leach	L	5,962	13.0
					11,932	26.0
1964	64,279*	80.9	J.A. Stodart	C	26,298	50.6
			J.K. Stocks	Lab	18,359	35.3
			J.R. Telfer	L	7,352	14.1
					7,939	15.3
1966	65,507	78.7	J.A. Stodart	C	24,882	48.2
			R.G. Douglas	Lab/Co-op	20,073	39.0
			J.R. Telfer	L	6,571	12.8
					4,809	9.2
1970	72,709	75.0	J.A. Stodart	C	26,864	49.2
			G. Foulkes	Lab	19,523	35.8
			D.C.E. Gorrie	L	4,467*	8.2
			Miss M.M. Gibson	SNP	3,711*	6.8
					7,341	13.4

Election	Electors	T'out	Candidate	Party	Votes	%
1950	44,382	76.9	†J. Carmichael	Lab	20,268	59.4
			F. Irwin	C	11,025	32.3
			R. Duncan	ILP	1,974*	5.8
			D. Kelly	Com	858*	2.5
					9,243	27.1
1951	43,570	76.9	J. Carmichael	Lab	21,307	63.6
			R.A. Thomson	C	10,382	31.0
			R. Duncan	ILP	1,796*	5.4
					10,925	32.6
1955	53,733**	66.0	J. Carmichael	Lab	20,476	57.7
			P.T. Cowcher	C	12,375	34.9
			G.W. Stone	ILP	2,619*	7.4
					8,101	22.8
1959	48,473	68.5	J. Carmichael	Lab	21,048	63.4
			I. Docherty	C	12,139	36.6
					8,909	26.8
[Resignation]						
1961 (16/11)	45,347	41.9	J. Bennett	Lab	10,930	57.5
			M. McNeill	C	3,935	20.7
			I.C.H. Macdonald	SNP	3,549	18.7
			G.W. Stone	ILP	586*	3.1
					6,995	36.8
1964	41,482	63.6	J. Bennett	Lab	18,879	71.6
			J. Hogg	C	7,492	28.4
					11,387	43.2
1966	37,159	58.8	J. Bennett	Lab	16,219	74.3
			J. Hogg	C	5,619	25.7
					10,600	48.6
1970	31,239	56.3	J. Bennett	Lab	11,056	62.9
			R. Gavin	C	3,801	21.6
			G. Wallace	SNP	1,550*	8.8
			Rev. J.T.A. Glass	Ind	1,180*	6.7
					7,255	41.3

Note:—

1970: Glass sought election as a 'Protestant' candidate.

lection	Electors	T'out	Candidate	Party	Votes	%
950	50,515	80.7	W. Reid	Lab	21,013	51.5
			†C.S. McFarlane	C	19,766	48.5
					1,247	3.0
951	49,732	82.4	W. Reid	Lab	20,994	51.3
			C.S. McFarlane	C	19,969	48.7
					1,025	2.6

This constituency was divided in 1955.

Election	Electors	T'out	Candidate	Party	Votes	%
1950	44,859	83.8	†J. Henderson	C	24,341	64.8
			I.R. Mitchell	Lab	10,269	27.3
			M.I. Shields	L	2,984*	7.9
					14,072	37.5
1951	44,881	82.5	J. Henderson	C	26,125	70.5
			Miss A.M. Patrick	Lab	10,912	29.5
					15,213	41.0
1955	45,969	75.7	J. Henderson	C	25,265	72.6
			L.P. Thomas	Lab	9,514	27.4
					15,751	45.2
1959	64,703	80.2	J. Henderson	C	30,743	59.2
			J. Jarvie	Lab	21,169	40.8
					9,574	18.4
1964	65,074	79.3	E.M. Taylor	C	27,299	52.9
			Mrs. E. McCulloch	Lab	24,294	47.1
					3,005	5.8
1966	65,759	79.7	E.M. Taylor	C	26,549	50.7
			F.L. Forrester	Lab	25,330	48.3
			G. Barlow	Ind	516*	1.0
					1,219	2.4
1970	71,952	74.6	E.M. Taylor	C	29,093	54.2
			D.C.H. Mackay	Lab	24,188	45.0
			J. McDonagh	Ind Lab	419*	0.8
					4,905	9.2

Note:—

1966: Barlow was the nominee of the Scottish Anti-Vivisection Society.

Election	Electors	T'out	Candidate	Party	Votes	%
1950	36,739	74.0	J. McInnes	Lab	14,861	54.6
			†J.R.H. Hutchison	C	11,857	43.6
			G.A. Aldred	Ind Soc	485*	1.8
					3,004	11.0
1951	36,379	74.3	J. McInnes	Lab	15,757	58.3
			W. Sinclair	C	10,875	40.2
			G.A. Aldred	Ind Soc	411*	1.5
					4,882	18.1
1955	42,068**	64.1	J. McInnes	Lab	16,674	61.8
			I.D. Barber-Fleming	C	10,307	38.2
					6,367	23.6
1959	36,540	67.4	J. McInnes	Lab	15,918	64.6
			I.D. Barber-Fleming	C	8,712	35.4
					7,206	29.2
1964	30,465	62.4	J. McInnes	Lab	13,343	70.1
			G.F. Boyd	C	5,679	29.9
					7,664	40.2
1966	26,579	58.7	T.M. McMillan	Lab	11,673	74.8
			R.B. Anderson	C	3,924	25.2
					7,749	49.6
1970	20,284	59.2	T.M. McMillan	Lab	7,936	66.1
			J.G.L. Rennie	C	2,394	19.9
			A. McIntosh	SNP	1,688	14.0
					5,542	46.2

Election	Electors	T'out	Candidate	Party	Votes	%
1955	48,067	79.1	J.N. Browne	C	19,120	50.3
			B. Millan	Lab	18,910	49.7
					210	0.6
1959	46,768	82.7	B. Millan	Lab	19,649	50.8
			J.N. Browne	C	19,047	49.2
					602	1.6
1964	46,118	80.9	B. Millan	Lab	21,775	58.4
			P.C. Hutchison	C	15,518	41.6
					6,257	16.8
1966	45,472	80.4	B. Millan	Lab	21,174	57.9
			P.C. Hutchison	C	11,970	32.7
			G.A. Leslie	SNP	3,425*	9.4
					9,204	25.2
1970	49,932	75.1	B. Millan	Lab	20,872	55.7
			W. Wober	C	13,661	36.4
			R.G. Edwards	SNP	2,946*	7.9
					7,211	19.3

ection	Electors	T'out	Candidate	Party	Votes	%
50	53,859	77.3	†Mrs. A. Cullen	Lab	24,137	58.0
			J.A. Young	C	13,078	31.4
			P. Kerrigan	Com	2,435*	5.9
			W. McGuinness	AP	1,959*	4.7
					11,059	26.6
51	53,795	76.0	Mrs. A. Cullen	Lab	25,288	61.9
			J.A. Young	C	13,069	31.9
			P. Kerrigan	Com	2,553*	6.2
					12,219	30.0
55	56,627**	65.2	Mrs. A. Cullen	Lab	22,567	61.1
			W.B. Thomson	C	11,839	32.1
			P. Kerrigan	Com	2,491*	6.8
					10,728	29.0
59	48,004	68.2	Mrs. A. Cullen	Lab	20,731	63.3
			W.C. Hunter	C	10,072	30.8
			P. Kerrigan	Com	1,932*	5.9
					10,659	32.5
64	36,768	64.5	Mrs. A. Cullen	Lab	16,931	71.4
			W.C. Hunter	C	5,455	23.0
			Mrs. M.A. Hunter	Com	1,339*	5.6
					11,476	48.4
66	32,050	61.7	Mrs. A. Cullen	Lab	14,453	73.1
			W.C. Hunter	C	4,513	22.8
			Mrs. M.A. Hunter	Com	819*	4.1
					9,940	50.3

[Death]

69 (30/10)	25,057	58.5	F.P. McElhone	Lab	7,834	53.4
			T. Brady	SNP	3,671	25.0
			W. Shearer	C	2,732	18.6
			J.R. Kay	Com	361*	2.5
			M. Lygate	WPS	72*	0.5
					4,163	28.4
970	24,749	59.8	F.P. McElhone	Lab	10,260	69.3
			W. Shearer	C	3,071	20.8
			T. Brady	SNP	1,089*	7.4
			J.R. Kay	Com	376*	2.5
					7,189	48.5

GLASGOW, GOVAN [598]

Election	Electors	T'out	Candidate	Party	Votes	%
1950	49,189	84.0	J.N. Browne	C	19,267	46.
			J. Davis	Lab	18,894	45.
			T.R.L. Fraser	L	1,628*	3.
			W. Lauchlan	Com	1,547*	3.
					373	1.
1951	49,025	84.9	J.N. Browne	C	20,936	50.
			J. Davis	Lab	20,695	49.
					241	0.
1955	55,743**	71.8	J. Rankin	Lab/Co-op	24,818	62.
			A.G. Hutton	C	15,216	38.
					9,602	24.
1959	51,084	75.0	J. Rankin	Lab/Co-op	23,139	60.
			A.G. Hutton	C	13,319	34.
			G. McLennan	Com	1,869*	4.
					9,820	25.
1964	44,517	70.3	J. Rankin	Lab/Co-op	20,326	65.
			P. Breuer	C	9,571	30.
			G. McLennan	Com	1,378*	4.
					10,755	34.
1966	40,481	67.5	J. Rankin	Lab/Co-op	18,533	67.
			P. Breuer	C	7,677	28.
			G. McLennan	Com	1,103*	4.
					10,856	39.
1970	35,322	63.3	J. Rankin	Lab/Co-op	13,443	60.
			G.F. Belton	C	6,301	28.
			J.M.T. Grieve	SNP	2,294*	10.3
			T. Biggam	Com	326*	1.
					7,142	31.

GLASGOW, HILLHEAD [599]

Election	Electors	T'out	Candidate	Party	Votes	%
1950	46,455	82.2	†T.G.D. Galbraith	C	23,181	60.8
			G.M. Thomson	Lab	12,920	33.8
			Miss P.M. Gibson	L	2,072*	5.4
					10,261	27.0
1951	46,238	82.2	T.G.D. Galbraith	C	24,654	64.9
			H. Shapiro	Lab	13,359	35.1
					11,295	29.8
1955	40,802**	72.9	Hon. T.G.D. Galbraith	C	20,106	67.6
			Mrs. J.B. Davidson	Lab	9,648	32.4
					10,458	35.2
1959	38,154	77.1	Hon. T.G.D. Galbraith	C	20,094	68.3
			T.B. Duncan	Lab	9,317	31.7
					10,777	36.6
1964	35,580	74.7	Hon. T.G.D. Galbraith	C	16,993	64.0
			D.D.T. Reid	Lab	9,572	36.0
					7,421	28.0
1966	34,388	73.5	Hon. T.G.D. Galbraith	C	15,899	62.9
			W. Boyle	Lab	9,384	37.1
					6,515	25.8
1970	34,407	69.6	Hon. T.G.D. Galbraith	C	14,674	61.3
			J.V. Cable	Lab	7,303	30.5
			G. Wotherspoon	SNP	1,957*	8.2
					7,371	30.8

GLASGOW, KELVINGROVE [600]

Election	Electors	T'out	Candidate	Party	Votes	%
1950	38,899	78.8	†Rt. Hon. W.E. Elliot	C	15,197	49.6
			†J.L. Williams	Lab	13,973	45.6
			S.J. Ranger	L	831*	2.7
			C.M. Grieve	Ind	639*	2.1
					1,224	4.0
1951	38,472	78.6	Rt. Hon. W.E. Elliot	C	15,837	52.4
			J.L. Williams	Lab	14,406	47.6
					1,431	4.8
1955	39,672**	67.6	Rt. Hon. W.E. Elliot	C	14,854	55.4
			J.L. Williams	Lab	11,966	44.6
					2,888	10.8
[Death]						
1958 (13/3)	35,138	60.5	Mrs. M.A. McAlister	Lab	10,210	48.0
			Mrs. K. Elliot	C	8,850	41.6
			D. Murray	Ind	1,622*	7.6
			W.C. Park	ILP	587*	2.8
					1,360	6.4
1959	34,319	70.9	F.J.P. Lilley	C	12,355	50.8
			Mrs. M.A. McAlister	Lab	11,254	46.2
			W.C. Park	ILP	740*	3.0
					1,101	4.6
1964	28,407	67.3	Dr. M.S. Miller	Lab	10,340	54.0
			F.J.P. Lilley	C	8,791	46.0
					1,549	8.0
1966	24,299	66.3	Dr. M.S. Miller	Lab	9,311	57.8
			H. Dykes	C	6,793	42.2
					2,518	15.6
1970	18,907	60.2	Dr. M.S. Miller	Lab	6,106	53.7
			R.E. Dundas	C	5,274	46.3
					832	7.4

Notes:—

1950: Grieve advocated a policy of Scottish nationalism.

1958: Murray sought election as a 'Liberal Home-Rule' candidate.

GLASGOW, MARYHILL [601]

Election	Electors	T'out	Candidate	Party	Votes	%
1950	44,903	80.0	†W. Hannan	Lab	21,990	61.2
			Miss J.S. Murray	C	11,559	32.2
			Miss E.T. Cowan	L	2,375*	6.6
					10,431	29.0
1951	45,032	80.7	W. Hannan	Lab	22,912	63.0
			P.T. Cowcher	C	13,076	36.0
			A.E. Pickard	Ind	356*	1.0
					9,836	27.0
1955	48,197	69.9	W. Hannan	Lab	21,174	62.8
			A.A. Bell	C	12,536	37.2
					8,638	25.6
1959	46,422	73.7	W. Hannan	Lab	21,893	64.0
			N.J. Adamson	C	12,311	36.0
					9,582	28.0
1964	43,190	70.5	W. Hannan	Lab	20,796	68.4
			N.J. Adamson	C	8,403	27.6
			G. Barlow	Ind	1,231*	4.0
					12,393	40.8
1966	42,912	68.5	W. Hannan	Lab	19,936	67.8
			R.S. Hay	C	6,075	20.7
			H. MacDonald	SNP	3,387*	11.5
					13,861	47.1
1970	45,127	63.9	W. Hannan	Lab	18,925	65.6
			A.K.R. Murchison	C	6,638	23.0
			A.C.W. Aitken	SNP	3,273*	11.4
					12,287	42.6

Note:—

1964: Barlow was the nominee of the Scottish Anti-Vivisection Society.

615

GLASGOW, POLLOK [602]

Election	Electors	T'out	Candidate	Party	Votes	%
1950	54,688	81.3	†T.D. Galbraith	C	25,052	56.4
			J.S. Clark	Lab	17,263	38.8
			A. Anderson	L	2,148*	4.8
					7,789	17.6
1951	62,961	82.5	T.D. Galbraith	C	28,787	55.4
			J.S. Clark	Lab	23,136	44.6
					5,651	10.8

[Seat Vacant at Dissolution (Resignation on appointment as Minister of State, Scottish Office, and elevation to the Peerage—Lord Strathclyde)]

Election	Electors	T'out	Candidate	Party	Votes	%
1955	51,800**	75.5	J.C. George	C	23,975	61.2
			A. MacArthur	Lab	15,130	38.7
					8,845	22.6
1959	52,472	78.9	J.C. George	C	24,338	58.8
			J.M. Smith	Lab	17,072	41.2
					7,266	17.6
1964	52,094	77.8	A. Garrow	Lab	18,089	44.6
			R.D. Kernohan	C	17,793	43.9
			R.N. Straker	L	4,670*	11.5
					296	0.7
1966	51,301	79.0	A. Garrow	Lab	21,257	52.4
			P.T. Telfer-Smollett	C	19,282	47.6
					1,975	4.8

[Death]

Election	Electors	T'out	Candidate	Party	Votes	%
1967 (9/3)	51,088	75.7	E. Wright	C	14,270	36.9
			R.G. Douglas	Lab/Co-op	12,069	31.2
			G.A. Leslie	SNP	10,884	28.2
			I.D. Miller	L	735*	1.9
			A.C. Murray	Com	694*	1.8
					2,201	5.7
1970	57,501	72.6	J. White	Lab	19,311	46.2
			E. Wright	C	18,708	44.8
			G.A. Leslie	SNP	3,733*	8.9
					603	1.5

Election	Electors	T'out	Candidate	Party	Votes	%
1955	41,326	74.7	W. Reid	Lab	15,533	50.3
			Sir C.S. McFarlane	C	15,353	49.7
					180	0.6
1959	49,284	78.8	W. Reid	Lab	21,608	55.6
			R.D. Kernohan	C	17,241	44.4
					4,367	11.2
1964	60,027	75.7	H.D. Brown	Lab	29,889	65.8
			K.B. Miller	C	15,524	34.2
					14,365	31.6
1966	59,575	70.8	H.D. Brown	Lab	28,201	66.9
			D.I. Fraser	C	12,986	30.8
			J. Jackson	Com	988*	2.3
					15,215	36.1
1970	64,852	65.6	H.D. Brown	Lab	25,864	60:9
			D.D.M. Masterton	C	11,881	27.9
			W. McRae	SNP	4,181*	9.8
			J. Jackson	Com	601*	1.4
					13,983	33.0

Election	Electors	T'out	Candidate	Party	Votes	%
1950	49,010	84.6	†Sir A.S.L. Young, Bt.	C	19,294	46.
			W. Bargh	Lab/Co-op	19,055	46.
			W. Ferguson	L	2,023*	4.
			R. McIlhone	Com	1,088*	2.
					239	0.
[Death]						
1950	49,321	73.7	J.R.H. Hutchison	C	18,494	50.
(25/10)			W. Bargh	Lab/Co-op	17,175	47.
			D.W. Gibson	ILP	680*	1.
					1,319	3.
1951	49,814	85.1	J.R.H. Hutchison	C	21,497	50.
			J. Robertson	Lab	20,872	49.
					625	1.
1955	46,370**	79.5	J.R.H. Hutchison	C	18,654	50.
			H. James	Lab/Co-op	18,226	49.
					428	1.
1959	56,278	81.8	W.W. Small	Lab	24,690	53.
			J. Bias	C	21,320	46.
					3,370	7.
1964	56,819	77.2	W.W. Small	Lab	27,036	61.
			R.B. Anderson	C	16,856	38.
					10,180	23.
1966	59,478	74.3	W.W. Small	Lab	27,320	61.
			Mrs. A.S. Douglas	C	14,493	32.
			H.D. Boyd	Com	2,395*	5.
					12,827	29.
1970	65,436	70.5	W.W. Small	Lab	26,492	57.
			N.J. Mountney	C	14,487	31.
			A. Mitchell	SNP	4,313*	9.
			H.D. Boyd	Com	846*	1.
					12,005	26.

lection	Electors	T'out	Candidate	Party	Votes	%
950	51,801	79.9	†J. McGovern	Lab	23,467	56.6
			T.C. Henderson	C	15,226	36.8
			M. MacEwen	Com	1,678*	4.1
			J.W. Graham	ILP	1,031*	2.5
					8,241	19.8
951	52,267	81.2	J. McGovern	Lab	25,359	59.8
				(Ind Lab)		
				(Lab)		
			J.O.M. Hunter	C	15,876	37.4
			J.W. Graham	ILP	1,195*	2.8
					9,483	22.4
955	53,533	69.3	J. McGovern	Lab	21,464	57.8
			J.O.M. Hunter	C	15,645	42.2
					5,819	15.6
959	49,987	75.3	M. Galpern	Lab	22,916	60.9
			D.E. Donaldson	C	14,743	39.1
					8,173	21.8
964	46,358	71.4	Sir M. Galpern	Lab	22,494	68.0
			Hon. G.A. Weir	C	10,598	32.0
					11,896	36.0
966	44,873	68.6	Sir M. Galpern	Lab	20,208	65.6
			W.J. Rennie	C	6,857	22.3
			W. Lindsay	SNP	3,732*	12.1
					13,351	43.3
970	46,822	63.7	Sir M. Galpern	Lab	17,840	59.9
			A.N. McCue	C	7,969	26.7
			W. Lindsay	SNP	3,995	13.4
					9,871	33.2

Election	Electors	T'out	Candidate	Party	Votes	%
1950	55,756	76.9	†J.C. Forman	Lab/Co-op	25,603	59.7
			J. McNicol	C	13,666	31.9
			D.W. Campbell	L	1,853*	4.3
			R.F. Horne	Com	1,764*	4.1
					11,937	27.8
1951	57,019	78.0	J.C. Forman	Lab/Co-op	27,749	62.4
			W.H. Bennett	C	16,748	37.6
					11,001	24.8
1955	40,537**	69.1	J.C. Forman	Lab/Co-op	16,131	57.5
			J.A. Young	C	10,358	37.0
			F. Hart	Com	1,532*	5.5
					5,773	20.5
1959	38,147	72.6	J.C. Forman	Lab/Co-op	16,297	58.8
			E.M. Taylor	C	10,167	36.7
			F. Hart	Com	1,235*	4.5
					6,130	22.1
1964	37,248	69.2	R. Buchanan	Lab	16,828	65.3
			R.B.J.D. Black	C	5,632	21.8
			A. McIntosh	SNP	2,366*	9.2
			N. McLellan	Com	950*	3.7
					11,196	43.5
1966	35,428	66.6	R. Buchanan	Lab	15,998	67.8
			D.H. Heatlie	C	4,499	19.1
			W.J. Morton	SNP	2,222*	9.4
			N. McLellan	Com	867*	3.7
					11,499	48.7
1970	37,986	61.3	R. Buchanan	Lab	14,968	64.3
			J. Sorbie	C	4,574	19.6
			W.J. Morton	SNP	3,323	14.3
			N. McLellan	Com	423*	1.8
					10,394	44.7

GLASGOW, TRADESTON [607]

ection	Electors	T'out	Candidate	Party	Votes	%
50	53,711	78.8	†J. Rankin	Lab/Co-op	26,598	62.9
			A. Hart	C	15,704	37.1
					10,894	25.8
51	53,404	80.0	J. Rankin	Lab/Co-op	26,966	63.1
			A. Hart	C	15,771	36.9
					11,195	26.2

This constituency was divided in 1955.

GLASGOW, WOODSIDE [608]

Election	Electors	T'out	Candidate	Party	Votes	%
1950	43,728	80.2	W.G. Bennett	C	17,075	48
			†W. Leonard	Lab/Co-op	15,996	45
			T.L. Woodside	L	2,005*	5
					1,079	3
1951	42,950	80.9	W.G. Bennett	C	18,553	53
			R. McCutcheon	Lab/Co-op	16,210	46
					2,343	6
1955	48,632**	72.8	W. Grant	C	19,846	56
			J. McGinley	Lab	15,543	43
					4,303	12
1959	44,746	75.2	Rt. Hon. W. Grant	C	16,567	49
			J. McGinley	Lab	14,483	43
			G.V. McLaughlin	L	2,583*	7
					2,084	6

[Resignation on appointment as Lord Justice Clerk—Lord Grant]

Election	Electors	T'out	Candidate	Party	Votes	%
1962	42,111	54.7	N.G. Carmichael	Lab	8,303	36
(22/11)			N.M. Glen	C	6,935	30
			J. House	L	5,000	21
			A. Niven	SNP	2,562*	11
			G.A. Aldred	Ind Soc	134*	0
			R. Vallar	SPGB	83*	0
					1,368	6
1964	40,035	74.0	N.G. Carmichael	Lab	13,521	45
			N.M. Glen	C	11,954	40
			J. House	L	2,443*	8
			Dr. D.J.D. Stevenson	SNP	1,600*	5
			R. Vallar	SPGB	88*	0
					1,567	5
1966	36,678	73.0	N.G. Carmichael	Lab	13,540	50
			N.M. Glen	C	11,202	41
			R.C. Fairlie	SNP	1,916*	7
			R. Vallar	SPGB	122*	0
					2,338	8
1970	35,676	63.8	N.G. Carmichael	Lab	10,785	47
			V.J. MacColl	C	9,457	41
			D.R. Rollo	SNP	1,912*	8
			G.R. McKay	Ind C	614*	2
					1,328	5

Note:—

1970: McKay was opposed to Britain entering the Common Market and also advocated the re-introduction of capital punishment.

GREENOCK [609]

Election	Electors	T'out	Candidate	Party	Votes	%
1950	48,792	83.2	†Rt. Hon. H. McNeil	Lab	20,548	50.6
			I. McColl	L	11,639	28.7
			J.S. Thomson	Ind	6,458	15.9
			J.R. Campbell	Com	1,228*	3.0
			W.O. Brown	AP	718*	1.8
					8,909	21.9
1951	49,494	83.0	Rt. Hon. H. McNeil	Lab	23,452	57.1
			W.R. McLean	C	17,615	42.9
					5,837	14.2
1955	48,400*	77.9	Rt. Hon. H. McNeil	Lab	19,378	51.4
			I. MacArthur	C	18,345	48.6
					1,033	2.8
[Death]						
1955 (8/12)	48,760	75.3	Dr. J.D. Mabon	Lab/Co-op	19,698	53.7
			I. MacArthur	C	17,004	46.3
					2,694	7.4
1959	48,366	78.9	Dr. J.D. Mabon	Lab/Co-op	19,320	50.6
			W.T.C. Riddell	L	10,238	26.8
			L.M. Turpie	C	8,616	22.6
					9,082	23.8
1964	46,549*	76.5	Dr. J.D. Mabon	Lab/Co-op	19,627	55.1
			C.M. Barclay	L	9,055	25.4
			D.R.G. Sillars	C	6,473	18.2
			J.S. Thomson	Ind	458*	1.3
					10,572	29.7
1966	45,164	73.6	Dr. J.D. Mabon	Lab/Co-op	18,988	57.2
			I.M. Will	L	7,727	23.2
			R.E. Dundas	C	5,835	17.5
			W. Dunn	Com	702*	2.1
					11,261	34.0
1970	47,385	76.0	Dr. J.D. Mabon	Lab/Co-op	19,334	53.7
			W.T.C. Riddell	L	16,100	44.7
			A.C. Murray	Com	559*	1.6
					3,234	9.0

Notes:—

1950: Thomson advocated a Coalition Government with Winston Churchill as Prime Minister.

Brown also advocated a policy of Scottish nationalism.

Election	Electors	T'out	Candidate	Party	Votes	%
1950	50,645	84.8	†T.F. Hubbard	Lab	25,756	60.0
			R. Bell	C	17,192	40.0
					8,564	20.0
1951	52,473*	84.6	T.F. Hubbard	Lab	26,885	60.6
			R. Harris	NL & C	17,484	39.4
					9,401	21.2
1955	53,553*	75.2	T.F. Hubbard	Lab	23,861	59.3
			D.D. Young	NL & C	16,392	40.7
					7,469	18.6
1959	54,232	80.5	H.P.H. Gourlay	Lab	25,428	58.3
			J. Law	C	14,186	32.5
			D. Blyth	L	4,020*	9.2
					11,242	25.8
1964	52,355	77.2	H.P.H. Gourlay	Lab	24,263	60.0
			N. Gow	NL & C	11,756	29.1
			Dr. J.C. Lees	SNP	4,423*	10.9
					12,507	30.9
1966	51,765	75.4	H.P.H. Gourlay	Lab	23,273	59.6
			N. Gow	C	10,539	27.0
			Dr. J.C. Lees	SNP	5,223	13.4
					12,734	32.6
1970	55,098	74.5	H.P.H. Gourlay	Lab	22,986	56.1
			A.M. Hogg	C	13,193	32.1
			Dr. J.C. Lees	SNP	4,863*	11.8
					9,793	24.0

PAISLEY [611]

lection	Electors	T'out	Candidate	Party	Votes	%
950	61,924	84.0	†D.H. Johnston	Lab	29,204	56.1
			H. Black	C	19,001	36.5
			V.M. Shaw	L	3,830*	7.4
					10,203	19.6
951	63,281	84.4	D.H. Johnston	Lab	29,570	55.3
			J.F. Wilson	C	16,545	31.0
			V.M. Shaw	L	7,291	13.7
					13,025	24.3
955	62,376	76.2	D.H. Johnston	Lab	26,823	56.4
			R.D. Kernohan	C	20,725	43.6
					6,098	12.8
959	63,097	78.9	D.H. Johnston	Lab	28,519	57.3
			G.R. Rickman	C	21,250	42.7
					7,269	14.6

[Resignation on appointment as a Senator of the College of Justice—Lord Johnston]

961 (20/4)	62,141	68.1	J. Robertson	Lab	19,200	45.4
			J.M. Bannerman	L	17,542	41.4
			G.R. Rickman	C	5,597	13.2
					1,658	4.0
964	62,336	79.8	J. Robertson	Lab	26,318	52.9
			J.M. Bannerman	L	16,837	33.9
			M. Crichton	C	6,583	13.2
					9,481	19.0
966	61,363	76.5	J. Robertson	Lab	28,160	60.0
			M. Crichton	C	10,892	23.2
			V.M. Shaw	L	7,889	16.8
					17,268	36.8
970	65,740	71.5	J. Robertson	Lab	25,429	54.1
			J. Workman	C	15,232	32.4
			Mrs. M. MacDonald	SNP	3,432*	7.3
			A. Sked	L	2,918*	6.2
					10,197	21.7

Election	Electors	T'out	Candidate	Party	Votes	%
1950	53,697	84.4	†M. MacPherson	Lab	22,186	49.0
			W.D.H.C. Forbes	C	20,632	45.5
			R. Curran	SNP	1,698*	3.7
			G. McAlister	Com	801*	1.8
					1,554	3.5
1951	54,300	86.1	M. MacPherson	Lab	24,421	52.3
			W.D.H.C. Forbes	C	22,313	47.7
					2,108	4.6
1955	53,832*	79.7	M. MacPherson	Lab	20,651	48.2
			J.R. McMillan	C	19,345	45.1
			J. Halliday	SNP	2,885*	6.7
					1,306	3.1
1959	55,759	81.1	M. MacPherson	Lab	22,423	49.6
			R.S. Johnston	C	19,797	43.8
			J. Halliday	SNP	2,983*	6.6
					2,626	5.8
1964	56,806	79.9	M. MacPherson	Lab	23,766	52.4
			J.A. Davidson	C	17,070	37.6
			W.A. Milne	SNP	4,526*	10.0
					6,696	14.8
1966	57,015	77.1	M. MacPherson	Lab	23,146	52.7
			I. Docherty	C	13,726	31.2
			W.A. Milne	SNP	6,322	14.4
			P.J. McIntosh	Com	767*	1.7
					9,420	21.5
1970	61,953	73.1	M. MacPherson	Lab	22,984	50.7
			D.R. Anderson	C	15,754	34.8
			I.M. Murray	SNP	6,571	14.5
					7,230	15.9

SCOTLAND --- COUNTIES

Election	Electors	T'out	Candidate	Party	Votes	%
1950	50,080	75.6	†R.J.G. Boothby	C	24,971	66.0
			J.G. MacKenzie	Lab	12,886	34.0
					12,085	32.0
1951	52,475	70.0	R.J.G. Boothby	C	24,985	68.1
			A.G.S. Whipp	Lab	11,730	31.9
					13,255	36.2
1955	45,423**	59.8	Sir R.J.G. Boothby	C	18,600	68.5
			C.M. Ross	Lab	8,543	31.5
					10,057	37.0

[Elevation to a Life Peerage—Lord Boothby]

Election	Electors	T'out	Candidate	Party	Votes	%
1958	44,694	65.9	P. Wolrige-Gordon	C	14,314	48.6
(20/11)			J.B. Urquhart	Lab	7,986	27.1
			M. Mackie	L	7,153	24.3
					6,328	21.5
1959	44,628	67.1	P. Wolrige-Gordon	C	18,982	63.4
			J.B. Urquhart	Lab	10,980	36.6
					8,002	26.8
1964	43,502	70.1	P. Wolrige-Gordon	C	14,621	48.0
			N.W. King	L	7,088	23.3
			D. McGibbon	Lab	6,840	22.4
			B.M. Cockie	SNP	1,925*	6.3
					7,533	24.7
1966	42,661	68.2	P. Wolrige-Gordon	C	12,067	41.4
			Hon. R.M. Sinclair	L	8,034	27.6
			I.S. Davidson	Lab	6,422	22.1
			B.M. Cockie	SNP	2,584*	8.9
					4,033	13.8
1970	45,711	68.8	P. Wolrige-Gordon	C	12,866	40.9
			A.R. Farquhar	SNP	9,377	29.8
			H.C. Grimes	Lab	5,656	18.0
			G.C. Hoyer-Millar	L	3,548*	11.3
					3,489	11.1

Election	Electors	T'out	Candidate	Party	Votes	%
1950	39,077	80.9	†H.R. Spence	C	17,550	55.5
			T. Oswald	Lab	7,298	23.1
			I.R.M. Davies	L	6,748	21.4
					10,252	32.4
1951	41,078	78.3	H.R. Spence	C	17,761	55.2
			N. Hogg	Lab	7,278	22.6
			M. Mackie	L	7,128	22.2
					10,483	32.6
1955	47,125**	72.6	H.R. Spence	C	20,216	59.0
			Miss M. MacNeil	Lab	9,288	27.2
			T.R.L. Fraser	L	4,705	13.8
					10,928	31.8
1959	46,429	72.1	A.F. Hendry	C	22,937	68.5
			W. Kemp	Lab	10,542	31.5
					12,395	37.0
1964	45,744	77.4	A.F. Hendry	C	16,429	46.4
			J.D.G. Davidson	L	11,754	33.2
			K.A. Munro	Lab	7,203	20.4
					4,675	13.2
1966	46,011	76.3	J.D.G. Davidson	L	15,151	43.2
			A.F. Hendry	C	13,956	39.7
			J.T. Henderson	Lab	6,008	17.1
					1,195	3.5
1970	52,108	75.8	C.C. Mitchell	C	18,396	46.7
			Mrs. L.M. Grimond	L	12,847	32.5
			W.W. Hay	Lab	6,141	15.5
			J.G. McKinlay	SNP	2,112*	5.3
					5,549	14.2

Election	Electors	T'out	Candidate	Party	Votes	%
1950	36,890	81.4	†C.N. Thornton-Kemsley	NL & C	15,485	51.5
			J.R. Justice	Lab	8,304	27.7
			T. Adam	L	6,233	20.8
					7,181	23.8
1951	37,836	76.3	C.N. Thornton-Kemsley	NL & C	18,515	64.1
			J. Mackie	Lab	10,356	35.9
					8,159	28.2
1955	37,146	72.3	C.N. Thornton-Kemsley	NL & C	18,516	69.0
			C. Buick	Lab	8,323	31.0
					10,193	38.0
1959	36,513	71.3	Sir C.N. Thornton-Kemsley	NL & C	17,536	67.4
			R. Hughes	Lab	8,486	32.6
					9,050	34.8
1964	35,324	77.0	Hon. A.L. Buchanan-Smith	C	13,401	49.3
			K.A.J. Barton	L	9,268	34.1
			Mrs. K.M.J. Klopper	Lab	4,513	16.6
					4,133	15.2
1966	34,583	76.2	Hon. A.L. Buchanan-Smith	C	13,286	50.4
			K.A.J. Barton	L	7,756	29.4
			C.T. Walker	Lab	5,318	20.2
					5,530	21.0
1970	37,058	74.7	Hon. A.L. Buchanan-Smith	C	14,687	53.1
			J. Gourlay	Lab	5,092	18.4
			J. McGugan	SNP	4,677	16.9
			J. Grimond	L	3,212*	11.6
					9,595	34.7

Election	Electors	T'out	Candidate	Party	Votes	%
1950	43,746	82.0	J.A.L. Duncan	NL & C	19,324	53.9
			N. Hogg	Lab	9,176	25.6
			J. Jenkins	L	7,360	20.5
					10,148	28.3
1951	45,073	76.6	J.A.L. Duncan	NL & C	24,478	70.9
			J. Harold	Lab	10,028	29.1
					14,450	41.8
1955	44,796	73.6	J.A.L. Duncan	NL & C	23,967	72.7
			H.P.H. Gourlay	Lab	8,996	27.3
					14,971	45.4
1959	44,840	75.9	Sir J.A.L. Duncan, Bt.	NL & C	19,435	57.1
			G.Y. Mackie	L	8,139	23.9
			J.L. Stewart	Lab	6,477	19.0
					11,296	33.2
1964	44,495	75.6	J. Bruce-Gardyne	C	19,566	58.2
			R.G. Douglas	Lab/Co-op	7,590	22.6
			C.B.H. Scott	L	6,472	19.2
					11,976	35.6
1966	44,705	71.2	J. Bruce-Gardyne	C	22,407	70.4
			F.C. McManus	Lab	9,404	29.6
					13,003	40.8
1970	49,293	73.9	J. Bruce-Gardyne	C	20,439	56.1
			C.G.M. Slesser	SNP	8,409	23.1
			H. Coutts	Lab	7,557	20.8
					12,030	33.0

ARGYLL [617]

Election	Electors	T'out	Candidate	Party	Votes	%
1950	38,563	75.1	†D. McCallum	C	19,259	66.5
			I.W. Nicholson	Lab	9,215	31.8
			Mrs. M.S.M. Holt	Ind	490*	1.7
					10,044	34.7
1951	46,357	67.1	D. McCallum	C	21,191	68.1
			R. Young	Lab	9,925	31.9
					11,266	36.2
1955	42,182	66.6	D. McCallum	C	19,006	67.6
			R. Young	Lab	9,091	32.4
					9,915	35.2
[Death]						
1958 (12/6)	39,962	67.1	M.A.C. Noble	C	12,541	46.8
			W.D. McKean	L	7,375	27.5
			R. Young	Lab	6,884	25.7
					5,166	19.3
1959	40,015	71.0	M.A.C. Noble	C	16,599	58.4
			D. Nisbet	Lab	7,356	25.9
			Hon. G.E. Noel	L	4,469	15.7
					9,243	32.5
1964	39,965	70.3	Rt. Hon. M.A.C. Noble	C	13,277	47.2
			D.L. McMillan	Lab	8,120	28.9
			J.J. Mackay	L	6,707	23.9
					5,157	18.3
1966	38,949	72.3	Rt. Hon. M.A.C. Noble	C	12,178	43.2
			J. McFadden	Lab	8,486	30.1
			J.J. Mackay	L	7,512	26.7
					3,692	13.1
1970	40,825	74.0	Rt. Hon. M.A.C. Noble	C	13,521	44.8
			I. MacCormick	SNP	9,039	29.9
			J. McFadden	Lab	7,633	25.3
					4,482	14.9

Note:—

1950: Mrs. Holt advocated a policy of Scottish nationalism.

Election	Electors	T'out	Candidate	Party	Votes	%
1950	42,462	84.7	†Sir T.C.R. Moore	C	21,094	58.6
			J. Pollock	Lab	14,880	41.4
					6,214	17.2
1951	43,574	86.5	Sir T.C.R. Moore	C	21,985	58.3
			Miss J.M.J. Auld	Lab	15,702	41.7
					6,283	16.6
1955	43,931	77.1	Sir T.C.R. Moore	C	20,006	59.1
			Miss J.M.J. Auld	Lab	13,866	40.9
					6,140	18.2
1959	45,444	79.1	Sir T.C.R. Moore, Bt.	C	19,659	54.7
			A. Eadie	Lab	16,303	45.3
					3,356	9.4
1964	46,269	83.0	Hon. G.K.H. Younger	C	20,047	52.2
			A. Eadie	Lab	18,346	47.8
					1,701	4.4
1966	46,285	85.3	Hon. G.K.H. Younger	C	19,988	50.6
			C.E. O'Halloran	Lab	19,504	49.4
					484	1.2
1970	51,691	81.6	Hon. G.K.H. Younger	C	22,220	52.7
			J.M. Craigen	Lab/Co-op	17,770	42.1
			L. Anderson	SNP	2,186*	5.2
					4,450	10.6

Election	Electors	T'out	Candidate	Party	Votes	%
1950	43,288	79.1	†Sir C.G. MacAndrew	C	22,019	64.3
			G. Aitken	Lab	12,243	35.7
					9,776	28.6
1951	45,110	77.3	Sir C.G. MacAndrew	C	22,361	64.2
			J.D. Mabon	Lab	12,492	35.8
					9,869	28.4
1955	44,065*	71.5	Rt. Hon. Sir C.G. MacAndrew	C	20,338	64.5
			D. Lambie	Lab	11,183	35.5
					9,155	29.0
1959	44,291	73.4	Sir F.H.R. Maclean, Bt.	C	20,270	62.4
			D. Lambie	Lab	12,218	37.6
					8,052	24.8
1964	44,352	74.6	Sir F.H.R. Maclean, Bt.	C	16,497	49.8
			D. Lambie	Lab	11,934	36.1
			R.J. Gammon	L	4,671	14.1
					4,563	13.7
1966	43,627	76.0	Sir F.H.R. Maclean, Bt.	C	16,138	48.6
			D. Lambie	Lab	13,482	40.7
			R.P. Cochrane	L	3,539*	10.7
					2,656	7.9
1970	47,786	73.6	Sir F.H.R. Maclean, Bt.	C	18,853	53.6
			H.G. Millar	Lab	12,459	35.4
			Mrs. M. Macrae	SNP	3,852*	11.0
					6,394	18.2

Election	Electors	T'out	Candidate	Party	Votes	%
1950	44,842	85.6	A.C. Manuel	Lab	18,792	49.0
			W.R. Milligan	C	16,830	43.8
			C.J. Coleman	L	2,760*	7.2
					1,962	5.2
1951	46,733	86.3	A.C. Manuel	Lab	21,003	52.1
			W.R. Milligan	C	19,310	47.9
					1,693	4.2
1955	47,112*	83.3	D.L.S. Nairn	C	19,713	50.2
			A.C. Manuel	Lab	19,546	49.8
					167	0.4
1959	48,596	86.7	A.C. Manuel	Lab	21,901	52.0
			D.L.S. Nairn	C	20,225	48.0
					1,676	4.0
1964	50,510	84.2	A.C. Manuel	Lab	23,999	56.4
			G.R. Rickman	C	18,523	43.6
					5,476	12.8
1966	50,744	82.1	A.C. Manuel	Lab	24,035	57.7
			J.A. Corrie	C	17,637	42.3
					6,398	15.4
1970	58,024	80.7	D. Lambie	Lab	24,536	52.4
			I.B. Lang	C	19,569	41.8
			Rev. A. Macdonald	SNP	2,383*	5.1
			T. Menzies	Ind	339*	0.7
					4,967	10.6

Note:—

19 70: Menzies advocated the re-introduction of capital punishment.

Election	Electors	T'out	Candidate	Party	Votes	%
1950	45,974	86.2	†W. Ross	Lab	22,412	56.6
			A.D.M. Shaw	C	14,179	35.8
			J.G. Thomson	L	2,157*	5.4
			Mrs. I. Brown	Com	860*	2.2
					8,233	20.8
1951	46,869	86.7	W. Ross	Lab	24,664	60.7
			N.M. Glen	C	15,955	39.3
					8,709	21.4
1955	47,256	81.1	W. Ross	Lab	23,324	60.9
			J. Sutherland	C	14,983	39.1
					8,341	21.8
1959	49,090	82.4	W. Ross	Lab	25,379	62.7
			R.I. McNaught	C	15,087	37.3
					10,292	25.4
1964	48,824	82.8	W. Ross	Lab	25,173	62.3
			G.H. Webster	C	10,796	26.7
			I.M. Will	·L	4,443*	11.0
					14,377	35.6
1966	48,073	79.0	Rt. Hon. W. Ross	Lab	26,036	68.5
			A. McQuarrie	C	11,949	31.5
					14,087	37.0
1970	52,092	79.2	Rt. Hon. W. Ross	Lab	24,477	59.3
			G. Law	C	11,476	27.8
			A. MacInnes	SNP	2,836*	6.9
			A.J. Wight	L	2,459*	6.0
					13,001	31.5

Election	Electors	T'out	Candidate	Party	Votes	%
1950	43,346	85.4	†E. Hughes	Lab	22,284	60.2
			J.C. George	C	14,717	39.8
					7,567	20.4
1951	44,999	82.9	E. Hughes	Lab (Ind Lab) (Lab)	22,576	60.5
			D.M.H. Smith	C	14,740	39.5
					7,836	21.0
1955	46,007	76.8	E. Hughes	Lab	21,778	61.6
			D.M.H. Smith	C	13,569	38.4
					8,209	23.2
1959	48,063	80.9	E. Hughes	Lab (Ind Lab) (Lab)	24,774	63.7
			W.H. Hunter	C	14,105	36.3
					10,669	27.4
1964	47,936	77.6	E. Hughes	Lab	24,795	66.7
			W.H. Hunter	C	12,392	33.3
					12,403	33.4
1966	46,505	75.1	E. Hughes	Lab	23,495	67.2
			C.R. Graves	C	11,442	32.8
					12,053	34.4
[Death]						
1970 (19/3)	50,089	76.3	J. Sillars	Lab	20,664	54.0
			C.R. Graves	C	9,778	25.6
			S.H. Purdie	SNP	7,785	20.4
					10,886	28.4
1970	50,324	76.9	J. Sillars	Lab	23,910	61.8
			N.D. Simpson	C	11,675	30.2
			S.H. Purdie	SNP	3,103*	8.0
					12,235	31.6

Election	Electors	T'out	Candidate	Party	Votes	%
1950	32,359	74.1	†W.S. Duthie	C	13,952	58.1
			J. Brown	Lab	6,303	26.3
			Sir G.J. Lethem	L	3,739	15.6
					7,649	31.8
1951	35,643	65.6	W.S. Duthie	C	16,562	70.9
			A.S. Flett	Lab	6,806	29.1
					9,756	41.8
1955	38,378	54.7	W.S. Duthie	C	14,643	69.8
			W. Paterson	Lab	6,337	30.2
					8,306	39.6
1959	32,129	63.3	Sir W.S. Duthie	C (Ind C) (C)	14,359	70.6
			R.W. Irvine	Lab	5,992	29.4
					8,367	41.2
1964	30,880	67.8	W.H.K. Baker	C	9,995	47.8
			H. Dickson	Lab	5,574	26.6
			T.A. MacNair	L	5,354	25.6
					4,421	21.2
1966	30,216	65.1	W.H.K. Baker	C	8,139	41.3
			B.F. Wishart	L	6,762	34.4
			R. Middleton	Lab	4,775	24.3
					1,377	6.9
1970	31,705	68.9	W.H.K. Baker	C	8,457	38.7
			H. Watt	SNP	5,006	22.9
			T.R.L. Fraser	L	4,589	21.0
			A.F. Walls	Lab	3,795	17.4
					3,451	15.8

Election	Electors	T'out	Candidate	Party	Votes	%
1950	50,514	82.8	†J.J. Robertson	Lab	17,105	40.
			W.J. Anstruther-Gray	C	15,377	36.
			J.A. Stodart	L	9,352	22.
					1,728	4.
1951	50,933	83.8	W.J. Anstruther-Gray	C	22,510	52.
			J.J. Robertson	Lab	20,152	47.
					2,358	5.
1955	50,764	80.3	W.J. Anstruther-Gray	C	21,739	53.
			P. Jones	Lab	19,029	46.
					2,710	6.
1959	50,569	83.2	Sir W.J. Anstruther-Gray, Bt.	C	22,472	53.
			P. Jones	Lab	19,622	46.
					2,850	6.
1964	50,251	85.0	Rt. Hon. Sir W.J. Anstruther-Gray, Bt.	C	21,669	50.
			J.P. Mackintosh	Lab	21,044	49.
					625	1.
1966	50,584	86.1	J.P. Mackintosh	Lab	22,620	51.
			Rt. Hon. Sir W.J. Anstruther-Gray, Bt.	C	20,931	48.
					1,689	3.
1970	55,252	83.8	J.P. Mackintosh	Lab	21,107	45.
			J.D.M. Hardie	C	20,466	44.
			Dr. D.R.F. Simpson	SNP	4,735*	10.
					641	1.

Note:—

1970: Simpson received the official support of the local Liberal Association.

Election	Electors	T'out	Candidate	Party	Votes	%
1950	25,400	76.5	†Sir D. Robertson	C	6,969	35.8
			Rt. Hon. Sir A.H.M. Sinclair, Bt.	L	6,700	34.5
			A. MacArthur	Lab	5,767	29.7
					269	1.3
1951	27,097	73.5	Sir D. Robertson	C	9,814	49.3
			R. Murray	Lab	6,799	34.1
			P.J.M. McEwan	L	3,299	16.6
					3,015	15.2
1955	26,619	69.5	Sir D. Robertson	C (Ind C)	10,453	56.5
			H.F. Sutherland	Lab	5,364	29.0
			J.S. Mowat	L	2,674	14.5
					5,089	27.5
1959	26,716	69.6	Sir D. Robertson	Ind C	12,163	65.4
			R.K. Murray	Lab	6,438	34.6
					5,725	30.8
1964	27,291	80.1	G.Y. Mackie	L	7,894	36.1
			J.B. Urquhart	Lab	6,619	30.3
			Hon. P.F. Maitland	C	4,550	20.8
			J.M. Young	Ind C	2,795	12.8
					1,275	5.8
1966	26,776	79.2	R.A.R. MacLennan	Lab	8,308	39.1
			G.Y. Mackie	L	8,244	38.9
			J.M. Watt	C	4,662	22.0
					64	0.2
1970	28,709	83.1	R.A.R. MacLennan	Lab	8,768	36.7
			G.Y. Mackie	L	6,063	25.4
			J.M. Young	C	5,334	22.4
			D.G. Barr	SNP	3,690	15.5
					2,705	11.3

Note:—

1964: Young was supported by Sir David Robertson the former MP and a breakaway (Independent) Conservative Association which was formed after Sir David relinquished the Conservative Whip in January 1959. The Association was dissolved early in 1965.

DUMFRIESSHIRE [626]

Election	Electors	T'out	Candidate	Party	Votes	%
1950	56,346	78.6	†N.M.S. Macpherson	NL & C	26,268	59.3
			H.S. Wilson	Lab	18,025	40.7
					8,243	18.6
1951	53,706	80.2	N.M.S. Macpherson	NL & C	26,386	61.3
			G.B.A. Douglas	Lab	16,669	38.7
					9,717	22.6
1955	54,285	73.7	N.M.S. Macpherson	NL & C	24,550	61.3
			H.S. Wilson	Lab	15,472	38.7
					9,078	22.6
1959	57,212	77.4	N.M.S. Macpherson	NL & C	25,867	58.4
			G.C. Moodie	Lab	18,437	41.6
					7,430	16.8

[Elevation to the Peerage—Lord Drumalbyn]

Election	Electors	T'out	Candidate	Party	Votes	%
1963	57,288	71.6	D.C. Anderson	C	16,762	40.9
(12/12)			I. Jordan	Lab	15,791	38.5
			C.L. Abernethy	L	4,491*	10.9
			J.H.D. Gair	SNP	4,001*	9.7
					971	2.4
1964	57,502	81.6	H.S.P. Monro	C	22,816	48.7
			I. Jordan	Lab	18,360	39.1
			J.H.D. Gair	SNP	5,726*	12.2
					4,456	9.6
1966	56,797	80.2	H.S.P. Monro	C	20,779	45.6
			T.C. Boyd	Lab	16,358	35.9
			J.H.D. Gair	SNP	5,727	12.6
			R. Semple	L	2,679*	5.9
					4,421	9.7
1970	60,939	76.2	H.S.P. Monro	C	24,661	53.1
			R.D. Donnelly	Lab	15,555	33.5
			J.H.D. Gair	SNP	6,211	13.4
					9,106	19.6

Note:—

1963: Anderson was Solicitor-General for Scotland.

DUNBARTONSHIRE, EAST [627]

lection	Electors	T'out	Candidate	Party	Votes	%
)50	57,309	86.0	†Rt. Hon. D. Kirkwood	Lab	25,943	52.6
			W.S.I. Whitelaw	C	21,367	43.4
			C.E. Forrester	L	1,952*	4.0
					4,576	9.2
)51	60,136*	86.6	C.R. Bence	Lab	26,678	51.3
			W.S.I. Whitelaw	C	23,252	44.6
			A.E. Henderson	Com	2,158*	4.1
					3,426	6.7
)55	61,003	81.6	C.R. Bence	Lab	24,216	48.7
			N.M. Glen	C	23,086	46.4
			A.E. Henderson	Com	2,448*	4.9
					1,130	2.3
)59	64,961	84.2	C.R. Bence	Lab	27,942	51.1
			D.C. Anderson	C	24,553	44.9
			A.E. Henderson	Com	2,200*	4.0
					3,389	6.2
)64	72,528	82.5	C.R. Bence	Lab	32,949	55.0
			T.W. Strachan	C	25,137	42.0
			J. Reid	Com	1,771*	3.0
					7,812	13.0
)66	78,453	80.6	C.R. Bence	Lab	32,985	52.2
			K.B. Miller	C	23,001	36.4
			W. Johnston	SNP	5,715*	9.0
			J. Reid	Com	1,548*	2.4
					9,984	15.8
970	93,683	77.8	H. McCartney	Lab	32,527	44.7
			J.S.B. Henderson	C	26,972	37.0
			G.S. Murray	SNP	8,257*	11.3
			J.G. Brown	L	3,460*	4.7
			J. Reid	Com	1,656*	2.3
					5,555	7.7

Election	Electors	T'out	Candidate	Party	Votes	%
1950	48,420	85.5	†A.S. McKinlay	Lab	20,398	49.
			R.A. Allan	C	19,785	47.
			F. Hart	Com	1,198*	2.
					613	1.
[Death]						
1950 (25/4)	48,462	83.4	T. Steele	Lab	20,367	50.
			R.A. Allan	C	20,074	49.
					293	0.
1951	49,058*	86.6	T. Steele	Lab	21,799	51.
			P.W.N. Fraser	C	19,292	45.
			L.L. Maitland	L	1,415*	3.
					2,507	5.
1955	49,217	84.8	T. Steele	Lab	21,854	52.
			Lady Huggins	C	19,902	47.
					1,952	4.
1959	50,277	83.7	T. Steele	Lab	22,105	52.
			N.M. Glen	C	19,964	47.
					2,141	5.
1964	50,608	82.1	T. Steele	Lab	21,079	50.
			P.T. Telfer-Smollett	C	15,448	37.
			A. Gray	SNP	5,004*	12.0
					5,631	13.
1966	50,522	81.9	T. Steele	Lab	21,636	52.
			W. Adams	C	13,724	33.
			R.O. Campbell	SNP	6,042	14.
					7,912	19.
1970	57,943	78.0	I. Campbell	Lab	23,009	50.
			W. Adams	C	16,783	37.
			R.O. Campbell	SNP	5,414*	12.
					6,226	13.

Election	Electors	T'out	Candidate	Party	Votes	%
1950	49,511	81.6	†J. Henderson-Stewart	NL & C	25,749	63.7
			S.P. McLaren	Lab/Co-op	10,694	26.5
			D.A. Freeman	L	3,975*	9.8
					15,055	37.2
1951	51,162	78.7	J. Henderson-Stewart	NL & C	28,446	70.6
			J. McGowan	Lab	11,844	29.4
					16,602	41.2
1955	50,522	73.2	J. Henderson-Stewart	NL & C	26,104	70.6
			J. McGowan	Lab	10,872	29.4
					15,232	41.2
1959	50,537	75.2	Sir J. Henderson-Stewart, Bt.	NL & C	26,585	69.9
			J. Nicol	Lab	11,421	30.1
					15,164	39.8
[Death]						
1961 (3/11)	49,931	67.3	Sir J.E. Gilmour, Bt.	C	15,948	47.5
			J. Smith	Lab	8,882	26.4
			D.F. Leach	L	8,786	26.1
					7,066	21.1
1964	49,782	77.8	Sir J.E. Gilmour, Bt.	C	21,001	54.2
			J. Smith	Lab	9,765	25.2
			D.C. Wood	L	5,075	13.1
			J. Braid	SNP	2,635*	6.8
			Miss L.M.C. Greene	Loyalist	257*	0.7
					11,236	29.0
1966	49,332	76.1	Sir J.E. Gilmour, Bt.	C	19,323	51.5
			H. Peaker	Lab	9,229	24.6
			J. Braid	SNP	5,394	14.4
			D.A. Barrie	L	3,574*	9.5
					10,094	26.9
1970	53,155	74.5	Sir J.E. Gilmour, Bt.	C	21,619	54.6
			H. Ewing	Lab	9,756	24.6
			J. Braid	SNP	4,666*	11.8
			W.R.S. Pickard	L	3,577*	9.0
					11,863	30.0

Note:—

1961: Gilmour joined the Liberal-Unionist Group in the House of Commons as an associate member.

Election	Electors	T'out	Candidate	Party	Votes	%
1950	50,684	84.9	W.W. Hamilton	Lab	23,576	54
			P.W.N. Fraser	NL & C	10,131	23
			†W. Gallacher	Com	9,301	21
					13,445	31
1951	52,558*	85.5	W.W. Hamilton	Lab	29,195	64
			J.P. Fyfe	NL & C	11,038	24
			W. Lauchlan	Com	4,728*	10
					18,157	40
1955	53,417*	80.3	W.W. Hamilton	Lab	26,849	62
			N.R. Wylie	C	10,638	24
			W. Lauchlan	Com	5,389	12
					16,211	37
1959	55,992	81.3	W.W. Hamilton	Lab	25,554	56
			A.L. Buchanan-Smith	C	11,257	24
			L. Daly	FSL	4,886*	10
			W. Lauchlan	Com	3,828*	8
					14,297	31
1964	55,948*	78.6	W.W. Hamilton	Lab	28,806	65
			J.B.M. Gall	C	11,880	27
			W. Lauchlan	Com	3,273*	7
					16,926	38
1966	56,023	76.8	W.W. Hamilton	Lab	27,123	63
			J.B.M. Gall	C	8,300	19
			R.R. Patrick	SNP	6,046	14
			A.D. MacMillan	Com	1,542*	3
					18,823	43
1970	65,968	74.3	W.W. Hamilton	Lab	29,929	61
			J.G. McLauchlan	C	12,837	26
			J. Halliday	SNP	5,386*	11
			A.D. MacMillan	Com	855*	1
					17,092	34

ection	Electors	T'out	Candidate	Party	Votes	%
▮50	51,490	68.6	Lord Malcolm Douglas-Hamilton	C	16,056	45.5
			D.P.D.N. Thompson	Lab	11,236	31.8
			J.M. Bannerman	L	8,023	22.7
					4,820	13.7
▮51	50,302	69.3	Lord Malcolm Douglas-Hamilton	C	22,497	64.5
			T.A. MacNair	Lab	12,361	35.5
					10,136	29.0
Resignation]						
▮54	50,755	49.2	N.L.D. McLean	C	10,329	41.4
▮1/12)			J.M. Bannerman	L	8,998	36.0
			W. Paterson	Lab	5,642	22.6
					1,331	5.4
▮55	51,197	67.6	N.L.D. McLean	C	14,352	41.4
			J.M. Bannerman	L	13,386	38.7
			D.P.D.N. Thompson	Lab	6,891	19.9
					966	2.7
▮59	49,546	71.6	N.L.D. McLean	C	15,728	44.3
			J.M. Bannerman	L	11,653	32.9
			J.F. Coulter	Lab	8,073	22.8
					4,075	11.4
▮64	50,067	71.4	D.R. Johnston	L	14,235	39.8
			N.L.D. McLean	C	12,099	33.9
			A.C. McLean	Lab	9,402	26.3
					2,136	5.9
▮66	50,462	72.1	D.R. Johnston	L	14,356	39.4
			D.A. Wathen	C	11,961	32.9
			A.C. McLean	Lab	10,069	27.7
					2,395	6.5
▮70	54,258	72.3	D.R. Johnston	L	15,052	38.4
			D.A. Wathen	C	12,378	31.5
			D. Macaulay	Lab	9,038	23.0
			Miss A.C. Cameron	SNP	2,781*	7.1
					2,674	6.9

Election	Electors	T'out	Candidate	Party	Votes	%
1950	27,626	63.1	†J. MacLeod	Ind L (NL & C)	10,912	62.
			A.C.B. Reid	Lab	6,521	37.
					4,391	25.
1951	29,706	57.5	J. MacLeod	NL & C	10,969	64.
			A.C.B. Reid	Lab	6,104	35.
					4,865	28.
1955	25,746	61.9	J. MacLeod	NL & C	9,929	62.
			Mrs. J.B. Saggar	Lab	6,003	37.
					3,926	24.
1959	25,350	65.3	J. MacLeod	NL & C	7,813	47.
			Mrs. J.B. Saggar	Lab	4,815	29.
			C. Murchison	L	3,918	23.
					2,998	18.
1964	24,777	69.4	A.R. Mackenzie	L	6,923	40.
			Sir J. MacLeod	NL & C	5,516	32.
			W.A. Ross	Lab	4,767	27.
					1,407	8.
1966	24,530	71.2	A.R. Mackenzie	L	7,348	42.
			W.A. Ross	Lab	5,304	30.
			A.J. Cameron	C	4,820	27.
					2,044	11.
1970	26,947	71.7	J.H.N. Gray	C	6,418	33.
			A.R. Mackenzie	L	5,617	29.
			R.D. MacLean	Lab	5,023	26.
			G. Nicholson	SNP	2,268*	11.
					801	4.

Note:—

1950: MacLeod was supported by the local Conservative Association.

ection	Electors	T'out	Candidate	Party	Votes	%
)50	28,290	55.7	†M.K. Macmillan	Lab	8,387	53.2
			H.M. Sinclair	L	6,950	44.1
			D. Murray	Ind	425*	2.7
					1,437	9.1
)51	27,263	60.5	M.K. Macmillan	Lab	8,039	48.7
			J. Mitchell	NL & C	6,709	40.7
			D. Murray	L	916*	5.6
			M.I. MacLean	SNP	820*	5.0
					1,330	8.0
)55	24,856	59.6	M.K. Macmillan	Lab	8,487	57.3
			J.C. Frame	NL & C	6,315	42.7
					2,172	14.6
)59	25,178	64.2	M.K. Macmillan	Lab	8,663	53.6
			D. Macleod	NL & C	7,496	46.4
					1,167	7.2
)64	23,699	66.9	M.K. Macmillan	Lab	8,740	55.1
			D. Macleod	L	4,894	30.9
			C.A. Cameron	C	2,217	14.0
					3,846	24.2
)66	22,821	61.5	M.K. Macmillan	Lab	8,565	61.0
			C.A. Cameron	C	2,832	20.2
			J.F.M. Macleod	L	2,638	18.8
					5,733	40.8
)70	23,518	64.8	D.J. Stewart	SNP	6,568	43.1
			M.K. Macmillan	Lab	5,842	38.4
			R.M. Macleod	C	2,822	18.5
					726	4.7

ote:—

1950: Murray sought election as a 'Hearth and Home' candidate and advocated a policy of Scottish nationalism.

Election	Electors	T'out	Candidate	Party	Votes	%
1950	46,338	63.0	†J.H. Mackie	C	19,136	65
			A.E. Thompson	Lab	10,056	34
					9,080	31
1951	34,896	75.6	J.H. Mackie	C	16,261	61
			A.E. Thompson	Lab	6,949	26
			R.T. Johnston	L	3,174*	12
					9,312	35
1955	34,396	69.1	J.H. Mackie	C	15,893	66
			W.S. Gray	Lab	7,879	33
					8,014	33
[Death]						
1959 (9/4)	35,980	72.7	H.J. Brewis	C	13,204	50
			Hon. S.B. Mackay	L	6,721	25
			W. Cross	Lab	6,250	23
					6,483	24
1959	36,296	75.6	H.J. Brewis	C	15,454	56
			Hon. S.B. Mackay	L	6,412	23
			J. Pickett	Lab	5,590	20
					9,042	32
1964	37,331	73.8	H.J. Brewis	C	14,530	52
			Hon. S.B. Mackay	L	6,619	24
			J.P. Gordon	Lab	6,401	23
					7,911	28
1966	36,683	66.6	H.J. Brewis	C	15,137	62
			D. Douglas	Lab	9,283	38
					5,854	24
1970	38,669	72.0	H.J. Brewis	C	14,003	50
			A. Donaldson	SNP	5,723	20
			D. Douglas	Lab	5,665	20
			C.B.H. Scott	L	2,461*	8
					8,280	29

Election	Electors	T'out	Candidate	Party	Votes	%
1950	53,604	84.5	†J. Timmons	Lab	25,715	56.7
			N.J.K. Cadzow	C	19,605	43.3
					6,110	13.4
1951	54,814	86.0	J. Timmons	Lab	26,529	56.3
			N.J.K. Cadzow	C	20,591	43.7
					5,938	12.6
1955	54,628*	78.9	J. Timmons	Lab	23,365	54.2
			W.G. Greig	C	19,755	45.8
					3,610	8.4
1959	55,845	82.2	J. Timmons	Lab	25,119	54.7
			W.G. Greig	C	20,767	45.3
					4,352	9.4
1964	56,718	80.4	J. Hamilton	Lab	27,556	60.4
			J.B. Highgate	C	18,068	39.6
					9,488	20.8
1966	57,137	78.0	J. Hamilton	Lab	27,166	61.0
			J.B. Highgate	C	16,198	36.3
			T. Woods	Com	1,209*	2.7
					10,968	24.7
1970	63,976	75.5	J. Hamilton	Lab	26,431	54.8
			J.B. Highgate	C	15,720	32.5
			T. McAlpine	SNP	6,157	12.7
					10,711	22.3

Election	Electors	T'out	Candidate	Party	Votes	%
1950	51,242	81.7	†T. Fraser	Lab	29,292	70.
			R.C.M. Monteith	C	12,555	30.
					16,737	40.
1951	51,606	80.6	T. Fraser	Lab	28,591	68.
			R.C.M. Monteith	C	13,015	31.
					15,576	37.
1955	51,066	76.1	T. Fraser	Lab	26,187	67.
			G.L. Dalzell-Payne	C	12,661	32.
					13,526	34.
1959	51,995	79.9	T. Fraser	Lab	27,423	66.
			J.A. Davidson	C	11,510	27.
			D.R. Rollo	SNP	2,586*	6.
					15,913	38.
1964	52,588	77.5	T. Fraser	Lab	28,964	71.
			I. Docherty	C	11,806	29.
					17,158	42.
1966	53,393	73.3	Rt. Hon. T. Fraser	Lab	27,865	71.
			I.J.A. Dyer	C	11,289	28.
					16,576	42.

[Resignation on appointment as Chairman of the North of Scotland Hydro-Electric Board]

Election	Electors	T'out	Candidate	Party	Votes	%
1967 (2/11)	54,226	73.7	Mrs. W.M. Ewing	SNP	18,397	46.
			A. Wilson	Lab	16,598	41.
			I.J.A. Dyer	C	4,986*	12.
					1,799	4.
1970	60,034	80.0	A. Wilson	Lab	25,431	52.
			Mrs. W.M. Ewing	SNP	16,849	35.
			J.R. Harper	C	5,455*	11.
			H.C. Taylor	Ind L	295*	0.
					8,582	17.

ection	Electors	T'out	Candidate	Party	Votes	%
50	46,156	84.7	Lord Dunglass	C	19,890	50.9
			†T. Steele	Lab	19,205	49.1
					685	1.8

[Seat Vacant at Dissolution (Succession to the Peerage—Earl of Home)]

51	47,281	87.0	P.F. Maitland	C	21,467	52.2
			W.L. Taylor	Lab	19,674	47.8
					1,793	4.4
55	49,726	85.9	Hon. P.F. Maitland	C (Ind C) (C)	21,828	51.1
			J. Mackie	Lab	20,870	48.9
					958	2.2
59	57,094	87.2	Mrs. J.C.M. Hart	Lab	25,171	50.5
			Hon. P.F. Maitland	C	24,631	49.5
					540	1.0
64	64,165	86.0	Mrs. J.C.M. Hart	Lab	30,242	54.8
			W.H. Beale	C	24,922	45.2
					5,320	9.6
66	68,763	83.7	Mrs. J.C.M. Hart	Lab	29,735	51.7
			W.H. Beale	C	21,995	38.2
			H.C.D. Rankin	SNP	5,838*	10.1
					7,740	13.5
70	84,973	78.9	Rt. Hon. Judith C.M. Hart	Lab	30,194	45.1
			A.C.S. MacDougall	C	27,721	41.3
			H.C.D. Rankin	SNP	7,859*	11.7
			D. McDowall	Com	1,273*	1.9
					2,473	3.8

Election	Electors	T'out	Candidate	Party	Votes	%
1950	49,325	84.5	†A. Anderson	Lab	22,608	54.3
			Dr. A.D. Robertson	NL & C	14,183	34.0
			Dr. R.D. McIntyre	SNP	3,892*	9.3
			R.B. Henderson	Com	1,007*	2.4
					8,425	20.3
1951	48,732	84.7	A. Anderson	Lab	23,641	57.3
			N.A. Sloan	NL & C	17,650	42.7
					5,991	14.6
[Death]						
1954 (14/4)	48,193	70.5	G.M. Lawson	Lab	19,163	56.4
			N.A. Sloan	NL & C	13,334	39.3
			J. Gollan	Com	1,457*	4.3
					5,829	17.1
1955	48,875*	76.5	G.M. Lawson	Lab	20,147	53.9
			A.M.C. Hutchison	C	17,262	46.1
					2,885	7.8
1959	50,503	81.1	G.M. Lawson	Lab	22,009	53.7
			B. Brogan	C	17,613	43.0
			D. Murray	Ind	1,331*	3.3
					4,396	10.7
1964	50,209	78.9	G.M. Lawson	Lab	23,281	58.8
			J.J. Young	C	14,789	37.3
			J. Sneddon	Com	1,565*	3.9
					8,492	21.5
1966	49,909	74.7	G.M. Lawson	Lab	22,658	60.8
			J.J. Young	C	13,100	35.2
			J. Sneddon	Com	1,508*	4.0
					9,558	25.6
1970	52,739	73.7	G.M. Lawson	Lab	20,683	53.3
			Miss G.S. Bell	C	12,509	32.3
			Miss I. Lindsay	SNP	3,861*	9.9
			J. Sneddon	Com	1,829*	4.7
					8,174	21.0

Note:—

1959: Murray advocated a policy of Scottish nationalism. He was a member of the Liberal Party.

Election	Electors	T'out	Candidate	Party	Votes	%
1950	44,863	84.7	†Miss M.M. Herbison	Lab	22,162	58.3
			T.D. Ross	C	14,812	39.0
			R.F.B. Nelson	L	1,023*	2.7
					7,350	19.3
1951	44,855	85.4	Miss M.M. Herbison	Lab	22,304	58.2
			W.S. How	C	16,000	41.8
					6,304	16.4
1955	43,050*	81.5	Miss M.M. Herbison	Lab	20,307	57.9
			A.F. Hendry	C	14,784	42.1
					5,523	15.8
1959	43,505	82.8	Miss M.M. Herbison	Lab	21,152	58.7
			Hon. G.K.H. Younger	C	14,883	41.3
					6,269	17.4
1964	47,032	82.0	Miss M.M. Herbison	Lab	23,385	60.6
			J.A. Corrie	C	15,192	39.4
					8,193	21.2
1966	47,972	79.2	Rt. Hon. Margaret M. Herbison	Lab	23,160	60.9
			R.B.J.D. Black	C	14,857	39.1
					8,303	21.8
1970	54,450	77.9	J. Smith	Lab	21,982	51.8
			R.B.J.D. Black	C	16,963	40.0
			J.B. Hutchison	SNP	3,486*	8.2
					5,019	11.8

LANARKSHIRE, RUTHERGLEN [640]

Election	Electors	T'out	Candidate	Party	Votes	%
1950	44,044	86.1	†G. McAllister	Lab	18,779	49.5
			R.C. Brooman-White	C	18,084	47.7
			Mrs. C.B. Goodfellow	L	1,055*	2.8
					695	1.8
1951	44,167	87.7	R.C. Brooman-White	C	19,554	50.5
			G. McAllister	Lab	19,202	49.5
					352	1.0
1955	43,016	84.1	R.C. Brooman-White	C	19,141	52.9
			G. McAllister	Lab	17,040	47.1
					2,101	5.8
1959	42,833	85.8	R.C. Brooman-White	C	19,146	52.1
			E.J. Milne	Lab	17,624	47.9
					1,522	4.2
[Death]						
1964 (14/5)	41,511	82.0	J.G. MacKenzie	Lab	18,885	55.5
			I.M. Sproat	C	15,138	44.5
					3,747	11.0
1964	41,769	86.0	J.G. MacKenzie	Lab	18,892	52.6
			I.M. Sproat	C	15,391	42.8
			R.N. Armstrong	SNP	1,648*	4.6
					3,501	9.8
1966	40,870	84.2	J.G. MacKenzie	Lab	18,621	54.1
			J.H. Young	C	13,607	39.5
			A. Peacock	SNP	2,194*	6.4
					5,014	14.6
1970	42,607	79.7	J.G. MacKenzie	Lab	17,751	52.3
			P.C. Hutchison	C	14,710	43.3
			D.N. Livingstone	Ind	1,490*	4.4
					3,041	9.0

Note:—

1970: Livingstone advocated a policy of Scottish nationalism.

ʃection	Electors	T'out	Candidate	Party	Votes	%
ɓ55	55,307	78.1	D.J. Pryde	Lab	25,994	60.2
			J.A. Stodart	C	17,208	39.8
					8,786	20.4
[Ŝeat Vacant at Dissolution (Death)]						
ɓ59	58,092	81.3	J.M. Hill	Lab	28,457	60.2
			W.S. How	C	18,797	39.8
					9,660	20.4
ɓ64	61,689*	78.9	J.M. Hill	Lab	29,820	61.3
			D.A.P. Buchanan	C	18,861	38.7
					10,959	22.6
ɓ66	62,940	77.5	A. Eadie	Lab	27,608	56.7
			J.L.G. Lamotte	C	13,192	27.0
			A.W.S. Rae	SNP	7,974	16.3
					14,416	29.7
ɓ70	76,931	75.6	A. Eadie	Lab	30,802	52.9
			J.L.G. Lamotte	C	18,328	31.5
			G. Park	SNP	9,047	15.6
					12,474	21.4

Election	Electors	T'out	Candidate	Party	Votes	%
1950	61,668	82.9	†D.J. Pryde	Lab	26,966	52.8
			Rt. Hon. Florence Horsbrugh	C	19,778	38.7
			W.W. Gilmour	L	4,365*	8.5
					7,188	14.1
1951	63,213	83.8	D.J. Pryde	Lab	29,271	55.3
			J.A. Stodart	C	23,681	44.7
					5,590	10.6

This constituency was divided in 1955.

Election	Electors	T'out	Candidate	Party	Votes	%
1950	34,476	75.0	†Rt. Hon. J. Stuart	C	15,478	59.9
			R. Murray	Lab	10,383	40.1
					5,095	19.8
1951	35,370	74.5	Rt. Hon. J. Stuart	C	15,881	60.2
			D.T. Hutchison	Lab	10,487	39.8
					5,394	20.4
1955	35,663	67.9	Rt. Hon. J. Stuart	C	14,667	60.6
			M. Mackay	Lab	9,538	39.4
					5,129	21.2
1959	35,487	73.6	G.T.C. Campbell	C	13,742	52.7
			M. Mackay	Lab	6,539	25.0
			D.C. Macdonald	L	5,831	22.3
					7,203	27.7
1964	36,098	69.4	G.T.C. Campbell	C	12,741	50.8
			G.C. McIntosh	Lab	6,830	27.3
			J.F.M. Macleod	L	5,478	21.9
					5,911	23.5
1966	36,151	68.0	G.T.C. Campbell	C	11,842	48.1
			D. MacKenzie	Lab	8,384	34.1
			T.A. MacNair	L	4,368	17.8
					3,458	14.0
1970	39,242	72.2	G.T.C. Campbell	C	13,994	49.4
			T.A. Howe	SNP	7,885	27.8
			P. Talbot	Lab	6,452	22.8
					6,109	21.6

ORKNEY and SHETLAND [644]

Election	Electors	T'out	Candidate	Party	Votes	%
1950	29,131	67.7	J. Grimond	L	9,237	46.8
			†Sir B.H.H. Neven-Spence	C	6,281	31.9
			H.R. Leslie	Lab	4,198	21.3
					2,956	14.9
1951	29,603	69.0	J. Grimond	L	11,745	57.5
			A. Tennant	C	5,354	26.2
			M.A. Fairnie	Lab	3,335	16.3
					6,391	31.3
1955	27,868	66.1	J. Grimond	L	11,753	63.8
			J.W. Eunson	C	3,760	20.4
			E.P.S. Ramsay	Lab	2,914	15.8
					7,993	43.4
1959	26,435	71.3	J. Grimond	L	12,099	64.2
			R.H.W. Bruce	C	3,487	18.5
			R.S. McGowan	Lab	3,257	17.3
					8,612	45.7
1964	25,481	72.8	Rt. Hon. J. Grimond	L	11,604	62.6
			Dr. J.L. Firth	C	3,704	20.0
			I. MacInnes	Lab	3,232	17.4
					7,900	42.6
1966	24,927	65.2	Rt. Hon. J. Grimond	L	9,605	59.1
			Dr. J.L. Firth	C	3,630	22.3
			H. Lynch	Lab	3,021	18.6
					5,975	36.8
1970	24,707	68.0	Rt. Hon. J. Grimond	L	7,896	47.0
			Dr. J.L. Firth	C	5,364	31.9
			W.M. Reid	Lab	3,552	21.1
					2,532	15.1

Election	Electors	T'out	Candidate	Party	Votes	%
1950	35,897	76.9	†W.M. Snadden	C	15,299	55.4
			I.A.D. Millar	L	7,183	26.0
			D. MacLaren	Lab	5,124	18.6
					8,116	29.4
1951	35,176	73.2	W.M. Snadden	C	19,625	76.2
			Mrs. I. McGregor	Lab	6,124	23.8
					13,501	52.4
1955	34,219	70.5	W.G. Leburn	C	18,133	75.2
			J. Bayne	Lab	5,975	24.8
					12,158	50.4
1959	33,582	71.0	W.G. Leburn	C	16,256	68.2
			J.G. MacKenzie	Lab	4,008	16.8
			A. Donaldson	SNP	3,568	15.0
					12,248	51.4
[Death]						
1963 (7/11)	32,428	76.1	Rt. Hon. Sir A.F. Douglas-Home	C	14,147	57.4
			I.A.D. Millar	L	4,819	19.5
			A. Forrester	Lab	3,752	15.2
			A. Donaldson	SNP	1,801*	7.3
			J.W.S. Smith	Ind C	78*	0.3
			W.G. Rushton	Ind	45*	0.2
			R. Wort	L & DBCP	23*	0.1
					9,328	37.9
1964	32,931	75.9	Rt. Hon. Sir A.F. Douglas-Home	C	16,659	66.6
			A. Forrester	Lab	4,687	18.8
			A. Donaldson	SNP	3,522	14.1
			C.M. Grieve	Com	127*	0.5
					11,972	47.8
1966	32,412	73.5	Rt. Hon. Sir A.F. Douglas-Home	C	14,466	60.8
			A. Donaldson	SNP	4,884	20.5
			B.K. Parnell	Lab	4,461	18.7
					9,582	40.3
1970	33,944	74.1	Rt. Hon. Sir A.F. Douglas-Home	C	14,434	57.3
			Mrs. E.Y. Whitley	SNP	4,670	18.6
			D.F. Leach	Lab	3,827	15.2
			J.M. Calder	L	2,228*	8.9
					9,764	38.7

Notes:—

1963: Douglas-Home was Prime Minister and First Lord of the Treasury.

Rushton retired on the eve of poll in favour of Millar.

1964: A petition was lodged relating to this election but was dismissed.

Election	Electors	T'out	Candidate	Party	Votes	%
1950	54,296	81.6	†A. Gomme-Duncan	C	24,850	56.1
			W. Hughes	Lab	11,706	26.4
			D. Stewart	SNP	4,118*	9.3
			J.L. Wilson	L	3,623*	8.2
					13,144	29.7
1951	55,507	78.3	A. Gomme-Duncan	C	25,798	59.4
			N. McBride	Lab	11,167	25.7
			Dr. R.D. McIntyre	SNP	6,479	14.9
					14,631	33.7
1955	55,054	73.5	A. Gomme-Duncan	C	22,948	56.7
			Dr. R.D. McIntyre	SNP	9,227	22.8
			J.B. Urquhart	Lab	8,313	20.5
					13,721	33.9
1959	55,064	75.6	I. MacArthur	C	24,217	58.2
			Dr. R.D. McIntyre	SNP	9,637	23.1
			T.W. Moore	Lab	7,781	18.7
					14,580	35.1
1964	54,582	75.6	I. MacArthur	C	23,912	57.9
			F.L. Forrester	Lab	10,184	24.7
			Dr. R.D. McIntyre	SNP	7,186	17.4
					13,728	33.2
1966	54,159	72.3	I. MacArthur	C	22,129	56.5
			J. Jennings	Lab	10,911	27.9
			M.B. Shaw	SNP	6,128	15.6
					11,218	28.6
1970	56,984	73.6	I. MacArthur	C	21,860	52.0
			Miss V.A. Friel	Lab	9,972	23.8
			D.C. Murray	SNP	7,112	17.0
			R.A.L. Livsey	L	3,011*	7.2
					11,888	28.2

Election	Electors	T'out	Candidate	Party	Votes	%
1950	61,325	78.9	†E.G.R. Lloyd	C	31,650	65.4
			W.L. Taylor	Lab	16,716	34.6
					14,934	30.8
1951	59,330*	81.7	E.G.R. Lloyd	C	31,908	65.8
			D.J. Phillips	Lab	16,588	34.2
					15,320	31.6
1955	58,024	78.1	Sir E.G.R. Lloyd	C	30,959	68.3
			D.J. Phillips	Lab	14,371	31.7
					16,588	36.6
1959	61,060	82.9	Miss M.B. Harvie Anderson	C	29,672	58.7
			A.J. Houston	Lab	14,579	28.8
			D.M.H. Starforth	L	6,339	12.5
					15,093	29.9
1964	64,146	82.6	Miss M.B. Harvie Anderson	C	27,846	52.6
			J.S. Gordon	Lab	16,503	31.1
			D.M.H. Starforth	L	8,655	16.3
					11,343	21.5
1966	65,971	79.9	Miss M.B. Harvie Anderson	C	28,017	53.1
			R. Lochrie	Lab	17,426	33.1
			J.W. McHardy	L	7,252	13.8
					10,591	20.0
1970	73,510	76.2	Miss M.B. Harvie Anderson	C	29,163	52.0
			Mrs. J.A. Carnegie	Lab	16,062	28.7
			Mrs. O.M. Watt	L	7,053	12.6
			J.M. Buchanan	SNP	3,733*	6.7
					13,101	23.3

Election	Electors	T'out	Candidate	Party	Votes	%
1950	49,754	77.6	†Hon. J.S. Maclay	NL & C	20,810	53.!
			†T. Scollan	Lab	17,780	46.
					3,030	7.!
1951	47,187*	84.9	Hon. J.S. Maclay	NL & C	21,546	53.!
			B. Millan	Lab	18,493	46.:
					3,053	7.!
1955	46,407*	83.0	Rt. Hon. J.S. Maclay	NL & C	21,283	55.:
			Dr. J.D. Mabon	Lab/Co-op	17,243	44.!
					4,040	10.!
1959	47,395	82.6	Rt. Hon. J.S. Maclay	NL & C	20,959	53.!
			C. Minihan	Lab	18,206	46.!
					2,753	7.!

[Seat Vacant at Dissolution (Elevation to the Peerage—Viscount Muirshiel)]

Election	Electors	T'out	Candidate	Party	Votes	%
1964	51,018*	82.9	N.F. Buchan	Lab	19,518	46.
			R.P. Paton	C	18,507	43.!
			G.E. McFadyean	L	4,253*	10.
					1,011	2.:
1966	53,796	81.6	N.F. Buchan	Lab	23,849	54.:
			R.P. Paton	C	20,060	45.
					3,789	8.!
1970	60,250	79.5	N.F. Buchan	Lab	22,999	48.!
			A.M. Fletcher	C	20,695	43.:
			W.J.A. Macartney	SNP	4,195*	8.!
					2,304	4.!

Election	Electors	T'out	Candidate	Party	Votes	%
1950	47,430	82.1	A.J.F. Macdonald	L	15,347	39.4
			†Lord William Scott	C	14,191	36.4
			L.P. Thomas	Lab	9,413	24.2
					1,156	3.0
1951	47,614	84.9	C.E.M. Donaldson	C	16,438	40.6
			A.J.F. Macdonald	L	15,609	38.6
			T. White	Lab	8,395	20.8
					829	2.0

This constituency was incorporated into the new constituency of Roxburghshire, Selkirkshire and Peeblesshire in 1955.

Election	Electors	T'out	Candidate	Party	Votes	%
1955	56,907	80.8	C.E.M. Donaldson	C	21,925	47.7
			S.E. Graham	L	14,755	32.1
			L.A. Morrison	Lab	9,296	20.2
					7,170	15.6
1959	55,459	80.0	C.E.M. Donaldson	C	22,275	50.2
			J.M. MacCormick	L	12,762	28.8
			T. Dalyell	Lab	9,336	21.0
					9,513	21.4
1964	53,753	82.2	C.E.M. Donaldson	C	18,924	42.8
			D.M.S. Steel	L	17,185	38.9
			R.K. Murray	Lab	7,007	15.8
			A.J.C. Kerr	SNP	1,093*	2.5
					1,739	3.9
[Death]						
1965 (24/3)	53,310	82.2	D.M.S. Steel	L	21,549	49.2
			R.L. McEwen	C	16,942	38.6
			R.K. Murray	Lab	4,936*	11.3
			A.J.C. Kerr	Ind	411*	0.9
					4,607	10.6
1966	53,180	84.9	D.M.S. Steel	L	20,607	45.6
			I.J. McIntyre	C	18,396	40.8
			C. Lindsay	Lab	6,131	13.6
					2,211	4.8
1970	57,180	80.8	D.M.S. Steel	L	19,524	42.3
			R. Fairgrieve	C	18,974	41.1
			L. Griffiths	Lab	4,454*	9.6
			H. Hastie	SNP	3,147*	6.8
			W.R. Cassell	Ind	103*	0.2
					550	1.2

Notes:—

1965: Kerr advocated a policy of Scottish nationalism.

1970: Cassell was opposed to the Abortion Act, 1967.

Election	Electors	T'out	Candidate	Party	Votes	%
1950	48,767	83.4	†Rt. Hon. A. Woodburn	Lab	22,980	56.5
			Hon. S.D. Loch	C	13,630	33.5
			C.H. Johnston	L	4,078*	10.0
					9,350	23.0
1951	50,142	85.7	Rt. Hon. A. Woodburn	Lab	25,231	58.7
			Hon. S.D. Loch	C	17,727	41.3
					7,504	17.4
1955	50,342*	79.8	Rt. Hon. A. Woodburn	Lab	23,588	58.7
			R.C. Aitchison	C	16,579	41.3
					7,009	17.4
1959	52,200	80.7	Rt. Hon. A. Woodburn	Lab	25,004	59.3
			R.C. Aitchison	C	17,132	40.7
					7,872	18.6
1964	52,424	79.8	Rt. Hon. A. Woodburn	Lab	23,927	57.2
			A. MacDonald	C	12,815	30.6
			C.D. Drysdale	SNP	5,106*	12.2
					11,112	26.6
1966	52,640	77.5	Rt. Hon. A. Woodburn	Lab	22,557	55.3
			A. MacDonald	C	10,037	24.6
			C.D. Drysdale	SNP	8,225	20.1
					12,520	30.7
1970	61,811	75.7	R.G. Douglas	Lab/Co-op	23,729	50.7
			J. Fairlie	C	13,178	28.2
			I.C.H. Macdonald	SNP	7,243	15.5
			R.E. Bell	L	2,640*	5.6
					10,551	22.5

Election	Electors	T'out	Candidate	Party	Votes	%
1950	41,817	85.7	†A. Balfour	Lab	19,930	55.6
			Miss M.B. Harvie Anderson	C	15,894	44.4
					4,036	11.3
1951	43,027	86.7	A. Balfour	Lab	20,893	56.0
			Miss M.B. Harvie Anderson	C	16,396	44.0
					4,497	12.0
1955	43,098*	80.4	A. Balfour	Lab	18,935	54.6
			W.A. Gay	C	15,721	45.4
					3,214	9.3
1959	43,686	83.6	W. Baxter	Lab (Ind Lab) (Lab)	21,008	57.5
			W.A. Gay	C	15,497	42.5
					5,511	15.0
1964	44,315	81.2	W. Baxter	Lab	21,144	58.8
			J.G.C. Barr	C	14,834	41.2
					6,310	17.6
1966	43,728	82.4	W. Baxter	Lab	17,513	48.6
			Dr. R.D. McIntyre	SNP	9,381	26.0
			J.D.M. Hardie	C	9,148	25.4
					8,132	22.6
1970	48,885	79.0	W. Baxter	Lab	18,884	48.9
			J. Glen	C	11,465	29.7
			Dr. R.D. McIntyre	SNP	8,279	21.4
					7,419	19.2

Election	Electors	T'out	Candidate	Party	Votes	%
1950	56,789	79.1	†Rt. Hon. G. Mathers	Lab	27,236	60.6
			W.M. Younger	C	15,999	35.6
			W.M. Hynd	Ind	1,039*	2.3
			J. Borrowman	Com	664*	1.5
					11,237	25.0
1951	56,259	84.9	J. Taylor	Lab	28,906	60.5
			H.E. Atkins	C	18,854	39.5
					10,052	21.0
1955	57,045	75.4	J. Taylor	Lab	25,654	59.7
			W.R. Grieve	C	17,347	40.3
					8,307	19.4
1959	58,457	77.9	J. Taylor	Lab	27,454	60.3
			W.I. Stewart	C	18,083	39.7
					9,371	20.6
[Death]						
1962 (14/6)	58,856	71.1	T. Dalyell	Lab	21,266	50.9
			W.C. Wolfe	SNP	9,750	23.3
			W.I. Stewart	C	4,784*	11.4
			D. Bryce	L	4,537*	10.8
			G. McLennan	Com	1,511*	3.6
					11,516	27.6
1964	62,328	79.5	T. Dalyell	Lab	24,933	50.4
			W.C. Wolfe	SNP	15,087	30.4
			R.A.G. Stuart	C	8,919	18.0
			Mrs. I. Swan	Com	610*	1.2
					9,846	20.0
1966	63,967	79.6	T. Dalyell	Lab	26,662	52.4
			W.C. Wolfe	SNP	17,955	35.3
			Dr. D.L. MacKinnon	C	5,726*	11.2
			Mrs. I. Swan	Com	567*	1.1
					8,707	17.1
1970	72,367	76.7	T. Dalyell	Lab	29,360	52.9
			W.C. Wolfe	SNP	15,620	28.2
			Earl of Ancram	C	10,048	18.1
			C. Bett	Com	459*	0.8
					13,740	24.7

Note:—

1950: Hynd advocated a policy of Scottish nationalism.

NORTHERN IRELAND — BOROUGHS

BELFAST, EAST [654]

Election	Electors	T'out	Candidate	Party	Votes	%
1950	61,561	76.6	A.J. McKibbin	C	29,844	63.3
			T.W. Boyd	Lab	17,338	36.7
					12,506	26.6
1951	62,798	74.5	A.J. McKibbin	C	28,881	61.7
			T.W. Boyd	Lab	17,910	38.3
					10,971	23.4
1955	61,258	70.4	A.J. McKibbin	C	26,938	62.5
			T.W. Boyd	Lab	13,041	30.2
			L. Mulcahy	SF	3,156*	7.3
					13,897	32.3
[Death]						
1959 (19/3)	58,388	57.9	S.R. McMaster	C	19,524	57.8
			J.S. Gardner	Lab	14,264	42.2
					5,260	15.6
1959	58,663	75.2	S.R. McMaster	C	26,510	60.1
			J.S. Gardner	Lab	16,412	37.2
			B. Boswell	SF	1,204*	2.7
					10,098	22.9
1964	58,196	72.5	S.R. McMaster	C	24,804	58.8
			S.J. Watt	Lab	15,555	36.9
			D. McConnell	Rep	1,827*	4.3
					9,249	21.9
1966	57,077	68.2	S.R. McMaster	C	21,283	54.7
			R.M. McBirney	Lab	17,650	45.3
					3,633	9.4
1970	59,524	75.7	S.R. McMaster	C	26,778	59.5
			D.W. Bleakley	Lab	18,259	40.5
					8,519	19.0

BELFAST, NORTH [655]

Election	Electors	T'out	Candidate	Party	Votes	%
1950	75,563	74.8	H.M. Hyde	C	36,412	64.4
			W.J. Leeburn	Lab	20,146	35.6
					16,266	28.8
1951	76,243	75.7	H.M. Hyde	C	34,995	60.7
			J. Morrow	Lab	22,685	39.3
					12,310	21.4
1955	76,990	69.3	H.M. Hyde	C	33,745	63.3
			W.R. Boyd	Lab	15,065	28.2
			F. McGlade	SF	4,534*	8.5
					18,680	35.1
1959	74,494	71.1	W.S. Mills	C	32,173	60.7
			J.W. McDowell	Lab	18,640	35.2
			F. McGlade	SF	2,156*	4.1
					13,533	25.5
1964	72,400	69.5	W.S. Mills	C	29,976	59.6
			J.W. McDowell	Lab	17,564	34.9
			F. McGlade	Rep	2,743*	5.5
					12,412	24.7
1966	71,434	65.5	W.S. Mills	C	26,891	57.4
			D.A. Overend	Lab	19,927	42.6
					6,964	14.8
1970	75,740	78.1	W.S. Mills	C	28,668	48.5
			J. Sharkey	Lab	18,894	31.9
			Rev. W.J. Beattie	Prot U	11,173	18.9
			J.D. McKeague	Ind C	441*	0.7
					9,774	16.6

BELFAST, SOUTH [656]

Election	Electors	T'out	Candidate	Party	Votes	%
1950	66,486	69.3	†C.H. Gage	C	34,620	75.2
			J.E. McKernan	Lab	11,428	24.8
					23,192	50.4
1951	66,212	73.8	C.H. Gage	C	37,046	75.8
			R. McBrinn	Lab	11,815	24.2
					25,231	51.6
[Resignation]						
1952	65,196	47.1	Sir D.C. Campbell	C	23,067	75.1
(4/11)			S. Napier	Lab	7,655	24.9
					15,412	50.2
1955	64,844	65.7	Sir D.C. Campbell	C	33,392	78.5
			E. Brown	Lab	7,508	17.6
			P. Kearney	SF	1,679*	3.9
					25,884	60.9
1959	59,864	72.1	Sir D.C. Campbell	C	30,164	69.9
			N. Searight	Lab	9,318	21.6
			Miss S.M. Murnaghan	L	3,253*	7.5
			B. O'Reilly	SF	434*	1.0
					20,846	48.3
[Death]						
1963	57,864	48.3	R.J. Pounder	C	17,989	64.3
(22/10)			N. Searight	Lab	7,209	25.8
			A. Hamilton	L	2,774*	9.9
					10,780	38.5
1964	57,558	68.3	R.J. Pounder	C	27,422	69.8
			J.H. Barkley	Lab	8,792	22.4
			Miss J.B. Rosenfield	L	1,941*	4.9
			R. McKnight	Rep	1,159*	2.9
					18,630	47.4
1966	56,381	63.3	R.J. Pounder	C	23,329	65.4
			J.E. Holmes	Lab	12,364	34.6
					10,965	30.8
1970	57,112	68.4	R.J. Pounder	C	27,523	70.4
			J. Coulthard	Lab	11,567	29.6
					15,956	40.8

Election	Electors	T'out	Candidate	Party	Votes	%
1950	78,896	83.6	Rev. J.G. MacManaway	C	33,917	51.!
			†J. Beattie	Irish LP	30,539	46.:
			J. Steele	SF	1,482*	2.:
					3,378	5.:

[Disqualification of MacManaway who at the time of his election was a Minister of the Church of Irelar

Election	Electors	T'out	Candidate	Party	Votes	%
1950	78,459	79.9	T.L. Teevan	C	31,796	50.:
(29/11)			J. Beattie	Irish LP	30,883	49.:
					913	1.4
1951	78,828	84.1	J. Beattie	Irish LP	33,174	50.(
			T.L. Teevan	C	33,149	50.(
					25	0.(
1955	78,589	74.7	Mrs. F.P.A. McLaughlin	C	34,191	58.:
			J. Beattie	Irish LP	16,050	27.:
			E. Boyce	SF	8,447	14.4
					18,141	31.#
1959	73,405	72.7	Mrs. F.P.A. McLaughlin	C	28,898	54.1
			J. Brennan	NI Ind Lab	20,062	37.#
			T.A. Heenan	SF	4,416*	8.:
					8,836	16.!
1964	69,399	74.7	J.A. Kilfedder	C	21,337	41.:
			H. Diamond	Rep LP	14,678	28.:
			W.R. Boyd	Lab	12,571	24.:
			L. McMillan	Rep	3,256*	6.:
					6,659	12.:
1966	67,575	74.8	G. Fitt	Rep LP	26,292	52.(
			J.A. Kilfedder	C	24,281	48.(
					2,011	4.(
1970	68,665	84.6	G. Fitt	Rep LP (SDLP)	30,649	52.8
			B.J.H. McRoberts	C ·	27,451	47.:
					3,198	5.#

Note:—

1950: MacManaway's disqualification is detailed in House of Commons Papers, 1950
(29/11) (Cmd. 8067) xviii, 415.

NORTHERN IRELAND —— COUNTIES

ANTRIM, NORTH [658]

Election	Electors	T'out	Candidate	Party	Votes	%
1950			†Rt. Hon. Sir R.W.H. O'Neill, Bt.	C	Unopp.	
1951			Rt. Hon. Sir R.W.H. O'Neill, Bt.	C	Unopp.	
[Resignation]						
1952 (27/10)			P.R.H. O'Neill	C	Unopp.	
1955	67,315	72.2	Hon. P.R.H. O'Neill	C	41,763	86.0
			J. Dougan	SF	6,809	14.0
					34,954	72.0
1959	69,880	64.5	H.M. Clark	C	42,807	94.9
			J. Dougan	SF	2,280*	5.1
					40,527	89.8
1964	70,762	63.3	H.M. Clark	C	40,372	90.1
			S. Caughey	Rep	4,424*	9.9
					35,948	80.2
1966	72,039	56.7	H.M. Clark	C	31,927	78.1
			R.G. Moore	L	8,941	21.9
					22,986	56.2
1970	79,930	73.4	Rev. I.R.K. Paisley	Prot U	24,130	41.1
			H.M. Clark	C	21,451	36.6
			P.J. McHugh	Lab	6,476*	11.0
			A. McDonnell	Nat DP	4,312*	7.4
			R.G. Moore	L	2,269*	3.9
					2,679	4.5

Election	Electors	T'out	Candidate	Party	Votes	%
1950	77,499	63.3	†Prof. D.L. Savory	C	41,023	83.6
			E. Brown	Lab	8,068	16.4
					32,955	67.2
1951			Prof. D.L. Savory	C	Unopp.	
1955	84,939	65.3	S.K. Cunningham	C	50,347	90.7
			M. Traynor	SF	5,155*	9.3
					45,192	81.4
1959	93,655	59.3	S.K. Cunningham	C	52,786	95.1
			M. Traynor	SF	2,745*	4.9
					50,041	90.2
1964	105,304	64.3	Sir S.K. Cunningham, Bt.	C	47,325	69.9
			S.A. Stewart	Lab	16,531	24.4
			L.F. Wilson	Rep	3,830*	5.7
					30,794	45.5
1966	113,645	55.9	Sir S.K. Cunningham, Bt.	C	40,840	64.3
			S.A. Stewart	Lab	22,672	35.7
					18,168	28.6
1970	143,274	68.0	J.H. Molyneaux	C	59,589	61.2
			R. Johnston	Lab	19,971	20.5
			T.H. Caldwell	Ind C	10,938*	11.2
			D.J. MacAllister	Nat DP	6,037*	6.2
			R.A.M. Smith	L	913*	0.9
					39,618	40.7

ARMAGH [660]

lection	Electors	T'out	Candidate	Party	Votes	%
950			†J.R.E. Harden	C	Unopp.	
951			J.R.E. Harden	C	Unopp.	
Resignation]						
954 (20/11)			C.W. Armstrong	C	Unopp.	
955	72,492	82.7	C.W. Armstrong	C	38,617	64.4
			T. MacCurtain	SF	21,363	35.6
					17,254	28.8
959	73,416	64.2	J.E. Maginnis	C	40,325	85.5
			J. Lynch	SF	6,823	14.5
					33,502	71.0
964	74,184	73.0	J.E. Maginnis	C	35,223	65.1
			J. Lynch	Rep	12,432	22.9
			S.D. Ewart	Lab	6,523*	12.0
					22,791	42.2
966	76,111	63.3	J.E. Maginnis	C	34,687	72.0
			C.E. McGleenan	Rep	13,467	28.0
					21,220	44.0
970	86,847	78.5	J.E. Maginnis	C	37,667	55.3
			H. Lewis	Unity	21,696	31.8
			J.E. Holmes	Lab	8,781	12.9
					15,971	23.5

Election	Electors	T'out	Candidate	Party	Votes	%
1950	77,316	68.1	†Sir W.D. Smiles	C	41,810	79.4
			A.H. McElroy	Lab	10,836	20.6
					30,974	58.8
1951	80,921	65.7	Sir W.D. Smiles	C	43,285	81.4
			A.H. McElroy	Lab	9,914	18.6
					33,371	62.8
[Death]						
1953 (15/4)			Mrs. P. Ford	C	Unopp.	
1955	84,968	61.1	G.B.H. Currie	C	50,315	96.8
			J. Campbell	SF	1,637*	3.2
					48,678	93.6
1959	89,886	58.8	G.B.H. Currie	C	51,773	98.0
			J. Campbell	SF	1,039*	2.0
					50,734	96.0
1964	97,151	63.1	G.B.H. Currie	C	45,091	73.5
			E. Bell	Lab	11,571	18.9
			Rev. A.H. McElroy	L	3,797*	6.2
			P.J. McGrattan	Rep	855*	1.4
					33,520	54.6
1966	100,755	48.9	G.B.H. Currie	C	38,706	78.5
			Miss S.M. Murnaghan	L	10,582	21.5
					28,124	57.0
1970	121,196	66.6	J.A. Kilfedder	C	55,679	69.1
			K. Young	Lab	14,246	17.6
			Dr. R.S. Nixon	Ind C	6,408*	7.9
			J.R. McGladdery	Ind	3,321*	4.1
			H. Simonds-Gooding	L	1,076*	1.3
					41,433	51.5

Note:—

1970: McGladdery sought election as an 'Independent Moderate' candidate.

Election	Electors	T'out	Candidate	Party	Votes	%
1950	79,125	76.7	L.P.S. Orr	C	38,508	63.5
			J. Macgougan	Irish LP	22,176	36.5
					16,332	27.0
1951	79,001	82.0	L.P.S. Orr	C	37,789	58.3
			G.F. Annesley	N	26,976	41.7
					10,813	16.6
1955	77,832	73.9	L.P.S. Orr	C	37,921	65.9
			K. O'Rourke	SF	19,624	34.1
					18,297	31.8
1959	77,627	56.4	L.P.S. Orr	C	36,875	84.2
			K. O'Rourke	SF	6,928	15.8
					29,947	68.4
1964	77,391	72.1	L.P.S. Orr	C	32,922	59.0
			G. Mussen	Rep	11,031	19.8
			S. Thompson	Lab	6,260*	11.2
			H. Simonds-Gooding	L	5,610*	10.0
					21,891	39.2
1966	78,096	65.8	L.P.S. Orr	C	32,876	63.9
			J.G. Quinn	L	9,586	18.7
			G. Mussen	Rep	8,917	17.4
					23,290	45.2
1970	87,079	73.9	L.P.S. Orr	C	34,894	54.3
			H.J. Golding	Unity	21,676	33.7
			J.G. Quinn	L	7,747*	12.0
					13,218	20.6

Note:—

1951: Annesley sought election as a 'Protestant Republican' although he was not supported by Sinn Fein or any other republican organisation. His campaign was conducted under the auspicies of nationalist organisations and the 'label' Nationalist has been used as it would appear to be the most accurate description of his sponsorship.

FERMANAGH and SOUTH TYRONE [663]

Election	Electors	T'out	Candidate	Party	Votes	%
1950	67,424	92.1	C. Healy	N	32,188	51.9
			H.S.C. Richardson	C	29,877	48.1
					2,311	3.8
1951	67,219	93.4	C. Healy	N	32,717	52.1
			F.G. Patterson	C	30,082	47.9
					2,635	4.2
1955	65,770	92.4	P.C. Clarke	SF	30,529	50.2
			R.G. Grosvenor	C	30,268	49.8
					261	0.4
1959	64,022	61.6	R.G. Grosvenor	C	32,080	81.4
			J.H. Martin	SF	7,348	18.6
					24,732	62.8
1964	63,642	85.6	Marquess of Hamilton	C	30,010	55.1
			A. Molloy	Rep	16,138	29.6
			G.E. FitzHerbert	L	6,006*	11.0
			B.W. Gamble	Lab	2,339*	4.3
					13,872	25.5
1966	63,188	86.0	Marquess of Hamilton	C	29,352	54.0
			J.J. Donnelly	Unity	14,645	26.9
			P.R.C. Brady	Rep	10,370	19.1
					14,707	27.1
1970	70,381	91.2	F. McManus	Unity	32,813	51.1
			Marquess of Hamilton	C	31,390	48.9
					1,423	2.2

Note:—

1955: As the result of an election petition, the Court found that Clarke (who was serving a term of ten years imprisonment for treason) was disqualified and that Grosvenor had been duly elected as Member of Parliament for the constituency.

LONDONDERRY [664]

lection	Electors	T'out	Candidate	Party	Votes	%
950	72,515	80.6	†Sir R.D. Ross, Bt.	C	36,602	62.6
			H.J. McAteer	SF	21,880	37.4
					14,722	25.2

[Resignation on appointment as Northern Ireland Government Agent in London]

| 951 (19/5) | | | W. Wellwood | C | Unopp. | |

| 951 | | | W. Wellwood | C | Unopp. | |

955	71,297	77.6	R. Chichester-Clark	C	35,673	64.5
			M. Canning	SF	19,640	35.5
					16,033	29.0

959	73,241	70.2	R. Chichester-Clark	C	37,529	73.0
			M. Canning	SF	13,872	27.0
					23,657	46.0

964	76,918	76.5	R. Chichester-Clark	C	37,700	64.1
			H.J. McAteer	Rep	21,123	35.9
					16,577	28.2

966	78,191	76.4	R. Chichester-Clark	C	34,729	58.1
			P.J. Gormley	N	22,167	37.1
			N. Gillespie	Rep	2,860*	4.8
					12,562	21.0

970	90,302	81.6	R. Chichester-Clark	C	39,141	53.1
			E.G. McAteer	Unity	27,006	36.6
			E.J. McCann	Ind Lab	7,565*	10.3
					12,135	16.5

Note:—

1970: McCann was the nominee of the Londonderry branch of the Northern Ireland Labour Party but he was refused endorsement as an official candidate of the party.

(North Tyrone, and the Magherafelt rural district of County Londonderry)

Election	Electors	T'out	Candidate	Party	Votes	%
1950	68,535	91.6	†A. Mulvey	N	33,023	52.6
			J.M. Shearer	C	29,721	47.4
					3,302	5.2
1951	68,412	91.8	M. O'Neill	N	33,094	52.7
			J.M. Shearer	C	29,701	47.3
					3,393	5.4
1955	66,847	88.6	T.J. Mitchell	SF	29,737	50.2
			C. Beattie	C	29,477	49.8
					260	0.4

[Disqualification of Mitchell who at the time of his election was serving a term of ten years imprisonment]

1955	66,847	89.7	T.J. Mitchell	SF	30,392	50.7
(11/8)			C. Beattie	C	29,586	49.3
					806	1.4

[Disqualification of Beattie who at the time of his election held an office of profit under the Crown]

1956	66,891	88.4	G. Forrest	Ind C (C)	28,605	48.3
(8/5)			T.J. Mitchell	SF	24,124	40.8
			M. O'Neill	N	6,421*	10.9
					4,481	7.5
1959	66,607	71.0	G. Forrest	C	33,093	70.0
			T.J. Mitchell	SF	14,170	30.0
					18,923	40.0
1964	67,647	85.1	G. Forrest	C	29,715	51.6
			T.J. Mitchell	Rep	22,810	39.6
			P.J. McGarvey	Lab	5,053*	8.8
					6,905	12.0
1966	67,796	83.9	G. Forrest	C	29,728	52.2
			T.J. Mitchell	Rep	27,168	47.8
					2,560	4.4

[Death]

1969	68,973	91.5	Miss J.B. Devlin	Unity	33,648	53.3
(17/4)			Mrs. A. Forrest	C	29,437	46.7
					4,211	6.6
1970	77,143	91.4	Miss J.B. Devlin	Unity	37,739	53.5
			W.N.J. Thornton	C	31,810	45.1
			M. Cunningham	Ind	771*	1.1
			P.F. O'Neill	Ind	198*	0.3
					5,929	8.4

Notes:—

1955: At the time of the election Mitchell was serving a term of imprisonment for treason and he was disqualified from being a Member of Parliament (see House of Commons Papers, 1955-56 (32) xxxii, 1131). A petition was not lodged and in due course the House of Commons authorised a new writ to be issued to fill the vacancy. Mitchell was once again nominated and elected but this time a petition was lodged and the Court found that as Mitchell was disqualified, Beattie had been duly elected as Member of Parliament for the constituency.

1956: Beattie's disqualification is detailed in House of Commons Papers, 1955-56 (145) vi, 457 and 1955-56 (145-1) vi, 463.

1969: Miss Devlin was the youngest woman ever to have been elected to the House of Commons. She was twenty-one years of age and had been born on April 23, 1947.

1970: Miss Devlin claimed to be the Unity candidate but the circumstances of her re-adoption are confused. Prior to the election she had announced that she would not seek re-election but subsequently changed her mind and decided to contest the seat. A meeting at Omagh on May 26 decided that there was no need to call a 'Unity convention' and endorsed her candidature. Despite this decision, it was announced on June 1 that a convention would be held at Cookstown on June 7 but this was subsequently cancelled at the last minute. After the declaration of the result Miss Devlin was quoted as saying: "Mid-Ulster may not have 37,000 socialists, but it has got a socialist Member of Parliament and before very long it will have a strong socialist organisation in the constituency". Subsequently an Independent Socialist Association was formed by her supporters.

Cunningham sought election as an 'Independent Unity and Farmers' candidate. He had nationalist sympathies.

O'Neill sought election as a 'National Socialist' candidate. He retired on the eve of poll in favour of Miss Devlin.

APPENDICES

CONSTITUENCY SWINGS

The swing (the average of the Conservative % gain and Labour % loss) between General Elections is given only where Conservative and Labour candidates shared the top two places in the poll at succeeding elections. Where this did not occur the letters NC have been used to indicate that the swing has not been calculated. By-election figures are not included here but will be found in *British Parliamentary Election Statistics 1918-1970*, pp. 29-38.

In cases where a major boundary change would have made the calculation of swing misleading, no figure is given but two asterisks (**) have been inserted. Minor boundary changes which took place in 1951, 1955, 1959 and 1964 are indicated by one asterisk (*) placed after the swing figure to denote that there may be a slight distortion of the percentage due to small changes in the constituency boundary. A dash (−) indicates that the constituency had either been abolished or not yet created.

As indicated above, the swing shown throughout this Appendix is to the Conservatives and a minus sign thus indicates a swing to Labour. It is the conventional calculation of swing based on the total votes cast in the constituency and not only on the votes cast for Conservative and Labour candidates (known as the "two-party swing").

In calculating the swing by computer, the number of votes rather than the percentage of votes for each candidate have been used. This procedure avoids the accumulation of rounding errors and provides a more precise swing figure than would be the case if the percentages (rounded to one decimal place) given in the pages of constituency results had been used.

The final column of the Appendix shows the total overall swing in each constituency.

LONDON—BOROUGHS

CONSTITUENCY	1950-1951	1951-1955	1955-1959	1959-1964	1964-1966	1966-1970	Total
BARONS COURT	−	−	1.3	−2.9	−3.5	3.3	−1.8
BATTERSEA							
North	−0.5	0.7	3.9	−1.5	−4.3	4.8	3.1
South	1.2	0.4	1.9	−6.1	−4.2	3.5	−3.3
BERMONDSEY	−1.9	0.8	3.9	−2.4	−1.3	3.7	2.8
BETHNAL GREEN	NC	**	4.3	−1.1	−3.1	5.8	5.9
CAMBERWELL							
Dulwich	1.8	1.1	0.4	−5.1	−3.7	5.6	0.1
Peckham	−0.2	2.1	2.5	1.0	−7.8	4.5	2.1
CHELSEA	1.5	3.5	0.3	−5.5	−2.3	4.9	2.4
CITIES of LONDON and							
WESTMINSTER	0.0	3.4	0.1	−6.5	−4.1	4.2	−2.9
DEPTFORD	1.5	−0.6	3.8	−4.7	−3.6	4.5	0.9
FULHAM	−	−	1.4	−3.3	−3.1	4.2	−0.8
East	0.4	−	−	−	−	−	0.4

CONSTITUENCY	1950-1951	1951-1955	1955-1959	1959-1964	1964-1966	1966-1970	Total
FULHAM (Cont.)							
West	NC	—	—	—	—	—	—
GREENWICH	0.6	1.5	2.7	−6.4	−2.3	4.4	0.5
HACKNEY							
Central	—	—	2.0	−4.8	−4.5	5.9	−1.4
South	−0.4	—	—	—	—	—	−0.4
HAMMERSMITH							
North	−11.8	**	1.8	−3.6	−5.9	6.1	−13.4
South	−0.9	—	—	—	—	—	−0.9
HAMPSTEAD	−0.3	1.4	0.5	−10.6	−4.3	2.8	−10.5
HOLBORN and ST. PANCRAS							
SOUTH	−0.6	0.8	2.3	−5.7	−4.8	4.3	−3.7
ISLINGTON							
East	0.2	−0.4	2.7	−4.4	−2.5	2.8	−1.6
North	0.7	−0.7	4.5	−6.0	−2.6	2.7	−1.4
South-West	0.2	0.1	3.0	−2.6	−2.9	5.8	3.6
KENSINGTON							
North	−0.6	0.9	2.7	−2.8	−4.9	2.2	−2.5
South	1.9	2.9	NC	NC	−3.0	3.1	4.9
LAMBETH							
Brixton	−0.5	−0.9	3.9	−5.0	−3.2	4.0	−1.7
Norwood	0.8	2.8	2.4	−7.4	−3.5	2.0	−2.9
Vauxhall	1.6	1.2	2.7	−2.1	−2.5	3.0	3.9
LEWISHAM							
North	0.7	0.5	1.5	−5.0	−3.5	1.6	−4.2
South	0.8	−0.2	3.8	−6.3	−3.4	5.1	−0.2
West	0.4	2.2	2.2	−6.1	−3.6	3.5	−1.4
PADDINGTON							
North	−0.3	2.3	2.0	−6.5	−5.2	5.9	−1.8
South	0.2	2.0	3.0	−6.5	−4.9	3.2	−3.0
POPLAR	−0.7	0.5	4.3	−0.5	−6.8	4.1	0.9
ST. MARYLEBONE	1.9	3.4	−0.2	−6.8	−0.6	3.3	1.0
ST. PANCRAS NORTH	−0.8	2.4	0.5	−5.1	−3.4	5.6	−0.8
SHOREDITCH and FINSBURY	−5.3	−0.9	6.4	−1.4	−5.0	6.5	0.3
SOUTHWARK	−0.5	0.8	5.7	−5.5	−4.6	6.3	2.2
STEPNEY	−1.7	1.2	4.8	−1.2	−4.4	2.0	0.7
STOKE NEWINGTON and							
HACKNEY NORTH	−1.0	**	1.6	−4.6	−5.1	5.4	−3.7
WANDSWORTH							
Central	0.8	2.1	0.9	−4.6	−4.4	2.9	−2.3
Clapham	−0.1	1.1	2.5	−2.9	−4.8	10.2	6.0
Putney	0.6	1.3	−2.6	−5.6*	−2.0	1.8	−6.5
Streatham	1.4	2.0	0.6	−6.3	−5.2	3.3	−4.2
WOOLWICH							
East	0.7	−0.7*	0.4	−4.4	−3.4	6.2	−1.2
West	1.3	0.6*	2.0	−6.0	−2.7	4.0	−0.8
Average	−0.2	1.2	2.3	−4.5	−3.8	4.3	−0.8

ENGLAND—BOROUGHS

CONSTITUENCY	1950-1951	1951-1955	1955-1959	1959-1964	1964-1966	1966-1970	Total
ACCRINGTON	2.2	0.8	0.9	−5.9	−1.9	7.8	3.9
ACTON	0.7	1.6	1.9	−5.0	−3.9	6.6	1.9
ALTRINCHAM and SALE	2.7	2.7	−3.9	−5.4	−2.8	4.1	−2.6
ASHTON-UNDER-LYNE	−0.9*	**	−0.8	−1.7	−4.2	4.2	−3.4
BARKING	0.8	2.0	4.4	−5.3	−2.1	2.8	2.6
BARNSLEY	NC	3.5	−0.9	−1.3*	−0.7	3.3	3.9
BARROW-IN-FURNESS	3.3	3.7	−1.5	−0.4	−5.2	4.2	4.1
BATH	1.4*	2.0	−0.4	−2.7	−3.2	5.5	2.6
BATLEY and MORLEY	0.3	−0.5	1.8	−2.8	−2.5	5.6	1.9
BEBINGTON	4.6	1.4	−0.2	−6.7	−3.8	2.6	−2.1
BECKENHAM	2.2	1.6	0.5	−4.6	−2.5	4.3	1.5
BEXLEY	1.3	2.8	3.5	−3.6	−2.1	5.8	7.7
BILSTON	0.8	4.2*	4.1	0.4	−3.8	6.0	11.7
BIRKENHEAD	0.8	1.5	−0.4	−3.1	−3.9	3.8	−1.3
BIRMINGHAM							
All Saints	−	−	1.8	−0.8	−7.7	−1.2	−7.9
Aston	−0.5	**	6.5	−1.6	−6.2	4.5	2.7
Edgbaston	1.6	3.4	2.0	−2.4	−6.6	3.5	1.5
Erdington	1.7	−	−	−	−	−	1.7
Hall Green	2.7	**	3.2	−4.4	−6.5	6.5	1.5
Handsworth	3.8	**	0.6	−6.3	−5.0	1.0	−5.9
King's Norton	2.5	−	−	−	−	−	2.5
Ladywood	1.9	**	2.0	0.5	NC	NC	4.4
Northfield	3.8	**	2.0	−2.6	−6.1	8.6	5.7
Perry Bar	1.7	5.8	2.1	0.7	−5.4	6.8	11.7
Selly Oak	−	−	2.6	−3.1	−5.9	1.1	−5.3
Small Heath	−0.1	**	3.4	−4.7	−8.3	5.2	−4.5
Sparkbrook	0.6	**	5.6	−3.3	−8.6	4.6	−1.1
Stechford	1.4	**	4.9	−3.3	−8.7	7.1	1.4
Yardley	1.3	**	5.0	−1.7	−6.2	6.5	4.9
BLACKBURN	−	−	−2.3	−4.7	−0.9	5.1	−2.8
East	2.9	−	−	−	−	−	2.9
West	1.1	−	−	−	−	−	1.1
BLACKPOOL							
North	2.8	1.0	−3.1*	NC	NC	4.9	5.6
South	3.6	−0.8	−0.5	−7.6*	−4.0	5.7	−3.6
BLYTH	0.9	0.6	−1.5	−1.3	−2.3	4.0	0.4
BOLTON							
East	3.7	3.3	−0.8	−6.1	−5.9	9.7	3.9
West	NC	NC	NC	NC	−2.7	8.1	5.4
BOOTLE	−0.1*	**	−1.7	−8.3	−1.4	−0.3	−11.8
BOURNEMOUTH							
East and Christchurch	3.3	2.0	0.2	−4.0*	−2.3	5.6	4.8
West	3.2	2.3	0.0	−6.1	−2.6	5.2	2.0
BRADFORD							
Central	2.9	−	−	−	−	−	2.9
East	3.5	**	3.6	−3.8	−7.7	2.1	−2.3
North	2.0	**	3.0*	−4.8	−3.6	3.2	−0.2
South	2.1	**	1.0	−1.0	−4.3	6.4	4.2
West	−	−	2.4	−2.2	−6.0	4.0	−1.8
BRENTFORD and CHISWICK	0.9	1.0	1.4	−3.6	−1.9	0.1	−2.1
BRIGHOUSE and SPENBOROUGH	−0.1	**	1.7	−0.9	−3.8	4.9	1.8
BRIGHTON							
Kemptown	2.3	0.8*	0.0	−6.4	−0.8	4.0	−0.1
Pavilion	1.8	−0.5*	1.9	−7.5	−4.3	5.3	−3.3

CONSTITUENCY SWINGS

CONSTITUENCY	1950-1951	1951-1955	1955-1959	1959-1964	1964-1966	1966-1970	Total
BRISTOL							
Central	1.9	**	6.9	−4.1	−3.7	4.7	5.7
North-East	2.3	**	3.5	−1.4	−5.4	4.7	3.7
North-West	1.1	**	3.9	−0.9	−1.8	1.7	4.0
South	0.7	**	3.3	−2.7	−3.7	5.3	2.9
South-East	2.8	**	3.2	−3.9	−1.2	6.0	6.9
West	2.9	**	−0.9	NC	NC	1.4	3.4
BROMLEY	2.1	2.8	1.8	−5.4	−1.8	4.5	4.0
BURNLEY	−0.1	0.9	−1.3	−7.5	−1.9	5.4	−4.5
BURY and RADCLIFFE	1.0	1.9	0.1	−4.8	−3.0	7.0	2.2
CAMBRIDGE	0.8	2.0	−0.4	−5.7	−2.5	6.4	0.6
CARLISLE	2.5*	4.3	1.9	−4.9	−3.6	2.9	3.1
CHELTENHAM	1.1	2.2	1.4	−4.5	−2.8	6.0	3.4
CHESTERFIELD	1.2	6.1	−4.8	−1.5	−3.8	3.9	1.1
COVENTRY							
East	0.8	6.1	−0.5	−4.0*	−4.7	5.4	3.1
North	1.6	6.1	2.1	−2.6*	−5.3	2.6	4.5
South	0.6	3.6	3.2	−3.3*	−3.2	3.0	3.9
CROSBY	3.5	**	−1.1	−8.6*	−4.3	2.6	−7.9
CROYDON							
East	1.0	—	—	—	—	—	1.0
North	1.1	—	—	—	—	—	1.1
North-East	—	—	0.4	−5.2	−3.8	4.2	−4.4
North-West	—	—	0.0	−4.7	−3.4	2.6	−5.5
South	—	—	1.2	−5.4	−2.8	3.6	−3.4
West	1.1	—	—	—	—	—	1.1
DAGENHAM	0.5	2.2	4.9	−4.1	−3.0	4.3	4.8
DARLINGTON	6.6	1.9	1.8	−6.4	−2.6	0.7	2.0
DARTFORD	1.0	—	—	—	—	—	1.0
DERBY							
North	2.1	**	3.0	−6.3	−2.7	7.1	3.2
South	1.9	**	3.6	−3.7	−5.1	8.4	5.1
DEWSBURY	1.8	**	4.3	−3.0	−5.3	7.4	5.2
DONCASTER	1.3*	1.4	1.9	−4.8	−5.5	3.1	−2.6
DROYLSDEN	2.2	—	—	—	—	—	2.2
DUDLEY	2.5	−1.3*	4.7	−4.1	−0.1	8.8	10.5
EALING							
North	2.3	0.4	4.0	−4.3	−2.6	2.3	2.1
South	1.2	1.9	0.9	−4.2	−4.3	3.6	−0.9
EAST HAM							
North	1.7	1.2	2.3	−3.6	−5.5	6.0	2.1
South	1.3	0.8	2.6	−4.5	−3.9	8.1	4.4
ECCLES	2.4	0.0	0.4*	−5.3*	−3.7	4.7	−1.5
EDMONTON	0.7	1.8	6.1	−4.7	−3.4	6.0	6.5
ENFIELD							
East	0.0	2.6	5.9	−4.3	−1.7	4.7	7.2
West	1.9	2.9	1.5	NC	NC	2.6	8.9
ERITH and CRAYFORD	—	—	3.8	−3.7	−0.2	4.7	4.6
ETON and SLOUGH	0.4	1.8	3.1	0.1	−4.8	2.1	2.7
EXETER	1.6	1.2	0.1	−4.8	−5.5	5.2	−2.2
FELTHAM	—	—	1.6	−4.3	−3.2	3.4	−2.5
FINCHLEY	0.2	1.0	3.0	NC	NC	2.6	6.8
GATESHEAD							
East	−5.1	**	−2.5	−5.6*	−5.1	4.8	−13.5
West	0.4	**	0.4	−4.1*	−5.8	6.7	−2.4
GILLINGHAM	1.0	1.8	3.9	−2.2	−3.3	5.0	6.2
GLOUCESTER	2.7*	1.7*	−2.3	−1.6*	−1.3	7.2	6.4

CONSTITUENCY SWINGS

CONSTITUENCY	1950-1951	1951-1955	1955-1959	1959-1964	1964-1966	1966-1970	Total
GOSPORT and FAREHAM	−0.1	2.4	1.9	−3.3	−2.6	3.7	2.0
GRIMSBY	−0.3	2.8	3.7	−4.2*	−4.6	2.1	−0.5
HALIFAX	6.3	2.0	0.9	−3.2	−4.6	5.4	6.8
HARROW							
Central	1.9	**	2.8	−6.6	−3.9	3.7	−2.1
East	1.6	**	2.8	−4.3	−3.4	5.7	2.4
West	3.0	**	1.0	−6.5	−2.3	3.9	−0.9
HARTLEPOOLS, THE	2.5	1.0*	1.8	−3.1	−6.4	1.5	−2.7
HASTINGS·	2.8	**	0.7	−5.0	−4.3	5.4	−0.4
HAYES and HARLINGTON	0.3	5.7	3.5	−4.5	−3.2	5.0	6.8
HENDON							
North	0.3	2.0	1.5	−4.8	−0.6	3.6	2.0
South	0.7	2.3	1.6	−5.4	−3.8	3.1	−1.5
HESTON and ISLEWORTH	1.0	**	2.6	−5.6	−3.2	4.8	−0.4
HORNCHURCH	0.6	1.9	3.9	−4.8	−2.2	6.1	5.5
HORNSEY	−0.1	2.8	−0.2	−7.1	−3.6	3.7	−4.5
HOVE	2.4	−0.1	0.6	−6.4	−2.6	2.9	−3.2
HUDDERSFIELD							
East	1.0	**	1.4	−6.6	−3.5	7.8	0.1
West	NC	**	NC	NC	NC	5.2	5.2
ILFORD							
North	1.3	1.4	2.6	−5.4*	−4.1	4.9	0.7
South	0.8	2.0	1.0	−6.0*	−4.6	4.5	−2.3
IPSWICH	0.1	0.4*	0.4	0.6	−3.7	5.7	3.5
JARROW	−	−	0.7	−1.6	−3.4	4.1	−0.2
KEIGHLEY	3.5	−1.4	4.3	−3.5	−1.7	5.8	7.0
KINGSTON UPON HULL							
Central	0.1	−	−	−	−	−	0.1
East	1.7	**	0.9*	−3.8	−7.0	0.5	−7.7
Haltemprice	2.5	−	−	−	−	−	2.5
North	2.0	**	0.1	−1.9	−7.8	0.0	−7.6
West	−	−	3.5	−4.4	−7.9	2.5	−6.3
KINGSTON UPON THAMES	1.0	**	1.4	−5.8*	−2.6	3.6	−2.4
LEEDS							
Central	1.2*	−	−	−	−	−	1.2
East	−	−	0.7	−3.3*	−3.7	3.9	−2.4
North	0.2*	−	−	−	−	−	0.2
North-East	0.3*	**	2.6	−3.4*	−3.9	0.2	−4.2
North-West	1.1*	**	−0.3	−6.0	−3.9	1.9	−7.2
South	0.7*	**	1.4	−0.7	−5.4	4.2	0.2
South-East	0.0*	**	2.0	−3.5	−4.1	5.3	−0.3
West	1.3*	**	1.9	−3.1	−4.1	3.9	−0.1
LEICESTER							
North-East	1.6	3.4	4.7	−3.0	−5.0	8.5	10.2
North-West	1.7	2.7	2.0	−3.7	−5.1	7.4	5.0
South-East	2.0	**	3.1	−2.7	−4.7	2.8	0.5
South-West	1.7	2.6	2.2	−2.3	−2.7	8.8	10.3
LEIGH	0.1	1.0	−2.8	−2.3	−1.1	6.3	1.2
LEYTON	1.1	0.4	3.7	−4.7	−0.3	2.1	2.3
LINCOLN	0.2	−2.1	1.0	−0.6*	−2.6	2.2	−1.9
LIVERPOOL							
Edge Hill	−0.4	**	0.5	−8.1	−4.0	5.3	−6.7
Exchange	−2.5	**	−0.9	−8.8	−3.6	1.0	−14.8
Garston	2.2	**	1.0	−7.8	−2.3	2.6	−4.3
Kirkdale	−0.2	**	1.1	−8.8	−3.7	2.8	−8.8
Scotland	−2.0	3.2*	3.2	−8.5	−3.8	−0.7	−8.6
Toxteth	1.2	2.0*	−0.6	−10.0	−2.2	2.2	−7.4

CONSTITUENCY SWINGS

CONSTITUENCY	1950-1951	1951-1955	1955-1959	1959-1964	1964-1966	1966-1970	Total
LIVERPOOL (Cont.)							
Walton	−0.4*	**	1.3	−8.2	−3.7	1.3	−9.7
Wavertree	1.3	**	0.1	−9.3	−2.8	NC	−10.7
West Derby	−0.3	**	0.7	−8.6*	−2.2	−0.4	−10.8
LUTON	1.6	1.9	0.5	−5.9	−1.8	4.1	0.4
MANCHESTER							
Ardwick	0.3	**	−5.7	−3.1	−3.5	8.5	−3.5
Blackley	2.3	3.8	−1.4	−6.0	−6.3	4.4	−3.2
Cheetham	0.6	**	−2.1	−1.9	−4.6	6.7	−1.3
Clayton	2.1	−	−	−	−	−	2.1
Exchange	1.4	**	−3.6	−4.5	−4.4	3.1	−8.0
Gorton	1.3	**	−0.6	−4.2	−5.0	3.2	−5.3
Moss Side	2.6	2.1	−2.0	−5.9	−4.6	1.1	−6.7
Openshaw	−	−	−0.4	−2.0	−5.0	6.1	−1.3
Withington	4.9	**	−3.5	−4.7	−5.4	3.7	−5.0
Wythenshawe	0.4	**	−1.7	−5.4	−4.4	3.4	−7.7
MERTON and MORDEN	1.7	2.7	2.3	−6.1	−2.9	4.2	1.9
MIDDLESBROUGH							
East	1.5	4.1	0.9	−8.0*	−5.6	4.1	−3.0
West	6.3	6.2	1.3	−11.0*	−3.2	4.9	4.5
MITCHAM	0.9	1.8	2.0	−4.9	−3.1	4.7	1.4
NELSON and COLNE	−0.1	2.0	1.2	−2.0	−2.6	8.0	6.5
NEWCASTLE-UNDER-LYME	−0.3	1.3	1.2	−2.4	−3.8	9.5	5.5
NEWCASTLE UPON TYNE							
Central	−0.7	**	0.8	−6.0	−5.6	3.1	−8.4
East	3.2	0.8	2.2	−2.1	−7.8	1.6	−2.1
North	−1.6	6.4	1.0	−4.0	−6.5	1.7	−3.0
West	0.7	**	0.9	−3.6	−4.3	3.9	−2.4
NORTHAMPTON	1.9	0.9	0.5	−1.6	−2.9	5.6	4.4
NORWICH							
North	5.1*	2.0	0.5	−0.7	−4.7	4.8	7.0
South	−0.8	−0.1	0.6	−4.0	−3.9	5.9	−2.3
NOTTINGHAM							
Central	1.9	**	1.4*	−5.0	−6.2	3.2	−4.7
East	2.3	−	−	−	−	−	2.3
North	−	−	1.4*	−3.7	−3.1	4.4	−1.0
North-West	2.5	−	−	−	−	−	2.5
South	1.5	**	0.2*	−4.6	−2.8	4.1	−1.6
West	−	−	4.3*	−2.8	−5.3	5.2	1.4
OLDBURY and HALESOWEN	4.2	0.9	2.7	1.3	−2.4	5.8	12.5
OLDHAM							
East	2.6*	−1.7*	−2.5	−2.8	−2.8	6.6	−0.6
West	0.6*	−0.1*	−0.4	−3.8	−2.5	8.7	2.5
OXFORD	2.9	1.3	0.7	−6.7*	−3.7	4.1	−1.4
PLYMOUTH							
Devonport	0.9*	**	6.3	−2.3	−3.7	1.3	2.5
Sutton	1.4*	**	2.4	−5.4	−4.9	3.9	−2.6
PONTEFRACT	−0.6	−0.1	−0.2	0.2	−2.2	3.5	0.6
POOLE	2.0	1.1	1.7	−3.6	−2.4	6.1	4.9
PORTSMOUTH							
Langstone	1.2	1.2*	1.2	−8.2*	−1.4	4.9	−1.1
South	−0.2	3.4*	2.7	−6.3	−3.0	2.7	−0.7
West	0.3	2.9*	3.5	−7.0	−2.4	0.3	−2.4
PRESTON							
North	0.2	2.3	1.6	−5.1	−3.0	6.7	2.7
South	0.1	0.6*	3.1	−4.1*	−3.2	5.3	1.8
PUDSEY	3.7	1.6	1.8	−1.3	−3.4	3.5	5.9

CONSTITUENCY SWINGS

CONSTITUENCY	1950-1951	1951-1955	1955-1959	1959-1964	1964-1966	1966-1970	Total
READING	—	—	4.3	−4.0*	−4.2	5.4	1.5
North	1.2	—	—	—	—	—	1.2
South	1.7	—	—	—	—	—	1.7
RICHMOND (Surrey)	0.7	0.2	1.3	−5.7*	−2.2	2.7	−3.0
ROCHDALE	4.1	1.1	NC	NC	NC	NC	5.2
ROCHESTER and CHATHAM	−0.3	−1.6*	3.4	−2.0*	−1.1	6.9	5.3
ROMFORD	−0.1	**	2.0	−4.8	−2.1	4.8	−0.2
ROSSENDALE	0.5	−1.6	0.3	−1.0	−1.4	7.8	4.6
ROTHERHAM	1.4	2.3	0.5	−3.7	−3.2	3.3	0.6
ROWLEY REGIS and TIPTON	2.3	1.4*	4.0	1.0	−5.6	4.1	7.2
RUISLIP-NORTHWOOD	1.7	1.6	0.7	−3.8	−3.1	6.9	4.0
ST. HELENS	1.7	−1.0*	2.2	−4.9	−3.8	5.1	−0.7
SALFORD							
East	1.4	4.7	−2.4	−6.5	−6.1	6.1	−2.8
West	1.6	2.4	−2.3	−2.2*	−3.7	4.9	0.7
SHEFFIELD							
Attercliffe	0.5	**	2.3	−3.4	−5.1	6.9	1.2
Brightside	−0.4	**	−0.5	−3.3	−4.8	4.1	−4.9
Hallam	1.4	**	2.1	−4.4	−4.6	5.5	0.0
Heeley	1.8	**	−1.9	−7.5	−5.5	4.6	−8.5
Hillsborough	0.4	**	2.3	−5.9	−5.5	5.8	−2.9
Neepsend	−0.2	—	—	—	—	—	−0.2
Park	−0.5	**	2.1	−4.5	−6.4	5.7	−3.6
SMETHWICK	1.5	2.5	3.5	7.2	−7.7	1.7	8.7
SOUTHALL	0.8	0.7	4.4	0.2	−4.6	1.3	2.8
SOUTHAMPTON							
Itchen	0.6	**	2.1	−5.7	NC	NC	−3.0
Test	0.9	**	2.6	−6.0	−2.7	4.1	−1.1
SOUTHEND							
East	2.8	**	1.1	−5.3	−3.4	7.9	3.1
West	3.2	**	NC	NC	NC	5.6	8.8
SOUTHGATE	0.4	1.4	NC	NC	NC	3.5	5.3
SOUTHPORT	2.9	2.6	NC	NC	−2.5	NC	3.0
SOUTH SHIELDS	3.7*	1.5	1.7	−4.4	−2.3	4.5	4.7
STOCKPORT							
North	1.3	0.2	−1.7	−5.9	−2.0	5.3	−2.8
South	1.6	1.3*	−2.2	−7.3	−1.8	3.0	−5.4
STOCKTON-ON-TEES	2.3	1.3*	0.8	−3.9	−3.2	5.4	2.7
STOKE-ON-TRENT							
Central	0.9	0.7*	2.7	−3.0	−3.9	5.5	2.9
North	0.1	4.6*	2.9	−0.8	−6.8	5.3	5.3
South	2.7	2.2*	4.3	−1.3	−3.6	3.4	7.7
STRETFORD	3.5	2.9	−2.6	−6.5	−5.0	7.0	−0.7
SUNDERLAND							
North	4.0	0.9*	0.7	−4.3	−4.0	0.1	−2.6
South	4.4	2.1*	−1.0	−2.5	−5.9	1.0	−1.9
SURBITON	—	—	2.5	−6.8	−2.7	2.4	−4.6
SUTTON and CHEAM	1.6	3.3	0.4	−3.7	−2.4	5.0	4.2
SUTTON COLDFIELD	—	—	1.0	NC	NC	0.6	1.6
SWINDON	2.7	2.1*	0.5	−6.7	−1.2	6.3	3.7
TORQUAY	2.0	1.8	−0.4	NC	NC	4.3	7.7
TOTTENHAM	0.5	2.4	2.3	−3.4	−4.2	4.0	1.6
TWICKENHAM	1.7	2.0	0.4	−3.6	−4.0	4.2	0.7
TYNEMOUTH	1.6	3.3	2.3	−5.7	−3.4	2.8	0.9
WAKEFIELD	2.4	**	0.8	−2.9*	−2.8	3.0	0.5
WALLASEY	0.7	0.2	0.0	−7.8	−5.1	2.3	−9.7
WALLSEND	1.4	0.9	1.3	−3.9	−4.8	3.9	−1.2

CONSTITUENCY SWINGS

CONSTITUENCY	1950-1951	1951-1955	1955-1959	1959-1964	1964-1966	1966-1970	Total
WALSALL	−2.2	—	—	—	—	—	−2.2
North	—	—	1.6	−0.4*	−3.7	7.4	4.9
South	—	—	5.8	−1.4*	−3.6	6.1	6.9
WALTHAMSTOW							
East	2.9	2.8	2.5	−3.5	−3.4	3.6	4.9
West	0.6	1.1	1.8	−0.9	−3.3	8.2	7.5
WANSTEAD and WOODFORD (formerly Woodford, *q.v.*)	—	—	—	—	NC	2.5	2.5
WARRINGTON	−0.1	2.4*	0.8	−6.6	−6.3	4.9	−4.9
WATFORD	1.0	2.5	1.2	−4.9	−2.7	4.3	1.4
WEDNESBURY	2.5	**	3.2	3.5	−5.2	5.1	9.1
WEMBLEY							
North	1.5	2.5	1.5	−5.4	−2.8	3.6	0.9
South	1.5	2.8	1.6	−3.9	−4.5	1.9	−0.6
WEST BROMWICH	1.2	2.4	4.4	2.3	−2.7	2.6	10.2
WEST HAM							
North	1.0	0.5	1.8	NC	NC	NC	3.3
South	0.2	1.9	2.4	NC	NC	5.1	9.6
WIGAN	−0.7	0.8	−1.3	−3.2	−3.3	5.6	−2.1
WILLESDEN							
East	1.4	1.1	3.3	−4.8	−6.5	2.5	−3.0
West	0.2	2.5	3.2	−5.8	−5.6	2.0	−3.5
WIMBLEDON	1.1	**	1.3	−5.3	−2.1	2.4	−2.6
WOLVERHAMPTON							
North-East	2.6	**	7.0	−0.9	−5.9	9.1	11.9
South-West	2.8	**	3.9	−0.9	−4.0	8.7	10.5
WOODFORD (Wanstead and Woodford from 1964, *q.v.*)	−0.5	**	−1.8	—	—	—	−2.3
WOOD GREEN	2.0	1.9	2.6	−5.4	−4.2	3.7	0.6
WORCESTER	1.0	1.3*	0.9	0.0	−4.1	4.8	3.9
WORTHING	2.6	2.5	−1.3	NC	NC	4.3	8.1
YORK	0.7	0.2	2.4	−2.4*	−6.2	3.3	−2.0
Average	**1.4**	**1.9**	**1.4**	**−4.0**	**−3.9**	**4.4**	**0.7**

ENGLAND—COUNTIES

CONSTITUENCY	1950-1951	1951-1955	1955-1959	1959-1964	1964-1966	1966-1970	Total
BEDFORDSHIRE							
Bedford	0.7	2.6*	1.8	−4.0	−3.7	5.4	2.8
Mid	−0.4	2.6*	1.0	−0.2	−2.4	6.4	7.0
South	2.7	1.8	1.5	−4.1	−3.2	6.1	4.8
BERKSHIRE							
Abingdon	1.1	3.7	1.4	−4.9	−3.0	7.1	5.4
Newbury	0.7	**	2.0	−4.6*	−1.8	5.8	2.1
Windsor	0.7	1.8	2.0	−3.8	−3.5	6.6	3.8
Wokingham	1.1	**	0.0	−3.5*	−4.6	6.3	−0.7
BUCKINGHAMSHIRE							
Aylesbury	1.8	1.0	3.1	−2.9	−3.6	5.4	4.8
Buckingham	1.9	1.2	0.6	−3.3	−0.7	4.3	4.0
South	1.7	0.4	−0.8	NC	NC	4.5	5.8
Wycombe	2.1	6.0	1.7	−1.8	−2.0	6.2	12.2

CONSTITUENCY SWINGS

CONSTITUENCY	1950-1951	1951-1955	1955-1959	1959-1964	1964-1966	1966-1970	Total
CAMBRIDGESHIRE	0.8	0.5	3.6	−0.9	−2.2	5.6	7.4
CHESHIRE							
Cheadle	2.4	1.3*	NC	NC	NC	NC	3.7
City of Chester	0.2	4.0	−1.1	−4.6	−3.8	4.1	−1.2
Crewe	1.1	**	3.2	−2.7	−3.8	6.7	4.5
Knutsford	3.1	**	NC	NC	NC	NC	3.1
Macclesfield	2.5	1.0	−0.4	−3.5	−2.1	5.4	2.9
Nantwich	—	—	−1.9	−1.2	−5.0	3.0	−5.1
Northwich	1.8	**	1.2	−4.6	−5.0	4.9	−1.7
Runcorn	2.5	1.7	1.7	−7.3	−2.6	3.8	−0.2
Stalybridge and Hyde	1.5	0.1	−1.4	−2.4	−2.9	3.9	−1.2
Wirral	2.3	2.2	0.5	−6.5	−3.9	4.2	−1.2
CORNWALL							
Bodmin	NC	NC	NC	NC	NC	NC	NC
Falmouth and Camborne	1.1	−0.1	−3.5	1.3	−0.1	5.2	3.9
North	NC	NC	NC	NC	NC	NC	NC
St. Ives	3.1	0.4	−0.6	NC	NC	6.7	9.6
Truro	2.1	−0.3	−0.4	−0.5	−2.8	6.4	4.5
CUMBERLAND							
Penrith and the Border	NC	2.7	0.3	−4.4	−1.9	5.6	2.3
Whitehaven	0.8	1.1	0.3	−2.3	−1.9	3.7	1.7
Workington	2.7	0.6	−0.8	−1.9	−1.2	1.7	1.1
DERBYSHIRE							
Belper	0.9	1.5	1.9	−1.2	1.6	4.8	9.5
Bolsover	0.7	1.0	0.7	−1.2	−2.7	4.5	3.0
High Peak	0.4	3.2	−0.9	−4.4	−2.6	2.7	−1.6
Ilkeston	NC	5.9	0.7	0.5	−2.0	4.6	9.7
North-East	−0.4	0.2	3.6	−1.3	−2.7	6.1	5.5
South-East	1.6	**	1.6	−0.8	−3.9	6.8	5.3
West	0.3	0.8	1.7	NC	NC	5.7	8.5
DEVON							
Honiton	NC	NC	NC	NC	NC	NC	NC
North	NC	NC	NC	NC	NC	NC	NC
Tavistock	2.4*	0.9	NC	NC	NC	NC	3.3
Tiverton	2.7	0.7	0.9	NC	NC	4.7	9.0
Torrington	NC	−1.2	NC	NC	NC	NC	−1.2
Totnes	1.4	0.4	2.2	−3.2	−2.3	5.0	3.5
DORSET							
North	NC	NC	NC	NC	NC	NC	NC
South	0.9	2.4	1.3	−6.6	0.9	4.6	3.5
West	0.9	−0.7	1.8	−1.5	−1.8	5.5	4.2
DURHAM							
Bishop Auckland	2.6	2.8*	−2.8	−1.3	−3.0	4.2	2.5
Blaydon	0.8	1.7	1.0	−1.3	−2.5	4.3	4.0
Chester-le-Street	0.3	0.7	0.5	0.6	−1.8	5.4	5.7
Consett	2.1	2.2	0.2	−1.3	−5.2	2.4	0.4
Durham	1.0	1.0	−0.3	−1.9	−2.3	3.7	1.2
Easington	0.3	1.7	−0.7	−0.7	−0.9	1.6	1.3
Houghton-le-Spring	1.3	−0.3*	0.2	1.1	−2.7	4.1	3.7
Jarrow	0.6*	—	—	—	—	—	0.6
North-West	1.0	1.2	−0.6	−1.7	−3.8	4.0	0.1
Sedgefield	0.2	2.6*	1.2	−2.2	−4.0	4.1	1.9
ESSEX							
Billericay	2.0	**	−0.9	−2.8	−2.0	3.1	−0.6
Chelmsford	0.4	**	4.2	−3.8	−2.0	5.7	4.5
Chigwell	—	—	4.2	−2.5	−1.4	6.6	6.9
Colchester	3.1	1.3	2.4*	−4.4	−2.5	7.9	7.8

CONSTITUENCY SWINGS

CONSTITUENCY	1950-1951	1951-1955	1955-1959	1959-1964	1964-1966	1966-1970	Total
ESSEX (Cont.)							
Epping	0.8	−1.7	0.0	−5.2	−2.6	6.2	−2.5
Harwich	2.2	2.3	2.4	−3.3	−3.9	4.2	3.9
Maldon	1.2	1.4	1.8*	−0.9	−1.1	4.9	7.3
Saffron Walden	0.3	2.0	0.2*	−2.7	−2.1	6.6	4.3
South-East	−	−	1.3	−4.0	−2.6	8.1	2.8
Thurrock	−4.5	−0.6	4.6	−3.3	−2.1	6.7	0.8
GLOUCESTERSHIRE							
Cirencester and Tewkesbury	0.5	**	NC	−3.7	−1.5	4.9	0.2
South	0.8	**	2.8	−1.6	−2.1	5.4	5.3
Stroud	−	−	1.1	−2.3*	−1.4	5.9	3.3
Stroud and Thornbury	1.3*	−	−	−	−	−	1.3
West	3.0*	3.0	−1.2	−1.7	−0.7	7.5	9.9
HAMPSHIRE							
Aldershot	2.7	1.6	3.0	−2.8	−3.7	3.6	4.4
Basingstoke	0.5	**	4.4	−4.2	−4.2	3.6	0.1
Eastleigh	−	−	2.8	−1.5	−1.4	6.1	6.0
New Forest	2.0	**	−0.1	−4.4*	−2.1	6.5	1.9
Petersfield	2.0	**	0.0	NC	NC	NC	2.0
Winchester	−0.3	**	1.8	−6.1	−0.5	4.1	−1.0
HEREFORDSHIRE							
Hereford	1.2	NC	NC	NC	3.9	5.7	10.8
Leominster	1.8	−1.3	NC	NC	NC	NC	0.5
HERTFORDSHIRE							
Barnet	2.0	**	1.9	−4.7	−2.8	3.2	−0.4
East	−	−	2.4	−2.9	−2.3	6.1	3.3
Hemel Hempstead	0.6	−2.3	0.7	−3.3	−2.1	6.5	0.1
Hertford	1.0	**	1.4	−5.0	−2.5	6.3	1.2
Hitchin	1.0	**	2.5	−5.7	−4.2	4.3	−2.1
St. Albans	2.2	**	2.2	−3.9	−2.8	5.2	2.9
South-West	−1.4	−1.9	1.9	−3.8	−2.3	3.9	−3.6
HUNTINGDONSHIRE	−0.2	1.0	2.6	−1.1	−3.6	3.5	2.2
ISLE of ELY	1.7	0.5	−0.4	−0.8	−4.3	8.0	4.7
ISLE of WIGHT	1.3	0.8	0.3	−2.0	−1.1	5.1	4.4
KENT							
Ashford	1.6	1.3	2.4	−2.3	−1.1	3.5	5.4
Canterbury	2.4	1.5	−0.3	−5.0	−0.4	4.2	2.4
Chislehurst	0.6	**	2.6	−5.0	−2.3	4.2	0.1
Dartford	−	−	3.2	−3.0	−1.7	6.3	4.8
Dover	1.1	−0.4	0.2	−3.5	−2.5	4.3	−0.8
Faversham	1.7	0.5	−0.2	−3.8	1.5	5.9	5.6
Folkestone and Hythe	2.8	0.1	1.1	−3.9	−2.6	6.2	3.7
Gravesend	−0.1	**	−1.0	−2.7*	−3.3	4.9	−2.2
Isle of Thanet	2.0	0.6	−1.2	−4.7	−2.3	5.1	−0.5
Maidstone	−0.2	1.2	2.7	−3.1	−2.7	5.9	3.8
Orpington	0.7	**	1.1	NC	NC	NC	1.8
Sevenoaks	2.5	1.5	2.0	−1.4	−3.4	5.2	6.4
Tonbridge	2.0	0.7	−0.5	−2.2	−1.8	5.7	3.9
LANCASHIRE							
Chorley	NC	**	0.7	−3.0	−1.1	6.2	2.8
Clitheroe	2.4	1.1	1.6	−2.5	−2.6	4.9	4.9
Darwen	−1.9	**	0.3	−4.0	−3.1	7.1	−1.6
Farnworth	3.2	1.6	−0.9*	−3.5	−4.1	7.7	4.0
Heywood and Royton	1.9	−0.5	−1.1	−3.0	−4.8	4.8	−2.7
Huyton	−0.4	−1.4*	−2.2	−9.7*	−2.3	2.3	−13.7
Ince	−0.5	−0.4	0.5	0.3	−1.6	5.2	3.5
Lancaster	−0.9	3.3	1.2	−4.1	−6.2	4.9	−1.8

CONSTITUENCY	1950-1951	1951-1955	1955-1959	1959-1964	1964-1966	1966-1970	Total
LANCASHIRE (Cont.)							
Middleton and Prestwich	2.1	1.3	−1.8	−7.7	−5.5	4.5	−7.1
Morecambe and Lonsdale	3.0	1.8	−3.3	−4.5	−2.4	3.0	−2.4
Newton	0.8	0.4*	0.5	−5.3	−0.1	6.0	2.3
North Fylde	2.4	3.0	−1.7*	−5.2	−4.0	7.6	2.1
Ormskirk	1.2*	**	0.8	−6.6*	−3.8	2.6	−5.8
South Fylde	2.1	1.2*	−0.7	NC	NC	6.1	8.7
Westhoughton	1.1	0.1	−0.2	−0.6	−3.2	9.5	6.7
Widnes	−0.1	2.3*	−0.1	−4.9	−3.9	3.0	−3.7
LEICESTERSHIRE							
Bosworth	5.1	3.1*	2.7	−3.9	−1.9	8.0	13.1
Harborough	1.1	**	0.9	−1.5	−4.4	7.1	3.2
Loughborough	0.5	2.1*	0.8	−0.6	−1.8	6.1	7.1
Melton	−0.1	4.7	0.3	−0.8	−4.5	7.0	6.6
LINCOLNSHIRE—PARTS of HOLLAND							
Holland with Boston	0.9	0.6	1.8	−5.0	−5.1	7.8	1.0
LINCOLNSHIRE—PARTS of KESTEVEN, and RUTLANDSHIRE							
Grantham	−2.8	0.2	4.3	−0.9*	−3.9	6.6	3.5
Rutland and Stamford	−0.1	0.2	3.1	−1.9	−2.1	6.7	5.9
LINCOLNSHIRE—PARTS of LINDSEY							
Brigg	2.0	2.5	3.1	−3.9	−4.3	6.7	6.1
Gainsborough	2.1	1.0	2.6	0.4	−4.0	3.9	6.0
Horncastle	0.7	0.4	−0.2	NC	NC	6.7	7.6
Louth	1.5	1.6	2.3	−3.0*	−3.4	4.8	3.8
MIDDLESEX							
Spelthorne	0.9	**	1.2	−3.8	−3.2	6.4	1.5
Uxbridge	1.1	0.8	2.4	−0.8	−1.6	4.8	6.7
NORFOLK							
Central	1.0*	1.4	0.5	−1.8	−1.7	7.7	7.1
King's Lynn	1.4	0.6	0.5	−2.2	−2.1	2.3	0.5
North	2.2	−1.2	0.7	0.8	−0.8	6.2	7.9
South	1.1	−2.4	1.8	−0.9	−2.8	6.1	2.9
South-West	1.1	−0.9	0.2	0.3	0.9	6.2	7.8
Yarmouth	2.5	−0.1	3.2	−2.0	−3.1	4.3	4.8
NORTHAMPTONSHIRE							
Kettering	1.3	0.7	2.4	−2.4	−3.4	5.6	4.2
Peterborough	0.2	2.9	1.3	−2.0	−2.5	4.1	4.0
South	1.3	1.8	1.6	−2.7	−1.4	4.1	4.7
Wellingborough	6.9	1.4	1.7	−0.7	−2.3	4.6	11.6
NORTHUMBERLAND							
Berwick-upon-Tweed	0.6	0.5	2.8	−1.1	−4.7	4.3	2.4
Hexham	NC	4.4	−1.0	−3.6	−3.9	2.8	−1.3
Morpeth	−0.4	1.3	−1.4	−0.8	−1.7	7.3	4.3
NOTTINGHAMSHIRE							
Ashfield	—	—	1.2	−2.2	−0.8	5.4	3.6
Bassetlaw	2.0	**	0.1	−1.0	−2.6	3.8	2.3
Broxtowe	−0.2	—	—	—	—	—	−0.2
Carlton	3.4	3.3	0.5	−2.2	−2.1	6.3	9.2
Mansfield	1.9	**	0.7	−2.9	−0.2	4.2	3.7
Newark	−0.2	**	0.5	−2.4	−2.4	5.5	1.0
Rushcliffe	1.7	**	2.6	−1.8	−3.0	5.5	5.0
OXFORDSHIRE							
Banbury	1.6	0.8	2.1	−2.0	−0.8	4.8	6.5

CONSTITUENCY SWINGS

CONSTITUENCY	1950-1951	1951-1955	1955-1959	1959-1964	1964-1966	1966-1970	Total
OXFORDSHIRE (Cont.)							
Henley	1.1	0.6	1.7	−2.1*	−2.8	5.9	4.4
SHROPSHIRE							
Ludlow	−0.3	1.5	−1.4	−1.4	−4.0	6.7	1.1
Oswestry	0.4	2.5	−0.8	−5.1	−2.4	5.5	0.1
Shrewsbury	1.4	1.5	0.6	−3.8	−3.8	7.1	3.0
The Wrekin	1.3	3.0	3.0	−0.6	−3.9	1.4	4.2
SOMERSET							
Bridgwater	0.0	2.8	−0.1	−2.5	−3.5	5.1	1.8
North	1.6*	1.8*	2.1	−3.0*	−1.4	6.2	7.3
Taunton	2.8	1.9	0.8	−1.9	−1.8	5.2	7.0
Wells	2.5	1.2	0.7	−1.4*	−2.1	5.0	5.9
Weston-super-Mare	1.5	−3.0*	4.7	−2.9	−2.9	4.9	2.3
Yeovil	1.3	1.4	1.8	−1.4	−2.6	4.4	4.9
STAFFORDSHIRE							
Brierley Hill	2.4	1.4*	4.5	−0.1	−2.3	9.5	15.4
Burton	−0.8	2.5	2.9	−2.9	−3.0	4.0	2.7
Cannock	1.0	**	2.4	−0.7	−2.3	11.0	11.4
Leek	2.1	0.7	0.0	−2.4	−2.9	7.4	4.9
Lichfield and Tamworth	1.6	**	2.1	−2.2	0.1	5.6	7.2
Stafford and Stone	1.1	3.3	1.0	−4.2	−1.8	3.9	3.3
SUFFOLK							
Bury St. Edmunds	−0.1	0.7	3.6	−3.8	−0.4	6.6	6.6
Eye	NC	NC	1.7	3.1	−1.9	4.6	7.5
Lowestoft	2.7	−1.2	3.7	1.1	−2.4	4.5	8.4
Sudbury and Woodbridge	1.5	1.5*	2.4	−1.8	−1.6	4.0	6.0
SURREY							
Carshalton	1.7	1.8	1.2	−2.4	−3.8	4.7	3.2
Chertsey	0.4	3.7	1.0	−3.4	−1.9	5.2	5.0
Dorking	1.1	1.3	1.2	−2.0	−3.7	4.6	2.5
East	4.2	1.8	NC	NC	NC	NC	6.0
Epsom	2.3	2.8	0.2	NC	NC	4.4	9.7
Esher	1.0	2.3	1.1	−4.0	−1.6	4.1	2.9
Farnham	2.1	1.6	2.3	NC	NC	NC	6.0
Guildford	2.6	0.0	1.0	−2.8*	−2.7	5.6	3.7
Reigate	0.8	0.3	0.9	−3.3	−1.9	5.0	1.8
Woking	1.6	−0.5	3.0	−6.3*	−0.8	3.8	0.8
SUSSEX (EAST)							
Eastbourne	2.8	**	0.8	NC	NC	NC	3.6
East Grinstead	1.5	**	3.2	NC	NC	NC	4.7
Lewes	2.0	**	2.6	−4.9	−1.9	3.6	1.4
Rye	−	−	NC	NC	NC	NC	NC
SUSSEX (WEST)							
Arundel and Shoreham	2.7	2.5	1.1	−4.4	−3.0	5.4	4.3
Chichester	2.0	1.1	1.7	NC	NC	5.0	9.8
Horsham	2.7	−3.7*	−1.8	−3.6	−2.9	4.8	−4.5
WARWICKSHIRE							
Meriden	−	−	1.5	−0.6*	−3.3	6.8	4.4
Nuneaton	0.2	**	1.4	−1.8	0.6	−1.1	−0.7
Rugby	1.1	−1.5	2.3	1.4*	−2.5	−2.6	−1.8
Solihull	3.1	1.8	1.7	−5.1	−3.0	5.2	3.7
Stratford	2.2	4.1	0.0	−6.3	−1.5	6.5	5.0
Sutton Coldfield	0.9	−	−	−	−	−	0.9
Warwick and Leamington	0.7	4.0	−1.9	−2.7*	−2.1	5.6	3.6
WESTMORLAND	NC	0.2	NC	NC	NC	NC	0.2
WILTSHIRE							
Chippenham	1.0	2.3	2.2	NC	NC	NC	5.5

CONSTITUENCY SWINGS

CONSTITUENCY	1950-1951	1951-1955	1955-1959	1959-1964	1964-1966	1966-1970	Total
WILTSHIRE (Cont.)							
Devizes	0.5	0.7*	2.1	−0.4	−1.7	4.6	5.8
Salisbury	0.6	3.0	−0.2	−2.9	−1.9	5.2	3.8
Westbury	0.4	1.7	2.6	−1.2	−2.4	5.7	6.8
WORCESTERSHIRE							
Bromsgrove	2.4	2.6	2.9	−2.4	−2.7	5.4	8.2
Kidderminster	1.5	3.7	0.8	−3.0	−3.8	5.4	4.6
South	2.1	0.6*	1.2	NC	NC	5.7	9.6
YORKSHIRE (EAST RIDING)							
Beverley	1.1	—	—	—	—	—	1.1
Bridlington	NC	**	2.3*	−6.1	−4.6	3.2	−5.2
Haltemprice	—	—	0.0	−1.9	−3.6	−0.7	−6.2
Howden	—	—	1.7	NC	NC	4.3	6.0
YORKSHIRE (NORTH RIDING)							
Cleveland	2.0	4.6	1.6	−4.9	−5.8	5.5	3.0
Richmond	2.2	3.0	1.9	−6.3	−3.1	2.3	0.0
Scarborough and Whitby	2.7	1.3	NC	NC	NC	NC	4.0
Thirsk and Malton	3.8	−3.1	−0.1	−2.6	−4.8	5.3	−1.5
YORKSHIRE (WEST RIDING)							
Barkston Ash	0.1	−0.3	1.1	0.4*	−2.5	3.3	2.1
Colne Valley	NC	**	−3.0	NC	NC	NC	−3.0
Dearne Valley	0.0	1.7	0.2	−3.1	−3.2	4.0	−0.4
Don Valley	0.8*	0.4	2.8	−1.0	−3.0	5.4	5.4
Goole	−0.1	−1.7	0.8	−0.4	−3.1	4.6	0.1
Harrogate	2.0	1.8	2.0	NC	NC	NC	5.8
Hemsworth	−0.3	**	1.1	−0.9	−2.3	4.6	2.2
Normanton	1.0	0.0	0.8	0.1	−3.9	8.0	6.0
Penistone	2.5	**	1.2	−5.2	−3.2	3.9	−0.8
Ripon	2.1	0.5	1.0	NC	NC	4.1	7.7
Rother Valley	0.9	0.1	1.5	−0.3	−2.4	5.0	4.8
Shipley	1.7	4.9	0.3*	−2.5	−2.6	3.9	5.7
Skipton	2.4	2.2	−0.4	−2.3	−3.1	5.4	4.2
Sowerby	2.0	−1.5	0.9	−2.0	−2.7	6.3	3.0
Average	**1.3**	**1.2**	**1.1**	**−2.7**	**−2.5**	**5.1**	**3.3**

WALES AND MONMOUTHSHIRE—BOROUGHS

CONSTITUENCY	1950-1951	1951-1955	1955-1959	1959-1964	1964-1966	1966-1970	Total
ABERDARE	−0.5	1.9	−0.1	−1.3	0.2	NC	0.2
CARDIFF							
North	3.7*	2.7	1.5	−7.0	−4.4	2.6	−0.9
South-East	1.5*	1.0	2.5	−6.7	−3.0	5.1	0.4
West	−0.8*	−0.1	2.0	−5.9	−1.8	4.4	−2.2
MERTHYR TYDFIL	1.3	2.3	0.1	−2.8	−0.3	NC	0.6
NEWPORT	1.0	3.3*	0.6	−4.4	−2.3	2.3	0.5
RHONDDA							
East	NC	NC	NC	NC	NC	NC	NC
West	0.8	NC	NC	NC	NC·	NC	0.8

CONSTITUENCY SWINGS

CONSTITUENCY	1950-1951	1951-1955	1955-1959	1959-1964	1964-1966	1966-1970	Total
SWANSEA							
East	1.7	1.1*	−0.3	−4.5	−2.7	5.6	0.9
West	1.6	1.0*	1.6	−3.2	−3.6	3.1	0.5
Average	**1.1**	**1.7**	**1.0**	**−4.5**	**−2.2**	**3.8**	**0.1**

WALES AND MONMOUTHSHIRE—COUNTIES

CONSTITUENCY	1950-1951	1951-1955	1955-1959	1959-1964	1964-1966	1966-1970	Total
ANGLESEY	NC	NC	NC	−0.5	1.8	2.5	3.8
BRECONSHIRE and							
RADNORSHIRE	0.9	−6.1	1.1	−3.0	−0.2	4.9	−2.4
CAERNARVONSHIRE							
Caernarvon	NC	−0.7	1.5	−3.5	−1.9	NC	−4.6
Conway	1.8	5.5	−0.2	−1.3	−5.5	1.9	2.2
CARDIGANSHIRE	NC	NC	NC	NC	NC	NC	NC
CARMARTHENSHIRE							
Carmarthen	NC	NC	NC	NC	NC	NC	NC
Llanelli	NC	3.0*	−0.7	−3.0	−1.6	NC	−2.3
DENBIGHSHIRE							
Denbigh	NC	NC	NC	NC	NC	NC	NC
Wrexham	2.8	1.5	−0.2	−0.6	−4.4	2.9	2.0
FLINTSHIRE							
East	3.8	1.2	2.5	−4.1	−4.7	5.0	3.7
West	2.3	0.3	−1.5	−3.1	−2.8	4.5	−0.3
GLAMORGANSHIRE							
Aberavon	2.9	2.4	0.5	−6.7	−1.5	4.9	2.5
Barry	2.8*	6.1	1.5	−5.3	−2.8	6.0	8.3
Caerphilly	0.4	1.9	−1.8	−0.6	−2.2	NC	−2.3
Gower	0.2	2.4	2.1	−2.8	−2.9	6.8	5.8
Neath	2.7	0.5	2.7	−2.8	−5.3	4.6	2.4
Ogmore	−1.4	3.0	0.9	−0.8	−2.8	5.2	4.1
Pontypridd	2.1	1.1	2.9	−3.1	−3.6	4.1	3.5
MERIONETHSHIRE	NC	NC	NC	NC	NC	NC	NC
MONMOUTHSHIRE							
Abertillery	0.1	2.2	−0.3	−0.9	−2.2	3.6	2.5
Bedwellty	0.1	0.8	0.6	−1.7	−2.7	6.7	3.8
Ebbw Vale	0.0	1.5	−1.8	−2.6	−1.5	NC	−4.4
Monmouth	0.3*	1.6*	−0.2	−6.3	−3.4	3.8	−4.2
Pontypool	1.9	2.8	−0.5	−3.0	−1.9	4.4	3.7
MONTGOMERYSHIRE	NC	NC	NC	NC	NC	NC	NC
PEMBROKESHIRE	−8.3	NC	NC	−3.4	2.5	7.1	−2.1
Average	**0.9**	**1.6**	**0.5**	**−2.8**	**−2.4**	**4.6**	**1.2**

704

SCOTLAND—BURGHS

CONSTITUENCY	1950-1951	1951-1955	1955-1959	1959-1964	1964-1966	1966-1970	Total
ABERDEEN							
North	0.5	−2.2*	−0.4	−1.6	−4.6	3.4	−4.9
South	−0.3	−1.0*	0.8	−4.7	−5.7	2.8	−8.1
COATBRIDGE and AIRDRIE	0.9	1.5*	5.0	−11.2	−2.1	2.3	−3.6
DUNDEE							
East	0.6	−0.4	0.0	−0.5	−1.5	3.3	1.5
West	NC	NC	1.1	−3.9	−3.9	1.7	−5.0
DUNFERMLINE BURGHS	0.2	0.1	−0.4	−0.1*	−4.3	3.4	−1.1
EDINBURGH							
Central	2.0	**	0.5	−3.0	−4.9	5.1	−0.3
East	3.2	1.6*	2.2	−5.8*	−4.3	4.0	0.9
Leith	3.0	−8.4	3.7	−0.6	−1.8	4.7	0.6
North	2.8	**	2.3	−5.8	−2.7	2.3	−1.1
Pentlands	2.0	**	0.8	−7.6*	−2.7	3.3	−4.2
South	2.4	−5.1	−3.0	−4.8*	−2.9	−1.0	−14.4
West	1.9	1.1	−4.1	−5.3*	−3.0	2.1	−7.3
GLASGOW							
Bridgeton	−2.8	**	−2.0	−8.2	−2.7	3.6	−12.1
Camlachie	0.3	−	−	−	−	−	0.3
Cathcart	1.8	2.1	−13.4	−6.3	−1.7	3.4	−14.1
Central	−3.5	**	−2.8	−5.5	−4.7	1.8	−14.7
Craigton	−	−	−1.1	−7.6	−4.2	3.0	−9.9
Gorbals	−1.6	**	−1.7	−7.9	−0.9	0.8	−11.3
Govan	−0.2	**	−0.8	−4.4	−2.7	3.9	−4.2
Hillhead	1.4	**	0.7	−4.4	−1.1	2.5	−0.9
Kelvingrove	0.4	**	−3.1	−6.3	−3.8	4.2	−8.6
Maryhill	1.0	0.7	−1.2	−6.4	−3.2	2.3	−6.8
Pollok	−3.3	**	−2.5	−9.1	−2.1	1.7	−15.3
Provan	−	−	−5.3	−10.2	−2.2	1.6	−16.1
Scotstoun	0.4	**	−4.2	−7.9	−2.9	1.5	−13.1
Shettleston	−1.2	3.3	−3.0	−7.1	−3.7	5.1	−6.6
Springburn	1.6	**	−0.8	−10.7	−2.7	2.1	−10.5
Tradeston	−0.2	−	−	−	−	−	−0.2
Woodside	1.8	**	−3.0	−5.7	−1.7	1.4	−7.2
GREENOCK	NC	5.7*	NC	NC	NC	NC	5.7
KIRKCALDY BURGHS	−0.6*	1.3*	−3.6	−2.6	−0.8	4.4	−1.9
PAISLEY	−2.4	5.8	−0.9	NC	NC	7.5	10.0
STIRLING and FALKIRK BURGHS	−0.5	0.7*	−1.4	−4.5	−3.3	2.7	−6.3
Average	0.4	0.4	−1.3	−5.7	−3.0	−2.9	−5.6

SCOTLAND—COUNTIES

CONSTITUENCY	1950-1951	1951-1955	1955-1959	1959-1964	1964-1966	1966-1970	Total
ABERDEENSHIRE							
East	2.1	**	−5.2	NC	NC	NC	−3.1
West	0.1	**	2.5	NC	NC	NC	2.6
ANGUS and KINCARDINESHIRE							
North Angus and Mearns	2.2	4.9	−1.6	NC	NC	NC	5.5
South Angus	6.8	1.8	NC	NC	2.6	NC	11.2
ARGYLL	0.8	−0.5	−1.4	−7.1	−2.6	NC	−10.8
AYRSHIRE and BUTE							
Ayr	−0.3	0.7	−4.4	−2.5	−1.6	4.7	−3.4
Bute and North Ayrshire	−0.1	0.4*	−2.1	−5.5	−2.9	5.1	−5.1
Central Ayrshire	0.5	2.3*	−2.2	−4.4	−1.2	2.4	−2.6
Kilmarnock	−0.3	−0.2	−1.8	−5.1	−0.8	2.8	−5.4
South Ayrshire	−0.3	−1.1	−2.1	−3.0	−0.6	1.4	−5.7
BANFFSHIRE	4.9	−1.1	0.8	−10.0	NC	NC	−5.4
BERWICKSHIRE and EAST LOTHIAN	4.8	0.6	0.1	−2.7	−2.7	1.2	1.3
CAITHNESS and SUTHERLAND	NC	6.2	NC	NC	NC	NC	6.2
DUMFRIESSHIRE	2.0	0.1	−3.0	−3.6	0.1	5.0	0.6
DUNBARTONSHIRE							
East	1.4*	2.2	−2.0	−3.4	−1.4	4.1	0.9
West	−2.2*	0.6	−0.2	−4.2	−2.8	2.7	−6.1
FIFE							
East	2.0	0.0	−0.6	−5.4	−1.1	1.5	−3.6
West	−4.6*	1.3*	3.2	−3.5*	−2.6	4.4	−1.8
INVERNESS-SHIRE and ROSS and CROMARTY							
Inverness	7.7	NC	NC	NC	NC	NC	7.7
Ross and Cromarty	NC	−1.9	−3.3	NC	NC	NC	−5.2
Western Isles	NC	−3.3	3.7	NC	NC	NC	0.4
KIRKCUDBRIGHTSHIRE and WIGTOWNSHIRE							
Galloway	2.1	−0.8	NC	NC	NC	NC	1.3
LANARKSHIRE							
Bothwell	0.4	2.1*	−0.6	−5.7	−1.9	1.2	−4.5
Hamilton	1.3	1.3	−1.8	−1.9	−0.1	NC	−1.2
Lanark	1.3	−1.1	−1.7	−4.3	−1.9	4.9	−2.8
Motherwell	2.8	3.4*	−1.5	−5.3	−2.1	2.3	−0.4
North	1.4	0.4*	−0.8	−1.9	−0.3	5.0	3.8
Rutherglen	1.4	2.4	−0.8	−6.9	−2.4	2.8	−3.5
MIDLOTHIAN	−	−	−0.1	−1.0*	−3.5	4.1	−0.5
MIDLOTHIAN and PEEBLESSHIRE	1.8	−	−	−	−	−	1.8
MORAY and NAIRNSHIRE	0.4	0.4	3.2	−2.0	−4.8	NC	−2.8
ORKNEY and SHETLAND	NC	NC	NC	NC	NC	NC	NC
PERTHSHIRE and KINROSS-SHIRE							
Kinross and West Perthshire	NC	−1.0	0.5	−1.7	NC	NC	−2.2
Perth and East Perthshire	2.0	NC	NC	NC	−2.3	−0.2	−0.5
RENFREWSHIRE							
East	0.4*	2.5	−3.4	−4.2	−0.7	1.6	−3.8
West	−0.1*	1.4*	−1.7	−4.7*	−3.1	1.9	−6.3
ROXBURGHSHIRE and SELKIRKSHIRE	NC	−	−	−	−	−	NC

CONSTITUENCY SWINGS

CONSTITUENCY	1950-1951	1951-1955	1955-1959	1959-1964	1964-1966	1966-1970	Total
ROXBURGHSHIRE, SELKIRKSHIRE and PEEBLESSHIRE	—	—	NC	NC	NC	NC	NC
STIRLINGSHIRE and CLACKMANNANSHIRE							
Clackmannan and East Stirlingshire	2.8	0.0*	−0.6	−3.9	−2.1	4.1	0.3
West Stirlingshire	−0.4	1.4*	−2.9	−1.2	NC	NC	−3.1
WEST LOTHIAN	2.0	0.9	−0.6	NC	NC	NC	2.3
Average	1.4	0.8	−1.0	−4.0	−1.7	3.0	−1.2

NORTHERN IRELAND—BOROUGHS

CONSTITUENCY	1950-1951	1951-1955	1955-1959	1959-1964	1964-1966	1966-1970	Total
BELFAST							
East	−1.5	4.4	−4.7	−0.5	−6.3	4.8	−3.8
North	−3.7	6.8	−4.7	−0.4	−4.9	0.8	−6.1
South	0.6	4.6	−6.3	−0.5	−8.3	5.0	−4.9
West	NC	NC	NC	NC	NC	NC	NC
Average	−1.5	5.3	−5.2	−0.5	−6.5	3.5	−4.9

NORTHERN IRELAND—COUNTIES

CONSTITUENCY	1950-1951	1951-1955	1955-1959	1959-1964	1964-1966	1966-1970	Total
ANTRIM							
North	NC	NC	NC	NC	NC	NC	NC
South	NC	NC	NC	NC	−8.4	6.0	−2.4
ARMAGH	NC	NC	NC	NC	NC	NC	NC
DOWN							
North	1.9	NC	NC	NC	NC	NC	1.9
South	NC	NC	NC	NC	NC	NC	NC
FERMANAGH and SOUTH TYRONE	NC	NC	NC	NC	NC	NC	NC
LONDONDERRY	NC	NC	NC	NC	NC	NC	NC
MID-ULSTER	NC	NC	NC	NC	NC	NC	NC
Average	1.9	NC	NC	NC	−8.4	6.0	−0.3

GENERAL ELECTION STATISTICS

	Votes	%	Candidates	MPs	T'out
950 *(Electorate: 34,412,255)*					
Conservative	12,492,404	43.5	619	298[†]	–
Labour	13,266,176	46.1	617	315	–
Liberal	2,621,487	9.1	475	9	–
Others	391,057	1.3	157	3	–
Total	28,771,124	100.0	1,868	625	83.9
951 *(Electorate: 34,919,331)*					
Conservative	13,718,199	48.0	617	321	–
Labour	13,948,883	48.8	617	295	–
Liberal	730,546	2.6	109	6	–
Others	198,966	0.6	33	3	–
Total	28,596,594	100.0	1,376	625	82.6
955 *(Electorate: 34,852,179)*					
Conservative	13,310,891	49.7	624	345[†]	–
Labour	12,405,254	46.4	620	277	–
Liberal	722,402	2.7	110	6	–
Others	321,182	1.2	55	2	–
Total	26,759,729	100.0	1,409	630	76.8
959 *(Electorate: 35,397,304)*					
Conservative	13,750,875	49.3	625	365	–
Labour	12,216,172	43.9	621	258	–
Liberal	1,640,760	5.9	216	6	–
Others	254,845	0.9	74	1	–
Total	27,862,652	100.0	1,536	630	78.7
964 *(Electorate: 35,894,054)*					
Conservative	12,002,642	43.4	630	304[†]	–
Labour	12,205,808	44.1	628	317	–
Liberal	3,099,283	11.2	365	9	–
Others	349,415	1.3	134	0	–
Total	27,657,148	100.0	1,757	630	77.1

GENERAL ELECTION STATISTICS

	Votes	%	Candidates	MPs	T'out
1966 *(Electorate: 35,957,245)*					
Conservative	11,418,455	41.9	629	253	—
Labour	13,096,629	48.1	622	364[†]	—
Liberal	2,327,457	8.5	311	12	—
Others	422,206	1.5	145	1	—
Total	**27,264,747**	**100.0**	**1,707**	**630**	**75.8**
1970 *(Electorate: 39,342,013)*					
Conservative	13,145,123	46.4	628	330	—
Labour	12,208,758	43.1	625	288[†]	—
Liberal	2,117,035	7.5	332	6	—
Others	873,882	3.0	252	6	—
Total	**28,344,798**	**100.0**	**1,837**	**630**	**72.0**

[†] Including the Speaker

Source: *British Parliamentary Election Statistics 1918-1970* (Political Reference Publications, 1971)

REDISTRIBUTION OF SEATS IN 1950
UNALTERED CONSTITUENCIES

The following eighty constituencies were unaffected by boundary changes:

† indicates a former county constituency

LONDON—BOROUGHS

Deptford
Fulham, East
Fulham, West
Greenwich
Hampstead
Islington, East
Islington, North

Kensington, North
Lambeth, Norwood
Paddington, North
Paddington, South
St. Marylebone
Wandsworth, Streatham

ENGLAND—BOROUGHS

†Acton
Altrincham and Sale
Barking
Bath
Birmingham, Edgbaston
Birmingham, Handsworth
†Brentford and Chiswick
Dagenham
East Ham, North
East Ham, South
Hendon, North
Hendon, South
Heston and Isleworth

†Hornchurch
Mitcham
Nelson and Colne
Southport
Sutton and Cheam
†Sutton Coldfield
Twickenham
Walthamstow, East
Walthamstow, West
Wembley, North
Wembley, South
Wigan
Woodford

ENGLAND—COUNTIES

Buckinghamshire, Wycombe
Essex, Epping
Essex, Thurrock
Huntingdonshire
Isle of Wight
Nottinghamshire, Bassetlaw

Somerset, Bridgwater
Somerset, Taunton
Somerset, Yeovil
Surrey, Carshalton
Warwickshire, Nuneaton
Westmorland

WALES AND MONMOUTHSHIRE—COUNTIES

Anglesey
Breconshire and Radnorshire
Cardiganshire
Denbighshire, Wrexham
Glamorganshire, Ogmore

Glamorganshire, Pontypridd
Merionethshire
Monmouthshire, Ebbw Vale
Montgomeryshire
Pembrokeshire

SCOTLAND—COUNTIES

Argyll
Banffshire
Berwickshire and East Lothian
(formerly Berwickshire and Haddingtonshire)
Caithness and Sutherland
Inverness-shire and Ross and Cromarty,
Inverness
Inverness-shire and Ross and Cromarty,
Ross and Cromarty
Inverness-shire and Ross and Cromarty,
Western Isles

Lanarkshire, Lanark
Moray and Nairnshire
Orkney and Shetland
Perthshire and Kinross-shire, Kinross and
West Perthshire (formerly Kinross and Western
Perthshire and Kinross-shire, Perth and
East Perthshire (formerly Perth)
Roxburghshire and Selkirkshire
West Lothian (formerly Linlithgowshire)

NORTHERN IRELAND—BOROUGHS

Belfast, East
Belfast, North

Belfast, South
Belfast, West

NORTHERN IRELAND—COUNTIES

Armagh

CONSTITUENCIES WITH MINOR BOUNDARY CHANGES

Although the Boundary Commissions reports did not distinguish between major and minor boundary changes, and the numerous alterations in local government areas made the task of comparing boundaries extremely hazardous, the following eight constituencies appear to have had only minor boundary changes:

ENGLAND—BOROUGHS

Carlisle
Ilford, North
Ilford, South

Nottingham, West
(formerly Nottingham, North-West)

ENGLAND—COUNTIES

Isle of Ely

WALES AND MONMOUTHSHIRE—COUNTIES

Denbighshire

SCOTLAND—COUNTIES

Dumfriesshire

Kirkcudbrightshire and Wigtownshire, Galloway
(formerly Galloway)

CONSTITUENCIES AMALGAMATED

The following eleven constituencies were created as the result of amalgamations with either no boundary alterations or very minor changes:

New Constituency: **Comprising former constituencies of:**

LONDON—BOROUGHS

New Constituency	Comprising former constituencies of
Bermondsey	Bermondsey, Rotherhithe Bermondsey, West Bermondsey
Bethnal Green	Bethnal Green, North-East Bethnal Green, South-West
Cities of London and Westminster	City of London (two seats) Westminster, Abbey Westminster, St. George's
Islington, South-West	Islington, South Islington, West
Poplar	Poplar, Bow and Bromley Poplar, South Poplar
Shoreditch and Finsbury	Finsbury Shoreditch
Southwark	Southwark, Central Southwark, North Southwark, South-East
Stepney	Stepney, Limehouse Stepney, Mile-End Stepney, Whitechapel and St. George's

ENGLAND—BOROUGHS

New Constituency	Comprising former constituencies of
Leyton	Leyton, East Leyton, West
West Ham, North	West Ham, Stratford West Ham, Upton
West Ham, South	West Ham, Plaistow West Ham, Silvertown

REDISTRIBUTION OF SEATS IN 1955

ABOLISHED CONSTITUENCIES

The following constituencies ceased to exist from the General Election of May 1955.

Former Constituency: **Contents transferred to:**

LONDON—BOROUGHS

Fulham, East	Barons Court Fulham
Fulham, West	Barons Court Fulham
Hackney, South	Bethnal Green Hackney, Central
Hammersmith, South	Barons Court Hammersmith, North

ENGLAND—BOROUGHS

Birmingham, Erdington	Birmingham, Aston Sutton Coldfield
Birmingham, King's Norton	Birmingham, Hall Green Birmingham, Northfield Birmingham, Selly Oak
Blackburn, East	Blackburn
Blackburn, West	Blackburn Lancashire, Darwen
Bradford, Central	Bradford, East Bradford, North Bradford, West
Croydon, East	Croydon, North-East Croydon, South
Croydon, North	Croydon, North-East Croydon, North-West
Croydon, West	Croydon, North-West Croydon, South
Dartford	Erith and Crayford Kent, Dartford
Droylsden	Ashton-under-Lyne Manchester, Gorton Manchester, Openshaw
Kingston upon Hull, Central	Kingston upon Hull, East Kingston upon Hull, North Kingston upon Hull, West
Kingston upon Hull, Haltemprice	Kingston upon Hull, West Yorkshire, Haltemprice

REDISTRIBUTION OF SEATS IN 1955

Former Constituency:	Contents transferred to:
Leeds, Central	Leeds, South-East Leeds, West
Leeds, North	Leeds, North-East Leeds, North-West
Manchester, Clayton	Manchester, Cheetham Manchester, Exchange Manchester, Openshaw
Nottingham, East	Nottingham, Central Nottingham, North Nottingham, South
Nottingham, North-West	Nottingham, North Nottingham, West
Reading, North	Reading Berkshire, Newbury
Reading, South	Reading Berkshire, Wokingham
Sheffield, Neepsend	Sheffield, Brightside Sheffield, Hillsborough Sheffield, Park
Walsall	Walsall, North Walsall, South

ENGLAND—COUNTIES

Durham, Jarrow	Gateshead, East Jarrow
Gloucestershire, Stroud and Thornbury	Gloucestershire, South Gloucestershire, Stroud
Nottinghamshire, Broxtowe	Nottingham, North Nottinghamshire, Ashfield Nottinghamshire, Rushcliffe
Warwickshire, Sutton Coldfield	Sutton Coldfield Warwickshire, Meriden
Yorkshire, Beverley	Yorkshire, Haltemprice Yorkshire, Howden

SCOTLAND—BURGHS

Glasgow, Camlachie	Glasgow, Bridgeton Glasgow, Provan
Glasgow, Tradeston	Glasgow, Gorbals Glasgow, Govan

SCOTLAND—COUNTIES

Midlothian and Peeblesshire	Midlothian Roxburghshire, Selkirkshire and Peeblesshire
Roxburghshire and Selkirkshire	Roxburghshire, Selkirkshire and Peeblesshire

NEW CONSTITUENCIES

New Constituency: Comprising areas formerly contained in:

LONDON—BOROUGHS

Barons Court
                                     Fulham, East
                                     Fulham, West
                                     Hammersmith, South

Fulham
                                     Fulham, East
                                     Fulham, West

Hackney, Central
                                     Hackney, South
                                     Stoke Newington and Hackney North

ENGLAND—BOROUGHS

Birmingham, All Saints
                                     Birmingham, Handsworth
                                     Birmingham, Ladywood

Birmingham, Selly Oak
                                     Birmingham, King's Norton
                                     Birmingham, Northfield
                                     Birmingham, Sparkbrook

Blackburn
                                     Blackburn, East
                                     Blackburn, West

Bradford, West
                                     Bradford, Central
                                     Bradford, North
                                     Bradford, South

Croydon, North-East
                                     Croydon, East
                                     Croydon, North

Croydon, North-West
                                     Croydon, North
                                     Croydon, West

Croydon, South
                                     Croydon, East
                                     Croydon, West

Erith and Crayford
                                     Dartford

Feltham
                                     Heston and Isleworth
                                     Middlesex, Spelthorne

Jarrow
                                     Durham, Jarrow

Kingston upon Hull, West
                                     Kingston upon Hull, Central
                                     Kingston upon Hull, Haltemprice

Leeds, East
                                     Leeds, North-East
                                     Leeds, South-East

Manchester, Openshaw
                                     Droylsden
                                     Manchester, Clayton
                                     Manchester, Gorton

Nottingham, North
                                     Nottingham, East
                                     Nottingham, North-West
                                     Nottinghamshire, Broxtowe

Nottingham, West
                                     Nottingham, North-West
                                     Nottingham, South

Reading
                                     Reading, North
                                     Reading, South

Surbiton
                                     Kingston upon Thames

Sutton Coldfield
                                     Birmingham, Erdington
                                     Warwickshire, Sutton Coldfield

Walsall, North
                                     Walsall
                                     Staffordshire, Cannock

New Constituency:	Comprising areas formerly contained in:
Walsall, South	Walsall Staffordshire, Lichfield and Tamworth

ENGLAND—COUNTIES

Cheshire, Nantwich	Cheshire, Crewe Cheshire, Northwich
Essex, Chigwell	Woodford Essex, Chelmsford
Essex, South-East	Southend, East Essex, Billericay
Gloucestershire, Stroud	Gloucestershire, Cirencester and Tewkesbury Gloucestershire, Stroud and Thornbury
Hampshire, Eastleigh	Hampshire, New Forest Hampshire, Petersfield Hampshire, Winchester
Hertfordshire, East	Hertfordshire, Hertford Hertfordshire, Hitchin
Kent, Dartford	Dartford Kent, Chislehurst Kent, Gravesend Kent, Orpington
Nottinghamshire, Ashfield	Nottinghamshire, Broxtowe Nottinghamshire, Mansfield
Sussex, Rye	Hastings Sussex, Eastbourne Sussex, East Grinstead Sussex, Lewes
Warwickshire, Meriden	Warwickshire, Nuneaton Warwickshire, Sutton Coldfield
Yorkshire, Haltemprice	Kingston upon Hull, Haltemprice Yorkshire, Beverley
Yorkshire, Howden	Yorkshire, Beverley Yorkshire, Bridlington

SCOTLAND—BURGHS

Glasgow, Craigton	Glasgow, Govan Glasgow, Pollok
Glasgow, Provan	Glasgow, Camlachie

SCOTLAND—COUNTIES

Midlothian	Midlothian and Peeblesshire
Roxburghshire, Selkirkshire and Peeblesshire	Midlothian and Peeblesshire Roxburghshire and Selkirkshire

INDEX TO CANDIDATES

This index lists the names of all candidates at General Elections from 1950 to 1970 and at intervening by-elections up to the end of August 1971. The number or numbers following the name of each candidate indicate the constituency reference number which is given, after the name of the constituency, at the top of each page. It does *not* refer to the folio number which appears in small type at the foot of each page.

An asterisk preceding the name of a candidate indicates that his or her name will also be found in the index to *British Parliamentary Election Results 1918-1949* (Political Reference Publications, 1969). It is felt that this information will be helpful to readers wishing to trace the activities of a candidate in both the pre-1950 and post-1950 periods. Where the entry in this index is in any way different from that in the 1918-1949 index (due perhaps to a change of surname or the acquirement of a courtesy title) this is indicated by repeating the 1918-1949 index entry in italic type within brackets.

Owing to the very limited biographical information which is available about many of the candidates during this period, there is no doubt that some errors must have occurred. Every entry has been verified as far as possible but compiling an index of this size is complicated by changes in surname (by marriage or deed poll), the adoption of additional hyphenated surnames and by the acquirement of courtesy titles.

The problems which arise in checking that a John Smith who contested a constituency in 1918 was the same, or a different person, who fought an election many years later will be appreciated by those who have researched information on candidates, especially prior to 1950.

Men and women candidates are listed in separate sections of the index and double surnames (hyphenated and un-hyphenated) have been cross-indexed for ease of reference.

SECTION ONE —— MEN

A

SECTION TWO – – – WOMEN

A

Abrahams, Lady, 222, 300, 415
Adams, Miss F.E., 418
Allison, Miss J., 40
Amory, Hon. Mrs. M.I.G.H.,
see Heathcoat-Amory
Anderson, Miss M.B. Harvie,
see Harvie Anderson
*Apsley, Lady, 97
*Archibald, Lady, (Mrs. D.H. Archibald), 476
Archibald, Mrs. D.H., see Archibald, Lady
Armitage, Mrs. P.A., 180
Arram, Miss J.M., 251, 380
Arrowsmith, Miss M.P., 11
Arundel, Miss H.M., 587
Ashley, Mrs. E., 274
Aspin, Mrs. M., 195, 337
Asquith, Miss J.P., 535
Auld, Miss J.M.J., 618
Ayliffe, Mrs. M.D., 412

B

*Bacon, Rt. Hon. Alice M., 176, 179
Baker, Mrs. J.E.M., 395, 499
Baker, Miss O.K.L.L., see Lloyd-Baker
Bartlet, Mrs. S.M., 314
Bateson, Mrs. R.W., 411
Bell, Miss G.S., 638
Bellamy, Mrs. J., 174
Beresford, Mrs. E., 160
Betteridge, Mrs. M., 23
Bevan, Mrs. J., see Lee, Miss J.
Beynon, Mrs. H.E.P., see Protheroe-Beynon
*Billson, Miss M.G., 113
Birk, Mrs. A.L., 237, 251
*Bliss, Miss B.E.M.S., 404
Bolam, Mrs. B., 368
*Bonham Carter, Lady Violet, 530
Boothroyd, Miss B., 183, 212, 248, 454
Bounevialle, Miss R.M. de, see de Bounevialle
Bowen, Miss M.C., 303
*Braddock, Mrs. E.M., 189
Bremner, Mrs. W.C.G., 55
Bridges, Mrs. F.M., 25
Brookes, Miss B.A., 202, 297, 433
Brookes, Mrs. P.S., 307
*Brown, Mrs. I., 621
Brown, Mrs. M.M., 327
Brown, Miss W.D., 178
*Buckmaster, Miss H.M.A., 20
Burns, Mrs. J.Y.L., 541
*Burton, Miss E.F., 111
Burton, Miss M.E., 228
Burwell, Miss B.S., 54
Butler, Mrs. J.S., 312
Bysouth, Mrs. O.E.M., 306

C

Cameron, Miss A.C., 631
Candy, Mrs. I.F., 391
Carnegie, Mrs. J.A., 647
Carson, Miss H.G., 379

Carter, Lady Violet Bonham, see Bonham Carter
*Castle, Rt. Hon. Barbara A., 76, 77
Castle, Dr. Maureen E., 341
Catlin, Miss S.V.T.B., see Williams, Mrs. S.V.T.B.
Chadwick, Mrs. D.P., 486
*Chaplin, Mrs. I., (Miss I. Marcousé), 43
Chipchase, Miss E.E.B., 286, 494
Clark, Mrs. A.P., see Kerr, Mrs. A.P.
Clark, Mrs. M., 353, 388
Clarke, Mrs. P., 523
Collard, Mrs. E.K., 387
Collis, Miss G.C.Z., 374
*Colman, Miss G.M., 287
Colquhoun, Mrs. M.M., 417
Cooper, Miss B.P., 39
Cope, Mrs. J., 49
*Corbet, Mrs. F.K., 7
Corn, Miss B., 129
Cowan, Miss E.T., 601
Crane, Mrs. M.M., 25
Craven, Miss V.S., 538
Crowther, Miss J.F., 297, 432
Cruchley, Mrs. O.R., 580
*Cullen, Mrs. A., 597
Curtis, Mrs. B.A.M., 42

D

Dangerfield, Mrs. E.T., 399, 580
*Dart, Miss V., 268
*Davidson, Viscountess, 397
Davidson, Mrs. H.B., 586
Davidson, Mrs. J.B., 599
Davies, Mrs. A.P. Llewelyn, see Llewelyn Davies
Davies, Mrs. B., 491
Davies, Mrs. J.E., 558
Dean, Miss F., 207
de Bounevialle, Miss R.M., 391
de la Motte, Mrs. M.L., 11, 304
Denby, Miss M.J., 468
Devlin, Miss J.B., 665
Dickinson, Miss G.W., 303
Dickinson, Miss M., 165
Dimson, Mrs. G.F., 155
Douglas, Mrs. A.S., 604
*Dower, Mrs. A.L.G., 531
Dowling, Miss I., 10
Draper, Mrs. G., 42
Dunmore, Mrs. B., 491
Dunwoody, Hon. Mrs. G.P., 138

E

Easton, Mrs. G.M., 2
Edmondson, Mrs. J.I., 375
Edwards, Mrs. E.M., 112
Edwards, Mrs. M.V., 223, 349, 352
Elliot, Mrs. K., 600
Elliott, Mrs. J.R., 102
Ellis, Dr. M. Jane, 527
Ellis, Miss N. Wyn, see Wyn Ellis
Emmet, Hon. Mrs. E.V.E., 500
English, Miss R.C., 487
Ewing, Dr. Catherine E.O., see Orr-Ewing
Ewing, Mrs. W.M., 636

INDEX TO CONSTITUENCIES

This index shows the constituency reference number which is given, following the name of the constituency, at the top of each page. It does *not* refer to the folio number which appears in small type at the foot of each page. The index has been extensively cross-indexed for ease of reference.

The names of borough constituencies are followed, within brackets, by the name of the administrative county in which they are situated. The only exceptions are boroughs which bear the same name as the county, and London Boroughs which are already grouped together in the pages of constituency results. This information will allow readers to collate election results on a county basis.

For those who may wish to compare 1950-1970 constituencies with those of pre-1950, it should be noted that the following counties have changed their names during this century: Angus (formerly Forfarshire), East Lothian (formerly Haddingtonshire), Hampshire (formerly Southampton-shire), Midlothian (formerly Edinburghshire), Moray (formerly Elginshire), West Lothian (formerly Linlithgowshire).

In addition to the changes noted above, two new administrative counties were created as a result of amalgamations on April 1, 1965. They were Cambridgeshire and Isle of Ely, and Huntingdon and Peterborough. On the same date a new administrative area of Greater London was formed comprising the former administrative counties of London and Middlesex plus parts of Essex, Hertfordshire, Kent and Surrey; the county boroughs of Croydon, East Ham and West Ham; 28 Metropolitian Boroughs; 39 non-county boroughs and 15 urban district councils. Constituencies (other than the London Boroughs listed on pages 1-48) which came wholly within Greater London from 1965 are prefixed in this index by an asterisk (*). Constit-uencies partly within the Greater London area are prefixed with a dagger (†).

On April 1, 1968, the borough of Torquay was incorporated into the new county borough of Torbay. On the same date the county borough of Teesside was created from the existing county borough of Middlesbrough and the boroughs of Redcar, Stockton-on-Tees and Thornaby-on-Tees.

The following county abbreviations have been used:

Beds.	Bedfordshire	Lancs.	Lancashire
Berks.	Berkshire	Lincs.	Lincolnshire
Bucks.	Buckinghamshire	Middx.	Middlesex
Glam.	Glamorganshire	Mon.	Monmouthshire
Glos.	Gloucestershire	Staffs.	Staffordshire
Hants.	Hampshire	Wilts.	Wiltshire
Herts.	Hertfordshire	Worcs.	Worcestershire

INDEX TO FOOTNOTES

The number or numbers indicate the constituency reference number which is given, after the name of the constituency, at the top of each page. It does *not* refer to the folio number which appears in small type at the foot of each page.

Where a candidate's name appears in a footnote relating to a constituency which he contested the entry will be found in the Index to Candidates and the name is not indexed again here.